A great number of the skills that contribute to solid biblical interpretation involve considering a text in one or another of its various contexts—linguistic, literary, historical, social, cultural, rhetorical, intertextual. But how often do we give adequate attention to the geographical and archaeological contexts of the events about which we read or the settings in which Jesus was raised, taught, acted, died, and rose again? This distinctive and clearly-focused commentary is replete with solid information about those geographical and archaeological contexts, and with connections to the Gospel texts (ranging from the secure to the suggestive, but always stimulating), that will admirably help us keep those physical contexts in view as we read, interpret, teach, and preach from the Gospels.

– DAVID A. DESILVA, Trustees' Distinguished Professor of New Testament and Greek, Ashland Theological Seminary

It is very rare for me to say in an endorsement that a work is "invaluable" and a "must purchase," but this is one of them. As one who has been writing commentaries for over thirty years, my only question is why someone didn't think of this a long time ago. My retirement project is doing a series of commentaries on the entire New Testament (nineteen volumes), and I just wish I had this five years ago when I started. Once I have this in hand, I will never write anything without consulting this "geographical commentary." I find it equally essential on general background issues as on geography itself. I am very impressed and cannot wait to start using it. Thank you, Barry, and thank you, Lexham Press! Now get me this material!

–GRANT OSBORNE, professor emeritus, Trinity Evangelical Divinity School

This commentary focuses on the nexus of space, sociology, and theology as reflected in the Gospel text. Highlighting the socio-spatial background of each pericope enhances exegesis. This is especially true in the Gospels where the narrative shifts from place to place. The Lexham Geographic Commentary on the Gospels should be part of every Bible students' library.

—PHILIP COMFORT, visiting professor of religion, Coastal Carolina University

LEXHAM GEOGRAPHIC COMMENTARY

on the Gospels

LEXHAM GEOGRAPHIC COMMENTARY
on the Gospels

Barry J. Beitzel, General Editor

Kristopher A. Lyle, Contributing Editor

LEXHAM PRESS

Lexham Geographic Commentary on the Gospels

Edited by Barry J. Beitzel with Kristopher A. Lyle

Copyright 2016, 2017 Lexham Press

Lexham Press, 1313 Commercial St., Bellingham, WA 98225
LexhamPress.com

Print ISBN 9781683590446

Lexham Editorial: Donna Huisjen, Douglas Mangum, and Joel Wilcox
Cover Design: Bryan Hintz
Back Cover Design: Brittany Schrock
Typesetting: ProjectLuz.com

CONTENTS

ABBREVIATIONS

AB   Anchor Bible

ABD   *Anchor Bible Dictionary.* Edited by David Noel Freedman. 6 vols. New York: Doubleday, 1992

Ag. Ap.   *Against Apion* (Josephus)

ANET   *Ancient Near Eastern Texts Relating to the Old Testament.* Edited by James B. Pritchard. 3rd ed. Princeton: Princeton University Press, 1969

ANF   *Ante-Nicene Fathers.* Edited by Alexander Roberts, James Donaldson, A. Cleveland Coxe, and Allan Menzies. 10 vols. American ed. New York: Christian Literature Publishing, 1885–97

Ant.   *Jewish Antiquities* (Josephus)

b.   Babylonian Talmud

BA   *Biblical Archaeologist*

BAR   *Biblical Archaeology Review*

BASOR   *Bulletin of the American Schools of Oriental Research*

BBR   *Bulletin for Biblical Research*

BDAG   Bauer, W., F. W. Danker, W. F. Arndt, and F. W. Gingrich, eds. *Greek-English Lexicon of the New Testament and Other Early Christian Literature.* 3rd ed. Chicago: University of Chicago Press, 2000

BECNT   Baker Exegetical Commentary on the New Testament

BTB   *Biblical Theology Bulletin*

CurTM   *Currents in Theology and Mission*

DDD   *Dictionary of Deities and Demons in the Bible.* Edited by Karel van der Toorn, Bob Becking, and Pieter W. van der Horst. 2nd rev. ed. Leiden: Brill, 1999

DJG   *Dictionary of Jesus and the Gospels.* Edited by Joel B. Green, Jeannine K. Brown, and Nicholas Perrin. 2nd ed. Downers Grove, IL: InterVarsity Press, 2013

EJ   *Encyclopaedia Judaica.* Edited by Fred Skolnik and Michael Berenbaum. 2nd ed. 22 vols. Detroit: Macmillan Reference USA, 2007

HA-ESI   *Ḥadashot Arkheologiyot–Excavations and Surveys in Israel (from 1999)*

ICC   International Critical Commentary

IEJ   *Israel Exploration Journal*

ISBE   *International Standard Bible Encyclopedia.* Edited by Geoffrey W. Bromiley. 4 vols. Grand Rapids: Eerdmans, 1979–1988

JAS   *Journal of Archaeological Science*

JBL   *Journal of Biblical Literature*

JETS   *Journal of the Evangelical Theological Society*

JSS   *Journal of Semitic Studies*

LCL   Loeb Classical Library
Life   *The Life* (Josephus)
m.   Mishnah
NEA   *Near Eastern Archaeology*
NEAEHL   *New Encyclopaedia of Archaeological Excavations in the Holy Land.* Edited by
            Ephraim Stern. 5 vols. Jerusalem: Israel Exploration Society, 1993, 2008
NICNT   New International Commentary on the New Testament
NIDB   *New Interpreter's Dictionary of the Bible.* Edited by Katharine Doob Sakenfeld.
            5 vols. Nashville, TN: Abingdon, 2006–2009
NIGTC   New International Greek Testament Commentary
NovT   *Novum Testamentum*
NPNF^1   *Nicene and Post-Nicene Fathers*, Series 1 (Vols. 1–8: Augustine; Vols. 9–14:
            Chrysostom). Edited by Philip Schaff. 14 vols. New York: The Christian
            Literature Company, 1886–1889
NPNF^2   *Nicene and Post-Nicene Fathers*, Series 2. Edited by Philip Schaff and Henry
            Wace. 14 vols. New York: The Christian Literature Company, 1890–1900
NTApoc   *New Testament Apocrypha.* 2 vols. Revised ed. Edited by Wilhelm
            Schneemelcher. English trans. ed. Robert McL. Wilson. Louisville:
            Westminster John Knox, 2003
NTS   *New Testament Studies*
PEQ   *Palestine Exploration Quarterly*
SBL   Society of Biblical Literature
SHBC   Smyth & Helwys Bible Commentary
t.   Tosefta
Tg. Neof. Targum Neofti
TJ   *Trinity Journal*
TS   *Theological Studies*
TynBul   *Tyndale Bulletin*
UF   *Ugarit-Forschungen*
War   *Jewish War* (Josephus)
WBC   Word Biblical Commentary

EDITOR'S PREFACE

To adapt a line from Ecclesiastes 12, "Of the writing of commentaries there is no end." Today's practitioners of biblical studies axiomatically regard the enterprise to be richly multi-faceted—even multidisciplinary. As a result of such breadth of inquiry, no one commentary series is capable of straddling the entire intellectual waterfront. When we see a "Layman's Commentary" series, or a "Critical Commentary" series, or an "Expositor's Commentary" series, we implicitly recognize and accept the fact that certain aspects of the biblical text will be emphasized while others may be treated more selectively or not at all. The same pretty much holds true for a "Theological Commentary" series, an "Exegetical Commentary" series, or a "Bible Backgrounds Commentary" series. Perhaps even more narrowly focused but still in this same tradition, one thinks of an "Arminian Commentary" series, a "Lutheran Commentary" series, and possibly even a "Woman's Commentary" series or a "South Asia Commentary" series. It has become understandably acceptable to us that no one commentary source can or should attempt to cover everything inherent in this widely diverse field. Accordingly, to refer to a "Geographic Commentary" series is merely to echo this same sentiment, while at the same time to attempt to identify and delineate something of a distinctive approach and to define a particular focus of textual explication.

The conceptual premise of this commentary holds that geography (space) is a legitimate, if commonly overlooked, hermeneutical category. Even cursory reflection leads one to the inescapable conclusion that words from God have been revealed in *real time* about *real people* in *real places*. And we think it *highly significant* that authors who spell out for us the biblical storyline in terms of "Who?", "What?", "How?", or "When?", often also add the element of "Where?", whether explicitly or implicitly. This tendency to incorporate the spatial dimension into a narrative actually sets the Bible apart from most other holy writings. For instance, the Bible contains references to hundreds of place names, in addition to several scores of mountain names, water names, desert/wilderness names, regional names, territorial names, and the like. Even beyond these casual spatial references, there are numerous occasions when geography is tellingly employed as the interpretive axis around which the narrative itself revolves; in which case geography functions as a nexus of interpretation. By way of contrast, the entire Qur'an contains fewer geographical citations than can be found in Genesis 1-20 alone. Little wonder, then, that an OCLC WorldCat bibliographic search for the entry "Atlas: Qur'an/Koran" yields but one entry.[1]

---

1. Abū Khalīl, Shawqī, *Atlas of the Qur'ān*, appearing in four language editions. I am making a formal distinction here between an Atlas of the Qur'an and an Atlas of Islam. The latter

As I have argued elsewhere,[2] many crucially important aspects of biblical history are said to have transpired *in very precise places on earth*—not in empty space nor even in heaven. In the New Testament alone, one thinks in this regard of the location of the birth, the crucifixion, the resurrection, and the ascension of Christ, and perhaps also of the early apostolic missionary expansion. If the Christian gospel were simply a matter of otherworldliness or were concerned only with spiritual or moral values, gaining an appreciation of the spatial dimension of the Bible would hardly matter, and seminal events in the Bible would hardly have been geographically encoded in the text by the inspired biblical writers. But it is neither of these! Central to the *kērygma*!! (κήρυγμα) of the New Testament is the foundational claim that God became man at a definite moment in time and at a precise point in space. To be unaware of or to neglect the geographical DNA of the Bible or the biblical world will therefore often mean that one may run afoul of the biblical argument or that reality may dissolve into sentimentalism. The *Lexham Geographic Commentary on the Gospels* seeks to address these "Where?" questions.

In the Gospels, for example, there is often a very clear and direct correlation between the substance of one of Jesus's teachings, conversations, or sermons and the spatial environment in which he chose to offer it. This is not always the case, to be sure, but it does occur with frequency and regularity. May I highlight a few of the more conspicuous and salient illustrations? Given the history of the site of Caesarea Philippi, and what its many prominent natural and architectural features represented in the classical world, it is surely significant that *while at Caesarea Philippi* Jesus first posed questions to his disciples about his true messianic identity, gave Peter a particular new name and a new authority over which not even the gates of Hades could prevail, and a new commission (Matt 16:13-20). In similar fashion, given what Herod Archelaus had callously and ruthlessly perpetrated on his Jewish subjects from near and around New Testament Jericho only a few years before the ministry of Jesus, it is doubtless spatially significant that *while on the Roman road between Jericho and Jerusalem* Jesus gave an eerily reminiscent "parable" about a ruthless and despotic nobleman who had obtained power, despite being opposed by local citizens (Luke 19:1, 11-27).[3] Examples like these can be multiplied in the Gospels within an individual pericope, where Jesus exploited his physical surroundings to punctuate and underscore his teaching point(s). This is the essence of what we hope to capture in our volume.

Beyond individual pericopes of this sort studied more-or-less in isolation, it is also useful to observe a basic overall cultural pattern of differences between Jesus' words and teachings while in Galilee, as over against what he spoke and how he spoke in

---

bibliographical category, describing and portraying the growth of Islam throughout the Arabian Peninsula, across the Middle East and the Mediterranean World, and into Europe and to points beyond, is well represented in literature and is very useful.

2. Barry J. Beitzel, *The New Moody Atlas of the Bible* (Chicago: Moody Press, 2009, 16-17); idem, *Biblica: The Bible Atlas: A Social and Historical Journey Through the Lands of the Bible* (London: Viking/Penguin, 2006), Foreword.

3. On this event and its significance, see, in this volume, Aubrey L. Taylor, "The Historical Basis of the Parable of the Pounds," on pg. 385, especially the section called "Who is the Unjust Nobleman?"

Judea and Jerusalem. Our contemporary world, and in particular our modern business world, has become increasingly fascinated with a concept known as "culture mapping," which is designed to help individuals and companies navigate the subtle, sometimes treacherous terrain where people from different backgrounds or cultures are expected to work together in harmony.

Given such a mode of thinking, I would say the Gospels present Jesus as knowing his cultural map quite intimately and using it very effectively. Thus for example, in the rustic and largely unstratified social simplicity of Galilee—with its farmlands, fields, and fishing grounds—Jesus' choice of imagery often had to do with salt, seed, and types of soil; with sizes of gates and spacious storage barns; and with calling disciples to become "fishers of men." By fairly stark contrast, while in Judea and Jerusalem—in an environment predominated by viticulture and pastoralism (with not much farming, and no fishing at all), and with the added layer of a complex, social stratification—Jesus spoke of shepherds, vine-dressers, and the religious elite; he spoke of public prayers and places of honor at festivals and synagogues; of fasting, tithing, and the giving of alms.[4] These cultural differences between Galilee and Judea/Jerusalem are not absolute or inviolable in the Gospels, to be sure, and I do not wish to oversimplify or to overstate the case. Nevertheless, they are reflected with sufficient frequency and pattern that one must conclude this was deliberate on Jesus' part. This broader sensitivity to how Jesus tailored his message to particular geographical regions is an aspect covered by a few contributors of this volume.

As one might imagine, I was keenly interested in recruiting contributors to this volume who possess a high level of geographical knowledge and proficiency, combined with a passion for and an interest in this sort of project. Towards that end, let me provide a profile of the 14 scholars selected to contribute to the volume. Each scholar has obtained at least one graduate degree "in the field," by which I mean specifically in Middle Eastern geography, historical-geography, human geography, archaeology, and/or biblical studies, whether in North America, Great Britain, or Israel. Almost all hold a terminal degree or are ABD in a terminal program. A great majority are or have been involved in archaeological field work in Israel, oftentimes for extended years and at multiple sites, and sometimes in field supervisory roles. Every contributor is or has been an active professional on-site field guiding instructor—more than half have beyond a dozen years' experience—providing either on-site education for credit to student study groups and/or to private groups of interested laypersons who are touring. These teaching and tour guiding experiences center in Israel and the West Bank, of course, but in some cases they also include Jordan, Egypt, and even Lebanon. Some of the contributors hold permanent faculty status at an Israeli or an American academic institution, while some others hold permanent adjunct faculty status in Israel. Almost all have published elsewhere on an aspect of biblical geography. I am pleased to present a cadre of well-rounded, fully-qualified writers for this volume.

Finally, as I write the words of this Preface, we in the United States are in the midst of a presidential political campaign. Through this process, candidates of all persuasions

---

4. Jesus does warn his Galilean listeners to beware of such public religiosity, but that is different from inveighing against those who actually engage in such practices.

have stood up and made grand promises on a wide range of topics they hope will help win over voters. This has prompted me to ask myself if I actually recall any political promises made only two or four years ago, and if, at the end of the day, this really even matters. Yet how strikingly and splendidly different are the promises of God found in these Gospels. Christ followers have an altogether predictable, unchanging, and promise-keeping God: we can be certain he will still be tomorrow what he was yesterday, and his promises will remain effectual and continue to be relevant—today, tomorrow, and beyond!

Barry J. Beitzel
Deerfield, Illinois
August, 2016

CHAPTER 1

THE BIRTHPLACE OF JESUS AND THE JOURNEYS OF HIS FIRST VISITORS

Matt 2:1-12; Luke 2:1-20

Paul H. Wright

KEY POINTS

- Bethlehem's topography naturally associated itself with shepherding despite its high elevation.

- There was no space for Mary and Joseph to stay in the "guest-room" (*katalyma*); it was not an "inn" (*pandocheion*).

- The shepherds' proximity to Bethlehem suggests Jesus was born in summer or early autumn.

- The journey of the magi was both dangerous and long, contrary to the somewhat romanticized version of the story we pass on today.

THE GEOGRAPHICAL SETTING OF BETHLEHEM

The ancient village of Bethlehem was located five miles (eight km) south of Jerusalem, one half mile (0.8 km) east of the watershed at the end of a short, narrow spur of chalky limestone angling southeastward. Its elevation, at just over 2500 feet (762 m), is about the same as Jerusalem, and the rainfall is virtually identical for Bethlehem and Jerusalem (twenty-four in, or sixty-one cm, per year, about the same as the wheat fields from central Nebraska to central Texas). The end of the spur on which ancient Bethlehem sat falls away quickly to the east, to the Beit Sahour basin. Here are wide tracts of land and rich, fertile fields suitable for grain. The soils of the Beit Sahour basin are a nice mixture of red clay (terra rosa) and softer, somewhat chalky rendzinas—a combination that ensures adequate nutrients and soil that can easily be plowed. Just beyond, where

1

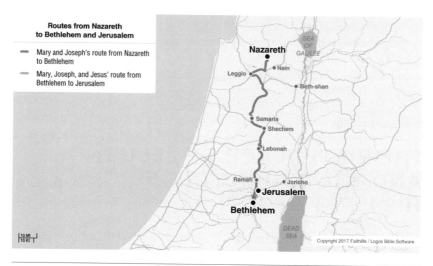

Routes from Nazareth
to Bethlehem and Jerusalem

— Mary and Joseph's route from Nazareth
to Bethlehem

— Mary, Joseph, and Jesus' route from
Bethlehem to Jerusalem

Nazareth

Nain

Leggio

Beth-shan

Samaria

Shechem

Lebonah

Ramah   Jericho

Jerusalem

Bethlehem

SEA OF GALILEE

DEAD SEA

Copyright 2017 Faithlife / Logos Bible Software

rainfall amounts drop below the twelve-inch (thirty cm) annual minimum necessary for wheat, the soils are immature and unproductive and the overall shape of the land morphs into the chalky, barren Wilderness of Judah. With it, permanent settlement gives way to transient encampments of sheep and goats as shepherds follow the seasons in search of watering holes and grazing land (compare Pss 23:2; 65:11–13). For the residents of Jerusalem, the view into this eastern wilderness is largely blocked by the Mount of Olives, a geographical reality that tends to isolate Jerusalem from its larger environment.[1] Bethlehem has no Mount of Olives-type ridge to the east, and the view afforded its residents is a wide open downward expanse, over the wheat fields of the Beit Sahour basin and into the pallid, undulating hills of the Judean Wilderness. This topography tends to associate Bethlehem with the natural environment of shepherds, even though the village itself sits high in the fertile hill country of Judea.

All textual and archaeological evidence—which is scant—indicates that the Bethlehem of the Old and the New Testaments was but a village. Very little archaeological work has been done at the site except in connection with the Church of the Nativity.[2] The oldest settlement seems to have been east of the biblical town in the Beit Sahour basin. Only with the advent of cistern technology in the Iron Age did settlement move to the top of the ridge now occupied by the Church of the Nativity and Manger Square. This is an area that otherwise lacks natural sources of water and where settlement is somewhat restricted by a topography which drops away to the east, north, and south. Rehoboam, the son of Solomon, strengthened Bethlehem's fortifications (2 Chr 11:5–6), but to what extent is unknown, and nothing indicating city walls from his time has been found. Bethlehem enjoyed a pleasant local economy and controlled an important crossroads on the watershed ridge

---

1. See Aubrey Taylor, "In the Garden of Gethsemane" on pg. 476

2. Kay Prag, "Bethlehem: A Site Assessment." *PEQ* 132 (2000): 169–81.

(where roads ascend from Tekoa and the Herodium in the southeast and from the Elah Valley in the southwest), but the city seems to always have sat in the shadow of Jerusalem and Hebron, its larger neighbors north and south. Micah's assessment, made in the mid-eighth century BC, fits the archaeological, geographical, and historical data: "But you, Bethlehem Ephrathah, though you are small among the clans of Judah" (Mic 5:2 NIV). All indications suggest that this was still the case at the time of Jesus.

THE NATURE OF A *KATALYMA*

The birth of Jesus is a Bethlehem story that fits nicely with what is known of the cultural and geographical context of the village in the first century AD. It starts with Joseph and Mary's journey to the village to register for the census (Luke 2:4). Travel in the region was a dangerous enterprise in ancient times, and finding a safe place to spend the night posed a particularly difficult challenge (see Judg 19:15). A traveler preferred to stay with extended family or, if that were not possible, where he or she could claim prior connections (e.g., with the friend of a friend). Most houses (be they of a commoner or a king) had a guest-room or lodging place (*katalyma*, κατάλυμα) where a traveler could pause to eat or sleep for a period of time. This is the word that is usually, though incorrectly, translated "inn" in Luke 2:7.[3] When in the *katalyma*,

the traveler received the hospitality and protection of the family who lived there (see Sir 14:25). There were proper inns (*pandocheion*, πανδοχεῖον) at certain places along the network of roads in the Roman Empire, though only one is mentioned in the Gospels: the inn of the parable of the good Samaritan (Luke 10:34). That story reflects travel conditions that could be found on the road between Jerusalem and Jericho, a route essentially absent of houses and hence guest-rooms.[4] The Mishnah (m. Yebamot 16:7) also mentions an inn on the road from Jerusalem to the Dead Sea, though likely from a later period. In any case, it seems as though proper inns were not a significant part of first century AD Judea, and that travelers who were fortunate enough not to overnight in the open typically stayed in a *katalyma* instead.

Village houses of the first century AD were composed of a number of small rooms and open courtyards with no fixed floor plan *per se*.[5] Styles of housing differed regionally (Galilee vs. Judea, for instance), but the functionality of space was rather consistent.[6] For instance, rooms that were more private in character (e.g., the place where the homeowner and his wife slept) tended to be toward the back of the housing compound, well out of view of visitors, while spaces for public activities such as wedding feasts or acts of hospitality were up front, closer to the street. Some of the rooms and/or court-

---

3. The only other mention of a *katalyma* in the Gospels is the room in which Jesus held the Passover as his Last Supper (Mark 14:14; Luke 22:11).

4. See A.D. Riddle, "The Passover Pilgrimage from Jericho to Jerusalem: Jesus' Triumphal Entry" on pg. 395.

5. John J. Rousseau and Rami Arav, "House," in *Jesus and His World: An Archaeological and Cultural Dictionary* (Minneapolis: Fortress Press, 1995), 128–31.

6. Yizhar Hirschfeld, *The Palestinian Dwelling in the Roman-Byzantine Period* (Jerusalem: Franciscan Press, 1995), 21–107.

yards were reserved for the family's animals (a donkey or two, perhaps, and the sheep and goats). Flocks and herds were brought into the household compound in times of danger or inclement weather, and their body heat slightly warmed the living spaces of its residents. In villages built in the hill country, houses could easily have multiple stories, especially if the building was located on a slope. In this case, the room for the animals was typically in the lower story while the family lived above. In any case, because the *katalyma* served guests rather than persons who were permanently attached to the household, it was likely a room close to the front of the house, near the street. Traditional village homes throughout the Middle East today are arranged the same way, and a visitor will invariably find himself or herself hosted in a place within the household compound that is somewhat detached from rooms where the regular daily activity of the household takes place.[7]

There was no room, we read, for Mary and Joseph in the *katalyma* of the house where they intended to stay in Bethlehem (Luke 2:7). All the protocols of hospitality operative in the ancient Near East suggest that this was the home of a relative, and it was blood ties that had brought Joseph (and Mary) to Bethlehem for the census in the first place (Luke 2:4). *Why* there was no room in the *katalyma* is a matter of speculation. Perhaps the homeowner was already using the space for other purposes. Perhaps other guests were already in town for the census. Or perhaps this was simply not an appropriate place for someone to give birth, reading Luke 2:7 idiomatically, "there was no room *there* for *that*." This latter suggestion is supported by birthing practices that have been documented in traditional village homes in places such as Bethlehem prior to the introduction of hospitals in modern times. At the moment of birth, the expectant mother would go to the room where animals were

---

7. Hirschfeld, *Palestinian Dwelling*, 109–215.

normally kept (the stable) to give birth, and only later was brought back up into the living spaces of the housing compound. Because this was a time of year when shepherds were out in the fields (Luke 2:8), the stable of the house likely would have been empty or used for storage, not filled with live animals.

In the mid-second century AD the church father Justin Martyr wrote that Jesus was born in a cave (*Dialogue with Trypho* 78). It is generally accepted that when Constantine first built the Church of the Nativity in Bethlehem some eighty years later, he located the altar of the church over that cave. Today there are a number of interconnected caves under the church; the one that is directly beneath the altar remembers the spot of Jesus' birth and the place of the manger in which he was laid. Village houses throughout the hill country of Judea often were built in front of or over caves, with the cave serving as the original room of the house and eventually becoming a place for storage or for animals. Other than through the collective weight of church tradition, it is impossible to know if the cave under the altar of the Church of the Nativity is actually the birth place of Jesus or not. At least the memory of Jesus having been born in a cave is consistent with the most reasonable understanding of living conditions in first century AD Judea. In all of this, Jesus' birth was quite unremarkable: the point is that God became a human, and the fact that he did so in a very normal birth process only heightens the intimacy of the incarnation (see photo of "Altar in the Church of the Nativity" on pg. 17).[8]

THE VISIT OF THE SHEPHERDS

Luke 2:8 provides some clues that help us understand the geographical setting of the visit of the shepherds and the time of year of Jesus' birth:

> And there were shepherds living out in the fields nearby, keeping watch over their flocks at night (NIV).

"Nearby" suggests that the shepherds were in Bethlehem's economic zone, the area which stretched mainly eastward into the Beit Sahour basin, a region dotted with grain fields although bordering the open Judean Wilderness. That the shepherds who visited Mary, Joseph, and Jesus were "living out in the fields" suggests several things. First, the shepherds must have had rights to be in fields that otherwise would have been sown with grain. Likely they were shepherds connected to the village of Bethlehem, like David (1 Sam 16:11; 17:15, 20; Ps 78:70–71), rather than shepherds of the semi-nomadic variety (i.e., Bedouin). If so, they likely would have known everyone in Bethlehem and been familiar with the community. Second, the shepherds must have been in the fields at a time when the fields were fallow, that is, after harvest and before plowing and planting. Theirs is a symbiotic relationship: sheep and goats (flocks are nearly always mixed) graze on the stubble of the harvested wheat and barley fields and in the process fertilize the field for the next cycle of plowing and planting. While not negating the age-old tension between farmers and shepherds over land use, within the confines of a village their relationship is mutually dependent and usually beneficial.

---

8. See Benjamin A. Foreman, "Luke's Birth Narrative: Reconstructing the Real Story" on pg. 10.

Based on the weather patterns of Israel, the season between harvest and plowing is summer through early autumn (June/July through September/October). Fields are plowed at the beginning of the rainy season, and grain (barley and wheat) is planted in November. Barley ripens by March/April (the time of Passover; Exod 23:15; Deut 16:1–8) and wheat a few weeks later in May/early June (the time of Shavuot/Weeks/Pentecost; Exod 23:16; Deut 16:9–12). Here we can place the story of Ruth, a Bethlehem harvest story (Ruth 2:1–3:18). In late December and January, when the rain is the heaviest, the grain is just beginning to sprout, its tender shoots promising a good harvest as long as shepherds keep their flocks out of the fields. If the rains are good, there is sufficient rainfall, meanwhile, for a thin covering of wild grasses to sprout in the Judean Wilderness and runoff rainfall to collect in wilderness depressions and pools. It is here where shepherds drive their flocks when the fields nearer Bethlehem are otherwise sprouting grain. As the rain tapers off in the spring and temperatures rise, the grasses of the wilderness burn off, and the shepherds bring their flocks back up into the hills, entering the fields after the wheat has been harvested in early summer. These seasonal patterns imply the birth of Jesus was a summertime event (see infographic "Agricultural Cycle of the Levant/Palestine" on pg. 530).

Luke's statement that the shepherds were keeping watch over their flocks "at night" suggests the same. In the rainy wintertime, nighttime temperatures in Bethlehem are typically in the low 50s (degrees Fahrenheit) at best, and can drop below freezing. This is the time of year that flocks would either be deep in the warmer wilderness, or if in Bethlehem, housed in stables, out of the cold and driving rain. In the summertime, temperatures in Bethlehem often rise to the high 80s and 90s (degrees Fahrenheit), hot enough to drive shepherds and flocks into shade and inactivity during the heat of the day. But summer nights out of doors are quite pleasant, a time when shepherding at night would be expected.

Rabbinic sources (m. Shekalim 7:4) indicate that certain fields at Migdal Eder (lit. "watchtower of the flock;" compare Gen 35:19–21) southeast of Bethlehem were reserved year-round as places where animals that were intended for temple sacrifice were raised. Such shepherds were, it is often supposed, more ritually clean than common shepherds and hence more fitting to be the ones chosen by the angels to visit the infant Jesus.[9] John the Baptist called Jesus "the Lamb of God who takes away the sin of the world" (John 1:29 NIV), and while it may be theologically tempting to associate his birth with shepherds who were already connected to the ritual of temple sacrifice, this can in no way be proven.

THE JOURNEY OF THE MAGI

Matthew 2:1–12 records a different account of Jesus' birth, focusing on the visit of the magi. This narrative contains very little detail about who the magi were, their homeland, or the routes that they traveled to and from Bethlehem. Two millennia of church tradition has filled in the gaps in a wide variety of ways. Most traditions that have reached the West speak

---

9. Alfred Edersheim, *The Life and Times of Jesus the Messiah* (New York: Longmans, Green, and Co., 1896), 1:186–87.

of three magi (one for each of the three gifts mentioned in Matthew 2:11), some even giving them names: Bithisarea, Melchior, and Gathaspa in a sixth century Latin tradition (*Excerpta Latina Barbari* 51b) and Balthasar, Melkon, and Gaspar in a fourteenth century Armenian tradition (*Armenian Infancy Gospel*). The latter three were remembered as kings of Persia, India, and Arabia, respectively. The Venerable Bede suggested that each of the magi hailed from a different son of Noah, hence representing the three human and geographical divisions of the world (*Matthaei Evangelium Exposito* 1.2). While these and other traditions help to personalize the narrative or connect it to larger theological themes, the sheer variety of ideas about the nature and origins of the magi confirms the difficulty of identifying pertinent geographical information within the narrative of Matthew itself.

Leaving the notice of the star aside (its identification belongs to celestial geography), a few clues prompt reasonable speculation about the origin and route of the magi. The first is the name, *magoi*. In ancient Greek texts the term *magos* (μάγος, sg.) denoted someone with the reputation of having special supernatural knowledge or abilities (e.g., Simon the magician and Bar-Jesus; Acts 8:9–11; 13:6). Whether such power was real or not is beside the point, as the reputation of having it was enough to confirm the title. More specifically, according to Herodotus (*Histories* 1.101, 107, 120; 3.65, 73, 79; 7.19, 37, 113) *magoi* were members of a Persian (originally Median) priestly class that specialized in astrology, magic, divination, and the interpretation of dreams. Most scholars have accepted this connection and

understood the magi of Matt 2 to have come from either Persia or Babylon, where they would have been immersed in an already ancient tradition that sought to understand how astrological phenomena might influence or presage events on earth. There they would have had contact with Jewish communities at least as old as the Babylonian exile (sixth century BC).

All of this fits nicely with Matthew's note that the magi were "from the east" (Matt 2:1), that is, as is usually supposed, from eastern Mesopotamia. If so, the route that the magi would have taken to Bethlehem approximated that trod by Abraham and by the Jews who had returned from Babylonian exile: up the Euphrates River, then southward along the eastern edge of the Anti-Lebanese mountain range and into Transjordan before turning westward into Judea.

A difficulty with a Persian or Babylonian origin of the magi is the gifts brought to the Christ child: gold, frankincense, and myrrh (Matt 2:11). None of these products are native to Persia or Babylon. The ancient world's gold supply originated in Nubia, south of Egypt (modern north Sudan), and frankincense and myrrh are distilled from the resin (sap) of desert shrubs native to south Arabia (Yemen) and East Africa. Frankincense and myrrh were carried to a waiting Roman world via the Spice Route, from southern Arabia northward along the eastern side of the Hejaz Mountains, then across the Negeb to ports at Gaza and Ashkelon or through the Sinai and Nile Delta to Alexandria. In the time of the New Testament, these routes were controlled by the Nabateans, the most recent of a long and generally nameless line of desert caravaneers who brought exotic goods to ports along the desert and sea (cf. Gen 37:25-28; Ezek 27:22-24).[10]

The visit to Solomon by the Queen of Sheba bearing spices and large amounts of gold (1 Kgs 10:1-25) provides historic and literary allusions to the journey of the magi. So too does the vision of Isa 60:3, 6:

> Nations will come to your light and kings to the brightness of your dawn ... Herds of camels will cover your land, young camels of Midian and Ephah. And all from Sheba will come, bearing gold and incense and proclaiming the praise of the LORD (NIV).

Except for the term *magos* (or its Hebrew equivalent, *ashshaph*), which could be used generically in Matt 2:1 as it is in Acts 8:9-11 and 13:6, all of the key elements of the journey of the magi are found in these verses. This gives an Arabian setting for the magi geographic merit.

Whether the magi of Matt 2 came from eastern Mesopotamia or southern Arabia, they would have entered Judea "from the east" (Matt 2:1). While identifying their exact route is impossible, geographical logic suggests that they crossed the Jordan Valley at the northern end of the Dead Sea and passed through Jericho, the administrative and tax center for caravan trade entering the Roman province of Judea from Transjordan (Perea). Here Herod maintained a sumptuous and imposing palace complex meant, among other things, to showcase his reputation to travelers passing through.[11] Matthew

doesn't say where the magi met Herod the Great, although Jerusalem seems most likely (Matt 2:3, 7); Herod may first have heard of their arrival into his realm via his tax authorities stationed in Jericho. From Jerusalem, the magi made a short five-mile (eight-km) journey south to Bethlehem, where they met Joseph, Mary, and the infant Jesus in a "house" (Matt 2:11). That the young family was in a house rather than a stable or an "inn" is inconsequential given first century AD village architecture and the birthing practices mentioned above.

The magi "returned to their country by another route" (Matt 2:12 NIV). This route, too, is unknown, but again geographical logic offers a suggestion. From Bethlehem the primary natural route traces the watershed ridge along the spiny backbone of the hill country of Judea on a north-northeast, south-southwest line. Heading back north would have taken the magi to Jerusalem; south would have led them to Hebron, then into the Negeb and out of Herod's kingdom. If they were heading to Arabia this route would have been both natural and tempting, as it would have immediately placed them on the Nabatean-controlled spice route connecting Petra with Gaza, where they could have blended in with moving caravans. Or, the magi could have left Bethlehem heading southeastward, following a natural ridge route to the oasis at En Gedi, then crossed the Dead Sea at its narrowest point (via the Lisan Peninsula that extends eastward from Moab), and from there connected to the Spice Route

---

10. The Nabateans are first mentioned by Diodorus of Sicily in the late first century BC, though he references as a source Hieronymus of Cardia, an officer of Alexander the Great from the late fourth century BC (Diodorus XIX 94.1-10).

11. Ehud Netzer, *The Architecture of Herod the Great Builder* (Grand Rapids: Baker Academic, 2006), 42-80.

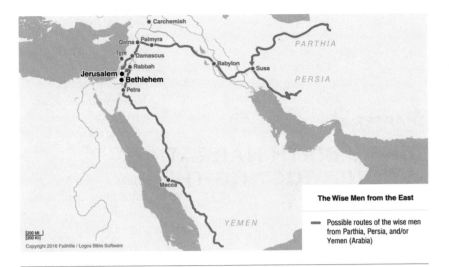

The Wise Men from the East

━━ Possible routes of the wise men from Parthia, Persia, and/or Yemen (Arabia)

on the Nabatean-controlled Moab Plateau above. This would have taken them past the Herodium and Masada, both Judean strongholds of Herod the Great, risking identification and capture (cf. Matt 2:12). Either of these routes could have been possible if the magi were heading to eastern Mesopotamia as well, although the track would have been circuitous. A third alternative has the magi dropping into the wilderness of Judah through the Beit Sahour basin directly east of Bethlehem, then following a more difficult track that makes a loop to Jericho through the Kidron wadi system, a bit south of the normal Jerusalem-Jericho road. This track was frequented during the Byzantine Period when that part of the wilderness became home to a number of monasteries and *laura* of the early church. It would, however, have taken the magi to the vicinity of the Hyrcania (another Herodian fortress) and Jericho, where again they might have been intercepted by Herod's soldiers. No route home was easy, though the way through the Negeb was least likely to attract Herod's attention. And whether the magi returned

to eastern Mesopotamia or to southern Arabia, they themselves undertook a journey of tremendous personal risk, a reality often lost in the majesty typically associated with their journey.

BIBLIOGRAPHY

Edersheim, Alfred. *The Life and Times of Jesus the Messiah.* 2 vols. New York: Longmans, Green, and Co., 1896.

Hirschfeld, Yizhar. *The Palestinian Dwelling in the Roman–Byzantine Period.* Jerusalem: Franciscan Press, 1995.

Netzer, Ehud. *The Architecture of Herod the Great Builder.* Grand Rapids: Baker Academic, 2006.

Prag, Kay. "Bethlehem: A Site Assessment." *PEQ* 132 (2000): 169–81.

Rousseau, John J., and Rami Arav. *Jesus and His World: An Archaeological and Cultural Dictionary.* Minneapolis: Fortress Press, 1995.

CHAPTER 2

LUKE'S BIRTH NARRATIVE: RECONSTRUCTING THE REAL STORY

Luke 2:1-7

Benjamin A. Foreman

KEY POINTS

- Jesus was born into a poor family, evidenced for example by his parents's offering of two turtle doves at the temple (a concessionary offering for those unable to offer a lamb).

- Some facts of Jesus' birth are inaccurate in the traditional narrative: e.g., there is no evidence Mary rode on a donkey (she probably walked),. and Jesus was not born in a stable (it was probably a cave attached to a house).

- Far from a cold rejection at birth, the first chapters of Luke tell a story of people welcoming Jesus with wonder.

CENSUS COMPLICATIONS (LUKE 2:1-2)

Writing to a Gentile audience, Luke sets the birth of Jesus in the context of secular history by stating that Jesus was born during the reign of Augustus Caesar. Augustus (born Octavian) is one of three Roman emperors mentioned in the New Testament.[1] He was born in 63 BC, the same year that Rome began to rule over the land of Israel.[2] Augustus was instrumental in Rome's transition from republic

---

1. The other two are Tiberius (Luke 3:1) and Claudius (Acts 18:2).

2. Pompey, Rome's chief military general, moved his forces into the land of Israel in 63 BC in order to settle a dispute between Alexandra Salome's two sons Hyrcanus and Aristobulus. Seizing most of the country with relative ease, Pompey turned to Jerusalem and overcame the city after a three-month siege (Josephus, *Ant.* 14.53, 66). Eventually the land was divided into

to empire.[3] Augustus' reign (27 BC–AD 14) was generally peaceful and prosperous for Rome. The period of peace and stability that began under Augustus continued for some 250 years and is called the *Pax Romana*.

Since the Roman Empire had no permanent borders, it is difficult to delineate its precise outer limits in Jesus' day.[4] Tacitus states that "the ocean and remote rivers were the boundaries of the empire" (*Annals* 1.9). In the region of the Levant, however, topography and climate helped to draw the lines. The Arabian Desert is a natural barrier, and thus the eastern fringe of the Roman Empire roughly followed the inner rim of the Fertile Crescent. The land of Israel (including territory east of the Jordan River), therefore, was the furthest frontier in the east. To the west, Augustus completed the annexation of Spain and pushed the western periphery of the empire to the Atlantic Ocean. In short, the Mediterranean was a Roman lake, and "by the time when Christ was born ... a traveler could go from Jerusalem to Lisbon on the Atlantic, or from the upper Nile to the English Channel, without leaving the empire."[5]

In late 5 BC, probably the year that Jesus was born,[6] there were some twenty-three provinces in the Roman Empire with twenty-eight military legions spread throughout its territory (totaling approximately 150,000 troops).[7] In Augustus' day the provinces were divided between "imperial" and "senatorial" provinces. Imperial provinces were under the direct jurisdiction of the emperor; he chose the governor and determined how long he held the office. Senatorial provinces reported to the senate and did not have any legions stationed in their territory (probably to prevent the governors from using the army for their own political advancement).[8] Their governors were selected by the senate and held their offices for only one year. In AD 6 Rome converted Judea and Samaria into an imperial province, but since it was a smaller territory it did not have a legionary garrison. If reinforcements were needed, the ruler (e.g., Pilate) had to appeal to the governor of Syria.

When Jesus was born Rome was ruling the land of Israel through its client-king Herod.[9] Luke, however, does not mention Herod. He states that Augustus' decree "was the first registration when

---

five districts, and Hyrcanus was allowed to rule over the Jews as ethnarch, but subject to the authority of the governor of Syria (see *Ant.* 14.34–76, 91).

3. Octavian was Julius Caesar's grandnephew and was named in Caesar's will as his adopted son and heir. When Julius Caesar was assassinated in 44 BC, Octavian was only nineteen years old, and a thirteen-year power struggled ensued. It was not until 31 BC that Octavian finally defeated his chief rival Mark Antony at the Battle of Actium. In 27 BC the senate bestowed on him the name "Augustus" (meaning "majestic") and declared him to be the supreme ruler of the empire. He ruled for just over forty years (27 BC–AD 14).

4. The one exception to this was Parthia in the east (modern Iran and southern Armenia).

5. Colin M. Wells, "Roman Empire," *ABD* 5:803.

6. See the compelling argument in Harold W. Hoehner, *Chronological Aspects of the Life of Christ* (Grand Rapids: Zondervan, 1977), 11–25.

7. Colin Wells, *The Roman Empire* (Stanford: Stanford University Press, 1984), 133.

8. Wells, *The Roman Empire*, 143–45.

9. See Benjamin A. Foreman, "Matthew's Birth Narrative" on pg. 19.

Quirinius was governor of Syria" (2:2 ESV). Josephus references a census that was taken in the first year of Quirinius' rule (*Ant.* 17.355; 18.1–2), but the problem is that Quirinius was appointed governor of Syria in AD 6—more than ten years after the date that many scholars assign to Jesus' birth.[10] Many commentators, therefore, believe that Luke made a historical blunder.

The issue of Quirinius is difficult and cannot be resolved here. It is unlikely, however, that Luke mistakenly connected Jesus' birth to the AD 6 census since in Acts 5:37 he refers to this census in its proper context. As for why Luke mentions Quirinius before he was officially governor of Syria, it may be that Quirinius completed a census begun by his predecessor. Admittedly, the issue is complicated, and a number of other reasonable solutions are available.[11]

Luke 2:1 seems to imply that Augustus requisitioned a census of the entire Roman Empire: "all the world should be registered." Readers, therefore, have typically envisioned hordes of people making their way back to their hometowns for registration. This verse is difficult because although we know of three censuses carried out by Augustus, we have no record of an empire-wide census in his days. The solution might simply be that the registration that brought Mary and Joseph to Bethlehem was a local census limited to the land of Israel, yet part of a larger effort to gather statistics for the entire empire.

THE JOURNEY TO BETHLEHEM (LUKE 2:3–5)

Jews typically took one of two routes when going from Galilee to the central Hill Country (i.e., to Jerusalem or further south). From Nazareth, the first option was to travel eastward through the Jezreel Valley to the Jordan Rift, south along the Jordan River to Jericho, then up the steep southern ridge of the Wadi Qilt (called the "Ascent of Adummim"; e.g., Josh 15:17) into the Hill Country. The distance from Nazareth to Bethlehem along this route is roughly ninety miles. This is the route that Jesus took on his final journey to Jerusalem, just over a week before he was crucified.[12] The second option was to walk directly south along the "spine" of the Central Hill Country. Wayfarers traveling along this route (known as the "Road of the Patriarchs" because it was frequently used by them) would pass through the important Old Testament cities of Shechem, Bethel, Mizpah, Ramah, Gibeah, Jerusalem, and Bethlehem. Although this route is more direct (about seventy miles in total), it cut through the heart of Samaritan territory. Jews did not have good relations with Samaritans (see John 4:9), but it was not unusual for them to use this road. Josephus, for example, says, "it was the custom of the Galilaeans at the time of a festival to pass through Samaritan territory on their way to the Holy City" (*Ant.* 20.118). It was along this route that Jesus, as he was moving from Judea to Galilee, boldly professed to the

---

10. In AD 6 Archelaus was exiled to Vienne in Gaul, Judea and Samaria were incorporated into the province of Syria, and Augustus made Quirinius the new ruler (Josephus, *Ant.* 17.342–44; 17.355; 18.1–2).

11. For a good overview and some proposed solutions, see Darrell L. Bock, *Luke 1:1–9:50* (Grand Rapids: Baker, 1994), 903–9.

12. See Luke 18:35–19:28.

Samaritan woman at the well that he was the Messiah (John 4:1–42[13]). Luke, however, does not give us any indication of which route Mary and Joseph took to register for the census.

Contrary to popular understanding, neither Luke nor Matthew say that Mary made the trip on a donkey (or any other animal). This may be significant since, as France points out, only the wealthy traveled on the backs of animals in the first century AD.[14] According to Keener, "A donkey could cost between two months' and two years' wages, depending on its age and condition, but most peasants who could save enough would buy one, as they were extremely important even in small-scale farming."[15] Luke, however, makes it clear that Jesus was born into a poor family—Joseph and Mary offered a sacrifice of two turtledoves when they presented Jesus to the Lord at the temple (Luke 2:24). According to Lev 12:6–8, this was the concessionary burnt offering for those who were too poor to offer up a lamb. Jesus was born to a family of humble stature, and the lack of reference to an animal contributes to this depiction.[16]

THE BIRTHPLACE OF JESUS IN CONTEXT (LUKE 2:6–7)

Sometime after arriving in Bethlehem, Mary gave birth to Jesus. Luke is the only Gospel writer who records the actual birth of Jesus. His account is surprisingly brief: "And she gave birth to her firstborn son and wrapped him in swaddling cloths and laid him in a manger, because there was no place for them in the inn" (Luke 2:7 ESV). What kind of a setting should we envision from this description?

One thing is clear: Mary gave birth to Jesus in a place where guests did not usually stay. Luke 2:7 tells us that Jesus was laid in a manger *because there was no room* for them in the "inn" (more on this word later). In other words, there did not "just happen" to be a manger (perhaps used as furniture) in the visitors' quarters. The location of Jesus' birth was unusual in some way.

Many who are familiar with the Christmas story imagine Mary giving birth to Jesus in a stable. The story is well-known: Mary and Joseph arrive in Bethlehem late at night and frantically search for a place to lodge. An angry innkeeper points to a "No Vacancy" sign hanging in the window, and in desperation Joseph leads Mary to a stable where she gives birth to Jesus that night. Some important clues in the text, however, suggest that this scene is inaccurate.

One key point to notice is Luke does not say that Jesus was born the same night they arrived in Bethlehem. Luke 2:6 says that "*while they were there* the time came for her to give birth." This implies that some time had elapsed (Luke does not say how much) between their arrival and Jesus' birth. This is significant because if Mary and Joseph had already been in Bethlehem for several days, or perhaps

13. See Perry G. Phillips, "At the Well of Sychar" on pg. 92.

14. R. T. France, *The Gospel of Matthew* (Grand Rapids: Eerdmans, 2007), 775.

15. Craig S. Keener, *The Gospel of Matthew: A Socio-Rhetorical Commentary* (Grand Rapids: Eerdmans, 2009), 490n91.

16. The only time that Jesus rode an animal was at the triumphal entry, where Jesus was presented as a king. Those donkeys did not belong to Jesus (or his disciples); they were borrowed for the occasion (Matt 21:2–3; Luke 19:30–34).

even weeks, the place where they were staying was not an "emergency" shelter found in the heat of the rapidly-increasing contractions of labor. A few days, or weeks, would have been plenty of time for Joseph to find a suitable place for his pregnant wife to give birth.

The reason Mary gave birth in that particular location was that "there was no room in the katalyma (κατάλυμα)." Most English translations render katalyma as "inn." But this translation is unfortunate because the word occurs also in Luke 22:11 where it clearly means "guest room" (e.g., NIV, NLT, ESV, NASB, NRSV, HCSB, NET). Had Luke meant "inn" (i.e., a traveler's lodge) he would have used the word pandocheion (πανδοχεῖον), as he does in Luke 10:34. Thus, a better translation of Luke 2:7 is, "There was no place for them in the guest room."[17]

Hospitality, in antiquity, was a bigger part of life than it is in today's western society. It was not unusual to invite travelers passing through the region into one's home, even if they were strangers (see Gen 18:1; 19:1-11; 24:1-49; Judg 19:16-30). This is the image behind Jesus' words in Rev 3:20 (ESV): "Behold, I stand at the door and knock. If anyone hears my voice and opens the door, I will come in to him and eat with him, and he with me." According to one scholar, "Jews of the Second Temple and rabbinic periods prized hospitality as a virtue (t. Zebaḥ. 6:4ff.; Jos. Ant. 1.250f.)."[18] Since visitors

were frequently entertained, house owners sometimes built a guest room on the top floor of the house (e.g., 2 Kgs 4:10; Luke 22:12). This is probably the room alluded to in Luke 2:7. Given this heavy emphasis on hospitality, why was there "no place" for Joseph and his pregnant wife Mary?

One answer might be that there simply was not an empty room to be found anywhere in the village because Bethlehem was inundated with individuals who had come to register for the census. But surely a woman who is nine months pregnant (or nearly so) would have been given special priority on lodging. Most people recognize this, and thus a more common explanation is that Mary was not welcomed into anyone's guest room because of the unusual circumstances of her pregnancy. From their perspective Mary was bearing an illegitimate child; inviting her into their home could be interpreted as an approval of her actions.[19] The problem with this understanding, however, is that Matthew states that when the magi arrived in Bethlehem to pay homage to Jesus, Joseph and his family were residing in a house (Matt 2:11). If the stigma of an illicit relationship had prevented Mary and Joseph from staying in a proper room before Jesus was born, why would anyone welcome them into their house after his birth? What had changed? If anything, Mary and Joseph would

---

17. "It is possible that Joseph had relied upon the hospitality of some friend in Bethlehem, whose 'guest-chamber,' however, was already full when he and Mary arrived" (Alfred Plummer, The Gospel According to St. Luke [London: T&T Clark, 1896], 54).

18. J. Koenig, "Hospitality," ABD 3:300.

19. Note that the Talmud calls Jesus a "bastard" in the true sense of the word (e.g., b. Sanhedrin 67a).

have been more ostracized after the birth.[20] Additionally, Matthew implies that Joseph and his family intended on settling in Bethlehem after coming back from Egypt and returned to Nazareth only after hearing that Archelaus was ruling over Judea in the place of Herod (Matt 2:22[21]). Had the hospitality in Bethlehem been so cold that Joseph was unable to find a proper room for his pregnant wife, it is unlikely that he would have wanted to relocate there. All of this suggests that the birth of Jesus in a neglected stable is unlikely.

Tradition places Jesus' birth in a cave. In AD 339 Constantine memorialized the cave in which Jesus was said to have been born by building a church over the site. Tourists today can still see the cave inside Bethlehem's Church of the Nativity. This tradition, however, goes back at least two hundred years before Constantine. Three second-century AD sources make reference to a cave. Justin Martyr (AD 100–165) claims in his *Dialogue with Trypho* (78.5) that, "Since Joseph could not find a lodging in that village [Bethlehem], he took up his quarters in a certain cave near the village; and while they were there Mary brought forth the Christ."[22] An anonymous work from the second half of the second century AD called *The Protevangelium of James* also maintains that Mary gave birth in a cave outside of Bethlehem (17.1–18.1):

And they came half the way, and Mary said to him: 'Joseph, take me down from the ass [from the she-ass], for the child within me presses me, to come forth.' And he took her down there and said to her: 'Where shall I take you and hide your shame? For the place is desert.' And he found a cave there and brought her into it, and left her in the care of his sons and went out to seek for a Hebrew midwife in the region of Bethlehem.[23]

According to this text, however, Mary gave birth to Jesus in the cave even before they arrived in Bethlehem, not because no lodging could be found in the village. Finally, Origen (AD 185–254) explains, "there is shown at Bethlehem the cave where he was born, and the manger in the cave where He was wrapped in swaddling-clothes."[24]

At first glance it may be tempting to reject the cave tradition since both Justin Martyr and the *Protevangelium* place Jesus' birth *outside* of Bethlehem, in clear contradiction of Matthew and Luke. But the tradition might not be so easily dismissed. Jerome (AD 342–420), who was a resident of Bethlehem for over forty years, asserts that Hadrian (ca. AD 135) converted the cave into a pagan shrine:

From the time of Hadrian to the reign of Constantine—a period

---

20. The response that this particular family (in Matt 2:11) probably welcomed Mary and Joseph because they had not heard about Mary's "miraculous" pregnancy is unlikely given that Bethlehem was a small village. Such juicy pieces of gossip have the tendency to spread.

21. See A. D. Riddle, "The Passover Pilgrimage from Jericho to Jerusalem" on pg. 395.

22. Translation from *ANF* 1:237. Justin believed that Jesus' birth in a cave fulfilled a prophecy found in Isaiah 33:16.

23. Translation from *NTApoc* 1:433.

24. *Against Celsus* 1.51. Translation from *ANF* 4:418.

of about one hundred and eighty years ... Bethlehem ... was overshadowed by a grove of Tammuz, that is of Adonis; and in the very cave where the infant Christ had uttered His earliest cry lamentation was made for the paramour of Venus.[25]

This text is important for two reasons. First, Hadrian's transformation of the cave into a pagan worship site is a strong indication that the tradition goes back even further than the time of Hadrian. Second, Christians were most likely not permitted to worship at the cave for that 180-year period of time—or at the very least they would have avoided the site. That the Bethlehemites did not select another cave, but preserved the tradition for nearly two hundred years, is significant because it means that they did not feel free to fabricate tradition.[26]

Caves were frequently used as stables in antiquity, and therefore the argument against a stable setting could be equally applied to the cave tradition: Why could Joseph not find a more suitable place for his wife to give birth? An understanding of the layout of houses in the first century AD may suggest a surprising answer (see infographic "First-Century Israelite House" on pg. 395).

Although in western culture it is unheard of for animals (aside from pets)

to be kept inside the house, this was fairly common in antiquity. The necromancer at Endor, for example, had a fattened calf *in the house* which she killed and gave to Saul (1 Sam 28:24; compare Amos 6:4; Ps 50:9; Judg 11:31).[27] This was the practice in New Testament times as well.[28] Unusual as this might seem for us today, there were several advantages to keeping animals inside the house. First, their body heat helped to keep the house warm in the winter. Second, animals were valuable in an agrarian society, and keeping them inside helped to prevent theft. Third, animal dung was used as fuel for cooking (e.g., Ezek 4:15); thus keeping them inside made it easier to gather their waste for burning. Typically, one room on the ground floor, often paved with cobbles or flagstones, was reserved for livestock. This room was separated from the other rooms of the house by pillars (called "fenestrated walls") that supported the ceiling of the second floor (which was sometimes converted into a guest room). Mangers were frequently placed between these pillars.

All of this suggests that Jesus was not born in a stable but in the main quarters of a house (which, given the early tradition of the cave, may have incorporated a cave into its living space). Since Bethlehem was very crowded because of the census, the guest room was probably already full of visitors when Mary and

---

25. *Epistle to Paulinus* 58.3. Translation from *NPNF*^2 6:120.

26. Jerome Murphy-O'Connor, "Where Was Jesus Born? Bethlehem ... Of Course" in *The First Christmas: The Story of Jesus' Birth in History and Tradition*, ed. Sarah Murphy (Washington, D.C.: Biblical Archaeology Society, 2009), 51.

27. See further in Philip J. King and Lawrence E. Stager, *Life in Biblical Israel* (Louisville, KY: Westminster John Knox, 2001), 28–35.

28. Bailey argues that Jesus' reference in Luke 13:10–17 to "untying your ox or donkey" on Shabbat implies that the animals were kept in the house. See Kenneth Bailey, *Jesus Through Middle Eastern Eyes: Cultural Studies in the Gospels* (Downers Grove, IL: InterVarsity, 2008), 31.

Altar in the Church of the Nativity

Joseph arrived. As a good middle-eastern host, the head of the house could not turn the couple away, nor would he ask his guests to find alternate lodging. The best solution, therefore, would have been to invite them to stay with his family in the main quarters of his·house.[29] Since the family's livestock was kept in the room adjacent to where Jesus was born, Jesus would have been placed in one of the mangers that stood between the pillars dividing the room.[30]

JESUS IS WELCOMED, NOT REJECTED

Luke's birth narrative is sometimes interpreted as a foreshadowing of the people's rejection of Jesus. The "no vacancy" sign which hung in the window of the inn is paradigmatic—so the argument goes—of Jesus' reception among his countrymen. They had no room for him in their hearts. But if our reconstruction is correct, a different theological trajectory emerges: Jesus was not initially rejected—he was accepted.[31] This is evident not only in Luke's account of Jesus' birth but in the following chapters of his book as well. The shepherds, after hastily making their way to Bethlehem to see the child announced by the host of angels, gladly receive Jesus and praise God for what they had seen and heard (Luke 2:20). Eight days later, Jesus is praised and blessed by Simeon and Anna when he is presented to the Lord at the temple (Luke 2:22–38). In the following pericope even the religious leaders are amazed at his understanding and answers (Luke 2:47). Several verses later, Luke comments that upon returning to Nazareth that Jesus increased in favor with God *and*

---

29. See the diagrams in Bailey, *Jesus Through Middle Eastern Eyes*, 29, 33.

30. For a more thorough discussion, see Kenneth E. Bailey, "The Manger and the Inn: The Cultural Background of Luke 2:7," *Theological Review* 2.2 (1979), 33–44.

31. This should not be taken in the wrong direction, however. Jesus nevertheless had a humble birth.

man (Luke 2:52), and even at the beginning of his ministry Jesus is "glorified by all" (Luke 4:15). In short, the flow of the first chapters of Luke is that of a warm initial reception, not a cold rejection. It is not until Jesus returns to Nazareth that the days of his amiable acceptance come to an end (Luke 4:28–30).[32]

BIBLIOGRAPHY

Bailey, Kenneth. *Jesus Through Middle Eastern Eyes: Cultural Studies in the Gospels*. Downers Grove, IL: InterVarsity Press, 2008.

———. "The Manger and the Inn: The Cultural Background of Luke 2:7." *Theological Review* 2.2 (1979): 33–44.

Bock, Darrell L. *Luke 1:1–9:50*. BECNT. Grand Rapids: Baker, 1994.

France, R. T. *The Gospel of Matthew*. NICNT. Grand Rapids: Eerdmans, 2007.

Hoehner, Harold W. *Chronological Aspects of the Life of Christ*. Grand Rapids: Zondervan, 1977.

Keener, Craig S. *The Gospel of Matthew: A Socio-Rhetorical Commentary*. Grand Rapids: Eerdmans, 2009.

King, Philip J., and Lawrence E. Stager. *Life in Biblical Israel*. Louisville, KY: Westminster John Knox, 2001.

Murphy-O'Connor, Jerome. "Where Was Jesus Born? Bethlehem … Of Course." *The First Christmas: The Story of Jesus' Birth in History and Tradition*. Edited by Sarah Murphy. Washington, D.C.: Biblical Archaeological Society, 2009.

Plummer, Alfred. *The Gospel According to St. Luke*. ICC. London: T&T Clark, 1896.

Wells, Colin M. *The Roman Empire*. Stanford: Stanford University Press, 1984.

---

32. See Elaine A. Phillips, "On the Brow of the Hill at Nazareth," on pg. 100.

CHAPTER 3

MATTHEW'S BIRTH NARRATIVE

Matt 2:1-18

Benjamin A. Foreman

KEY POINTS

- Many expected the messiah to be born in Jerusalem—home of Israel's greatest king—not the modest village of Bethlehem.

- The magi probably travelled around nine hundred miles (over roughly four months) in search of the newly born messiah.

- Joseph, Mary, and Jesus' flight to Egypt likely took them forty-five days.

- Jesus is the ideal Israel whose story does not end with exile in Egypt but begins the final exodus.

JESUS' BIRTH IN BETHLEHEM OF JUDEA (MATT 2:1-6)

It may come as a surprise that only Matthew and Luke state that Jesus was born in Bethlehem (Matt 2:1; Luke 2:6-7).[1] None of the other New Testament books even allude to Jesus' birthplace, and the word Bethlehem only occurs eight times

in the New Testament.[2] Nevertheless, the location of Jesus' birth is theologically significant.

In addition to the Bethlehem in the land of Judah, the Old Testament mentions another Bethlehem in Galilee in the territory allotted to the tribe of Zebulun (Josh 19:15).[3] This Galilean Bethlehem

---

1. This lack of emphasis on the village of Jesus' birth has caused some to assert that Jesus was not even born in Bethlehem; see, for example, Steve Mason, "Where Was Jesus Born?" *The First Christmas: The Story of Jesus' Birth in History and Tradition*, ed. Sarah Murphy (Washington, D.C.: Biblical Archaeological Society, 2009), 33-48.

2. Matt 2:1, 5, 6, 8, 16; Luke 2:4, 15; John 7:42.

3. The site has been identified with an Arab village (abandoned in 1948) located on a low mound on the northwestern rim of the Jezreel Valley, just west of Sepphoris. Although it has a strong toponymic connection, it is problematic in that excavations have only uncovered

may have been the hometown of Ibzan, one of the minor judges who led Israel for seven years (Judg 12:8–10).[4] The Bible clearly distinguishes between these two cities, and although the Old Testament predicted that the messiah would be active in Zebulun and the greater Galilee region (Isa 9:1; compare Matt 4:14–16), it also foretold that he would be born in Bethlehem of Judah (Mic 5:2; compare Matt 2:6; John 7:42).

The Messiah's earthly origin from the tribe of Judah is integral to the biblical drama of redemption. Even before the establishment of the monarchy, Judah was singled out as the tribe that would supply Israel's rulers (Gen 49:10). God promised David—the king from the tribe of Judah *par excellence*—that he would raise up from his offspring a kingdom that would last forever (2 Sam 7:12–16). Isaiah speaks of a figure who would rule on the throne of David with justice and righteousness (Isa 9:6–7), and Micah even states that a ruler with eternal origins would come from Bethlehem of Judah (Mic 5:2). Given this trajectory,

it is not surprising that Matthew highlights Bethlehem of Judah as the city of Jesus' birth since one of Matthew's main concerns is to present Jesus as the king.

From a theological perspective, however, it is remarkable that Jesus was born in Bethlehem. One would expect the "King of the Jews" to be born in Jerusalem— this was where the magi came looking for Jesus (Matt 2:1). But the Messiah was not born in the ancient capital of the kingdom of Judah, the place where nineteen Judahite kings had resided and the center of Israel's religious worship. Instead, he was born in a small village five miles to the south. While Bethlehem was the hometown of David, Israel's greatest king, and was known from a handful of biblical stories,[5] the hamlet itself was politically and religiously insignificant in Jesus' day.[6] Even the prophecy in Mic 5:2 highlights this: "But you, O Bethlehem Ephrathah, who are too little to be among the clans of Judah, from you shall come forth for me one who is to be ruler in Israel, whose coming forth is from of old, from ancient days."[7] In short, the

---

finds from the Persian period onward. See Aviram Oshri, "Bethlehem of Galilee," *NEAEHL* 5:1609–11.

4. Though some believe that Ibzan was from Bethlehem in Judah, it is more likely that he was from Bethlehem in Galilee since this is the only place in the book of Judges where the village is called simply "Bethlehem." (Everywhere else in the book it is referred to as "Bethlehem of Judah.")

5. Bethlehem was the hometown of: (1) the Levite who joined the Danite migration (Judg 17:7–9), (2) the concubine who was violently raped (Judg 19:1–2, 18), and (3) Naomi's family (Ruth 1:1–2). Also, Rachel died near Bethlehem (Gen 35:19; 48:7).

6. Only limited excavations have been carried out in Bethlehem. The Old Testament site most likely is to be identified with the mound east of the Church of the Nativity (where the present-day open market is). Excavations in the Church of the Nativity have uncovered remains of the church built in the days of Constantine. See Michael Avi-Yonah, "Bethlehem," *NEAEHL* 1:203–10.

7. Biblical quotations in this article are from the ESV. Matthew's rendering of this text appears to be a free translation of the Hebrew and not a direct quotation of the Septuagint. His change from "are too little" to "are by no means least" does not contradict the original meaning of Micah's prophecy. Matthew's point is that Bethlehem is significant only in that it is the birthplace of the messiah.

Messiah's entrance onto the stage of history was geographically unpretentious. This modest arrival contributes to a major theme in Jesus' ministry, namely the humble nature of his first coming. He was born to an unassuming family (Luke 2:24), in an unconventional dwelling (Luke 2:7), in an insignificant village. He grew up in an unremarkable town (John 1:46), and came to serve not to be served (Matt 20:28). He was a humble king (Matt 21:5; Zech 9:9); a suffering servant (Isa 53), not a conquering emperor.

Although Jesus was born in Bethlehem, he is never referred to as "Jesus of Bethlehem" in the Bible. Nineteen times in the New Testament, however, he is called "Jesus of Nazareth" (one time by Jesus himself).[8] His close association with Nazareth can be explained historically: Jesus spent the first thirty years of his life there (Luke 3:23), and thus people would have naturally connected him to Nazareth, not Bethlehem. Although this historical situation might initially be troubling given Micah's prophecy, a close tie to Nazareth is also prophetically satisfying. As Matthew later notes, his move to Nazareth fulfilled Scripture as well (Matt 2:23).[9]

The arrival of the Messiah was not a grand entrance. Jesus was a kingly figure from David's hometown, but Bethlehem itself was a modest village. Put differently, he was a humble king (see Zech 9:9). Both of these threads, which run throughout Jesus' ministry, converge in the village of Bethlehem.

EXCURSUS:
BETHLEHEM AS THE
BIRTHPLACE OF THE MESSIAH
IN EARLY JUDAISM

The messianic interpretation of Mic 5:2 was not simply an overzealous christological exegesis promoted by the early followers of Jesus to justify their belief that he was the messiah. The conviction that the messiah would be born in Bethlehem was also current in (at least some streams of) Jewish theology in the first and second centuries AD.

In John 7:42 Jesus' opponents countered the claim of some in the crowd that he was the messiah with the argument that he did not have the correct geographical origins. Believing that he was born and raised in Galilee (Nazareth), they objected: "Has not the Scripture said that the Christ comes from the offspring of David, and comes from Bethlehem the village where David was?"

The Aramaic Targum of Mic 5:2 (Heb. 5:1), whose composition and editing is probably to be dated to sometime after AD 70, interprets the passage messianically and even inserts the word *messiah* ("anointed one") into its translation: "And you, O Bethlehem Ephrathah, you who were too small to be numbered among

---

8. Matt 21:11 (crowds); 26:71 (servant girl); Mark 1:24 (unclean spirit); 10:47 (crowd); 16:6 (angel); Luke 4:34 (unclean spirit); 18:37 (crowd); 24:19 (Cleopas and companion); John 1:45 (Philip); 18:5, 7 (chief priests and Pharisees); 19:19 (Pilate); Acts 2:22 (Peter); 3:6 (Peter); 4:10 (Peter); 6:14 (Stephen); 10:38 (Peter); 22:8 (Jesus); 26:9 (Paul).

9. If, as seems likely, Matthew sees Jesus' move to Nazareth as a fulfillment of the messianic "shoot" image (which in Hebrew sometimes uses the word *netser* [e.g., Isa 11:1]), then from a prophetic point of view it is almost more fitting that Jesus is associated with Nazareth not Bethlehem since messianic shoot imagery is abundant in the Old Testament: e.g., Isa 11:1 (*netser*); 4:2 (*tsemach*); 53:2 (*yoneq*); Jer 23:5 (*tsemach*); 33:15 (*tsemach*); Zech 3:8 (*tsemach*); 6:12 (*tsemach*). Only one passage explicitly connects the messiah's origin to Bethlehem.

the thousands of the house of Judah, from you shall come forth before me the anointed One, to exercise dominion over Israel, he whose name was mentioned from of old, from ancient times."[10]

The Jerusalem Talmud, compiled in approximately the fifth century AD, records a conversation between a Jew and an Arab in which the latter tells the Jew that the "messiah-king" was born on the same day that the temple was destroyed (y. Berachot 2:3, 4b). After inquiring about the messiah's name, the Jew then asks where the messiah is from, to which the Arab responds: "From the royal capital of Bethlehem in Judea."[11] Although the story is meant to justify the belief that the Scriptures teach that the messiah will be born on the same day that the temple is destroyed, it nevertheless shows that the belief in the birth of the messiah in Bethlehem was current in some strands of Jewish thinking.

Genesis 35:19–21 records that after Rachel's death and burial near Bethlehem, Jacob journeyed to the tower of Eder. The Aramaic Targum of Gen 35:21 adds that the tower of Eder is "the place from which the King Messiah will reveal himself at the end of days."[12] Although Genesis does not say where the tower of Eder is, the context suggests that it

is somewhere near Bethlehem. This is confirmed by the highly messianic language of Mic 4:8 (the only other place where the tower of Eder is mentioned in the Old Testament) and its proximity to the Bethlehem reference in Mic 5:2. The Mishnah also implies that it is south of Jerusalem near Bethlehem (m. Shekalim 7:4). Thus, this text also seems to reflect the Jewish belief that the messiah would be born in Bethlehem.[13]

HEROD AND HIS KINGDOM (MATT 2:1)

Six individuals from the Herodian family are mentioned in the New Testament.[14] Herod (popularly called "the Great"), the first and most powerful of these, ruled from 37–4 BC. Having been appointed governor of Galilee in 48 BC (by his father Antipater), Herod distinguished himself as a successful ruler and military leader. In 40 BC he was nearly killed by the Parthians, and leaving his family behind at Masada, he fled to Rome in search of more power. Working through Mark Antony and Octavian, he convinced the Roman senate to grant him the throne, and in the summer months of that year he was pronounced king of Judea, Galilee, Perea, and Idumea. It took him three years to gain control of

---

10. English translation from Kevin J. Cathcart and Robert P. Gordon, *The Targum of the Minor Prophets* (Collegeville, MN: The Liturgical Press, 1989), 122.

11. English translation from Tzvee Zahavy, *The Talmud of the Land of Israel: A Preliminary Translation and Explanation*, vol. 1 (Chicago: University of Chicago Press, 1982), 88.

12. English translation from Michael Maher, *Targum Pseudo-Jonathan: Genesis* (Collegeville, MN: The Liturgical Press, 1992), 121.

13. Evidently this was Rashi's belief as well. Commenting on Mic 5:1 (Eng. 5:2) he states that the phrase "from you shall come forth for me" speaks of the messiah the son of David. Some Jewish commentators (e.g., Metzudat David, 18th century), however, contend that although the passage speaks of the messiah, it does not say that he will be born in Bethlehem, only that his roots (through David his ancestor) are in this city.

14. Herod (e.g., Matt 2:1), Archelaus (Matt 2:22), Antipas (e.g., Matt 14:1), Philip (e.g., Matt 14:3), Agrippa I (Acts 12), Agrippa II (Acts 25–26).

these territories, and thus scholars consider 37 BC to be the beginning of his rule. Over the next 20 years Augustus added to Herod's kingdom the territories of Samaritis, Hulitis, Gaulanitis, Batanea, Auranitis, and Trachonitis. In late 5 BC—probably the year that Jesus was born—Herod ruled over a kingdom that "rivalled [sic] the kingdoms of David and Solomon."[15] The exact borders of his kingdom are difficult to determine, though at its peak it stretched roughly from Paneas (Caesarea Philippi) on the slopes of Mount Hermon to Beer-Sheba, and from Joppa to Philadelphia.

Herod ruled over a mixture of Jewish and non-Jewish residents. In the far north, Gaulanitis, Batanea, Auranitis, and Trachonitis were sparsely settled by mostly non-Jews. The residents of Samaria were mostly Samaritan; Galilee, Perea, Idumea, and Judea were the most heavily Jewish-populated areas in the region. Undoubtedly, this diverse ethnic population contributed to the religious tensions that prevailed in Herod's day.

Herod was severely disliked by the majority of his Jewish constituents. At least three factors contributed to their animosity. First, the Jews were suspicious of his commitment to Judaism. Although his devotion to the Jewish religion cannot be seriously questioned (he never would have invested so much time and effort to refurbishing the temple had he not had some religious fervor),[16] he was also equally committed to the Emperor Cult

and built three temples to Augustus: one in Sebaste, one in Caesarea, and one in Panias. (Note that all three of these temples were built in mostly non-Jewish areas.) Second, Herod ruled with an iron fist. Josephus records multiple stories of Herod's harsh treatment of the Jews and states that "he was a man who was cruel to all alike and one who easily gave in to anger and was contemptuous of justice" (*Ant.* 17.191). Third, the Jews were suspicious of his pedigree. His mother Cypros was a Nabatean and thus was not Jewish, and his father Antipater was an Idumean. Although the Idumeans were considered to be Jewish in the first century AD, they were not ethnically related to the nation. They were, rather, descendants of Edomites who had crossed over the Jordan Rift sometime in the Second Temple period and settled in the region of the biblical Negev (i.e., roughly from Hebron to Beer-Sheba). In the late second century BC they were forced to convert to Judaism by John Hyrcanus. Thus, Herod did not have the ancestry to be the ruler of the Jews: he was not from the tribe of Judah nor even a descendant of the Hasmoneans (who were from the tribe of Levi). At best, he had a dubious connection to the Jewish nation (Antigonus, the final Hasmonean king, called him a "half-Jew" [*Ant.* 14.403]).

Herod knew that he was disdained by the Jews.[17] As the years of his rule progressed, he became increasingly fearful of potential usurpers. Therefore, it is no

---

15. Peter Richardson, *Herod: King of the Jews and Friend of the Romans* (Minneapolis: Fortress Press, 1996), 131.

16. "It is almost impossible to imagine he [Herod] wanted to undertake the work [of refurbishing the temple]—or was able to get agreement from the priestly authorities—without a strong personal commitment to Judaism" (Richardson, *Herod*, 195).

17. To ensure that there would be mourning on the day of his death, Herod imprisoned a number of important Jewish leaders in Jericho and ordered that they be killed the moment

wonder that "he was troubled" (Matt 2:3) when he heard that the magi were looking for "he who has been born king of the Jews" (Matt 2:2). Herod had been given the kingdom by the Roman senate. From a Jewish perspective, he had no legal right to the throne. Learning that this ruler was born in Judah, in the ancestral village of Israel's greatest king, would have only exacerbated his fears.

THE MAGI FROM THE EAST (MATT 2:7-12)

Matthew, unfortunately, does not give us many details concerning the men who came looking for the newly-born Jesus. The term *magos* (μάγος, pl. *magoi*) can refer to magicians, sorcerers, astrologers, or dream interpreters. In the Persian period the magi were a priestly caste that interpreted dreams, and the Septuagint uses the term as such in the book of Daniel (e.g., Dan 1:20; 2:2). The *magoi* in Acts 8:9-24 and 13:6-11 are magicians. However, given their mention of the star in Matt 2, they are probably astrologers.

Scholars have not shied away from speculating where the magi came from. Since gold, frankincense, and myrrh abounded in Yemen, Justin Martyr (second century AD) and others after him contended that they came from the Arabian Peninsula. Because the Greek of Matt 2:2 can be translated "We saw his star in the east" (e.g., KJV, NASB), others have suggested that they originated in Asia Minor since the magi would have seen a star in the west had they been in Persia. But the Greek simply means "when it rose," and Matthew explicitly

says in Matt 2:2 that they came from the east. Thus, Arabia and Asia Minor are ruled out by Matthew's own words. Although *magoi* were closely associated with the Persians, which therefore might place their origins in Persia, it is slightly more likely that they came from Babylon given the Babylonians' strong interest in astrology and astronomy. Additionally, Babylon had a larger community of Jews than Persia, and it is probable that their association of a star with the king of the Jews stemmed from conversations with the exiled Jewish community concerning their expected messiah.[18] If the magi indeed came from Babylon, their roughly 900-mile journey may have taken about four months (this is how long it took Ezra to make the trip; Ezra 7:9).

Matthew does not explicitly state that the magi came directly to Herod upon

Bible Word Study: μάγος, *magos*

their arrival in Jerusalem. According to the narrative, Herod "heard" that the magi were looking for the newborn king,

---

Herod died. News of their execution, then, was to be leaked before the population was informed of his death (Josephus, *War* 1.660).

18. See Raymond Brown, *The Birth of the Messiah* (New York: Doubleday, 1977), 167-69.

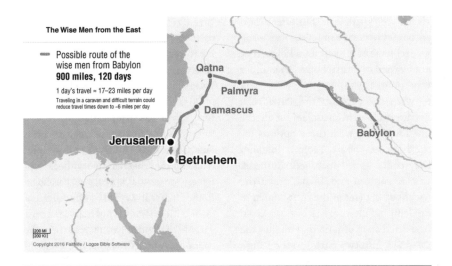

The Wise Men from the East

━ Possible route of the
  wise men from Babylon
  900 miles, 120 days

  1 day's travel ≈ 17–23 miles per day
  Traveling in a caravan and difficult terrain could
  reduce travel times down to ~6 miles per day

Qatna
Palmyra
Damascus
Jerusalem
Bethlehem
Babylon

200 MI
200 KI
Copyright 2016 Faithlife / Logos Bible Software

inquired of the chief priests and scribes as to what the Scriptures had to say about this, and only then summoned the magi to ascertain when they sighted the star (Matt 2:3–7). It is reasonable to assume, therefore, that the magi's search for the messiah initially began in the temple area. But given the sensitivity of the subject and Herod's involvement in the religious affairs of the day,[19] they almost certainly would have been quickly summoned to Herod's palace, 750 yards to the west (perhaps even on the same day).

A good case can be made for dating this event to late 5 BC, several months before Herod's death. According to Josephus, Herod was deathly ill at this point and extremely paranoid about conspiracies to seize his throne (e.g., *Ant.* 17.167–168). A short while earlier he had killed his sons Alexander and Aristobulus after suspecting them of plotting his assassination, and in the final days of his life he executed his son Antipater, outliving him by only five days (*War* 1.664–5). After exe-

cuting his son Antipater, he changed his will for the seventh time and named his sons Archelaus, Philip, and Antipas as his successors. In short, talk of a newly-born king of the Jews could not have come at a worse time.

The star did not actually lead the magi to Jerusalem. They travelled to the city because they saw a rising star. (It might be argued that they did not need a star to lead them forward since from their perspective it would be obvious that the king of the Jews would be born in the nation's capital.) Once Herod sent them to Bethlehem, however, Matthew states that the star actually led them to the house where Jesus was (Matt 2:9). The relatively level five-mile journey down the "Road of the Patriarchs" (the main north-south artery that runs through the heartland of the country) would have taken them a couple of hours at the most.

The passage does not indicate how long the magi remained in Bethlehem, though a quick succession of events seems likely

---

19. For example, Herod appointed the Jewish high priests (Josephus, *War* 1.437).

given Herod's paranoia. Thus, after a short encounter with the King of the Jews—and an exchange of gifts fit for a king—they are warned to return home "by another way" (Matt 2:11–12).

With the Road of the Patriarchs northward toward Jerusalem cut off, the magi were left with three options for their journey home. From Bethlehem they could have continued southeast past Herodium and Tekoa, taken the Ascent of Ziz (see 2 Chr 20:16) down to En Gedi, and then crossed over the Lisan (the dried strip of land that divides the Dead Sea into two parts) to the King's Highway in Transjordan. Another option was to move south along the Road of the Patriarchs past Hebron to Arad, from there cut southeast through the southern Judean Wilderness, and cross over to the King's Highway south of the Dead Sea. The third option was to travel west down the Hushah Ridge, through the Elah Valley (see 1 Sam 17:15–19), and out to the International Highway on the Coastal Plain. Although we can only speculate, option one seems to be the least likely since the route runs close to Herod's fortress at Herodium and cuts through very rough terrain. Option two involves a detour to the south and rough terrain as well. The third option, therefore, is the most logical and perhaps the most likely.

FLIGHT TO EGYPT (MATT 2:13–14)

Shortly after the departure of the magi an angel of the Lord appeared to Joseph in a dream (the first of three that he would receive) instructing him to flee to Egypt with his family. Evidently Herod had not yet been informed of the magi's depar-

ture ("Herod is about to search for the child"), though given Herod's proclivity to react irrationally, a quick departure was essential. Leaving in the night, Joseph and his family departed for Egypt.

Since the beginning of Israel's history Egypt has been a place of refuge in times of trouble. Abraham, and later Jacob, descended to Egypt to find relief from famines that had struck the land of Israel (Gen 12:10; 42:3; 43:2; 46:6). Jeroboam found shelter in Egypt after he fell out of favor with Solomon (1 Kgs 11:40), and pressures in the land of Israel forced the exilic community to flee to Egypt in the days of Jeremiah (Jer 42–43). In the mid-seventh century BC (during the reign of Manasseh), a Jewish community began to form on the island of Elephantine near Aswan. They eventually built a temple there like the one in Jerusalem, offering up sacrifices and celebrating the Jewish festivals there rather than in Jerusalem. A cache of papyrus letters written in Aramaic (called the "Elephantine Papyri") was discovered at the end of the 19th century and provides some insight into what Jewish life was like for the Elephantine Jews in the Second Temple period. According to Josephus, after Alexander the Great conquered Egypt in ca. 330 BC he permitted the Jews to settle in Alexandria and even gave them equal rights with the Greeks (Ant. 12.8–9). Over the next several centuries Jews continued to immigrate to Egypt so that by the time of Christ, there were, according to Philo, over one million Jews in Alexandria and the rest of Egypt (Flacc. 43).[20]

The Way of Shur, which crossed through the northern Sinai to the Nile Delta, was the main route that con-

---

20. Not all the Jews living in Egypt, however, had settled there voluntarily. According to Josephus, Ptolemy I took 120,000 Jews as prisoners of war and forcibly settled them in Egypt (Ant. 12.7, 11).

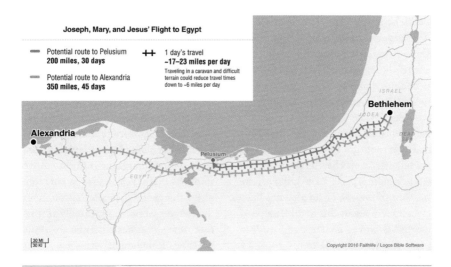

Joseph, Mary, and Jesus' Flight to Egypt

— Potential route to Pelusium
200 miles, 30 days

— Potential route to Alexandria
350 miles, 45 days

┼┼ 1 day's travel
~17–23 miles per day

Traveling in a caravan and difficult
terrain could reduce travel times
down to ~6 miles per day

Bethlehem

Alexandria

Pelusium

Copyright 2016 Faithlife / Logos Bible Software

nected Egypt to Israel (compare Gen 16:7). Roughly following this route, Alexandria is about 350 miles from Bethlehem. Matthew does not tell us where they settled in Egypt, but if Alexandria (which had the largest Jewish population in Egypt) was their final destination, the journey may have taken about forty-five days (following Ezra's travel time average from Babylon to Jerusalem). In Jesus' day the Roman occupied territory of Egypt extended up to Gaza, and since it is unlikely that they would have settled in the barren upper Sinai Peninsula, their closest destination would have been Pelusium or Avaris in the eastern Nile Delta, about 200 or 230 miles from Bethlehem, respectively. A journey to either of these cities may have taken close to a month.

Matthew's purpose in mentioning Jesus' descent into Egypt, however, is not simply to satisfy the historical curiosity of his readers. This geographical detail, rather, is part of a larger theological argument, namely that Jesus is the ideal Israel.

He is the true Son of God who came out of Egypt. And he, like Moses, also narrowly escaped the murderous machinations of a wicked ruler. This typological presentation of Jesus strengthens Matthew's overall argument that Jesus is the messiah by tightening the connection between Jesus and the Old Testament story. Jesus' life is evidence that God has once again begun to work. The Old Testament story is once again playing itself out in the life of Jesus, the ideal Israel. God has begun to work in the same way, with the same people, and in the same place. Egypt, therefore, is theologically suggestive in Matthew's birth narrative.

HEROD'S SLAUGHTER OF THE BABIES IN BETHLEHEM (MATT 2:16–18)

News of the magi's secret departure eventually reached Herod's ears, and with predictable rage, he ordered that all the male children of the region two years old and under be put to death.[21] As noted earlier,

---

21. The Greek does not specifically determine that the infants were male, though this can be assumed since Herod was seeking to do away with a threat to his kingship. A girl

Bethlehem was a small village in Jesus' day. Population estimates range from three hundred to one thousand, and even if the larger number is taken, there probably would not have been many more than twenty male babies under the age of two.[22] This being the case, it is not entirely surprising that Josephus does not mention Herod's slaughter of the infants. He may have only mentioned Herod's more "spectacular" killings (like his sons or wives), or he may not have even known about this at all (Josephus wrote his works nearly one hundred years after Herod died).[23]

Herod's killing prompts Matthew to quote from Jer 31:15, which mentions weeping and lamentation in Ramah. Situated about ten miles north of Bethlehem in the tribal allotment of Benjamin, this village figured prominently in a number of Old Testament stories.[24] Jeremiah, however, does not mention the city to recall a past event. Rather, he references Ramah because this was where the Babylonians gathered all of the Judahites before parading them off to Babylon (Jer 40:1). For Jeremiah, there-fore, Ramah is a cypher for exile. But why mention Rachel? The answer may be found in the rhetorical strategy of Jer 31. Rachel was the mother of Joseph, who fathered Manasseh and Ephraim (Gen 30:24)—the founders of the two most influential tribes of the northern kingdom. This is significant because in Jer 31, the northern kingdom of Israel is used as an a fortiori argument for the asser-tion that there is hope for the kingdom of Judah beyond the exile. Throughout the chapter Jeremiah repeatedly affirms that Yahweh has not forgotten about the northern kingdom of Israel (see espe-cially Jer 31:20). This statement would have been rhetorically powerful for the Judahites who were about to be sent off to exile: If Yahweh has not forgotten about Israel, then how much more can Judah be assured of a future.[25] Jeremiah's ref-erence to Ramah and Rachel, therefore, signifies both the tragedy of exile and the hope that lies beyond it.

Matthew's use of Jer 31:15 is difficult to understand. What does seem to be clear, however, is that while the geographi-cal location of Ramah is significant in

---

would not be a threat. See R. T. France, *The Gospel of Matthew* (Grand Rapids: Eerdmans, 2007), 82n2.

22. Although Matthew mentions that Herod's slaughter extended beyond Bethlehem, there are no villages or cities in the immediate vicinity of Bethlehem. "All that region" prob-ably refers to the farmers or shepherds who, though "residents" of Bethlehem, did not dwell in the village itself.

23. This event is mentioned by a fifth century AD Latin philosopher called Macrobius (though he wrote that Herod killed all of the babies of *Syria* who were under the age of two). Beitzel argues that Macrobius found this historical tidbit in the Roman imperial records. Thus, Herod's slaughter of the babies may have extra-biblical confirmation after all. See Barry Beitzel, "Herod the Great: Another Snapshot of His Treachery?" *JETS* 57.2 (2014): 309–22.

24. For example, Deborah was active between Ramah and Bethel (Judg 4:5); Samuel was born in Ramah, ministered there throughout his life, and was buried there (1 Sam 1:19; 7:17; 25:1); and Baasha king of Israel provocatively built Ramah, starting a war with Asa king of Judah (1 Kgs 15:17).

25. A more detailed exegesis of this chapter can be found in Benjamin A. Foreman, *Animal Metaphors and the People of Israel in the Book of Jeremiah* (Göttingen: Vandenhoeck & Ruprecht: 2011), 63–66.

Jer 31:15, it is not in Matt 2:18. Jesus was not marched off to Babylon from Ramah. Matthew appeals to a similar situation, not location, in his quotation of the text. Just as there was weeping when Judah was taken into exile, so there was weeping when Jesus—the ideal Israel—was forced into exile. Although the people of Bethlehem did not weep because of his exile (they mourned the death of the infants), the result was the same. At the same time, the hopeful overtones of Jer 31 can be detected by the careful reader of Matt 2. Matthew 2:18 is sandwiched between two references to Jesus' exodus from Egypt. As Matthew states, it is "out of Egypt" that Yahweh has called his Son (Matt 2:15), and should anyone have missed that, Matthew continues with Jesus' return to the land of Israel in the very next verses. Although the full intent of Matthew's use of Jer 31:15 may be difficult to grasp, at the very least the trajectory of Matt 2 conforms to that of Jer 31: Israel's story does not end in exile, and neither does that of Jesus, the ideal Israel.

BIBLIOGRAPHY

Avi-Yonah, Michael. "Bethlehem," NEAEHL 1:203–10.

Beitzel, Barry. "Herod the Great: Another Snapshot of His Treachery?" JETS 57.2 (2014): 309–22.

Brown, Raymond. The Birth of the Messiah. New York: Doubleday, 1977.

Cathcart, Kevin J. and Robert P. Gordon. The Targum of the Minor Prophets. The Aramaic Bible. Vol. 14. Collegeville, MN: The Liturgical Press, 1989.

Foreman, Benjamin A. Animal Metaphors and the People of Israel in the Book of Jeremiah. Göttingen: Vandenhoeck & Ruprecht, 2011.

France, R. T. The Gospel of Matthew. NICNT. Grand Rapids: Eerdmans, 2007.

Maher, Michael. Targum Pseudo-Jonathan: Genesis. The Aramaic Bible. Vol. 1B. Collegeville, MN: The Liturgical Press, 1992.

Mason, Steve. "Where Was Jesus Born? O Little Town of ... Nazareth?" Pages 33–48 in The First Christmas: The Story of Jesus' Birth in History and Tradition. Edited by Sarah Murphy. Washington, D.C.: Biblical Archaeological Society, 2009.

Oshri, Aviram. "Bethlehem of Galilee," NEAEHL 5:1609–11.

Richardson, Peter. Herod: King of the Jews and Friend of the Romans. Minneapolis: Fortress Press, 1996.

Zahavy, Tzvee. The Talmud of the Land of Israel: A Preliminary Translation and Explanation. Vol. 1. Chicago: University of Chicago Press, 1982.

CHAPTER 4

THE SIZE AND MAKEUP OF NAZARETH AT THE TIME OF JESUS

Matt 2:23

Paul H. Wright

KEY POINTS

- The Nazareth of Jesus' time was a small agricultural village with limited opportunities beyond subsistence living for its residents.

- The name Nazareth does not appear in any text from the Early Roman Period (outside of the New Testament), which corroborates its geographical and archaeological insignificance.

- The geographical landscape of Nazareth provided Jesus with opportunities to familiarize himself with the ways of the land as well as the tumultuous history of Israel played out in the surrounding valleys.

FIRST IMPRESSIONS OF NAZARETH

Jesus spent nearly thirty years in Nazareth, "where he had been brought up" (Luke 4:16 NIV; compare Luke 3:23). Other than a reference to his profession as a carpenter (τέκτων; Mark 6:3), there is no mention in the Gospels about what he did there all those years (the *Infancy Gospel of Thomas* provides fanciful details).[1] Luke mentions on two occasions that Jesus grew up, but only in terms that

---

1. All sorts of stories about Jesus' formative years developed in the early church. Among the best known are those recorded in the *Infancy Gospel of Thomas*, a collection of traditions that dates to around AD 125. According to this gospel, Jesus fashioned birds from clay and made them fly; lengthened a board that Joseph cut too short; carried water in a cloak after he broke the jar his mother had provided to fetch it; healed his young brother James of a venomous snake bite, and so on. The popularity of these traditions is attested by the fact that they

are provocatively brief (his growth was normal, yet blessed):

> And the child grew and became strong; he was filled with wisdom, and the grace of God was upon Him (Luke 2:40 NIV).

> And Jesus grew in wisdom and stature, and in favor with God and men (Luke 2:52 NIV).

The only story in the canonical Gospels about Jesus' growing-up years took place in Jerusalem where, when he was twelve, he engaged in discussion with religious teachers in the temple and impressed everyone with his insight (Luke 2:41–50). Jesus may have already received an extensive education in Torah, and it is possible that Nazareth was populated by Jews who were interested in things of the Bible (the Hebrew Bible or Old Testament).

This positive image of Nazareth must be balanced, however, by two incidents that happened as Jesus began his public ministry: his violent rejection in the synagogue (Luke 4:16–30) and the comment of Nathanael of Cana: "Nazareth! Can anything good come from there?" (John 1:45–46 NIV; compare John 21:2). These have given Nazareth a rather negative reputation in the eyes of interpreters of the Bible in the centuries since.

Today Nazareth is the largest urban center in Galilee, the seat of government for Israel's Northern District and the economic hub of the region. Visitors to its downtown core are shown structures that preserve memories of the Holy Family; most were built in the last one hundred years, although some preserve remains from the time of the Crusades or the Byzantine Period. Nazareth is now home to a number of thriving Christian communities of various traditions as well as a large Muslim population (the Jewish city of Nazareth Illit, Upper Nazareth, is to the east). These realities, too, tend to subtly shape our impressions of Jesus' home town, and we need to look past them to recover the nature of the Nazareth of the Gospels.

What might be known, or at least reasonably supposed, of the character of Nazareth in the first century AD? Relevant data can be drawn from geography, archaeology, and texts, including the New Testament. In this, it is helpful to take a quick view of the larger geographical context of Galilee first in order to have a meaningful point of comparison with Nazareth itself.

EVIDENCE FROM GEOGRAPHY

THE LARGER GEOGRAPHICAL CONTEXT OF GALILEE

Nazareth—the modern city and the site of the ancient town—is located high on a ridge that marks the line between Galilee and the Jezreel Valley. The Jezreel Valley is the largest of the agricultural valleys of modern (and ancient) Israel. It is also the only level connector between the Mediterranean Sea and Transjordan, and as such served as Rome's primary gateway into the southern Levant, connecting the natural port of Ptolemais (Akko) with Gilead. Writers from the Hellenistic, Roman, and Byzantine periods called the Jezreel Valley "the Great Plain" (Judith 1:8; Josephus, *Life* 115; *War* 2.188; Eusebius,

---

were translated into numerous languages. See David R. Cartlidge and David L. Dungan, eds., *Documents for the Study of the Gospels*, rev. and enlarged ed. (Minneapolis: Fortress Press, 1994), 86–90.

Jezreel Valley

Onomasticon 108.12–14), a description that is deceptive in its simplicity. The combination of ready agriculture and favored trade served to make the Jezreel Valley a zone of international priorities in the time of the New Testament. Indeed, the western end of the valley, one of its most fertile areas, belonged to Bernice, wife of Herod Agrippa II, only to be expropriated by Josephus, commander of the Jewish forces during the Great Revolt, for the war effort (*Life* 118–119).

Much of Galilee proper, the hilly region to the north, is also a zone that by nature lies open to international influences. The land divides easily between Upper and Lower Galilee, based primarily on elevation (m. Shevi'it 9:2). Upper Galilee, with elevations reaching over two thousand feet (610 m), is the southern end of the soaring Lebanese range. At the time of Jesus a portion of Upper Galilee belonged to the region of Tyre and, though dotted with small villages, the region felt the tug of Hellenistic cul-

ture and Roman political might. The first century AD historian Flavius Josephus describes Cydasa in eastern Upper Galilee as "a strong inland village of the Tyrians, always at feud and strife with the Galilaeans" (*War* 4.104–105). Jesus was likely somewhere up in these Upper Galilee hills "in the region of Tyre and Sidon" when he met the Syro-Phoenician woman (Matt 15:21–28 NIV).

Nazareth is in Lower Galilee where elevations stay below two thousand feet (610 m). The heartland of Lower Galilee, once territory belonging primarily to the tribes of Zebulun and Naphtali (Josh 19:10–16, 32–39), is composed of a series of east-west ridges of hard limestone. A long, fertile valley nestles between them. The terrain offers wonderful conditions for prosperous agricultural village life: rich, fertile alluvial soil; plentiful rainfall with abundant sources of surface water; broad fields for grain; and terraced slopes for orchard crops.[2] Josephus described it best, though with his usual flair for exaggeration:

---

2. B. Golomb and Y. Kedar, "Ancient Agriculture in the Galilee Mountains" *IEJ* 21 (1971): 136–40.

For the land is everywhere so rich in soil and pasturage and produces such variety of trees, that even the most indolent are tempted by these facilities to devote themselves to agriculture. In fact, every inch of the soil has been cultivated by the inhabitants; there is not a parcel of waste land. The towns, too, are thickly distributed, and even the villages, thanks to the fertility of the soil, are all so densely populated that the smallest of them contains above fifteen thousand inhabitants (*War* 3.42–43).

References to "Galilee" in texts from the time of the New Testament refer mostly to the political district that was governed by the tetrarch Herod Antipas, son of Herod the Great, the Herod of Jesus' adult ministry (Luke 3:1). Josephus gave a brief border description of this Galilee in *Jewish War* (3.35–39). Its territory included southeastern Upper Galilee, all of Lower Galilee between the Ptolemais / Akko Plain and the Sea of Galilee, and much of the Jezreel Valley. Nazareth lay just south of its geographical center.

Because the economic and political center of the New Testament world lay in the Mediterranean rather than Mesopotamia, as had been the case prior to the conquest of Alexander the Great, most of the significant traffic in the region no longer moved north-south between Egypt and Assyria but west-east, between the Mediterranean ports of Tyre, Ptolemais, Dor, and Caesarea, on the one hand, and the fields and land routes of Transjordan on the other. As a result, the Jezreel Valley and the valleys of Lower Galilee served the larger world as corridors connecting the vibrant, emerging world of the Mediterranean with

the old, established world of the ancient Near East: important for economic control, military penetration, and cultural influence. The prophet Isaiah already had sensed this international tendency seven centuries before when he called the region Galilee of the Gentiles (*gelil haggoyim*). Indeed, the first time that the region was called Galilee in the Old Testament at all, it was with the moniker "... of the Gentiles" (Isa 9:1). In Isaiah's day, the context was the imminent invasion of Israel by Assyria from the northeast, striking Galilee first in the process. In Jesus' day this basic characterization had not changed, although the direction of influence and threat had swung around to the west. Matthew quoted Isaiah early in his Gospel to help explain Jesus' move from Nazareth (in the land of Zebulun) to Capernaum (in the land of Naphtali), both towns that lay within the territory of "Galilee of the Gentiles" (Matt 4:13–15). All of this sets a context for Nazareth, "the city where he had been brought up," as a place adjacent to corridors of tremendous opportunity. In doing so, it heightens by stark contrast what is known of Nazareth itself from the time of the New Testament.

THE IMMEDIATE GEOGRAPHICAL CONTEXT OF NAZARETH

First, an important detail regarding the specific geographical setting of Nazareth within Lower Galilee. The ancient village of Nazareth sat within a broad, shallow basin atop the ridge that separates Lower Galilee from the Jezreel Valley. This ridge, today called the Nazareth Ridge, is a tipped block of limestone that rises sharply out of the Jezreel Valley along an earthquake fault line. The rise, 800 feet (244 m) in elevation, is too steep to be used for agricultural terraces and virtu-

Mount Tabor and Jezreel Valley from Nazareth Ridge

ally impassable to traffic other than via narrow, tortuously slow switchbacks. This geographical reality tended to isolate historic Nazareth from the Jezreel Valley, although the view down into the valley from atop the ridge is nothing short of magnificent.

To the north, the Nazareth Ridge slopes much more gradually into the Beth-Netofa Valley, a broad and immensely fertile east-west corridor that carried the international route between Ptolemais on the Mediterranean and Tiberius on the Sea of Galilee. This is the largest of the interior valleys of Lower Galilee and, for all intents and purposes, was the heartland of the tribal inheritance of Zebulun. It was also the economic center of the political district of Galilee at the time of Jesus. During the time of the Old Testament the largest city here was Hannathon (T. el–Bediwiya; Josh 19:14), while in the first century AD it was Sepphoris, a place well known to Josephus but not mentioned in the Gospels. Both cities were located at the valley's wetter, western end, with con-

venient highway connections to the coast. The economic opportunities in the Beth-Netofa Valley were as promising as those of the Jezreel Valley, though on a smaller scale, and it was to this direction, due to the gradual northern slope of the Nazareth Ridge, that the village of Nazareth most naturally faced.

Because ancient Nazareth was located in an oval basin atop a high, rocky ridge, its horizon line was tight. This tended to disengage the residents of Nazareth from opportunities offered in the better connected valleys below. The walk to Sepphoris probably would have taken only a couple of hours, but this is not the point. While a good argument can be made that the residents of Nazareth were drawn toward the Beth-Netofa Valley out of economic necessity, there is no reason to suppose that the people of Sepphoris (or anyone else for that matter) would have wanted to make the journey the other way. Nazareth was not on a through route of any kind, nor was it home to resources that attracted much attention. As such, its inhabitants had to seek out ways to connect with the rest of Galilee. This reality shaped the kind of interaction that they had with outsiders, as well as the perceptions each likely had of the other.

The basin atop the Nazareth Ridge, as well as the slope of the ridge facing the Beth-Netofa Valley, are made of a soft type of limestone (Senonian) that has benefits but also drawbacks for human settlement. The soils produced from this type of limestone, called rendzinas, are lime rich but fertile if well watered (there is ample rainfall in the region). The fields encircling Nazareth, though, are rocky and not very large. This made them adequate for small village agriculture but not for supporting the sort of large, profitable estates that could be found in the broad, alluvial valleys below (the kind that needed many day laborers, or where landowners might be tempted to tear down their barns to build bigger ones; compare Matt 20:1–16; Luke 12:16–20). Underground water resources in areas of soft limestone tend to be small, and while there are some springs in the Nazareth basin, they are not particularly strong. Moreover, soft limestone makes for inferior building materials, a matter that would be of interest to stonemasons and builders such as Joseph or Jesus (on this, see below). All of this means that on geographical criteria alone, we would expect that Nazareth would be a small agricultural village inhabited by relatively poor people who were pretty much left alone by the rest of the world. There were plenty of places a few miles away where living conditions were much better and where persons who were looking to become someone or do something could have chosen to settle instead. One can easily argue that these geographical realities alone would have tended to make the inhabitants of first century AD Nazareth provincial, or at the least overlooked by the rest of Galilee.

EVIDENCE FROM ARCHAEOLOGY

Archaeological evidence suggests the same. Substantive archaeological remains in and around the site of ancient Nazareth from the time of Jesus are scanty, partly because the bedrock is high, partly because the area has been subject to continuous rebuilding, and partly because there appears to have been nothing of substance from the first century AD to have been preserved anyway. Most of the archaeological work has been done in connection with the Basilica of the Annunciation, an imposing but welcoming structure in the oldest part of the town, tucked up into the northeastern end of the basin.[3] The current church, consecrated in 1969, was built over the remains of a church from the time of the Crusades; it mostly preserves the Crusader outlines. Below are remains of a much smaller church dating to the fifth century AD. This seems to have been the earliest church at the site, as around AD 384, a half a century after Constantine, the pious pilgrim Egeria mentioned a "big and very splendid cave" in which Mary lived, with an altar, but not a church.[4] Egeria's comments on Nazareth are quite brief and suggest that the village was not yet a place of common veneration by Christians. In any case, under the current basilica and in its immediate vicinity archaeologists

---

3. Bellarmino Bagatti, "Nazareth: Excavations," *NEAEHL* 3:1103–5.

4. John Wilkinson, *Egeria's Travels to the Holy Land* (Jerusalem: Ariel, 1981), 193–94.

have found a number of cavities hewn into bedrock that can be dated to the first century AD. These seem to have been silos, granaries, cisterns, wells, cellars, or depressions for storing jars of oil or wine. In a few places traces of house foundations from the first century AD have also been found, but not much more than that, and certainly nothing palatial or anything from earlier periods. It is impossible to know which, if any, of these remains might have been part of a housing compound belonging to the family of Joseph and Mary.[5]

The basilica, under and around which these scant finds are concentrated, was built on a low natural hill with shallow valleys to the east and west, now nearly completely filled in and on which buildings of modern Nazareth have been constructed. The ancient village seems to have been located atop this hill, and this is where the concentration of archaeological material has been found. There are a number of ancient tombs a few hundred feet beyond, to the north, west, and south. Because first century AD Jewish tombs were built outside of villages rather than within, the empty space between the archaeological remains of a village and its tombs must demark the size of the village, which in the case of first century Nazareth was small. The main water source was three springs on the slopes northwest of the village. Already in ancient times—exactly when is unknown—one of these was channeled to a spot on the eastern side of Nazareth that is remembered as Mary's Well (the current structure over that

spot was erected in 1862). Excavations about a third of a mile to the west have uncovered evidence of a first century AD farmstead that included a wine press, watchtowers, terraces, and a spring-fed irrigation system. Today, this is the site of Nazareth Village, a newly constructed reconstruction of a Galilee village at the time of Jesus.

What hasn't been found archaeologically is evidence of any kind of large public structure from the first century AD, including a synagogue. That Nazareth had a synagogue is known from Matt 13:54 and Luke 4:16. Many of the towns and villages of Jesus' Galilee, including Capernaum (Luke 7:1–5), had synagogues (Matt 12:9; Mark 3:1), although archaeological remains of a synagogue building dating specifically to the time of Jesus have been found so far only at Magdala.[6] It is likely that many of the synagogues to which Jesus sent his disciples were dual-use buildings that served as meeting places for Torah reading and study on the Sabbath but as normal living spaces the rest of the week. The lack of archaeological evidence for a synagogue at Nazareth dating to the first century AD may indicate the same. Taken together, the meager archaeological evidence suggests that the Nazareth of Jesus' day was a small agricultural village with limited opportunities beyond subsistence living for its residents.

TEXTUAL EVIDENCE

The textual evidence is similar. The most striking thing about primary source material for Nazareth in the first cen-

---

5. Ken Dark, "Has Jesus' Nazareth House Been Found?" *BAR* 41.2 (Mar–Apr 2015): 54–63, 72.

6. Mordechai Aviam, "The Decorated Stone from the Synagogue at Migdal: A Holistic Interpretation and a Glimpse into the Life of Galilean Jews at the Time of Jesus," *NovT* 55 (2013): 205–20.

tury AD is that the name Nazareth doesn't appear in any text from the Early Roman Period, including the works of Josephus, outside of the New Testament. That Nazareth was literally "off the map" in the time of Jesus corroborates its geographical and archaeological insignificance. When the name Nazareth finally does appear in early texts, in the late third and early fourth centuries AD, it is in works of the early church fathers. The exception is a fragment of a broken dark gray marble slab unearthed in the remains of the third-fourth century AD synagogue at Caesarea in 1962.[7] This slab lists the twenty-four priestly courses, or groups, named in 1 Chr 24:7-18, with the name of the city to which each course moved after the destruction of the temple in AD 70. The eighteenth line of the inscription reads: "[the 18th] co[urse, Happizzez], Nazareth." The village of Nazareth may have been a religiously observant town even prior to AD 70 to have attracted the priestly course afterwards, and the town may have prided itself on its ability to remain so in spite of Galilee's natural connectedness to Hellenism and Roman political might. It is in this context that Jesus learned Torah to such an extent that as a youth he could converse with the religious leaders in the Jerusalem temple (Luke 2:41-50), and that the men of the synagogue reacted harshly to his inclusion of the Gentiles in God's plan (Luke 4:16-30).

EVIDENCE FROM NEIGHBORING CITIES AND TOWNS

The picture of Jesus' Nazareth can be brought into clearer focus by comparing it to other nearby cities and towns. The more prosperous and populous settlements in the vicinity were located in or in very close proximity to the broad alluvial valleys. Nain (Luke 7:11) and Bethlehem of Zebulun (Josh 19:15) edged the Jezreel Valley, for example, while Cana (Kh. Qana; John 2:1) and Sepphoris (*Life* 38 and elsewhere in Josephus) were adjacent to the Beth-Netofa Valley. Residents of cities and towns such as these were able to benefit directly from the rich agricultural and commercial resources at their doorstep, and it was in places such as these, rather than villages such as Nazareth, where Galilee's Jewish (and Gentile) elite would have lived.

Large-scale excavations at Sepphoris have uncovered vast areas of that city's infrastructure.[8] Most of what has been found and preserved for public display dates from the Late Roman through the Byzantine Periods, well after the time of the New Testament. However, enough has been excavated to suggest that Sepphoris was a thriving city at the time of Jesus as well. Sepphoris had been made the capital of the district of Galilee by the Roman proconsul Gabinius in the early 50s BC (*Ant.* 14.91; *War* 1.170). Herod the Great incorporated the city into his kingdom in 37 BC, continuing to use it as the administrative capital of Galilee and the symbolic presence of Roman imperial might in the region. When Herod died in 4 BC, Sepphoris was attacked by the Jewish rebel Judas the Galilean (Josephus called him a "brigand-chief"; *War* 2.56) who was bent on restoring Jewish sovereignty to the region. Rome responded by destroying the city (*War* 2.68). When

---

7. Michael Avi-Yonah, "A List of Priestly Courses from Caesarea," *IEJ* 12 (1962): 137-39.

8. Zeev Weiss, "Sepphoris," *NEAEHL* 4:1324-28; 5:2029-35.

Colonnaded Street in Sepphorus

Herod Antipas succeeded his father as ruler of Galilee he rebuilt Sepphoris, making it the "ornament of all Galilee" (*Ant*. 18.27).

Much has been made of the natural association of Nazareth with Sepphoris—at four miles apart, the journey between the two would have taken less than two hours—and that in the early years of the first century AD this is the place where construction jobs could be found. Joseph the father of Jesus was a *tektōn* by trade (Matt 13:55), as quite naturally was his oldest son, Jesus (Mark 6:3). Though nearly all English translations of the Gospels render the term *tektōn* as "carpenter," a *tektōn* was a skilled worker in local building materials of all kinds, be they wood, stone, or metal.[9] In first century AD Galilee that meant someone who

was primarily a stonemason. Typically a *tektōn* was hired to build the parts of a building or house that were beyond the skill of his fellow townspeople (e.g., set the corners, align the walls so that roof would hold, build the door and the lock, etc.) and to oversee the entire construction process. This made the *tektōn* part builder, part architect, part contractor, and part artisan. Anthropological studies of pre-industrialized Palestinian towns suggest that every town, village, or group of villages had a *tektōn* to service its specialized building needs.[10] If this model is correct, Joseph and then Jesus was the *tektōn* for Nazareth. Like many similarly skilled workers from other small villages, they would have found work in neighboring towns and cities. This reasonable assumption brings Joseph and

---

9. Ken M. Campbell, "What Was Jesus' Occupation?" *JETS* 48.3 (2005): 501–19.

10. Yizhar Hirschfeld, *The Palestinian Dwelling in the Roman-Byzantine Period* (Jerusalem: Franciscan Press, 1995), 112–43.

Jesus to Sepphoris where they not only would have found gainful employment but been exposed to a cultural and ethnic world much larger than that of Nazareth. It also gives a realistic context to many of Jesus' teachings that reference structures and construction techniques known to a *tektōn* (Matt 7:24–27; 16:18; 21:33, 42; Mark 2:1–4; Luke 12:18; 14:28–30; John 14:2–3).

Another town to which Nazareth should be compared is Cana. The weight of church tradition locates Cana at Kafr Kana, a large town on the northern slope of the Nazareth Ridge facing the Beth-Netofa Valley which, like Sepphoris, was about a two-hour walk from Nazareth. This is the site that is visited by busloads of pilgrims today, with churches of various traditions remembering the wedding attended by Jesus (John 2:1–11). A more likely candidate for the Cana visited by Jesus, however, is Kh. Qana, a prominent mound on the northern edge of the Beth-Netofa Valley one-half days' walk from Nazareth. This site is difficult to access today because it is three miles off the nearest paved road. Here is archaeological evidence of a large and prosperous town from the first century AD. The remains of several *miqve'ot* (ritual immersion pools) found at the site show that it also had a large Jewish population.[11] The presence of six large stone storage jars that held the water

that Jesus turned to wine suggests that the family of the groom in Cana was likely wealthy, and that they kept Jewish ritual purity laws.[12][13]

Lying five miles from each other on opposite sides of the valley, Sepphoris and Cana seem to have been the two main cities in the Beth-Netofa Valley at the time of Jesus. Sepphoris carried a reputation gained by being the Roman administrative center of Galilee, while Cana may well have been the Jewish counterpoint: wealthy enough, though with its heart oriented toward Jerusalem. In either case, Nazareth stood apart, a small, off-road village on the periphery of the economic and cultural centers of Galilee. Nathanael's comment "Nazareth! Can anything good come from there?" (John 1:46 NIV) may have been simply natural incredulity by the native of a prosperous town (John 21:2) directed against a village that in position and promise was very much the opposite.

CONCLUSION

All available evidence suggests that the population of first century AD Nazareth was at best a few hundred people and maybe as few as one hundred. In Luke 2:39 the place is called a "city" (*polis*, πόλις), but here *polis* is used only in its most general sense as a "settled area." The lack of archaeological and textual

---

11. Peter Richardson, *Building Jewish in the Roman East* (Waco, TX: Baylor University Press, 2004), 55–71, 91–107.

12. Stone vessels of all types were related to Jewish ritual purity laws (unlike pottery, stone was considered to retain ritual purity; m. Kelim 10:1; m. Parah 3:2). As such, when found in archaeological excavations they seem to be a marker of ethnicity, indicating the presence of Jews. Stone vessels dating to the first and second centuries AD have been found at sites throughout Judea and Galilee, including Nazareth, as well as on the coastal plain. Stone vessels were more costly than their pottery counterparts; six large stone storage jars especially so. See Yitzhak Magen, *The Stone Vessel Industry in the Second Temple Period* (Jerusalem: Israel Exploration Society, 2002), 148–62.

13. See also Emily J. Thomassen, "Jesus' Ministry at Cana in Galilee" on pg. 74.

evidence for Nazareth prior to the first century AD suggests that Nazareth was not only a small village at the time of Jesus, but a relatively new one as well. It is likely that Nazareth was settled in the late second century or early first century BC, after Galilee was brought back under Jewish political control at the time of the Hasmonean kingdom. If so, this may have been part of an attempt—either government sponsored or just demographic in nature—to re-Judaize the region, an effort, in effect, to negate the term "Galilee *of the Gentiles.*" This would explain why Jews would settle in an area that was not otherwise naturally attractive for settlement, and why the men of the synagogue of Nazareth responded so negatively to Jesus' suggestion that God had a plan for Gentiles (Luke 4:24-30).

The physical setting of Nazareth also allows us to see a geographical context for two important aspects of Jesus' ministry. As seen, Nazareth's main connections lay northward, into the Beth-Netofa Valley. Jesus must have entered and crossed this valley often, if not to work at Sepphoris, to visit Cana and other places in the vicinity (one is not invited to the wedding of someone who is not already a close acquaintance or relative). On these early journeys he would have become familiar with the agricultural landscape of the Beth-Netofa Valley, as well as the day-to-day rhythm of the people of the land. Jesus' parables burst with language of the land and are a sure witness to his tight connections with the people of the agricultural villages of Galilee.

Jesus' connections to the Jezreel Valley are equally important. It was in and around the Jezreel Valley that many critical events recorded in the Old Testament, Jesus' own Bible, took place. In a great counter-clockwise sweep of sites around

the valley, Elijah defeated the prophets of Baal on Mount Carmel (1 Kgs 18:20-46); Josiah lost his life at Megiddo (2 Kgs 23:28-30); Elijah rebuked Ahab for killing Naboth and confiscating his ancestral land (1 Kgs 21:1-14); Saul and Jonathan, the king and crown prince of Israel, lost their lives at Mount Gilboa (1 Sam 31:1-13); Gideon drove back the Midianites from the spring of Harod (Judg 7:1-25); Elisha raised a boy to life at Shunem (2 Kgs 4:9-37); Saul consulted a witch at En Dor (1 Sam 28:3-25); and Deborah and Barak defeated the forces of Sisera beneath Mount Tabor (Judg 4:1-24). The exact setting or at least the general proximity of all these events can be seen from the top of the Nazareth Ridge, and it is likely that from there Jesus had ample opportunity to consider ways that the kings, prophets, and military leaders of his own past responded to the call of God back in the rough-and-tumble days of early Israel. As Jesus "grew in wisdom and stature, and in favor with God and men" (Luke 2:52 NIV) he, too, must have seized opportunities to become resolved to the call of God on his life before leaving his village to enter a world of need (see map "Old Testament Events in Jezreel Valley" on pg. 534).

BIBLIOGRAPHY

Aviam, Mordechai. "The Decorated Stone from the Synagogue at Migdal: A Holistic Interpretation and a Glimpse into the Life of Galilean Jews at the Time of Jesus." *NovT* 55 (2013): 205-20.

Avi-Yonah, Michael. "A List of Priestly Courses from Caesarea." *IEJ* 12 (1962): 137-39.

Bagatti, Bellarmino. "Nazareth: Excavations." *NEAEHL* 3:1103-5.

Campbell, Ken M. "What Was Jesus'
    Occupation?" *JETS* 48.3 (2005):
    501–19.
Cartlidge, David R., and David L.
    Dungan, eds. *Documents for the Study
    of the Gospels*. Rev. and enlarged ed.
    Minneapolis: Fortress Press, 1994.
Dark, Ken. "Has Jesus' Nazareth House
    Been Found?" *BAR* 41.2 (Mar–Apr
    2015): 54–63, 72.
Golomb, B., and Y. Kedar. "Ancient
    Agriculture in the Galilee
    Mountains." *IEJ* 21 (1971): 136–40.
Hirschfeld, Yizhar. *The Palestinian
    Dwelling in the Roman–Byzantine
    Period*. Jerusalem: Franciscan Press,
    1995.
Magen, Yitzhak. *The Stone Vessel
    Industry in the Second Temple Period*.
    Jerusalem: Israel Exploration
    Society, 2002.
Richardson, Peter. *Building Jewish in
    the Roman East*. Waco, TX: Baylor
    University Press, 2004.
Weiss, Zeev. "Sepphoris." *NEAEHL*
    4:1324–28; 5:2029–35.
Wilkinson, John. *Egeria's Travels to the
    Holy Land*. Jerusalem: Ariel, 1981.

CHAPTER 5

MINISTRY IN THE WILDERNESS

Matt 3:1-12; Luke 3:1-20

Aubrey L. Taylor

KEY POINTS

- The ministry of John the Baptist was located in the wilderness near Bethany beyond the Jordan.

- This land was rugged and empty, but it was filled with symbolism.

- The wilderness paradoxically symbolizes chaos and distance from God, as well as a place for God to create new life and order.

- In the wilderness God created a people and bound them to himself, laying a foundation for the future nation.

- John likely believed he was initiating God's return by enacting prophetic passages in a literal way within the wilderness.

SETTING THE SCENE FOR JOHN'S MINISTRY

Winding down the difficult but well-traveled eastern descent from Jerusalem to Jericho, the ancient road follows a continuous ridgeline that traces south of the Wadi Qelt as it cuts deep canyons into the soft limestone.[1] This route descends nearly four thousand feet (1219 m) in elevation over fifteen miles (twenty-four km) as it plunges into the depths of the Rift Valley. The surrounding countryside, known as the Judean Wilderness, is exceedingly inhospitable due to its rugged terrain, poor soil, and arid conditions. Lying under a rain shadow, only the sparsest of desert vegetation is possible, springs are exceedingly rare, and apart from a few hardy shepherds and their flocks, the region is incapable of sustaining life. As a result, this is an empty land, "formless and void," and few but the trav-

---

1. The biblical name of this road, Ascent of Adummim, is found in Josh 15:7, 18:17.

Judean Wilderness

elers making the necessary trek between Jerusalem and Jericho would venture out into this rugged wasteland of pale chalky hills and deep ravines.

Jerusalem itself stands at the crest of the Judean Hill Country, overlooking this local desert, but also shielded from it by the Mount of Olives range. Isolated in the hills, the unlikely capital city has few connections to the outside world, and those that do exist are critical. Though unappealing, the Jericho road represents Jerusalem's only direct route eastward.[2] And Jericho itself holds many important connections to the larger world that a capital city like Jerusalem must control for both prosperity and security. Other routes from Jericho westward connect to the Benjamin Plateau and the coastal highway beyond—the main route for international trade and traffic through the land of Israel, connecting to Egypt, Mesopotamia, and

the Phoenician ports. To the east, Jericho aligns with one of four primary Jordan River fording points and provides access up onto the Madaba Plateau and thus the King's Highway, another critical international artery, which traces north-south along the watershed of the Transjordan, connecting Arabia with Damascus. It is through here that Joshua first brought the Israelites into the land of promise, that Elijah ascended to heaven in a fiery chariot and Elisha received a double portion of his prophetic spirit, and it is here that we begin our search for not only the location of John's ministry, but also the complex meanings associated with a prophet in these unusual and desolate surroundings.

THE LOCATION OF JOHN'S MINISTRY

Geographical markers for the ministry of John the Baptist are both plentiful and

---

2. See A.D. Riddle, "The Passover Pilgrimage from Jericho to Jerusalem" on pg. 395.

vague. Matthew 3:1–6 places John in the "wilderness (erēmos, ἔρημος) of Judea" and along the Jordan River, with people coming to him from "Jerusalem and all Judea and the whole region of the Jordan." Mark 1:4 simply locates him in the "wilderness," but with a similar contingent of followers from "the whole Judean countryside and all the people of Jerusalem" coming out to him at the Jordan River. Luke 3:2–3 indicates that John may be found both in the "wilderness" and in "all the country around the Jordan." Only the Gospel of John offers precise toponyms, placing John at Bethany beyond the Jordan (Bēthania ... peran tou Iordanou; John 1:28) and at Aenon near Salim (Ainōn engys tou Saleim; John 3:23). These locations are not without difficulty, however, as their exact locations are unknown, and there are several possible candidates for both. Aenon, meaning "spring," is likely near either the Salim by ancient Shechem (associated today with the Arab village Salim, within the political district of Samaria, or at Umm el-ʿUmdan, eight miles south of Scythopolis [ancient Beth Shean]).[3] The latter lies within the Decapolis and along the Jordan Valley, in association with another significant Jordan River ford. It is this northern option that is most often preferred, fitting as it does within John's Jordan Valley scope, and

perhaps also serving to position him outside of Herod Antipas' territory at a time when John's criticism of this ruler had begun to place him in danger.

The location of Bethany beyond the Jordan has also been widely debated.[4] However, based upon the geographical details provided by the Gospel writers related to John's association with the wilderness and about the places his audience came from, it is perhaps most convincingly sought along the eastern banks of the Jordan River, just north of the Dead Sea. Near the Judean Wilderness and accessible to those coming from Jerusalem and Judea, long standing church tradition places John's ministry in proximity to the ford opposite Jericho, and both banks claim association. The "beyond Jordan" suffix strongly indicates that the eastern bank was intended, placing John in the political district of Perea.[5] The current consensus is that—though any archeological evidence has long since been erased by shifting water courses, and the precise location may never be found—Bethany beyond the Jordan is most likely located within proximity to the Hajlah ford and the mouth of Wadi el-Kharrar.[6] It is in this region that we place, if not the entirety of John's ministry, at least those most significant moments recorded in our Gospel accounts.

---

3. Carl G. Rasmussen, Zondervan Atlas of the Bible (Grand Rapids: Zondervan, 2010), 213. Scripture quotations in this paragraph and throughout this article are from the NIV.

4. Origen amended Bēthania in the original text to Bēthabara, "the place of crossing over," in an early attempt to identify the site (Origen, Commentary on John [ANF 9:370]). See also J. Carl Laney, "The Identification of Bethany Beyond the Jordan," in "Selective Geographical Problems in the Life of Christ" (ThD diss., Dallas Theological Seminary, 1977), 50–70. For an alternative view, in favor of a northerly location, see Anson F. Rainey and R. Steven Notley, The Sacred Bridge (Jerusalem: Carta, 2006), 350–51; L. J. Perkins, "Bethany Beyond the Jordan," ABD 1:703.

5. Perea (Peraia) is a shortened form of a Greek phrase which can be translated "other side [of the Jordan]."

6. Yohanan Aharoni, Michael Avi-Yonah, Anson F. Rainey, and Zeʾev Safrai, The Carta Bible Atlas, 4th ed. (Jerusalem: Carta, 2002), 169; Paul H. Wright, Greatness Grace & Glory: Carta's Atlas of Biblical Biography (Jerusalem: Carta, 2008), 153–54; Rasmussen, Atlas, 213.

REASONS FOR MINISTERING FROM THIS LOCATION

Thus we may begin to ask ourselves why? Why would John have chosen to locate his ministry here? First, there may be some very practical reasons for John's location. The Jordan River itself offers the running water necessary for ritual immersion as defined by rabbinic law. Additionally, both the location near Salim and that of our proposed Bethany lie along important east-west crossroads that would have carried significant traffic in John's day. The ford across from Jericho connected Livias, the capital of Perea, to Jerusalem, the capital of Judea. Such a location afforded any would-be prophet a ready audience, and the larger network of trade and travel would soon spread the word, attracting people from the surrounding regions. Luke 3:7 indicates that crowds had gathered to be baptized by John, including tax collectors and soldiers, and Matt 3:7 mentions religious authorities in his list—just the sort of people likely to travel an important road such as this.[7] However, likely much more significant to John's choice of location is the potent symbolism evoked by associating himself with the wilderness and, in particular, with this southernmost fording point along the Jordan River. These associations then reflexively bolster the identification of this site as the mostly likely location for his ministry.

1. Provided the right type of water for baptism

2. Provided heavy foot traffic and high exposure

3. Imbued with powerful symbolism

The wilderness has ambivalent symbolism, both in the Hebrew Bible and in the larger ancient world. Cosmological constructs often depicted the created order as a central disk of land, emerging from primordial waters, with the temple of the supreme deity at its center.[8] This land disk was surrounded by the forces of chaos, "un-created" and unlivable regions, often represented by water and desert, far from God's presence and sometimes linked with the underworld. From this, associations develop in which bodies of water and unsettled, inhospitable wilderness regions in the literal landscape become symbols for their cosmic counterparts and accrue similar connotations. They are liminal zones, unclean places, apart from the land of the living, and perhaps apart from the Creator God (see infographic "Ancient Herew Conception of the Universe" on pg. 529).[9]

Drawing on this imagery, John's position in the wilderness is then a striking statement. Likely raised to take his place among the priesthood (see Luke 1:5-13), John has left behind the accepted dwelling place of God and positioned himself

---

7. Also John 1:19 indicates that priests and Levites were sent "from Jerusalem" to see John.

8. For example, Isa 40:22, Gen 1:1-9, Job 26:10; Prov 8:27. For sources related to the ancient Near Eastern perception of the cosmos, see Othmar Keel, *The Symbolism of the Biblical World: Ancient Near Eastern Iconography and the Book of Psalms* (Winona Lake, IN: Eisenbrauns, 1997); Wayne Horowitz, "The Babylonian Map of the World," *Iraq* 50 (1988): 147-65; John H. Walton, *Ancient Near Eastern Thought and the Old Testament: Introducing the Conceptual World of the Hebrew Bible* (Grand Rapids: Baker Academic, 2006), 165-99.

9. See Josh 22:19; Lev 16:8-10, 21-22; Ps 78:19.

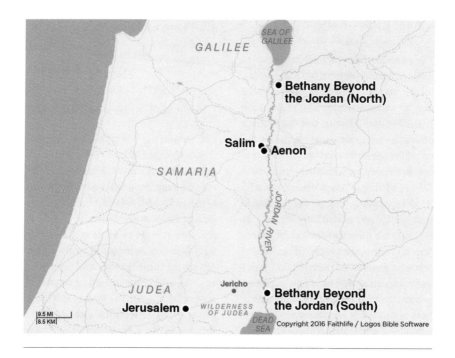

instead along the periphery. A priest and a prophet, he has forsaken his role in the temple, the very center of the created order, to take up residence in the God-forsaken wilderness. This is the world upside-down, and it delivers a subversive critique of the Jerusalem elite and the temple establishment, suggesting that YHWH can no longer be found in the center.[10] If this is an accurate interpretation of John's position vis-à-vis the temple, he was not alone. Many of his contemporaries believed the temple establishment was corrupt beyond redemption and it was time for a radical step toward renewal. John's actions suggest he may have agreed with this perspective, as he drew attention away from the routine of the temple and refo-

cused his audience on the spirit of God's law or Torah.

In line with this, John's message has an apocalyptic flavor that resonated both with the frustrated expectations of his day and with the larger prophetic canon. John's call to repentance is framed as a necessary preparation in light of a coming judgment, stating that "the kingdom of heaven has come near" (Matt 3:2). Also known as the Day of the Lord within the Hebrew Bible, it is an eschatological concept with a range of meanings. Generally, it anticipated YHWH's judgment upon his enemies and the reestablishment of Israel. He would then return and fill his temple, ruling over a restored creation. There are also passages that suggest Israel, too, will face judgment and those who have lived

---

10. Carl R. Kazmierski, *John the Baptist: Prophet and Evangelist* (Collegeville, MN: The Liturgical Press, 1996), 35.

in disobedience to God will not be part of the renewed Israel.[11]

In the first century AD, these ideas held particular potency in light of what seemed to many to be the ongoing state of exile in which they lived. The exile itself was seen as a just punishment for national sin—God's people had failed to follow Torah and had thus broken their covenant with God. Passages such as Isa 41, Mic 4:1–4, Hag 2:4–9, and Zech 8:1–15 had encouraged the returning exiles with hopeful visions of God's future forgiveness and the ascendancy of Israel. However, the expected restoration had not come; instead, Roman occupation and priestly corruption were constant indicators that Israel was still at odds with God. Speculation abounded regarding when and how God might finally act to redeem his people and fulfill his promises. Though most people were focused on Rome as the enemy, when John preached the imminent advent of YHWH, he indicated that many in Israel would also stand condemned. However, John's message was not merely one of apocalyptic doom, but ultimately one of hope and rebirth, imagery again drawn out of the wilderness in which he dwelt.

Just as the wilderness can, through its affinity with the concept of the uncreated or chaotic periphery, acquire negative associations, so too can it attain positive associations. The "formless and void" quality on the outskirts of the created order represents, not just chaos, but also the potency of pre-creation, the potential available within the, as yet, unordered. As such, the wilderness is not just a region of death, but holds hope for new life. Coupled with Israel's memory of

the exodus, it is this imagery that makes John's actions comprehensible within the larger traditions of Israel. Passages such as Jer 2:1–8, Hos 2:14–23, and Deut 32:8–14 recall Israel's formative wilderness experience following the exodus from Egypt as an ideal time in which Israel dwelt in an utterly reliant state with their God and he faithfully met their needs and dwelt in their midst. In the wilderness, YHWH created a people and bound them to himself, laying a foundation for the future nation. Though, in actuality, not a perfect time in Israel's history, it was recalled with fondness in the years leading up to the Assyrian and Babylonian invasions, as spiritual compromises had begun to take their toll on the hearts and souls of Israel's leaders. There was a sense that Israel needed to return to this simple and dependent state in an act of recreation and thus reinvigorate their faith and live their calling. The wilderness became a symbol for spiritual renewal, and in John's day, his position within the wilderness would have been a comprehensible reference to this tradition within prophetic literature.

Additionally, on the anticipated Day of the Lord, life is imagined breaking forth in the wilderness in the form of springs and vegetation as the spirit of God returns from the east to restore his people (Isa 32:15–16; 41:18–19; 43:19–20; Jer 31:2; Zech 14:4; Isa 41:2; Bar 5:5–7; Ezek 43:2–4). Isaiah 40:3–5, uniformly associated with John's ministry by the Gospel writers, states:

> A voice cries out: "In the wilderness prepare the way of the LORD, make straight in the desert a highway for our God. Every valley shall

---

11. Amos 5, esp. vv. 18–20; Ezek 7; Zeph 1:7–18; 2:1–3; Mal 3:1–4; 4:1–3; Joel 2:1–2.

be lifted up, and every mountain and hill be made low; the uneven ground shall become level, and the rough places a plain. Then the glory of the LORD shall be revealed, and all people shall see it together, for the mouth of the LORD has spoken."

In it, one can imagine the Rift Valley lifted and the hills of the Judean wilderness smoothed as the well-known road from Jericho becomes a wide, level avenue leading YHWH to Jerusalem. Employing this passage, the Gospel writers indicate they believed that John's ministry was preparing the way for YHWH's return, and John's own message indicates that he saw himself in this role. His choice to, in many ways, literally enact these passages in the landscape refers to current expectations as well as biblical tradition. The associations drawn between John and Elijah have similar intent.[12] Malachi 4:5-6 states that the prophet Elijah will be sent prior to the Day of the Lord, in order to prepare Israel before God's return and thus divert his wrath. The few examples we have of John's specific teachings indicate that he, like many prophets before him, understood this preparation required a return to God through obedience to Torah, which would manifest itself in righteous living.[13] Choosing to stage his ministry in the very wilderness from which these hopeful images emerge would have communicated the immedi-

acy and intent of his message in ways that words could not have.

JOHN'S METHOD AND MESSAGE

Uniquely, John's call appears to have been meant for everyone, even those in professions often thought irredeemable.[14] This is one way in which John critically differs from the Essenes, who maintained an exclusive community and claimed God's future redemption for themselves alone.[15] Though in many ways similar to the Essenes—both left Jerusalem for the wilderness, both are critical of the current temple establishment, and both perform unique ritual immersions—it is perhaps better to see the similarities as evidence that they shared a common spiritual heritage. Rather, given what John considered the crucial historical moment in which they dwelt, he called all Israel to consider their relationship with God and their fellow man, and to make whatever corrections were necessary in order to be found righteous in the coming day of judgment and therefore included in the redeemed Israel.

Indeed, it has been suggested that in the first century AD a renewed obedience to Torah might have been expected to initiate the return of YHWH and bring an end to exile.[16] John's call to repentance, though certainly individual in many ways, should likely still be understood in light of the larger concerns over the corporate sins that had led to the exile and the hopes for national restoration that

---

12. 2 Kgs 1:8, which is echoed in Matt 3:4 and Mark 1:6; Luke 1:16-17, 76-79.

13. Luke 3:10-14; Josephus, *Ant.* 18.117; compare Ezek 36:26, Hos 6:6, Ps 51:16-17, Isa 1:11-20; Isa 58.

14. Tax collectors, soldiers, even prostitutes (Luke 3:12, 14; Matt 21:32).

15. George W. E. Nickelsburg, "Eschatology: Early Jewish Literature," *ABD* 2:587.

16. Joan E. Taylor, *The Immerser: John the Baptist within Second Temple Judaism* (Grand Rapids: Eerdmans, 1997), 147.

were prevalent in his day.[17] Those who responded to his call were participating in a national revival intended to bring about the restoration of Israel and the advent of God. Through confession and repentance, those who underwent John's baptism stood not just for themselves, but symbolically for the whole. They hoped to both precipitate the redemption of Israel and to insure their place within it as true children of Abraham when the kingdom of heaven finally appeared.[18]

Baptism, then, was a fitting symbol that John drew upon to communicate his message. Ritual immersions had a role in most ancient religions. Within Judaism there already existed a tradition of immersion associated with ritual purity, and proselyte baptism was adopted sometime in the first century as well.[19] John's baptism seems unique in that, according to his message, immersion for purity would not be efficacious apart from evidence of true repentance. However, the act of baptism itself still likely drew upon the symbolism common to all other traditions which made use of the practice. Water, associated with the chaos from which all matter was extracted and ordered, evokes images of both death and birth, destruction and creation. Rites which utilize water are often ones marking change or transition, as the participant moves from one status to another, whether it be from impure to pure, or from initiate to community member, or, in John's case, from sinner to obedient child of God. And not only this, but the symbol of creation might

be further applied to the group of penitents as a whole. John was preparing a holy people for YHWH's return. A new, obedient Israel was being born.

It is perhaps also significant to note that prophetic action, such as preaching in a specific location or baptizing people, held complex meaning. It not only symbolically communicated an intended message, but like a visual teaching device, it was considered capable of bringing about the reality to which it referred. Thus, by enacting these prophetic passages in a literal way within the literal landscape, John, and others of his day, likely believed that they were actively initiating YHWH's return. For some, this was thrillingly momentous, so John drew a wide following, eager to participate. However, for others, an overthrow of the current system would be less desirable, so John also made enemies who feared his prophetic acts might shift the balance—and not in their favor.[20]

There were those in Israel who would be a part of this new movement of God and those who would not. According to John, those who repent and bear fruit in accordance with that repentance are the true children of Abraham. They are the Israel whom God will redeem. And what better place to call out and give birth to a renewed Israel than at the place where Israel took its first steps toward nationhood, at the border of the promised land, east of Jericho. Performing his baptism here, at the the Jordan River, John reenacts the original exodus "baptism" of

---

17. N. T. Wright, *Jesus and the Victory of God* (Minneapolis: Fortress Press, 1996), 268–74.

18. Robert L. Webb, "Jesus' Baptism: Its Historicity and Implications," *BBR* 10.2 (2000): 283–85.

19. Lars Hartman, "Baptism," *ABD* 1:583–84.

20. Herod Antipas, for one, did not appreciate John's message. The Jerusalem elite were likely not fond of him either (Matt 3:7–12; 14:3–5; Luke 3:7–9, 19–20).

Israel under Joshua in a prophetic act of creating a new people, a new Israel (compare Josh 3–5). Standing in the wilderness, John declares that the time has come for a new exodus and a new people of God, bringing them through the waters of chaos to emerge as a new creation. This new people of God—repentant, righteous, and purified—are now prepared for God to act and bring to completion his promised salvation. His message rings out boldly: "the kingdom of heaven has come near" (Matt 3:1).

Such a message was bound to create enemies, and John made a powerful one—Herod Antipas, the tetrarch of Galilee and Perea. The Gospels indicate that Antipas imprisoned John because he criticized the lawfulness of Antipas' marriage to Herodias, who was both his niece and his sister-in-law.[21] However, both in the Gospels and in Josephus' account of John's death, there is a hint that something more than moral law was at stake. Remember that, in John's eschatological scheme, inclusion in the coming kingdom of God is achieved via demonstrated righteousness. John's message of the imminent advent of YHWH in conjunction with his censure of Antipas essentially communicated a vote of no-confidence in the ruler and anticipated his downfall

in the emerging new order. So too, the righteous behavior he prescribed for soldiers, tax-collectors, and the like was an implicit condemnation of existing power structures and threatened to undermine the economy.[22] Attracting large crowds, if John were to choose to take practical action to initiate the social revolution and divine judgment he preached, Antipas would be a likely target. Indeed, Josephus recounts that Antipas saw John as a political enemy who could not be ignored, powerful enough to raise a rebellion.[23]

Better safe than sorry, Antipas had John arrested and imprisoned in Machaerus, a Herodian fortress in southern Perea, overlooking his border with Nabatea.[24] Not far from the proposed location of Bethany beyond Jordan and the only one of the several such Herodian fortresses within Antipas' territories, this site boasted of a lavish palace and quarters for political prisoners. So too, having broken faith with King Aretas of Nabatea, his former father-in-law, through insult and border dispute, Antipas had reason to expect conflict on his vulnerable southeastern frontier and may have moved to this site in preparation.[25] Therefore, it is likely here, in the fortress of Machaerus, that the infamous birthday feast took place in which Herodias claimed the

---

21. Matt 14:3–4, Mark 6:17–18; cf. Lev 18:13, 16; Lev 20:21.

22. Wright, *Greatness Grace & Glory*, 167.

23. Josephus, *Ant.* 18:118.

24. Josephus, *Ant.* 18:119. It is worth noting that Flusser regarded Josephus' identification of Machaerus as the site of John's imprisonment inaccurate. Thus, he offers the suggestion that John's beheading took place at Antipas' palace in Tiberius. Notley cites this as support for a northern location for John's ministry, including identifying Bethany beyond the Jordan with the region of Batanea (Rainey and Notley, *Sacred Bridge*, 351; citing David Flusser, *Jesus* [Jerusalem: Hebrew University Magnes Press, 2001], 278).

25. Josephus, *Ant.* 18:109–15. It is unclear which action, the border dispute or the divorce of Aretas' daughter, precipitated the conflict. Marriage and divorce of the elite were often politically motivated, and thus these two elements may be inseparable.

head of John the Baptist, perhaps as much for political expediency as spite.[26] His disciples removed his body. Although there is no textual reference to the place of John's burial, a tradition emerged in the fourth century AD placing his burial near Sebaste, another Herodian palace in Samaria, but the site has little to recommend it besides its distance from Antipas' territory.

Ironically, in their attempt to evade John's prophetic predictions, Antipas and Herodias seem to have secured their place on the losing side. Josephus tells us that Antipas' army was soon destroyed in battle by King Aretas and that the defeat was popularly attributed to God's judgment of Antipas for his treatment of John.[27] Popular support for John and criticism of Antipas did not subside with John's death. Antipas' ignominy appeared cemented while John's reputation as a prophet and his message of hope persisted unabated, regardless of his personal fate, or even his doubts.[28] Later, as Jesus' own ministry began to attract attention, it did so initially in light of John's. Contemplating what must have been an unusual answer to the questions regarding Jesus' identity, Antipas and others wondered whether Jesus might actually be John back from the dead.[29] Jesus seems only to have emerged from John's shadow

following John's death, likely indicating a strong correspondence between their two ministries. Perhaps thanks to John's own words, "he must become greater; I must become less," the stage was set for Jesus to bring to fullness the restoration of Israel for which John had so earnestly labored.[30]

BIBLIOGRAPHY

Aharoni, Yohanan, Michael Avi-Yonah, Anson F. Rainey, and Ze'ev Safrai. *The Carta Bible Atlas.* 4th ed. Jerusalem: Carta, 2002.

Flusser, David. *Jesus.* Jerusalem: Hebrew University Magnes Press, 2001.

Hartman, Lars. "Baptism." ABD 1:583–94.

Horowitz, Wayne. "The Babylonian Map of the World." *Iraq* 50 (1988): 147–65.

Kazmierski, Carl R. *John the Baptist: Prophet and Evangelist.* Collegeville, MN: The Liturgical Press, 1996.

Keel, Othmar. *The Symbolism of the Biblical World: Ancient Near Eastern Iconography and the Book of Psalms.* Winona Lake, IN: Eisenbrauns, 1997.

Laney, J. Carl. "The Identification of Bethany Beyond the Jordan." Pages 50–70 in "Selective Geographical Problems in the Life of Christ." ThD diss., Dallas Theological Seminary, 1977.

---

26. Matt 14:6–11; Mark 6:21–18. Herodias may have thought she was acting in Antipas' (and certainly her own) best interests. She is known to have played the political game as avidly as any man. Her remarriage to Herod Antipas was certainly a step up on the political food chain, and Josephus tells us that it was her machinations that ultimately led to Herod's downfall, as she attempted to force his hand to claim the title of king (*Ant.* 18:240–55). John's execution may have been a similarly intentioned move to protect their position where she saw Antipas lacking in political will.

27. Josephus, *Ant.* 18.116–20.

28. Matt 14:1–2; 16:14; 17:10–13; Mark 8:28; Luke 9:19. Regarding John's doubts, see Matt 11:2–6; Luke 7:18–23.

29. Matt 14:1–2; Mark 6:14–16; Luke 9:7–9; Matt 16:13–14; Mark 8:27–28.

30. John 3:30.

Nickelsburg, George W. E. "Eschatology: Early Jewish Literature." *ABD* 2:579–94.

Origen. *Commentary on John*. In vol. 9 of *The Ante-Nicene Fathers*. Edited by Alexander Roberts and James Donaldson. 10 vols. American ed. New York: Christian Literature Publishing, 1896–97.

Perkins, L. J. "Bethany Beyond the Jordan." *ABD* 1:703–5.

Rainey, Anson F., and R. Steven Notley. *The Sacred Bridge*. Jerusalem: Carta, 2006.

Rasmussen, Carl G. *Zondervan Atlas of the Bible*. Grand Rapids: Zondervan, 2010.

Taylor, Joan E. *The Immerser: John the Baptist within Second Temple Judaism*. Grand Rapids: Eerdmans, 1997.

Walton, John H. *Ancient Near Eastern Thought and the Old Testament: Introducing the Conceptual World of the Hebrew Bible*. Grand Rapids: Baker Academic, 2006.

Webb, Robert L. "Jesus' Baptism: Its Historicity and Implications." *BBR* 10.2 (2000): 261–309.

Wright, N. T. *Jesus and the Victory of God*. Minneapolis: Fortress Press, 1996.

Wright, Paul H. *Greatness Grace & Glory: Carta's Atlas of Biblical Biography*. Jerusalem: Carta, 2008.

CHAPTER 6

WILDERNESS EVENTS: THE BAPTISM AND TEMPTATION OF JESUS

Matt 3:13-4:11; Luke 3:21-4:15

Aubrey L. Taylor

KEY POINTS

- The rich history of the Judean wilderness where Jesus was baptized and tempted imbues these inaugural events of his ministry with powerful symbolism.

- At the waters of the Jordan, Jesus identifies himself with Israel's complicated history and hope-filled future, and rises as a figure who seeks to finally usher in the kingdom of God.

- Jesus' temptation in the wilderness echoes other key biblical figures who emerged from this barren and trying land with new purpose and identity.

Down on the banks of the Jordan River, crowds gathered as a "voice in the wilderness" invited repentant sinners to a unique baptism that would usher in the kingdom of God. Jesus, too, joined the ranks of those baptized, yet Christian tradition has understood his experience at the Jordan River in very different terms from those of his companions. Jesus' baptism by John and subsequent temptation in the wilderness mark a critical turning point in his life and serve to inaugurate his public ministry. Though interpre-tively complex, Jesus' baptism and temptation gain in richness and clarity when viewed through the lens of their physical surroundings.

THE EVENT AND SIGNIFICANCE OF JESUS' BAPTISM

Jesus' baptism is recorded explicitly in the Synoptic Gospels, while in the Gospel of John, it is referenced indirectly through the testimony of John the Baptist. This testimony takes place in Bethany beyond Jordan (John 1:28), one of two locations named in association with the Baptist's ministry.[1] John's Gospel is the only one to provide specific place names for John the Baptist's activities, but both named locations have proved difficult to identify. The Synoptics provide contextual clues that suggest Jesus' baptism and likely a significant portion of John's ministry took place near the Jordan River ford across from Jericho. Due to its association with the baptism of Jesus, Bethany beyond Jordan has been generally sought in this same vicinity. However, based on a perceived chronological puzzle within the Gospel of John, some have suggested that Bethany beyond Jordan be sought

elsewhere or perhaps disassociated from the baptism of Jesus entirely.[2] Conversely, John's unique approach to chronology can be seen as undermining a literalist reading of the timeline presented in John 1:43–2:1.[3] However, the ongoing debate over whether the location of Jesus' baptism should also be associated with Bethany beyond Jordan is beyond the scope of this article.

Rather, the site of Jesus' baptism has been generally sought on the eastern side of the Jordan River, just north of the Dead Sea, near the mouth of the Wadi el-Kharrar.[4] Here an early and reliable tradition places the events in the vicinity of

---

1. Aenon near Salim is the other location specifically named (John 3:23).

2. John 1:43 states that the day after Jesus' baptism and subsequent interactions with John and his disciples that "Jesus decided to go to Galilee." It then immediately records Jesus' calling of the disciples from the town of Bethsaida, on the shore of the Sea of Galilee. So too, John 2:1 records that "on the third day" there was a wedding in Cana, in lower Galilee, which Jesus attended. Seeing in these passages an indication that Galilee and the baptismal site must be within a day's walk, some have suggested Bethany be sought in the north of Israel. Proponents of this approach include Rainer Riesner, "Bethany Beyond the Jordan (John 1:28): Topography, Theology and History in the Fourth Gospel," *TynBul* 38 (1987): 29–63; "Bethany Beyond the Jordan," *ABD* 1:703–5; William H. Brownlee, "Whence the Gospel According to John?," in *John and Qumran*, ed. James H. Charlesworth (London: Geoffrey Chapman, 1972), 166–74; David Flusser, *Jesus* (Jerusalem: Hebrew University Magnes Press, 2001), 43; Anson F. Rainey and R. Steven Notley, *The Sacred Bridge* (Jerusalem: Carta, 2006), 350–51; Douglas S. Earl, "'(Bethany) Beyond the Jordan': The Significance of a Johannine Motif," *NTS* 55 (2009): 279–94. Hutton specifically counters Riesner's position in Jeremy M. Hutton, "'Bethany Beyond the Jordan' in Text, Tradition, and Historical Geography," *Biblica* 89 (2008): 305–28.

3. Rudolf Bultmann, *The Gospel of John: A Commentary*, trans. R. Alan Culpepper and G. R. Beasley-Murray (Eugene, OR: Wipf & Stock, 2014), 10; Raymond E. Brown, *The Gospel According to John (I–XII)* (Garden City, NY: Doubleday, 1966), xxiv–xxxiv; Charles H. H. Scobie, "Johannine Geography," *Studies in Religion* 11 (1982): 77–84; R. T. Fortna, "Theological Use of Locale in the Fourth Gospel," in *Gospel Studies in Honor of Sherman Elbridge Johnson*, ed. M. H. Shepherd and E. C. Hobbs (Evanston, IL: Anglican Theological Review, 1974), 58–95; J. Ramsey Michaels, *The Gospel of John* (Grand Rapids: Eerdmans, 2010), 139–41. This position does not require an ahistorical approach to the Gospel of John; see, for example, Paul N.Anderson, "Why This Study Is Needed, and Why It Is Needed Now," in *John, Jesus, and History, Volume 1: Critical Appraisals of Critical Views*, ed. Paul N. Anderson, Felix Just, and Tom Thatcher (Atlanta: Society of Biblical Literature, 2007), 13–74; Craig L. Blomberg, *The Historical Reliability of John's Gospel: Issues and Commentary* (Downers Grove, IL: InterVarsity Press, 2001), 77–78, 80.

4. Yohanan Aharoni, Michael Avi-Yonah, Anson F. Rainey, and Ze'ev Safrai, *The Carta Bible Atlas*, 4th ed. (Jerusalem: Carta, 2002), 169; Paul H. Wright, *Greatness Grace & Glory: Carta's Atlas of Biblical Biography* (Jerusalem: Carta, 2008), 153–54; Carl G. Rasmussen, *Zondervan*

the southernmost fording point along the Jordan River, a location that accords with the geographical referents found in Matt 3:1-6, 13; 4:1; Luke 3:3; 4:1; Mark 1:4-5, 9-12.[5] Accessible from Jerusalem and the Judean hill country (Matt 3:10; Mark 1:5), the site would have been busy with traffic in John's day. The road from Jerusalem to Jericho continues on eastward to Livias, the capital of Perea, connecting the two political districts and bringing religious leaders, soldiers, tax-collectors, and many others through this funnel along the trade network (Matt 3:7, Luke 3:7, 10-14). This location also carries symbolic associations that are clearly intended by the Gospel writers and likely by John the Baptist himself (Mark 1:2-3, 6-7; Matt 3:3-4; Luke 3:4-6; cf. Mal 3:1; 4:5-6; Is 40). John's ministry is set within the larger "wilderness" around the Jordan River and east of the Judean hills. This wilderness is where Israel took its first steps toward nationhood as the people entered the promised land under Joshua (Josh 3-5). This region was where Elijah was taken up to heaven in a fiery chariot (2 Kgs 2). Israel expected the return of YHWH following the exile to come from this direction, as promised in passages such as Ezek 43:2-4. With these rich historical associations and eschatological expectations, it is likely that John chose this location for its communicative function as well as its general accessibili-

ty.[6] Wordlessly, it tied his message to the heritage of the Jewish people and their hopes for Israel's renewal as he invited his listeners to prepare for the advent of YHWH through a baptism for the repentance of sins.

Jesus, too, participates in the baptism of John, and it marks the beginning of his public ministry. Matthew 3:13 indicates that Jesus traveled from Galilee to be baptized by John at the Jordan, perhaps participating in a mass baptism (Luke 3:21). Jesus was probably familiar with John's ministry before this time, perhaps as one of John's disciples.[7] However, the Gospels all record this moment as one which distinguishes Jesus' preeminence. Also, somewhat problematically, Christian tradition has faced a difficult question (as did, apparently, the Baptist himself; see Matt 3:14-15): Why would a sinless Jesus participate in a baptism explicitly associated with repentance? What did this baptism mean to Jesus?

Jesus' baptismal experience as recorded in the Gospels resonates with several Old Testament narratives that provide some initial insight into the significance of Jesus' baptism. Linked through location, each story recounts authority passing from mentor to disciple in the vicinity of the Jordan River across from Jericho. In Numbers 27:18-23, Moses, who had led Israel through the

---

Atlas of the Bible (Grand Rapids: Zondervan, 2010), 213; John F. McHugh, *A Critical and Exegetical Commentary on John 1-4* (London: T&T Clark, 2009), 144-47; J. Carl Laney, "The Identification of Bethany Beyond the Jordan," in "Selective Geographical Problems in the Life of Christ" (ThD diss., Dallas Theological Seminary, 1977), 50-70.

5. Though Origen is often faulted for generating this association, there is manuscript evidence that he was relying on a genuine local tradition that preceded him (Origen, *Commentary on John* [ANF 9:370]; Riesner, "Bethany Beyond the Jordan," ABD 1:704; Hutton, "Bethany Beyond the Jordan," 305-28).

6. McHugh, *John 1-4*, 124-25; Aubrey L. Taylor, "Ministry in the Wilderness" on pg. 42.

7. Daniel S. Dapaah, *The Relationship between John the Baptist and Jesus of Nazareth: A Critical Study* (Lanham, MD: University Press of America, 2005), 95.

wilderness to the borders of the promised land overlooking the southern ford of the Jordan River, laid hands on Joshua, commissioning him to bring Israel into the land. So too, in 2 Kings 2:1–15, Elijah is taken up in a chariot of fire at the Jordan River, across from Jericho, where his mantle and a double portion of his spirit then fell upon his disciple Elisha. And now Jesus receives a similar commissioning in this area, recalling important moments of transition and new beginnings in the life of Israel, under the oversight of his mentor John, thought by many to be Elijah returned from the dead. The correspondence would probably not have been lost on the original audience.

In all four Gospels, a vision accompanies Jesus' baptism. In John 1:32, it is John who sees "the Spirit come down from heaven as a dove" to remain on Jesus. In Luke, Jesus is in prayer following his baptism when he receives the vision. In both Matthew and Mark, Jesus experiences the vision as he comes up from the baptismal waters. In it, the heavens are opened and the spirit of God "like a dove" alights upon him. A voice then announces "This is my Son, whom I love; with him I am well pleased."[8]

This experience is often interpreted as Jesus' anointing prior to ministry, but it may also help clarify the meaning of the baptism itself. Within the narrative, the vision marks Jesus as the recipient of God's special favor and indicates a unique relationship between God and Jesus, but the vision also communicates acceptance of, or pleasure in, the baptismal act itself. The words spoken by the voice echo several Old Testament passages, though direct quotation is unlikely. Psalm 2:7— "You are my son; today I have become your father"—is one possible source text. Isaiah 42:1 is also a good candidate. Similar in wording, it also references the Spirit's descent:

> Here is my servant, whom I uphold,
> my chosen one in whom I delight;
> I will put my Spirit on him, and he
> will bring justice to the nations.

These passages both have messianic overtones, and on that basis, Christian tradition has interpreted the vision as a sort of messianic announcement. However, since neither of these passages is precisely quoted, the answer may lie with other examples in Scripture where an individual is set apart as especially beloved of God.[9] The Greek word agapētos (ἀγαπητός), often translated into English as "beloved," may be used to render several Hebrew words, one of which is associated with Daniel.

The book of Daniel was very popular in the Second Temple period, and Jesus himself frequently identifies himself using the phrase "Son of Man" found in Dan 7:13.[10] Apocalyptic in genre and set in

---

8. Matt 3:16–17: compare Mark 1:10–11 and Luke 3:22. Scripture quotations in this article are from the NIV. In Matthew's Gospel, this announcement appears to be public. However, both Mark and Luke record it in such a way as to suggest a more private experience.

9. Joan E. Taylor, *The Immerser: John the Baptist within Second Temple Judaism* (Grand Rapids: Eerdmans, 1997), 268–72.

10. Peter W. Flint, "The Daniel Tradition at Qumran," in *The Book of Daniel: Composition and Reception*, ed. John J. Collins and Peter W. Flint (Leiden: Brill, 2002), 329, 363–65; Daewoong Kim, "The Use of Daniel in the Gabriel Revelation," in *Hazon Gabriel: New Readings of the Gabriel Revelation*, ed. Matthias Henze (Atlanta: Society of Biblical Literature, 2011), 153.

Babylon, it addresses concerns regarding the restoration of Israel following the national tragedy of exile. In Daniel 9, Daniel is interceding on behalf of his people by means of corporate confession: "[I] was praying and confessing my sin and the sin of my people Israel and making my request to the LORD my God for his holy hill" (Dan 9:20) when the angel Gabriel appeared to him. Gabriel tells Daniel that he is *hamudoth*, beloved of God, and as a result, his prayers were received, and he is granted a vision (Dan 9:23). So, too, Jesus is called beloved of God and granted a vision. Is it possible that in his baptism, he was also making corporate confession and interceding on behalf of his nation?

There are two items of context that support this conclusion. In Israelite thought, a king is thought to act the part of representing the nation as a whole before God or other nations, offering petitions or even making atonement on its behalf.[11] Throughout the Gospels, there is an indication that Jesus saw his calling in light of this concept.[12] Additionally, in Jesus' day, a discussion of sins likely referenced, at least in part, the corporate sins that led to Israel's exile.[13] According to the prophets, Israel had failed to

remain faithful to the covenant they made with YHWH at Sinai, and as a result, YHWH had allowed Babylon to overrun his people. However, the prophets also taught that in the future, YHWH would forgive Israel and restore them, rescuing them from their enemies and coming again to dwell in their midst.[14] Daniel's own corporate confession is in reference to this theological tradition.[15] The fact that conditions had not improved for the Jewish people in subsequent years indicated to many that Israel's guilt remained and God's forgiveness was still withheld. They were, in essence, still in exile and alienated from their God.[16] John's own ministry was likely focused on this issue, as he called forth a new, repentant Israel, seeking God's forgiveness, not just for themselves but for the nation, in order to initiate the return of YHWH and the end of exile.[17]

Therefore, when Jesus is baptized under John, it is perhaps best understood in light of his role as a "representative of Israel." Passing through the waters of the Jordan, in harmony with his ancestors and the hopeful pilgrims of his own day, he participates in the same symbolic act that characterized John's ministry. Jesus identifies himself with corporate Israel,

---

11. Keith W. Whitelam, "King and Kingship," *ABD* 4:40; Henri Cazelles, "Sacral Kingship," *ABD* 5:865.

12. For example, the symbol of the vine in John 15:1–5; compare Ps 80:8–19; Isa 5:1–10. The well-known title "Son of God" should be understood first as a reference to Israel and then as a reference to Jesus as a representative of Israel (Exod 4:22–23; Jer 31:9; Wis 18:13; Matt 2:15; Mark 1:1; Luke 1:35); see N. T. Wright, "Jesus, Israel and the Cross," in *SBL 1985 Seminar Papers*, ed. K. H. Richards (Chico, CA: Scholars Press, 1985), 83–84; Jeannine K. Brown, "Matthew, Gospel of," *DJG* 580–81.

13. For example, Deut 28:58–68; 29:10–30:10; Jer 11:6–11; 22:8–9; Zech 7:8–14.

14. For example, Hos 2:14–23; Mic 4:1–4; Zeph 3:14–20; Zech 8:1–8.

15. Dan 9:1–19.

16. N. T. Wright, *Jesus and the Victory of God* (Minneapolis: Fortress Press, 1996), 268–74. Lam 5:19–22 is a poignant expression of this sense of abandonment.

17. For further discussion, see Taylor, "Ministry in the Wilderness" on pg. 42.

its calling, its failings, and its hope—and participates in a movement that sought to usher in the kingdom of God. Like Daniel, his confession of sins, which necessarily accompanied baptism under John, was likely in the tradition of corporate guilt and confession, as he represented his people before God.[18] And God responds favorably due to the beloved status of the one petitioning. In those words, Jesus' identity and role are confirmed and so, too, the hopeful expectations of many in Israel.[19]

THE EVENT AND SIGNIFICANCE OF JESUS' TEMPTATION

Jesus' temptation, too, can in many ways be seen in light of this representative role. Following his baptism and vision, Matthew records that Jesus was "led by the Spirit into the wilderness to be tempted by the devil" (Matt 4:1; compare Luke 4:1-2).[20] The Greek word *erēmos* (ἔρημος) in this context is almost certainly referring to the Judean Wilderness, as it does in Matt 3:1 in reference to John's ministry; and its proximity to the baptismal site makes this identification quite clear. Imbued with historical and cosmological associations in Israelite thought, this setting plays an important role within the narrative.

Lying east of the watershed of the Judean hills, under the rain shadow, only sparse desert vegetation grows. The rare spring trickling out at the base of a steep ravine provides the only source of water. A stark and awe-inspiring place, the seemingly endless undulating chalk hills overwhelm the viewer with both strange beauty and hostility as they tumble precipitously eastward into the Rift Valley. Were it not for the Jericho road, Jerusalem's only direct eastern access, few would venture here. In summer, the pale hills glare under a cloudless sky and even shepherds find the region inhospitable. Reminiscent of Deuteronomy 32:6, it is "a land that no one passes through, where no one lives." This region became a local repository for Israelite memories of their formative years prior to entering the promised land as well as a rich cultural reservoir of creation imagery associated with unlivable regions such as this.

Similar to water, the unformed and unlivable nature of the wilderness may evoke ideas of chaos and thus pre-creation.[21] It is unordered matter, unsuitable for life, perhaps even opposed to it. As such, wilderness regions are conceivably godforsaken and, sometimes, associated with the underworld or evil spirits.[22] However, that same chaos also represents potential. As exhibited in Genesis 1, it awaits only the Creator's word to give it a name, form, and purpose.

This same creative potential is then symbolically present for those who pass through the wilderness. Throughout the Bible, there are numerous instances in which a figure is tested and honed in diffi-

---

18. See also Ezra 9-10.

19. Luke 1:46-55, 67-79; 2:25-38.

20. Deut 8:2 also sees YHWH as the active agent, initiating the testing.

21. See Gen 1:2; Isa 21:1; N. Wyatt, "Sea and Desert: Symbolic Geography in West Semitic Religious Thought," *UF* 19 (1987): 375-89.

22. For example, Isa 13:21; 34:14. Othmar Keel, *The Symbolism of the Biblical World: Ancient Near Eastern Iconography and the Book of Psalms* (Winona Lake, IN: Eisenbrauns, 1997), 76-77, 83; G. J. Riley, "Demon," *DDD* 236.

cult circumstances, often literally in the wilderness, before returning to his community with renewed power and purpose to do God's work. Moses' wilderness exile preceded his calling and ministry. Israel was set apart through the covenant at Mount Sinai, yet subsequently led through the wilderness in preparation for nationhood. David, anointed king in his youth, endured a protracted time hiding from Saul in the wilderness before taking the throne. Finally, John the Baptist, like Elijah before him, became a renowned prophet of God in the wilderness itself, both ministries expanding exponentially from that unlikely beginning. All these figures draw life from seeming death, power from obscurity, and emerge with a newfound strength and clarity of purpose, prepared for their new, public role.

Jesus also participates in this rich heritage. Following his baptism, he enters into the wilderness, mirroring the experiences of Israel and the great leaders that went before him prior to launching his public ministry. Reference to Israel's own wilderness sojourn in Sinai and southern Transjordan is explicit throughout. The setting elicits correspondence, as does the forty day period of fasting, the nature of the temptations themselves, and the Scriptures quoted.[23] In each case, Jesus,

as the newly recognized "son of God" and representative of Israel, faces the same struggles that Israel faced in the wilderness, but this time "Israel" triumphs.[24]

Jesus' temptation is recounted through three interactions with a spiritual foe.[25] Associated with evil spirits, the wilderness is a fitting setting for this encounter, and the first temptation, to change stones to bread, takes place on site. The two subsequent incidents are located elsewhere, perhaps through a visionary experience.[26] In Matthew's Gospel, the next temptation takes place at the pinnacle of the temple. Here, the Tempter suggests that Jesus throw himself down, perhaps as a means of announcing himself and his new name, "son of God," to the people through a spectacular display.[27] Likely envisioning a specific location, we must consider first-century Jerusalem's layout and architecture to pinpoint the site. In Jesus' day, the Temple Mount was walled in with a great retaining wall to create a level platform surrounding the temple as part of Herod the Great's enlargement of the Jewish holy precinct. The southeastern corner of this retaining wall towers over a precipitous drop into the Kidron Valley, so many have connected this location with the "pinnacle" mentioned in the temptations.[28] However, the southwestern side, though less dra-

---

23. Num 14:33–34; Exod 34:28. The temptations themselves reference Exodus 16, 17, 32. Jesus' answers are taken from Deut 8:3; 6:13; 6:16.

24. R. T. France, *The Gospel of Matthew* (Grand Rapids: Eerdmans, 2007), 126.

25. Each Gospel account uses a different name for this figure. In Matthew, he is "the tempter" (*ho peirazōn*); in Mark, "the Satan" (*ho Satan*); in Luke, "the devil" (*ho diabolos*). See Raymond F. Collins, "Temptation of Jesus," *ABD* 6:382.

26. Not unlike Daniel, fasting precedes a vision. Donald A. Hagner, *Matthew 1–13* (Dallas: Word Books, 1993), 63; Ben Witherington III, *Matthew* (Macon, GA: Smyth & Helwys, 2006), 90.

27. Witherington, *Matthew*, 90–93.

28. Witherington, *Matthew*, 94; Hagner, *Matthew 1–13*, 66; France, *The Gospel of Matthew*, 132.

Southwest Corner of the Temple Mount

matic, had a unique function that better fits the proposed purpose of this temptation. Known to us from Josephus as the "place of the trumpeting," this spot was used to announce Jewish holy days.[29] Temple personnel would, upon observing the appropriate celestial signs, blow a shofar to announce to the community the beginning of Shabbat or other festivals. Because first-century residential Jerusalem was settled on the hills south and west of the Temple Mount (and not on the east), this was the most logical location from which to make announcements. Archeologically, within the rubble of the Roman destruction of Jerusalem (AD 70), a stone was found

fallen from near the southwest corner of the Temple Mount with a fragmentary inscription "to the place of the trumpeting to …" It was beautifully carved to sit as a corner piece atop the Temple Mount retaining wall with space for a man to stand and look out over the city.[30] The function of this stone and its location overlooking Jerusalem makes it a more probable site for the temptation as an attempt to elicit a miraculous sign from God.

Finally, in Matthew's account, Jesus is led to a very high mountain so that he could see "all the kingdoms of the world (Matt 4:8)." Impossible in reality, any attempt to connect this to a literal loca-

---

29. Josephus, *War* 4.580–83.

30. Benjamin Mazar, "Hebrew Inscription from the Temple Area in Jerusalem," *Qadmoniot* 12.4 (1970): 142–44; Aaron Demsky, "When the Priests Trumpeted the Onset of the Sabbath: A Monumental Hebrew Inscription from the Ancient Temple Mount Recalls the Sacred Signal," *BAR* 12.6 (1986): 50–52.

Trumpeting Stone

tion is unhelpful.[31] Rather, mountains often have a symbolic function in a literary context, and Matthew's Gospel regularly presents significant moments in Jesus' ministry on mountain tops (Matt 5:1; 17:1; 28:16). In the ancient Near East, mountains were potent symbols of the divine, and in the Hebrew Bible they carried royal and eschatological significance. Delivered from the mountain top, the Tempter's invitation to world domination in exchange for idolatrous worship has an air of power and authority, and it marks the climax of our story. Undoubtedly an allusion to Israel's disastrous fall into idolatry in the wilderness (Exod 32-33), the temptation to worship other gods continued to plague Israel throughout its history, and eventually led to the exile. The mountaintop setting may have also alluded to eschatological expectations such as those found in Mic 4:1–4 that spoke of the longed-for restoration of Israel and envisioned a day to come in which Mount Zion "shall be established as the highest of the mountains, and shall be raised up above the hills." In this day, the nations—no longer oppressors—will come to worship YHWH and all will live in peace.[32] If intentional, this temptation appears to offer Jesus a means by which to accomplish this goal. However, Jesus

31. Similar to Moses' own mountaintop view in Deut 34:1–4, which is also literally impossible. Hagner, *Matthew 1–13*, 68.

32. Other examples include Isa 2:1:4; 25:6–9; Zech 2:11; 9:10; 14:8–11; Pss 2:8; 72:8–9; Dan 7:13–14; Rev 21:10. This correspondence is also noted by France, *The Gospel of Matthew*, 134–35.

responds as the faithful Israelite. He rejects the Tempter's alternative path to meet Israel's needs and accomplish YHWH's goals, in turn, preparing himself for the greater temptation still to come in Gethsemane.

Through all these trials, Jesus' faithfulness is revealed and his identity confirmed, and when he emerges, he does so filled with the power of the Holy Spirit (Luke 4:14). So too, in this encounter, something about the true nature of the wilderness is revealed. Far from godforsaken, the Creator God is present and active. Rather than a region of chaos and death, it is a place of creative renewal, brimming with anticipation. For those who pass through it, the hope of new life lies just below the surface, calling to mind Isa 41:18–20:

> I will make rivers flow on barren heights, and springs within the valleys. I will turn the desert into pools of water, and the parched ground into springs ... so that people may see and know, may consider and understand, that the hand of the LORD has done this, the Holy One of Israel has created it.

One of the great biblical symbols, the wilderness requires dependence on God, refines and forms God's people for their intended purpose, and ultimately reveals God's glory. Jesus too takes part in this imagery and emerges with his calling clarified and his dependence on God tried and tested. He is now prepared to bear his new name, Son of God, and to begin his public ministry.

BIBLIOGRAPHY

Aharoni, Yohanan, Michael Avi-Yonah, Anson F. Rainey, and Ze'ev Safrai. *The Carta Bible Atlas*. 4th ed. Jerusalem: Carta, 2002.

Anderson, Paul N. "Why This Study Is Needed, and Why It Is Needed Now." Pages 13–74 in *John, Jesus, and History, Volume 1: Critical Appraisals of Critical Views*. Edited by Paul N. Anderson, Felix Just, and Tom Thatcher. Atlanta: Society of Biblical Literature, 2007.

Blomberg, Craig L. *The Historical Reliability of John's Gospel: Issues and Commentary*. Downers Grove, IL: InterVarsity Press, 2001.

Brown, Jeannine K. "Matthew, Gospel of." *DJG* 570–84.

Brown, Raymond E. *The Gospel According to John (I–XII)*. AB 29. Garden City, NY: Doubleday, 1966.

Brownlee, William H. "Whence the Gospel According to John?" Pages 166–94 in *John and Qumran*. Edited by James H. Charlesworth. London: Geoffrey Chapman, 1972.

Bultmann, Rudolf. *The Gospel of John: A Commentary*. Translated by R. Alan Culpepper and G. R. Beasley-Murray. The Johannine Monograph Series. Edited by Paul N. Anderson. Eugene, OR: Wipf & Stock, 2014.

Cazelles, Henri. "Sacral Kingship." *ABD* 5:863–66.

Collins, Raymond F. "Temptation of Jesus." *ABD* 6:382–83.

Conder, C. R., and H. H. Kitchener. *The Survey of Western Palestine*. 3 vols. London: The Committee of the Palestine Exploration Fund, 1881–83.

Conder, C.R. "Bethany Beyond Jordan." *PEQ* 9 (1877): 184–86.

Dapaah, Daniel S. *The Relationship between John the Baptist and Jesus of Nazareth: A Critical Study*. Lanham, MD: University Press of America, 2005.

Demsky, Aaron. "When the Priests Trumpeted the Onset of the Sabbath: A Monumental Hebrew Inscription from the Ancient Temple Mount Recalls the Sacred Signal." *BAR* 12.6 (November/December 1986): 50–52.

Earl, Douglas S. "'(Bethany) Beyond the Jordan': The Significance of a Johannine Motif." *NTS* 55 (2009): 279–94.

Flint, Peter W. "The Daniel Tradition at Qumran." Pages 329–67 in *The Book of Daniel: Composition and Reception*. Edited by John J. Collins and Peter W. Flint. Leiden: Brill, 2002.

Flusser, David. *Jesus*. Jerusalem: Hebrew University Magnes Press, 2001.

Fortna, R. T. "Theological Use of Locale in the Fourth Gospel." Pages 58–94 in *Gospel Studies in Honor of Sherman Elbridge Johnson*. Edited by M. H. Shepherd and E. C. Hobbs. Evanston, IL: Anglican Theological Review, 1974.

France, R. T. *The Gospel of Matthew*. NICNT. Grand Rapids: Eerdmans, 2007.

Hagner, Donald A. *Matthew 1–13*. WBC 33a. Dallas: Word Books, 1993.

Hutton, Jeremy M. "'Bethany Beyond the Jordan' in Text, Tradition, and Historical Geography." *Biblica* 89 (2008): 305–28.

Keel, Othmar. *The Symbolism of the Biblical World: Ancient Near Eastern Iconography and the Book of Psalms*. Winona Lake, IN: Eisenbrauns, 1997.

Kim, Daewoong. "The Use of Daniel in the Gabriel Revelation." Pages 153–72 in *Hazon Gabriel: New Readings of the Gabriel Revelation*. Edited by Matthias Henze. Atlanta: Society of Biblical Literature, 2011.

Laney, J. Carl. "The Identification of Bethany Beyond the Jordan." Pages 50–70 in "Selective Geographical Problems in the Life of Christ." ThD diss., Dallas Theological Seminary, 1977.

Mazar, Benjamin. "Hebrew Inscription from the Temple Area in Jerusalem." *Qadmoniot* 12.4 (1970): 142–44.

McHugh, John F. *A Critical and Exegetical Commentary on John 1–4*. ICC. London: T&T Clark, 2009.

Michaels, J. Ramsey. *The Gospel of John*. NICNT. Grand Rapids: Eerdmans, 2010.

Origen. *Commentary on John*. In vol. 9 of *The Ante-Nicene Fathers*. Edited by Alexander Roberts and James Donaldson. 10 vols. American ed. New York: Christian Literature Publishing, 1896–97.

Rainey, Anson F., and R. Steven Notley. *The Sacred Bridge*. Jerusalem: Carta, 2006.

Rasmussen, Carl G. *Zondervan Atlas of the Bible*. Rev. ed. Grand Rapids: Zondervan, 2010.

Riesner, Rainer. "Bethany Beyond the Jordan." *ABD* 1:703–5.

———. "Bethany Beyond the Jordan (John 1:28): Topography, Theology and History in the Fourth Gospel." *TynBul* 38 (1987): 29–63.

Riley, G. J. "Demon." *DDD* 235–40.

Scobie, Charles H. H. "Johannine Geography." *Studies in Religion* 11 (1982): 77–84.

Taylor, Joan E. *The Immerser: John the Baptist within Second Temple Judaism*. Grand Rapids: Eerdmans, 1997.

Whitelam, Keith W. "King and Kingship." *ABD* 4:40–48.

Witherington, Ben, III. *Matthew*. SHBC. Macon, GA: Smyth & Helwys, 2006.

Wright, N. T. *Jesus and the Victory of God*. Minneapolis: Fortress Press, 1996.

———. "Jesus, Israel and the Cross."
    Pages 75–95 in *SBL 1985 Seminar*
    Papers. Edited by K. H. Richards.
    Chico, CA: Scholars Press, 1985.
Wright, Paul H. *Greatness Grace & Glory:*
    Carta's Atlas of Biblical Biography.
    Jerusalem: Carta, 2008.
Wyatt, N. "Sea and Desert: Symbolic
    Geography in West Semitic Religious
    Thought." *UF* 19 (1987): 375–89.

CHAPTER 7

LOCATING THE BAPTISM OF JESUS

John 1:19-2:1

Benjamin A. Foreman

KEY POINTS

- It is possible that Jesus was not baptized at Bethany beyond the Jordan because John the Baptist was active at different venues throughout his ministry.

- Bethany beyond the Jordan is only mentioned once in the entire New Testament, making it understandably more difficult to locate.

- Two sites along the Jordan River—one north and one south—have gained the most attention; however, the northern option makes more sense when geographical constraints on travel are considered.

Some of the best-known stories from Jesus' life are found only in the Gospel of John. John 1:19-2:1 is one such example. Were it not for this chapter we would have no record of Jesus' early presence at Bethany beyond the Jordan, nor of the defining events that took place there. It was here that John the Baptist declared Jesus to be "the Lamb of God, who takes away the sin of the world" (John 1:29 ESV; compare Isa 53:4-7). According to the Gospel record, this was the first time Jesus was presented as the sacrifice that would achieve the long-awaited salvation.[1] Jesus also chose three of his initial followers there (John 1:35-42), two of whom would later become pillars in the early church.[2] Thanks to this

---

1. The original intention of this significant statement has been fiercely debated. But as Carson rightly notes, "As a writer who holds that all (Old Testament) scripture points to Jesus (5:39-40), John might well see adequate warrant for the application of this title to Jesus, sacrificially understood, in the lamb of Isaiah 53:7, 10" (D.A. Carson, *The Gospel According to John* [Grand Rapids: Eerdmans, 1991], 150).

2. Andrew and Peter are explicitly named in John 1:35-42. The third, unnamed disciple (John 1:35, 40) was probably John, as many commentators recognize (e.g., Leon Morris, *The Gospel According to John*, rev. ed. [Grand Rapids: Eerdmans, 1995], 136).

passage we also know that after a short stay at Bethany beyond the Jordan, Jesus travelled to Cana of Galilee for a wedding (1:43–2:1) where he performed the first miracle of his public career (2:2–11), calling two more disciples—Philip and Nathanael (1:43–51)—along the way.

While this passage is familiar to many, its chronological and geographical details have generated much discussion. What is the relationship between John 1 and the account of Jesus' baptism in the Synoptics? And is there anything in the text suggesting where Bethany beyond the Jordan is? These two questions are the subject of our discussion below.

THE TIMING OF THE EVENTS IN JOHN 1:19–2:1

Because of similarities with the Synoptics,[3] many believe John 1:19–34 is a parallel account of Jesus' baptism.[4] Those who attempt to harmonize the Synoptics with John 1 usually place Jesus' baptism somewhere between John 1:25–29.[5] However, the chronology of Jesus' move-

ments in John 1 makes this implausible. In John 1 Jesus travels to Galilee two days after his encounter with John (John 1:35, 43), and then to a wedding in Cana two days later (John 2:1; see list below). In the Synoptics, Jesus is "immediately" (Mark 1:12) led into the wilderness after his baptism to be tempted by the devil for forty days (Matt 4:2; Mark 1:13; Luke 4:2).

A common way to account for these chronological variances is to maintain John 1 has been structured thematically. The time sequence, it is argued, should be interpreted symbolically rather than chronologically.[6] Clearly some of John's Gospel is organized thematically.[7] But what common idea binds all of John 1:19–2:11 together? And even if a topical thread is detected, why would the author repeatedly emphasize that each of the events in John 1 occurred on chronologically sequential days? A thematic presentation of the events could have been achieved without these chronological notices.[8] On the contrary, time is demonstrably important in the Gospel

---

3. Compare Matt 3:1–12; Mark 1:2–8; Luke 3:3–22; and John 1:19–34.

4. Anson Rainey and Steven Notley, *The Sacred Bridge* (Jerusalem: Carta, 2006), 350: "At points the evangelist parallels the Synoptic Gospels, and at other points he presents independent traditions." See also Yohanan Aharoni, Michael Avi-Yonah, Anson F. Rainey, and Ze'ev Safrai, *The Carta Bible Atlas*, 4th ed. (Jerusalem: Carta, 2002), 169; Barry J. Beitzel, *The New Moody Atlas of the Bible* (Chicago: Moody, 2009), 240; Raymond E. Brown, *The Gospel According to John (i–xii)* (New York: Doubleday, 1966), 45; C. K. Barrett, *The Gospel According to St. John* (London: SPCK, 1960), 142.

5. Carson, *John*, 148; Barrett, *John*, 146; Rainey and Notley, *Sacred Bridge*, 350.

6. E.g., Brown, *John*, 45.

7. See, for example, Jesus' use of the sheep metaphor in John 10:11 and 10:27, or his statement "I am the light of the world" in John 8:12 and 9:5.

8. A number of interpreters (e.g., Carson, *John*, 167–68) believe seven (not six) days should be detected in 1:19–2:1. Since Andrew and the unnamed disciple first met Jesus at 4:00 PM and then spent the rest of the day with him (John 1:39), they argue Andrew introduced Peter to Jesus (John 1:40–42) on the *next* day. Having an extra day for John 1:40–42, therefore, yields seven days when the "third day" (John 2:1) is calculated by inclusive reckoning. A seven-day sequence of events is theologically significant and echoes (in their view) the creation week. But this interpretation is unlikely. If the author wished to draw parallels to the seven days of creation why would he omit a day in his sequence of events?

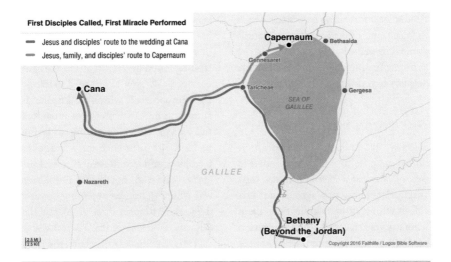

First Disciples Called, First Miracle Performed

— Jesus and disciples' route to the wedding at Cana
— Jesus, family, and disciples' route to Capernaum

of John. Jesus' activities on particular days are frequently emphasized (John 4:40, 43; 6:22; 7:37; 11:6, 17, 39; 12:1, 12; 19:14, 31, 42; 20:1, 19, 26). Throughout the Gospel, John uniquely highlights the time of year by mentioning five festivals by name (three Passovers [John 2:13; 6:4–5; 11:55–56], the Feast of Booths [John 7:2], and Hanukkah [John 10:22]), and he occasionally even records details about the hour of the day (John 1:39; 4:6, 52; 19:14).[9] On this basis, John 1 is best understood sequentially.[10] Since Jesus

travelled to Cana of Galilee a few days after his encounter with John the Baptist at Bethany beyond the Jordan, all of John 1:19–2:1 must have happened *after* Jesus' baptism and forty-day temptation.[11]

If this is the case, then Jesus may not have been baptized at Bethany beyond the Jordan. Because we know John the Baptist was active at different venues throughout his ministry (Matt 3:1; John 3:23), it is possible Jesus was baptized elsewhere (the Synoptics do not name the baptismal site).[12] This is a crucial point. If Jesus was bap-

---

9. Another unnamed feast is mentioned in John 5:1.

10. See also Beitzel, *New Moody Atlas*, 240.

11. There are two similarities between John 1:19–28 and the Synoptics. In both accounts (1) reference is made to Isa 40:3–5, and (2) John the Baptist denies he is the messiah and confesses he is unworthy to even untie his sandals (Luke 3:15–16; John 1:20, 25). These correspondences, however, are not strong enough to imply they relate to the same event. First, in John 1:23 the Baptist himself cites Isa 40:3–5 in response to a question; in the Synoptics the narrator quotes the passage to introduce John the Baptist. Second, it is not unlikely that John would give the same answer to a question on two separate occasions. Jesus frequently repeated himself (e.g., Matt 12:39; 16:4), and there is no reason to think John the Baptist would not have as well. (The baptism of the Holy Spirit is also referenced in all four accounts, but in John it occurs in John 1:33, which clearly relates to a time after Jesus' baptism.)

12. Since the focus of this article is on Jesus' movement from Bethany beyond the Jordan to Cana of Galilee, the location of Jesus' baptism will not be pursued here. The question is addressed directly in Aubrey Taylor's article on pg. 42 ("Ministry in the Wilderness").

tized at least forty days before the events in John 1, then the geographical details gleaned from the baptism account in the Synoptics cannot be used to help locate Bethany beyond the Jordan.[13]

THE LOCATION OF BETHANY BEYOND THE JORDAN

Bethany beyond the Jordan is only mentioned once (John 1:28) and alluded to twice (John 3:26 and 10:40) in the New Testament. These passages do not provide us with very many indications about where it was situated, and its location has been uncertain since the late Roman Period. In any case, two suggestions have the most merit.[14]

WADI EL-KHARRAR

Many scholars locate the site five miles north of the Dead Sea at the intersection of Wadi el-Kharrar with the Jordan River (just across from Jericho).[15] The strongest argument for this identification is tradition—which can be traced back at least as far as Origen (ca. AD 184–253). In his commentary on the Gospel of John, he argues that although Bethany is the reading found in "almost all" of the manuscripts, "We should not read 'Bethany' but 'Bethabara,'" which he implies is across from Jericho on the east bank of the Jordan River.[16] His interpretation had a major influence on subsequent tradition and scholarship.[17] Eusebius (ca. AD 260–340) noted that Bethabara was where "John was baptizing, beyond the Jordan" (*Onomasticon* 58:19), and the Pilgrim of Bordeaux (ca. AD 333) wrote that it is five Roman miles from the Dead Sea to the place "where the Lord was baptized by John."[18] The Medaba mosaic map (ca. AD 560) positions Bethany beyond the Jordan at Bethabara, but on the western bank of the Jordan.[19] Later tradition situated Bethabara more specifically near the mouth of Wadi el-Kharrar, and over time churches were built on both banks of the Jordan River to commemorate Jesus' baptism.[20]

---

13. It is frequently noted, for example, that Bethany beyond the Jordan must be close to Jerusalem because according to Mark "all the country of Judea and Jerusalem" were going out to be baptized by John (Mark 1:5).

14. At least eight identifications have been proposed by scholars but only the two main candidates are discussed below. Critical evaluations of the other suggestions can be found in Rainer Riesner, "Bethany Beyond the Jordan (John 1:28): Topography, Theology and History in the Fourth Gospel" *TynBul* 38 (1987): 34–43; J. Carl Laney, "Selective Geographical Problems in the Life of Christ" (ThD diss., Dallas Theological Seminary, 1977), 50–63.

15. For example, Laney, "Geographical Problems," 63–69; Jeremy M. Hutton, "'Bethany Beyond the Jordan' in Text, Tradition, and Historical Geography," *Biblica* 89 (2008): 305–28; John McHugh, *A Critical and Exegetical Commentary on John 1–4* (London: T & T Clark, 2009), 144–47.

16. Origen, "Commentary on the Gospel of John," *ANF* 9:370.

17. "Bethabara" is found in the KJV and NKJV.

18. The Pilgrim of Bordeaux, *Itinerary from Bordeaux to Jerusalem*, trans. Aubrey Stewart, ed. Charles W. Wilson (London: Palestine Pilgrims' Text Society, 1887), 26.

19. See Michael Avi-Yonah, *The Madaba Mosaic Map: With Introduction and Commentary* (Jerusalem: Israel Exploration Society, 1954), 35.

20. For a more in-depth overview of the tradition, see Rami Khouri, "Where John Baptized: Bethany Beyond the Jordan," *BAR* 31.1 (Jan/Feb 2005): 34–43; Laney, "Geographical Problems," 67–69.

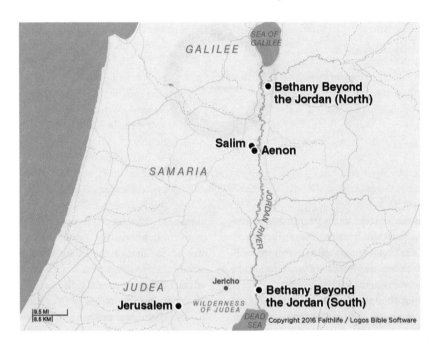

Bethany beyond the Jordan (north and south)

In support of this lengthy tradition, some point to the description of John the Baptist's overall ministry: he is the voice of one crying in the wilderness.[21] A location across from Jericho, therefore, is thought to be a good fit since the area is on the fringe of the Judean Wilderness. The Baptist's close association with Elijah is also referenced in support of this vicinity since early tradition connected the region to Elijah.[22] Some believe John the Baptist purposefully chose the area to highlight this connection.[23]

Furthermore, Josephus specifies Antipas imprisoned John the Baptist in Machaerus (*Ant.* 18.116–19). Because of this some scholars deduce the Baptizer was active primarily in Perea, so they conclude it would be natural for him to begin his ministry in the area of Wadi el-Kharrar, which is in Perea.[24] It is also pointed out that Wadi el-Kharrar is near one of the fords of the Jordan River, and since "Bethany" may mean "house of the boat," some argue the village was located near a ford.[25] Finally, recent

---

21. Clearly the geography of at least part of John's ministry is theologically significant since his quotation of Isa 40:3–5 would have fallen flat in Jerusalem.

22. The Pilgrim of Bordeaux located a hill in the area as the place where Elijah ascended into heaven (*Itinerary*, 26), and the Pilgrim from Piacenza (ca. AD 570) identified Wadi el-Kharrar as the brook Cherith (*Itinerarium* 9).

23. E.g., Mc Hugh, *John 1–4*, 124–25.

24. Laney, "Geographical Problems," 64–65.

25. Laney, "Geographical Problems," 66.

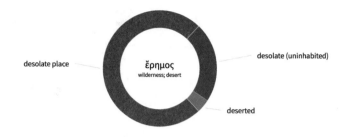

desolate place — ἔρημος wilderness; desert — desolate (uninhabited)

deserted

Bible Word Study: ἔρημος, erēmos

archaeological excavations have uncovered remains from the first century AD on Tell el-Kharrar, as well as a large multichurch complex from the Byzantine period adjacent to the Jordan River.[26]

Although all this evidence appears impressive, none of it is persuasive upon further examination. First, Origen's reading of Bethabara and his assumption that it was near the Dead Sea was not based on any personal knowledge of the site. He himself admits, "*They say* that Bethabara is pointed out on the banks of the Jordan, and that John *is said* to have baptized there."[27] Since his subscription to the local tradition was based on hearsay, its historical reliability is dubious.[28]

Second, "wilderness" in popular English usage might evoke the image of a desert, but the Greek word (*erēmos*, ἔρημος) is broader and simply means an uninhabited place. Matthew not only uses the term for the wilderness of Judea (Matt 3:1, 3), but also for the uninhabited area at the foot of the Golan Heights near Bethsaida (Matt 14:13), which is not a desert. The term *erēmos* is also used for the desolate places of Galilee (Mark 1:45; Luke 5:16), the unpopulated area of New Testament Judea near Ephraim (John 11:54), and an open stretch somewhere between Jerusalem and Gaza (probably on the Coastal Plain; Acts 8:26). The word "wilderness" (*erēmos*), therefore, does not point to a specific geographical region.[29] Isaiah 40:3-5 means nothing more than that John the Baptist—somewhat ironically—trumpeted the coming of the messiah in unpopulated areas. As for the Baptist's close association with Elijah, it is important to note that at Bethany beyond the Jordan, John *distanced* himself from the prophet by expressly denying he was Elijah (John 1:19-28).

---

26. See Khouri, "Where John Baptized," 35-43.

27. Origen, "Commentary on John," *ANF* 9:370.

28. Even lengthy traditions are sometimes wrong (compare "The Geographical Significance of the Transfiguration" on pg. 298). Tradition is by nature uncritical, and as Laney points out: "Later writers who used the name 'Bethabara' appear to simply be following the suggestion of Origen" ("Geographical Problems," 64).

29. John 3:23 even says John was baptizing at Aenon near Salim. The location of Aenon has also been debated, but it should probably be identified with Umm el-'Umdan, eight miles south of Beth-Shean on the west side of the Jordan River. But according to any identification, it is not in a desert. See further in Rainey and Notley, *Sacred Bridge*, 350-51.

Third, it is gratuitous to assume John the Baptist was primarily active in Perea. There is simply not enough evidence for us to know where he spent most of his time ministering.[30] Fourth, Bethany might mean "house of the boat," but this need not imply it was near a ford in the Jordan. The Bethany near Jerusalem certainly was not. Finally, although there may have been settlement in the area of Wadi el-Kharrar in the first century AD, this does not mean it is Bethany beyond the Jordan. Tell el-Kharrar may simply be an unknown site from the first century AD. As for the remains of the multichurch complex from the Byzantine period, this proves nothing more than what we already know from written texts: some Byzantine Christians believed this was where John the Baptist began his baptism ministry.

BATANEA

There is evidence for locating Bethany beyond the Jordan away from Wadi el-Kharrar. One observation that suggests a northern location is that Bethany beyond the Jordan is never called a city or village.[31] The description of the two places called Bethany in John 10 and 11 indicates this is deliberate. John 10:40 tells us Jesus "went away again across the Jordan to the *place* where John had been baptizing at first" (ESV).[32] In John 11:1 (see also John 11:30), however, Lazarus is from Bethany, the *village* of Mary and Martha. Since John 10:40 refers to Bethany as a *place* (not a village), this suggests it was a region. This interpretation gains merit when juxtaposed with Josephus and other ancient writers' designation of "Batanea" for the Old Testament region of Bashan (e.g., Josephus, *Life* 54; *Ant.* 9.159; Tg. Neof. Deut 32:14; Eusebius, *Onomasticon* 44:9–11), which is repeatedly said to be "beyond the Jordan" (e.g., Num 32:32; Deut 3:8). The rendering "Batanea" for Bashan can be explained linguistically.[33] Since the proto-Semitic *th* appears as *sh* in Hebrew but as *t* in Aramaic,[34] "Batanaea is a Hellenized form of the Aramaic equivalent of the Hebrew name Bashan."[35]

The chronology of events in John 1:19–2:1 also suggests a northern location (see list below). In John 2:1 Jesus arrives in Cana of Galilee "on the third day," which is almost certainly a reference to the third day after the previously-mentioned event (i.e., Philip and Nathanael's call on the sixth day; John 1:43–51). If the author is calculating the days by inclu-

---

30. The only two other specific geographical locations where John is said to have been active are the Judean Wilderness (Matt 3:1) and Aenon near Salim (John 3:23), neither of which is in Perea.

31. See Riesner, "Bethany," 55.

32. In the Gospel of John, the first place where John baptizes is Bethany beyond the Jordan (John 1:25). Jesus' baptism occurred before this, but it is not mentioned in John.

33. See C. R. Conder, "Bethany Beyond Jordan," *Palestine Exploration Quarterly Statement* 9 (1877): 184–87; Riesner, "Bethany," 53–54.

34. See the phoneme chart in A. F. Rainey, "The Toponymics of Eretz-Israel," *BASOR* 231 (1978): 9.

35. W. H. Brownlee, "Whence the Gospel According to John?" in *John and Qumran*, ed. James H. Charlesworth (London: Geoffrey Chapman, 1972), 169. Building on Riesner's work, Earl makes a theological case for locating Bethany beyond the Jordan in the Bashan of the Old Testament (Douglas S. Earl, "'[Bethany] Beyond the Jordan': The Significance of a Johanine Motif," *NTS* 55.3 [2009]: 279–94).

Location and Timing between Jesus' Baptism and First Miracle	
Day 1 (John 1:19–28)	Bethany beyond the Jordan: John testifies that he is the "voice of one crying in the wilderness" (Isa 40:3–5)
Day 2 (John 1:29–34; 1:29, "The next day …")	Bethany beyond the Jordan: John declares Jesus to be the Lamb of God and reflects on Jesus' baptism
Day 3 (John 1:35–42; 1:35, "The next day …")	Bethany beyond the Jordan: Jesus calls Andrew and Peter
Day 4 (John 1:43–51; 1:43, "The next day …")	Bethsaida: Jesus calls Philip and Nathanael
Day 5 (implied)	Cana of Galilee: Jesus travels from Bethsaida to Cana
Day 6 (John 2:1–11; 1:1, "The next day …")	Cana of Galilee: Jesus changes water to wine

sive reckoning, this allows two full days of travel at most between Bethany beyond the Jordan and Cana of Galilee.[36] Traveling through the Rift Valley, Wadi el-Kharrar is about eighty miles from Cana of Galilee (Khirbet Cana). It would have been impossible to make this trip in two—or even three—full days. As Beitzel has shown, "The evidence is generally uniform and mutually corroborating that one day's journey in the ancient world incorporated between 17 and 23 miles."[37] Bethany beyond the Jordan cannot be more than a two- or three-day walk from Cana of Galilee (i.e., somewhere between forty to sixty miles).

John 1:43–44 also implies Bethany beyond the Jordan is in the north, less than one day away from Bethsaida. In

John 1:43 Jesus decides to go to Galilee, and then immediately finds Philip who was from Bethsaida. Although it is possible Philip was not in his hometown when Jesus met him, the text suggests he was (or was somewhere nearby). According to John 1:43 and 1:45, Jesus *found* Philip, who then *found* Nathanael. Since both had to be found, neither was part of a crowd that had gone out to see Jesus or John the Baptist. If they were not traveling with a curious crowd of onlookers, there is no reason to locate them anywhere other than in their hometown.[38] This suspicion is strengthened by the calling of Andrew and Peter, who were also from Bethsaida, the day before. Within two days, Jesus called four people who were from Bethsaida on the northern shore of the

36. Half a day after the events of John 1:43–51, half a day on the day of arrival to allow time for Jesus to prepare for the wedding and recuperate after the trip, and one full day in between.

37. Barry J. Beitzel, "Travel and Communication: The Old Testament World," *ABD* 6:646. Based on statements made in Josephus, the Mishnah, and the Talmud, Riesner ("Bethany," 44–45) estimates the average full day's march was about forty kilometers or twenty-five miles. Even using this larger number, three full days is not enough time to make the journey.

38. It seems safe to assume Nathanael was also from Bethsaida (or a neighboring village) since the two were close acquaintances.

Sea of Galilee. As Riesner notes, "Such a gathering of Galileans as John 1 supposes appears astonishing at the lower reaches of the Jordan, and improbable, when we take into consideration our discussion of the distances."[39]

In the end, the evidence favors equating Bethany beyond the Jordan with the region of Batanea, to the northeast of the Sea of Galilee. Since Jesus apparently traveled to Cana via Bethsaida, it is most logical (geographically) to locate the events in John 1:19–42 somewhere in the modern-day Golan Heights, north of the Decapolis.[40]

BIBLIOGRAPHY

Aharoni, Yohanan, Michael Avi-Yonah, Anson F. Rainey, and Ze'ev Safrai. *The Carta Bible Atlas.* 4th ed. Jerusalem: Carta, 2002.

Avi-Yonah, Michael. *The Madaba Mosaic Map: With Introduction and Commentary.* Jerusalem: Israel Exploration Society, 1954.

Barrett, C. K. *The Gospel According to St. John.* London: SPCK, 1960.

Beitzel, Barry J. *The New Moody Atlas of the Bible.* Chicago: Moody, 2009.

Brown, Raymond E. *The Gospel According to John (i–xii).* New York: Doubleday, 1966.

Brownlee, W. H. "Whence the Gospel According to John?" Pages 166–94 in *John and Qumran.* Edited by J. H. Charlesworth. London: Geoffrey Chapman, 1972.

Carson, D. A. *The Gospel According to John.* Grand Rapids: Eerdmans, 1991.

Conder, C. R. "Bethany Beyond Jordan." *Palestine Exploration Fund Quarterly Statement* 9 (1877): 184–87.

Earl, Douglas S. "'(Bethany) Beyond the Jordan': The Significance of a Johanine Motif." *NTS* 55.3 (2009): 279–94.

Hutton, Jeremy M. "'Bethany Beyond the Jordan' in Text, Tradition, and Historical Geography." *Biblica* 89 (2008): 305–28.

Khouri, Rami. "Where John Baptized: Bethany Beyond the Jordan." *Biblical Archaeology Review* 31.1 (Jan/Feb 2005): 34–43.

Laney, Carl J. "Selective Geographical Problems in the Life of Christ." ThD diss., Dallas Theological Seminary, 1977.

McHugh, John. *A Critical and Exegetical Commentary on John 1–4.* London: T&T Clark, 2009.

Morris, Leon. *The Gospel According to John.* Rev. ed. NICNT. Grand Rapids: Eerdmans, 1995.

The Pilgrim of Bordeaux. *Itinerary from Bordeaux to Jerusalem: 'The Bordeaux Pilgrim' (333 A.D.).* Translated by Aubrey Stewart. Edited by Charles W. Wilson. London: Palestine Pilgrims' Text Society, 1887.

Rainey, Anson F. "The Toponymics of Eretz-Israel." *BASOR* 231 (1978): 1–17.

Rainey, Anson F., and R. Steven Notley. *The Sacred Bridge.* Jerusalem: Carta, 2006.

Riesner, Rainer. "Bethany Beyond the Jordan (John 1:28): Topography, Theology and History in the Fourth Gospel." *TynBul* 38 (1987): 29–63.

---

39. Riesner, "Bethany," 48.

40. The Zavitan and Yehudia springs, northeast of the Sea of Galilee, secrete a solid stream of water and would have been ideal for baptizing.

CHAPTER 8

JESUS' MINISTRY AT CANA IN GALILEE

John 2:1–11; 4:46–54; 21:2

Emily J. Thomassen

KEY POINTS

- The Gospel of John is the only book in the New Testament to mention Cana, making its location difficult to identify.

- Jesus performed two miracles early in his ministry at Cana: turning water to wine and healing a sick child miles away.

- Historical sources, physical geography, and archaeology all converge to suggest that modern Khirbet Qana is the strongest candidate for the location of Cana of Galilee.

CANA IN THE WRITTEN SOURCES

In the New Testament, Cana is only mentioned in the Gospel of John. John highlights Cana as an important locale for Jesus' early ministry. According to John, Jesus' first two "signs" (*sēmeion*, σημεῖον, John 2:11; 4:54) occurred at Cana in Galilee: changing water into wine (John 2:1–11) and the healing from a distance of the son of a royal official (John 4:46–54). Cana is also the city of origin of Jesus' disciple Nathanael (John 1:45–49; 21:2). The

multiple references to Jesus' presence in Cana may suggest that the village was a regular stopping point for Jesus during his travels through Lower Galilee.

Cana is also known from the writings of the first century Jewish historian Flavius Josephus. During the First Jewish Revolt against Rome, Josephus served as general of the Jewish forces in Galilee. In his autobiography, *Life*, Josephus described his time in the region, stating that he spent time (*dietribon*)[1] in "a vil-

---

1. The Greek verb *diatribō* (διατρίβω) can mean spend time, employ oneself, or abide. Thackeray's translation of "my quarters at the time" is perhaps close to what Josephus meant, a temporary stay for a military purpose (Josephus, *Life* 86 [Thackeray, LCL]).

lage of Galilee which is called Cana" (*Life* 86 [Thackeray, LCL]). Later, Josephus made reference to Cana's location on the great plain of Asochis (*Life* 207), which is known today as the Beth Netofa Valley.

Both the Gospel of John and Josephus refer to Cana as "Cana of Galilee" (*Kana tēs Galilaias*, Κανὰ τῆς Γαλιλαίας), perhaps in order to distinguish it from the Old Testament site Kanah (*Qanah*) in the territory of Asher, located southeast of Tyre (Josh 19:28) and from the Kanah River (*nahal qanah*; Josh 16:8; 17:9), a stream on the border between Manasseh and Ephraim.[2] While there may have been multiple villages with the name Cana, there is no reason to doubt Josephus' identification of "Cana of the Galilee" with the same Cana in the Gospel of John.

The numerous references to Cana in both Josephus and the Gospel of John may indicate that Cana was not a small and obscure town, but a well-known village in a prominent locale. Although John does not specify the size or stature of the village of Cana, Nathanael's initial attitude towards Jesus may suggest that Cana was more affluent or cosmopolitan than Nazareth. Upon hearing that Jesus was from Nazareth, Nathanael from Cana replied, "Nazareth, can anything good come from there?" (John 1:46 NIV).

Nathanael's gut reaction may offer a lens through which to consider the worldview and socio-economic status of the residents of Cana.

THE MIRACLE OF WATER TO WINE

John's choice to repeat the location "Cana of Galilee" (John 2:1, 11) at the beginning and end of the narrative of Jesus' turning water into wine bookends the account by highlighting the place where it occurred. John's conscious repetition of the setting shows he was concerned with reminding his readers of the geographic details of Jesus' early Galilean ministry. John shows no concern for the details of who was getting married, who invited Jesus to the wedding, or why the wine had run out. However, John is careful to report the conditions of the miracle, which involved turning an enormous amount of water into wine. John records that the water within six stone water jars—each of which held two or three measures, equivalent to twenty to thirty gallons (John 2:6)—was turned into wine. The large amount of water mentioned in the text might lead one to suggest that Cana was situated near a spring[3] or that the residents were able to effectively collect and store rainwater using cisterns.

Yardenna Alexandra translates the phrase, "At the time my headquarters were at Cana" (Yardenna Alexandre, "Karm er-Ras Near Kafr Kanna," in *The Archaeological Record from Cities, Towns, and Villages*, vol. 2 of *Galilee in the Late Second Temple and Mishnaic Periods*, ed. David A. Fiensy and James Riley Strange [Minneapolis: Fortress Press, 2015], 152).

2. The name Qanū is known from El-Amarna letter 204:4, and the site is likely identified with Qanah southeast of Tyre (Josh 19:28; see Anson F. Rainey and R. Steven Notley, *The Sacred Bridge* [Jerusalem: Carta, 2006], 86). In addition, a third century AD mosaic from Caesarea Maritima, which contains a list of the twenty-four priestly families of Galilee, suggests that a town called Cana was the home place of the course of Eliashib (see Samuel Klein, *Beiträge zur Geographie und Geschichte Galiläas* [Leipzig: R. Haupt, 1909], 56–57; and Michael Avi-Yonah, "A List of Priestly Courses from Caesarea," *IEJ* 12 [1962]: 137–39).

3. This may account for the identification of 'Ain Kana, which means Spring of Cana, as the location of the miracle. See the discussion below.

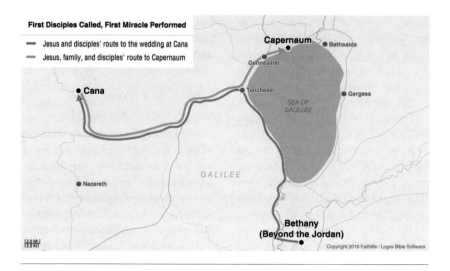

First Disciples Called, First Miracle Performed

━━ Jesus and disciples' route to the wedding at Cana

━━ Jesus, family, and disciples' route to Capernaum

Capernaum
● Bethsaida
Gennesaret
● Cana
Taricheae ●
● Gergesa
SEA OF
GALILEE
GALILEE
● Nazareth
Bethany
(Beyond the Jordan)
●

Copyright 2016 Faithlife / Logos Bible Software

John records that the six stone water jars served the purpose of the Jewish custom of purification (John 2:6). Unlike clay vessels, stone vessels would not catch impurities if they came into contact with an unclean object or person. During the Second Temple Period, segments of the Jewish population were concerned with ritual purity. Stone vessels have been found in mansions in the Jewish quarter in Jerusalem, at the Qumran settlement, and in numerous towns in Judea and Galilee.[4] The presence of stone vessels may attest to the observance of purity laws relating to practices of the Jerusalem temple.

Jesus' command to fill the jars with water would not have been a simple task. If the jars had been partially or completely empty, the servants would have needed to fetch a large amount of drinking water from a nearby location, perhaps a cistern or a spring. John does not tell us more about the jars, where they were kept, or how they were filled with water.

Yet, the narrator reports that Jesus told them to *fill* the water jars (John 2:7). The fact that "they filled them to the brim," (John 2:7 NIV) suggests a considerable amount of time and effort on the servants' part.

THE MIRACLE OF HEALING FROM A DISTANCE

John's introduction of Jesus' second sign at Cana contains a deliberate reminder that Cana of Galilee is where Jesus turned the water into wine (John 4:43). During the time between these two Cana episodes, Jesus traveled to several locations. After his initial miracle at Cana, Jesus had been to Capernaum (John 2:12), to the temple in Jerusalem for Passover (John 2:13–3:21), to the Judean country side at Aenon near Salim (John 3:22–36), and back to Galilee by way of Samaria (John 4:1–45). By the time Jesus returned to Galilee, he had begun to develop a reputation based on what he had done in Jerusalem (John 4:45). By describing

---

4. Yitzhak Magen, *The Stone Vessel Industry in the Second Temple Period: Excavations at Hizma and the Jerusalem Temple Mount* (Jerusalem: Israel Exploration Society, 2002), 148–62.

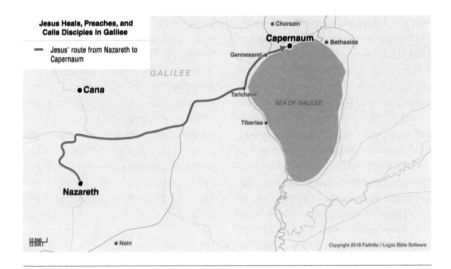

Jesus' return to Cana, John gives special attention to Cana as a city central to the beginning of Jesus' public ministry.

The royal official who traveled to see Jesus in Cana had come from Capernaum, a village on the northwestern shore of the Sea of Galilee. Matthew and Mark record that after Jesus began his ministry, he moved to Capernaum, which served as the base of his Galilean ministry (Matt 4:13; Mark 2:1).[5] Capernaum was a border town, situated between the regions of Galilee and Gaulanitis, territory ruled by Herod Antipas and Philip, respectively. Capernaum was probably home to a number of royal officials, soldiers, and tax collectors: among them was

Jesus' disciple Matthew (Matt 9:9-10). John does not indicate whether the royal official who traveled from Capernaum to see Jesus was a Jewish Herodian or a Gentile. His journey from Capernaum to Cana gave Jesus the opportunity to demonstrate his power to heal someone at a distance.

Within the narrative, John hints at the location of Cana in relation to Capernaum. After arriving at Cana, the royal official asked Jesus to *come down* (*katabainō*, καταβαίνω; John 4:49) to Capernaum to heal his son. After Jesus told the man that his son would live, John describes the man as on his way "coming down" (*katabainō*, John 4:51), when he

5. The synoptic accounts of the believing centurion from Capernaum in Matt 8:5-13 and Luke 7:1-10 share a similar theme of Jesus' healing from a distance, but a number of details differ from the Johannine account. Matthew and Luke record that the miracle took place while Jesus was in Capernaum and that it was a centurion (ἑκατόνταρχος; Matt 8:5; Luke 7:2) rather than a royal official (βασιλικός; John 4:46) who approached Jesus. In Matthew's account, Jesus healed the centurion's boy (*pais*, παῖς), which can mean "servant" or "child" (Matt 8:6), and in Luke's account Jesus cured the centurion's "slave" (*doulos*, δοῦλος; Luke 7:2). In John, Jesus heals the "son" of the royal official (*huios*, υἱός [John 4:46]). For further discussion of the synoptic parallel, see Raymond E. Brown, *The Gospel According to John* (Garden City, NY: Doubleday, 1966), 190-98; Ernest Haenchen, *John 1*, trans. R. W. Funk (Philadelphia: Fortress Press, 1984), 232-38.

was met by his servants. When traveling from Cana to Capernaum, one must
head east across the hills of Lower Galilee
and descend to the Sea of Galilee, which
sits roughly seven hundred feet (213 m)
below sea level. The Sea of Galilee is the
lowest point in the region. Considering
the walk from Cana to Capernaum was
roughly a day's journey of fifteen miles
(twenty-four km), it is not surprising
that when the man's servants met him
the next day, the time of the boy's healing the day before aligned with the time
that Jesus said he would be well (John
4:51–53). John's accurate description of
the geographic details may indicate that
he was quite familiar with the geography
of Galilee.

THE LOCATION OF CANA

The more serious problem is the identification of Cana and its exact location in
Lower Galilee. Cana may have been forgotten already during the Late Roman
period. Eusebius identified the New
Testament village of Cana with Kanah
(*qanah*) of Josh 19:28, which is rendered
in the Septuagint as *Kanthan* (Κανθαν).[6]
Eusebius did not offer additional topo-

graphical information about Cana's location, which may indicate that the actual
site was not known to him.[7] Since then, at
least four additional sites have been suggested by pilgrims, explorers, and archaeologists: ʿAin Kana, Kefr Kenna, Karm
er-Ras, and Khirbet Qana. Historical, geographical, archaeological, and toponymic
evidence favor Khirbet Qana as the strongest candidate, but some have questioned
this identification as additional archaeological work has been carried out in the
region.[8]

ʿAIN KANA

ʿAin Kana, which means "Spring of Cana,"
sits about 1.5 miles (2.4 km) northeast of
Nazareth. The site was suggested to be
Cana of Galilee by Claude R. Conder in
1878 based on the toponymic connection
and the perennial water source nearby.[9]
Near the spring sits the modern Arab
village of Reineh. The site does not fit
Josephus' geographic description that the
village was in the Beth Netofa valley, but
the water source accounts for the early
pilgrim reports that mention a spring
at the site. Archaeological work has not
been done in the modern village, and

---

6. Eusebius, *Onomasticon* 116:4.

7. Rainey and Notley, *Sacred Bridge*, 352.

8. While there is not complete scholarly consensus that Khirbet Qana is the correct identification, James F. Strange suggests that Khirbet Qana "has the consensus of scholarship
since Dalman," citing the third edition of Dalman's book *Orte und Wege Jesu*, published in 1924
(James F. Strange, "Cana of Galilee," *ABD* 1:827). Mackowski also suggests that Khirbet Qana
has scholarly consensus (Richard M. Mackowski, "Scholar's Qanah: A Re-examination of the
Evidence in Favor of Khirbet Qana," *Biblische Zeitschrift* 23 (1979): 278–84. However, Mordechai
Aviam asserts, "there is no way to make a clear decision on which of the three candidates is
the "real" Cana." He suggests the best candidate is Kefr Kenna followed by Karm er-Ras as
next most likely and with Khirbat Qana the third and least likely of the options (Mordechai
Aviam, "Cana," *Oxford Encyclopedia of the Bible and Archaeology*, ed. Daniel M. Master [New
York: Oxford University Press, 2013], 1:168).

9. Claude R. Conder, *Tent Work in Palestine: A Record of Discovery and Adventure* (New York,
D. Appleton: 1878), 1:150–55.

there is no report of ancient ruins at the site, suggesting ʿAin Kana is an unlikely candidate for Cana of Galilee.

KEFR KENNA

Kefr Kenna, a modern Arab village, sits three miles (4.8 km) northeast of Nazareth, and three miles (4.8 km) east of Sepphoris, the city that served as the capital of Galilee from 4 BC–AD 19. Because of its close proximity to Nazareth, Kefr Kenna is conveniently accessible to tourists and pilgrims coming from Nazareth who want to see the place where Jesus turned water into wine. Only limited archaeological excavations have been carried out in the modern village. Under the Franciscan church, archaeologists uncovered remains from the Crusader, Byzantine, Roman, and Hellenistic periods with very few pieces dating to the Hellenistic and early Roman periods.[10] Excavations unearthed a large public building, perhaps a synagogue, dated to the fourth or fifth century AD, as well as walls, pottery, and shards of stone vessels dating to the first century AD.[11] As will be discussed below, the strongest indicators against the identification of Kefr Kenna as Cana of Galilee are the weak top-

onymic connection between Cana and Kenna and the lack of evidence of early Christian pilgrimage to the site.

KARM ER-RAS

The modern town Karm er-Ras sits on a small hill approximately 0.6 miles (1 km) northwest of central Kefr Kenna. As the neighborhood developed during the 1980s through 2011, a series of salvage excavations were carried out by the Israel Antiquities Authority, primarily under the direction of Yardenna Alexandre. Final publication of the excavation is still forthcoming, but so far the finds have revealed remains from the Iron Age, Persian, Hellenistic, and Roman periods. The salvage excavations have turned up houses, floors, cisterns, hiding complexes, ritual baths, stone vessels, Hasmonean coins, and a potter's workshop with two kilns.[12] Alexandre believes the first century Jewish village at the site should be identified as Cana of the Galilee.[13] However, there is not a strong toponymic connection to support her claim. Mordechai Aviam has suggested that Karm er-Ras may be a good candidate for Garis, a city mentioned by Josephus in the same area (Life 395).[14]

10. F. Massimo Luca, "Kafr Kanna (The Franciscan Church)," in The Archaeological Record from Cities, Towns, and Villages, vol. 2 of Galilee in the Late Second Temple and Mishnaic Periods, ed. David A. Fiensy and James Riley Strange (Minneapolis: Fortress Press, 2015), 158–66.

11. The excavator D. Barshad suggests that no traces of dwellings were found on the hill above due to massive erosion. However, Barshad excavated an underground hiding complex which he believed was used during the First Jewish Revolt. The final reports have still not been published (see Aviam, "Cana," 165–68, esp. 166).

12. Yardenna Alexandre, "The Archaeological Evidence of the Great Revolt at Karm er-Ras (Kfar Kanna) in the Lower Galilee," in The Great Revolt in the Galilee (Haifa: Hecht Museum, University of Haifa, 2008), 73–79; Rami Arav, "Cana in Galilee," Encyclopedia of the Historical Jesus, ed. Craig A. Evans (New York: Routledge, 2008), 89–91.

13. Alexandre, "The Archaeological Evidence," 73–79; Alexandre, "Karm er-Ras," 154.

14. Aviam, "Cana," 168.

KHIRBET QANA

Khirbet Qana is located 8.5 miles (13.7 km) north of Nazareth, 1.2 miles (1.9 km) southeast of Jotapata, and 4.4 miles (7.1 km) north-northeast of Sepphoris. The site is a small ruin nestled atop a prominent hill, 330 feet (101 m) high, on the northeastern edge of the Beth Netofa Valley. Khirbet Qana held a strategic position as a fairly isolated village, connected only to the hills to the north by a low neck. The village was easily defendable from attackers in the valley below.

Khirbet Qana was suggested as the location of Cana of Galilee by Edward Robinson on June 18, 1838. Analyzing the historical sources and the toponymic connection, Robinson rejected the popular notion that ancient Cana of Galilee should be located at Kefr Kenna. He favored Khirbet Qana since he was told that the locals called it "Kana el-Jelil," a name Robinson argued was a more accurate preservation of the ancient name "Cana of Galilee."[15] Robinson also noted that pilgrim traditions locating the site at Kefr Kenna occurred with greater frequency after the sixteenth century. Perhaps out of monastic convenience, the traditional site was moved to Kefr Kenna. Since then, Kefr Kenna has remained the traditional site for pilgrims and tourists alike. Therefore, when one visits Galilee today, the churches recalling Jesus' miracle are all found at Kefr Kenna and not Khirbet Qana.

Beginning in 1998, archaeological excavations at Khirbet Qana have revealed an active village during the early Roman period.[16] The excavators, Douglas R. Edwards and C. Thomas McCollough, have provisionally dated a domestic quarter, public buildings, and industrial features to the early decades of the first century AD, suggesting the village consisted of an unwalled settlement of five hectares with a population of about twelve hundred.[17] Edwards and McCollough suggest that a large public building with distinct architectural features, including a plastered floor, two rows of columns, and a bench, may be a synagogue. They have provisionally dated the building to the late first cen-

---

15. Robinson wrote, "Now as far as the prevalence of an ancient name among the common people, is any evidence for the identity of an ancient site—and I hold it to be the strongest of all testimony, when, as here, not subject to extraneous influences, but rather in opposition to them—so far is the weight of evidence in favour of this northern Kana el-Jelil, as the true site of the ancient Cana of Galilee. The name is identical, and stands the same in the Arabic version of the New Testament; while the form Kefr Kenna can only be twisted by force into a like shape" (Edward Robinson and Eli Smith, *Biblical Researches in Palestine, Mount Sinai and Arabia Petraea: A Journal of Travels in the Year 1838* [Boston: Crocker and Brewster: 1841], 3:205). However, there is some question over how widespread the use of the name Kana el-Jalil for Khirbet Qana actually was (E. W. G. Masterman, "Cana of Galilee," *The Biblical World* 36 [1910]: 80–81).

16. C. Thomas McCollough, "City and Village in Lower Galilee: The Import of the Archeological Excavations at Sepphoris and Khirbet Qana (Cana) for Framing the Economic Context of Jesus," in *The Galilean Economy in the Time of Jesus*, ed. David A. Fiensy and Ralph K. Hawkins (Atlanta: Society of Biblical Literature, 2013), 58.

17. C. Thomas McCollough, "Khirbet Qana," in *The Archaeological Record from Cities, Towns, and Villages*, vol. 2 of *Galilee in the Late Second Temple and Mishnaic Periods*, ed. David A. Fiensy and James Riley Strange (Minneapolis: Fortress Press, 2015), 2.127-45, esp. 137; compare McCollough, "City and Village in Lower Galilee," 58.

tury AD.[18] The suggestion of the building's function as a synagogue is strengthened by comparison to the first century synagogue at Gamla.[19] The archaeological evidence suggests that Khirbet Qana was a thriving Jewish village during the first century.

LOCATION AND ROUTES

The strategic position of Khirbet Qana, its close proximity to Jotapata, and its location near the Beth Netofa Valley fit the description of Josephus' Cana of Galilee. Khirbet Qana is a plausible location for Josephus' headquarters as commander of Galilee because the site guarded the ascent to Jotapata.[20] The high and isolated location of Khirbet Qana would have provided Josephus with a good vantage point into the Beth Netofa Valley. Josephus' report of an overnight march from Cana to Tiberius with two hundred men fits the physical geography of Khirbet Qana and demonstrates the importance of a strategic location (Life 86–90).

Khirbet Qana is strategically located on an important east-west corridor of Lower Galilee, the ancient road connecting Ptolemais to Magdala (Tericheae). It was also near a branch of the International Coastal Highway as it continued north

through the Jezreel Valley, around Nazareth towards Sepphoris, past Cana, Arbela, to the Sea of Galilee, past Magdala, Capernaum, Bethsaida, and north along the Rift Valley. The description of the royal official's journey from Capernaum to Cana (John 4:46–53) also fits the physical geography of Khirbet Qana, a site about a day's walk from Capernaum.

The journey from Nazareth to Capernaum is nearly thirty miles (48.3 km), making Khirbet Qana an ideal stopping point along the way. The historical sources, physical geography, and archaeology all converge to make the site of Khirbet Qana the strongest candidate for Cana of Galilee. The two miracles Jesus performed in Cana may suggest that Jesus regularly stopped in Cana during his travels through Lower Galilee. As the location of his first two signs, the village played an important role in Jesus' early Galilean ministry.

BIBLIOGRAPHY

Alexandre, Yardenna. "The Archaeological Evidence of the Great Revolt at Karm er-Ras (Kfar Kanna) in the Lower Galilee." Pages 73–79 in *The Great Revolt in the Galilee*. Haifa:

18. McCollough suggests that the synagogue may have been built after AD 70 to accommodate the influx of refugees from the south after the First Jewish Revolt (McCollough, "Khirbet Qana," 141). Both ceramic evidence and radio carbon dating point to a first century date for the building (Jason A. Rech, Alysia A. Fischer, Douglas R. Edwards, and A. J. Timothy Jull, "Direct Dating of Plaster and Mortar Using AMS Radiocarbon: A Pilot Project from Khirbet Qana, Israel," *Antiquity* 77 [2009]: 155–64).

19. McCollough, "City and Village in Lower Galilee," 62; Douglas R. Edwards, "Khirbet Qana: From Jewish Village to Christian Pilgrim Site," in *The Roman and Byzantine Near East*, ed. J. H. Humphrey (Portsmouth, RI: Journal of Roman Archaeology, 2002), 3:101–32.

20. Mordechai Aviam argues against the idea that Josephus would live at Khirbet Qana when his headquarters, Jotapata, were only 1.6 miles away. On the contrary, lodging at Khirbet Qana would give Josephus the opportunity to abide in a flourishing Jewish village in an isolated and secure location near his headquarters (see Aviam, "Cana," 168; see also E. W. G. Masterman, "Cana of Galilee," *Palestinian Exploration Fund Quarterly Statement* 46 (1914): 179–83.

Hecht Museum, University of Haifa, 2008.

———. "Karm er-Ras Near Kafr Kanna." Pages 146-57 in *The Archaeological Record from Cities, Towns, and Villages.* Vol. 2 of *Galilee in the Late Second Temple and Mishnaic Periods.* Edited by David A. Fiensy and James Riley Strange. Minneapolis: Fortress Press, 2015.

Arav, Rami. "Cana in Galilee." Pages 89-91 in *Encyclopedia of the Historical Jesus.* Edited by Craig A. Evans. New York: Routledge, 2008.

Avi-Yonah, Michael. "A List of Priestly Courses from Caesarea." *IEJ* 12 (1962): 137-39.

Aviam, Mordechai. "Cana." Pages 165-68 in *The Oxford Encyclopedia of the Bible and Archaeology.* Edited by Daniel M. Master. Vol. 1. New York: Oxford University Press, 2013.

Brown, Raymond E. *The Gospel According to John.* AB 29. Garden City, NY: Doubleday, 1966.

Conder, Claude R. *Tent Work in Palestine: A Record of Discovery and Adventure.* Vol. 1. New York: D. Appleton, 1878.

Edwards, Douglas R. "Khirbet Qana: From Jewish Village to Christian Pilgrim Site." Pages 101-32 in *The Roman and Byzantine Near East.* Edited by J. H. Humphrey. Vol. 3. Portsmouth, RI: Journal of Roman Archaeology, 2002.

Haenchen, Ernest. *John 1.* Hermeneia 57. Translated by R. W. Funk. Philadelphia: Fortress Press, 1984.

Josephus. Translated by Henry St. J. Thackeray et al. 10 vols. LCL. Cambridge, MA: Harvard University Press, 1926-1965.

Klein, Samuel. *Beiträge zur Geographie und Geschichte Galiläas.* Leipzig: R. Haupt, 1909.

Luca, F. Massimo. "Kafr Kanna (The Franciscan Church)." Pages 146-57 in *The Archaeological Record from Cities, Towns, and Villages.* Edited by David A. Fiensy and James Riley Strange. Vol. 2 of *Galilee in the Late Second Temple and Mishnaic Periods.* Minneapolis: Fortress Press, 2015.

Mackowski, Richard M. "Scholar's Qanah: A Re-examination of the Evidence in Favor of Khirbet Qanah." *Biblische Zeitschrift* 23 (1979): 278-84.

Magen, Yitzhak. *The Stone Vessel Industry in the Second Temple Period: Excavations at Hizma and the Jerusalem Temple Mount.* Jerusalem: Israel Exploration Society, 2002.

Masterman, E. W. G. "Cana of Galilee." *Palestinian Exploration Fund Quarterly Statement* 46 (1914): 179-83.

———. "Cana of Galilee." *The Biblical World* 36 (1910): 79-92.

McCollough, C. Thomas. "City and Village in Lower Galilee: The Import of the Archeological Excavations at Sepphoris and Khirbet Qana (Cana) for Framing the Economic Context of Jesus." Pages 49-74 in *The Galilean Economy in the Time of Jesus.* Edited by David A. Fiensy and Ralph K. Hawkins. Atlanta: Society of Biblical Literature, 2013.

———. "Khirbet Qana." Pages 127-45 in *The Archaeological Record from Cities, Towns, and Villages.* Edited by David A. Fiensy and James Riley Strange. Vol. 2 of *Galilee in the Late Second Temple and Mishnaic Periods.* Minneapolis: Fortress Press, 2015.

Rainey, Anson F., and R. Steven Notley. *The Sacred Bridge.* Jerusalem: Carta, 2006.

Rech, Jason A., Alysia A. Fischer, Douglas R. Edwards, and A. J. Timothy Jull. "Direct Dating of

Plaster and Mortar Using AMS
Radiocarbon: A Pilot Project from
Khirbet Qana, Israel." *Antiquity* 77
(2009): 155–64.

Robinson, Edward, and Eli Smith.
*Biblical Researches in Palestine, Mount
Sinai and Arabia Petraea: A Journal
of Travels in the Year 1838.* 3 vols.
Boston: Crocker and Brewster, 1841.

Strange, James F. "Cana of Galilee." *ABD*
1:827.

CHAPTER 9

CAPERNAUM: A STRATEGIC HOME FOR THE MESSIAH

Matt 4:12-17; Luke 4:14-41; John 4:43-45

Aubrey L. Taylor

KEY POINTS

- While Nazareth was Jesus' hometown, Capernaum came to function as the hub of his ministry, so much so that Matthew called it "his own town" (9:1).

- Matthew described Jesus' move to Capernaum as though he was withdrawing to a remote and isolated region, which is hardly true for that part of Galilee, a busy intersection of international trade and travel.

- Galilee's location made its Jewish population vulnerable to influence and pressure from foreign peoples, but at the same time, Galilee proved to be an opportune location for its people to be a blessing.

- Jesus's move from Nazareth to Capernaum was not a retreat into remoteness but a deliberate move into a more diverse region where his message and impact could have a wider and more receptive audience.

FROM NAZARETH TO CAPERNAUM

All four Gospels locate a significant part of Jesus' ministry around the Sea of Galilee, and specifically in the village of Capernaum. Luke records Jesus teaching in Capernaum's synagogue following his rejection in Nazareth, performing healings and casting out demons there.[1] Mark speaks of Jesus living there, and John says he was welcomed in Galilee, seemingly in contrast to the treatment he received in his hometown.[2] However, Matthew writes the most about Jesus' relationship

---

1. Luke 4:14-41; 7:1-10.
2. Mark 1:14-15; 2:1; John 2:12; 4:43-46; 6:17, 24, 59.

The Synagogue at Capernaum

Nave

to Capernaum, calling it "his own town" (Matt 9:1)[3] and recording that, following the death of John the Baptist, Jesus "withdrew" to Galilee, leaving Nazareth for Capernaum (Matt 4:12). A potentially confusing turn of phrase, it conjures up images of Galilee as a remote location, isolated and peaceful, and gives the impression that Jesus' move there was motivated by a desire for seclusion, perhaps in an attempt to escape the same fate as John.[4] Though distinctly contradicted by historical and geographical data, this connotation has continued to adhere to Jesus' Galilean ministry and has implications not only for our interpretation of Matthew 4:12-17 but for Jesus' ministry as a whole.

Additionally, Matthew states that this move takes place "to fulfill what was said through the prophet Isaiah" (Matt 4:14). He goes on to present a slightly modified quotation of Isa 9:1-2 (Heb 8:23-9:1). Matthew's Gospel is known for these types of fulfillment citations, though it is not entirely clear in what way he understands Jesus' move to Capernaum to fulfill this passage.[5] Furthermore, Isaiah 9:1-7 contains a number of linguistic puzzles and historical and geographical references that have confounded scholars and complicated the passage's interpretation. Though a thorough analysis of Isa 9:1-7, particularly its linguistic anomalies, lies outside the scope of this article, we must attempt to address the references found in Isa 9:1 (compare Matt 4:15) and consider how Matthew may have understood them in light of Jesus' ministry.[6]

---

3. Scripture quotations in this article are from the NIV.

4. See W. D. Davies and Dale C. Allison Jr., *A Critical and Exegetical Commentary on the Gospel According to Saint Matthew* (Edinburgh: T&T Clark, 1988), 1:376.

5. For example, Matt 1:22-23; 2:14-15, 17-18, 23; 8:17.

6. For more information regarding the unique difficulties posed by this passage, see J. A. Emerton, "Some Linguistic and Historical Problems in Isaiah VIII. 23," *JSS* 14 (1969): 151-75; Patricia K. Tull, *Isaiah 1-39* (Macon, GA: Smyth & Helwys, 2010), 186-88.

MAKING SENSE OF ISAIAH 9:1-2

There is a general consensus regarding the events referenced in Isa 9:1-2. In 733 BC, the Assyrian ruler Tiglath-pileser III began a two-year invasion of the kingdom of Israel, conquering the northern portion of the country, specifically Upper and Lower Galilee, the Jezreel Valley, and Gilead.[7] Though Assyria went on to conquer the rest of Israel in subsequent years, these regions were the first to fall. They were closer to Assyria, making them the nearest conquest; but they were also a uniquely vulnerable and strategic target due to their position along the main international road connecting Egypt to Mesopotamia and their accessible topography.

Upon leaving Egypt, the dominant path of travel ran north-south, following the flat ground of Israel's coastal plain, which lies just west of the rugged hill country which formed Judah and Samaria's interior. Though near this important roadway, these mountainous regions were essentially isolated from it. As a result, they generally lay outside the interests of invaders, who were more concerned with securing the trade route than with conquering the small kingdoms that existed alongside it. North of this, however, the topography changes and is no longer a singular core of rocky highlands. With a plain on the periphery, the north is comprised of interspersed hills and valleys that draw traffic through its interior.

The Carmel Mountain Range, which runs northwest-southeast, projects out into the Mediterranean, cutting off the coastal plain and forcing traffic inland via a few well-worn mountain passes. These, in turn, funnel travelers around the Jezreel Valley like a great

Judean Central Hill Country

traffic circle, with roads like spokes projecting out into the Galilean countryside, carrying the wealth (and the armies) of the ancient world. From here, one can travel eastward to the King's Highway in Transjordan and Arabia to the south, westward to the Phoenician ports, or north and east to Damascus and Mesopotamia beyond. This latter destination frequently brought traffic down to the shore of the Sea of Galilee itself, tracing its northern shoreline before continuing on across the open plain of the Bashan to Damascus.

HEAVY FOOT TRAFFIC THROUGH GALILEE

For the Galilee, the implications of this traffic pattern were far-reaching. Unlike its southern neighbors in Judah and

---

7. Though there have been alternative suggestions for the historical context referenced in this verse, this is the general consensus. See Brevard S. Childs, *Isaiah* (Louisville, KY: Westminster John Knox, 2001), 79; Davies and Allison, *Matthew*, 380. For a historical reconstruction, see Anson F. Rainey and R. Steven Notley, *The Sacred Bridge* (Jerusalem: Carta, 2006), 230–32).

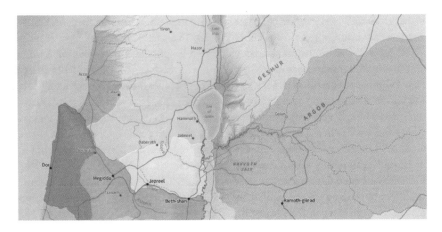

Hazor, Megiddo, and Beth-shan

Samaria, Galilee was both desirable and vulnerable, and the inhabitants could not retreat to a defensible core. The geographical features that consistently channeled traffic through the heart of the local population laid the inhabitants open to conquest, both culturally and militarily. In Israel's early history they struggled to control this region, and cities like Hazor, Megiddo, and Beth-shan, which governed lucrative points along the trade route, remained in more powerful hands.[8] Once Israel conquered these sites, they benefited economically yet faced other problems. With the trade route came foreign influences in the form of diplomatic and economic relationships and, of course, religion.[9] This eventually led to a crisis of apostasy, idolatry, and injustice that, according to the prophets, incurred YHWH's judgment against the nation of Israel in the form of the Assyrian conquest and exile.[10] It is this event to which our passage alludes.

Though there are interpretive complexities connected to the places identified in Isa 9:1, it is plausible they are all referencing the north-west portion of Israel, generally referred to as the Galilee, and its conquest by Assyria in 733-34 BC. But beyond this, and likely more to the point, Isaiah is making use of the known character of the Galilee to communicate a theological concept. Vulnerable to outside influence and conquest, the Israelites who settled here faced the dilemma of how to live in this international environment, with all its inherent risks and opportunities, and yet remain faithful to YHWH. In Isaiah's day this internationalism could be directly associated with the presence of foreign invaders. However, the invasion itself was framed as the result of external influences. Israel had followed the nations

8. Josh 17:16; Judg 1:27; 4:2; 1 Sam 31:1-10.

9. 1 Kgs 9:11; 12:26-31; 16:31-33.

10. Hos 7:11-13; Isa 9:8- 10:6; Deut 29:10-29.

rather than YHWH in matters of justice, righteousness, and worship.

Tragically, the intention had been just the reverse. Many texts within the Hebrew Bible suggest that Israel's calling was to be a blessing or light to the nations.[11] Though vulnerable in many ways, the Galilee was uniquely situated to fulfill this role.[12] As susceptible as those living here were to external influences, there was a similar capacity to influence others as people and ideas moved through in a continuous stream and out into the rest of the known world. From this underlying reality, Isaiah recognizes hope (Isa 9:2). One day, YHWH will forgive and restore his people, and this area will no longer be held in contempt, a place of darkness where God's people are drawn off into apostasy and exile. Rather, it will serve its purpose as a source of illumination, and YHWH will complete his promise of restoration, not only for Israel but for all nations.

From this we can see that Jesus' move from Nazareth to Capernaum was not a withdrawal to a remote and uncomplicated region. Rather, he was moving into a sphere ripe with historical associations

and eschatological implications. Of the two communities, Nazareth was the more remote village. Tucked behind a ridge north of the Jezreel Valley, Nazareth had surprisingly little contact with the internationalism so prevalent in the Galilee.[13] On the other hand, Capernaum, located on the shore of the Sea of Galilee, was a busy town along one of the branches of the international road that connected the Jezreel Valley, Phoenicia, and Damascus.[14]

In Jesus' day, Palestine had also been divided into political districts by the Roman Empire. Capernaum was in the district of Galilee, governed by Herod Antipas, but it lay on the border with the political district of Gaulanitis, part of Herod Phillip's territory, and opposite the Decapolis, a predominantly Roman and Gentile district that controlled the whole eastern shoreline. As a result, Capernaum had a customs office and a military presence, and those living there interacted with Jews and Gentiles alike.[15] In light of this, Jesus' "withdrawal" is perhaps best explained as a move away from the conservative community where he was raised to a region that was more open to his message.[16] Though likely a contro-

---

11. Gen 12:1-3; Isa 2:2-4; 11:1-10; 19:23-25; 49:5-6; Jer 3:11-18; Zech 8:20-23.

12. Perhaps this perspective within Hebraic theology arose from a consideration of their geographical circumstances alongside the tradition that YHWH purposefully placed them in this difficult environment, yet called it good (e.g., Deut 8:7-10).

13. See Paul H. Wright, "The Size and Makeup of Nazareth at the Time of Jesus" on pg. 30.

14. Estimates vary, but the population may have been around 1,500, whereas Nazareth was perhaps 400. Certainly not of a size to be considered a polis (πόλις), it was still an active and sizable community. See Jonathan L. Reed, *Archaeology and the Galilean Jesus: A Re-Examination of the Evidence* (Harrisburg, PA: Trinity, 2000), 152.

15. Matt 9:1, 9-10; Mark 2:1, 13-15. There is much discussion regarding the Gentile centurion in Matt 8:5-13; Luke 7:1-10. It seems unlikely that there was a permanent garrison of Roman soldiers in Capernaum. It is more likely that Antipas used Roman terminology and organizational structures for his army and had Gentiles serving in leadership roles (Mark A. Chancey, *Greco-Roman Culture and the Galilee of Jesus* [Cambridge: Cambridge University Press, 2005], 50-56).

16. See Luke 4:16-30; John 4:43-45.

Tribal Regions around the Sea of Galilee

versial choice, the very qualities that contributed to the Galilee's worldly reputation allowed for a positive reception of Jesus' message. And from Capernaum, that message found a wider audience than if he had remained in Nazareth or moved to Jerusalem, spreading along the international road and attracting people from the Decapolis, Transjordan, and even Tyre and Sidon (see map "Kingdom of Herod the Great" on pg. 531).[17]

Therefore, it becomes apparent that Matthew's citation of Isa 9:1-2 is about more than geographical correspondence. The larger historical and theological connotations of this passage and this region form a critical backdrop to Matthew's message. Beginning in Matthew 4:13 he draws the link between the text of Isaiah and Jesus' ministry by noting Nazareth's location in the ancient Israelite territory of Zebulun and Capernaum's within the territory of Naphtali. However, this is not the climax of the quote. Just as in

Isaiah's version, "Galilee of the Gentiles" is the focal point of the geographical citations, and the hope of restoration the true climax and intended message.

CONCLUSION

Matthew 4:17 states, "From that time on Jesus began to preach, 'Repent, for the kingdom of heaven has come near.'" In the first century, this phrase was evocative of the hoped-for restoration of Israel that prophets like Isaiah had taught the Jewish people to expect, and through the ministry of Jesus, Matthew sees this coming to pass. The Galilee, which had failed to remain faithful to the Mosaic covenant and as a result had been the first to go into exile, was the first to see the dawn of the coming kingdom, and the very things which had made it vulnerable in the past now brought it blessing.

Notably, Matthew often quotes Isaiah when he speaks of Jesus' minis-

---

17. Mark 3:8; Luke 6:17; Matt 4:25; see Emily J. Thomassen, "Jesus' Journey into Gentile Territories" on pg. 247.

try extending to the Gentiles.[18] It would
seem that, through Jesus' ministry in
Galilee, Matthew sees something more
than just YHWH's promised restoration
of Israel. Isaiah's "people who sat in darkness" for whom the "light has dawned" is
expanded to encompass the Gentiles as
well.[19] Just as Israel was intended to serve
this role of a light to the nations, Jesus,
as Israel's true representative, completes
this calling. Placing himself on the international road, accessible yet vulnerable,
his message spreads and God's larger
work of restoration has begun.[20]

BIBLIOGRAPHY

Aharoni, Yohanan. *The Land of the Bible:
A Historical Geography*. Philadelphia:
Westminster, 1979.

Alter, Robert. *The Art of Biblical Poetry*.
New York: Basic Books, 1985.

Beitzel, Barry J. "The *Via Maris* in
Literary and Cartographic Sources."
BA June (1991): 64–65.

Chancey, Mark A. *Greco-Roman Culture
and the Galilee of Jesus*. Cambridge:
Cambridge University Press, 2005.

Childs, Brevard S. *Isaiah*. Old Testament
Library. Louisville, KY: Westminster
John Knox, 2001.

Davies, W. D., and Dale C. Allison Jr. *A
Critical and Exegetical Commentary on
the Gospel According to Saint Matthew*.
3 vols. ICC. Edinburgh: T&T Clark,
1988.

Emerton, J. A. "Some Linguistic and
Historical Problems in Isaiah VIII.
23." *JSS* 14 (1969): 151–75.

Forrer, Emilio O. *Die Provinzeinteilung
Des Assyrischen Reiches*. Leipzig: J. C.
Hinrichs, 1920.

Healey, Joseph P. "Am Ha'arez." *ABD*
1:168–69.

Luz, Ulrich. *Matthew 1–7: A Commentary*.
Translated by James E. Crouch.
Hermeneia. Minneapolis: Fortress
Press, 2007.

Meshel, Ze'ev. "Was There a 'Via Maris'?"
IEJ 23.3 (1973): 162–66.

Neyrey, Jerome H. "The Idea of Purity
in Mark's Gospel." *Semeia* 98 (1986):
91–129.

Nolland, John. *The Gospel of Matthew: A
Commentary on the Greek Text*. The
New International Greek Testament
Commentary. Grand Rapids:
Eerdmans, 2005.

Rainey, Anson. "Toponymic Problems
(Cont.), the Way of the Sea,
Shim'on—Shimron Once Again." *Tel
Aviv* 8 (1981): 146–51.

Rainey, Anson F., and R. Steven Notley.
The Sacred Bridge. Jerusalem: Carta,
2006.

Reed, Jonathan L. *Archaeology and the
Galilean Jesus: A Re-Examination of
the Evidence*. Harrisburg, PA: Trinity,
2000.

Ritter, Carl. *Die Erdkunde im Verhältniss
zur Natur und zur Geschichte des
Menschen*. Vol. 15. Berlin: G. Reimer,
1850.

Schumacher, G. *The Jaulân*. Palestine
Exploration Fund No. 19. London:
Richard Bentley and Son, 1888.

———. "The 'Via Maris': A Reply."
Palestine Exploration Fund Quarterly
22 (1889): 78–79.

---

18. Davies and Allison, *Matthew*, 1:379.

19. In fact, Matthew's use of the word "dawned" instead of Isaiah's "shined" may be intentional to evoke Isa 58:6–10; 60:1–7 (Nolland, *Matthew*, 174; compare Luke 2:32; Acts 13:47; 26:23).

20. Matt 28:16–20; Mark 16:15.

Slingerland, H. Dixon. "The Trans
Jordanian Origin of St. Matthew's
Gospel." *JSOT* 2.3 (1979): 18–28.
Tull, Patricia K. *Isaiah 1–39*. SHBC 14a.
Macon, GA: Smyth & Helwys, 2010.
Watts, John D. *Isaiah 1–33*. WBC 24.
Rev. ed. Nashville, TN: Thomas
Nelson, 2005.

CHAPTER 10

AT THE WELL OF SYCHAR

John 4:1-42

Perry G. Phillips

KEY POINTS

- Jesus and his disciples had traveled roughly forty miles (64.4 km) from Judea to Samaria.

- Jews generally went the long way around to avoid Samaria, but Jesus "had to" go through Samaria.

- Jews and Samaritans had a complicated past with strained social relations in the present.

- None of this prevented Jesus from offering a Samaritan woman living water at Jacob's Well.

TRAVELING TO SYCHAR

In John 4, Jesus and his disciples are in Samaria at a town called Sychar, located east of present-day Nablus and about one mile from the ancient site of Shechem (Tel Balata). The contemporary village of Askar preserves the ancient name Sychar.[1]

They had traveled from Judea to Samaria on their way to Galilee (John 4:3-4). John states that Jesus "had to ["must needs" KJV] go through Samaria" (John 4:4), but Jesus did not "have to" from a geographical standpoint.[2]

He could have taken the longer route across the Jordan River to Perea (at Jericho), traveled north along the Jordan Rift, and then crossed back into Cis-Jordan near Scythopolis (Old Testament Beth Shean). Jesus and his disciples made

---

1. The authenticity of this site is well-attested (see Stephen Langfur, "Nablus [Shechem]: Jacob's Well," accessed July 14, 2016, http://www.netours.com/content/view/113/25/1/2).

2. Unless otherwise indicated, Scripture quotations in this article are from the NIV.

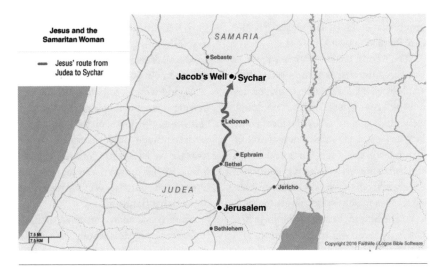

that longer trek on his final journey to Jerusalem.[3]

The route through Samaria, however, was shorter and popular during the Jewish feasts when hordes of Galileans traveled to Jerusalem (Josephus, Ant. 20.118). Although one cannot rule out geographical and temporal reasons, it appears that traveling through Samaria was a divine necessity, especially since John uses the Greek word *edei* (ἔδει, "to be necessary"). The contracted form of *edei—dei* (δεῖ)—appears several times in other contexts for divine mission (e.g., John 3:14; 9:4; 10:16; 12:34; 20:9).

AT JACOB'S WELL

Jesus waited outside Sychar, resting by the well, while his disciples went into town to buy food (John 4:4–8). The well

was on the land that the patriarch Jacob had purchased from the Canaanites (Gen 33:18–19; Josh 24:32). While he was at the well, a Samaritan woman came out to draw water. Jesus asked her for a drink of water, a request that surprised her due to the historical animosity between Jews and Samaritans.[4]

To answer her question of why a Jew would ask a Samaritan woman for water, Jesus replied that she should have asked *him* for "living water" (John 4:10). The Greek for "living water," *hydōr zōn* (ὕδωρ ζῶν), represents the Hebrew idiom *maim chayim* ("living water"), used to refer to running or flowing water. Of all water sources, living water represents the most fresh and the most satisfying. Springs bring forth living water, but so can wells that penetrate flowing, under-

---

3. Compare Luke 9:55, 56, where they leave Samaria, and Luke 18:35, where they are in Jericho.

4. See the excursus below on Jewish-Samaritan relations. The statement in John 4:9 that "Jews do not associate with Samaritans" may have been a comment from the narrator, but we cannot rule out that the woman spoke these words either as a reminder to Jesus to keep his distance or as an exclamation of surprise that a Jew would initiate such a request. The Greek phrase could also mean "Jews do not use dishes Samaritans have used" as in the NIV footnote.

ground water, and this appears to be the case for Jacob's Well.[5]

The region boasts of eighty springs, but the only well is Jacob's Well. Why would Jacob dig a well when many springs dot the area? These springs, no doubt, were already claimed by the local populace, so Jacob had to find a new source of water. Jacob was a foreigner in the land and had to purchase a plot of ground near Shechem from the sons of Hamor for his camp. Presumably, springs were too valuable to include in the sale, so the only alternative for Jacob was to dig a well.[6]

While Jesus was using "living water" as a metaphor for salvation, the Samaritan woman remained focused on physical water and whether Jesus could deliver any water since the well was deep (about one hundred thirty feet or forty meters), and he had nothing with which to draw water (John 4:11–12).

Perhaps the fact that the Samaritans accepted only the five books of Moses as Scripture limited the woman's appreciation of the living water metaphor as referring to God. In Jeremiah, Yahweh is "the spring of living water" (Jer 2:13a; 17:13) rejected by the Israelites for "broken cisterns that cannot hold water" (2:13b). The time will come when "living water will flow out from Jerusalem, half of it east to the Dead Sea and half of it west to the Mediterranean Sea, in summer and in winter" (Zech 14:8; compare Ezek 47:8–12). Isaiah invites "all you who are thirsty, come to the waters" (Isa

55:1), which Isaiah uses as a metaphor to imbibe freely of God's grace, for the Lord will freely pardon those who forsake their sin (55:7).

Living water symbolizes new life: a flowing, overwhelmingly refreshing river of life freely bestowed on the believer. No work required—unlike in drawing water from the well. Jesus has done all the work for us. He has drawn the living water in himself and poured it over us in the giving of the Spirit (John 4:13–14).

Since the woman continued to think in terms of physical water, Jesus made a more direct effort to reveal himself—asking her to fetch her husband and return to the well.

"I have no husband," she replied. Jesus said to her, "You are right when you say you have no husband. The fact is, you have had five husbands, and the man you now have is not your husband. What you have just said is quite true." (John 4:17–18)

With this revelation, she finally recognized Jesus as, at least, a prophet, so she changed the subject from her personal life to the dispute between Samaritans and Jews over sacred space.

"Sir," the woman said, "I can see that you are a prophet. Our ancestors worshiped on this mountain, but you Jews claim that the place where we must worship is in Jerusalem." (John 4:20)

---

5. See Barry J. Beitzel, *The New Moody Atlas of the Bible* (Chicago: Moody, 2009), 62–63, for a list of varying sources of water. Interestingly, the aquifer under Samaria is Israel's largest source of non-desalinated water (Aryeh Savir, "Rains from Samaria—The Largest Source of Water in Israel," *The Algemeiner* [website], April 3, 2012, accessed July 14, 2016, https://www.algemeiner.com/2012/04/03/rains-from-samaria—the-largest-source-of-water-in-israel).

6. Frédéric L. Godet, *Commentary on the Gospel of John*, trans. Timothy Dwight, vol. 1 (New York: Funk & Wagnalls, 1886), 421.

The statement formally is not a question, but from the context, it is obvious that the woman seeks clarification. When she realized Jesus was a prophet, she decided to take the opportunity to straighten out a perennial question she and other members of her community had pondered for centuries.

> "Woman," Jesus replied, "believe me, a time is coming when you will worship the Father neither on this mountain nor in Jerusalem. You Samaritans worship what you do not know; we worship what we do know,[7] for salvation is from the Jews. Yet a time is coming and has now come when the true worshipers will worship the Father in the Spirit and in truth, for they are the kind of worshipers the Father seeks. God is spirit, and his worshipers must worship in the Spirit and in truth." (John 4:21–24)

Jesus answers the temporal question: Jerusalem has primacy over Mount Gerizim. But from an eternal perspective, none of this is going to matter, for worshiping the Father is a matter of the heart, not of location. God wants worship in spirit and in truth. The choice of Sychar as the location for this teaching was no accident. Jesus was echoing the statement of Joshua in the Old Testament who had reaffirmed the Sinai Covenant at nearby Shechem with these words: "Now,

therefore, fear the LORD and serve Him in sincerity and truth" (Josh 24:14 NASB). Joshua's covenant renewal reminded his listeners of God's faithfulness to an obedient people. Jesus' words reverberate with the same promise of a faithful father to those who worship him properly.

Jesus' answer may have led the woman to suspect he was the coming Messiah since she replied that they were waiting for the Messiah to "explain everything" to them; Jesus confirms her suspicion (John 4:25–26).

It is also possible that John the Baptist's ministry had taken place near the region of Samaria. If so, the Samaritan woman's notion that Jesus might be the messiah could have come from John's teachings. John was baptizing at Aenon near Salim (John 3:23). This location may be near the present Arab village of Salim, which is in Samaria. We cannot know for sure, however, since evidence exists for three other possible locations for Aenon.[8] Whatever the source of her knowledge, her question brought about Jesus' first declaration that he was the messiah, the Christ.

The woman left her water jar,[9] ran to town, and told the people what had occurred—leading many from the town to come out to see Jesus themselves (John 4:28–30).

After two days in Samaria, and leaving numerous Samaritan believers behind, Jesus and his disciples return to welcoming crowds in Galilee. Unfortunately, in

---

7. Jesus may be directing this statement to the Samaritans who rejected all but the five books of Moses (Torah). Besides the Torah, the Jews had the Psalms, the wisdom literature, the prophets, and the historical books to give them a greater knowledge of God than the Samaritans.

8. See Anson F. Rainey and R. Steven Notley, *The Sacred Bridge* (Jerusalem: Carta, 2006), 350–51.

9. A vessel attributed to the woman is on display at the recently constructed Greek Orthodox Church at Sychar. A tradition—recounted by the senior priest of the church—relates

time the Samaritans forgot this interaction with Jesus, and later, when he "set his face to go to Jerusalem" (Luke 9:51 KJV), they refused him passage, whereupon Jesus crossed the Jordan into the Decapolis before crossing back near Jericho on his last ascent to Jerusalem (Luke 9:51–56).

Jesus' encounter with the Samaritan woman shows that Jesus was willing to break cultural taboos in order to reach people with the gospel. He also did not hesitate to discuss deep spiritual issues with ordinary people. As it turned out, they were far more responsive to him than were the elites of his day.

EXCURSUS: A SHORT HISTORICAL BACKGROUND OF THE SAMARITANS

One first encounters the Samaritans[10] in Scripture after the Jews' return from the Babylonian Exile. Initially, the Samaritans offered to help the Jews with the building of the temple in Jerusalem. The Jewish leaders rebuffed them, and the Samaritans retaliated by attempting to stop the building through mocking (Neh 4:1–3), threats (Ezra 4:4; Neh 4:11–13), and appeals to the governing Persian authorities (Ezra 4:7–24). Needless to say, the people dwelling in Samaria did not ingratiate themselves to the Jewish population.

Second Kings 17 provides clues to the origin of Samaria's population at that time. In 722 BC the northern kingdom of Samaria[11] fell to the Assyrians. The Assyrians—in order to prevent rebellion amongst their conquered peoples—mixed up populations by exiling one ethnic group and replacing it with another. Second Kings 17:24 states:

> The king of Assyria brought people from Babylon, Kuthah, Avva, Hamath and Sepharvaim and settled them in the towns of Samaria to replace the Israelites.

---

how Helena, Emperor Constantine's mother, recovered the jug from Sychar and took it to Constantinople. The Crusaders took the jar with them to Rome where it remained until Father Abouna Jeremias, senior priest and present archon of the church, asked Pope Benedict for permission to transfer the vessel back to Sychar. Pope Benedict agreed, and about five years ago the vessel returned to Sychar where it is prominently displayed half-way up one of the church's pillars (Father Jeremias, in discussion with the author, May 27 2016).

10. Not called Samaritans *per se*, but the context makes it clear that those who discouraged and later openly opposed the building of Jerusalem and the temple were from Samaria (Ezra 4:17; Neh 4:2). In the Bible, the term "Samaritans" first appears in Matt 10:5. In Jesus' day, the term "Samaritan" referred to one that lived in the Roman province of Samaria, not necessarily one from the city of Samaria. The woman no doubt originated from Sychar, for the city of Samaria would be about a two-hour walk from the well.

11. Samaria became the name of the northern kingdom of Israel after King Omri bought the hill of Samaria from Shemer for two talents of silver (1 Kgs 16:24). Omri built here the third capital of the northern kingdom. So important was this city that its name became a metonymy for the northern kingdom (Isa 9:9–12: Hos 8:5; Amos 3:9). The Old Testament calls the pre-exilic dwellers of the northern kingdom *hashomronim* ("Samaritans" ESV, KJV; "people of Samaria" NASB, NIV), named after their capital city Samaria. Later, the term "Samaritan" denoted a disparaged group of inhabitants considered foreigners to the Jews. (Note that Jesus separated the Samaritans from both the Gentiles and from the Jews (Matt 10:5, 6). See R. T. Anderson, "Samaritans," *ISBE* 4:303–8; idem, "Samaritans," *ABD* 5:940–47.

They took over Samaria and lived in its towns.[12]

At first, the new inhabitants did not know of the God of Israel, let alone honor him. The Lord, apparently still jealous for his land, sent lions to attack them. Upon learning of this danger to the new occupants, the king of Assyria ordered that a priest be sent to teach them "the custom of the god of the land" (2 Kgs 17:27).[13] Unfortunately, the teaching of the priest made little impact. The peoples continued to worship their own gods:

> The men of Babylon made Succoth-benoth, the men of Cuth made Nergal, the men of Hamath made Ashima, and the Avvites made Nibhaz and Tartak; and the Sepharvites burned their children in the fire to Adrammelech and Anammelech the gods of Sepharvaim (2 Kgs 17:29-31).

Still frightened of the lions, the people covered their bets by serving Israel's God alongside their own gods. They even appointed priests from among themselves to offer sacrifices at the high places. They continued following the religious customs of their homelands (2 Kgs 17:29-33). This blending of idolatry with reverence for God was not an acceptable compromise.

> To this day they persist in their former practices. They neither worship the LORD nor adhere to the decrees and regulations, the laws and commands that the LORD gave the descendants of Jacob, whom he named Israel. ... They would not listen, however, but persisted in their former practices. Even while these people were worshiping the LORD, they were serving their idols. To this day their children and grandchildren continue to do as their ancestors did. (2 Kgs 17:34, 40-41)

Ezra and Nehemiah, aware of the background of Samaria's populace, spurned Samaria's offer of help.[14] This religious dispute over theological purity led to political animosity between the Jews of Judah and the dwellers of Samaria that continued through the intertestamental period.

SAMARITAN/JUDEAN RELATIONSHIPS BETWEEN THE TESTAMENTS

Events in the intertestamental period exacerbated the enmity between the

---

12. From the context, it is clear that some Israelites from Samaria remained in the land. Otherwise, why would the Lord be anxious for his land if it were totally devoid of Israelites? Concomitantly, 1 Kings 17:34-35 makes it clear that some Israelites remained. If not, why would the Lord rebuke the inhabitants for not following "the statutes and the ordinances and the laws and the commandments" the Lord laid down for them at Sinai (see 1 Kgs 17:35-39)?

13. Note that the priest originated from Samaria, so he probably resided at Dan or at Bethel where Jeroboam I initially set up golden calves as proxies for Yahweh. One legitimately wonders, therefore, about the orthodoxy of the priest. If imbued with heterodoxy himself, is there any wonder why the people slouched towards syncretism?

14. The Samaritans, of course, advance a different, more favorable history. They consider themselves descendants of Jacob and the true followers of Yahweh. In their view, Eli, the priest at Shiloh mentioned in 1 Samuel, corrupted Yahweh worship when he took the ark from Mount Gerizim to Shiloh (see Wayne Brindle, "The Origin and History of the Samaritans," *Grace Theological Journal* 5.1 [1984]: 50-54).

Jews and the Samaritans.[15] Samaritans sold Jews into slavery during the reign of Antiochus III (the Great).[16] The Samaritans also interfered with the signal fires that announced the new moon to the Jewish inhabitants outside of Judea.[17] During Jesus' early years, the Samaritans defiled the temple in Jerusalem by scattering dead men's bones in the temple courtyard just as the priests opened the gates for the celebration of Passover.[18]

Lest one think the animosity was one-sided: The Jews under John Hyrcanus reduced the Samaritan city of Shechem and conquered the city of Samaria, selling its inhabitants into slavery. Hyrcanus also committed the ultimate desecration against Samaritan religion by destroying their temple on Mount Gerizim.[19]

According to Yehoshua M. Grintz, "the Samaritans considered this temple to be their most holy spot, and their tradition ascribes nearly all of the biblical account of the patriarchs' deeds and the places associated with them (the land of Moriah, Beth-El, etc.) to Mt. Gerizim."[20] In spite of the temple's destruction, Mount Gerizim continued as the Samaritan place of worship.

BIBLIOGRAPHY

Anderson, Robert T. "Samaritans." ABD 5:940–47.

Anderson, Robert T. "Samaritans." ISBE 4:303–8.

Beitzel, Barry J. The New Moody Atlas of the Bible. Chicago: Moody, 2009.

Brindle, Wayne. "The Origin and History of the Samaritans." Grace Theological Journal 5.1 (1984): 47–75.

Edersheim, Alfred. The Life and Times of Jesus the Messiah. 2 vols. New York: Longmans, Green, and Co., 1896.

Godet, Frédéric L. Commentary on the Gospel of John. Translated by Timothy Dwight. Vol. 1. New York: Funk & Wagnalls, 1886.

Grintz, Yehoshua M., and Shimon Gibson. "Gerizim, Mount." EJ 7:507–9.

Har-El, Menashe. Golden Jerusalem. Jerusalem: Gefen Publishing House, 2004.

---

15. Key aspects of the conflict between Jews and Samaritans are summarized by Alfred Edersheim, The Life and Times of Jesus the Messiah (New York: Longmans, Green, and Co., 1896), 1:399.

16. Josephus, Ant. 12:154–59.

17. Upon the word of two witnesses that they had seen the new moon, the ruling priesthood in Jerusalem lit a bonfire announcing the beginning of the month. Subsequently, a line of signal fires brought the message all the way to Babylonia (see Menashe Har-El, Golden Jerusalem [Jerusalem: Gefen Publishing House, 2004], 99–101).

18. Josephus, Ant. 18:17–23. This incident occurred while Coponius was procurator of Judea, AD 6–9.

19. Dates uncertain, but sometime in the late 2nd century BC.

20. Yehoshua M. Grintz and Shimon Gibson, "Gerizim, Mount," EJ 7:507. For a collection of excerpts from primary sources illustrating Judean/Samaritan tensions over the location of the legitimate temple of God, see Mahlon H. Smith, "Judean-Samaritan Feud," Into His Own: Perspectives on the World of Jesus (website), accessed July 14, 2016, http://virtualreligion.net/iho/samaria.html. See also Yitzhak Magen, "Gerizim, Mount," NEAEHL 2:484–87. Interestingly, in spite of the plethora of references to the temple on Mount Gerizim, archaeological excavations have not yielded evidence of a temple.

Jeremias, Abounas, interview by Author. (May 27, 2016).

Langfur, Stephen. "Nablus (Shechem): Jacob's Well." Accessed July 14, 2016. http://www.netours.com/content/view/113/25/1/2.

Magen, Yitzhak. "Gerizim, Mount." NEAEHL 2:484–91.

Morris, Leon. The Gospel According to John. NICNT. Grand Rapids: Eerdmans, 1971.

Rainey, Anson F., and R. Steven Notley. The Sacred Bridge. Jerusalem: Carta, 2006.

Savir, Aryeh. "Rains from Samaria— The Largest Source of Water in Israel." The Algemeiner (website). April 3, 2012. Accessed July 14, 2016. https://www.algemeiner. com/2012/04/03/rains-from- samaria---the-largest-source-of- water-in-israel/.

Smith, Mahlon H. "Judean – Samaritan Feud." Into His Own: Perspectives on the World of Jesus (website). Accessed July 14, 2016. http://virtualreligion. net/iho/samaria.html.

CHAPTER 11

ON THE BROW OF THE HILL AT NAZARETH

Luke 4:16–20

Elaine A. Phillips

KEY POINTS

- Upper Galilee was a home to rebels, bandits, and radical resistance movements that opposed Roman occupation.

- Gentile inhabitants of Upper Galilee had been forced to convert to Judaism over a century before the time of Christ.

- Seen from Nazareth Ridge, the Jezreel Valley provided a view into the rough and tumble past of Israel's journey with their God.

- Jesus' rebuke of his hometown is made more pungent when this history is kept in mind as he teaches and is, subsequently, driven to the precipice.

AN OVERVIEW OF NAZARETH

"Can anything good come out of Nazareth?" (John 1:46). This brash question from Nathanael sets the stage for our exploration of the narrative in Luke 4:16–30. The question itself suggests a number of interpretive levels. Does it refer to the size of the town, the location, or something about its intrinsic character? Nazareth was in the Galilee, a region viewed with some suspicion by

Jews in Jerusalem (John 7:41: "Surely the Messiah does not come from the Galilee, does he?" NRSV). There were reasons for this. As part of the old northern kingdom, this region had endured the resettlement policy of the Assyrian Empire (2 Kgs 17:24–41), and the population in the centuries just before Christ was primarily Gentile. In 104–103 BC, however, Aristobulus I imposed conversion to Judaism on these people (Josephus, *Ant.*

13.318).[1] No doubt, this history influenced how some people from Jerusalem and Judea viewed the inhabitants of Galilee, even in the early first century AD.

Perhaps because of the more rugged topography and isolation of Upper Galilee (about ten miles north of Nazareth), the region was also home to rebels and bandits. As part of his initial brutal subjugation of his kingdom (40–37 BC), Herod the Great went to war to defeat them (Josephus, War 1.290–316). After Herod's death in 4 BC, a revolt against Rome broke out in the Galilee, and Sepphoris, center of the Roman presence in the Galilee region, was burned (Josephus, War 2.68). In the decades that followed, radical resistance movements opposed to Roman occupation emerged; many of the notable leaders were from towns in the Galilee.[2] This was "home" to the Son of God.

In all four Gospels, we read variations on a further stinging comment about Nazareth from Jesus himself. The one in Luke comes from this very narrative: "No prophet is accepted in the prophet's home town" (Luke 4:24 NRSV).[3] Mark's version is the strongest: "A prophet is not without honor, except in his hometown and among his relatives and in his own household" (Mark 6:4 ESV). And yet, he was acknowledged by the crowds to be "Jesus of Nazareth,"[4] (though this is perhaps because the Hebrew form of his name, Joshua, was so common that further identification was important). With these observations in mind, we will continue to explore Nazareth from geographical and geopolitical angles.

GEOGRAPHICAL AND GEOPOLITICAL CONTEXTS

During the first century AD, Nazareth was a small town, nestled in a chalk basin atop a high ridge that served as the northern boundary of the Jezreel Valley.[5] The precipice edge overlooking the valley is somewhat higher in elevation than the town and would have provided a sense of seclusion and protection for that small village in the first century. Nevertheless, climbing to that precipice affords dramatic views of the immense arena that had served for millennia as a highway and a battleground. Both the commercial and military traffic during the first centuries BC and AD shaped the character of Nazareth considerably. The Jezreel Valley was Jesus' backyard as he was growing up.[6]

From that Nazareth Ridge overlooking the valley, he would have seen to the east Mount Tabor, jutting up from the valley floor. We sense echoes of Deborah and Barak contending with the forces of Jabin and Sisera (Judg 4–5). Just to the south of Mount Tabor were Mount Moreh and, across the opening of the

1. Kenneth E. Bailey, *Jesus Through Middle Eastern Eyes: Cultural Studies in the Gospels* (Downers Grove, IL: InterVarsity Press, 2008), 152.

2. The most notable was Judas the Galilean (Josephus, War 2.118).

3. See also Matt 13:57; Mark 6:4; John 4:44.

4. Matt 21:11; 26:71; Mark 1:24; 16:6; Luke 4:34; 18:37; 24:19; John 1:45; 18:5, 7; 19:19.

5. Paul H. Wright, *Greatness Grace & Glory: Carta's Atlas of Biblical Biography* (Jerusalem: Carta, 2008), 175; Steven P. Lancaster and James M. Monson, *Regional Study Guide*, Version 5.0 (Rockford, IL: Biblical Backgrounds, Inc., 2011), 44–45.

6. George Adam Smith, *The Historical Geography of the Holy Land* (1931; repr., London: Fontana Library, 1974), 282–83.

Jezreel Valley from Nazareth Ridge

Harod Valley, Mount Gilboa. Additional narratives from the Hebrew Bible were set in these contexts: Gideon's battle with the Midianites (Judg 6–8), Saul's final days on Mount Gilboa, his disastrous visit to the witch at Endor behind enemy lines (1 Sam 28), and his choice of death in the face of the Philistine defeat (1 Sam 31). The city of Shunem where the prophet Elisha brought a young man back to life (2 Kgs 4) was at the foot of Mount Moreh. Jesus would later perform the same miracle in Nain, just around the corner from Shunem (Luke 7:11–17).

At the critical intersection of the Jezreel and Harod Valleys was the city of Jezreel. It was poised to monitor traffic from major power centers in Syria and points farther east, often in the form of hostile armies. These battlefields stretched from Ramoth Gilead, across the Jordan River to the east, into the heart of the Jezreel Valley. In addition to the bloodshed during wartime, the name of Jezreel was associated with inno-cent blood as well. Elijah condemned the treachery of Jezebel against Naboth, who refused to relinquish his family-owned vineyard to the petulant king Ahab and was executed after a trumped-up charge (1 Kgs 21). Jezebel met her death at Jezreel at the order of Jehu (2 Kgs 9), but Jehu went on a bloody rampage against Ahab's family, having the heads of his seventy sons delivered to Jezreel (2 Kgs 9). The history of these places that Jesus knew was blood-soaked.

Turning west and gazing across the Jezreel Valley brought additional dramatic narratives to the fore. The contest between Elijah and the prophets of Baal took place on Mount Carmel (1 Kgs 17–18). Elisha later lodged there when the Shunammite traveled to him for help (2 Kgs 4). It was to Mount Carmel that Naaman, the Syrian general, likely came to Elisha for healing from leprosy (2 Kgs 5). At the base of Mount Carmel lay Megiddo, the plum that many tried to capture and hold. What a backdrop for this stage on which centuries of world history unfolded![7]

As if this were not enough, residents of Nazareth could climb the slight rise to the north of their village and survey the fertile Beth Netofa Valley. Across that valley was the small town of Cana (John 2). Just about three and a half miles to the northwest was Sepphoris, the largest city in the Galilee and well-positioned for Rome to guard the whole region (Josephus, *War* 3.30–34.). Although it is not mentioned at all in the Gospels, it would have been a major part of the cultural setting of Jesus' day. He no doubt knew it very well, and possibly even worked there with Joseph in the days before his public ministry. Just to the east of Nazareth was Gath Hepher, the hometown of Jonah (2 Kgs 14:25; Jonah 1:1). It is no wonder that Jesus referred to "the sign of Jonah" and expected his audiences to understand (Matt 12:38–41; compare Matt 16:4; Luke 11:29–32).[8]

The Beth Netofa Valley provided a significant east-west corridor from the coast into the interior of the Galilee, to Sepphoris and beyond. Thus, even though Nazareth was in a protected basin to the south of that main route, it was close enough to access and experience the effects of military and commercial traffic west to Acco and then north to Phoenicia. In addition, connections to the east led to the major international highway that passed the Sea of Galilee and the lake-side towns of Magdala, Genneseret, and Capernaum. That route led on toward Mount Hermon, beyond to

Damascus, and to points even farther east. While this land was the eastern frontier of the Roman Empire in the first century, there was a whole world in Mesopotamia as well, and it had affected God's people in the centuries past.

Nazareth was in the tribal allotment of Zebulun, one of the four northernmost tribes that often felt the isolation of being separated from the rest of the tribes by the expanse of the Jezreel Valley. Both Zebulun and Naphtali are mentioned by Isaiah as lands viewed with contempt ("Galilee of the Gentiles"), but the prophet went on to declare "the people who walked in darkness have seen a great light" (Isa 9:1–2 ESV). The dismissive tone of Isa 9:1 may have contributed to the negative assessment that Nazareth experienced. Nevertheless, Matthew returned to that text and emphasized the light. Both Nazareth in Zebulun and Capernaum in Naphtali would be rehabilitated with the light dawning upon them (Matt 4:12–17).

JESUS IS REJECTED
(LUKE 4:16–30)

PREACHING IN THE SYNAGOGUE

Jesus returned to the Galilee following his baptism and temptation, and he was teaching in the synagogues (Luke 4:14–15). He visited his hometown of Nazareth and went to the synagogue on the Sabbath. Luke reminds us that this was his custom. Perhaps his growing reputation as a popular teacher won for him the privilege of reading the Hebrew Scriptures for the day.[9] Luke tells us that Jesus read from Isa

---

7. See Smith, *Historical Geography*, 253.

8. See map "Old Testament Events in Jezreel Valley" on pg. 534.

9. On the basis of Acts 13:15, Bailey suggests, "It was customary for worship leaders to invite a worthy person in the congregation to read from the Scriptures and comment on

61:1–2. It seems that the scroll was already prepared for him to read. It may be that the Torah reading that preceded Isaiah was Lev 25 which covered the regulations for the Jubilee. The emphasis in the Isaiah passage on freedom for prisoners and release for the oppressed suggests that connection. This combination of texts might have ignited sparks of nationalistic hope for that moment. After all, the inhabitants of Nazareth were living under the ever-present Roman presence in Sepphoris.

When Jesus had finished the reading, he rolled up the scroll and sat down. This did not mean he was finished; it meant now the instruction would start. Jesus set right out to astonish the gathered congregation. In fact, if this is the same incident that Mark briefly reports (Mark 6:1–6; see also Matt 13:53–58), the people were disagreeable right from the beginning. They were incredulous at his teaching and actions, scoffed at his family connections, and, as Mark indicates, "took offense" or "stumbled" on his account. All of this prompted Jesus to exclaim that a prophet was not without honor except in his hometown.

Luke gives us a fuller account of the rhetorical developments up to this point. Once Jesus declared that the Scripture he had just read was fulfilled that day in their hearing, they "bore witness" (*martyreō*, μαρτυρέω), were astonished, and asked the same incredulous question:

given that his father was Joseph, who did he think he was anyway? Many translations interpret "bearing witness" in a positive sense; the people spoke well of him but then shortly turned entirely against him. It might be, however, that "bearing witness" had negative undertones from the outset. The Greek grammar of the sentence allows that, and it fits better with the development of the story and the parallels in Matt and Mark. In any case, if there had been any veneer of admiration in their words to this point, Jesus straightway exposed them as skeptics who were unconvinced unless they saw a dramatic demonstration of miraculous power that was designed to give them what they expected from a messianic figure.[10]

This volley was followed by his declaration that no prophet was accepted in his hometown. While the other Synoptic Gospels comment at this point on the lack of faith of the people and the fact that Jesus did not do many miracles, Luke forges ahead with more of Jesus' teaching on the occasion. His mention of Israel's signature prophets—Elijah and Elisha—was not merely a literary link with what he just said about honor for prophets; these were also geopolitical and religious allusions—stinging ones for that time.

In the days of Elijah and Elisha, the Israelites who lived in the northern part of the land were caught in pincers between two hostile political entities:

the reading" (*Jesus Through Middle Eastern Eyes*, 147). However, we know too little about customary synagogue practices in the first century to say with certainty *why* Jesus was allowed to read. Marshall notes Jesus may have "informally requested permission to read before the service began" (I. Howard Marshall, The Gospel of Luke, NIGTC [Exeter: Paternoster, 1978], 182). It appears that most men would have been eligible to read and that several men likely read during a service (m. Megillah 4:1–4; compare Darrell L. Bock, *Luke: 1:1–9:50*, BECNT [Grand Rapids: Baker Academic, 1994], 403–4).

10. Bailey, *Jesus Through Middle Eastern Eyes*, 150–51.

to testify approvingly

μαρτυρέω
testify; bear witness

to bear witness

to be approvingly testified of

to be testified

Bible Word Study: μαρτυρέω, martyreō

Phoenicia to the northwest and Aram (Syria) to the northeast. Phoenicia had been the source of Baal worship, an ongoing temptation for the Israelites in this land that depended on rain from the heavens (Deut 11:11–15). In Elijah's time, Ahab and Jezebel ruled the northern kingdom and had essentially established Baal worship as the state religion right in the heart of Samaria. When Elijah declared that there would be neither rain nor dew except at his word (1 Kgs 17:1), he was confronting Baal head-on. Baal was supposedly the god of storm, rain, agricultural fertility, and economic well-being. At the same time, Elijah was directed to go to Sidon and provide sustenance and life for a widow and her son in the name of the Lord God of Israel.

As if that were not enough, Jesus went on to remind his audience of the other major thorn in Israel's flesh following the reign of Ahab; it was Aram to the northeast. The high-ranking commander of the Aramean army, Naaman, was in good standing because the Lord had given Aram victory over Israel. (There is a sub-text here: Israel's disobedience under Ahab meant God's chastisement via enemy forces.) Because Naaman was suffering from leprosy, however, he was likely living on the fringes of good society. Nevertheless, a young Israelite woman who had been taken captive was serving in Naaman's household. Rather than wishing ill on her master, she informed him of the possibility of being healed if he appealed to the Lord God of Israel. His journey eventually landed him on Elisha's doorstep, then dipping in the muddy Jordan River, and finally heading back home as a cleansed person (2 Kgs 5).

We need one more detail to understand the powerful rebuke behind the words of Jesus. People of the ancient Near East connected gods with specific lands and did not expect those gods to operate outside territorial boundaries.[11] The widow from Sidon was gathering sticks to cook her last morsels because she expected to die. Baal had failed; what else was left? Her switch of allegiance from

---

11. A striking example appears in 2 Kgs 17:24–41. Following the fall of the northern ten tribes to Assyria, the empire-wide exile and resettlement policy meant non-Israelites were moved into the land. When they experienced severe attacks from lions (sent by the Lord), they presumed they needed education regarding the "law of the god of the land" (17:26–27). The same world view is evident in the messages from Sennacherib to the defenders of Judah and Jerusalem (2 Chr 32:9–15).

Baal to the Lord God of Israel was a radical demonstration of faith. The same was true of Naaman. Immediately following his healing, he wanted to take two mule-packs of earth back to Syria so that he could shape a context in which to worship the Lord (2 Kgs 5:17). It would probably take time for his worldview to shift gears entirely (see 2 Kgs 5:18–19)

The people in Nazareth who had gathered in the synagogue that day were waiting for a dramatic messianic demonstration, but they were not at all inclined to believe—unlike those detested outsiders had done centuries before.[12] Jesus called them on their self-serving motives and nationalistic arrogance. Perhaps there were reverberations of contemporary oppression from outsiders coming in from the sea—the Romans. No doubt Jesus' audience would much rather have been reminded about how Elijah called down judgment on all the prophets of Baal at the later event on Mount Carmel. But Jesus said nothing of this.

Although reminders of the sign of Jonah were not part of Jesus' history lesson from the Hebrew Bible on that day, they would have had the same effect. Jonah preached repentance to Nineveh, a major city of the Assyrian Empire. Their leaders boasted of brutality against conquered peoples.[13] Jonah's initial flight upon hearing the call to preach was likely due at least partly to fear. His later response of anger at God's mercy likewise betrayed his desire to see the enemy flattened. Fear and anger against the powerful oppressor in Jesus' day burst forth in their fury at him.[14]

THE CROWD'S REACTION

In their rage, the mob drove Jesus out of town and up to the crest of the hill on which the town was built. The intent was to pitch him over the edge. The early rabbinic legal discussions give us insight into the requirements for capital punishment by means of stoning. The guilty party was taken to a place that was twice his height and was pushed at the hips by one of the witnesses. This detail was important because the individual's legs would be knocked out from under him and he would land in a way that would be more likely to be fatal. If he survived, the second witness placed a stone (probably a large one) on his heart in order to bring about his end. If he managed to live through that, then all the witnesses would take up stones against him (m. Sanhedrin 6:4). This applied to a number of offenses deemed serious enough to warrant death. It seems that Jesus' words verged on blasphemy in the mind of the crowd and tipped them into the death penalty mode. Offenses that warranted death by stoning included having improper sexual relations, committing blasphemy, practicing idolatry or divination, profaning the Sabbath, and cursing parents (m. Sanhedrin 7:4).

Given the rugged precipice, the crowd's mentality, and this ready process, disaster was imminent—but Jesus simply walked right through the crowd. It was

12. Bailey, *Jesus Through Middle Eastern Eyes*, 164–65.

13. The records from Year 1 of Assurnasirpal II's annals are just one example (see Daniel David Luckenbill, *Ancient Records of Assyria and Babylonia* [Chicago: The University of Chicago Press, 1926], 1:141–45).

14. Paul H. Wright, *Greatness Grace & Glory*, 175–77.

Nazareth's loss. After this, Jesus moved his base of operations to Capernaum (Luke 4:31; see Matt 4:13; John 2:12).

BIBLIOGRAPHY

Bailey, Kenneth E. *Jesus Through Middle Eastern Eyes: Cultural Studies in the Gospels.* Downers Grove, IL: InterVarsity Press, 2008.

Baly, Denis. *The Geography of the Bible.* Rev. ed. New York: Harper and Row, 1974.

Beck, John A. *The Land of Milk and Honey: An Introduction to the Geography of Israel.* Saint Louis, MO: Concordia, 2006.

Bock, Darrell L. *Luke: 1:1–9:50.* BECNT. Grand Rapids: Baker Academic, 1994.

Josephus. *The Jewish War.* 2 vols. Translated by H. St. J. Thackeray. LCL. Cambridge, MA: Harvard University Press, 1927–28.

Lancaster, Steven P., and James M. Monson. *Regional Study Guide.* Version 5.0. Rockford, IL: Biblical Backgrounds, Inc., 2011.

Luckenbill, Daniel David. *Ancient Records of Assyria and Babylonia.* 2 vols. Chicago: The University of Chicago Press, 1926.

Marshall, I. Howard. *The Gospel of Luke: A Commentary on the Greek Text.* NIGTC. Exeter: Paternoster Press, 1978.

Neusner, Jacob. *The Mishnah: A New Translation.* New Haven, CT: Yale University Press, 1988.

Orni, Efraim, and Elisha Ephrat. *Geography of Israel.* 3rd ed. Jerusalem: Keter, 1971.

Rasmussen, Carl G. *Zondervan Atlas of the Bible.* Grand Rapids: Zondervan, 2010.

Smith, George Adam. *The Historical Geography of the Holy Land.* 1931. Reprint, London: Fontana Library, 1974.

Wright, Paul H. *Greatness Grace & Glory: Carta's Atlas of Biblical Biography.* Jerusalem: Carta, 2008.

CHAPTER 12

THE DOMESTIC ARCHITECTURE OF CAPERNAUM AND BEYOND
A WINDOW INTO FIRST CENTURY LIFE

Matt 8-9 with Synoptic Parallels (Matt 9:1-8; Mark 2:1-12; Luke 5:17-26; Matt 8:5-13; Luke 7:1-10; Matt 9:10-13; Luke 5:29; Mark 9:33-37)

Elaine A. Phillips

KEY POINTS

- Capernaum was Jesus' home base of operation; more specifically Jesus made Simon Peter's home his own.

- Five of Jesus' disciples lived in Capernaum: Peter, Andrew, James, John, and Matthew.

- The homes from this area were all built from basalt, which made the inside gloomier than those built from limestone—a fact that provides more context for Jesus' words about light and lamps.

Even though Jesus declared that the Son of Man had nowhere to lay his head (Matt 8:20), he did nevertheless make Capernaum his home base (Mark 2:1). The town was near the border between territorial holdings of Herod Antipas and Herod Philip, both sons of Herod the Great. In addition, the northern reaches of the Greek-speaking Decapolis region were also nearby. Capernaum was at a crossroad point on the route between Asia, Africa, and Europe. All of these factors meant the presence of tax collectors and a garrison of troops to keep order.

What a choice for Jesus! It was important enough that Matthew collected the events that took place in Capernaum's homes into two chapters of place-based narratives (Matt 8-9). The dwelling places of those who are named have a high profile in these chapters, and the theological significance of Jesus' choice to make his home in the midst of his people is unmistakable; it is another reflection of God with us.

We can also investigate these homes for a small window into the daily life of the first century. In several cases, the very architecture of the home determined the shape of the narrative and the lessons embedded therein. Further, we learn who owned those homes and what their social status might have been. As Jesus approached or entered into these homes, he was entering a dwelling that would afford some sense of stability to his itinerant band of disciples. One additional level of symbolism may lie in those events that take place inside as opposed to outside.

CAPERNAUM: PROPERTY OWNERS AND SOCIAL STATUS

In Matthew 8–9, we read of four real estate owners in Capernaum. The best known is Simon Peter. Early on in Jesus' Galilean ministry, he chose Simon Peter and Andrew as disciples (Matt 4:18–20; Mark 1:16–18). It was not long before Peter's home became Jesus' home as well. He healed Simon Peter's mother-in-law (Matt 8:14–15; Mark 1:29–30; Luke 4:38) and seems to have been welcomed into the home, even though it was modest. From the archaeological finds in small Galilean towns such as Capernaum and Korazin, we know that homes were constructed so that it was easy to add small rooms onto the complex when necessary. This is called the *insula* house structure. We also know that crowds from the whole town and beyond gathered around the door of this house on multiple occasions (Mark 1:33).

In the second half of the first century, Christians began to visit Capernaum, and particularly a large room (21 x 23 ft / 6.5 x 7 m). Perhaps it was used as a house church (*domus ecclesia*), carrying on an already honored tradition. It seems unlikely the early believers would have allowed that place to slip into oblivion. Several clues from the archaeologists' work are also illuminating.[1] The main room was plastered which seems to have been unusual in the first century. While normal ceramic remains would have been household pots of various shapes, here they found large storage jars. Oil lamps were also part of the assemblage. It is possible the house was used for communal gatherings. In the fourth century, this central large room was expanded.[2] In one of the rooms, markings on the walls like what we might call graffiti mention "Jesus," "Lord," and "Messiah." Signs of a fish and a crucifix were etched on the plastered walls. The inscriptions in Hebrew, Greek, Syriac, and Latin suggest pilgrims. Egeria, a late fourth century pilgrim, noted the presence of a substantial church in Capernaum. In the fifth century it was converted to an octagonal church, the architectural style that signified a memorial church. Five of Jesus' disciples lived in Capernaum: Peter, Andrew, James, John, and Matthew.

The other three Capernaum homeowners seem to have been significantly wealthy. They represented the mili-

---

1. On the archaeological details of this site, see James F. Strange and Hershel Shanks, "St. Peter's House: Has the House Where Jesus Stayed in Capernaum Been Found?" in *Ten Top Biblical Archaeology Discoveries* (Biblical Archaeology Society, 2011), 68–85.

2. See also Paul H. Wright, *Greatness Grace & Glory: Carta's Atlas of Biblical Biography* (Jerusalem: Carta, 2008), 182.

tary, bureaucratic, and religious strata of Capernaum's social scene. The first was a centurion who was "at home" in Capernaum (Matt 8:5–13; Luke 7:1–10). Jesus never entered that house because the centurion was sensitive to the social divide that separated most Jewish people from the foreign occupiers. Nevertheless, he asked Jesus for healing for his servant, and his plea was granted. Roman officers stationed in this town near the border between Herod Antipas' Galilee and Herod Philip's territories would no doubt have had comfortable lodgings with sufficient space for servants. Luke also adds details regarding the centurion's good standing with the Jewish elders, especially since he had built their synagogue.

The converted tax-collector, Matthew (called Levi in Luke's Gospel), held a banquet in his house (Matt 9:10–13; Luke 5:29). We learn that many tax collectors and "sinners" were eating with Jesus and his disciples on that occasion. In other words, this was a luxurious and large dwelling, in contrast to what the disciples and others in Jesus' following were accustomed to. Tax collectors turned over quite a profit from their heavy-handed measures. Levi's guests were reclining at table, another hint of the upper-class lifestyle. It is also worth noting that the Pharisees were in a position to see this happening—perhaps lingering outside the doors.

Jairus was ruler of the local synagogue in Capernaum, another high-profile position. That no doubt meant his house was likewise substantial. When Jesus finally got there, after a brief healing detour en route, the place was filled with mourners and was noisy. Jesus entered the house and sent the whole lot outside. They would not be privy to this miracle (Matt 9:23–26; Mark 5:35–43; Luke 8:49–56).

Although Matthew does not provide substantial details of these narratives, Luke mentions Pharisees, one named Simon (Luke 7:36–50), who invited Jesus to dine with them (see also Luke 11:37–54; 14:1–6). In the first two cases, they reclined at a table and were expected to engage in washing rituals before dining. While the text does not indicate the setting was Capernaum, these events still seem to be located in the Galilee. By the third narrative, it is a ruler of the Pharisees, and Jesus is journeying toward Jerusalem (Luke 13:22; 14:1).

SIGNATURE EVENTS IN CAPERNAUM

It was high drama when the friends of a paralytic man removed the roof of the place Jesus called home in Capernaum (Matt 9:1–8; Mark 2:1–12; Luke 5:17–26). Jesus was preaching the word to the crowds milling outside the doorway. Pharisees and teachers of the law were sitting there as well (Luke 5:17). There was no way to get through to Jesus with the paralyzed man, so his friends removed the roof, having dug through it (Mark 2:4). Luke has a bit of a different twist on the roof modification, saying they removed the clay tiles (Luke 5:17). Luke's addition might be a narrative reflection of his own Graeco-Roman background where roof tiles would have been a common feature. The detail in the story of digging through the roof fits well with the customary roof construction in which long poles spaced about 18 inches apart would have been covered with more slender branches and mud that was rolled each season to pack it together. It might not be too much of a stretch to suggest there were tiles as well, but it is impossible to be certain. The emphasis of the narrative is instead on the faith and faithfulness of the friends. It is also on the truth that Jesus could heal both the physical paralysis and the spiritual disorder of sin that needed to be dealt with. At the word of Jesus, the man took up his mat and went outside, making his way through the crowds at the door as a walking demonstration of Jesus' power to do both.

As to the other events in Capernaum, Jesus never entered the centurion's residence; he did not have to. Instead, the exchange served as a platform to celebrate the steady and reasoned faith of the foreign military man, an outsider to be sure, but one who had the trust of the local leaders (Matt 8:5-13; Luke 7:1-10). The perspective shifted as Jesus and his disciples dined with the tax collectors and other sketchy persons—"sinners" (Matt 9:10-13; Luke 5:29). This scene would be repeated in Jericho when Jesus dined at Zacchaeus' house (Luke 19:1-10). In both cases, the religious establishment—the Pharisees—did not approve. Those Jesus dined with were outsiders. The narrative of Jairus, however, brought Jesus right into the center of the synagogue ruler's home where his daughter had died. Jesus expelled all the mourners so that only he, Peter, James, John, and the girl's parents were left in the room. They were privileged to witness the restoration of her life and then were ordered not to speak of it (Luke 8:56).

Lest Jesus be accused of avoiding Pharisees, that was not the case. He ate with them as well (Luke 11:37-54; 14:1-24). In both instances recorded by Luke, the dining environment was high class; foot washing was an expected demonstration of hospitality, and there were designated places of honor to sit at, suggesting a notable number of guests. Of course, these presumed religious models tripped-up in both cases, prompting rebukes from Jesus.

On at least one occasion, the home in Capernaum was the scene of an argument. The disciples had been out and about in Galilee. After arriving back in Capernaum, they were disputing who among them was the greatest. The room was large enough to hold the Twelve, plus

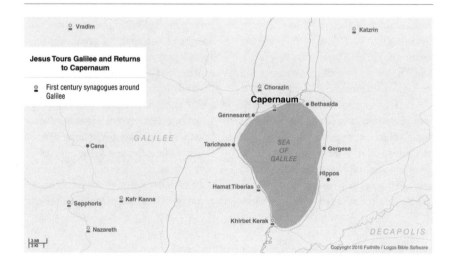

Jesus Tours Galilee and Returns to Capernaum

First century synagogues around Galilee

at least the child who stood in their midst when Jesus made his point (Mark 9:33–37).

HOUSEHOLD EQUIPMENT AT CAPERNAUM (AND ELSEWHERE)

The follow-up to the previous narrative teaches us about domestic and perhaps industrial equipment. Jesus said that anyone who caused a child to sin would be better off if a millstone were tied around his neck and he were cast into the sea (Matt 18:6; Mark 9:42; Luke 17:2). This was a dramatic declaration. The Sea of Galilee was right there and was viewed as an abyss that would have been terribly frightening. As for millstones, they were huge and heavy. Excavations in Capernaum have turned up numerous large stones used for olive pressing (perhaps evidence of an olive pressing industry). There could have been no better visual aids.[3][4]

Additional home implements and utensils included domestic grindstones, winnowing forks, threshing boards (Amos 1:3; Isa 41:15–16) and yokes. These would all have been intrinsic to Jesus' daily life. Grinding grain was the job of women, and it took about one hour to grind a kilo of flour. For a family, that might mean upwards of three hours of grinding per day. "Give us this day our coming day's bread" takes on a new meaning. The yoke was used to both direction and control animals. The symbolism is obvious. Jesus said "Take my yoke upon you ... my yoke is easy and my burden is light" (Matt 11:29–30 NIV). Jews knew well the figure of the "yoke of Torah." One final indispensable item was the water storage jar. At the wedding feast in Cana, there were six of these stone water jars,

each holding up to thirty gallons. These were used for ceremonial cleansing (John 2:1–11).

Millstone found at Capernaum

RESIDENCES IN JERUSALEM

Moving beyond the parameters of Jesus' Galilean ministry, we can learn important details about home architecture and ownership by visiting Jerusalem. These dwellings also span a significant social status range. In a village near Jerusalem, Martha owned a home into which she invited Jesus. It seems to have been small enough that she was unsettled when her sister, Mary, sat at the feet of Jesus without a care for helping Martha (Luke 10:38–42). Clearly, there were no servants here.

Additional details about family homes come to light as we piece together nar-

---

3. See Cyndi Parker, "Millstones in Capernaum" on pg. 308.
4. Wright, *Greatness Grace & Glory*, 172.

rative snippets in the Gospels. We learn from John that Lazarus was also in Martha's home, which was located in Bethany on the east side of the Mount of Olives (John 11:1). Just days before Jesus celebrated Passover with his disciples, Mary (unnamed in Matthew and Mark) poured oil on Jesus' head as he reclined at a table with Simon the Leper (Matt 26:6–13; Mark 14:3–9; John 11:2; 12:1–11). That event also took place in Bethany. Perhaps Bethany was something of a colony for those who suffered from leprosy; it was out of view of the temple but still close to Jerusalem.[5][6]

In Jerusalem, Jesus instructed the disciples to prepare the Passover in an upstairs guest room; in fact, Jesus called it "*my* guest room" (Mark 14:14), suggesting that perhaps he had made arrangements ahead of time. Mark tells us it was large (*megas*, μέγας); it had to be since all the disciples would be reclining around the Passover table (Matt 26:19; Mark 14:14–15; Luke 22:7–14).

In another social stratum altogether was the palace of the high priest Caiaphas (Matt 26:3). This might cross the border between domestic and institutional structures. As Jesus was enduring this first phase of the trial, Peter was below (Mark 14:66) in the courtyard (see also Matt 26:57–75; Luke 22:54–62; John 18:15–18). It was a sufficiently large and open space for the guards to light a fire to keep warm. During the course of his denials, Peter was on the move from the courtyard to the gate, and then finally outside (Matt 26:69–75; Luke 22:54–62).

A SIGNIFICANT HOME IN BETHLEHEM

Both Mark and Luke mention preparing the "guest room" for Passover. This is our connection to one more architectural design feature of first century housing. When Mary and Joseph arrived in Bethlehem, Luke tells us there was no room in the "inn." The Greek word used there is *katalyma* (κατάλυμα; Luke 2:7). The same term is used in conjunction with the large upper room prepared for Passover for Jesus and his disciples. Homes often had a separate, somewhat raised, guest room at one end. Between that raised room and a lower space where animals sheltered at night was a living space that may have opened into the animal shelter. This would have been complete with feeding troughs hollowed out in the bedrock floor. Many homes were built into natural caves.[7]

Mary and Joseph came to Bethlehem in response to the mandated census. Because the royal line of David was so significant, an even larger number of people may have been returning to Bethlehem. No doubt Joseph's lineage assured the couple treatment that was as honorable as possible in the crowded conditions. It is unlikely they would have been shunted into a remote cattle-shed, even though all the guest rooms in the local houses were

5. See A. D. Riddle, "The Passover Pilgrimage from Jericho to Jerusalem: Jesus' Triumphal Entry" on pg. 395.

6. See the XLVI:13–18 (Florentino García Martínez, *The Dead Sea Scrolls Translated: The Qumran Texts in English*, 2nd ed., trans. Wilfred G.E. Watson [Grand Rapids: Eerdmans, 1996], 168).

7. Kenneth E. Bailey, *Jesus Through Middle Eastern Eyes: Cultural Studies in the Gospels* (Downers Grove, IL: InterVarsity Press, 2008), 25–37.

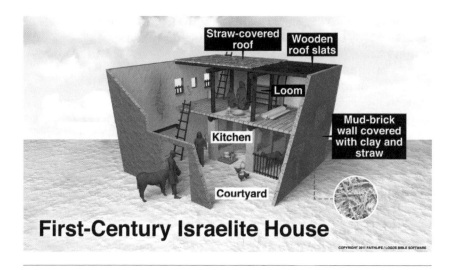

First-Century Israelite House

COPYRIGHT 2011 FAITHLIFE / LOGOS BIBLE SOFTWARE

taken. Instead, Mary and Joseph found themselves in the lower room of a house near the animals' nighttime shelter. As an addendum, we read that when the magi came following the star, they arrived at the "house" (Matt 2:10–11).[8]

SYMBOLISM AND LESSONS

Having explored the domestic contexts of these significant events, we can unpack additional interpretive layers. Being inside as opposed to outside may have carried symbolic overtones. Jesus' disciples asked him to explain challenging kingdom teachings to them once they had withdrawn "inside" (Matt 13:36). At one point, his mother and brothers arrived when he was at home. Mark's version of the narrative emphasizes that they were outside while he surveyed those who were inside with him and said that whoever did God's will was family (Mark 3:19–35; see also Matt 12:46–50; Luke 8:19–20). Jesus went indoors to heal two

blind men (Matt 9:28), perhaps so that the initial burst of light into their eyes would not be overpowering. And the most harrowing reference: Judas left the scene of the last supper, went out, and it was night (John 13:30).

Viewing housing symbolism from another angle, buildings around the Sea of Galilee were constructed of the local stone, dark gray basalt. That meant that the inside of these homes was gloomier than the interior of houses elsewhere that were constructed of limestone. Rasmussen suggested a possible connection with Isa 9:1–2, a prophetic declaration to the tribes that inhabited this area, Zebulun and Naphtali. They were in spiritual gloom, a people walking in darkness.[9] In these dark interiors, lamps were essential and needed to be put on their stands in order to give light to all in the house; it was foolhardy to hide them. Both Mark and Luke use the word "hidden" (*kryptos*, κρυπτός), indicating a

---

8. See Paul H. Wright, "The Birthplace of Jesus and the Journeys of His First Visitors" on pg. 1.

9. Carl G. Rasmussen, *The Zondervan Atlas of the Bible* (Grand Rapids: Zondervan, 2010), 42.

dark and hidden place, a crypt or underground room.[10] Jesus used the lamp figure in a rich texture of implications: "let your light shine ... that they may see your good deeds and glorify your Father who is in heaven" (Matt 5:16 NIV); "your eye is the lamp of your body; when your eyes are healthy, your whole body also is full of light ... see to it, then, that the light within you is not darkness" (Luke 11:34–36 NIV).

Additional home structures occasionally peppered Jesus' teaching. No doubt his audiences knew well the difference between houses built on rock and those on sand, especially in the face of the flash floods that occur during the rainy season in the land (Matt 7:24–27). Luke's account of Jesus' words refers to the river or torrent bursting against the house (Luke 6:48–49). In his parables, Jesus also alluded to home owners, those who had slaves and a manager (Luke 12:35–48), those who would lock their doors (Luke 13:25–27), and the woman who swept her dirt floor looking for the lost coin (Luke 15:8–10). The somewhat irregular-shaped, dull coin would have blended into the grimy floor. Finding it again was fraught with uncertainty and patient perseverance; the light of a lamp would have been essential.

We save the most compelling lesson for last. We have already introduced the idea of the insula housing with inter-connected rooms that were added to accommodate extending families. Bringing a new bride into the family would be a celebrated event, and the home would expand with the growth of the household. As Jesus prepared his small band of disciples for the forthcoming tumult of his arrest, trial, and death, he comforted them with the assurance that in his Father's house there were many rooms. Better yet, he was going to prepare a place for them, and he promised them that ultimately, they would be with him there (John 14:1–3). In other words, they were assured that they were added to God's family. The symbolism of the bridegroom preparing a place for his bride, the church, is powerful and enduring.

BIBLIOGRAPHY

Bailey, Kenneth E. *Jesus Through Middle Eastern Eyes: Cultural Studies in the Gospels*. Downers Grove, IL: InterVarsity Press, 2008.

García Martínez, Florentino. *The Dead Sea Scrolls Translated: The Qumran Texts in English*. 2nd ed. Translated by Wilfred G. E. Watson. Grand Rapids: Eerdmans, 1996.

Lancaster, Steven, and James M. Monson. *Regional Study Guide*. Version 5.0. Rockford, IL: Biblical Backgrounds, Inc., 2011.

Rasmussen, Carl G. *The Zondervan Atlas of the Bible*. Grand Rapids: Zondervan, 2010.

Strange, James F., and Hershel Shanks, "St. Peter's House: Has the House Where Jesus Stayed in Capernaum Been Found?" Pages 68–85 in *Ten Top Biblical Archaeology Discoveries*. Washington, DC: Biblical Archaeology Society, 2011.

Wright, Paul H. *Greatness Grace & Glory: Carta's Atlas of Biblical Biography*. Jerusalem: Carta, 2008.

10. Matt 5:15–16; Mark 4:21–22; Luke 8:16–18; 11:33–36; 15:8. See Edwin M. Yamauchi and Marvin R. Wilson, *Dictionary of Daily Life in Biblical and Post-Biblical Antiquity*, 2 vols. (Peabody, MA: Hendrickson, 2015), 2:219.

Yamauchi, Edwin M., and Marvin R. Wilson. *Dictionary of Daily Life in Biblical and Post-Biblical Antiquity.* 2 vols. Peabody, MA: Hendrickson, 2015.

CHAPTER 13

THE CROWDS THAT FOLLOWED JESUS

Mark 3:7-8; see also Matt 4:24-25; Luke 6:17-18

Perry G. Phillips

KEY POINTS

- Jesus chose Capernaum as his home base of operation, even though Nazareth was his hometown.

- Capernaum was a bustling city with a diverse population, due in part to its strategic location for trade and travel.

- The location of Jesus' ministry and accompanying miracles are the key factors that contributed to his ability to draw such huge crowds.

CROWDS FROM HITHER AND YON

No Facebook, no Twitter, no news media, yet Jesus' reputation spread hither and yon seemingly with the ease of modern communications technology. And his reputation kept growing, astounding his friends and confounding his enemies. He's not just the "talk of the town." He's the talk of all of Galilee!

Jesus has returned to Capernaum, his adopted hometown, after a tormenting (literally!) time in Judea: three satanic temptations, vexation and animosity from the temple authorities, and a "so-so" discussion with Nicodemus.[1] But no rest for the weary. Time to get down to business; time to teach and to proclaim the good news of the kingdom. Time to make the rounds to the synagogues,[2] teaching and healing, sticking primarily with Jewish audiences, careful to bear the good news first to the Jews (Matt 10:5).

---

1. At least his trek through Samaria was pleasant. See my article "At the Well of Sychar" on pg. 92.

2. Josephus states, "Moreover, the cities lie here very thick ... that the very least of them contain above fifteen thousand inhabitants" (*War* 3.43 [Whiston]). The number may be inflated, but the point is clear—there were plenty!

But Galilee cannot contain his fame; it spreads like wildfire to regions beyond— some close, some far; some Jewish, some not. Crowds far and wide beat a path towards him, straining to hear his words and to be cured by his healing touch. But where were these crowds from and, more importantly, how did they hear about Jesus? The list below gives us a clue.

ORIGIN OF CROWDS THAT SOUGHT JESUS ACCORDING TO THE SYNOPTICS[3]

- Jerusalem: Matt 4:25[4]; Mark 3:8[5]; Luke 6:17[6]; 7:17[7]

- Judea: Matt 4:25; Mark 3:7; Luke 6:17; 7:17

- Idumea: Mark 3:8

---

3. Useful information for the entries in this list appear below under "Excursus: Capernaum's Surrounding Regions."

4. Jesus no doubt exemplified good teaching and clear proclamation of the good news of the kingdom, both of which attracted many listeners. It appears, however, that most of the crowds came to him for his healing ministry. Note Matthew's emphasis on bringing the sick to him (4:24). Jesus healed "those suffering severe pain, the demon-possessed, those having seizures, and the paralyzed" (Matt 4:24 NIV). In this author's opinion, no finer exposition of these maladies exists than that of Albert Barnes, *Notes, Explanatory and Practical, on the Gospels*, vol. 1 (New York: Harper & Brothers, 1858), 56–58. Barnes' notes are widely available online. A PDF version of vol. 1 of his notes on the Gospels is available at https://archive.org/details/notesexplanator04unkngoog (accessed June 16, 2017).

5. Mark also brings out Jesus' miraculous healing power (2:1–12; 3:1–5) and his teaching to crowds (2:13). But Mark makes a point of showing that Jesus is "Lord of the Sabbath" (2:27–28). First, Jesus' actions in the grain field with his disciples underscore that religious conventions (in this case, those of the Sabbath mandated by the religious authorities) do not trump human physical needs. Here, Mark highlights the same theme by relating the healing of a man with a withered hand on the Sabbath. (Luke reports another Sabbath miracle intended to provoke the religious authorities [4:31–36].) Both actions discomfit the Jewish leaders, Pharisees and Herodians in this case, who seek to destroy him. So Jesus and his disciples exit the premises. As with Matthew, Mark notes that many crowds followed him from surrounding areas that included Jerusalem. Why from Jerusalem? Jesus, humanly speaking, made a spectacle of himself at the temple, and now the Jewish leaders learn that he is desecrating the Sabbath. No doubt the Jewish leaders sent their representatives to Galilee to scope out further what this "troublemaker" was doing.

6. Similar to Matthew's "Sermon on the Mount" but not the same sermon. See Walter L. Liefeld and David W. Pao, "Luke," in *The Expositor's Bible Commentary: Revised Edition*, eds. Tremper Longman III and David E. Garland, vol. 10 (Grand Rapids: Zondervan, 2007), 132–33.

7. Luke's account of the healing at Nain mentions two crowds—those already following Jesus and those attending the funeral. Upon raising the young man (Jesus ruined every funeral he attended!), "This news about Jesus spread throughout Judea and the surrounding country" (7:17 NIV). Why does Luke mention Judea when the miracle took place at Nain? Nain was on the north side of Mount Moreh in the Jezreel Valley, far from the geographical territory of Judea and only a stone's throw from the southern border of Lower Galilee, which, according to Josephus, started at Xaloth (present day Iksal) at the base of the Nazareth ridge (*War* 3.35–40). Luke may be indicating the geographical extent of the news by singling out Judea from the surrounding country: "Even the Judeans heard about this miracle—and from tiny Nain up north!" Or, in this author's opinion, Luke is using "Judea" in place of "Galilee" in the same spirit as

- Galilee: Matt 4:25; Mark 3:7; Luke 6:17 (implied)

- Decapolis: Matt 4:25

- Perea (Beyond the Jordan): Matt 4:25; Mark 3:8

- Tyre: Mark 3:8; Luke 6:17; 7:17

- Sidon: Mark 3:8; Luke 6:17; 7:17

- Syria: Matt 4:24

- Samaria: not mentioned[8]

What is the common element that motivates the crowds to visit Jesus? What is the one thing that jumps out in each case? *Jesus performed miracles!* That was the magnet that attracted the crowds — local and foreign.[9] A withered hand — restored! Anyone in pain, or paralyzed, or epileptic, or demon-possessed — healed! A widow's dead son — raised![10] How could anyone keep silent?

Jesus' miracles not only impressed the ocals but also propelled his fame far and wide from a tiny neighborhood around Capernaum[11] to regions as far

---

his use of "Judea" (preferred reading, MSS. ℵ, B) in 4:44. The parallel passage in Mark 1:36-39 makes it clear the synagogues in which Jesus is preaching at this time are in Galilee. One also should not lose the connection between the raising of the widow's son at Nain (modern Nein), on the north side of Mount Moreh, and Elisha's raising of the son of the woman from Shunem (modern Sulam) on the south side of Mount Moreh, a mere two-mile distance. No wonder the people exclaimed after the miracle, "A great prophet has appeared among us" (Luke 7:16 NIV). They had Elisha's earlier miracle in mind. For other parallels between the miracles of Elisha and Jesus, see Bruce Waltke, "Meditating on Scripture," *Tabletalk*, September 1, 2009, accessed August 20, 2016, http://www.ligonier.org/learn/articles/meditating-scripture. In this volume, see also Emily J. Thomassen, "Shared Memories of Resurrection on the Hill of Moreh" on pg. 149 and Elaine A. Phillips, "On the Brow of the Hill at Nazareth" on pg. 100.

8. Note the glaring omission of Samaria from the accounts even though Samaria is closer to Galilee than, say, Idumea or Syria. This may show the antipathy between Jews and Samaritans (Jesus tells his disciples to avoid the place, Matt 10:24), or it may be that the Samaritans had their own "facetime" with Jesus and did not feel inclined to visit Jesus on his home turf where they would not have been welcomed with open arms (see my article, "At the Well of Sychar" on pg. 92, especially the section "Excursus: A Short Historical Background of the Samaritans").

9. Two points here: First, this is not an exhaustive list of Jesus' mass healings. For a detailed listing, see "The Healings of Christ" at the website *Strong In Faith*, accessed August 18, 2016, http://stronginfaith.org/article.php?page=9. Second, as for the "Sermon on the Plain" (Luke 6), Jesus and his disciples wandered into a preexisting crowd, yet one can reasonably deduce that the crowds were drawn by the news of the Sabbath healing of the man with the withered hand just days prior (Luke 6:1-10).

10. On how Jesus' miracles echoed those of the Old Testament, see Paul H. Wright, *Greatness Grace, and Glory: Carta's Atlas of Biblical Biography* (Jerusalem: Carta, 2008), 182.

11. Scripture mentions that Jesus performed most of his miracles in the tri-city precincts of Capernaum, Bethsaida, and Chorazin (Matt 11:21; Luke 10:13). These three cities encompass an area of 3.5 miles square (8.9 kilometers square), which is slightly less than one fifth the area of Washington, DC.

as Syria, Tyre and Sidon to the north, and to Idumea way to the south. And Capernaum was indispensable for the spread of his fame. Why Capernaum? The answer is simple: location.

THE MOVE TO CAPERNAUM

Capernaum, on the northwest shore of the Sea of Galilee, boasted of great fishing,[12] excellent farming,[13] a tax office (Matt 9:9), a centurion and his contingent (Matt 8:5–9; Luke 7:1[14]), and a royal [unknown] official (John 4:46). Capernaum was no mean city![15] And— very importantly—Capernaum had excellent connections to surrounding districts[16] from which visitors and transients came in contact with Jesus.[17][18] Overwhelmed by Jesus, they returned to their homeland as his emissaries, her-

---

12. Josephus describes the fishing around Capernaum: "The people of the country call it Capharnaum [that is, Capernaum]. Some have thought it to be a vein of the Nile, because it produces the Coracin fish as well as that lake does which is near to Alexandria" (*War* 3.519–20 [Whiston]; see also, in this volume, J. Carl Laney, "Fishing the Sea of Galilee" on pg. 165). Archaeological investigations around the shore of the sea reveal numerous harbors at Capernaum (see map 14 in Barry J. Beitzel, *The New Moody Atlas of the Bible* [Chicago: Moody Publishers, 2009], 63). Flora and fauna around the Sea of Galilee similar to that of the Nile Delta led ancients to believe an underground river connected the two. Fascination with the wildlife in the Nile Delta continued into the fifth and sixth centuries AD for the inhabitants of Galilee (see Ehud Netzer and Zeev Weiss, "New Mosaic Art from Sepphoris," *BAR* 18.4 [Nov/Dec 1992]: 36–43).

13. Again, from Josephus: "The country also that lies over against this lake hath the same name of Gennesareth; its nature is wonderful as well as its beauty; its soil is so fruitful that all sorts of trees can grow upon it, and the inhabitants accordingly plant all sorts of trees there; for the temper of the air is so well mixed, that it agrees very well with those several sorts, particularly walnuts, which require the coldest air, flourish there in vast plenty; there are palm trees also, which grow best in hot air; fig trees also and olives grow near them, which yet require an air that is more temperate. One may call this place the ambition of nature, where it forces those plants that are naturally enemies to one another to agree together; it is a happy contention of the seasons, as if every one of them laid claim to this country; for it not only nourishes different sorts of autumnal fruit beyond men's expectation, but preserves them a great while; it supplies men with the principal fruits, with grapes and figs continually, during ten months of the year" (*War* 3.516–19 [Whiston]).

14. Luke 7:5 states that the centurion built the synagogue in Capernaum. Today, one can view a basalt foundation below the remains of a fifth century (or third century, depending on the archaeologist) limestone synagogue. Whether the basalt foundation existed during the time of Jesus is a matter of dispute (see Stanislao Loffreda, "Capernaum," *NEAEHL* 1:292–95).

15. The Gospels mention the city of Capernaum sixteen times, second only to Jerusalem.

16. For maps showing detailed connections between Capernaum and its surrounding regions, see Richard Cleave, *The Holy Land: Satellite Atlas*, vol. 1 (Nicosia: Rohr Productions, 1999), 66–67, 70–71. For an excellent, wider view of the connections between Capernaum and other regions like Idumea, Tyre, and Sidon, see map 27 in Beitzel, *Atlas*, 85.

17. See Cyndi Parker, "Millstones in Capernaum" on pg. 308.

18. The topography of Capernaum also afforded natural amphitheaters that aided Jesus' ability to speak to very large crowds (see my article "Natural Amphitheaters along the Sea of Galilee" in this volume on pg. 265).

alding their incredible experiences as they went.[19]

Capernaum was the key (humanly speaking) to the spreading fame of Jesus: comfortable living conditions, a friendly, diverse populous, a constant flow of foreigners, and exceptional connections. No wonder Jesus chose Capernaum as his headquarters! No wonder from there his fame spread and intensified like a tsunami![20]

CONCLUSION

Jesus became very popular very quickly. His teachings and his miraculous healings left people speechless, but these activities would have remained localized had it not been for a central, well-connected location from which news of his teachings and of his miracles could expand. Capernaum served as the central location, and with its excellent connections to surrounding regions, Jesus' reputation radiated from there with ease, thereby precipitating an influx of crowds near and far in return.

EXCURSUS: CAPERNAUM'S SURROUNDING REGIONS[21]

THE TETRARCHY OF PHILIP

Heading east from Capernaum and crossing the Jordan River meant leaving Galilee, ruled by Herod Antipas, and entering into Herod Philip's[22] territory, mainly inhabited by Gentiles, and consisting of the districts of Batanea, Gaulanitis, Trachonitis, and Auranitis, (Josephus, *War* 2:93–100; *Ant.* 18:106–108). Its capital was Caesarea Philippi,[23] a major city that collected lots of traffic from its surroundings and funneled it west to the coastal cities of Tyre and Sidon, and south to the Sea of Galilee. Heavy travel between Caesarea Philippi and Capernaum afforded travelers ample opportunity to encounter Jesus at Capernaum and to disseminate the news in Caesarea Philippi and beyond, even all the way north to Damascus in Syria.

TYRE AND SIDON

One did not have to travel from Capernaum to Tyre and Sidon via Caesarea

19. It is not unreasonable to presume that those whom Jesus healed enthusiastically proclaimed all that Jesus had done for them to their kinfolk and to their neighbors, just as in the example of the healed Gadarene/Gerasene/Gergesene demoniac (Matt 8:28–34; Mark 5:1–20; Luke 8:26–39).

20. One may wonder why Jesus didn't choose Bethsaida (also named Julias) for his headquarters. It had all the advantages of Capernaum's geographical connections, and the disciples Philip, Andrew, and Peter originated from there (John 1:44). Bethsaida also received the status of *polis* (πόλις) by Herod Philip (Josephus, *Ant.* 18.28), and as a *polis* its commerce no doubt exceeded that of Capernaum. Most likely, the main reason was that Bethsaida was not a Jewish city; and in keeping with Jesus' intent on first preaching to the Jews (Matt 10:5), Bethsaida—in the lap of the Gentile Gaulanitis—simply would not do.

21. An interactive map of the regions under discussion is available at the website *Bible History Online*, accessed August 17, 2016, http://www.bible-history.com/geography/ancient-israel/israel-first-century.html.

22. Both of these rulers were sons of Herod the Great and inherited these regions upon Herod's death. (Herod Antipas also inherited Perea.) For a history of the Herodian period, see "The Herods: Magnificent to a Fault," in Wright, *Greatness Grace & Glory*, 121–46.

23. See Elaine A. Phillips, "Peter's Declaration at Caesarea Philippi" on pg. 286.

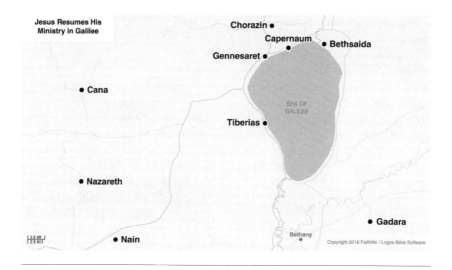

Philippi. More direct routes existed, including the route presumably taken by Jesus to visit this region, but he then returned to Galilee via Caesarea Philippi and the Decapolis (Matt 15:21–29; 16:13–20; Mark 7:24–31).[24] [25]

Tyre and Sidon were great port cities. It is interesting to contemplate how many members of the crowds from Tyre and Sidon likely consisted of sailors and travelers from distant regions of the Mediterranean. How far west did Jesus' reputation reach before Paul even began his missionary journeys?

THE DECAPOLIS

Literally, Decapolis means "ten cities," although more than ten cities dotted the region.[26] The Decapolis lay south of

Philip's territory and was another Gentile area from which Jesus received crowds (Matt 4:24). Besides traveling though the Decapolis on his return from Tyre and Sidon (see above), Jesus also visited the Decapolis and performed the miracle of casting out a legion of demons from one of the inhabitants (Matt 8:28–34; Mark 5:1–20; Luke 8:26–39). Unfortunately, the inhabitants considered the monetary loss of the swine more important than the spiritual benefits they may have received had Jesus stayed, so they urged him to leave. Although the healed man desired to follow Jesus, Jesus urged him to stay and to witness to his own people what God had done for him (Mark 5:20; Luke 8:39).[27]

24. See Yohanan Aharoni, Michael Avi-Yonah, Anson F. Rainey, Ze'ev Safrai, and R. Steven Notley, *The Carta Bible Atlas*, 5th ed. (Jerusalem: Carta, 2011), 178.

25. See Emily J. Thomassen, "Jesus' Journey into Gentile Territories" on pg. 247.

26. One of the cities, Scythopolis, was west of the Jordan River at the ancient site of Beth Shean (see John D. Wineland, "Decapolis," *NIDB* 2:77–80). A helpful map is available at *Bible History Online* (website): "The Decapolis and its Cities," accessed August 21, 2016, http://www.bible-history.com/maps/decapolis_cities.html.

27. See Todd Bolen, "Where Did the Possessed-Pigs Drown?" on pg. 196.

PEREA

The name "Perea" appears to be a shortened form of the Greek *peran ho Iordanēs* (πέραν ὁ Ἰορδάνης, "beyond the Jordan").[28] Although distant from Galilee, Perea fell under the jurisdiction of Herod Antipas. Its inhabitants were mainly Jewish, and Jesus spent a good bit of time there (Luke 9:51–18:34), where he may have been baptized by John the Baptist (see map "Kingdom of Herod the Great" on pg. 531).[29] [30]

IDUMEA

Mentioned only once in the Gospels, Idumea, south of Judea, most likely appears in Mark 3:8 as a designation of the farthest southern extent of the crowds approaching Jesus (see map above). Idumea is the Greek form of "Edom." After the exile of Judah by the Babylonians, the Edomites moved into the area, but during the time of the Hasmoneans, John Hyrcanus (2nd century BC) forced them to be circumcised and to obey Jewish laws, thereby becoming part of the Jewish commonwealth. Herod the Great's father, Antipater, was Idumean although his mother was Jewish.

BIBLIOGRAPHY

Aharoni, Yohanan, Michael Avi-Yonah, Anson F. Rainey, Ze'ev Safrai, and R. Steven Notley. *The Carta Bible Atlas.* 5th ed. Jerusalem: Carta, 2011.

Barnes, Albert. *Notes, Explanatory and Practical, on the Gospels.* Vol. 1. New York: Harper & Brothers, 1858. Accessed June 16, 2017 at Archive.org. https://archive.org/details/notesexplanator04unkngoog.

Beitzel, Barry J. *The New Moody Atlas of the Bible.* Chicago: Moody Publishers, 2009.

Cleave, Richard. *The Holy Land Satellite Atlas.* Vol. 1. Nicosia, Cyprus: Rohr Productions, 1999.

"The Healings of Christ." *Strong In Faith* (website), 2007. Accessed August 18, 2016. http://stronginfaith.org/article.php?page=9.

Josephus, Flavius. *The Works of Josephus: Complete and Unabridged.* Translated by William Whiston. Peabody, MA: Hendrickson, 1987.

Liefeld, Walter L., and David W. Pao. "Luke." Pages 19–355 in *The Expositor's Bible Commentary: Revised Edition.* Edited by Tremper Longman III and David E. Garland. Vol. 10. Grand Rapids: Zondervan, 2007.

Loffreda, Stanislao. "Capernaum." *NEAEHL* 1:292–95.

"Map of New Testament Israel." *Bible History Online* (website). Accessed August 22, 2016. http://www.bible-history.com/geography/ancient-israel/israel-first-century.html.

Netzer, Ehud, and Zeev Weiss. "New Mosaic Art from Sepphoris." *BAR* 18.6 (Nov/Dec 1992): 36–43.

Rainey, Anson F., and R. Steven Notley. *The Sacred Bridge.* Jerusalem: Carta, 2006.

---

28. See Paul J. Ray, Jr., "Perea," *NIDB* 4:442–43.

29. Of course, that depends upon the location of "Bethany beyond the Jordan." For discussion of the possible locations, see the articles by Aubrey L. Taylor in this volume: "Ministry in the Wilderness" on pg. 42 and "Wilderness Events: The Baptism and Temptation of Jesus" on pg. 53.

30. See Aubrey L. Taylor, "Wilderness Events: The Baptism and Temptation of Jesus" on pg. 53.

Ray, Paul J., Jr. "Perea." *NIDB* 4:442–43.

Waltke, Bruce. "Meditating on Scripture." *Tabletalk*, September 1, 2009. http://www.ligonier.org/learn/articles/meditating-scripture.

Wineland, John D. "Decapolis." *NIDB* 2:78–80.

Wright, Paul. *Greatness Grace & Glory: Carta's Atlas of Biblical Biography*. Jerusalem: Carta, 2008.

CHAPTER 14

JESUS AT THE POOL OF BETHESDA[1]

John 5:1–9

Gordon Franz

KEY POINTS

- Location and timing are key factors in appreciating the significance of the healing miracle Jesus performed on the man crippled for thirty-eight years.

- The sick man placed his hope for healing in the waters of a pagan shrine; yet he found healing in heeding the words of Jesus.

- Thirty-eight years of sickness parallels the time Israel spent wandering the wilderness after refusing to have faith and claim the promised land (they had already wandered for two years).

- The healing took place during the feast of Purim, at a time when Jews are expected to give gifts to the poor—which Jesus gave in the form of physical and spiritual healing.

INTRODUCTION

The healing of the man crippled with an infirmity for thirty-eight years at the Pool of Bethesda is the third miracle mentioned in the Gospel of John (5:1–18). The apostle John records the purpose of his Gospel at the end of the book:

And truly Jesus did many other signs [miracles] in the presence of his disciples, which are not written in this book, but these are written that you may believe that Jesus is the Christ, the Son of God, and that believing you may have life in his name. (John 20:30–31 NKJV)

---

1. This chapter is a revised version of an article published in *Archaeology and Biblical Research*. The original article was Gordon Franz, "Divine Healer: Jesus vs. Eshmun," *Archaeology and Biblical Research* 2.1 (1989): 24–28. Used by permission.

John selects certain miracles, of the many that Jesus did, to bring people to faith in the Lord Jesus Christ as their Savior and also to point out that the Lord Jesus is God manifest in human flesh. This sign was chosen to demonstrate that the Lord Jesus is infinitely superior to any pagan healing god.

This essay addresses itself to the background of the third miracle or sign, the incident which took place at Bethesda (John 5). When did the event take place? Where did it take place? How do the archaeological discoveries shed light on this passage? And what are the practical and theological implications of this event?

TEXTUAL PROBLEMS

There are several textual problems within the first four verses of the chapter. Without going into detail, a suggested translation of these verses is given below. The italicized words indicate the variant readings that are followed in this article.

"1) After this there was *a* feast of the Jews; and Jesus went up to Jerusalem. 2) Now there is at Jerusalem by the sheep pool, a (place) which is called in the Hebrew tongue, Bethesda, having five porches. 3) In these lay a great multitude of impotent folk, of blind, lame, paralyzed, *waiting for the moving of the water.* 4) *For an angel went down at a certain season into the pool, and troubled the water;*

whosoever then first after the troubling of the water stepped in was made whole of whatsoever disease he had."[2]

WHEN DID THE HEALING HAPPEN?

Scholars have debated the identification of the feast mentioned in John 5:1. Almost every major and minor Jewish feast has been suggested.[3] John's Gospel, as well as Mark's, appears to be arranged in chronological order. Within the Gospel of John, there are some chronological indicators as to which feast is mentioned in John 5:1.

The encounter with the Samaritan woman (John 4) took place during the Samaritan feast of *Zimmuth Pesah* (Preparation for Passover). This, in turn, takes place sixty days before the Samaritan Passover to commemorate Moses meeting Aaron, after the burning bush experience, to redeem the people of Israel from Egypt. John 4:35 states that there were four months before the grain harvest. The wheat harvest begins around the time of *Shavuot* (Pentecost). John 6:4 states that the Passover was near at hand. The only feast of the Jews which falls between *Zimmuth Pesah* and the Jewish Passover is the feast of Purim, connected with the events recorded in the book of Esther.[4] In the year AD 28, the feast of Purim fell on Shabbat (see John 5:9, 15, 18). The only feast day to fall on a Sabbath between AD 25 and AD 35 was Purim of AD 28 (see info-

---

2. On the textual difficulties with this passage, see Zane Hodges, "The Angel of Bethesda—John 5:4," *Bibliotheca Sacra* 136.541 (1979): 25–39.

3. John Bowman, "Identity and Date of the Unnamed Feast of John 5:1," in *Near Eastern Studies in Honor of William Foxwell Albright*, ed. Hans Goedicke (Baltimore, MD: Johns Hopkins University, 1971), 43–56.

4. Bowman, "Identity and Date of the Unnamed Feast of John 5:1"; idem, *The Fourth Gospel and the Jews* (Eugene, OR: Pickwick, 1975).

graphic "Agricultural Cycle of the Levant/ Palestine" on pg. 530).[5]

John 5:1 simply says it was "a feast"; thus it *should* be one of the minor feasts. Some have objected to Purim *because* it is a "minor" feast. Would the Lord Jesus be going up to Jerusalem for a minor feast, when only the major ones are required (Deut 16:16)? However, later in the Gospel, the Lord Jesus appears at the Feast of Dedication (Hanukkah), another minor feast (John 10:22).[6] In John's Gospel, the Bethesda incident is the first time that the Lord Jesus publicly declared himself to be God (5:18). Earlier in the Gospel, when he was in Jerusalem for the Passover (2:23–3:21), he did not publicly present himself to the people (2:23–25).

WHERE DID THE HEALING TAKE PLACE?

John 5:2 states that there is "by the sheep pool, a [place] which is called in the Hebrew tongue, Bethesda." The sheep pool has been identified by most biblical and archaeological scholars as the twin pools in the area of St. Anne's Church just north of the Temple Mount. The construction of the north pool most likely began during the Iron Age as a dam across the Bethesda Valley to catch the run-off from the rain. This has been identified as the Upper Pool where the prophet Isaiah met King Ahaz (Isa 7:3) and where the Assyrian military leadership besieging Jerusalem met the Judean leadership (Isa 36:2 // 2 Kgs 18:17).[7]

Urban von Wahlde[8] has argued that the "Upper Pool" was the pool that was partially excavated by David Adan in 1977[9] in the Kidron Valley. From a strategic military perspective it does not make sense for the Upper Pool to have been located down in the Kidron Valley, contrary to von Wahlde's view. It would have been a death trap for the Assyrian military leaders to go into the Kidron Valley, even with a host of armed bodyguards. The Judeans had the upper positions overlooking the pool from the city wall. They would also have been able to set up an ambush and cut off the Assyrian escape route out of the Kidron Valley.

Shimon Gibson identified the two large pools at St. Anne's Church as a *mikveh* complex (Jewish ritual bath). He said, "The Bethesda Pool consists of two large basins, the 'northern pool' (53 x 40 meters) serving as the upper reservoir (the *otsar*) for the collected rainwater and the 'southern pool' (47 x 52 meters) as the lower place of purification (the *mikveh*)." Gibson suggested that the date

5. Eugene W. Faulstich, *Calendar Conversion*, computer software (Spencer, IA: Chronology-History Research Institute, 1986).

6. Bowman, "Identity and Date of the Unnamed Feast of John 5:1"; idem, *The Fourth Gospel and the Jews*, 111–32.

7. Dan Bahat, *The Illustrated Atlas of Jerusalem* (New York: Simon and Schuster, 1989), 28, 33; idem, "The Fuller's Field and the 'Conduit of the Upper Pool,'" *Eretz-Israel* 20 (1989): 253–55, 203*–4*.

8. Urban C. von Wahlde, "The 'Upper Pool,' Its 'Conduit,' and 'The Road of the Fuller's Field' in Eighth Century BC Jerusalem and their Significance for the Pools of Bethesda and Siloam," *Revue Biblique* 113.2 (2006): 242–62.

9. David Adan, "The 'Fountain of Siloam' and 'Solomon's Pool' in First-Century C.E. Jerusalem," *IEJ* 29.2 (1979): 92–100.

of construction was about 25 BC, during the reign of Herod the Great.[10] Urban von Wahlde has also advocated for this position.[11]

But, in all probability, the incident of John 5 did not take place in the *mikveh* or *otsar*. The verse says it was in a place called "Bethesda." This word is made up of two Hebrew words, *beth* ("house") and *hesed* ("mercy"). This means that "Bethesda," the "House of Mercy," was some building or structure near the Sheep Pool.[12]

INSIGHTS FROM ARCHAEOLOGY

Excavations have been conducted in the area of St. Anne's Church that have shed light on this passage. In the area of the pools there was a large Byzantine church built at the beginning of the fifth century AD. The church is east-oriented with the entrance from the west. Such an orientation is typical of almost all the churches built in the Holy Land during this period. The altar area, which is over the place being venerated, is at the east end of the church and not over the pools. This was the place being venerated in connection with John 5 by the early church. Under this area, four occupation levels were found: two from the Jewish period (i.e.,

Hasmonean and Herodian, second century BC to AD 70) and two from the Late Roman period (i.e., second to fourth centuries AD).

It is known that there was a healing shrine in the area during the Late Roman period. This shrine, connected to the healing cult, was in rock hewn caves, with three or four steps leading down to them. A clay votive foot, thanking the god for healing, and a statue of a human head with the body of a snake, probably representing Asclepius, the Greek god of healing, were discovered in the excavations. Other finds also indicate the existence of a healing shrine.[13] Was there a healing shrine in the area during the time of Christ? There seems to be evidence that there was. Caves with water in them were connected with the healing cult of Asclepius. How the water was used in the ritual is not certain. This seems to be the background to the events of John 5.[14] Von Wahlde challenged this idea when he reported that the French archaeologists working at the site and studying it said there was "no archaeological evidence that the eastern baths functioned as religiously oriented healing baths in that period."[15] But generally, sacred areas remain sacred areas throughout their

10. Shimon Gibson, "The Pool of Bethesda in Jerusalem and Jewish Purification Practices of the Second Temple Period," *Proche-Orient Chrétien* 55 (2005): 270–93.

11. Von Wahlde, "Archaeology and John's Gospel," in *Jesus and Archaeology*, ed. James Charlesworth (Grand Rapids: Eerdmans, 2006), 523–86; idem, "The 'Upper Pool,' Its 'Conduit,' and 'The Road of the Fuller's Field,'" 242–62; idem, "The Pool(s) of Bethesda and the Healing in John 5: A Reappraisal of Research and of the Johannine Text," *Revue Biblique* 116.1 (2009): 111–36; idem, *The Gospel and Letters of John*, 3 vols. (Grand Rapids: Eerdmans, 2010), 2:215–28; idem, "The Puzzling Pool of Bethesda: Where Jesus Cured the Crippled Man," *BAR* 37.5 (2011): 40–47, 65.

12. John Wilkinson, *Jerusalem as Jesus Knew It* (London: Thames and Hudson, 1978), 95–97.

13. *St. Anne's Jerusalem* (Jerusalem: Sainte-Anne, 1963).

14. Pierre Benoit, "Découvertes Archéologiques Autour de la Piscine de Béthesda," in *Jerusalem through the Ages* (Jerusalem: Israel Exploration Society, 1968), 48–57; Joachim Jeremias, *The Rediscovery of Bethesda* (Louisville, KY: Southern Baptist Theological Seminary, 1966).

15. Von Wahlde, "The Pool(s) of Bethesda and the Healing in John 5," 128.

occupational history. Furthermore, the Romans looted the place for souvenirs before they destroyed it during the First Jewish Revolt (AD 66–70), so it is unlikely that any archaeological evidence would be found from before the revolt.

What was the identity of the healing god at the shrine? Archaeological data suggests that it was Asclepius during the Late Roman period, from the second century AD and onward. During the New Testament period, however, this deity may still have been called by the name of Eshmun, the Semitic healing god. If so, the Lord Jesus entered the healing shrine "Bethesda" (or "House of Mercy") of the pagan Semitic healing god, Eshmun. He found a man who had an infirmity for thirty-eight years and asked him, "Do you want to be made well?" The man responded that he had no one to help him into the pool (the small healing cubicles in the shrine) when it was stirred up by the angel. His answer makes much more sense if the incident occurred in a healing shrine of rock hewn caves having only three or four steps leading down to them.

Some might object to a pagan healing shrine being so close to Herod's Temple in Jerusalem. However, this shrine was outside the city wall of Jerusalem at the time and was situated close to the Roman garrison stationed at the Antonia fortress in the northwest corner of the Temple Mount.

THEOLOGICAL IMPLICATIONS

When the Lord Jesus walked into "Bethesda," he brought about a confrontation between himself and the pagan healing deity. With just the words of the Lord Jesus, the man took up his bed and walked away without touching the water,

and without the angel of the pagan deity stirring up the water in the pool.

Jesus won the confrontation. He truly was and is the Great Physician, because he is the only true God. The others, be they Asclepius or Eshmun, are not gods at all (Isa 45:20–22; 44:9). This event fulfilled the first part of the theme of John's Gospel, to show that "Jesus is the Christ, the Son of God."

The second part was fulfilled in the man with the infirmity. He had a choice: stay on his bed and not be healed or believe the words of the Lord Jesus and take up his bed and walk and thus receive "life." The man responded positively (John 5:9) and was made well. He then worshipped the Lord in the Temple (John 5:14).

The issue at stake in this showdown was: Who really is the Great Physician? And more important: Who really is God? The Lord Jesus did not depend on any shrine, or ritual, or even an angel. While, a few manuscripts read "Angel of the Lord" in John 5:4, the proper rendering of the text should be simply "angel." That being the case, the angel would have to be a fallen angel, a demon. There are several reasons for this. First, it would not be logical for God to use a good angel in a pagan healing shrine. Second, the word "angel" is a neutral term and is used of both good and fallen angels (Matt 25:41; 2 Cor 11:14). The context must determine which it is, and it makes sense that it would be a fallen angel that stirred up the water in a pagan healing shrine. A rabbinic example of this is found in *Midrash Rabbah Leviticus* 24:3 where an evil spirit stirs up water.[16] Finally, Satan, the "angel of light," can perform pseudo-healings to deceive people (2 Cor 11:13–15; Rev 19:20).

---

16. Freedman and Simon, *Midrash Rabbah Leviticus*, Vol. 4 (New York: Soncino, 1983), 305–6.

The Geography of Esther

Yet the Lord Jesus simply commanded the man to take up his bed and walk. This was something Eshmun or Asclepius could not do. The pagan deity's "healing power" issued forth at a "certain season," whereas the Lord Jesus was able to heal *anytime, anywhere*. The man responded positively and was healed instantly.

THE SIGNIFICANCE OF THE FEAST OF PURIM

Why did the Lord Jesus choose to go into this pagan healing shrine on Purim? The theme of the book of Esther is this: "God's preservation of His unbelieving people, and the celebration of that event in the feast of Purim."[17] This theme is crucial for understanding the book of Esther and for understanding why John included this "sign" done on Purim in his Gospel. The theme explains why neither the Name of God nor prayer are mentioned in the book of Esther. It explains why Mordecai is still in Susa on the thirteenth of Nisan

when he should have been back in Jerusalem for Passover on the fourteenth (Esth 3:12; Lev 23:5; Deut 16:16). It also addresses why there is a "lack of spiritual awareness in Esther and Mordecai, and the vengeful spirit so apparent at the end of the book."[18]

Esther and Mordecai were outside the will of God and in unbelief. The expression of faith for an Israelite—in this case Mordecai, who was from the tribe of Benjamin (Esth 2:5)—was to "flee the Chaldeans" (Isa 48:20,21; 52:7-12; Deut 28:64-67) and return to Zion when Cyrus made the decree allowing the people to return to Judah (Ezra 1:1-4). Yet a large number of Israelites and Judeans chose to remain outside the land of Israel, in Babylon and Susa, rather than return to Zion and the hardships that existed there. When a person is out of God's will, the last person they want to talk about is the Lord. Thus the name of God is not mentioned in the book. Sometimes a person

---

17. G. Edwin Shepperson, "The Role of the Book of Esther in Salvation History" (ThM thesis, Dallas Theological Seminary, 1975), 26.

18. Shepperson, "The Role of the Book of Esther," 25.

in unbelief or out of the will of God will perform religious rituals, just as the Jewish people did in Susa by fasting for three days, but they did not pray to the Lord their God (Esth 4:16–17; compare Isa 58:1–7). They were still part of God's covenant people, but they were in unbelief.

The Lord used Mordecai and Esther, outside the land of Israel in unbelief, in order to preserve the messianic line that had already returned to Judah in faith during the First Return. The messianic line returned in the person of Zerubbabel (Ezra 2:2; Matt 1:12–13; Luke 3:27). Haman's decree to annihilate *all* the Jews also affected the Jews living in the land of Judah (Esth 3:12–13; 4:3; 8:5, 9, 13). This was God's hand of providence at work.

THE SIGNIFICANCE OF "THIRTY-EIGHT YEARS"

Why does the Lord Jesus go into this pagan shrine and pick out one man to heal? Why didn't he just heal everybody? Jesus probably selected this one man because he was using the man as an object lesson.

The Lord Jesus, in John's Gospel, refers to the wilderness wanderings several times. In his conversation with Nicodemus he likens himself to the serpent in the wilderness (John 3:14–16; compare Num 21:9). As the Israelites looked at the serpent and lived, so any individual who looks to the Lord Jesus in faith has eternal life. In John 6 Jesus refers to the manna in the wilderness (6:31–40; compare Exod 16:15; Num 11:7; 1 Cor 10:3). In this passage Jesus likens himself to manna as bread come down from heaven. At the end of his discussion with the religious leaders, the Lord Jesus said that Moses wrote of him (John 5:45–47).

It seems reasonable to think that Jesus explained the significance of this miracle in this same analogical fashion. The number thirty-eight is used only one other place, by implication, in the Scriptures. The children of Israel wandered for forty years in the wilderness. It took them two years to go from Egypt to Kadesh-Barnea. At Kadesh-Barnea, Moses sent twelve spies into the land of Canaan. When they came back, they all

The Bronze Serpent

Numbers 21:4–9

Israelites spoke against God

God sent serpents, many died

Some healed by looking at the bronze serpent

COPYRIGHT 2011 FAITHLIFE / LOGOS BIBLE SOFTWARE

The Healing Bronze Serpent

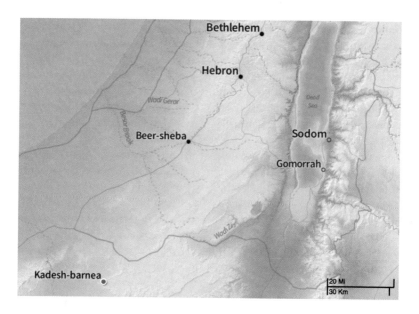

Kadesh-Barnea

gave an accurate report of what the land of Canaan was like. However, ten of them said it was impossible to take the land. The other two, Joshua and Caleb, said in essence, "God has given this land to us, let's go in and take it" (Num 12–13). The Israelites listened to the majority report, and God said, by implication, "Because of your unbelief, you will wander for thirty-eight more years" (Num 14:29–30). They were to wander in the wilderness for a total of forty years, one year for each day the spies were in the land (Num 14:33–34). However, at this point in their wanderings, they had already been in the wilderness for two years (Num 10:11). They had thirty-eight more years to go. Hebrews 4:19 says that that generation did not enter into the land because of unbelief.

The over-riding theme of the Gospel of John is faith and unbelief. Over ninety times John uses the words "believe" or "faith" to describe the condition for sal-

vation. John selects certain miracles and shows the reaction of the people. Do they trust the Lord Jesus or do they reject him? On Purim, Jewish people are commanded to give gifts to the poor (Esth 9:22). The Lord Jesus gave this poor sick man the gift of physical health and presumably eternal life.

SUMMARY

The Lord Jesus healed a man who had an infirmity for thirty-eight years, and he performed this miracle at a pagan healing shrine to the east of a large Jewish *mikveh* outside the walls of Jerusalem. This man was—like the nation of Israel—wandering in the wilderness for thirty-eight years because of unbelief. He had a choice to make. He trusted the words of the Lord Jesus, God manifest in human flesh, and received the Purim gift that the Lord offered to him—physical healing, the forgiveness of sin, and thus eternal life.

BIBLIOGRAPHY

Adan, David. "The 'Fountain of Siloam' and 'Solomon's Pool' in First-Century C.E. Jerusalem." *IEJ* 29.2 (1979): 92–100.

Bahat, Dan. "The Fuller's Field and the 'Conduit of the Upper Pool.'" *Eretz-Israel* 20 (1989): 253–55.

———. *The Illustrated Atlas of Jerusalem.* New York: Simon and Schuster, 1989.

Benoit, Pierre. "Découvertes Archéologiques Autour de la Piscine de Béthesda." Pages 48–57 in *Jerusalem through the Ages: The 25th Archaeological Convention October 1967.* Jerusalem: Israel Exploration Society, 1968.

Bowman, John. *The Fourth Gospel and the Jews: A Study in R. Akiba, Esther, and the Gospel of John.* Pittsburgh Theological Monograph Series. Eugene, OR: Pickwick, 1975.

———. "Identity and Date of the Unnamed Feast of John 5:1." Pages 43–56 in *Near Eastern Studies in Honor of William Foxwell Albright.* Edited by Hans Goedicke. Baltimore: Johns Hopkins Press, 1971.

Faulstich, Eugene W. *Calendar Conversion.* Spencer, IA: Chronology-History Research Institute, 1986. Computer software.

Franz, Gordon. "Divine Healer: Jesus vs. Eshmun." *Archaeology and Biblical Research* 2.1 (1989): 24–28.

Freedman, H., and Maurice Simon. *Midrash Rabbah Leviticus.* Vol. 4. New York: Soncino, 1983.

Gibson, Shimon. "The Pool of Bethesda in Jerusalem and Jewish Purification Practices of the Second Temple Period." *Proche-Orient Chrétien* 55 (2005): 270–93.

Jeremias, Joachim. *The Rediscovery of Bethesda.* Louisville, KY: Southern Baptist Theological Seminary, 1966.

Hodges, Zane. "The Angel of Bethesda—John 5:4," *Bibliotheca Sacra* 136.541 (1979): 25–39.

Shepperson, G. Edwin. "The Role of the Book of Esther in Salvation History." ThM thesis, Dallas Theological Seminary, 1975.

St. Anne's Jerusalem. Jerusalem: Sainte-Anne, 1963.

Wahlde, Urban C. von. "Archaeology and John's Gospel." Pages 523–86 in *Jesus and Archaeology.* Edited by James H. Charlesworth. Grand Rapids: Eerdmans, 2006.

———. *Commentary on the Gospel of John.* Vol. 2 of *The Gospels and Letters of John.* Eerdmans Critical Commentary. Grand Rapids: Eerdmans, 2010.

———. "The Nature and History of the Birkat Isra'il and Its Relation to the Pool 'With the Expanse of the Sea' (Sir. 50:3): Rereading Charles Warren." *PEQ* 142.3 (2010): 159–81.

———. "The Pool(s) of Bethesda and the Healing in John 5: A Reappraisal of Research and of the Johannine Text." *Revue Biblique* 116.1 (2009): 111–36.

———. "The Puzzling Pool of Bethesda: Where Jesus Cured the Crippled Man." *BAR* 37.5 (2011): 40–47, 65.

———. "The 'Upper Pool,' its 'Conduit,' and 'The Road of the Fuller's Field' in Eighth Century BC Jerusalem and Their Significance for the Pools of Bethesda and Siloam." *Revue Biblique* 113.2 (2006): 242–66.

Wilkinson, John. *Jerusalem as Jesus Knew It: Archaeology as Evidence.* London: Thames and Hudson, 1978.

CHAPTER 15

THE WORDS AND TEACHINGS OF JESUS IN THE CONTEXT OF GALILEE

Matt 5:13–16; 6:25–33; 7:13; 7:24–27;
13:3–9; 13:24–30; Luke 15:11–15

Alexander H. Vernon

KEY POINTS

- Jesus often adapted his teachings to take advantage of his immediate surroundings.

- Attention to Galilean geography strengthens our ability to hear Jesus' teachings as his original audience did.

- Many parables and analogies of Jesus find their concrete origins in the terrain and climate of the Galilee.

- Jesus used these concrete realities to teach his followers about forgiveness, repentance, the kingdom of God, and salvation.

INTRODUCTION

In fulfillment of Scripture, Jesus taught his audiences in parables (Matt 13:35). These metaphoric stories conveyed abstract concepts such as forgiveness, repentance, the kingdom of heaven, righteousness, and salvation, in the concrete, tangible, lived realities of the land of Galilee. Thus, the land itself is an invalu-

able hermeneutical tool for a better and richer understanding of Jesus' parables, for in these stories, we see that "all of Galilee is a stage."

According to the Synoptic Gospels, the bulk of Jesus' life and public ministry took place in Galilee, referring to the geographic region and Roman political district which lies to the west of the Sea of Galilee.[1] Jesus was raised in Nazareth, a small village in Lower Galilee, and later relocated and settled down in Capernaum, a large town situated along the northern shore of the Sea of Galilee. As a result of his Galilean residency, Jesus' dialect, accent, and parlance would necessarily be Galilean. Galilee itself was a great storehouse of imagery and examples, providing ample resources for weaving a verbal tapestry. The land of Galilee is a powerful interpreter of Jesus' teachings (see map "Kingdom of Herod the Great" on pg. 531).[2]

PARABLES AND METAPHORS

A key aspect of Jesus' teaching was the use of the parable (*mashal*). J. Dominic Crossan says, "The word *mashal*, with its most usual Greek translation, *parabole*, meant a similitude or comparison and the expression had a very wide range of application. In fact it is almost synonymous with metaphor."[3] A metaphor is a comparison where a word or phrase that is normally used to depict one thing or idea is applied to another. For example, "all the world's a stage." We know that the world is not literally a raised platform, constructed to give a commanding view of some sort of performance. But, in a sense, the world is the place where the grand human drama is being acted out. Within a metaphor are two components: the *source* and the *target* (see *Lexham Figurative Language of the Bible*

Glossary, section 2, for more details). In our example above, the stage is the source and the world is the target. Thus, in order to best understand a metaphor, a wise interpreter will explore as many potential meanings, both overt and nuanced, of both the source and the target.[4] This allows the interpreter to probe deeper meanings of the metaphor.

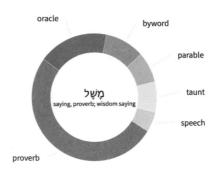

oracle
byword
parable
מָשָׁל
saying, proverb; wisdom saying
taunt
speech
proverb

Bible Word Study: *mashal*

When dealing with a historical metaphor, in this case a parable spoken some two thousand years ago, the historical context of the metaphor becomes crucially important. Levine notes that,

> In order better to hear the parables in their original contexts and so to determine what is normal

1. Anson F. Rainey and R. Steven Notley, *The Sacred Bridge*, 2nd. ed. (Jerusalem: Carta, 2014), 347.

2. For a parallel article in this volume on the Judean influence on Jesus' teachings, see Chris McKinny, "The Words and Teachings of Jesus in the Context of Judea" on pg. 338.

3. J. Dominic Crossan, "Parable," *ABD* 5:146.

4. Ed Greenstein, "Some Metaphors in the Poetry of Job," in *Built by Wisdom, Established by Understanding. Essays on Biblical and near Eastern Literature in Honor of Adele Berlin*, ed. Maxine L. Grossman (Bethesda, Maryland: University Press of Maryland, 2013), 179–83.

Highland Plateaus of Upper Galilee

and what is absurd, what is conventional and what is unexpected, we need to do the history ... The parables are open-ended in that interpretation will take place in every act of reading, but they are also *historically specific*. When the historical context goes missing or we get it wrong, the parables become open to problematic and sometimes abusive readings.[5]

A cursory reading of many of Jesus' parables reveals metaphoric imagery that is heavily "grounded": roads, rocks, soil, flora, and fauna. Levine is correct in noting that the parables are historically specific. But they are also very *locus specific*: they are physically situ-

ated in Galilee during the first century AD. Utilizing a working knowledge of Galilee's geography, we can expand our vocabulary to further probe the depth and meaning of Jesus' parables. The land itself is a vivid, living, active, and present character. The land affected much of Jesus' audience in very primal and basic ways: provision of food and water, travel, the kinds of shelter and resources available, and the kinds of livestock that one could own. Much more so than today, the people of first century Galilee were intimately connected to the land and therefore must have had a very visceral response to Jesus' parable. In order to experience Jesus' teachings in a similarly visceral way, we shall explore the land of

5. Amy-Jill Levine, *Short Stories by Jesus: The Enigmatic Parables of a Controversial Rabbi* (New York: Harper One, 2014), 9. Emphasis mine.

Galilee and see how its shape, character, climate, flora, and fauna can open up more entryways into the parables.

GEOGRAPHY

During the Roman era, "Galilee" referred to a particular political district to the west of the Sea of Galilee. This district encompassed the regions of Upper Galilee (northwest of the Sea of Galilee) and Lower Galilee (including Nazareth), and bordered the Rift Valley, with the Jordan River and the Sea of Galilee forming its eastern border. Galilee is the most geologically complex region within the Holy Land.[6] It is a mixture of hard, soft, and chalky limestones, basalt, and alluvial soils. These various rock types create very distinct geographic features: long, mountain ridges, intermontane valleys, and high plateaus.

UPPER GALILEE

Upper Galilee is a highland plateau, composed primarily of hard limestone (Cenomanian), with portions of soft and chalky limestones (Eocene and Senonian respectively) along its eastern front facing the Huleh Basin.[7] Upper Galilee was a remote and sparsely populated region during the biblical periods, as the erosion patterns of the hard limestone made travel difficult, with only small, provincial roads crisscrossing the area.[8] The villages were more remote and the

agriculture focused upon narrow, terraced plots of soil that supported summer crops of vines, figs, pomegranates, and olives. Life there would have been very slow, cyclical, and quiet.

LOWER GALILEE

Lower Galilee can be divided into two sections: east and west. The eastern section, primarily south of the Sea of Galilee and the city of Tiberias, is a zone of soft limestone (Eocene) that has been covered by basalt.[9] Lower Eastern Galilee encompasses several notable landmarks: Mount Arbel and its associated pass that connects to the northwestern alluvial plain of the lake and to ancient Magdala, on the western shore of the lake; to the west of Arbel lie the Horns of Hattin, site of Saladin's victory over the Crusaders; to the south of the Horns lies Mount Moreh, locale of Shunem and Nain. During the New Testament era, this region, like Upper Galilee, was sparsely populated due to the difficulties of navigating over basalt.[10]

Western Lower Galilee is a region of sites familiar to readers of the Bible: it is home to the mountains of Carmel and Tabor and the sites of Megiddo and Nazareth. The northern portion of this region, bordering Upper Galilee to the north, is marked by several east-west ridges (e.g., Nazareth, Tur'an, Jotapata) and their accompanying valleys.[11] These ridges are the result of several faults

---

6. Denis Baly, *The Geography of the Bible*, rev. ed. (New York: Harper & Row, 1974), 152.

7. Yohanan Aharoni, *The Land of the Bible: A Historical Geography* (London: Burns & Oates, 1979), 27–28; James M. Monson and Steven P. Lancaster, *Geobasics in the Land of the Bible* (Rockford, IL: Biblical Backgrounds, Inc., 2008), 3, 24–25.

8. Baly, *Geography*, 154–57.

9. Paul H. Wright, "The Illustrated Guide to Biblical Geography," (Jerusalem University College, 2012), 274–75.

10. Wright, "Biblical Geography," 160.

11. Wright, "Biblical Geography," 273.

View into Lower Galilee from Mount Carmel

within the region and are comprised of a mixture of hard (Cenomanian), soft (Eocene), and chalky (Senonian) limestones.

JEZREEL VALLEY

Bordering the southern end of Lower Galilee is the Jezreel Valley, which spans twenty miles (thirty-two km) from near the tip of Mount Carmel to the site of Tel Jezreel to the southeast. The valley is essentially flat, rising only eighty-five feet (twenty-six meters) in elevation along the entire west-east span. The valley is bordered on the south by the Carmel Range, which cuts off Galilee and the other northern regions from the Central and Southern Highlands that comprised the districts of Samaria and Judea. The Carmel Range is bookended by Mount Carmel on its northwestern end and Mount Gilboa on its southeastern flank.

These various geographic formations resulted in a region that was both remote and isolated in the villages at higher elevations, and open and cosmopolitan along the wider valleys and low lying areas where the major highways were situated. Further, most of the region is marked by exposed limestone bedrock and the volcanic deposits of basalt. Topsoil outside of the intermontane valleys is thin and sparse (see map "Old Testament Events in Jezreel Valley" on pg. 534).

SEA OF GALILEE AND ITS ENVIRONS

According to the Synoptic Gospels, the primary geographic focus of Jesus' ministry was in the area around the Sea of Galilee from near Tiberias along the western shore, wrapping around the northern shoreline, crossing over into the Bethsaida Plain on the northeastern corner of the lake and the political district of the tetrarchy of

Philip.[12] The northern shore of the lake is marked by two major alluvial plains at either end: Genneseret on the northwest end and Bethsaida on the northeast. These plains are capable of supporting a wide variety of crops. During the New Testament era, farmers would likely have focused upon wheat and barley as their main staples. Flat, open land is at a premium in the region, and grain is absolutely necessary for daily life.[13] Roads near these plains would run along the edges in order to not occupy precious farmland. The northern basin of the lake is surrounded (west to east) by the heights of Lower Eastern Galilee, the Rosh Pinna Sill, and the Golan Heights.

THE AGRICULTURAL YEAR

Galilee's yearly weather pattern is cyclical and fairly predictable: generally, Galilee experiences a cold, wet winter followed by a dry, hot summer. The transitional seasons of spring and fall are brief, but they provide ample opportunity for planting and harvesting between the two harsher seasons of summer and winter. During the early winter season, wheat and barley are planted, allowing them to soak up the winter rains. These rains provide Galilee with a lush, green, floral springtime landscape. This beauty rapidly gives way to a pale, yellowed landscape during the summer as the growing heat, combined with the *sirocco* east winds, dry out and kill off the grasses and flowers, while simultaneously preparing the barley and wheat for harvesting.[14]

During the long, hot summer months, fruit crops feast upon the evening dew, preparing them for harvest in the fall. As the year progresses in the fall months, grapes, figs, dates, pomegranates, and olives are harvested (see infographic "Agricultural Cycle of the Levant/Palestine" on pg. 530).

METAPHORS AND ANALOGIES OF JESUS

METAPHORS OF SALT AND LIGHT (MATT 5:13–16)[15]

"You are *the salt of the earth*" (Matt 5:13): This statement from the Sermon on the Mount makes an allusion to the city of Magdala, also known as Taricheae ("salted fish").[16] Magdala was the lakeside center for the salting and preservation of fish.[17] Magdala was 3.5 miles (5.6 km) north of Tiberias. From any vantage point along the northern shoreline, the area of Magdala is easily visible, particularly given its location along the shore below the striking profile of Mount Arbel.[18]

---

12. The tetrarchy of Philip spanned the region north/northeast of the lake (including Bethsaida), through the Golan Heights to the base of Mt. Hermon (including Caesarea Philppi) near the modern borders between Israel, Syria, and Lebanon.

13. Thus the allusions to "daily bread" and Jesus' specific reference to being the Bread of Life.

14. Baly, *Geography*, 51–53.

15. Biblical references are from the New Revised Standard Version (nrsv).

16. Josephus, *Life*, 188.

17. Pesachim 46a; Rainey and Notley, *The Sacred Bridge*, 355; Strabo, *Geography*, xvi.2.45.

18. The traditional site of the Sermon on the Mount is the Mount of Beatitudes, which is on the northwestern corner of the lake, above Tabgha's Church of the Loaves and Fishes, the adjacent Church of The Primacy of Peter, and the hot springs of Heptapegon. The hill is

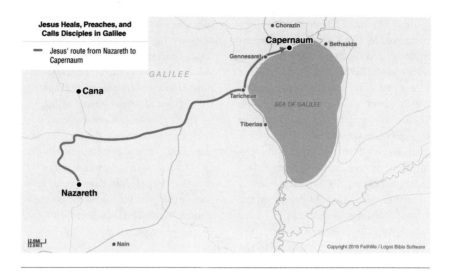

Like the salt utilized at Magdala, Jesus' listeners both add flavor to and preserve the created order. But, Jesus admonishes his listeners to persevere and maintain their unique quality as his disciples, lest they lose their ability to influence human affairs.

"A city located on top of a hill" (Matt 5:14): Approximately midway along the eastern shoreline of the lake is the ancient Decapolis city of Hippos. Hippos sits atop a prominent hill with only a small saddle connecting it to the Golan Heights plateau to its east. As a Decapolis city, Hippos was fully Roman: likely containing temples, bathhouses, gymnasia, and a nymphaeum.[19] In effect, Hippos' position allowed it to broadcast and proclaim to the basin surrounding the lake the wonder and glory of Rome. At night, its lights would have been very distinct and visible. Likewise, Jesus makes the comparison between his followers and Hippos: just as Hippos is high, prominent, visible, and proclaiming *Pax Romana* to all, Jesus' disciples are to be high, prominent, and visible, proclaiming *Pax Christus* to the world.

ANALOGIES AGAINST
ANXIETY (MATT 6:25–33)

"They neither sow nor reap nor gather into barns" (Matt 6:26): Jesus refers to grain agriculture with the mention of these activities. Because of the many large valleys and alluvial plains, much of Galilee was a locus of wheat and barley fields, unlike the hills of Samaria and Judea which were unsuitable for large scale grain farming, but were suitable

approximately three miles (4.8 km) west of Capernaum, which was the next destination on Jesus' itinerary after delivering the sermon (Matt 8:1–5).

19. The excavations at Hippos have revealed a nymphaeum, along with the remains of many large architectural elements (column, capitals, flagstones, pilasters, and lintels) that indicate edifices of substantial size. See Claire Epstein, "Hippus (Sussita)," *NEAEHL* 2:634–36; Arthur Segal, "Hippus (Sussita)," *NEAEHL* 5:1782–87.

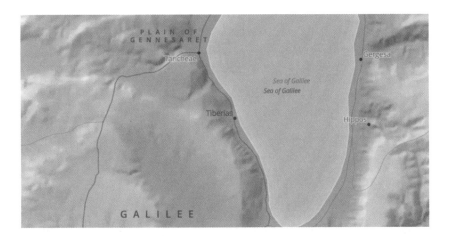

Locations of Taricheae (Magdala) and Hippos

for the fruit crops of grapes, olives, figs, and pomegranates.[20]

"Lilies of the field" (Matt 6:28-30): Jesus refers to the vast array of flowers that appear every spring during the rainy season. Rainfall in the Holy Land is heavier in higher elevations, further west, and further north. Due to its prime location in the north and close to the coast, Galilee receives larger amounts of rainfall than do Samaria and Judea.[21] The result is a landscape covered with a broad palate of vivid and brilliantly colored flowers, directly contrasted to the dry, barren brown and yellow floral remains of summer and fall. These vibrant colors, according to Jesus, would have been far more luxurious than anything Solomon could have imported for himself. Yet, these flowers and grasses are only alive for a few weeks before the east winds (*sirocco*) and the heat of summer scorch the earth.

Here, Jesus portrays God as being extravagantly wasteful in his provision of beauty and color, given that it will only be present for a brief amount of time. So if he places much more value upon human life than grass and flowers, then Jesus' disciples should expect that the Father will give them the provision they need.

ANALOGIES OF GATE SIZE (MATT 7:13)

In contrast to Samaria and Judea, Galilee was wide open to large scale, ancient international traffic. Galilee lies in a large, east-west geological depression that runs nearly perpendicular to the Central Hill Country. The Hill Country's hard, rugged limestone makes travel difficult and undesirable. Throughout the Old Testament period, Jerusalem remained relatively isolated, accessible via one primary road, which began in the Aijalon Valley (near Ben Gurion Airport), went up the steep

20. It is telling that the only references to vines in the Gospels are during the Last Supper in Jerusalem. See also Baly, *Geography*, 162, 183.

21. Even Galilee's drier, eastern areas receive as much rainfall as Jerusalem (approximately 24 inches).

Hippos (center hill)

slopes of the Judean Hills, and emptied out onto a small plateau some five miles (eight km) north of Jerusalem. During the New Testament era, Jerusalem remained isolated and primarily religiously important. The center of political gravity had shifted to Herod the Great's crown jewel: Caesarea Maritima.

Due to its more dynamic geography, Galilee possesses wide, open valleys, and fewer obstacles to traffic. Portions of the main trade route connecting Mesopotamia to Egypt (*Via Maris*) ran along the northwestern shore of the Sea of Galilee, heading west-southwest beneath the mountain and cliffs of Arbel towards Mount Tabor and the Jezreel Valley and through the Carmel Range via the Megiddo Pass.

During Jesus' day, this major road would have been visible running along the shore line, passing by Magdala on its way towards the Jezreel Valley. Further, the city of Tiberias was Herod Antipas' capital city and as such would have had a major artery connecting it with the Jezreel Valley, enabling it to interact with the port areas of Caesarea Maritima and Acco/Ptolamais.

Gentiles from all over the world traveled along these major roads.[22] Along with them, they carried trade goods, money, influence, and their pagan cultures. The broad, international roads represented the world that did not worship Israel's God. These roads allowed the Jewish "kings" to enjoy the fruits of their alliances with Caesar and his panoply of deities.

Unlike the large, grand roads leading to the glory of Caesar, small roads and footpaths criss-crossed Galilee's conservative Jewish interior. Travel was chal-

---

22. It is not by accident that Isaiah referred to Galilee as "Galilee of the Gentiles" (Isa 9:1).

Hippos (aerial view)

lenging and difficult, requiring purpose and dedication. Ultimately, Jesus may have been alluding to a smaller, narrow road that led up to Jerusalem, to the city of YHWH, and to life.

THE PARABLE OF TWO HOUSES (MATT 7:24–27)

"House on a rock ... house on the *sand*" (Matt 7:24, 26): Galilee is marked by the prominence of both bedrock in the hills and alluvial soils in the valleys. During the rainy winter season, the valleys would flood and also be inundated with soils running off from the hills. Unlike the southern Central Hill Country, which is almost exclusively hard limestone (Cenomanian), Galilee is a mixture of hard (Cenomanian), soft (Eocene), and chalky (Senonian) limestones.[23] The soils of the limestones are more susceptible to being washed away by Galilee's heavy winter rains, leaving the bedrock, particularly of the hard limestone, intact. Wise Galileans would build off the valley floor, along the rocky feet of the hills and ridges.[24]

Further, "rock" is a common metaphor for YHWH throughout the Old Testament. Thus, the wise man would use the solid and ever-present rock as the foundation for his house. Likewise, a spiritually wise man will build his "house" upon the rock—both the words of Jesus and, by inference, upon God himself. Conversely, the fool will build upon the loose soils and sands, which during the rainy season are subject to being swept

---

23. It should be noted that the Judean Wilderness, east of Jerusalem, Bethlehem, and Hebron, is also comprised of chalky (Senonian) limestone. Thus, any Judean who had traveled to Galilee to see Jesus would be able to relate to his metaphors (compare Mark 3:8).

24. Baly, *Geography*, 162.

Southern Plains of the Sea of Galilee

away as the waters rush down the hill-sides and through the gullies. Similarly, a fool's "spiritual" house that is built upon false gods and teachings will also be left in ruins.

THE PARABLE OF THE
SOWER (MATT 13:3–9)

In this famous parable, Jesus utilized the very ground of Galilee as his metaphorical source. Unlike Judea and Samaria, which had limited areas to sow grain, Galilee possessed large valleys and plains.[25] Fields of grain are much more common in Galilee than in Judea or Samaria. Roads and paths near a grain field would typically have run along the edges of the field.[26] These roads would be hard and packed down before the rains came.[27] Thus, as the sower was casting his seed, many would have fallen onto the road itself, remaining exposed to any ravenous birds. As previously mentioned, bedrock is usually visible, or just under much of the surface of the topsoil. So, the "rocky ground" can indicate either ground where the bedrock is exposed and occupying valuable space, or topsoil that is

---

25. The southern hills had small intermontane valleys, along with the Salim, Farah, and Tamun valleys in Samaria, and the Benjamin and Hebron Plateaus and the Rephaim Valley in Judea. More suitable grain farmland was available in the Shephelah and Coastal Plain westward of the Judean Hills.

26. Baly, *Geography*, 152.

27. It is possible that the seeds could have become embedded in the roads/paths after the rains had softened the road, but nonetheless, what grain grasses would have survived would be trod down again in early spring after the roads dried up and heavier traffic returned.

saturated with boulders, stones, and pebbles which occupy space in the arable soil.

A common and constant nuisance to Galilean farmers are thorns and thistles. These grow rapidly during the rainy season, absorbing excessive amounts of water. Thorns and thistles emerge from the soil at the same time as wheat and barley, competing with them for the limited water resources and space in the ground. As a result, the grain grasses would very literally be starving for water and whither away and die.

The estimated yield of a grain crop was ten to fifteen times the amount of grain sown.[28] Here, Jesus says that, at a minimum, the good soil will return an astonishing yield, double the normal amount. Jesus goes even further to suggest that good soil can produce a mind-boggling harvest two to ten times the normal yield.

An important issue to note is that the setting that Jesus painted was normal for ancient Galilean agriculture—some seed was always lost to the road, most fields contained bedrock and other stones of various size, and thorns and thistles were ubiquitous within and alongside the fields. The sower *was not being careless* in his casting of the seed. These four scenarios were common to practically every field and would have been a common sight to Jesus' audience, most of whom had fields of their own.[29] Thus, they could identify themselves with one locus of the sown field almost immediately.

Those like the seed on the path are like people who are exposed to and involved in the larger cosmopolitan world. The danger of being carried away by the birds of the world is high. Those who possess only a thin and shallow soil for their faith are those whose faith is most likely to wilt under the pressures and persecutions of this world (the scorching heat of the summer sun). Those who lie along the edge of the field, whose connection to the good soil is limited, will be choked out rapidly by thorns and thistles (the cares of this world).

In contrast to the previous three kinds of "soil," good soil—a heart trusting in the Lord and obeying the word of Jesus— will not just simply bring about a good yield. A trusting and obedient believer brings forth abundance, even a gratuitous amount, of good works.

THE PARABLE OF THE WEEDS AMONG THE WHEAT (MATT 13:24–30)

To purposefully sow weeds (e.g., darnel) amongst a neighbor's wheat crop was an act of agricultural terrorism. Darnel has almost the exact same appearance as wheat during the growth cycle. It is only after the heads appear that the two can be distinguished. At this point, it is too late to attempt to remove the darnel because of the risk of damaging the wheat. So, the householder commands his slaves to leave the weeds in the soil until the harvest time, where the two can be properly and safely separated. Given the limitations of Galilean fields, every square inch is vital and valuable. Weeds absorb precious water and will choke out the precious grain. In a subsistence economy, to lose portions of one's harvest to weeds placed the entire community in danger: grain is finite and must

---

28. K. C. Hanson and Douglas E. Oakman, *Palestine in the Time of Jesus* (Minneapolis: Fortress Press, 1998), 105.

29. An estimated eighty to ninety percent of Galilean society would have been involved in agriculture (Hanson and Oakman, *Palestine*, 104).

Judean Highlands

be rationed. Any loss during the harvest threatens life itself.[30]

To attempt to cleanse the kingdom of heaven of "weeds" is to run the larger risk of damaging individuals within the community of faith.[31] Before the full fruition of a life, often one cannot discern the fruit of that life. It is only after maturation and time that the true self is revealed—what might look like a weed is in fact a life of trust and faith, or vice-versa. To leave both together is to sustain the world and to allow the kingdom to grow and preserve human life.

THE PARABLE OF THE PRODIGAL SON (LUKE 15:11–15)

In the famous parable of the prodigal son, Jesus illustrated the extravagant grace and joy of the Father over a lost son. In setting up the story, Jesus mentions three salient points that indicate a potential regional setting for the parable. First, he mentions a "distant country" (chōran makran, χώραν μακράν). The Greek word chōra (χώρα) is alternately translated by the NRSV as "country" or "region." Thus, the chōra need not be hundreds of miles away. Second, he mentions pigs in the fields. The reference to pigs immediately identifies the distant region as Gentile. Third, he mentions "pods" (keration, κεράτιον), normally understood as referring to carob pods. Carob trees are very plentiful in Galilee and adjacent regions and would have been a very familiar sight to first century Jews. In referencing the pods, Jesus seems to assume that many of his kosher, Jewish

---

30. For example, note the response of the Timnites in Judg 15:6 after Samson destroys their fields. Samson's in-laws had unwittingly spurred Timnah's economic ruin.

31. In the rabbinic work Tanna debe Eliyahu (Zuta 5), there is a parallel teaching where if a vineyard has weeds in it, but still has one hundred or two hundred viable vines, then the vineyard will be tended regardless of the presence of the weeds. The interperation is that righteous people (the vines) will uphold the world (the vineyard) and preserve it (from the fire). See R. Steven Notley and Ze'ev Safrai, Parables of the Sages: Jewish Wisdom from Jesus to Rav Ashi (Jerusalem: Carta, 2011), 276.

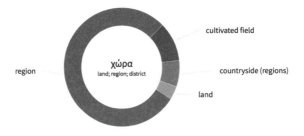

Bible Word Study: χώρα, chōra

audience would be aware of the dietary habits of domesticated swine. How is this possible? On the eastern side of the Sea of Galilee lay the Roman political district of the Decapolis, a Gentile region whose citizens would have had herds of swine. Although the Decapolis lay outside the borders of Jewish regions during the first century, it was in close enough proximity that Jews in Galilee would have had commercial dealings with the people of the Decapolis. In these encounters, Galilean Jews could have witnessed pork husbandry first hand. In fact, Luke describes how Jesus and the disciples found themselves in the region/country (chōra) of the Gerasenes, after a large storm blew their boat off course. In the course of Jesus' encounter with the demoniac, he sent the demons into a herd of swine (Luke 8:32–33). Specifically, the swine herd "rushed down the steep bank into the lake and was drowned."

The ideal geographic location for this event is the site of Kursi, along the eastern shore of the Sea of Galilee.[32] Approximately one mile (1.6 km) south of the site of this ancient first century fishing village is a steep embankment that runs down nearly into the water. The geographic feature of the slope, situated in the Decapolis, makes the connection between Kursi and the demoniac event logical and geographically likely.

Carob Pods

Later, when Jesus referred to the "distant country/district" in the parable of

---

32. Other suggested sites include: Umm Qais (Gadera, see Matt. 8:28) in modern Jordan, approximately six miles (9.7 km) southeast of the Sea of Galilee, and Jerash (Gerasa; see Mark 5:1), another Jordanian city, approximately thirty-three miles (53.1 km) southeast of the Sea of Galilee. For a fuller treatment on the geography of Gergesa/Gerasa/Gadera, see Rainey and Notley, *The Sacred Bridge*, 359–60. For a counterargument in this volume, see Todd Bolen, "Where Did the Possessed-Pigs Drown? Challenging Tradition and Respecting Textual Evidence" on pg. 196.

the prodigal son, it is possible that he is referring to the Decapolis. It was outside the predominant Jewish settlement, most certainly seeming far away to a Galilean villager in Lower Galilee. Swine were present, yet Jews living around the Sea of Galilee would likely have made economic forays and connections there.[33] This "distant" *chōra* area was socially and metaphorically distant: one far away from the love and grace of the Father.[34]

BIBLIOGRAPHY

Aharoni, Yohanan. *The Land of the Bible: A Historical Geography*. London: Burns & Oates, 1979.

Baly, Denis. *The Geography of the Bible*. Rev. ed. New York: Harper & Row, 1974.

Crossan, J. Dominic. "Parable." *ABD* 5:146–52.

Epstein, Claire. "Hippus (Sussita)." *NEAEHL* 2:634–36.

Greenstein, Ed. "Some Metaphors in the Poetry of Job." Pages 179–95 in *Built by Wisdom, Established by Understanding: Essays on Biblical and Near Eastern Literature in Honor of Adele Berlin*. Edited by M. L. Grossman. Bethesda, MD: University Press of Maryland, 2013.

Hanson, K. C., and Douglas E. Oakman. *Palestine in the Time of Jesus*. Minneapolis: Fortress Press, 1998.

Josephus. Translated by Henry St. J. Thackeray et al. 10 vols. LCL. Cambridge, MA: Harvard University Press, 1926–1965.

Levine, Amy-Jill. *Short Stories by Jesus: The Enigmatic Parables of a Controversial Rabbi*. New York: Harper One, 2014.

Monson, James M., and Steven P. Lancaster. *Geobasics in the Land of the Bible*. Rockford, IL: Biblical Backgrounds, Inc., 2008.

Notley, R. Steven, and Ze'ev Safrai. *Parables of the Sages: Jewish Wisdom from Jesus to Rav Ashi*. Jerusalem: Carta, 2011.

Rainey, Anson F., and R. Steven Notley. *The Sacred Bridge*. 2nd. ed. Jerusalem: Carta, 2014.

Segal, Arthur. "Hippus (Sussita)." *NEAEHL* 5:1782–87.

Strabo. *Geography*. Translated by Horace Leonard Jones. 8 vols. LCL. Cambridge, MA: Harvard University Press, 1917–1932.

Wright, Paul H. "The Illustrated Guide to Biblical Geography." Jerusalem University College, 2012.

---

33. See Chris McKinny, "Pig Husbandry in Israel during the New Testament" on pg. 183.

34. The apostle Paul states that Gentiles were "aliens from the commonwealth of Israel, and strangers to the covenants of promise, having no hope and without God in the world" (Eph 2:12).

CHAPTER 16

SHARED MEMORIES OF RESURRECTION ON THE HILL OF MOREH

Luke 7:11–17

Emily J. Thomassen

KEY POINTS

- Luke presents Jesus as a great prophet by means of literary and geographical allusions to the ministries of Elijah and Elisha.

- All three prophets resurrected an only son: Elijah at Zarephath, Elisha at Shunem, and Jesus at Nain.

- The miracles performed by Jesus and Elisha were performed on the slopes of the same hill—a connection Jesus' audience was sure to make.

- The parallel miracles and locations of these events strengthen Luke's presentation of Jesus as the fulfillment of Israel's prophetic expectations.

LOCATION OF NAIN: NORTHERN SLOPE OF THE HILL OF MOREH

The New Testament town Nain was located on the northern slopes of the Hill of Moreh, on the eastern edge of the Jezreel Valley. The modern Arab village Nein preserves the ancient toponym. Edward Robinson correctly identified modern Nein as Nain of the New Testament when he visited the site in 1838. Robinson noted that Nein had "dwindled to a small hamlet, occupied at most by a few families."[1] The ancient core of Nain lies within the modern village, six miles (9.7 km) southeast of Nazareth, Jesus' hometown, on the southern border of Lower Galilee.

---

1. Edward Robinson and E. Smith, *Biblical Researches in Palestine and the Adjacent Regions: A Journal of Travels in the Years 1838 & 1852*, 3rd ed., vol. 2, reprint with additional notes and a new introduction by William G. Dever (Jerusalem: The Universitas Booksellers: 1970), 361.

View of Mount Moreh from Mount Gilboa

Lower Galilee is characterized as a region of low hills and wide, open valleys. The Galilee region receives abundant rainfall, and its riverbeds are well watered. The abundant rainfall and fertile soil has allowed local communities to thrive in Lower Galilee. Towns like Nain were located near the alluvial valleys so that they could utilize the fertile soil and water supply for irrigation.[2] However, after heavy rains during the winter months, valleys became swampy. To avoid overflowing seasonal streams that could cause erosion or flooding, many settlements in Lower Galilee were located on sloping ridges above valley floors.

Nain sat perched on a northern slope of the Hill of Moreh, a basalt ridge rising to an elevation of 1690 feet (515 m) above the Jezreel Valley. The Hill of Moreh is situated between Mount Tabor (1929 ft / 588 m), an oval mound of hard Cenomanian limestone to the north, and Mount Gilboa (1640 ft / 500 m), a softer Eocene lime-

stone ridge to the south. The Hill of Moreh was an ideal location for a small town of Galilee because of its prime position on the Jezreel Valley, a fertile plain with thick alluvial soil.

Furthermore, Nain sat within reach of the international coastal highway as it passed through the Jezreel Valley. Yet Nain was slightly removed from the major passes of the international route. As the route continued from the coastal plain, traversed Mount Carmel, and dropped into the Jezreel Valley, travelers heading northeast via the Rift Valley would have passed by the Hill of Moreh, around Mount Tabor, and towards the Sea of Galilee. Travelers heading to the Rift Valley south of the Sea of Galilee near Beth Shean would have followed the Harod Valley, skirting around south of the Hill of Moreh.

The international highway connected major towns, but Nain, like other local Galilean settlements, was not directly on the main route. Perhaps Nain was

2. Sean Freyne, *Galilee: From Alexander the Great to Hadrian 323 BCE to 135 CE* (Edinburgh: T&T Clark, 1998), 11.

View of Mount Tabor, Moreh, and Gilboa from across the Jezreel Valley

intentionally a bit isolated and secluded from the larger world, yet it was able to view those passing by and see the possibilities brought by the nearby international route.

LUKE'S DESCRIPTION OF NAIN

Nain is mentioned only once in the New Testament (Luke 7:11), in a miracle account unique to Luke's Gospel. Luke indicates that Nain may have been a large settlement, not merely a small rural village of Galilee. Three times in the pericope Luke refers to Nain as a city, *polis* (πόλις) (7:11–12) rather than a village, *kōmē* (κώμη).[3] Several other towns are also referred to as a *polis* (πόλις) in

Luke: Nazareth (1:26; 2:39), Bethlehem (2:4), Capernaum (4:31), Bethsaida (9:10), Jerusalem (19:41; 22:10; 23:19; 24:49), and Arimathea (23:51). This may indicate that Nain was a settlement of considerable size during the first century. Luke records that Nain had a city gate (7:12), used by the crowd and those carrying the coffin of the dead young man because burial took place outside the city walls.

Before Jesus approached the city gate at Nain, the last place Luke had mentioned was Capernaum (7:1), a city about twenty-five miles (40.2 km) northeast of Nain. Perhaps Jesus had stopped at Cana or Nazareth on his way from Capernaum to Nain.[4]

---

3. Luke frequently uses the term *kōmē* (κώμη) for village so his choice to call Nain a *polis* (πόλις) should be regarded as intentional. See Luke 5:17; 8:1; 9:6, 12, 52, 56; 10:38; 13:22; 17:12; 19:30; 24:13; 24:28.

4. Luke's use of the phrase Καὶ ἐγένετο ἐν τῷ ἑξῆς with a finite verb (ἐπορεύθη) can be translated "soon afterwards" but literally means "and it happened in the following [time] that he made his way." The adverb *hexēs* (ἑξῆς, "next") is used as an adjective with the masculine article which is meant to be understood with a noun in mind, like *chronos* (χρόνος, "time"; Luke 7:11). See Joseph

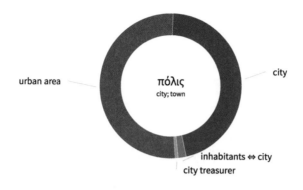

Bible Word Study: πόλις, *polis*

ARCHAEOLOGICAL REMAINS AT NAIN

In 1982, James F. Strange directed a survey of Lower Galilee on behalf of the University of South Florida.[5] The survey confirmed that the topography of Nain includes a ruined and eroded circular wall around the city which was completely covered with soil and debris. Northwest of the city is a spring with ancient cut stones and fragments of Roman sarcophagi found around it. On the east side of the village, the survey revealed a cemetery of rock-cut tombs.

In March 2007, Fadi Abu Zidan, on behalf of the Israel Antiquities Authority, directed a salvage excavation in the ancient nucleus of Nein.[6] The excavation revealed that the site was first inhabited during the Hellenistic period. A structure dated to the Roman period showed evidence of a massive conflagration during the second half of the first century AD, perhaps related to the Jewish War against

the Romans which began in AD 66. The destruction layer contained fragments of vessels, imported ceramics such as *terra sigillata*, fine quality glass ware, metal objects, and gold jewelry dating to the first century AD. This may indicate that some residents of Nain were wealthy, but because the site has not been further excavated, it is difficult to draw concrete conclusions about the socio-economic status of the residents of Nain during the first century.

JESUS' MIRACLE AT NAIN AND THE SIMILAR MIRACLES OF ELIJAH AND ELISHA

All four of the Gospels depict Jesus as a great prophet of Israel's past, but the connections between the ministry of Jesus and those of Elijah and Elisha are especially prominent in Luke.[7] Luke's use of literary allusions and geographical references calls to mind the stories of Elijah and Elisha. Luke recalled specific events

---

A. Fitzmyer, *The Gospel According to Luke I–IX*, AB 28 (Garden City, NY: Doubleday, 1986), 658.

5. James F. Strange, "Nain," *ABD* 4:1000–1001.

6. Fadi Abu Zidan, "Nein," *HA-ESI* 126 (2014), http://www.hadashot-esi.org.il/report_detail_eng.aspx?id=13691&mag_id=121.

7. For further discussion, see Jonathan Huddleston, "What Would Elijah And Elisha Do?: Internarrativity In Luke's Story Of Jesus," *Journal of Theological Interpretation* 5.2 (2011): 265–81;

in Israel's past in order to portray Jesus as the ultimate fulfillment of those events.[8] Luke's description of Jesus' visit to the synagogue in his hometown, Nazareth, explicitly compares Jesus to Elijah and Elisha (Luke 4:24–27). Like the ministries of Elijah and Elisha, Jesus' ministry also included helping the poor and oppressed and bringing the kingdom of God to non-Israelites. Jesus is depicted like a great prophet of Israel's past, yet as the divine Son of God, he surpasses the prophets who came before him. Luke cleverly weaves this theme into his narrative by means of literary allusion and geography.

Luke's account of Jesus raising to life a widow's "only son" (*monogenēs huios*, μονογενὴς υἱός, Luke 7:12) at Nain parallels similar miracle accounts of Elijah and Elisha set in the Galilee region during the ninth century BC: Elijah raising a widow's only son in Zarephath (1 Kgs 17:8–24) and Elisha raising the only son of a woman and her elderly husband in Shunem (2 Kgs 4:8–37).

PARALLEL ACCOUNTS OF ELIJAH,
ELISHA, AND JESUS RAISING
AN ONLY SON TO LIFE

The parallel Old Testament accounts of Elijah and Elisha raising to life a dead boy are strikingly similar. The account of Elisha raising the Shunammite's son was intended to portray Elisha as a prophet like his predecessor, Elijah. First, both miracle accounts describe a prophet raising an only son to life (1 Kgs 17:12; 2 Kgs 4:16–17). Second, both accounts shared the same setting: an upper-room chamber upon the prophet's own bed (1 Kgs 17:19; 2 Kgs 4:21). Third, in both accounts the prophet stretched himself out upon the dead boy multiple times (Elijah three times, 1 Kgs 17:21; Elisha two times, 2 Kgs 4:34–35). Afterward, each prophet restored the son to his mother (1 Kgs 17:23; 2 Kgs 4:36–37).[9]

A similar account of Jesus raising to life the only son of a widow at Nain draws to mind both Old Testament events, but the similarities between Jesus' miracle at Nain and Elijah's miracle at Zarephath are especially striking.[10] In each pericope, the prophet spoke to a *widow* at the *city gate* (Luke 7:12; 1 Kgs 17:10), felt compassion for her dire situation (Luke 7:12; 1 Kgs 17:20), and raised to life her only son (Luke 7:12; 1 Kgs 17:12). Furthermore, as Fitzmyer has argued, Luke's statement that Jesus gave him back to his mother is an explicit allusion to the Elijah narrative (Luke 7:15; compare 1 Kgs 17:23).[11] Afterward, the Phoenician woman recognized Elijah as God's messenger (2 Kgs 17:24), and the people of Nain recognized Jesus as a great prophet and acknowledged that God had visited his people (Luke 7:16).

José Severino Croatto, "Jesus, Prophet like Elijah, and Prophet-Teacher like Moses in Luke-Acts," *JBL* 124 (2005): 451–65.

8. Emily J. Thomassen, "An Investigation into the Geographical Movements of Elijah with Reference to Those of Jesus" (MA Thesis, Jerusalem University College, 2012), 122–55.

9. In 2 Kings 4:36–37, only the Shunammite woman is mentioned. Her husband is absent from the account of the boy's restoration, making the parallel to 1 Kings 17:23 even more apparent.

10. Fitzmyer, *The Gospel According to Luke I–IX*, 656.

11. Fitzmyer, *The Gospel According to Luke I–IX*, 656.

Zarephath: An Old Testament Town in Phoenicia

However, one key difference between the accounts of Elijah's miracle and Jesus' miracle is the geographical setting. Elijah's miracle is set in Zarephath (modern Sarafand in Lebanon), a city on the northern coastal plain of Phoenicia, approximately fifty miles (80.5 km) north of Mount Carmel, fourteen miles (22.5 km) north of Tyre and eight miles (12.9 km) south of Sidon. Ironically, Yahweh commanded Elijah to go to Phoenicia (1 Kgs 17:8–9), the homeland of Jezebel and the source of the Baal worship that Elijah was fighting against. One significant feature of the pericope's conclusion is the statement made by the Phoenician women: "Now I know that you are a man of God and that the word of Yahweh in your mouth is truth" (1 Kgs 17:24 LEB). At a crisis point in which Israel was wavering between Yahweh and Baal, it was a Phoenician widow, probably herself a Baal-worshipper, who proclaimed her trust in Yahweh.

The location of Elijah's miracle at Zarephath emphasizes the prophet's mission to people outside of the territory of Israel during the Old Testament.[12] Jesus' own ministry in the Gentile region of the Decapolis (Luke 8:26–39) and Tyre and Sidon[13] models this aspect of the ministries of Elijah and Elisha, particularly the inclusion of Gentiles. The mission of Jesus was not restricted to Israel alone (see map "Kingdom of Herod the Great" on pg. 531).[14]

Shunem: An Old Testament Town on the Slopes of the Hill of Moreh

In terms of geographic setting, Jesus' miracle at Nain calls to mind Elisha's miracle at Shunem, both of which were set on the slopes of the Hill of Moreh, overlooking the Jezreel Valley. The similarity in geographical setting between Shunem and Nain must have been in Luke's mind when he recorded the story of Jesus' miracle at Nain.

On the southern slopes of the Hill of Moreh, opposite Nain, sat the Old Testament town Shunem (modern Sulam; Josh 19:18; 1 Sam 28:4; 2 Kgs 4:8). During the ninth century BC, Shunem was a sizeable farming village, frequented by the prophet Elisha (2 Kgs 4:8), who passed by as he traveled between his family home, Abel-meholah[15] (1 Kgs 19:16) and Mount Carmel (2 Kgs 2:25; 4:25). This journey was a two-day trip which would require an overnight stop. Shunem, located half-

12. The traditional boundaries of Israel during the Old Testament period are frequently referred to by biblical authors as the territory between Dan in the north and Beersheba in the south (Judg 20:1; 1 Sam 3:20; 2 Sam 3:10; 17:11; 1 Kgs 4:25).

13. Luke does not include the account of Jesus' journey to Tyre and Sidon which is recorded in Matthew and Mark (Matt 15:21–28; Mark 7:24–30). For discussion of the so-called "Great Omission" in Luke, see Anson F. Rainey and R. Steven Notley, *The Sacred Bridge* (Jerusalem: Carta, 2006), 360–61.

14. See John A. Beck, "The Geography of Forgiveness" on pg. 258.

15. The identification of Abel-meholah is not certain. The name means "meadow of dancing" which may suggest an agricultural location. The town is listed as a point on Gideon's route in the flight of the Midianites (Judg 7:22). In addition, the town is listed in the fifth Solomonic district along with Beth Shean (1 Kgs 4:12). These two references suggest the site may be near the Jordan River south of Beth Shean. Eusebius and Jerome also place it ten milestones south of Scythopolis (Beth Shean). The strongest possibility for the location of the site is Tell Abu

way between Abel-meholah and Mount Carmel, served as a convenient rest stop for Elisha.[16]

On one occasion when he was passing by, a well-to-do woman (*ishah gedolah,* 2 Kgs 4:8) of Shunem persuaded Elisha to stop there for a meal. Elisha regularly stopped there when he was passing through (2 Kgs 4:8). Recognizing Elisha as a holy man of God, the Shunammite woman and her husband made him an upper-room with a bed, a table, a chair, and a lamp (2 Kgs 4:10) where he could spend the night when he traveled through Lower Galilee.

Perhaps as an expression of gratitude, Elisha blessed the childless couple with a son (2 Kgs 4:13-17), but the boy died tragically at a young age (2 Kgs 4:18-20). As a display of God's power, Elisha raised the boy to life. Undoubtedly the people of Shunem would not have forgotten that a great prophet had visited their city and God's power had been made manifest as the boy who had been dead was raised to life. When the main population center at the base of the Hill of Moreh moved from Shunem to Nain, perhaps the memory of the visit of the prophet and the power of God moved with it.[17]

THE REACTION OF THE CROWDS AT NAIN

When Jesus approached the village of Nain, he felt compassion on the widow whose only son had just died. His act of bringing her son back to life revealed the power of God and elicited a great response of fear and awe from the crowd gathered there. The people's response, "A great prophet has arisen among us" and "God has visited his people" (7:16 ESV) suggests that the people of Nain remembered the last time a great prophet, Elisha, had performed a very similar miracle on the slopes of the same hill. And now, in their day, God had visited his people again. Luke records that this news (*ho logos houtos,* ὁ λόγος οὗτος) about Jesus spread from Nain all the way to Judea and the surrounding country (7:17).

CONCLUSION

By means of literary allusion and a nuanced use of geography, Luke reminds his readers of stories from Israel's history as he portrays Jesus as the long awaited prophet of Israel's past. In his description of Jesus' miracle at Nain, Luke draws to mind two similar miracle accounts from the Old Testament: Elijah at Zarephath and Elisha at Shunem. There are strong literary parallels between all three accounts, but the geographic setting of Nain and Shunem suggests that those present must have been aware of the similar event at a similar location. The people at Nain who witnessed the miracle would have made the geographic connection. At the same time, Luke's telling of the miracle at Nain also draws on important literary allusions to the Elijah narrative. A thorough knowledge of history and geography sheds further light upon Jesus as the fulfillment of Israel's prophetic expectations.

Sus, ten miles (sixteen km) south-southeast of Beth Shean. For further discussion, see Emily J. Thomassen, "Investigation into the Geographical Movements."

16. Paul Wright, *Rose Then and Now Bible Map Atlas with Biblical Background and Culture* (Torrance, CA: Rose Publishing, 2012), 86, 195.

17. Wright, *Rose Then and Now Bible Map Atlas,* 195.

BIBLIOGRAPHY

Dowling, Elizabeth V. *Taking Away the Pound: Women, Theology, And The Parable* of the Pounds in The Gospel of Luke. London: T&T Clark, 2007.

Fitzmyer, Joseph A. *The Gospel According to Luke I–IX*. AB 28. Garden City, NY: Doubleday, 1986.

Freyne, Sean. *Galilee: From Alexander the Great to Hadrian 323 BCE to 135 CE*. Edinburgh: T&T Clark, 1998.

Huddleston, Jonathan. "What Would Elijah And Elisha Do?: Internarrativity In Luke's Story Of Jesus." *Journal of Theological Interpretation* 5.2 (2011): 265–81.

Rainey, Anson F., and R. Steven Notley. *The Sacred Bridge*. Jerusalem: Carta, 2006.

Robinson, Edward, and E. Smith. *Biblical Researches in Palestine and the Adjacent Regions: A Journal of Travels in the Years 1838 & 1852*. Vol. 2. 3rd ed. 1867. Reprinted with additional notes and a new introduction by William G. Dever. Jerusalem: The Universitas Booksellers, 1970.

Severino Croatto, José. "Jesus, Prophet like Elijah, and Prophet-Teacher like Moses in Luke-Acts." *JBL* 124 (2005): 451–65.

Thomassen, Emily J. "An Investigation into the Geographical Movements of Elijah with Reference to those of Jesus." MA Thesis, Jerusalem University College, 2012.

Wright, Paul. *Rose Then and Now Bible Map Atlas with Biblical Background and Culture*. Torrance, CA: Rose Publishing, 2012.

Zidan, Fadi Abu. "Nein." *HA-ESI* 126 (2014). http://www.hadashot-esi.org.il/report_detail_eng.aspx?id=13691&mag_id=121.

CHAPTER 17

CROSSING TO "THE OTHER SIDE" OF THE SEA OF GALILEE

Matt 8:18–22; Mark 5:1–20; Luke 8:26–39

Cyndi Parker

KEY POINTS

- Much of Jesus' ministry was centered in and around the Sea of Galilee, a bustling area of industry, trade, and access to international peoples.

- The major cities along the shoreline belonged to different political regions, leading to a diverse socio-political demographic.

- The topography of the sea allowed crowds to follow Jesus' travels from one shoreline to the other.

- The phrase "to the other side" aids in determining the locations of various events in Jesus' ministry around the Sea of Galilee.

Although Jesus based his public ministry in a town called Capernaum located along the northern shoreline of the Sea of Galilee, he traveled from "one town and village to another, proclaiming the good news of the kingdom of God" (Luke 8:1 NIV). Walking was the common mode of transportation, but the Gospels record that sometimes when traveling around the Sea of Galilee, Jesus and the disciples get into a boat and cross "to the other side" (*eis to peran*). This phrase, repeated in each Gospel, helps the

reader geographically place the following narratives:

- the healing of a demon-possessed man (Matt 8:28–34; Mark 5:1–20; Luke 8:26–39)

- the feeding of the five thousand (Matt 14:13–21; Mark 6:30–44; John 6:1–14)

- the feeding of the four thousand (Matt 15:32–38; Mark 8:1–9)

157

- Jesus' final journey to Caesarea Philippi (Matt 16:5; Mark 8:13)

Each of these narratives is discussed below, but, first, to understand the geographical movement signaled by the phrase "crossing to the other side," the reader should understand the shape and size of the Sea of Galilee, along with the political complexities of the first century.

THE GEOGRAPHY OF THE SEA OF GALILEE

The land of the Bible is split down the middle by the north-south fault line of the Rift Valley—a massive geographical trench stretching between the southeastern region of modern day Turkey in the north and Mozambique in southeastern Africa.[1] The Sea of Galilee and the Dead Sea are nestled in the Rift Valley and connected by the Jordan River. The Sea of Galilee has a lopsided shape that is sometimes described as a harp or a heart. The wide northern shoreline slants at a northeastern angle, and the southern shoreline pulls together in a narrow U-shape. From north to south, the lake is thirteen miles long, and from east to west at the widest point, the lake is eight miles across. At the southern end of the Sea of Galilee one can see down the Jordan Valley, a continuation of the Rift Valley south to the Dead Sea. To the north, however, the view up the Rift Valley is drastically limited by the rise of the Rosh Pina Sill—a large segment of basalt rock acting like a plug in the narrow neck of the Rift Valley.

North of the Rosh Pina Sill in the Rift Valley is a long, fertile, open land

called the Hula Valley. Water from four major springs in the northern part of the valley, along with the runoff rain water from the western hills of Upper Galilee and the eastern hills of Bashan (modern day Golan Heights), pours into the valley and slowly drains to the south until the Rosh Pina Sill prevents further progress south. Here, the waters collect to form the Jordan River. The river cuts a narrow passage between the Rosh Pina Sill and the hills of Bashan to the east and flows south into the northeastern portion of the Sea of Galilee. The river forms again on the opposite end of the Sea where it continues its journey through the Jordan Valley to the Dead Sea. Both the northern and southern branches of the river create breaks in the geography around the Sea of Galilee that became natural and easily identifiable political borders during the first century. Likewise, rainwater draining off the hills along the eastern edge of the Sea of Galilee etched a wide V-shaped canyon through the hills. This is the Samak wadi, which is located roughly one-third of the way down the eastern shoreline of the lake. Like the two branches of the Jordan River, the Samak wadi is a distinct geographical feature useful for creating an identifiable political border.

THE POLITICAL CONTEXT AROUND THE SEA OF GALILEE

When Herod the Great died, his kingdom was divided among his sons.[2] Archelaus inherited the southern hill country regions of Samaria, Judea, and Idumea, but he was later exiled and his

---

1. See Barry Beitzel, *The New Moody Atlas of the Bible* (Chicago: Moody, 2009), 48–54; Anson F. Rainey and R. Steven Notley, *The Sacred Bridge* (Jerusalem: Carta, 2005), 40–41; Carl G. Rasmussen, *Zondervan Atlas of the Bible*, rev. ed. (Grand Rapids: Zondervan, 2010), 24–27.

2. As described by Josephus in *Ant.* 17.11.4.

territory was given to Roman governors. Herod Antipas inherited the regions of Perea and Galilee. Herod Philip inherited Gaulanitis and the territories expanding outwards to the northeast, while Rome maintained direct control of the Decapolis—a collection of Hellenized cities east of the Rift Valley that were valued by Rome for protecting significant trade routes and guarding their eastern frontier.

Of these territories, three political units shared the shoreline of the Sea of Galilee—Galilee, Gaulanitis, and the Decapolis—and geographical features defined the political borders of each. From the northern branch of the Jordan River on the northeastern shoreline of the Sea of Galilee, along the western shoreline to the south to where the Jordan exits the lake, was the eastern border of the political unit of Galilee—a region including towns such as Capernaum, Magdala, and Tiberias. Although interspersed with large Hellenistic cities, the worldview of the local Galilean population remained primarily Jewish.

From the southern branch of the Jordan River, around the southern end of the lake, and north along two-thirds of the eastern shoreline to the Samak wadi, was Decapolis territory where the general worldview of the inhabitants was Hellenistic. Decapolis cities around the Sea of Galilee, such as Hippus and Gadara, were large Roman cities representing the imperial might of Rome (see map "Kingdom of Herod the Great" on pg. 531).

Gaulanitis absorbed the remaining small portion of the Sea of Galilee's shoreline between the Samak wadi and the northern branch of the Jordan River. Although Gaulanitis was compressed along the Sea of Galilee, the territory expanded like a fan outward to the northeast.[3] The region was home to a mixture of small Jewish towns such as Gamala (which developed resistance ideas against Rome), larger Jewish cities such as Bethsaida (which became a Roman polis), and large Hellenized cities such as Caesarea Philippi (which was designed and built around Hellenistic ideology). Gaulanitis required a skilled leader to maintain order among such complex and diverse population groups.

The area surrounding the Sea of Galilee is a limited geographical arena, yet in the first century this is where worldviews converged. Galilee was primarily Jewish, the Decapolis was primarily Hellenistic, and Gaulanitis was a mixture of both. Three political units, controlled by different rulers and representing a variety of lifestyles and worldviews, shared the small shoreline of the Sea of Galilee. The residents of these areas enjoyed the same freshwater resources: fish from the lake, a temperate climate allowing for abundant agriculture, and international roads providing opportunities to trade outside the region. The fact that each political unit included sizable cities around the shoreline of the Sea of Galilee emphasizes that the entire area was full of industry, trade, and access to international peoples.

CROSSING TO "THE OTHER SIDE"

The Sea of Galilee is small, and its location in the Rift Valley, surrounded on most sides by steep hillsides, provided

---

3. Philip was tetrarch over Gaulanitis, Auranitis, Trachonitis, Batanea, and Iturea, but only the territory of Gaulanitis touched the shoreline of the Sea of Galilee (Luke 3:1; Josephus, *Ant.* 17.11.4).

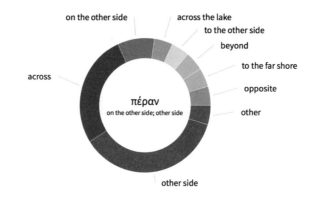

on the other side

across the lake

to the other side

beyond

to the far shore

across

opposite

πέραν
on the other side; other side

other

other side

Bible Word Study: πέραν, peran

the local inhabitants with a view of the entire surface area of the lake. From most places along the shoreline, one could follow the progress of a small boat as it sailed from one harbor to another. Such a vantage point allowed crowds to follow the travels of Jesus and his disciples. Although those who travelled by foot took longer to reach a destination than those traveling by boat, the crowds were able to keep track of Jesus' whereabouts.[4]

The Gospel narratives trace the movements of Jesus geographically, and when Jesus uses a boat for transportation, the narratives refer to Jesus and the disciples as crossing to "the other side" (to peran). The word peran (πέραν) is a preposition that can be translated "across," "beyond," "over," or "other side." When used with the Greek article to, peran functions as a noun meaning "the other side" or "the farther side." The phrase to peran has less to do with sailing across the lake from

east to west or from north to south, and more to do with moving from one political unit into another, as is exemplified in the narratives below.

JESUS HEALS A DEMON-POSSESSED MAN

Each Synoptic Gospel describes Jesus healing a demon-possessed man from the Decapolis (Matt 8:28–34; Mark 5:1–20; Luke 8:26–39). The narratives begin with Jesus in the political region of Galilee, but when evening comes, Jesus gives orders to his disciples to go to "the other side" (Matt 8:18; Mark 4:35; Luke 8:22). When they arrive, they are in a city in the Decapolis where Jesus restores the demon-possessed man and casts the demons into a herd of swine.[5] Notably, both "Legion," the name of the demons (Mark 5:9; Luke 8:30), and the presence of swine on the hillside reflect the Hellenistic context of the people in

---

4. Crowds monitored Jesus' movements and sometimes were able to arrive at the destination point before Jesus (Mark 6:33).

5. Complex textual and topographical data makes identifying the exact location of this miracle difficult. See Notley's summary of the challenging issues in Rainey and Notley, *Sacred Bridge*, 359–60.

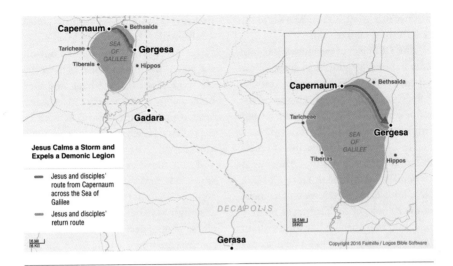

Jesus Calms a Storm and Expels a Demonic Legion

— Jesus and disciples' route from Capernaum across the Sea of Galilee

— Jesus and disciples' return route

the Decapolis.[6] At the end of the narrative, Jesus and the disciples get into a boat to cross to "the other side" (Mark 5:21).[7] Matthew records Jesus arriving at his hometown of Capernaum (Matt 9:1), and although Mark and Luke do not specify where Jesus lands, his interactions with a synagogue leader and with a woman considered unclean by her community support Matthew's record of Jesus returning to the Jewish area of Galilee.

JESUS FEEDS FIVE THOUSAND

The geographical setting of Jesus' miraculous feeding of the five thousand is complex since each Gospel gives different geographical clues for his movements. In Matthew 14, Jesus hears that Herod Antipas (the ruler of Galilee and Perea) beheaded John the Baptist, and so he withdraws to an unnamed solitary place (Matt 14:13). Likewise, Mark records Jesus withdrawing from the crowds to a desolate place (Mark 6:45), and while John states that Jesus goes to "the other side," he does not specify where the place is (John 6:1). Therefore, the location of this solitary place is not named in Matthew, Mark, or John. Luke, however, specifies that Jesus retreats to Bethsaida in Gaulanitis (Luke 9:10). Therefore, according to Luke's narrative, Jesus leaves Herod Antipas' territory and goes to Herod Philip's territory. The crowd is able to see the small boat sailing along the northern shoreline of the lake, and they race ahead to greet Jesus when he pulls into the harbor (Luke 9:11). In this location (the unspecified place of Matthew, Mark, and John, or Bethsaida in Luke's narrative), Jesus feeds the crowd of over five thousand people with five loaves

---

6. See Chris McKinny, "Pig Husbandry in Israel during the New Testament" on pg. 183.

7. Luke records that Jesus "got into the boat and returned" (8:37 ESV). Although he does not use the phrase "to the other side," the narrative began with Jesus in the Galilee region, so the implication is that Jesus crossed from the Decapolis to the Galilee. This conclusion is confirmed four verses later with specifically Jewish cultural references when Jesus interacts with the synagogue leader and the woman with the issue of blood.

and two fish (Matt 14:13–21; Mark 6:30–44; Luke 9:11–17; John 6:1–14).

Since the place of the miracle is named only in Luke, geographical clues following each of the other miracle accounts are helpful for further determining where the miracle took place. After feeding the multitudes and collecting the leftover bread and fish, Jesus tells the disciples to cross over to the other side while he finds a solitary place to pray (Matt 14:22–23; Mark 6:45; John 6:16). Matthew's placement of the miracle of the feeding of the five thousand is unspecified, so the direction to cross over to the other side does not clarify for the reader if Jesus' geographical movement is to the east or to the west. John specifies that the disciples crossed the sea to Capernaum in Galilee (John 6:17), suggesting John is in agreement with Luke regarding the miracle's location in Gaulanitis (this will be explored further below). Mark says that Jesus told his disciples to cross over to Bethsaida, suggesting that Mark's account of the feeding of the five thousand happened in Galilee since the disciples are to cross to Gaulanitis (Mark 6:45).

Matthew and Mark both state that the disciples struggled to reach their destination because the wind was against them (Matt 14:24; Mark 6:48). Since weather systems typically come from the Mediterranean Sea, the fierce wind causing the terrifying storm was likely coming from the west. This small detail suggests the disciples were traveling from the eastern side of the Sea of Galilee to the western side, further supporting the suggestion that the miracle took place in Gaulanitis but becoming a point of contradiction to Mark's account

that suggestively places Jesus in Galilee. Additionally, Matthew and Mark's narratives state that Jesus walks out on the water during the storm to meet the disciples. He enters the boat, and they immediately arrive at Gennesaret, a city located on the northwestern shoreline in the political region of Galilee (Matt 14:34; Mark 6:53).

From these geographical clues, it is possible to conclude that Matthew's account is similar to Luke's. Therefore, although Matthew's original "solitary place" is not specified, Jesus may have gone to Gaulanitis, fed the five thousand, sent the disciples ahead of him to Galilee, and arrived in Gennesaret after entering the boat. However, if Matthew's account follows Mark's Gospel, then the "solitary place" is in Galilee where the feeding of the five thousand takes place. The disciples are then encouraged to cross over to Bethsaida (in Gaulanitis), but when Jesus meets the disciples on the water, they arrive at Gennesaret in Galilee. As such, they arrive on the same side of the lake from which they departed. In this case, Mark's geographical indicators do not match his otherwise consistent use of "to cross over."[8]

Returning to John's account of the miracle, the geographical details following the narrative further suggest that Jesus was in Gaulanitis when he fed the five thousand, because following the miracle, Jesus set off across the lake for Capernaum (John 6:16). Due to the evening hour, the crowds cannot follow his progress across the lake, so they wait until morning for boats to arrive from Tiberius. The crowd that stayed on the opposite shore of the lake

---

8. Steven Notley suggests that the surprisingly disjointed geographical clues in Mark point to a larger literary construct (Rainey and Notley, *Sacred Bridge*, 360).

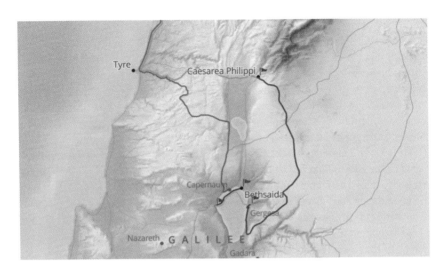

Jesus' Journey to Caesarea Philippi

(in Gaulanitis) discovered in the morning that Jesus did not disembark at Tiberius, so they go to Capernaum, where they find Jesus "on the other side of the lake" (John 6:25 NIV). If Jesus departed from a harbor in Gaulanitis and then landed in Capernaum, which is just west of the political boundary of the Jordan River, then this narrative is a great example of how little a distance can be covered and still be considered traveling "to the other side" (see "Ancient Harbors of the Sea of Galilee" map on pg. 170 for reference).

JESUS FEEDS FOUR THOUSAND

The same careful attention to geographical details is necessary when reading Matthew and Mark's accounts of Jesus feeding the crowd of four thousand with seven loaves and a few small fish (Matt 15:32–39; Mark 8:1–9). Matthew begins the narrative in an undetermined location, so Mark's account gives the reader the most helpful geographical clues. Mark 7:31 locates Jesus in the region of the Decapolis, and since there

is no mention of Jesus moving to a new location, the reader might assume Jesus is still in the Decapolis when he feeds the crowd of over four thousand people. This tentative conclusion is further supported when after the miracle, Jesus gets into a boat with his disciples and crosses to the region of Dalmanutha (Mark 8:10). This town is mentioned only in Mark's Gospel and is thought to be within the vicinity of Magdala on the northwestern side of the lake (in Galilee). Matthew, likewise, records that following the feeding of the four thousand, Jesus travels to Magdala (Matt 15:39), suggesting that Matthew agrees with Mark's geographical placement of this miracle in the region of the Decapolis.

JESUS TRAVELS TO CAESAREA PHILIPPI

Shortly after visiting and teaching in towns in Galilee, Jesus again enters a boat and crosses to "the other side" (Matt 16:5; Mark 8:13). The reader would not be amiss to understand that both Matthew and Mark are referring to Gaulanitis. Mark specifically states that Jesus goes to Bethsaida (Mark 8:22) and then continues his travels to Caesarea Philippi (Mark 8:27). Matthew does not record where Jesus lands when he crosses to "the other side," but he does note that Jesus immediately goes to Caesarea Philippi (Matt 16:5, 13). This suggests that when crossing the lake in Matt 16:5, Jesus travels from Galilee to Gaulanitis, from where he takes the primary trunk route north from Bethsaida to Caesarea Philippi.

As is evident in the above examples, not all of the Gospel narratives specify Jesus' point of origin in his travels nor his point of destination, but by following the geographical indicators, especially the phrase to "the other side," the reader is able to track Jesus' movements from one region to the other.

BIBLIOGRAPHY

Beitzel, Barry. *The New Moody Atlas of the Bible*. Chicago: Moody, 2009.

Rainey, Anson F., and R. Steven Notley. *The Sacred Bridge*. Jerusalem: Carta, 2006.

Rasmussen, Carl G. *Zondervan Atlas of the Bible*. Rev. ed. Grand Rapids: Zondervan, 2010.

CHAPTER 18

FISHING THE SEA OF GALILEE

Matt 13:47–50; Luke 5:1–11; John 21:6

Carl J. Laney

KEY POINTS

- Some symbols of early Christianity found their origins in the fishing industry.

- The Sea of Galilee, which is the lowest freshwater lake in the world, was the first pick for Jews to fish from in ancient times.

- Understanding how different types of fishing nets were used enriches our understanding of certain events and parables of Jesus.

Four of Jesus' disciples were fishermen before they became followers of Jesus: Peter, Andrew, James, and John (Matt 4:18–21). Jesus was familiar with their work as fishermen on the Sea of Galilee. When he called them as his disciples he invited them to become "fishers of men" (Matt 4:19). The fish became a symbol in early Christian art because the Greek word for "fish" (*ichthys*, ἰχθύς) provides the initial letters of the words in an early Christian creed. The first letter, *iota*, is the initial letter in the Greek word for "Jesus" (*Iēsous*, Ἰησοῦς). The second letter, *chi*, is the first letter in the word for "Christ" (*Christos*, Χριστός). The third letter, *theta*, is the first letter in the Greek word for "God" (*theos*, θεός). The fourth letter, *upsilon*, represents the Greek word for "son" (*huios*, υἱός). And the last letter, *sigma*, is the first letter in the Greek word for "Savior" (*sōtēr*, σωτήρ). Taken together the letters in the Greek word for "fish" symbolize the message "Jesus Christ, God's Son, Savior." As it does today, the early symbol of the fish could be used to identify a believer in Jesus without the need for verbal communication.

Another early Christian symbol taken from the fishing industry was the anchor: a symbol of security and hope in turbulent times (Heb 6:19). Images of the anchor and the fish appear in early Christian art and inscriptions. These symbols, along with the biblical references to fishing and fishermen, make it imperative for interpreters of the Bible

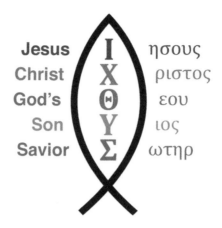

FISH	Jesus	Ι	ησους
IXΘΥΣ	Christ	Χ	ριστος
	God's	Θ	εου
	Son	Υ	ιος
	Savior	Σ	ωτηρ

to be familiar with the fishing industry of ancient times.

THE HISTORICAL CONTEXT

Luke 5:1–11 records Jesus' early ministry in Galilee. His baptism and temptation had already taken place (Luke 3:21–4:13). John the Baptist had identified Jesus as the "Lamb of God" and "Son of God" (John 1:29–34). Andrew, Peter, Philip, and Nathaniel had followed Jesus to Galilee and were present with Jesus in Cana when he performed his first miracle (John 2:1–11). They had traveled with Jesus to Jerusalem for Passover (John 2:23) and had returned to Galilee after their excursion through Samaria (John 4:3–42). Jesus had called Peter, Andrew, James, and John to become fishers of men (Matt 4:18–22). Luke 5:1–11 records a second call to follow Jesus.

While some scholars regard Matt 4:18–22, Mark 1:16–20, and Luke 5:1–11

as parallel accounts,[1] Robert Thomas and Stanley Gundry believe the features of Luke 5:1–11 are sufficiently distinct to regard it as a different event. In Matthew and Mark's account, the brothers Peter and Andrew were casting their nets, probably from the shore. In Luke's account the brothers were lowering the nets from their boat. Luke's account records that they took a great catch of fish. Matthew and Mark say nothing about a catch. It appears that the brothers went back to their fishing work after the first call by Jesus (Matt 4:18–22). But after responding to Jesus' second call (Luke 5:1–11), they remained with Jesus permanently.[2]

FISHING IN BIBLICAL TIMES

During biblical times, fish came mainly from the Mediterranean Sea, the Nile River, the Jordan River, and the Sea of Galilee. The people of Tyre fished the

---

1. A. T. Robertson, *Word Pictures in the Greek New Testament* Vol. 2 (Nashville, TN: Broadman Press, 1930), 68.

2. Robert L. Thomas and Stanley N. Gundry, *A Harmony of the Gospels* (Chicago: Moody, 1978), 52.

Mediterranean (Ezek 26:5) and sold their salted or dried fish in Jerusalem (Neh 13:16). The Nile was an important fishing grounds for the Egyptians, as indicated by the judgment on Egypt in Isa 19:8: "all those who cast a line into the Nile will mourn" (NASB). Various methods of fishing are illustrated in ancient Egyptian art.³ That the Jordan River contained fish is evident from the Medeba mosaic map which shows fish swimming upstream away from the salty waters of the Dead Sea. However, the tamarisk trees growing along the banks of the Jordan—the "thickets by the Jordan" (Jer 12:5; 49:19; 50:44)—made access difficult and dangerous. In the end, the Sea of Galilee was the most important local fishery for the Jews in ancient times.

THE SEA OF GALILEE

The Sea of Galilee is located in the Rift Valley between the Hula Basin and the Jordan Valley. This harp-shaped freshwater lake is fed by the Jordan River which flows into the sea at the north and exits at the southern end to continue its journey south to the Dead Sea. It was known as "Chinnereth" ("harp") in the Old Testament period (Num 34:11, Josh 13:27). The New Testament refers to it as the Lake of Gennesareth (Luke 5:1) due to its proximity to the plain of Gennesareth along its northwestern shore. It also takes the name "Sea of Tiberius" from the name of the new capital of Galilee built by Herod Antipas in honor of the emperor. The name most

familiar to readers of the Gospels is the "the Sea of Galilee" (Matt 4:18, 15:29; Mark 1:16, 7:31, John 6:1). In modern Israel it is called Yam ["sea"] Kinneret or simply "the Kinneret."

The Sea of Galilee is approximately thirteen miles from north to south and eight miles from east to west, covering an area of sixty-four square miles. The maximum depth is 150 feet. Situated in a basin six hundred eighty feet below sea level with the Golan Heights on the east and steep hillsides on the west, the Sea of Galilee is the lowest freshwater lake on earth. During the summer months the airstream rising off the surrounding hills comes in contact with the cooler sea-to-land breeze from the Mediterranean, creating high winds and unexpected storms. The Jewish historian Flavius Josephus provides a helpful description of the sea and comments that "its water is sweet to the taste and excellent to drink: ... it is perfectly pure" (War 3.506–507).⁴ He also reports that the region around the lake is "rich in soil and pasturage" (War 3.42). The sea was surrounded in ancient times by numerous cities, including Tiberias, Magdala, Capernaum, and Bethsaida, as well as fifteen active harbors.

FISH IN THE SEA OF GALILEE

Most of what we know about fish and fishing in the Sea of Galilee comes from the experience and expertise of a Galilean fisherman, Mendel Nun, who immigrated to Palestine from Latvia in 1939 and lived at Kibbutz En Gev until his

3. For pictures see https://commons.wikimedia.org/wiki/Category:Fish_in_Ancient_Egyptian_art; http://www.reshafim.org.il/ad/egypt/timelines/topics/fishing_and_hunting.htm.

4. Quotations of Josephus are from Thackeray's translation in The Loeb Classical Library: Josephus II: The Jewish War, Books I–III, trans. H. St. J. Thackeray (Cambridge, MA: Harvard University Press, 1927).

Types of Fish in the Sea of Galilee

Musht   **Barbels**   **Sardines**

death in 2010. Having spent his life fishing and exploring the ancient harbors of the Kinneret, Mendel became the foremost expert on this subject. His books and articles are primary resources for research on fishing the Sea of Galilee.

Fishing has always been an important commercial activity on the Sea of Galilee. Josephus reports that "the lake contains species of fish different, both in taste and appearance, from those found elsewhere" (*War* 3.508–509).

There are eighteen species of indigenous fish in the Sea of Galilee, ten of which are important commercially. These can be divided into three groups: the musht, the barbels, and the sardines.[5] The word "musht" is Arabic for "comb," referring to the long dorsal fin on this group of fish. The Hebrew name is "amnun," meaning "nurse fish," because even when the young fish are hatched the parent fish keep watch over them for a few days. The most important species of this group are the Talapia Galilea, which can grow to about sixteen inches in length. These tasty but boney fish are

served today in Israel's restaurants as "St. Peter's fish." The musht gather in the shallow shoals in the northern part of the Sea of Galilee during the winter months and disperse when the water warms in the spring. This probably accounts for the disciples being engaged in a fishing enterprise near Capernaum before being called by Jesus.

The second group of fish are the "barbels," which are members of the carp family. The classic characteristic of this variety are the barbs at the corners of their mouths. The Long Headed Barbel has a narrow silvery body and a pointed head. It can reach about thirty inches in length. The Barbus Canis is slightly smaller in size but features larger scales. Both species have been fished commercially since the biblical period and remain popular for Sabbath meals and Jewish feasts.

The third group of fish in the Sea of Galilee are the Kinneret sardines. These are the smallest commercial fish in the Kinneret, yet they amount to about half the yearly catch. The Kinneret sardines resemble saltwater sardines and are

5. Mendel Nun, *The Sea of Galilee and Its Fishermen in the New Testament* (Kibbutz Ein Gev: Kinnereth Sailing Co., 1989), 6.

found in large schools. The sardines are preserved by pickling and can be found today on the breakfast buffet at Israeli hotels.

Catfish are the largest indigenous fish found in the Kinneret, but since they have skin instead of scales, they are not kosher and cannot be eaten according to Mosaic law (Lev 11:9–11). Referring to it by its Greek name (korokinos, "Water Raven"), Josephus reports that fish of this variety can be found by the springs near Capernaum (War 3.521).

FISHING AND FISH NETS

More than a dozen ancient harbors have been located along the shores of the Sea of Galilee. These harbors provided safe havens for fishing and passenger boats when strong winds and storms stirred the otherwise placid sea. During the years between 1973 and 1986 when the water level on the Kinneret was quite low, the foundations of these ancient harbors and anchorages were exposed and carefully surveyed.[6][7] Discoveries included ancient stone anchors, mooring stones, fishing net sinkers, and a well preserved two thousand year-old wooden boat.[8]

While English translations of the Bible typically use just one word to refer to fishing nets, there are several different kinds of nets which can be distinguished in the Gospels. The dragnet (sagēnē, σαγήνη) is the oldest type of net. It is made up of a long wall of net, about a football field in length and about ten feet wide. The net has floats on the top and sinkers on the bottom. The dragnet is spread out about a hundred yards off shore and

parallel to it. The net is then dragged ashore by ropes on either end, surrounding and capturing the fish as it is pulled ashore. After the catch, the net must be dried and mended. In Matthew 13:47–48 Jesus refers to the dragnet in his parable about the kingdom of heaven. After the catch, the fishermen must remove the bad fish (those without scales) that cannot be eaten from those that can be offered for sale.

The cast-net (diktyon, δίκτυον) is a circular net, something like a parachute, with weights around the outer edge to make the net sink into the water. This net is used by a single fisherman who arranges the net on his arm and then casts the net into the water with his opposing arm. The net spreads out like a parachute and falls into the water. The weights attached to the outer edges of the net pull it to the bottom, trapping the fish.

There are two ways fish can be retrieved from the cast-net. First, the fisherman may wade around the perimeter of the net, removing the fish one-by-one. Second, he may wade around the net, gathering the sinkers and then pulling the net with the fish to shore or hoisting the net into the boat. Although cast-nets are no longer used commercially on the Kinneret, they are often used in a demonstration for tourists enjoying a boat ride across the lake. The cast-net is mentioned in Mark 1:16–18 where Jesus saw Peter and Andrew casting a net into the sea. Jesus said, "Follow me and I will make you become fishers of men." The two left their cast-nets and followed Jesus.

---

6. See Gordon Franz, "Ancient Harbors of the Sea of Galilee" on pg. 219.

7. Mendel Nun, Ancient Anchorages and Harbours Around the Sea of Galilee (Kibbutz Ein Gev: Kinneret Sailing Co., 1988).

8. Shelley Wachsmann, "The Galilee Boat," BAR 14.5 (Sept/Oct 1988): 18–33.

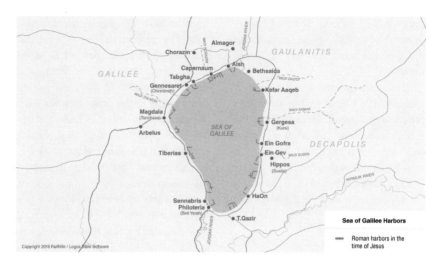

Ancient Harbors of the Sea of Galilee

The trammel net is the only kind that was used in ancient times and continues in use by commercial fishermen on the Sea of Galilee today. The trammel net is a compound net consisting of three layers of nets connected together. There are two exterior walls that have large mesh. The middle layer is a net made of much smaller mesh, about an inch or an inch and a half square. While there is no distinct Greek word for the trammel net, the plural "nets" (*diktya*), rather than the singular "net" (*diktyon*), distinguishes them in the Gospels. Trammel nets are about a hundred feet long, but are always attached together in a series. A set of trammel nets can extend for a distance of a hundred or more yards.

Fishing with a trammel net in ancient times was always done during the night when the fish could not see the threads of the net. Modern fishermen have nylon nets which can be used during the day. Weights on the trammel net pull it down into the water while floats keep the top

side of the wall near the surface. After setting the net, fishermen enter the water near the shore making noise and splashing with their oars. The fleeing fish attempt to swim away but become trapped in the small mesh net of the trammel. The trammel net is probably the type referred to in Mark 1:19–20 and Matt 4:21–22 where the Gospel writers report that James and John were mending their nets. The plural "nets" suggests that they were working on the three layered trammel net. The trammel net also appears to be the one referred to in Luke's account of the great catch of fish (Luke 5:1–7) and John's account of the miraculous catch during Jesus' third resurrection appearance (John 21:3–11).

The most familiar means of fishing for modern sports enthusiasts is with a hook and line. This method is well attested in ancient Assyrian reliefs and Egyptian art. When the tax collectors asked Peter, "Doesn't your teacher pay the temple tax?" (Matt 17:24 NIV), Peter replied, "Yes," and

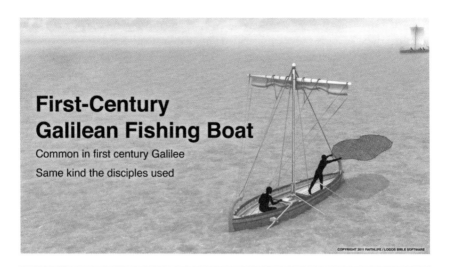

First-Century Galilean Fishing Boat

Common in first century Galilee

Same kind the disciples used

COPYRIGHT 2011 FAITHLIFE / LOGOS BIBLE SOFTWARE

then went to consult Jesus to see if he had answered correctly. Jesus told Peter, "Go to the lake and throw out your line. Take the first fish you catch; open its mouth and you will find a four-drachma coin" (Matt 17:27 NIV). Peter did as he was told and found a coin sufficient to pay the tax for both himself and Jesus.

Commercial fishing has always been hard work. Rowing heavy wooden boats and hauling in heavy nets with weights and floats was a job fit only for men with strength and stamina. The fishermen worked most of the night and then cared for the fish and mended their nets during the day. The catch could be sold fresh in local markets. To transport the catch to more distant markets, the fish could be sun-dried, pickled, or preserved with salt. Magdala (the home of Mary Magdalene) became a central point for processing the salted Kinneret sardines for shipping out of Galilee.[9]

LUKE 5:1-11

While some scholars believe this text is a variant of the story of the miraculous catch in John 21, the differences are too many and too great to identify it as such. Luke is recounting an event that took place at the beginning of Jesus' ministry in connection with his call of Peter, James, and John to become fishers of men. John 21, on the other hand, records an event that took place at a meeting of Jesus and his apostles after his resurrection.

Luke describes the situation in Luke 5:1, where Jesus is standing "by the lake of Gennesaret" while teaching a crowd that is pressing in on him. Luke uses the name "lake of Gennesaret" (*limnēn Gennēsaret*)—as does Josephus in his description (*War* 3.506)—whereas the other Gospels refer to it as a "sea" (*thalassa*, θάλασσα). Luke 5:1 is also the only place in the Gospels where the name Gennesaret is used rather than Galilee. Josephus explains that the lake

---

9. Nun, *Sea of Galilee and Its Fishermen*, 51.

takes its name from the "adjacent territory," clearly referring to the broad fertile plain along the northwest shore south of Capernaum (*War* 3.506).

As the eager listeners were "crowding around" (*epikeisthai*) him to hear the word of God, Jesus saw two boats at the water's edge. The fishermen had returned from a night of fishing and were washing their nets in preparation for the next day's work. Luke records that Jesus got into Peter's boat and asked him to push it out a little way from the land (Luke 5:3). Then he sat down and continued his teaching from the boat. While most people stand while teaching in modern times, it was customary in the biblical period for rabbis to sit and teach (see Matt 23:2).

When Jesus had finished speaking to the crowd on the shore, he instructed Peter, "Put out into deep water, and let down the nets for a catch" (Luke 5:4 NIV). The words of Jesus reveal clearly the kind of net Peter was using. It was a trammel net with weights on the bottom and floats (probably gourds) on the top. The trammel net would be lowered into "deep water," and the fishermen would splash with their oars, driving the fish toward the net to become trapped by the small mesh in the middle layer of the net. Peter's reply—"Master, we've worked hard all night and haven't caught anything" (Luke 5:5 NIV)—reflects the fact that fishing with a trammel net was customarily done at night when the fish could not see the net. Yet in obedience to Jesus, Peter and his companions maneuvered the boat into deep water and lowered the net.

As any fisherman will tell you, catching fish is a thrilling and memorable experience; and what a memorable day this was for Peter! The trammel net captured such a quantity of fish that it began to break apart! Mendel Nun reports that a good night's catch with a trammel net can result in a hundred to two hundred pounds of fish and even more during the peak of the musht season.[10]

A trammel net is usually lowered a dozen times during a night's work. The wiggling fish are extracted individually from the narrow mesh of the net. But with a large catch, the trammel net is hauled into the boat like a bundle with the fish tangled inside. This was the case described by Luke here. In fact, the catch was so large that two boats were required, and even then, the boats began to sink under the weight of the nets and the catch.

Peter immediately recognized that this was no ordinary night's catch! To catch such a quantity of fish *during the day* with a trammel net was nothing short of miraculous. Peter spoke to Jesus saying, "Go away from me Lord, for I am a sinful man" (Luke 5:8 NASB). This is reminiscent of Isaiah's response when he saw the vision of the Lord (Isa 6:5). Leon Morris observes, "Peter recognized the hand of God and that drove him to realize his own sinfulness."[11] It is probably significant that Peter goes from addressing Jesus as "Master" (*epistatēs*, ἐπιστάτης) in Luke 5:5 to addressing him as "Lord" (*kyrios*, κύριος) in Luke 5:8. While the designation *kyrios* may have the sense of "sir," referring to any person in high position, Peter's use of the term "raises Jesus above the human

---

10. Nun, *Sea of Galilee and Its Fishermen*, 32.

11. Leon Morris, *The Gospel According to St. Luke* (Grand Rapids: Eerdmans, 1974), 113.

level."[12] As a career fisherman on the Sea of Galilee, Peter recognized the significance of the enormous catch. It was a miracle.

Peter's partners in his fishing enterprise were "James and John, the sons of Zebedee" (Luke 5:10). Luke then records the sequel to the miracle. First, Jesus commands Peter, "Don't be afraid." The present imperative of prohibition could be rendered "Stop being afraid." Peter's reaction to the miracle in Luke 5:8 recalls the response of Manoah and his wife when they encountered the Angel of the Lord: "We will surely die, for we have seen God" (Judg 13:22). Having been reassured by Jesus, Peter is now informed of his new calling: "From now on you will be catching men" (Luke 5:10 NASB). The present tense of the participle "catch" (zōgrōn) indicates continuous action. The Greek word ζωγρέω (zōgreō) means "capture alive."[13] Peter's new career would be "catching" living souls for the kingdom instead of carrying dead fish to the market.

Luke brings his record of this encounter to a conclusion in Luke 5:11. Convinced of the worthiness of the call they had been given, Peter and his partners "pulled their boats up on shore, left everything and followed" Jesus (NIV). As noted above, this was not Jesus' first call of these fishermen. The first call is recorded in Matt 4:18-22. Luke 5:1-11 records their second call to become fishers of men. They appear to have returned to their fishing after the first call. But now they "left everything" and became permanent followers of Jesus.

MATTHEW 13:47-50

The parable of the dragnet likens the kingdom of heaven to the capture of "every kind" of fish (Matt 13:47). A dragnet does not distinguish the kinds of fish it captures. Among the "good" or edible fish are the "bad" or non-kosher fish, the ones that lack fins or have skin instead of scales (Lev 11:9-12). After the catch, the fishermen must separate the fish that can be sold in the market from those which do not have value and must be thrown away. The parable teaches the lesson that during the present age there will be a gathering of all kinds of people, the righteous along with the wicked. But at the end of the age there will be a judgment which will separate the wicked from the true believers.

JOHN 21:6

The miraculous catch of fish when Jesus met his disciples in Galilee after his resurrection illustrates the use of the trammel net. Similar to the situation described in Luke 5:1-11, the disciples have spent a night fishing and with no success. Jesus appears on the shore and directs them to "Throw your net on the right side of the boat" (John 21:6 NIV). Following his instructions, they have such success that they cannot get the net into the boat and must drag it ashore with the miraculous catch of fish. Peter was so stirred by this experience that he counted out the fish, and John records that they numbered 153 "large fish" (John 21:11).

While the three layered trammel net appears to have been used for this catch, Nun suggests that the net may have been

---

12. BDAG, s.v. "κύριος," 578.

13. BDAG, s.v. "ζωγρέω."

used to encircle the fish and then the cast net used to capture the fish within the enclosure.[14] He points out that the net that Peter drew ashore himself with the 153 fish could have only been the cast net.

Christian tradition places this event near the warm springs at Tabgha where schools of musht fish gather during the winter months. A small Franciscan chapel called The Church of the Primacy of Peter marks the traditional place where Jesus served his disciples breakfast and instructed Peter to "shepherd my sheep" (John 21:15–17).

BIBLIOGRAPHY

Josephus, Flavius. *Josephus II: The Jewish War, Books I-III*. Translated by H. St. J. Thackeray. LCL. Cambridge, MA: Harvard University Press, 1927.

Morris, Leon. *The Gospel According to St. Luke*. Grand Rapids: Eerdmans, 1974.

Murphy-O'Conner, Jerome. "Fishers of Fish, Fishers of Men." *Bible Review* 15.3 (June 1999): 22–27, 48–49.

Nun, Mendel. *Ancient Anchorages and Harbours Around the Sea of Galilee*. Kibbutz Ein Gev: Kinnereth Sailing Co., 1988.

———. "Cast Your Net Upon the Waters: Fish and Fishermen in Jesus' Time." *BAR* 19.6 (Nov/Dec 1993): 46–56.

———. *Sea of Galilee: Newly Discovered Harbours from the New Testament Days*. 3rd ed. Kibbutz Ein Gev: Kinnereth Sailing Co., 1992.

———. *The Sea of Galilee and Its Fishermen in the New Testament*. Kibbutz Ein Gev: Kinnereth Sailing Co., 1989.

Robertson, A. T. *Word Pictures in the Greek New Testament* Vol. 2. Nashville: Broadman Press, 1930.

Thomas, Robert L., and Stanley N. Gundry. *A Harmony of the Gospels*. Chicago: Moody, 1978.

Wachsmann, Shelley. "The Galilee Boat." *BAR* 14.5 (Sept/Oct 1988): 18–33.

---

14. Nun, *Sea of Galilee and Its Fishermen*, 43.

CHAPTER 19

WHAT TYPE OF STORMS DID JESUS CALM: WIND OR RAIN?

Matt 8:23-27; 14:22-33; Mark 4:35-41;
6:45-52; Luke 8:22-25; John 6:15-21

Gordon Franz

KEY POINTS

- Different types of storms develop over the Sea of Galilee, each type dependent upon the surrounding geography and time of year (temperature).

- The Gospels record Jesus calming two storms that threatened the lives of his disciples as they sailed across the sea.

- The landscape, the climate, and key textual details suggest Jesus calmed a windstorm—not a thunderstorm.

COMMON (MIS)CONCEPTIONS

Two storm events are recorded in the Gospels. The first, when the Lord Jesus takes his disciples to the harbor of Gadara on the southeastern part of the Sea of Galilee (Matt 8:23-27; Mark 4:35-41; Luke 8:22-25); and the second, after the feeding of the five thousand on the north shore of the sea (Matt 14:22-33, Mark 6:45-52, John 6:15-21). Our natural inclination is to think of storms as being accompanied by rain and dark skies, thunder and lightning. So it is not surprising if this is the way we visualize the Lord Jesus calming the storms on the Sea of Galilee. This common assumption is only reinforced by famous paintings like Rembrandt's masterpiece "Christ in the Storm on the Sea of Galilee" (see Excursus below). There is, however, good reason to believe that the two storms the Lord Jesus calmed were nothing like what we have grown so familiar with. There was neither rain nor dark skies, and no thunder or lightning. But how can this be? To those accustomed to sailing on the Sea of Galilee the answer would be obvious: they were windstorms, not thunderstorms.

In the remainder of the article, we will look at why this meteorological

Rembrandt's "Christ in the Storm on the Sea of Galilee"

reading is the most likely. First, we will explore the general weather patterns of the area. Second, we will take a closer look at each storm account, paying attention to the clues provided and remaining open to the portrait that might be painted of the storms that Jesus calmed.

EXCURSUS: REMBRANDT'S "CHRIST IN THE STORM ON THE SEA OF GALILEE" PAINTING

In 1633 the famous Dutch master Rembrandt van Rijn (1606–1669) painted his masterpiece "Christ in the Storm on the Sea of Galilee." It is the only seascape picture that he painted. This painting was in the Isabella Stewart Gardner Museum in Boston until it was stolen by art thieves in March of 1990.

The painting depicts the panic stricken disciples in their fishing boat trying to regain control of the vessel after being caught in a sudden fierce storm on the Sea of Galilee. A huge violent wave is crashing over the bow, and the sail is ripping as the boat draws perilously close to some rocks.

There are fourteen people in the boat: the Lord Jesus, his twelve disciples, and a fourteenth individual, most likely Rembrandt himself because he was known to paint himself into his pictures. One of the disciples is shown leaning over the edge of the boat, apparently sea-sick and vomiting. It was probably Judas, since he was the only non-Galilean among the twelve disciples, from the city of Keriot south of Hebron in the Negev of

Judah. He was not accustomed to sailing in a boat; the Galileans were.

But can Rembrandt's painting be considered an accurate depction of the storms recounted by the Gospels? Does it distort or illuminate our understanding of the Lord Jesus calming the storms on the Sea of Galilee? Unfortunately, Rembrandt painted this picture in Amsterdam and not at the Sea of Galilee during a winter storm. This is not to detract from the powerful imagery of the painting, but there are major mistakes in this painting (and similar renditions) that depart from the reality experienced by the disciples on those turbulent waters.

GENERAL WEATHER PATTERNS

In Israel there are only two seasons: the wet season and the dry season. The wet season begins a few weeks after Succoth (Feast of Tabernacles). These rains are called the early rains (*yoreh* in Hebrew; Deut 11:13, 14; Jer 5:24; Hos 6:3; Ps 84:6; Joel 2:23), and they generally fall during the months of October and November. The early rain loosens the hard soil so the plowing can commence and the farmer can sow the seeds for the new agricultural year.[1] Then there are the winter rains (Song 2:11) which usually last from December to February. These storms last for two or three days and come every seven to ten days. They bring thunderstorms, rain, hail, and sometimes even snow in the higher elevations (Ps 18; 2 Sam 23:20). The latter rains (*malqosh* in Hebrew) fall during March and April and usually bring heavy showers (Deut 11:14; Job 29:23; Prov 16:15; Jer 3:3; 5:24; Hos 6:3; Joel 2:23; Zech 10:1). The Mosaic

Law clearly states that the early rain and latter rain will come in their proper seasons if the people are obeying the commandments that God gave them and not following after other gods (Deut 11:13–17).

The dry season begins after Shavuot (Feast of Pentecost) and lasts from May until October. It is not completely dry because there is dew in the early hours before sunrise (Gen 27:28, 39; Deut 33:13–28; Hos 6:4; 13:3; Hag 1:10; Zech 8:12). On a number of occasions I experienced the dew before the sun came over the horizon when I was working on the Tel Lachish excavations. Sometimes the dew was quite thick, driving to the tel. In our Area S, the tarps over the area were heavy with large puddles of water on them. Once the sun came up, the dew dissipated very quickly. This dryness also causes wildfires to the forests and brush (Isa 5:24; 19:18; Joel 1:19, 20; 2:3). (See also "Excursus: Other Weather Patterns" below and infographic "Agricultural Cycle of the Levant/Palestine" on pg. 530.)

STORMS ON THE SEA OF GALILEE

The two storm events recorded in the Gospels on the Sea of Galilee were both winter windstorms. Such storms come from the east off the Golan Heights, unlike rainstorms which come from the west or the north. Due to the nature of how rainstorms develop, it is highly unlikely the disciples would have been caught in such a storm. Indeed, "caught" implies the storms develop with a sense of suddenness, but this is not the case. If the storms were rainstorms, the disciples—many of whom were seasoned fishermen—would have recognized the developing rain clouds and impending

---

1. Oded Borowski, *Agriculture in Iron Age Israel* (Winona Lake, IN: Eisenbrauns, 1987), 47–48.

threat and sought shelter in one of the harbors around the lake.

The eastern winter windstorms, on the other hand, come off the Golan Heights suddenly, without warning and with fierce winds. This explains why the veteran fishermen were so terrified of the storms on each occasion. The windstorms develop quickly and fiercely—yet end suddenly as well.

THE FIRST WINDSTORM

The first winter windstorm recorded in the Gospels took place about November of AD 28.[2] This was a pivotal event in the ministry of the Lord Jesus. He had just been rejected by some of the religious establishment (Matt 12:22-37; Mark 3:22-30; Luke 11:14-23) and decided to take his disciples and "cross over to the other side." In this case he was going to take his disciples to the Decapolis city of Gadara on the southeast side of the Sea of Galilee.[3] This was the first time in Jesus' public ministry that he was going to visit Gentile territory.

On the way to Gadara, Jesus and his disciples were in a small fishing vessel when they encountered a windstorm, causing the waves to come over the side and fill the boat (Matt 8:23-27; Mark 4:35-41; Luke 8:22-25).[4] Even the veteran fishermen among the disciples were terrified, but Jesus was fast asleep on a pillow in the stern of the boat! What a striking contrast.

The disciples woke up the Lord Jesus and asked, "Teacher, do you not care that we are perishing?" (Mark 4:38) and prayed, "Lord, save us! We are perishing!" (Matt 8:25). The Lord Jesus rebuked the winds and the waves and questioned the disciples about their faith.

The Gospels record that there is a great calm. The impression one gets is that the lake went from a violet tempest to mirror-flat within a matter of seconds. It is no wonder the disciples said, "Who can this be, that even the winds and the sea obey him?" (Matt 8:27). They were awestruck by the power of the Lord Jesus. But more importantly for our purposes, notice there is no mistake as to what Jesus is understood as controlling: "even the winds (anemos, ἄνεμος) and the sea obey him." The specific reference to "winds" strengthens our assessment that the disciples were dealing with a winter windstorm, and that it was the fierce winds that stuck out most in the disciples' minds.

THE SECOND WINDSTORM

The second winter windstorm recorded in the Gospels takes place the evening after the Lord Jesus fed the five thousand men, plus women and children right before Passover of AD 29 (John 6:4). This feeding, I believe, took place near Kibbutz Almagor, just to the west of the area of Bethsaida. After the Lord Jesus fed the multitudes, he dismissed

---

2. Assuming an AD 30 date for the crucifixion / resurrection of the Lord Jesus and an approximately four year earthly ministry.

3. See Todd Bolen, "Where Did the Possessed-Pigs Drown?" on pg. 196.

4. Their vessel was probably like the boat found near Magdala in 1986. See Shelley Wachsmann, "First Century CE Kinneret Boat Classes," in The Excavations of an Ancient Boat in the Sea of Galilee (Lake Kinneret), 'Atiqot 19 (Jerusalem: Israel Antiquities Authority, 1990), 119-24. Scripture quotations in this section and throughout the article are from the NKJV unless otherwise indicated.

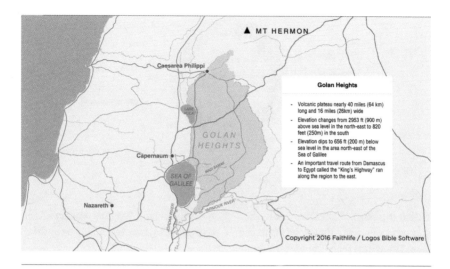

Copyright 2016 Faithlife / Logos Bible Software

the crowd and sent his disciples to their boat anchored in the Aish harbor. Jesus went further up the mountain to pray. The disciples headed "to the other side, to Bethsaida" (Mark 6:45) in an eastward direction. The storm came up and the winds were "against them" (*enantios autois*, ἐναντίος αὐτοῖς)—coming from the east off the Golan Heights.[5] At the fourth watch (between 3 AM and 6 AM) the Lord Jesus walked on the water to the disciples in the boat. They saw him and were afraid, thinking he must be a ghost; but he calmed them saying, "Be of good cheer! It is I, do not be afraid" (Matt 14:22–33; Mark 6:45–52; John 6:15–21).

Matthew's Gospel is the only one to record Peter's desire to walk on water to the Lord Jesus. The Lord Jesus bid him to come to him. Peter got out of the boat and walked on water as long as he had his eyes fixed on the Lord Jesus. When he took his eyes off the Lord and saw the storm, he began to sink. Peter prayed the shortest prayer in the Bible: "Lord,

save me!" (Matt 14:30). Jesus immediately reached out and caught Peter, chiding him for his "little faith" (Matt 14:31). When they got into the boat, the winds ceased. The disciples who stayed in the boat were amazed and worshiped Jesus and said, "Truly You are the Son of God" (Matt 14:33).

Again, the important facts to notice concerning the type of storm the disciples were engaging and that the Lord Jesus calmed are (1) the references to the direction the disciples were sailing (east), (2) the direction the wind was blowing (west), and (3) the explicit references to wind as the element that was of utmost concern to the disciples. All such clues point to the fierce windstorms that roll off the Golan Heights and across the Sea of Galilee—not a thunderstorm.

Ancient and Modern Testaments to Golan Height Winds

I had a study-group once that went out on a tourist boat ride on the Sea of Galilee.

---

5. See also Cyndi Parker, "Crossing to "The Other Side" of the Sea of Galilee" on pg. 157.

We left from the Kibbutz Ein-Gev harbor and went out just a little ways into the lake. The winds from the eastern windstorms were blowing down from the Golan Heights to the lake, and the wind was tossing the boat roughly. I can only imagine what it would have been like in a wooden vessel.

Josephus, the first-century AD Jewish historian, describes a winter windstorm that occurred during the siege of Gamla, located in the Golan Heights, in AD 67.[6] The Jewish defenders were shooting arrows and missiles from the towers and walls of Gamla eastward towards the Romans down below them. The Romans were attacking from the east. Josephus tells us: "Here the Jews worked havoc among the advancing enemy with missiles of all kinds and rocks which they rolled down upon them, being themselves from their elevated position no easy mark for an arrow. However, to seal their ruin, a storm miraculously arose which, blowing full in their faces [from the east], carried against them the arrows of the Romans and checked and deflected their own. Owing to the force of the gale they could neither stand on the edge of the precipices, having no firm foothold,

nor see the approaching enemy" (*War* 4.75–78 [LCL]; brackets added by author).

AN UNCOMMON CONCEPTION

The Gospels record two storms where the Lord Jesus calms the Sea of Galilee. Unlike the cirumstances we may naturally impose upon these events, there was neither rain nor thunder or lightning threatening the disciples' lives. Instead, the disciples had been suddenly confronted with the winter windstorms that come off the Golan Heights. The disciples were terrified because they knew how deadly these storms could be. Yet the Lord Jesus, the master of the sea, calmed the sea and the lake became mirror flat and uncannily quiet. The disciples were awestruck by this power. Instead of allowing conventional hunches or famous paintings to guide our reconstruction of these events, we have relied on the landscape, the climate, and key textual details to provide us with a more accurate picture of the storms that Jesus stilled.

EXCURSUS: OTHER WEATHER PATTERNS

When I was a little boy, my mother taught me this little ditty: "Red sky in

---

6. This siege ended on November 10, AD 67.

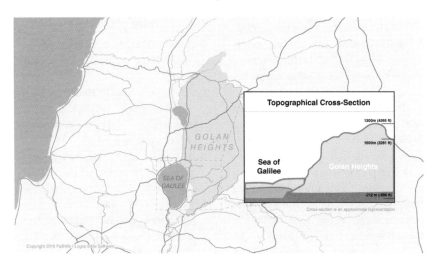

Cross-section of the Golan Heights

the morning, sailors take warning; Red sky at night, sailors delight." I had no idea that ditty had its basis in the Bible. The Lord Jesus was chiding the Pharisees and Sadducees about their ability to discern the next day's weather, but not the signs of the times. He said to them: "When it is evening you say, 'It will be fair weather, for the sky is red'; and in the morning, 'It will be foul weather today, for the sky is red and threatening.' Hypocrites! You know how to discern the face of the sky, but you cannot discern the signs of the times" (Matt 16:1-3).[7]

Mendel Nun, a lifelong fisherman on the Sea of Galilee, observed:

A red sunset indicates a stable atmosphere; because there are no upward air currents, dust in the atmosphere remains close to earth and these particles refract rays of light into red. This is also true for the morning forecast: the atmosphere is stable, but the appearance of low clouds signifies a possible change from fair weather to rainy.[8]

The Lord Jesus gives another weather forecast, but this time in Jericho. He is speaking to a multitude of people when he says to them: "When you see a cloud rising out of the west, immediately you say, 'A shower is coming'; and so it is. And when you see the south wind blow, you say, 'There will be hot weather'; and there is." (Luke 12:54-55). Again, Mendel Nun observed:

The first part of this forecast, with rain clouds coming from the west, is generally true for all the country. The second part, however, does not fit the Kinneret region. It does hold true for the southern part of

---

7. See Elaine A. Phillips, "Jesus' Interpretation of Weather Patterns" on pg. 278.

8. Mendel Nun, *The Sea of Galilee and its Fisherman in the New Testament*, (Kibbutz Ein-Gev: Kinnereth Sailing, 1989), 57; idem, "Fish, Storm and a Boat, *Jerusalem Perspective* 3.2 (1990): 4.

Israel, where the winds from the south, coming from the hot and dry Negev region, brings warm days during spring and autumn.[9]

This statement fits well with Jesus chiding the people in Jericho. It should be pointed out that the rain also comes from the north during the winter season. In Psalm 29:5-8 the psalmist describes the direction of a mighty storm as going from the Lebanon mountain range that includes Sirion (Mount Hermon) down to the Wilderness of Kadesh (Barnea). The storm was going from north to south. Proverb 25:23 states that "the north wind brings forth rain and a backbiting tongue an angry countenance." That is literally true of the winter rains in Israel. When the wind blows from the north, it brings rain, and sometimes very heavy rains. During the summer months, however, when it is not the rainy season, there is no rain when the wind blows from the north.

BIBLIOGRAPHY

Borowski, Oded. *Agriculture in Iron Age Israel.* Winona Lake, IN: Eisenbrauns, 1987.

Josephus. Translated by Henry St. J. Thackeray et al. 10 vols. LCL. Cambridge, MA: Harvard University Press, 1926-1965.

Nun, Mendel. "Fish, Storms and a Boat." *Jerusalem Perspective* 3.2 (March/April 1990): 3-5.

———. *The Sea of Galilee and its Fishermen in the New Testament.* Kibbutz Ein-Gev, Israel: Kinnereth Sailing, 1989.

Wachsmann, Shelley. "First Century CE Kinneret Boat Classes." Pages 119-24 in *The Excavations of an Ancient Boat in the Sea of Galilee (Lake Kinneret).* 'Atiqot 19. Jerusalem: Israel Antiquities Authority, 1990.

---

9. Nun, *Sea of Galilee and its Fishermen,* 57.

CHAPTER 20

PIG HUSBANDRY IN ISRAEL DURING THE NEW TESTAMENT

Matt 7:6; 8:28-34; Mark 5:1-20;
Luke 8:26-39; 15:11-32

Chris McKinny

KEY POINTS

- Textual and zooarchaeological evidence point to a disdain for and abstinence from pork by Jews since the time of ancient Israel.

- The almost total absence of pig bones in first century Judea stands in sharp contrast to the widespread consumption of pork in the surrounding Roman world.

- First century Jews were likely familiar with pig husbandry—as different teachings of Jesus demonstrate—despite their aversion to pork.

- The Synoptic Gospels present the healing of the demoniac in such a way that compares Jesus to Jonah, and the former as far superior.

- The presence of pig-herds in Gentile settings were clear ethnic boundary markers between Jews and Gentiles throughout the Early Roman period.

BIBLICAL PROHIBITION AND REACTIONS AGAINST PORK CONSUMPTION

From the biblical era until today, abstinence from pork has been viewed by outsiders as one of the most peculiar aspects of the Jewish dietary code, which, in turn, has remained one of the the single most defining religious markers of Judaism. From a wider anthropological perspective, Judaism's (as well as Islam's) abstinence from pork is peculiar, because of the widespread consumption of pork in most cultures throughout the world in both modern times and in antiquity. Pork's global popularity is due in large part to the fact that the pig (*sus scrofa*) is easily domesticated[1] and highly economical,[2] and its meat is considered to be one of the world's "best-tasting flesh and provides good-quality protein in large amount."[3] Besides their pleasant taste, pigs are perhaps most well-known for their voracious appetite of almost every type of consumable food, including human garbage. Historically, this reality has often led to pigs being used as garbage cleaners, either in the streets or in a pig sty, which has played a dominant role in the rejection of or abstinence from pork consumption in some cultures and religions.

Jewish abstinence from pork is rooted in Mosaic law (Lev 11:7–8; Deut 14:7–8), which prohibits pork consumption on the basis that despite the fact that the pig "parts the hoof" it does not "chew the cud." To this rationale the following command is added: "Their flesh you shall not eat, and their carcasses you shall not touch." With these prohibitions in the background, Prov 11:22 compares a "beautiful woman without discretion" to a "gold ring in a pig's snout."[4] The prophet Isaiah makes ref-

erence to pigs' blood or flesh on three separate occasions (Isa 65:4; 66:3, 17). In Isaiah 66:3, the offering of pigs' blood is compared negatively to a grain offering. It is worth noting that this verse compares sacrifices/offerings to crimes/sins on a greater to lesser scale of costliness. The scale can be reconstructed as follows: killing an ox versus murdering a man, sacrificing a lamb versus breaking a dog's neck, presenting a grain offering versus offering pigs' blood, and making a memorial offering of frankincense versus blessing an idol. This scale would place pigs' blood between the death of a dog (a despised animal in its own right; e.g., 1 Sam 17:43; 24:14; 2 Sam 3:8; 16:9; 1 Kgs 16:4; Prov 26:11; Matt 7:6; Luke 16:21) and blessing an idol. According to Isaiah 66:17, eating pigs' flesh and mice was apparently part of a pagan ritual in "the gardens" of Jerusalem. Finally, the reference to pigs' flesh in Isa 65:4 and its surrounding context may help illuminate the perceived ethical problem with Jesus' sending the demons from the demoniac (Legion) into the "large herd of pigs" (Matt 8:30–32; Mark 5:11–13, 16; Luke 8:32–33). In connection with this,

---

1. In the Levant, swine domestication began as early as 8000 BC. See D. W. Gade, "Hogs (Pigs)," in *The Cambridge World History of Food*, ed. K.F. Kiple and K.C. Ornelas, vol. 1 (Cambridge: Cambridge University Press, 2000), 537.

2. Besides the famous "omnivory" of pigs, which makes feeding them inexpensive, they also reproduce at a startlingly rapid rate. With regards to this Gade writes, "from a contemporary utilitarian perspective, the pig is one of the glories of animal domestication. It is prolific. After a gestation period of only 4 months, a sow gives birth to an average of 10 piglets, though litter size may, on occasion, be as large as 30. Growth is rapid. In a 6-month period, piglets of 1.2 kilograms can potentially increase in weight by 5,000 percent" (Gade, "Hogs [Pigs]," 537).

3. Gade, "Hogs (Pigs)," 536–37.

4. While dietary restrictions against pork consumption certainly would have played a role in ancient Israel's negative feelings towards pigs, this passage is primarily comparing a pig's ugliness to a beautiful woman by simply substituting the pig for the woman wearing a nose ring.

some commentators have suggested that Jesus appears to have acted unjustly,[5] because in causing the demons to enter into the pigs he would have played a role in the drowning of the pigs and the loss of property to the owner of the pigs. We will return to this issue in our discussion of these passages below.

JEWISH PERSPECTIVES ON PIGS AND PORK CONSUMPTION FROM THE SECOND TEMPLE PERIOD AND THE MISHNAH

The most famous and significant references to pigs in the Second Temple period relate to the Hasmoneans and the abominable practices of the Seleucid king Antiochus IV Epiphanes (175-164 BC). As part of a litany of charges against Antiochus, the writer of 1 Macc states that Antiochus "set up altars, sacred groves, shrines of idols, and sacrificed swine flesh and unclean beasts" (1 Macc 1:47; compare *War* 1.34; 12). With regards to this practice, Josephus states that Antiochus "sprinkled the temple with the broth of their (sacrificed swine) flesh, in order to violate the laws of the Jews" (*Ant.* 13.243), as well as actually sacrificing pigs on the altar of the temple (*Ant.* 12.253). In 2 Maccabees (which often expands on the events presented in 1 Maccabees), Antiochus is charged with torturing and executing Eleazar the scribe (2 Macc 6:18-31) and "seven brothers and their mother" (2 Macc 7:1-42; compare 4 Macc 5:1-13) for their refusal to consume pork.

Besides these references to the consumption of pork in the context of the

Maccabean Revolt, Jewish abstinence from pork is also mentioned in several philosophical treatments by Josephus (*Ag. Ap.* 2.137) and Philo of Alexandria (e.g., *Animals* 1.144-145; *Special Laws* 1 1.148; *Special Laws* 4 1.101).[6] These passages present an allegorical attempt to provide the rationale for pork abstinence that is rooted in the pig's delight "in wallowing in the mire." Philo understood there to be an ontological value in the Mosaic dietary system that stood in contrast to other systems, which could be quantified in comparing the character of a person to the type of animal that they consumed. With regards to this, Philo wrote the following: "for which reason the lawgiver very admirably compares those of the sophists who live in this manner to the race of swine, who live a life in no respect pure or brilliant, but confused and disorderly, and who are devoted to the basest habits" (*Animals* 1.144-145). These texts, along with the Seleucid attacks against the Jewish elite in 1-2 Maccabees and Josephus, provide the contemporary background of the Gospel references to pork consumption and pig husbandry.

The Mishnah, which was codified over a century after the life of Jesus, includes several references to pigs and pork abstinence in Jewish life. In m. Bava Qamma 6:7, it is stated that "none may rear swine anywhere." Interestingly, this passage is connected with a law concerning the keeping of dogs that reads, "a man may not rear a dog unless it is kept bound by a chain." Swine are "reckoned a kind of cattle" in the broader category

---

5. Including the philosopher Voltaire; see e.g., H. Clarke, *The Gospel of Matthew and Its Readers: A Historical Introduction to the First Gospel* (Bloomington, IN: Indiana University Press, 2003).

6. In this passage, Philo states that part of the rationale for abstaining from shellfish and pork is their "good taste," which would cause Israel to become "slavish of all outward senses."

of "wild animals" (also including dogs) by R. Meir (m. Kil'ayim 8:6). Vows connected with "swine's flesh" were considered to be non-binding oaths, along with a long list of other vows (m. Nedarim 2:1). Pig's skin was considered to be unclean even after tanning and processing (m. Hullin 9:2). The pig's mouth and tail were used as a comparison for blemishes on clean animals unfit for sacrifice (m. Bekhorot 6.8–9). In Jewish Alexandria, sows' wombs were removed in order to limit the swine population (m. Bekhorot 4:4). This final reference highlights attempts to completely remove pigs from all aspects of Jewish life, but also demonstrates Jewish familiarity with pig husbandry.

ZOOARCHAEOLOGICAL EVIDENCE RELATING TO PORK CONSUMPTION AND PIG HUSBANDRY IN ANCIENT ISRAEL

Animal bone remains from excavated archaeological contexts (zooarchaeology) are another important avenue for understanding Jewish perspectives on pork consumption during the biblical era. In broad terms, it seems clear that Israelite/Judahite aversion to pork consumption was practiced throughout the First Temple period/Iron Age, as pig bones are typically absent at many excavated Iron Age sites in Israel and Judah.[7] On the other hand, it seems that this aversion actually pre-dated Israel, as pig bones make up a very small part of the entire faunal assemblage in many excavated Late Bronze Age (1550–1200/1150 BC) Canaanite sites. This is particularly true for several large sites on the coastal plain (e.g., Ekron, Gath, Ashkelon) that were inhabited by Canaanite populations in the Late Bronze Age but were then settled by Philistines during the twelfth century BC.[8] With regards to this archaeological evidence, it has been suggested that the Israelite taboo against pig bones (as noted in the hill country of Ephraim, Manasseh, and Judah) can be understood as an ethnic boundary that separated them from their Philistine neighbors.[9] A recent multi-disciplinary study has shown that the modern wild pigs (i.e., hogs or wild boars) in Israel possess the same DNA sequence as

---

7. See e.g., Brian Hesse, "Animal Use at Tel Miqne-Ekron in the Bronze Age and Iron Age," *BASOR* 264 (1986): 17–27, doi:10.2307/1357016; idem, "Can Pig Remains Be Used for Ethnic Diagnosis in the Ancient Near East?," in *The Archaeology of Israel: Constructing the Past, Interpreting the Present*, ed. Neil Asher Silberman and David Small (Sheffield: Sheffield Academic Press, 1997), 238–70; Brian Hesse and Paula Wapnish, "Iron I: A Problem of Identity," *Near Eastern Archaeology* 62.2 (June 1, 1999): 61; Lidar Sapir-Hen et al., "Pig Husbandry in Iron Age Israel and Judah: New Insights Regarding the Origin of the Taboo," *Zeitschrift Des Deutschen Palästina-Vereins* 129.1 (2013): 1–20; Meirav Meiri et al., "Ancient DNA and Population Turnover in Southern Levantine Pigs-Signature of the Sea Peoples Migration?," *Scientific Reports* 3 (4 November 2013), doi:10.1038/srep03035; J. S. E. Lev-Tov, "Pigs, Philistines, and the Ancient Animal Economy of Ekron from the Late Bronze Age to the Iron Age II" (Ph.D dissertation, University of Tennessee, Knoxville, 2000); Avraham Faust and Justin Lev-Tov, "The Constitution of Philistine Identity: Ethnic Dynamics in Twelfth to Tenth Century Philistia," *Oxford Journal of Archaeology* 30.1 (2011): 13–31, doi:10.1111/j.1468-0092.2010.00357.x.

8. Lev-Tov, "Pigs, Philistines, and the Ancient Animal Economy," 196.

9. Israel Finkelstein, "Pots and People Revisited: Ethnic Boundaries in the Iron Age I," in *The Archaeology of Israel: Constructing the Past, Interpreting the Present*, eds. Neil Asher Silberman and David Small (Sheffield: Sheffield Academic Press, 1997), 216–37.

Dogs and Boar Statue, 1st Century AD

European wild boars and domestic pigs that seem to have been introduced to the region in the Iron Age by Sea Peoples (including the Philistines) who migrated to the Southern Levant during the twelfth century BC.[10] Conversely, DNA from pig bones from Late Bronze Age contexts shows clear similarities with other Near Eastern wild boars, which seems to indicate that new pig populations were introduced into the southern Levant during the early part of the Iron Age (c. 1175–1000 BC) when both the Philistines (and perhaps other Sea Peoples) and the Israelites were settling the Southern Levant.[11] On the other hand, and although pork consumption remained very low in Judah throughout the Iron Age, it seems to have diminished in Philistia during the latter part of the Iron II (c. 800–586 BC) while actually increasing in kingdom of Israel[12] sites in the north and Shephelah (e.g., Gezer, Tel Hamid).[13] This evidence demonstrates that cultural boundaries can be fluid and change over time; however, it is interesting that both the textual and archaeological evidence for the lack of pork consumption in Judah remains constant throughout the First Temple period. With regards to later periods, there are not many faunal assemblages that have been published from sites in first century Judea or Galilee (or the preceding Persian and Hellenistic periods), but the available evidence points to an almost total absence of pig bones in these

---

10. Meiri et al., "Ancient DNA and Population Turnover."

11. Meiri et al., "Ancient DNA and Population Turnover."

12. This could be related to Neo-Assyrian activity in Israel during the eighth century BC, as pork was a main component of the Assyrian diet.

13. Sapir-Hen et al., "Pig Husbandry in Iron Age Israel and Judah," 9–13.

regions,[14] which stands in sharp contrast to the widespread consumption of pork in the surrounding Roman world, as seen in literary, iconographic,[15] and archaeological contexts.

EXCURSUS: PIG HUSBANDRY IN MODERN ISRAEL

Since 1962, the Israeli Knesset has outlawed the raising of pigs in the State of Israel ("The Pig-Raising Prohibition Law"). Before this law passed, Segev states that "pork accounted for around 17 percent of the amount of meat from four-legged animals in the country."[16] The ban was supported by the "National Religious Party" and similar religious groups, but was opposed by many in the Israeli government, including then-Prime Minister David Ben-Gurion. Over time, pigs were euthanized by several different mean,s including burning (after being shot), drowning at sea(!), and

transferring to scientific institutions for testing.[17] The ban was opposed by both Druze and Christian communities (particularly at the Convent of Saint Vincent de Paul in Ein Karem), and the latter was defended by the Vatican who protested the ban through diplomatic channels.[18] Eventually, much of Israel's pig population was brought to two regions: the northern Negev (at Kibbutz Lahav for scientific testing) and the northern Galilee (I'blin and Meilia for Christian communities).[19] Ever year, over 200,000 pigs are slaughtered in these locations.[20] Besides these scientific/Christian pig-farming zones, Kibbutz Mizra in the Jezreel Valley specialized in pig farming (until 2010) and supplied many different pork products to the Israeli-Russian supermarket Tiv-Ta'am (who bought Kibbutz Mizra's pig-raising farm), which caters to Israel's large Russian and pork-consuming Russian population.[21]

---

14. See e.g., J. L. Reed, *Archaeology and the Galilean Jesus: A Re-Examination of the Evidence* (London: Bloomsbury T&T Clark, 2002), 117–19; B. W. Root, *First Century Galilee: A Fresh Examination of the Sources* (Tübingen: Mohr Siebeck, 2014), 101; R. Deines, "Religious Practices and Religious Movements in Galilee: 100 BCE– 200 CE," in *Life, Culture, and Society*, ed. D.A. Fiensy and J.R. Strange, vol. 1 of *Galilee in the Late Second Temple and Mishnaic Periods* (Minneapolis: Fortress, 2014), 53; E. M. Meyers, C. L. Meyers, and B. D. Gordon, "Sepphoris - Residential Area of the Western Summit," in *The Archaeological Record from Cities, Towns, and Villages*, ed. D.A. Fiensy and J.R. Strange, vol. 2 of *Galilee in the Late Second Temple and Mishnaic Periods* (Minneapolis: Fortress, 2015), 49.

15. See e.g., the stamped impressions on bricks of the tenth Roman Legion, which typically included the inscription "LEG X FR" and the relief of a pig.

16. Giora Goodman, "Pig Farming in Israel and Its Opponents, 1948–1962" (Heb.), *Cathedra: For the History of Eretz Israel and Its Yishuv*, 134 (2009): 65–90, http://www.jstor.org/stable/23408356; Tom Segev, "The Makings of History Pork and the People," *Haaretz*, January 27, 2012. http://www.haaretz.com/israel-news/the-makings-of-history-pork-and-the-people-1.409478.

17. Segev, "The Makings of History Pork and the People."

18. Segev, "The Makings of History Pork and the People."

19. D. Ben-Dov et al., "Guidelines for Pig Welfare in Israel," *Israel Journal of Veterinary Medicine* 69 (2014): 4.

20. Ben-Dov et al., "Guidelines for Pig Welfare in Israel," 4–5.

21. See discussion in Daphne Barak-Erez, *Outlawed Pigs: Law, Religion, and Culture in Israel* (Madison, WI: The University of Wisconsin Press, 2007), 102.

A PROVERB AND A PARABLE ABOUT FEEDING PIGS (MATT 7:6; LUKE 15:15)

In Matthew's version of the Sermon on the Mount (Matt 5–7), Jesus gave the following proverb: "Do not give dogs what is holy, and do not throw your pearls before pigs, lest they trample them underfoot and turn to attack you" (Matt 7:6 ESV). This proverb, which has clear similarities with synonymous parallelism in biblical Hebrew poetry (compare Prov 11:22), should probably be read chiastically with the pigs' reaction being related to the trampling of the pearls and the dogs' reaction being associated with their attacking those who foolishly gave them "what is holy."[22] As Carson points out, Jesus used the natural actions of unclean pigs and dogs in a metaphorical sense to temper the statement to "love your enemies" (Matt 5:43–47) by showing the foolishness of "proclaiming the gospel of the kingdom (i.e., "what is holy") to those designated as dogs and pigs."[23] In this regard, the parallel "pearls" should probably be understood as being trampled by the pigs, because they were not the food that the pigs had expected or wanted. Therefore, it seems that Jesus was deftly illustrating the foolishness of presenting the gospel to those who were unable to hear it (compare a similar line of thought, albeit with a different animal metaphor, in Matt 10:16). While wild dogs would have been a common aspect of life in ancient Jewish societies, it is unclear how much knowledge or interaction Jesus' audience would have had with domesticated pigs (see above). Nevertheless, Jesus' usage of pigs in this proverb (to a presumably majority Jewish audience) implies that domesticated pigs were widespread among the Gentile regions of the Decapolis and the nearby southern regions of Syria.

Jewish familiarity with pig husbandry can also be observed in the parable of the prodigal son (Luke 15:11–32). In the parable, the younger son demanded his inheritance from his father and after receiving his share traveled to a "far country" where he "squandered his property in reckless living" (Luke 15:13). After losing his inheritance, famine struck the land and the son was forced to hire "himself out to one of the citizens of that country who sent him into his fields to feed pigs" (Luke 15:15). The usage of pigs in the story indicates that the Jewish son had been living like a Gentile in Gentile territory (i.e., eating non-kosher food). Moreover, the son was so famished and destitute that he longed "to be fed with the pods (keration, χεράτιον) that the pigs ate, and no one gave him anything" (Luke 15:16 ESV). These "pods" are typically identified with the pods of the carob tree (Ceratonia siliqua), which are high in fat and grow throughout the southern Levant, the Mediterranean, and southern Europe.[24] One of the few drawbacks of raising pigs is their inability to digest fibrous plant material, which means that they cannot

---

22. It is unclear if Jesus or his audience would have understood pigs to be metaphorically related to the lifestyle of non-Jews in the same allegorical sense as Philo (see above). See discussion in R. T. France, *The Gospel of Matthew* (Grand Rapids: Eerdmans, 2007), 277–78.

23. D. A. Carson, "Matthew," in *The Expositor's Bible Commentary*, ed. Frank E. Gaebelein, vol. 8 (Grand Rapids: Zondervan, 1984), 185.

24. See e.g., L.J. Musselman, *A Dictionary of Bible Plants* (Cambridge: Cambridge University Press, 2011), 33–36.

survive only on pasturage (i.e., grass, hay, etc.) like sheep/goats and cattle can.[25] On account of this, the carob pod would have served as a good, cheap source of food for raising pigs for slaughter. Therefore, their occurrence in the parable is particularly fitting in demonstrating how far the wayward, previously wealthy, young Jewish man had fallen. At the beginning of the story, the young man had presumably eaten kosher food in abundance from his father's table.

Carob Pods

In the turning point of the parable, the famine was so severe (Luke 15:14) that he actually thought of eating the wild growing carob pods that were meant for the un-kosher swine herd for whom he had been caring (Luke 15:16). From this low point, the young man remembered his father's sufficient provision (bread) for his servants and decided to return and request to be a servant (Luke 15:17-19). The younger son returned to his father, who welcomed his second son by dressing him in expensive attire and killing a kosher and expensive "fat-

tened calf" in celebration of the return of his son (Luke 15:22-24). The food imagery (and its hierarchy in different social settings) continues into the conclusion of the parable with the older son's complaint to his father that despite his obedience he had never been given "a young goat, that I might celebrate with my friends" (Luke 15:25-32).

Without going into the theological or moral interpretations of the parable, it is clear that the pigs' food (pods), which would have only been known in a society that was aware of pig husbandry, was the lowest possible form of food, particularly when it is compared with a "young goat" or a "fattened calf." It is interesting that the parable does not make reference to the young man consuming pork, as this framing would seem to present a nice symmetry with the meat of the fattened calf and young goat that are referenced in the conclusion of the parable. However, this is probably because the consumption of pigs' food would be considered just as unclean as consuming pork itself, and the young man would have been too destitute to afford to buy a pig. In this sense, eating food designated for pigs may be understood as being even worse than eating pork.

CASTING DEMONS INTO PIGS (MATT 8:28-34; MARK 5:1-20; LUKE 8:26-39)

Jesus healing Legion and his companion by casting out demons from them into two thousand pigs "in the country of the Gerasenes/Gadarenes"[26] is the most significant Gospel reference to pigs and pig husbandry. It is another piece of textual

---

25. Gade, "Hogs (Pigs)," 537.

26. For a discussion of this textual critical and historical geographical problem see Todd Bolen, "Where Did the Possessed-Pigs Drown?," on pg. 196.

evidence that points to pig-herding/pork consumption as a clear ethnic boundary marker in the Early Roman period between Jews and Gentiles. Moreover, it also demonstrates that pig-herding was both common in the Roman Decapolis, a region quite close to Jewish populations, and consisted of roaming herds in very large numbers (see Mark 5:13). This event is recorded in each of the Synoptic Gospels with varying degrees of detail (Matt 8:28–34; Mark 5:1–20; Luke 8:26–39). Before examining the specific references related to the pigs, it is worth noting that each version of the account is preceded by Jesus calming the storm (Matt 8:23–27; Mark 4:35–41; Luke 8:22–25)—an event that has strong intertextual allusions to the calming of the sea in the story of Jonah.[27] In fact, this clear intertextual parallel may help explain one of the reasons for the casting of the demons into the pigs. While this is not the place to develop in detail the connection between Jonah and the Gospels' "calming of the seas," the list below illustrates the close parallels between the texts of Jonah 1 and the synoptic accounts.

INTERTEXTUAL PARALLELS AND CONTRASTS BETWEEN THE CALMING OF THE SEA(S) WITH JONAH AND JESUS

Incident	Jonah Reference	Gospel References
Board a ship	Jonah 1:3	Matt 8:23; Mark 4:36; Luke 8:22
Sail away from/to ministry	Jonah 1:2–3	Matt 8:28; Mark 5:1; Luke 8:22
Storm arises on the sea	Jonah 1:4	Matt 8:24; Mark 4:35; Luke 8:23
Fear grips sailors/disciples	Jonah 1:5	Matt 8:25, Mark 4:37–38; Luke 8:23
Jonah/Jesus are asleep	Jonah 1:5	Matt 8:24; Mark 4:38; Luke 8:23–24
Sailors/disciples request one who sleeps to save them	Jonah 1:6	Matt 8:25, Mark 4:38; Luke 8:24
Sea is calmed through different means	Jonah 1:16	Matt 8:26; cited from Mark 1:38; Luke 8:24
Sailors/disciples recognize the power of God/Jesus	Jonah 1:16, cf. 1:9	Matt 8:27, cited from Mark 4:41; Luke 8:25
Three days and three nights	Jonah 1:17	Matt 12:39–41; 16:4; Luke 11:29–32

---

27. Following the casting of the demons into pigs Mark and Luke record that Jesus "crossed again in the boat to the other side" where he healed Jairus' daughter and the woman with the discharge of blood (Mark 5:21–43; Luke 8:40–56; compare Matt 9:18–26).

With these listed parallels in mind, it is my opinion that the subsequent Synoptic Gospel narratives continue the parallels and contrasts between Jesus and Jonah by comparing their respective prophetic ministries to great Gentile cities (Nineveh/country of the Gerasenes/Gadarenes). In this vein and by using clear contrasting parallels between the attitudes of the prophets towards specific individuals (the Neo-Assyrian king versus Legion) and their respective cities, the Gospel writers demonstrate that Jesus was a far greater prophet than Jonah, and his contemporary "Decapolis" (see Mark 5:20) was a more wicked and unrepentant entity than Nineveh (see Matt 12:41; Luke 11:32). On the other hand, the obvious difference between the two narratives is the status and position of Jesus compared to Jonah after the calming of the seas. Jesus actually calmed the sea by his own authority and remained on the boat, whereas in the Jonah account, Yahweh calmed the sea after he was appeased because of Jonah's disobedience, after which Jonah was swallowed by a great fish (see above for references). However, the parallels resume as both Jonah and Jesus were brought to the shores of their respective Gentile cities (Jonah 3:1; Matt 8:28; Mark 5:1-2; Luke 8:26-27), but, once again, the link between the two narratives is interrupted with the introduction of the demon-possessed man who approached Jesus.

In Jonah 3, Jonah continued to Nineveh after being "vomited on dry land" and preached repentance to the city and its king—who repented. Conversely, Jesus encountered a demon-possessed man (and his companion, according to Matt 8:28), who had several distinct characteristics that have clear intertextual parallels in Isaiah 65:1-7. In my opinion, these intertextual parallels, together with the continuation of the Synoptics' Jonah story reversals is the primary basis for Jesus' rationale in casting the demons into the pigs. In connection with this line of thought, there are five clear parallels between Isaiah 65:1-7 and the story of the demon-possessed man/the casting of the demons into pigs. These include the following: (1) the Gentile audience (Isa 65:1; compare to Mark 5:1[28]), (2) the location and setting in the mountains and among the tombs at night (Isa 65:4, 7; compare to Mark 5:3-5), (3) the sin of the pagan sacrifice and consumption of pork (Isa 65:3, 5; compare to Mark 5:11-12), (4) the judgment of the wicked people/demons who had taken part in this activity (Isa 65:6-7; compare to Mark 5:12-13), (5) the salvation of Gentile(s) who had previously been oppressed by their pagan worship (Isa 65:1; compare to Mark 5:7, 15, 20).

These parallels serve both to demonstrate the prophetic significance of Jesus and the disciples' future ministry to Gentiles that had been predicted in Isa 65:1 and partially fulfilled in Mark 5:20 as well as to show Jesus' authority over demonic forces as he triumphed over them by casting them into the "sea" using their own medium (i.e., pigs). In other words, and with regards to the Isaiah parallels, pig sacrifice was a pagan rite that was undertaken in secret, at night, on sacrificial bricks, and presumably directed at demons. In the Roman world, pigs were widely used as sacrifices to dei-

---

28. Mark's account is the longest and most detailed of the three synoptic accounts.

ties and were often considered to be holy animals.[29]

However, in the context of Isaiah 65:1–7, pig sacrifice and subsequent pork consumption may be related to the ritual associated with the protection from Lamashtu, the Mesopotamian female demon who killed unborn human and animal children.[30] If so, Jesus' casting of the demons into the pigs and, subsequently, into the sea (which he had just calmed) may be understood as an expression of his authority not only over the specific demons who had inhabited the demon-possessed men but also of his cosmic power and authority over every demon behind pagan gods and goddesses. Moreover, by casting the demons into the sea via the animal vehicle of the pigs, Jesus continued the cosmological imagery from the preceding calming of the sea and the allusions to Jonah 1–2 by demonstrating his power over demons, unclean animals, and chaos itself (i.e., the sea). Whereas Jonah was saved by being cast into the sea/chaos and swallowed by a large fish at the behest of Yahweh, Jesus allowed the demons to avoid the apocalyptic abyss (cf. Luke 8:31; 2 Pet 2:4; Rev 20:3) by casting the demons into the sea using a large herd of pigs. The drowning of the pigs, as financially difficult as it must have been for their Gentile owners (see above), concludes the Jonah contrast by reversing Jonah's salvation from the sea by means of

a large fish to the demons' defeat into the sea by means of a large herd of pigs. After witnessing this event, the pigs' herdsman spread the news to the surrounding cities, who upon observing the results of Jesus' prophetic power promptly begged[31] that he withdraw from their territory (Mark 5:17). Finally, Jesus completes the reversal of the story of Jonah by acting in the role of Yahweh and sending the formerly demon-possessed man to proclaim God's mercy to the Decapolis (Mark 5:19–20); he is obedient (unlike Jonah) to Jesus' command despite the fact that he wants to stay with his healer and Lord.

In summary, we can describe the parallels and contrasts between Jonah and Jesus as follows: Jonah disobeyed Yahweh and fled by sea to Tarshish because of his hatred for Gentile Assyrians and his knowledge that Yahweh would be merciful to them. However, Jonah was supernaturally brought to Nineveh by means of a calmed sea and a great fish, which carried him through the sea/abyss (Jonah 2). Nineveh then repented and was mercifully saved from destruction (Jonah 3) while Jonah harbored hatred for them outside of the city (Jonah 4). In paralleled contrast, Jesus came to preach repentance to the country of the Gerasenes/Gadarenes, because of his love for the Gentile Decapolis, and supernaturally brought himself to the "other side" by means of his power and authority over

---

29. F. J. Simoons, *Eat Not This Flesh: Food Avoidances from Prehistory to the Present* (Madison, WI: The University of Wisconsin Press, 1994), 28.

30. Simoons, *Eat Not This Flesh*, 26; David R. West, *Some Cults of Greek Goddesses and Female Demons of Oriental Origin* (Kevelaer: Butzon & Bercker, 1995), 253; Roland De Vaux, *The Bible and the Ancient Near East*, trans. Damian McHugh (New York: Doubleday, 1971), 255–57; David Bryan, *Cosmos, Chaos and the Kosher Mentality* (London: Bloomsbury, 2015), 145–47. It is worth noting that Lamashtu rites continued into and beyond the Roman period even within Jewish ritual practice.

31. The demons (Mark 5:12), the people from the city (Mark 5:17), and the man formerly possessed by demons (Mark 1:18), each "begged" Jesus.

the sea in the role of Yahweh the Creator of heaven and earth (cf. Jonah 1:9; Mark 4:41). In a role reversal in which Jesus further eclipses Jonah the prophet and remains in the role of Creator, Jesus reversed the story of Jonah by healing the demon-possessed man, sending the demons into the sea/abyss by means of unclean pigs (compared to Jonah's salvation inside the large fish), and mercifully commanding the restored man to be a Jonah-like prophet to the Decapolis (Mark 5:20), despite the fact that they had already rejected him (Mark 5:17).

CONCLUSION

In this essay, we have examined the Old Testament prohibitions and attitudes against pork consumption, later Jewish perspectives on pigs, zooarchaeological evidence related to pork consumption in ancient Israel, and three specific Gospel contexts that make reference to pigs and/or pork consumption. The combined evidence clearly demonstrates that pork consumption and the presence of pig-herds in Gentile settings were clear ethnic boundary markers between Jews and Gentiles throughout the Early Roman period. Finally, it has been argued that the "casting of demons into pigs" episode in the Synoptic Gospels demonstrates this cultural background, but also has deep intertextual connections to the story of Jonah and Isaiah 65:1–7.

BIBLIOGRAPHY

Barak-Erez, Daphne. *Outlawed Pigs: Law, Religion, and Culture in Israel.* Madison, WI: The University of Wisconsin Press, 2007.

Ben-Dov, D., Y. Hadani, A. Ben-Simchon, L. Alborali, and P. S. Pozzi. "Guidelines for Pig Welfare in Israel." *Israel Journal of Veterinary Medicine* 69.1 (2014): 4–15.

Bryan, David. *Cosmos, Chaos and the Kosher Mentality.* London: Bloomsbury Publishing, 2015.

Carson, D. A. "Matthew." Pages 1–599 in vol. 8 of *Expositor's Bible Commentary.* Edited by Frank E. Gæbelein. Grand Rapids: Zondervan, 1984.

Clarke, H. *The Gospel of Matthew and Its Readers: A Historical Introduction to the First Gospel.* Bloomington, IN: Indiana University Press, 2003.

Deines, R. "Religious Practices and Religious Movements in Galilee: 100 BCE–200 CE." Pages 78–111 in *Life, Culture, and Society.* Edited by David A. Fiensy and James Riley Strange. Vol. 1 of *Galilee in the Late Second Temple and Mishnaic Periods:.* Minneapolis: Fortress, 2014.

De Vaux, Roland. *The Bible and the Ancient Near East.* Translated by Damian McHugh. New York: Doubleday, 1971.

Faust, Avraham, and Justin Lev-Tov. "The Constitution of Philistine Identity: Ethnic Dynamics in Twelfth to Tenth Century Philistia." *Oxford Journal of Archaeology* 30.1 (2011): 13–31. doi:10.1111/j.1468-0092.2010.00357.x.

Finkelstein, Israel. "Pots and People Revisited: Ethnic Boundaries in the Iron Age I." Pages 216–37 in *The Archaeology of Israel: Constructing the Past, Interpreting the Present.* Edited by Neil Asher Silberman and David Small. Sheffield: Sheffield Academic Press, 1997.

France, R. T. *The Gospel of Matthew.* Grand Rapids: Eerdmans, 2007.

Gade, D. W. "Hogs (Pigs)." Pages 536–41 in vol. 1 of *The Cambridge World*

History of Food. Edited by K. F. Kiple and K.C. Ornelas. Cambridge: Cambridge University Press, 2000.

Goodman, Giora. "Pig Farming in Israel and Its Opponents, 1948–1962." [Heb.] *Cathedra: For the History of Eretz Israel and Its Yishuv* 134 (2009): 65–90. http://www.jstor.org/stable/23408356.

Hesse, Brian. "Can Pig Remains Be Used for Ethnic Diagnosis in the Ancient Near East?" Pages 238–70 in *The Archaeology of Israel: Constructing the Past, Interpreting the Present*. Edited by Neil Asher Silberman and David Small. Sheffield: Sheffield Academic Press, 1997.

———. "Animal Use at Tel Miqne-Ekron in the Bronze Age and Iron Age." *BASOR* 264 (1986): 17–27. doi:10.2307/1357016.

Hesse, Brian, and Paula Wapnish. "Iron I: A Problem of Identity." *Near Eastern Archaeology* 62.2 (June 1999): 61. http://www.jstor.org/stable/3210702.

Lev-Tov, J. S. E. "Pigs, Philistines, and the Ancient Animal Economy of Ekron from the Late Bronze Age to the Iron Age II." PhD dissertation, University of Tennessee, Knoxville, 2000.

Meiri, Meirav, Dorothée Huchon, Guy Bar-Oz, Elisabetta Boaretto, Liora Kolska Horwitz, Aren M. Maeir, Lidar Sapir-Hen, Greger Larson, Steve Weiner, and Israel Finkelstein. "Ancient DNA and Population Turnover in Southern Levantine Pigs—Signature of the Sea Peoples Migration?" *Scientific Reports* 3 (4 November 2013). doi:10.1038/srep03035.

Meyers, E. M., C. L. Meyers, and B. D. Gordon. "Sepphoris - Residential Area of the Western Summit." Pages 39–52 in *The Archaeological Record from Cities, Towns, and Villages*. Edited by David A. Fiensy and James Riley Strange. Vol. 2 of *Galilee in the Late Second Temple and Mishnaic Periods*. Minneapolis: Fortress, 2015.

Musselman, L. J. *A Dictionary of Bible Plants*. Cambridge: Cambridge University Press, 2011.

Reed, J. L. *Archaeology and the Galilean Jesus: A Re-Examination of the Evidence*. London: Bloomsbury T&T Clark, 2002.

Root, B. W. *First Century Galilee: A Fresh Examination of the Sources*. Tübingen: Mohr Siebeck, 2014.

Sapir-Hen, Lidar, Guy Bar-Oz, Yuval Gadot, and Israel Finkelstein. "Pig Husbandry in Iron Age Israel and Judah: New Insights Regarding the Origin of the Taboo." *Zeitschrift Des Deutschen Palästina-Vereins* 129.1 (2013): 1–20.

Segev, Tom. "The Makings of History Pork and the People." *Haaretz*. January 27, 2012. http://www.haaretz.com/israel-news/the-makings-of-history-pork-and-the-people-1.409478.

Simoons, F. J. *Eat Not This Flesh: Food Avoidances from Prehistory to the Present*. Madison, WI: The University of Wisconsin Press, 1994.

West, David R. *Some Cults of Greek Goddesses and Female Demons of Oriental Origin*. Kevelaer: Butzon & Bercker, 1995.

CHAPTER 21

WHERE DID THE POSSESSED-PIGS DROWN?
CHALLENGING TRADITION AND RESPECTING TEXTUAL EVIDENCE

Matt 8:28-34; Mark 5:1-20; Luke 8:26-39

Todd Bolen

KEY POINTS

- Each of the Synoptic Gospels records the healing of the demoniac and subsequent "swine dive," but three different places names are given for the location of the event among the ancient manuscripts: Gadara, Gerasa, and Gergesa.

- Tradition favors Gergesa, but a critical evaluation of both Origen's influence and the excavations at Kursi prove Gergesa to be a dubious candidate.

- The geography and archaeology of the regions of Gadara and Gerasa not only permit but favor the early manuscripts' identification of the miracle at those locations.

One of the most interesting geographical difficulties in the Gospels is the location of the "swine dive" or "pig plunge" into the Sea of Galilee. As Jesus was about to set a man free of demon possession, the evil spirits requested to enter into a herd of swine feeding on the nearby hillside. When the request was granted, the demons caused the herd to run down the slope and to be drowned in the waters below. The miracle is recorded in each of the Synoptic Gospels (Matt 8:28-34; Mark 5:1-20; Luke 8:26-39), but three different place names are attested in ancient manuscripts for the location of the event. Textual scholars are in general agreement on the best readings of each Gospel, but many biblical geographers today reject those place names in favor of a third site on the grounds of topography. This approach is similar to that of the church father Origen, who reasoned that the places as written in the texts must be incorrect and proposed an alternative.[1] However, further analysis demonstrates that the readings of the earliest manuscripts are indeed accurate and that attempts to locate the miracle at a third site are ultimately unsuccessful.

TEXTUAL EVIDENCE

This issue is particularly difficult because it is recorded in three Gospels, and three variant readings exist in each Gospel. Many combinations of readings exist, including the possibilities that (1) each Gospel wrote a different place name, (2) that two agreed against one, or (3) that all three were originally the same. According to the Editorial Committee of the United Bible Societies, the best reading in Matthew is "Gadarenes" (*Gadarēnōn*, Γαδαρηνῶν), on the basis of "superior external attestation ... and the probability that "Gergesenes" (Γεργεσηνῶν) is a correction, perhaps proposed originally by Origen."[2] The reading of "Gerasenes" was judged to be very unlikely because it is "supported only by versional evidence."[3] On the other hand, in Mark and Luke, "Gerasenes" (*Gerasēnōn*, Γερασηνῶν) has strong attestation among "early representatives of both the Alexandrian and

Western types of text" and is accepted as the best reading by the Committee.[4]

Most scholars who prefer the reading of "Gergesenes" do not dispute the manuscript evidence or the decision of the Committee. They generally acknowledge the "strong textual witnesses for either Gadara or Gerasa"[5] but suggest that either (1) the Gospel writers were ignorant of the places and made "an obvious geographical mistake,"[6] (2) the earliest scribes tried to correct errant manuscripts,[7] or (3) the presence of the variants makes any attempt at reconstruction of the original impossible.[8] Another approach is to recognize that the best readings include two different place names among the three Gospels, and to conclude that the lack of unanimity undermines the earliest manuscript evidence. Many simply dismiss the best readings because they believe they are obviously incorrect.

OBJECTIONS TO GADARA AND GERASA

The approach of modern scholars in rejecting the manuscript readings is remarkably similar to the approach of Origen. The church father read the same two place names that the Committee

1. E.g., Origen's dismissal of "Bethany" in favor of "Bethabara" (*Commentary on John*, 6.24).

2. Bruce M. Metzger, *A Textual Commentary on the Greek New Testament*, 2nd ed. (Stuttgart: Deutsche Biblegesellschaft, 1994), 19.

3. Metzger, *A Textual Commentary*, 19.

4. Metzger, *A Textual Commentary*, 18, 72, 121.

5. R. Steven Notley, *In the Master's Steps: The Gospels in the Land* (Jerusalem: Carta Jerusalem, 2014), 46.

6. Gerd Theissen, *The Gospels in Context: Social and Political History in the Synoptic Tradition* (Minneapolis: Fortress, 1991), 109; compare Lucas H. Grollenberg, *Atlas of the Bible*, trans. Joyce M. H. Reid and H. H. Rowley (London: Nelson, 1957), 122.

7. Notley, *In the Master's Steps*, 51.

8. James C. Martin, *Exploring Bible Times: The Gospels in Context* (Amarillo, TX: Bible World Seminars, 2003), 122.

today believes are original, but he rejected them because they were incompatible with his knowledge of the geography. It is important to consider what Origen wrote:

> Thus we see that he who aims at a complete understanding of the Holy Scriptures must not neglect the careful examination of the proper names in it. In the matter of proper names the Greek copies are often incorrect, and in the Gospels one might be misled by their authority. The transaction about the swine, which were driven down a steep place by the demons and drowned in the sea, is said to have taken place in the country of the Gerasenes. Now, Gerasa is a town of Arabia, and has near it neither sea nor lake. And the Evangelists would not have made a statement so obviously and demonstrably false; for they were men who informed themselves carefully of all matters connected with Judaea. But in a few copies we have found, "into the country of the Gadarenes;" and, on this reading, it is to be stated that Gadara is a town of Judaea, in the neighborhood of which are the well-known hot springs, and that there is no lake there with overhanging banks, nor any sea. But Gergesa, from which the name Gergesenes is taken, is an old town in the neighborhood of the lake now called Tiberias, and on the edge of it there is a steep place abutting on the lake, from which it is pointed out that the swine

were cast down by the demons. Now, the meaning of Gergesa is "dwelling of the casters-out," and it contains a prophetic reference to the conduct towards the Savior of the citizens of those places, who "besought Him to depart out of their coasts." The same inaccuracy with regard to proper names is also to be observed in many passages of the law and the prophets, as we have been at pains to learn from the Hebrews, comparing our own copies with theirs which have the confirmation of the versions, never subjected to corruption, of Aquila and Theodotion and Symmachus.[9]

Origen's first observation is that the proper names in the Greek manuscripts cannot be trusted. Second, he recognizes two place names that are known to him in manuscripts, Gerasa and Gadara, and he gives reasons against these sites being correct. Third, he suggests Gergesa as a more suitable alternative. Several points are not clear from Origen's testimony. First, it is not evident if Gergesa was known to Origen from a manuscript or only from local tradition. Second, it is uncertain whether Gergesa was an existing city or if only its ruins existed. Third, it is not clear if Origen had personally visited the sites in question or was relying on the testimony of others. It may be noted that Origen's use of geographical terminology is rather loose, placing Gerasa in Arabia and Gadara in Judea. Most interpreters today cringe when reading Origen's argument for the location based upon Gergesa's etymology,

---

9. Origen, *Commentary on John*, 6.24. Translation from *ANF* vol. 10.

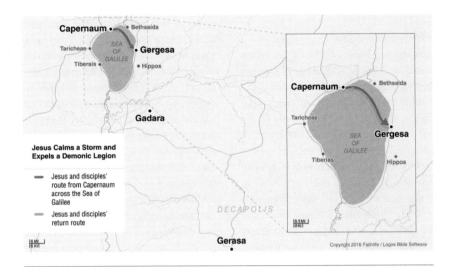

either rejecting its accuracy or denying its relevancy. These issues should give us pause before accepting Origen as a trustworthy authority.

Many scholars, however, agree with Origen on three points: (1) Gerasa and Gadara are mentioned in the earliest manuscripts; (2) neither city is located near the Sea of Galilee; and (3) neither city has a steep cliff running into the lake. Furthermore, they are two distinct sites, and clearly the Synoptics are only recording a single event.

THE CASE FOR GERGESA

Origen's preference for Gergesa was based on its location near the lake, the steep hill nearby, the fact that it was pointed out as the site of the miracle, and the prophetic reference of the name to the event. Scholars today identify Origen's Gergesa with modern Kursi.[10] Some believe that Kursi preserves the name Gergesa,[11] while others suggest it may preserve Gerasa.[12] Archaeological excavations are cited as providing confirmation of the identification, and occasionally a proponent will advocate that tombs were found in the area. The strongest argument in favor of locating the miracle at Kursi is the steep hillside located one mile (1.6 km) south of the site. For many, this single factor outweighs any other consideration.[13]

---

10. Rainer Riesner, however, suggests that Gergesa is the Semitic name for Hippos ("Archeology and Geography," *DJG* 51). This seems to be nothing more than a guess, and he seems to be unaware that the Semitic name for Hippos is Susita.

11. G. E. Wright and F. V. Filson believe that Gergesa is original, but observe that Kursi "is not the exact equivalent of the Greek word 'Gergesa'" (*The Westminster Historical Atlas to the Bible* [Philadelphia: Westminster Press, 1945], 86).

12. James A. Brooks, *Mark* (Nashville, TN: Broadman and Holman, 1991), 89; C. E. B. Cranfield, *The Gospel According to Saint Mark* (Cambridge: Cambridge University Press, 1972), 176.

13. More precisely, Gergesa is usually accepted because it has a slope, and the other two sites are too far from the lake. John McRay sums it up this way: Gergesa is "the only reasonable possibility, if any credence is to be given to the geographical statements of the gospels"

TEXTUAL EVIDENCE AGAINST GERGESA

The single greatest difficulty for proponents of a Gergesa location is the lack of evidence that Gergesa existed in the first century. The site is not mentioned by Josephus, the New Testament (except for later manuscripts at the point in question), or any other ancient source before Origen. Many scholars believe that Origen invented this place name in order to resolve the difficulty.[14] Eusebius and the Palestinian Talmud locate the Girgashites in this area, possibly indicating that Gergesa preserved the name of the Old Testament people group.[15] More likely, the identification was made based on a mistranslation in the Septuagint. Joshua 12:5 locates the Geshurites in this general vicinity, but the Septuagint renders it as "Gergesites." Thus in one tradition the Girgashites were relocated from the land west of the Jordan River (Josh 24:11) to the eastern side of the Sea of Galilee.[16] It is possible that Origen knew of this tradition and used it as the basis for identifying a Gergesa in this area.[17]

A midrash mentions "Gergeshta" east of the Sea of Galilee, which Safrai suggests is a village and thus proves "that a place called Gergesa really existed east of the lake."[18] This midrash is dated to the tenth century, and while it contains earlier material, it is unlikely that this material pre-dates Origen. Nor does the midrash say that Gergeshta is a settlement. It is more likely that, rather than this being the sole reference to a village by this name, it is simply perpetuating the tradition of the Septuagint, followed by Eusebius and the Palestinian Talmud, which mistakenly located the Girgashite people here. Textually, there is no clear evidence that a settlement named Gergesa existed in the time of Christ.[19]

While some assert that Origen invented the name of Gergesa, this case can only be made from circumstantial evidence, as Origen does not state this directly. It is true, however, that the easiest explanation that accounts for all of the readings of the Gospels is that Origen influenced copyists of the manuscripts. On the basis of manuscript

("Gerasenes," *ABD* 2:991). Unfortunately, his rejection of Gadara and Gerasa is based on a significant error: he claims that the latter sites are on the south*western* side of the lake, and this rules them out because "the event could not have taken place *in Galilee*" (John McRay, *Archaeology and the New Testament* [Grand Rapids: Baker, 1991], 167; emphasis mine).

14. Raymond G. Clapp, "A Study of the Place-Names Gergesa and Bethabara," *JBL* 26.1 (1907): 62–66; Grollenberg, *Atlas of the Bible*, 150; I. Howard Marshall, *The Gospel of Luke: A Commentary on the Greek Text* (Grand Rapids: Eerdmans, 1978), 336; J. Carl Laney, *Answers to Tough Questions from Every Book of the Bible* (Grand Rapids: Kregel, 1997), 214.

15. One problem with this view is that Josephus declares that "the name Girgashites had disappeared without leaving traces" (Clapp, "Place-Names," 66).

16. David W. Baker, "Girgashite," *ABD* 2:1028.

17. T. Baarda, "Gadarenes, Gerasenes, Gergesenes and the 'Diatessaron' Traditions," in *Neotestamentica et Semitica: Studies in Honour of Matthew Black*, ed. E. Earle Ellis and Max Wilcox (Edinburgh: T&T Clark, 1969), 186.

18. Ze'ev Safrai, "Gergesa, Gerasa, or Gadara? Where Did Jesus' Miracle Occur?," *Jerusalem Perspective* 51 (1996): 18.

19. See R. T. France, *The Gospel of Matthew* (Grand Rapids: Eerdmans, 2007), 340.

evidence, Matthew originally had Gadara or Gergesa, as the evidence for Gerasa is very late and limited.[20] The manuscripts for Gergesa are also later and can best be explained as adjustments to align with Origen's view. For instance, Codex Sinaiticus was apparently corrected from Gadara to Gergesa in Matthew and Mark.[21] Codex Ephraemi (C) reads Gadara in the text but Gergesa in the margin. It is difficult to explain why post-Origen scribes would change the text from Gergesa, which Origen advocated, to a site that is not on the lake and was rejected by the church father.

The best manuscripts of Mark and Luke have Gerasa, but the same later manuscripts which have Gergesa in Matthew also have Gergesa in Mark and Luke (א^c L f¹ cop^{bo}). Readings of Gadara in Mark and Luke are significant, but easily explained as assimilation to the popular Matthew.[22] It is not clear why, if Gergesa was original in all three Gospels, it would be changed in the earliest manuscripts of Matthew to Gadara and Mark/Luke to Gerasa. Such a shift would go against scribal tendencies to harmonize the text and to resolve difficult readings. Some suggest that scribes replaced Gergesa with Gadara and Gerasa because Gergesa was so little known. We certainly

cannot argue that it was not well known (we doubt that it existed!), but we consider it implausible that scribes would change the name to two different sites that they knew were not near the Sea of Galilee, thus creating a greater difficulty.[23] Gerasa and Gadara were major cities of the Roman and Byzantine periods, and just as Origen recognized the problem with their location, it is unlikely that multiple scribes would independently and arbitrarily change the names from a site they did not know to a site they knew but which was so distant from the lake. There are, in fact, many names in Scripture that scribes did not know, but the scribes' work was generally careful and accurate, or else geographical studies today would be utterly futile. Since we know Origen publicly preferred Gergesa, and the available manuscript evidence best comports with scribes acting under his influence, the most reasonable conclusion is that Gergesa was not in the manuscripts known to him.[24]

Most scholars in this debate, including those advocating Gergesa, agree that Gergesa was not found in manuscripts in Origen's day.[25] They advocate, instead, a very early mistake in transmission. Unable to find evidence of an early reading of Gergesa, some suggest the error

---

20. Metzger, *Textual Commentary*, 19.

21. This was apparently the work of correctors working in Origen's city of Caesarea in the sixth or seventh century (Bruce M. Metzger, *The Text of the New Testament: Its Transmission, Corruption, and Restoration*, 3rd ed. [New York: Oxford University Press, 1992], 46).

22. R. T. France, *The Gospel of Mark: A Commentary on the Greek Text* (Grand Rapids: Eerdmans, 2002), 226.

23. As France notes, "The wide and early attestation of the geographically embarrassing Γερασηνῶν in Mark is in its favour" (*Gospel of Mark*, 406).

24. Joseph A. Fitzmyer is alone in arguing that Gergesenes is "attested in numerous mss. that antedate Origen," but he gives no evidence for this claim, and those who cite him do not evaluate it (*The Gospel According to Luke (I–IX)* [Garden City, NY: Doubleday, 1981], 736–37).

25. E.g., Notley, *In the Master's Steps*, 51. McRay also acknowledges that the best readings do not include Gergesa ("Gerasenes," 991).

Aerial view of the Kursi Monastery

existed already in pre-Markan sources.[26] Thus they say that Mark's sources read "Gerasa" and he included it as such in his Gospel. Assuming Markan priority, they contend that Luke copied the obvious error from Mark, but Matthew noted the geographical problem and tried to relieve it by moving the site somewhat closer to the lake at Gadara.[27] The advantage of this theory is that it (1) recognizes the weight of the textual evidence, (2) explains the presence of the two place names, and (3) resolves the geographical difficulty (by noting that the name was wrong from the start). This approach is much better than that of the numerous scholars who effectively ignore the manuscript evidence. The problem with this view is that while it sounds logical, it is purely hypothetical. It also requires that all three Gospel writers, and their communities, were ignorant of sites in the land of Israel. Given that the evidence is strong that eyewitnesses were alive during the time when these Gospels were written, it is improba-

ble that such mistakes would be made and perpetuated, particularly for a miracle as dramatic as this one. Had the memory of the eyewitnesses dimmed, it would make more sense to omit the place name, but each Synoptic is careful to record it, suggesting they were confident of its location and that the location was significant.

Evidence for Gergesa's existence on the ground and in early Gospel manuscripts is very weak. The most reasonable hypothesis is that the location of the Girgashites in this area led Origen to propose this was the area of the "Gergesenes" and to recommend this manuscript correction to later scribes.

ARCHAEOLOGICAL EVIDENCE AGAINST GERGESA

The textual argument against Gergesa seems to have prevailed among scholars until excavations began at Kursi in 1970. Since that time, many scholars have hailed the archaeological work as definitive proof that Kursi/Gergesa was

26. W. D. Davies and Dale C. Allison Jr., *A Critical and Exegetical Commentary on the Gospel According to Saint Matthew* [London: T&T Clark, 1988–97], 2:79.

27. Richard B. Vinson, "Gadara, Gadarenes," *NIDB* 2:505.

the site of the miracle. In the words of the excavator Vassilios Tzaferis, "The discovery of a large and impressive church, together with a sizeable settlement, provided conclusive evidence for the location of the elusive scene of the gospel story."[28] In the twenty-five years since the publication of the excavation report, Tzaferis's work is cited as definitive by nearly all who advocate the location of Kursi. Yet a closer look demonstrates that the conclusions are not warranted by the evidence.

In excavations during the years 1970–73 and 1980, Tzaferis uncovered a monastery, a hillside chapel, and a small settlement near the shore. The monastery was built in approximately AD 500 and was finally abandoned ca. 750. The assumption made by Tzaferis and those who cite him is that the presence of a monastery proves that Kursi was a holy site that commemorated the miracle of the swine.[29] There are two problems with this view. First, Byzantine monasteries were built by the hundreds all over the land of Israel, and most of them do not commemorate holy sites.[30] The Kursi monastery is said to commemorate this miracle, but there is no evidence of this. For instance, the mosaics in the monastery depict flora and fauna, with typical motifs found throughout the Byzantine world, but there is no representation of swine.[31] By contrast, the Byzantine monastery at Tabgha has a mosaic floor with fishes and loaves to commemorate the feeding of the 5,000. An inscription found in the Kursi church makes no mention of the site's alleged significance. Second, if we assume the monastery was built to commemorate a holy site, it only proves that Christians in AD 500 held to such a view. But there are plenty of Byzantine churches on sites that biblical scholars know are inauthentic, including the fish and loaves mosaic just mentioned.[32] It is inappropriate, then, to suggest the Byzantine monastery provides any sort of independent or reliable evidence to the location of the miracle. No one disputes

---

28. Vassilios Tzaferis, *The Excavations of Kursi-Gergesa* (Jerusalem: Department of Antiquities and Museums, 1983), 43–44.

29. Thus Carl G. Rasmussen: "There a monastery was founded to commemorate the healing" (*Zondervan Atlas of the Bible*, rev. ed. [Grand Rapids: Zondervan, 2010], 211). The only one to question this that I have found is Leslie J. Hoppe, who writes, "Nothing was found at Kursi that indicates that the site was venerated in connection with the exorcism" ("Gerasa, Gerasenes," *NIDB* 2:557).

30. McRay argues that Gerasa cannot be the place of the miracle because "nothing has been found at Gerasa which would indicate early Christian interest in the city as a holy place. However, at El Kursi, a lavish church was built in the 5th century." Yet in the same article, McRay says, "Gerasa was graced with many Christian churches in the Byzantine Period," including several that were built before the Kursi church ("Gerasenes," 991).

31. Vassilios Tzaferis, "A Pilgrimage to the Site of the Swine Miracle," *Biblical Archaeology Review* 15.2 (1989): 51.

32. The biblical evidence indicates that the multiplication miracle took place in the vicinity of Bethsaida (Luke 9:10) which was on the northeastern side of the lake and not at Tabgha on the northwestern side. The mistake apparently arose from the error that there were two places named "Bethsaida," and that "Bethsaida of Galilee" should be located at Tabgha. Another incorrect site identification with an impressive Byzantine church is Mount Tabor, which was identified as the Mount of Transfiguration. The Gospel accounts indicate that the Transfiguration occurred closer to Caesarea Philippi (Matt 16:3).

that Origen's influence on Byzantine Christianity in the Holy Land was significant, so it is not at all surprising if the Byzantines built a church at this site because of Origen's belief.

In close proximity to the monastery is the slope of Wadi Samakh, and here Tzaferis excavated a hillside chapel. Again, the declared conclusions do not match the evidence. Tzaferis found a chapel with a mosaic floor, but nothing that identified it with a miracle. The chapel was built against a partial cave in the rock, so it has been stated that this may have been a tomb in which the demoniac lived.[33] The chapel is built around a large rock, and so Tzaferis concludes, "It is evident that the Christians who built the monastery at Kursi identified the rock shelter and 7 m [22 ft] high boulder with the site on which Jesus healed the demoniac."[34] But the mere presence of a boulder does not prove a particular religious identification. One can think of

dozens of possible significances, including the event where Jesus, possibly in this same region, went up on a hillside and sat down before feeding the four thousand (Matt 15:29–39).[35] One who has visited many Byzantine sites, however, knows that they are often built over "holy rocks" or inside "sacred caves." The value of these traditions is dubious, and Tzaferis's circular reasoning renders his identification unsound.

Perhaps the best reason for identifying this hillside chapel with the swine miracle is the hillside itself.[36] Several points should be noted in this regard. First, it simply is an assumption that the chapel was built on a hill to commemorate a hillside miracle. There is no evidence that the chapel was built to commemorate a miracle of any kind.[37] Second, and ignored by most today, is the location of this hillside in relation to the sea. The slope is nearly 550 yards (500 m) from the water's edge.[38] Recent

---

33. Mendel Nun, *Gergesa (Kursi): Site of a Miracle, Church and Fishing Village* (Kibbutz Ein Gev: Tourist Department and Kinnereth Sailing, 1989), 27. The excavator, however, never stated that the cave was a tomb.

34. Tzaferis, *Excavations*, 51.

35. In this regard, it should be noted that "Kursi" means "chair" (E. W. G. Masterman, "A Three Days' Tour around the Sea of Galilee," *The Biblical World* 26.3 [1905]: 172). The name could be a reference to Jesus' sitting down before feeding the four thousand. Most scholars agree that the feeding of the four thousand took place in the Decapolis, and so it should be considered whether this church may in fact commemorate this miracle. Gordon Franz notes that the Kursi monastery has mosaics depicting fish and baskets with handles, both suggestive of the feeding miracle ("Ancient Harbors on the Sea of Galilee," *Archaeology and Biblical Research* 4.4 [1991]: 119). The tenth-century pilgrim Eutychius identified Kursi as the location of both the feeding of the four thousand and the healing of the demoniac (Jack Finegan, *The Archeology of the New Testament*, rev. ed. [Princeton: Princeton University Press, 1992], 115).

36. Tzaferis says, "The early Christians chose to build the monastery here, directly at the foot of the 'steep' hill, on which the tower was also located" (Tzaferis, *Excavations*, 48).

37. The character of the site is a "monastic settlement" (Tzaferis, *Excavations*, 43), and it could have been that a group of monks simply were looking for an area along the Sea of Galilee that was not already occupied (as Tabgha, Magdala, and Capernaum were). The chapel may have been built for private prayers of either the monks or pilgrims on their way to Capernaum.

38. This difficulty was noted by early explorers, such as Masterman, "Three Days' Tour," 172, and Gustaf Dalman, *Sacred Sites and Ways*, trans. Paul P. Levertoff (New York: Macmillan,

Inside remains of the Kursi Monastery

advocates take Tzaferis' claim that "we discovered that this [tower] was the very site of the miracle"[39] but use it as support for a location one mile (1.6 km) away where the hillside nearly reaches the lake. Some might claim we are being too precise in this matter, but when the basis of the claim that the hillside chapel commemorates the miracle is a "sacred rock," but yet this sacred rock is far from what is judged a "suitable" hillside, then our precision is justified. It may well be that the miracle took place on a hillside 550 yards (500 m) from the lake, and that the swine ran down a hillside and across a plain before drowning. But that is decidedly not what Kursi advocates are suggesting, because the very basis for the Gergesa identification—from the time of Origen until today—is that this is the single place on the eastern side where the hillside reaches the shore.[40] Once this criterion is surrendered, suddenly many options on the eastern shore are available, including several in the "region of the Gadarenes." In other words, Kursi advocates can have either the commemorative Byzantine monastery and chapel, or the

1935), 179. This distance is not significantly affected by the water level in ancient times as it was only about three feet (1 m) below today's maximum height. See Mendel Nun, *Sea of Galilee: Newly Discovered Harbours from New Testament Days*, 3rd ed. (Kibbutz Ein Gev: Kibbutz Ein Gev Tourist Department, 1992), 7.

39. Tzaferis, "Pilgrimage," 48.

40. Wilson's testimony is quite clear on this matter: "On the shore of the lake are a few ruined buildings, to which the same name [Khersa] was given by the Bedawin. About a mile south of this, the hills, which everywhere else on the eastern side are recessed from a half to three quarters of a mile from the water's edge, approach within forty feet of it; they do not terminate abruptly, but there is a steep even slope, which we would identify with the 'steep place' down which the herd of swine ran violently into the sea ... . it is equally evident, on an examination of the ground, that there is only one place on that side where the herd of swine could have run down a steep place into the lake" (Charles W. Wilson and Charles Warren, *The Recovery of Jerusalem* [London: Richard Bentley, 1871], 368–69).

steep hillside next to the lake, but not both.[41] And since their case rests upon the combination of these items, their argument is significantly weakened.[42]

Unfortunately, it is what the excavator chose to ignore that is most interesting. Byzantine monasteries and chapels ultimately do no more than prove a fourth to sixth century tradition at the site, and many of these traditions are clearly based on less-than-convincing evidence. More important is the question of a first-century village here that was named Gergesa. Of this, Tzaferis says very little:

> On the shore, about 300 m from the monastery, was Tell Kh. el-Kursi, with remains of a khan of the Late Arabic period, and evidence of occupation in the Roman, Byzantine, Early Arabic and Crusader periods. North of the tell were the remains of an artificial harbour, explored in an underwater archaeological survey. The harbour was tentatively assigned to the Roman-Byzantine period.[43]

The Early Roman period is usually considered to extend from the first century BC until AD 70, and the Late Roman period concludes about AD 325. Tzaferis does not clarify when in the Roman period the site was in use. Dan Urman, however, in his survey of the Golan, gives greater detail.

> An excavation of an experimental trench [in Tell el-Kursi] revealed pottery of the Late Roman, Byzantine, and Early Medieval and Late Arab periods.[44]

On the basis of what has been found and published, then, there is no evidence for a settlement in this area during the time of Jesus' ministry. Nor is there any foundation for Notley and Safrai's view that Origen's "ancient city" of Gergesa was abandoned ruins, for in Origen's time the settlement at Kursi was neither abandoned nor ancient.[45]

The lack of tombs in the area of Kursi is further evidence against the site as the location of the miracle. The Gospels record that the demon-possessed man lived in tombs in the area (Matt 8:28; Mark 5:3; Luke 8:27), and so contemporary tombs are an important criterion in locating the site of the miracle. This is another matter in which too many have been content to recite the observations of a traveler a hundred years ago, assuming this constitutes sufficient and reliable evidence. Closer

---

41. Most writers who cite Vassilios Tzaferis are arguing for the steep hill one mile distant, but this misreads him: "*The location of these remains on the slope*, only about 200 m southeast of the church, supports the identification of the site with the locale of the miracle of the Gadarene swine because *the topographical conditions are so similar to those described in the Gospel account*" ("Kursi," *NEAEHL* 3:896; emphasis mine).

42. An additional point that seems to have been missed is that the local Bedouin called the tower Kursi, explaining it as a reference to a chair or stool, but they had a different name for the ruins on the shore, es-Sûr (W. Sanday, *Sacred Sites of the Gospels* [Oxford: Clarendon Press, 1903], 27).

43. Tzaferis, *Excavations*, 2. Tzaferis modifies this, without comment, in a popular publication, suggesting the settlement existed in the "early Roman period" (Tzaferis, "Pilgrimage," 47).

44. Dan Urman, *The Golan: A Profile of a Region During the Roman and Byzantine Periods*, ed. A. R. Hands and D. R. Walker (Oxford, England: British Archaeological Reports, 1985), 204.

45. Safrai, "Gergesa, Gerasa, or Gadara," 18; Notley, *In the Master's Steps*, 49.

Ground view of the Kursi Monastery

investigation, however, indicates that no tombs have been found in the area. One of the most vocal advocates for Kursi is McRay, who says there are tombs in the area, but the only evidence he gives is the report of Sanday, who made one visit to Palestine but never visited the area of Kursi.[46] Thomson said there were tombs in the mountain above,[47] but other explorers reported there were none in the area, including Wilson and Dalman.[48] More significant is the silence of Tzaferis in this regard. With the great attention the former Greek Orthodox monk Tzaferis gives to positively identifying Kursi as the location of the miracle, one cannot doubt he would have carefully searched the area for tombs and made a major point of the discovery in his publication. But in fact, Tzaferis says only, "The New Testament story relates the presence of caves in the vicinity, still preserved on the slopes above Nahal Samakh."[49] In short, he found no tombs. This is corroborated by the survey of Urman, which notes tombs in other areas, including the vicinity of the Gadara harbor, but none are noted in the area of Kursi.[50] The fact that no tombs have been found does not mean that none existed, but it should certainly give us pause before deciding that Gergesa is a perfect match, and it should halt the citation of false reports of long-ago travelers.

46. Alfred J. Hoerth and John McRay, *Bible Archaeology* (Grand Rapids: Baker, 2005), 166. Standing in Tiberias and looking across the lake, Sanday observed, "At the mouth of this ravine I had pointed out to me a tiny patch darker in colour than its surroundings. These are the ruins of *Khersa* or *Kersa*. I have practically no doubt that these ruins mark the place which gave its name to the miracle" (*Sacred Sites*, 25–26). For his mention of tombs, see page 27.

47. William M. Thomson, *The Land and the Book* (London: T. Nelson and Sons, 1894), 376. Robert H. Gundry reports that in 1893 Christie claimed that a number of tombs were found covered by a collapsed hillside, but two years later Lagrange rejected this claim (*Mark: A Commentary on His Apology for the Cross* [Grand Rapids: Eerdmans, 1992], 256).

48. Wilson and Warren, *Recovery*, 369; Dalman, *Sacred Sites*, 179.

49. Tzaferis, *Excavations*, 42.

50. Urman, *Golan*, 204.

One additional point may be noted before concluding that Gergesa lacks sufficient evidence to be a possible location of the miracle. Nun comments on the discovery of a synagogue at Kursi, which he suggests makes the settlement Jewish.[51] Tzaferis believes that the site was always known as Kursi, except in Christian literature where it was called Gergesa.[52] A site known as Kursi is mentioned multiple times in the Talmud, but without clear indication of its location. If the Kursi of the Talmud is identified with this Kursi, then this would provide further evidence against this identification, as it is very unlikely that swine were being raised by Jewish people.[53] In any case, it should be noted that Kursi sits next to the southern border of the territory of the Jewish ruler Herod Philip, which apparently ran along the Wadi Samakh.[54] It might be surprising then, if this characteristic "Decapolis" story occurred on its very northern edge, that Gentile herdsmen had such a large herd grazing so close to Jewish lands. This does not itself disprove the possibility, but it should keep us open to the idea that the place names given by the Gospel writers need not be improved upon because of "geographical logic."[55]

THE CASE FOR GADARA

The burden of proof for locating the miracle at a site where the textual evidence is weak surely rests on the site itself.

Gergesa fails to have sufficient evidence that it was originally in any Gospel manuscripts or that the location of Kursi meets the necessary geographical and archaeological requirements. This, however, does not solve the original difficulties of Gadara and Gerasa as noted by Origen and his modern followers. In this section, I will argue that the objections usually advanced against the Gadara reading are unconvincing and that a location on the southeastern shore of the lake has significant advantages.

The first objection raised by scholars against the reading of Gadara or Gerasa is that the sites are too distant from the shore. Indeed, Gadara (modern Umm Qeis) is six miles (10 km) southeast of the Sea of Galilee, and Gerasa (modern Jerash) is 34 miles (55 km) southeast of the same. As Notley observes, "At such remote distances from the lake, these cities are not suitable candidates."[56] But the Gospel writers do not locate the event in a city, but in the "region" (chōra, χώρα) of the city. The issue, then, is not where the city was located, but what the region comprised.

Most today recognize that the city of Gadara held territory as far as the Sea of Galilee. Josephus says that Gadara's territory stretched to the Jordan River, so there can be no argument in terms of distance alone that the Sea of Galilee is too far removed (War 3.37). In addition, the

---

51. Nun, Gergesa, 11

52. Tzaferis, Excavations, 46

53. See Chris McKinny, "Pig Husbandry in Israel during the New Testament" on pg. 183.

54. This seems to be the most likely place for the border, and the large size of the Wadi Samakh certainly would be a natural border.

55. Paul H. Wright considers the "geographical logic" in this case to outweigh the testimony of the earliest manuscripts (Understanding the New Testament: An Introductory Atlas [Jerusalem: Carta, 2004], 24).

56. Notley, In the Master's Steps, 47.

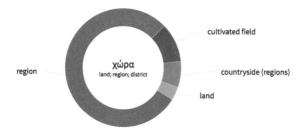

Bible Word Study: χώρα, chōra

famous baths on the north side of the Yarmuk River were under the jurisdiction of Gadara and known as "Hammat Gader." In fact, there is no geographical reason why Gadara's territory would include Hammat Gader but not land along the shore of the Sea of Galilee.[57]

The most compelling evidence that Gadara's territory extended to the Sea of Galilee is the recently discovered harbor along the southeastern shore. With an 800-foot (250-m) long breakwater, the harbor is the largest known on the Sea of Galilee.[58] The harbor of the nearby Decapolis city of Hippos is smaller than this one,[59] indicating that this harbor should not be associated with some small agricultural village but indeed belonged

to the great city of Gadara. This view is supported by the discovery of city coins of Gadara which depict ships on them for use in naval games. Michael Avi-Yonah has suggested that the ships were used in amphitheaters in the city,[60] and Dalman proposed that the battles took place on the Yarmuk River,[61] but no evidence has been found to support either view.[62] This large harbor was an ideal place for spectators to watch the competition. The harbor was useful as well for visitors traveling across the lake to visit the famous hot springs. Although the city was six miles (10 km) distant, the harbor, the baths, and the surrounding countryside would reasonably be known as the region of the Gadarenes.[63]

---

57. Compare Vita 9.42, where Josephus records that Justus "set the villages that belonged to Gadara and Hippos on fire; which villages were situated on the borders of Tiberias, and of the region of Scythopolis."

58. Mendel Nun, The Land of the Gadarenes: New Light on an Old Sea of Galilee Puzzle [Kibbutz Ein Gev: Sea of Galilee Fishing Museum, 1996], 21–22.

59. The breakwater is 385 feet (120 m) long (Nun, Sea of Galilee, 16).

60. Michael Avi-Yonah, The Holy Land, from the Persian to the Arab Conquests (536 B.C. to A.D. 640): A Historical Geography, rev. ed. (Grand Rapids: Baker, 1977), 174.

61. Dalman, Sacred Sites, 178–79.

62. In particular, in order to hold such games on the Yarmuk River, a dam would be required, but no traces of an ancient dam near Hammat Gader have been discovered (Nun, Gadarenes, 18).

63. Contra Safrai, who writes, "At that point on the lake's coast there was a large harbor that would naturally have served as Gadara's port. Though visited by vessels transporting goods to and from Gadara, geographically and administratively the port belonged to

The primary reason for dismissing the region of the Gadarenes as the possible location of the miracle is the alleged lack of a steep slope running into the water.[64] But the Gospel writers do not make such a claim. Mark's description that "the herd ran down the slope and into the water" (*hōrmēsen hē agelē kata tou krēmnou eis tēn thalassan*) does not require that the slope descended into the lake. Mark's use of prepositional phrases here emphasizes the destination (the lake) and not the path.[65] There could have been some distance between the slope and the lake, and in fact there is at least 50 feet (15 m) of level ground at the Kursi location.

There are three options near the Gadara harbor that satisfactorily meet the narrative's description. The first candidate is an embankment south of the Gadara harbor with a drop of 20–40 feet (6–12 m). Dalman's observations are relevant, particularly in light of the many who have come after him and denied any possibility of suitable geography in the area. He writes,

> The southern shore of the lake suits the story in that there, as on no other part of the shore, does water eat into the land, and has thereby formed a steep shore 6–12 meters in height. A herd wildly rushing over the shore-plain might easily be drowned here, coming so suddenly to the precipice.[66]

A second possible slope is at Tel Qatzir, a hill south of the Gadara harbor, located about half a mile (0.8 km) from the water's edge. The hill is sufficiently steep and the herd could have run down the slope and across the plain into the water. A third option is that the herds were grazing on the slopes of the Golan Heights to the northeast of the harbor. These slopes come within 550 yards (500 meters) of the lake, approximately the

Susita's territory; consequently, we should not expect the gospels to refer to this area as 'the land of the Gadarenes'" ("Gergesa, Gerasa, or Gadara," 18). The first problem with Safrai's argument is that he assumes that the Gospel writers must be using the term in a strict administrative sense, rather than in a practical sense. The second problem is that his basis for including the Gadara harbor in Hippos-Susita's administrative territory is the questionable assumption that ancient Kefar Tsemah was located at the Arab village of Samakh at the southern end of the lake. Nun refutes this by observing that the names are not as similar as they might appear and that no ancient ruins have been found at Samakh (*Gadarenes*, 15).

64. Some have adopted the Gergesa location from an inaccurate reading of the Greek text. For instance, several times Nun refers to the swine who "jumped off a precipice into the Sea of Galilee" (*Gadarenes*, 7), and Hoppe says they "rushed off the side of a cliff" ("Gerasa, Gerasenes," 557). Masterman was disappointed in the slope *at Kursi* ("Three Days' Tour," 172), and Thomson gives an appropriate assessment: "In studying the details of the miracle, I was obliged to modify one opinion or impression which had grown up with me from childhood. *There is no bold cliff overhanging the lake* on the eastern side, nor, indeed, on any other, except just north of Tiberias. Everywhere along the north-eastern and eastern shores, a smooth beach declines gently down to the water. There is no *'jumping-off place,'* nor, indeed, is any required" (*Land and the Book*, 377).

65. The prepositional phrases only assert that the pigs ran down the slope and into the lake without any demand that one immediately led to the other. Cf. the use of *hormaō*, ὁρμάω with *eis*, εἰς in Acts 19:29. If Mark had intended his readers to understand that the slope ended in the lake, he would have used *en*, ἐν or *epi*, ἐπί instead of *eis*, εἰς (cf. Acts 7:57).

66. Dalman, *Sacred Sites*, 178.

same distance as the Kursi monastery to the water. Any of these three options refute the claim that "no nearby slopes ... fit the topographical description."[67]

In terms of textual evidence, Gadara is an excellent candidate. With regard to an appropriate slope, Gadara is certainly possible. Concerning the presence of tombs, the region of Gadara is significantly better than the Kursi location. In travels in the area, I noted a Roman-era sarcophagus on the grounds of the HaOn holiday village, not far from the Gadara harbor. The sarcophagus was being used as a planter in the parking lot, suggesting that it had been discovered locally and re-purposed by someone not concerned with antiquities. Gordon Franz saw three sarcophagi in the same general area in a visit in the early 1990s.[68] In his archaeological survey, Urman observed "graves from Roman period SE of site" of Samra.[69] Samra is located immediately north of the ancient Gadara harbor and near the HaOn holiday village.

Another little-known fact is that a Byzantine church was built in this area. Nun reports that Samra had a "Byzantine chapel, with mosaics and inscriptions ... . It was found that the chapel had been part of a monastery."[70] Samra was occupied throughout the Arab periods until 1948,

and thus preservation of the Byzantine church is poor. One can certainly speculate that this church commemorated the site of a miracle in Jesus' ministry, though, as with the Kursi monastery, there is not enough evidence to prove this idea.

One objection raised against the Gadara (and Gerasa) location concerns the report of the herdsmen to the city, as well as the residents coming out to evict Jesus. Gadara, they claim, is simply too far for the men to travel there and return to see Jesus on the same day. Gadara is about six miles (10 km) from the harbor area, and because of the steep hill on which the city is located, a reasonable travel time would be three hours each way. Does the narrative allow for such an amount of elapsed time? Matthew records the incident as follows:

> The herdsmen fled, and going into the city they told everything, especially what had happened to the demon-possessed men. And behold, all the city came out to meet Jesus, and when they saw him, they begged him to leave their region (Matt 8:34).[71]

One of the problems in dealing with any narrative is that we can make assumptions about the text that are not neces-

---

67. Notley, *In the Master's Steps*, 48. This description contradicts Safrai's observation, which notes of the Gadara harbor area, "The shore there is steep; thus the plunging of the herd of swine into the waters of the lake is plausible" (Yohanan Aharoni Michael Avi-Yonah, Anson F. Rainey, and Ze'ev Safrai, *The Carta Bible Atlas*, 4th ed. [Jerusalem: Carta, 2002], 173).

68. Franz, "Ancient Harbors," 116.

69. Urman, *Golan*, 209.

70. Nun, *Gadarenes*, 19.

71. Matthew is cited here because he is the writer that locates the event in the region of the Gadarenes. Mark and Luke's accounts are essentially the same on this issue, except that each mentions that the report was made to those in the city and the country (Mark 5:14–17; Luke 8:34–37). At the conclusion of the narrative, Luke adds that "all the people of the surrounding country of the Gerasenes asked him to depart from them" (8:37). They simply note that the concern was held by more than those in the city.

sarily accurate. In this case, interpreters often assume Jesus was told to leave the region immediately after the death of the swine. But this is not required by any of the Synoptic Gospels. The context of this story in Jesus' life is that he traveled to the "other side" after a busy and discouraging season of ministry among the Jewish people.[72][73] He was tired and apparently seeking some time away for rest and possibly instruction of his disciples (Matt 8:18; Mark 4:38). After healing the demoniac, Jesus could have traveled to a nearby resting place and spent time there. Hours later, the crowd found him and asked him to leave. In any case, some amount of elapsed time is required for the crowd to be collected. How much time is too much? Even the passage of several days would correspond with the narrative and its conclusion that because of his miracle, the people of the area rejected his presence among them, and he left.

While it is possible that Matthew intends to suggest the herdsmen traveled to Gadara and returned with residents of the city, it is also possible that the "city" in view here is not Gadara. The fact that this is the "region of the Gadarenes" does not preclude the possibility that there were other cities, of lesser status, in the area. The word *polis*, πόλις in the Gospels can mean a city or a village,[74] and so Matthew may be suggesting only that the inhabitants of the nearest settlement came out to chase Jesus away.[75] It certainly seems more likely that local residents would be traumatized by the death of the pigs and urge Jesus' departure than would city-dwellers at a greater distance.[76] Roman period villages have been noted in the area by Urman, and one reasonable possibility is Samra, already noted above. In sum, the geography and archaeology of the Gadara region are consistent with Matthew's identification of the this area as the place of the miracle.

THE CASE FOR GERASA

It seems likely that the real cause of this entire debate originally goes back to Mark and Luke's choice of desig-

---

72. See Cyndi Parker, "Crossing to 'The Other Side' of the Sea of Galilee" on pg. 157.

73. Nun argues that the Gadara harbor was not "on the other side" but was "on the other end" of the Sea of Galilee (*Gergesa*, 14–15). Nun further suggests that skilled fishermen would not travel such a great distance during the winter. But the narrative explains that the disciples were caught in a storm, which could have changed their intended destination. And, in any case, basing a view on what one would ordinarily do is not a strong argument. Whether the Gospel writers would have felt the need to distinguish "other side" from "other end" is also questionable. They were traveling from the northwest side of the lake, and the Gadara harbor is on the southeast side of the lake. Many commentators note that the significance of "other side" is probably related to the Gentile presence (e.g., Michael J. Wilkins, "Matthew," in *Zondervan Illustrated Bible Backgrounds Commentary*, ed. Clinton E. Arnold, vol. 1 [Grand Rapids: Zondervan, 2002], 61).

74. Gergesa, if such a settlement existed, would fit our description of a village, and those who favor Kursi cannot easily object to the idea that a small village is in mind, unless they postulate that the Decapolis city of Hippos is intended.

75. "The πόλις of v. 33 was not necessarily that which gave it its name; it may have been any village near the eastern shore" (A. H. McNeile, *The Gospel According to St. Matthew* [Grand Rapids: Baker, 1915; reprint, 1980], 111–12).

76. Albrecht Alt, *Where Jesus Worked: Towns and Villages of Galilee Studied with the Help of Local History*, trans. Kenneth Grayston (London: Epworth Press, 1961), 26.

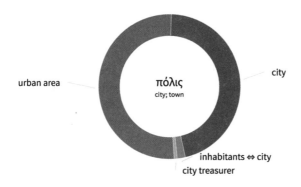

urban area — πόλις city; town — city

inhabitants ⇔ city
city treasurer

Bible Word Study: πόλις, polis

nating the place of the miracle as the "region of the Gerasenes." Because the city of Gerasa is so distant from the lake, and because the reading differs from Matthew's Gospel, questions arose. If the Synoptics had unanimously located the miracle in the "region of the Gadarenes," Origen and later scribes probably would never have questioned the identification, given Gadara's territory on the lake.[77] But the mention of Gerasa, one of the most well-known cities of the Decapolis, created an immediate tension with Matthew and the geography.

Origen's approach in rejecting both Gadara and Gerasa is not the only way that scholars have tried to resolve this problem. Cranfield suggested that the Gerasa mentioned by Mark and Luke was a small site near the shore in the region of Gadara.[78] Brooks believes that Gerasa was the ancient name of Kursi.[79] Nolland thinks that scribes mistook a similar place name by the lake for the Decapolis city of Gerasa.[80] The difficulty with all these is they are speculative. It seems unlikely that a second city with the same name would exist in close proximity to the well-known Gerasa.[81] The idea that scribes corrected the reading to Gerasa but left no evidence for it cannot be preferred. The simplest conclusion is that Mark and Luke referred to the area of the miracle as the region of the large

---

77. Nolland is alone in suggesting that Matthew originally read "Gerasenes," though "it is not at all the best-attested reading," thus harmonizing the three Gospel accounts (John Nolland, *The Gospel of Matthew: A Commentary on the Greek Text*, New International Greek Testament Commentary [Grand Rapids: Eerdmans, 2005], 373). This view attests to the strength of the reading of "Gerasenes" in Mark and Luke, and recognizes the unlikelihood of Gergesa, but must still explain why Gerasa is a suitable descriptor.

78. Cranfield, *Mark*, 176.

79. Brooks, *Mark*, 89. The advantage of this view is that it dispenses with the need for a "Gergesa," but it does not resolve the conflict with Gadara many miles to the south. Compare Cranfield, *Mark*, 176.

80. Nolland, *Gospel of Matthew*, 375–76.

81. Merrill F. Unger, *Archaeology and the New Testament* (Grand Rapids: Zondervan, 1962), 141.

Decapolis city of Gerasa. This is similar to Matthew's practice of mentioning not the closest village to the miracle but the most prominent Gentile city. But why did Mark and Luke mention Gerasa instead of Gadara? It would seem that Gadara would be both accurate and appropriate.

Several possibilities can be suggested, but they cannot be proven, and their strength is that they accord with the earliest manuscript readings. The first suggestion is that Gerasa, as a leading city of the Decapolis, had some territory in the vicinity of the lake.[82] The Sea of Galilee is the closest body of water to Gerasa, and its trade and fishing capabilities might have been lucrative to the city and its residents. Possibly Gerasa utilized Gadara's harbor in accomplishing its own commercial interests. A second possibility is that a group of residents of Gerasa had settled in the area near the harbor. They may have been facilitating business for their hometown, or may have simply taken advantage of the freedom to live near the lake. A third proposal is that Gerasa was a capital of the Decapolis, and this was a suitable way to identify that the miracle took place in this Gentile area.[83] A fourth possibility is that this was "a loose use of the term generally for the whole of the Decapolis."[84] A fifth hypothesis is that Mark and Luke designated this as the region of the Gerasenes because that city would have been more familiar to their readers in Greece and Rome than the city of Gadara.[85] Gerasa enjoyed an impressive era of building in the first century, and there is no doubt that Gerasa was better known throughout the empire than Gadara.

The reader will have to decide for himself whether any of these suggestions is plausible, or whether it is preferable to reject the earliest manuscripts of the Gospels in favor of Origen's solution.[86] It seems to this writer that one of these suggestions could be accurate and reasonably explain Mark and Luke's reference. Certainly adopting one of these is preferable to assuming the Gospel writers were simply ignorant of geography. Of all the geographical references in the Gospels, the one that would be the least likely to be confused is one that mentions swine running into the Sea of Galilee. If this idea was "demonstrably false" to Origen, then it certainly could not have escaped the notice of the Gospel writers and their earliest readers. It is reasonable to assume that Mark and Luke were emphasizing that this was the *region* of a well-known Decapolis city, which explains the presence of swine as well as the reaction

---

82. David E. Garland, "Mark," in *Zondervan Illustrated Bible Backgrounds Commentary*, ed. Clinton E. Arnold, vol. 1 (Grand Rapids: Zondervan, 2002), 234; J. Carl Laney, "Geographical Aspects of the Gospels," in *Essays in Honor of J. Dwight Pentecost*, ed. Stanley D. Toussaint and Charles H. Dyer (Chicago: Moody Press, 1986), 84. Laney asserts that "the historical and biblical data suggests that Gerasa shared the jurisdiction over the southeast lakeshore with Gadara," but it is not clear what historical data he has in mind (Laney, *Answers*, 214).

83. Theissen, *Gospels in Context*, 109.

84. France, *Mark*, 227.

85. Craig S. Keener, *A Commentary on the Gospel of Matthew* (Grand Rapids: Eerdmans, 1999), 282. Darrell L. Bock uses the Dallas suburb of Denton to explain how one writer might use a more general location than another (*Luke 1:1–9:50* [Grand Rapids: Baker, 1994], 782).

86. Another suggestion is that "region of the Gerasenes" should be translated as "land of the foreigners" (Riesner, "Archeology and Geography," 40).

of the residents.[87] Maybe the problem is not that the writers were too general, but that they were too specific. If only they had written "the region of the Decapolis," we might have been spared 1,800 years of wrangling over this issue.

CONCLUSION

While the solution to this problem is difficult, it must be acknowledged that certain aspects of the debate have been misleading and have obscured the real issues. The textual superiority of Gadara and Gerasa cannot be denied, and it accords with Origen's testimony of the existence of these readings. Claims for the existence of a Gergesa have been greatly overstated, and until today there is no clear evidence that there was an inhabited site in the first century or that it was ever known as Gergesa except in Byzantine literature. The discovery of the large harbor can only be attributed to Gadara, and this explains why Matthew would refer to this area by this name. As for Mark and Luke's reading, there are a number of possible ways to explain their reference to the region of the Gerasenes.

At the end of the discussion, the issue is how best to understand the manuscript evidence. Those who believe that Gergesa was original in the three Synoptics cannot satisfactorily explain why multiple alternate readings would arise before Origen if the Gospels were unanimous in this reading and a real site known as Gergesa existed. Those who accept Gergesa and another site, in any combination, cannot reconcile the geographical differences.[88] If the intent was to locate Gergesa in the region of a Decapolis city, the nearby Hippos would not have been displaced for Gadara.[89] A unanimous reading of Gadara would certainly resolve all difficulties, but the evidence is clear that readings of Gadara in Mark and Luke were motivated by assimilation to Matthew. A unanimous reading of Gerasa is unlikely given the poor manuscript evidence for it in Matthew. It is telling that the best explanation for the development of the reading of the manuscripts accords with the evidence of the earliest and best manuscripts of the three Synoptics. These too fit the geographical and archaeological requirements of the area in which the miracle occurred. While further evidence at both Kursi and around the Gadara harbor should be sought, there is no reason to continue to perpetuate the error of Origen in locating the miracle at a hypothetical Gergesa.

BIBLIOGRAPHY

Aharoni, Yohanan, Michael Avi-Yonah, Anson F. Rainey, and Ze'ev Safrai. *The Carta Bible Atlas.* 4th ed. Jerusalem: Carta, 2002.

Alt, Albrecht. *Where Jesus Worked: Towns and Villages of Galilee Studied with the Help of Local History.* Translated by

---

87. It may also be noted that Jesus was never expelled by the Jews from Jewish territory.

88. Thus Fitzmyer, who seems to accept Gergesa for Matthew, but "scarcely" so for Luke, is then left to caution "one against trying too hard to reconstruct what actually happened" (*Luke*, 736–37).

89. This is the combination preserved in the Majority Text (Matt: Gergesa; Mark=Luke: Gadara). Is it possible that the Gospel writers could have accurately located the event at both Gergesa and Gerasa, given Gerasa's prominence over Hippos? Possibly, but the manuscript evidence does not support such a combination.

Kenneth Grayston. London: Epworth Press, 1961.

Avi-Yonah, Michael. *The Holy Land, from the Persian to the Arab Conquests (536 B.C. to A.D. 640): A Historical Geography*. Rev. ed. Grand Rapids: Baker, 1977.

Baarda, T. "Gadarenes, Gerasenes, Gergesenes and the 'Diatessaron' Traditions." Pages 181–97 in *Neotestamentica et Semitica: Studies in Honour of Matthew Black*. Edited by E. Earle Ellis and Max Wilcox. Edinburgh: T. & T. Clark, 1969.

Baker, David W. "Girgashite." *ABD* 2:1028.

Bock, Darrell L. *Luke 1:1–9:50*. BECNT. Grand Rapids: Baker, 1994.

Brooks, James A. *Mark*. New American Commentary. Nashville, TN: Broadman and Holman, 1991.

Brown, J. W. "A Voyage to the Country of the Gadarenes." *Theology Today* 54.2 (1997): 226–27.

Clapp, Raymond G. "A Study of the Place-Names Gergesa and Bethabara." *JBL* 26.1 (1907): 62–83.

Cranfield, C. E. B. *The Gospel According to Saint Mark*. Cambridge Greek Testament Commentary. Cambridge: University Press, 1972.

Dalman, Gustaf. *Sacred Sites and Ways*. Translated by Paul P. Levertoff. New York: Macmillan, 1935.

Davies, W. D., and Dale C. Allison Jr. *A Critical and Exegetical Commentary on the Gospel According to Saint Matthew*. 3 vols. ICC. London: T&T Clark, 1988–97.

Finegan, Jack. *The Archeology of the New Testament*. Rev. ed. Princeton: Princeton University Press, 1992.

Fitzmyer, Joseph A. *The Gospel According to Luke (I–IX)*. AB. Garden City, NY: Doubleday, 1981.

France, R. T. *The Gospel of Mark: A Commentary on the Greek Text*. Grand Rapids: Eerdmans, 2002.

Franz, Gordon. "Ancient Harbors on the Sea of Galilee." *Archaeology and Biblical Research* 4.4 (1991): 111–21.

Garland, David E. "Mark." Pages 204–317 in vol. 1 of *Zondervan Illustrated Bible Backgrounds Commentary*. Edited by Clinton E. Arnold. Grand Rapids: Zondervan, 2002.

Grollenberg, Lucas H. *Atlas of the Bible*. Translated by Joyce M. H. Reid and H. H. Rowley. London: Nelson, 1957.

Guelich, Robert A. *Mark 1–8:26*. WBC. Dallas: Word Books, 1989.

Gundry, Robert H. *Mark: A Commentary on His Apology for the Cross*. Grand Rapids: Eerdmans, 1992.

Hoerth, Alfred J., and John McRay. *Bible Archaeology: An Exploration of the History and Culture of Early Civilizations*. Grand Rapids: Baker, 2005.

Holm-Nielsen, Svend, Ute Wagner-Lux, and K. J. H. Vriezen. "Gadarenes." *ABD* 2:866–67.

Hoppe, Leslie J. "Gerasa, Gerasenes." *NIDB* 2:577–59.

Keener, Craig S. *A Commentary on the Gospel of Matthew*. Grand Rapids: Eerdmans, 1999.

Laney, J. Carl. *Answers to Tough Questions from Every Book of the Bible*. Grand Rapids: Kregel, 1997.

———. "Geographical Aspects of the Gospels." Pages 75–88 in *Essays in Honor of J. Dwight Pentecost*. Edited by Stanley D. Toussaint and Charles H. Dyer. Chicago: Moody Press, 1986.

Lawrence, Paul. *The IVP Atlas of Bible History*. Downers Grove, IL: IVP Academic, 2006.

Marshall, I. Howard. *The Gospel of Luke: A Commentary on the Greek Text*.

NIGTC. Grand Rapids: Eerdmans, 1978.

Martin, James C. *Exploring Bible Times: The Gospels in Context*. Amarillo, TX: Bible World Seminars, 2003.

Masterman, E. W. G. "A Three Days' Tour around the Sea of Galilee." *The Biblical World* 26.3 (1905): 167–83.

———. "The Upper Jordan Valley." *The Biblical World* 32.5 (1908): 302–13.

McCown, Chester Charlton. "Gospel Geography: Fiction, Fact, and Truth." *JBL* 60.1 (1941): 1–25.

McNeile, A. H. *The Gospel According to St. Matthew*. Grand Rapids: Baker, 1915. Reprint, 1980.

McRay, John. *Archaeology and the New Testament*. Grand Rapids: Baker, 1991.

———. "Gerasenes." *ABD* 2:990–91.

Metzger, Bruce M. *The Text of the New Testament: Its Transmission, Corruption, and Restoration*. 3rd ed. New York: Oxford University Press, 1992.

———. *A Textual Commentary on the Greek New Testament*. 2nd ed. Stuttgart: Deutsche Biblegesellschaft, 1994.

Nolland, John. *The Gospel of Matthew: A Commentary on the Greek Text*. New International Greek Testament Commentary. Grand Rapids: Eerdmans, 2005.

———. *Luke 1–9:20*. WBC. Dallas: Word Books, 1989.

Notley, R. Steven. *In the Master's Steps: The Gospels in the Land*. Jerusalem: Carta Jerusalem, 2014.

Notley, R. Steven, and Ze'ev Safrai. *Eusebius, Onomasticon: The Place Names of Divine Scripture: Including the Latin Edition of Jerome*. Jewish and Christian Perspectives 9. Leiden: Brill, 2005.

Nun, Mendel. *Gergesa (Kursi): Site of a Miracle, Church and Fishing Village*. Kibbutz Ein Gev: Tourist Department and Kinnereth Sailing, 1989.

———. "Gergesa: Site of the Demoniac's Healing." *Jerusalem Perspective* 50 (1996): 18–25.

———. *The Land of the Gadarenes: New Light on an Old Sea of Galilee Puzzle*. Kibbutz Ein Gev: Sea of Galilee Fishing Museum, 1996.

———. *Sea of Galilee: Newly Discovered Harbours from New Testament Days*. 3rd ed. Kibbutz Ein Gev: Kibbutz Ein Gev Tourist Department, 1992.

Origen. "Commentary on John." Pages 297–411 in vol. 10 of *The Ante-Nicene Fathers: Translations of the Writings of the Fathers Down to A.D. 325*. Edited by Alexander Roberts, James Donaldson, A. Cleveland Coxe, and Allan Menzies. 10 vols. American ed. New York: Christian Literature Publishing, 1885–97.

Rasmussen, Carl G. *Zondervan Atlas of the Bible*. Rev. ed. Grand Rapids: Zondervan, 2010.

Riesner, Rainer. "Archeology and Geography." *DJG* 45–59.

Rousseau, John J., and Rami Arav. *Jesus and His World: An Archaeological and Cultural Dictionary*. Minneapolis: Fortress, 1995.

Safrai, Ze'ev. "Gergesa, Gerasa, or Gadara? Where Did Jesus' Miracle Occur?" *Jerusalem Perspective* 51 (1996): 16–19.

Sanday, W. *Sacred Sites of the Gospels*. Oxford: Clarendon Press, 1903.

Stein, Robert H. *Luke*. New American Commentary. Nashville, TN: Broadman and Holman, 1992.

Strauss, Mark. "Luke." Pages 318–515 in vol. 1 of *Zondervan Illustrated Bible*

Backgrounds Commentary. Edited by Clinton E. Arnold. Grand Rapids: Zondervan, 2002.

Theissen, Gerd. *The Gospels in Context: Social and Political History in the Synoptic Tradition*. Minneapolis: Fortress Press, 1991.

Thomson, William M. *The Land and the Book*. London: T. Nelson and Sons, 1894.

Tzaferis, Vassilios. "The Early Christian Monastery at Kursi." Pages 77–79 in *Ancient Churches Revealed*. Edited by Yoram Tsafrir. Jerusalem: Israel Exploration Society, 1993.

———. *The Excavations of Kursi-Gergesa*. 'Atiqot 16. Jerusalem: Department of Antiquities and Museums, 1983.

———. "Kursi." *NEAHL* 3:893–96.

———. "A Pilgrimage to the Site of the Swine Miracle." *BAR* 15.2 (1989): 44–51.

Unger, Merrill F. *Archaeology and the New Testament*. Grand Rapids: Zondervan, 1962.

Urman, Dan. *The Golan: A Profile of a Region During the Roman and Byzantine Periods*. BAR International Series 269. Edited by A. R. Hands and D. R. Walker. Oxford: British Archaeological Reports, 1985.

Vinson, Richard B. "Gadara, Gadarenes." *NIDB* 2:505.

Wilkins, Michael J. "Matthew." Pages 2–203 in vol. 1 of *Zondervan Illustrated Bible Backgrounds Commentary*. Edited by Clinton E. Arnold. Grand Rapids: Zondervan, 2002.

Wilson, Charles W., and Charles Warren. *The Recovery of Jerusalem*. London: Richard Bentley, 1871.

Wright, George Ernest, and Floyd Vivian Filson. *The Westminster Historical Atlas to the Bible*. Philadelphia: Westminster Press, 1945.

Wright, Paul H. *Understanding the New Testament: An Introductory Atlas*. Jerusalem: Carta, 2004.

CHAPTER 22

ANCIENT HARBORS OF THE SEA OF GALILEE[1]

Matt 4:18–22; 8:28–34; 14:15–21; 15:32–39;
Mark 1:16–20; 5:1–20; 6:32–44; 8:1–9, 8:10;
Luke 8:26–40; 9:12–17; John 6:1–14; 21:1–17

Gordon Franz

KEY POINTS

- The ancient harbors around the Sea of Galilee used by Jesus and his disciples have recently been revealed due to unusually low water levels.

- Of the sixteen harbors and anchorages that have been identified, a handful provide significant insight with respect to locating various events and places recorded in the Gospels.

- For example, Jesus called his first disciples at Tabgha, and likely healed the demoniac of multiple demons near Gadara.

- The remains at Kursi, as well as a knowledge of the surrounding harbors, lends credibility to the possibility that Kursi commemorates the feeding of the four thousand—not the healing of the demoniac as tradition suggests.

INTRODUCTION

The Lord Jesus spent much time on and around the Sea of Galilee with his fishermen-disciples. These disciples, who gave up all to follow him (Luke 5:11), were good

sailors. They knew the lake and its harbors well. The Gospels often refer to their maritime activities and the harbors they used. Now, for the first time in recent history, information on the harbors used by

---

1. This chapter is a revised version of an article published in *Archaeology and Biblical Research*. The original article was Gordon Franz, "Ancient Harbors on the Sea of Galilee," *Archaeology and Biblical Research* 4.4 (1991): 111–21. Used by permission.

Jesus and his disciples is coming to light. Sixteen harbors and anchorages have been identified and surveyed by Mendel Nun, a fisherman from Kibbutz Ein Gev on the east side of the Sea of Galilee. I am deeply indebted to him for sharing his wealth of knowledge concerning the lake and its history. In this essay I will discuss some of the lake's ancient harbors and their implications for Gospel geography.

THE HISTORY OF RESEARCH

In the past, explorers have searched in vain for harbors along the Sea of Galilee from the New Testament period. They have been unsuccessful because two millennia of wind and wave action have eroded the harbor superstructures. Only the foundations remain, and they were, until just over two decades ago, hidden beneath the water.

Mendel Nun has determined that the water level of the lake varied between 687 and 691 feet (209.5 and 210.5 meters) below sea level in the New Testament period.[2] In 1932, a dam was built at the southern outlet of the Jordan River allowing the maximum level to be controlled. It is normally maintained at -686 feet (-209 m); however, due to the drought between 1989 and 1991, the level dropped to a dangerously low -699 feet (-213 m) — a 13 foot (4 m) difference.[3] Since one-third of all the drinking water for modern Israel comes from the Sea of Galilee, this is a

serious problem. There could be adverse ecological effects as well. For those doing research on the antiquities of the lake, however, the drop proved to be a boon. Many ancient harbors were exposed for the first time in the modern era.

The first ancient harbor to be found was at Kursi on the eastern shore of the lake. Excavations were conducted here by the Department of Antiquities in the early 1970s. The harbor was discovered in an underwater survey carried out by S. Shapira and A. Raban of the Society for Underwater Archaeological Research. During the ensuing summer, the water level dropped and the harbors became visible from the shore.[4] Nun has since surveyed the entire lake, documenting fifteen additional ancient harbors and anchorages.[5] We will consider several of these harbors in relation to their geographical importance for the Gospel narratives.

A BRIEF SURVEY OF THE HARBORS AROUND THE SEA OF GALILEE

We will do a brief "tour" around the Sea of Galilee as we survey the sixteen Roman period harbors that have been discovered. We begin our tour at Kursi, the first harbor to be discovered on the lake, and travel around the lake in a clockwise direction. Our tour depends primarily on two sources: Mendel Nun's book *Sea*

---

2. Mendel Nun, *The Sea of Galilee: Water Levels, Past and Present* (Kibbutz Ein-Gev: Kinnereth Sailing, 1991), 10.

3. Nun, *Sea of Galilee: Water Levels*, 23–24.

4. Vassilios Tzaferis, *The Excavations of Kersi–Gergesa*, 'Atiqot 16 (Jerusalem: Department of Antiquities and Museums, 1983); Mendel Nun, *Gergesa (Kursi): Site of a Miracle, Church and Fishing Village* (Kibbutz Ein-Gev: Kinnereth Sailing, 1989).

5. Mendel Nun, *Sea of Galilee: Newly Discovered Harbours from New Testament Days*, 3rd ed. (Kibbutz Ein-Gev: Kinnereth Sailing, 1992); idem, *Sea of Galilee: Newly Discovered Harbours from New Testament Days* (Kibbutz Ein-Gev: Kinnereth Sailing, 1989).

Ancient Harbors of the Sea of Galilee

of Galilee: *Newly Discovered Harbours*[6] and Stefano DeLuca and Anna Lena's important essay, "The Harbor of the City of Magdala/Taricheae on the Shores of the Sea of Galilee, from the Hellenistic to the Byzantine Times: New Discoveries and Preliminary Results."[7]

THE KURSI HARBOR

The first harbor we will look at is the Kursi harbor surveyed by Mendel Nun.[8] The harbor is situated just to the north of Tel Kursi and south of the Wadi Samak. *Samak* is a Semitic word for fish. This wadi is well named because the best sardine fishing is at the mouth of this wadi. During the Second Temple period there was a fishing village in the area and a harbor that was about 492 feet (150 m) long. The remains of a fish tank measuring 10 by 11.5 feet (3 by 3.5 meters) was discovered. An aqueduct from the Wadi Samak brought fresh water to this fish tank. Most likely this is the harbor Jesus and his disciples left from after the feeding of the four thousand.

THE EIN GOFRA HARBOR

Ein Gofra, the spring of sulphur, had a small harbor, about 55 yards (50 meters)

---

6. Nun, *Sea of Galilee: Newly Discovered Harbours.*

7. Stefano DeLuca and Anna Lena, "The Harbor of the City of Magdala/Taricheae on the Shores of the Sea of Galilee, from the Hellenistic to the Byzantine Times. New Discoveries and Preliminary Results," *Harbors and Harbor Cities in the Eastern Mediterranean from Antiquity to the Byzantine Period: Recent Discoveries and Current Approaches* (Istanbul: Osterreiches Archaologisches Institut, 2014), 1:113–63. Their essay has a complete and up to date (2014) bibliography for those who would like to pursue this subject further.

8. Nun, *Sea of Galilee: Newly Discovered Harbours*, 3rd ed., 8–11; idem, *Gergesa (Kursi)*, 9–11; idem, "Ports of Galilee," *BAR* 25.4 (1999): 22–23; DeLuca and Lena, "Harbor of the City," 118.

long, associated with an agricultural settlement on shore.[9]

THE HIPPOS HARBOR

Susita/Hippos[10] was one of the Decapolis cities above the Sea of Galilee. It was visible from any point on the Sea of Galilee and was probably the city Jesus pointed to when he described his disciples as a "city set on a hill" (Matt 5:14).[11] It had a marine suburb and two harbors. The larger one had a breakwater that was about 131 yards (120 m) long. The smaller harbor had a breakwater of about 55 yards (50 m) long.[12]

THE DUERBAN HARBOR

The Duerban harbor was about 1.9 miles (3 km) to the south of the maritime suburb of Susita. It was connected to a prosperous ancient settlement but its identity remains elusive. There are fragmentary remains of a breakwater so not much is known of this harbor.[13]

THE GADARA HARBOR

Gadara is the second Decapolis city with a harbor on the Sea of Galilee. The ancient city of Gadara was located on the south side of the Yarmuk River, but it had lakefront property on the Sea of Galilee. The harbor, situated to the south of the modern Ha'on camping ground, had a promenade on the shore that was about 219 yards (200 m) long with a breakwater that measured 273 yards (250 m) long. Coins were minted by Gadara commemorating naval sea battles, called Naumachia, that took place near the harbor. Most likely this is the harbor the Lord Jesus landed in and then cast the demons into a herd of swine nearby (Matt 8:28–34; Mark 5:1–20; Luke 8:26–39; see "Casting the Demons into the Swine" on pg. 227).[14]

THE BEIT YERAH HARBOR

Near the ancient outlet of the Sea of Galilee is the Beit Yerah harbor. It belonged to the ancient site of Philoteria. Sections of this breakwater have been found, but its full length cannot be determined.[15]

THE SENNABRIS HARBOR

The Sennabris harbor consisted of a manmade lagoon with a breakwater of about 55 yards (50 m) long.[16]

---

9. Nun, *Sea of Galilee: Newly Discovered Harbours*, 3rd ed., 15; DeLuca and Lena, "Harbor of the City," 118.

10. *Susita* is the Aramaic word for horse, and *Hippos* is the Greek word for the same.

11. See Vernon H. Alexander, "The Words and Teachings of Jesus in the Context of Galilee" on pg. 122.

12. Nun, *Sea of Galilee: Newly Discovered Harbours*, 3rd ed., 16–18; idem, "Ports of Galilee," 30–31; DeLuca and Lena, "Harbor of the City," 118.

13. Nun, *Sea of Galilee: Newly Discovered Harbours*, 3rd ed., 19.

14. Nun, *Sea of Galilee: Newly Discovered Harbours*, 3rd ed., 20–23; DeLuca and Lena, "Harbor of the City," 118.

15. Nun, *Sea of Galilee: Newly Discovered Harbours*, 3rd ed., 24; DeLuca and Lena, "Harbor of the City," 119.

16. Nun, *Sea of Galilee: Newly Discovered Harbours*, 3rd ed., 25–26; DeLuca and Lena, "Harbor of the City," 119.

Hippos (center hill)

THE TIBERIAS HARBOR

The harbor for ancient Tiberias was elusive for many years. In the 1989 edition of Mendel Nun's book it was described as "lost."[17] But in his 1992 edition it was "found."[18] Tiberias was founded by Herod Antipas in AD 19 and was the capital of the province of Galilee. The size of the harbor changed with the changing size, and location, of the city over time. Nun, in his survey of the shoreline of Tiberias, found many stone net sinkers, net anchors, basalt anchors, and mooring stones. He realized there is still more work to be done on the harbor of Tiberias.[19] It is from this harbor that people departed to find the Lord Jesus after the feeding of the five thousand (John 6:23).

THE AMMAUS HARBOR

The Ammaus harbor is found in the area of the "Russian garden" about 1.9 miles (3 km) to the north of Tiberias. Warm mineral springs flow into the lake at this point, and it attracts the musht fish to the area in the winter and spring. It has a breakwater with two small piers connected with it.[20]

17. Nun, *Sea of Galilee: Newly Discovered Harbours* (1989), 15.

18. Nun, *Sea of Galilee: Newly Discovered Harbours*, 3rd ed., 27-31; Nun, "Ports of Galilee," 28-29; DeLuca and Lena, "Harbor of the City," 119.

19. Nun, *Sea of Galilee: Newly Discovered Harbours*, 3rd ed., 30-31; Nun, "Ports of Galilee," 28-29; DeLuca and Lena, "Harbor of the City," 119.

20. Nun, *Sea of Galilee: Newly Discovered Harbours*, 3rd ed., 32-33.

Hippos (aerial view)

THE MAGDALA HARBOR

The Magdala harbor is the only one to be scientifically excavated.[21] Magdala was also known as Taricheae, the place of the salting of the fish. It was here that fishermen would bring their catch of fish in order for it to be salted and shipped throughout the Roman world. The fishermen-disciples knew this harbor well, and when Jesus said that they were the "salt of the earth" (Matt 5:13), they understood the preservative quality of salt for preserving fish.[22]

THE GENNESAR HARBOR

The Gennesar harbor was built slightly to the east of Tel Kinneret, the city that gives its name to the lake. It has two breakwaters that are perpendicular to the shore and one breakwater parallel to the shore about 77 yards (70 m) long.[23] This is the harbor in the "land of Gennessaret" where Jesus and his disciples landed after the feeding of the five thousand and Peter's attempt to walk on water (Matt 14:34; Mark 6:53).

THE TABGHA HARBOR

The Tabgha harbor was nicknamed the "St. Peter's harbor" by Mendel Nun because this was the harbor that the fishermen from Capernaum used when they were fishing in the area. It is located to the northeast of the Church of the Primacy

21. DeLuca and Lena, "Harbor of the City"; Nun, *Sea of Galilee: Newly Discovered Harbours*, 3rd ed., 34–35; Nun, "Ports of Galilee," 26–27.

22. See also Vernon H. Alexander, "The Words and Teachings of Jesus in the Context of Galilee" on pg. 134.

23. Nun, *Sea of Galilee: Newly Discovered Harbours*, 3rd ed., 36–37; DeLuca and Lena, "Harbor of the City," 117.

and is only visible when the water level drops to -231.3 yards (-211.50 m). The harbor is comprised of two breakwaters. The first, 66 yards (60 m) long, is parallel to the shore and curves to the entrance on the east side. The second, perpendicular to shore, is 44 yards (40 m) long.[24]

THE CAPERNAUM HARBOR

The most important harbor for Gospel geography is the Capernaum harbor. The Lord Jesus called this city "his own city" (Matt 9:1). The length of the harbor is approximately 875 yards (800 m) with piers projecting from the promenade on the shore.[25] This harbor is where the Zebedee family and the other disciples moored their boats. It was also the place of the Galilean tax office run by Matthew (Matt 9:9; Mark 2:14; Luke 5:27).

THE AISH HARBOR

The Aish harbor is situated in the Amnun Bay about 0.9 miles (1.5 km) to the west of the Jordan River. It apparently served a small settlement nearby that had an abundant spring at the northwest foot of the settlement. There were two parallel breakwaters about 22 yards (20 m) apart. Most likely the Lord Jesus and his disciples landed here to go to the "deserted place" of Bethsaida and the eventual feeding of the five thousand.[26]

THE KEFAR AQAVYA HARBOR

The Kefar Aqavya harbor is located 2.5 miles (4 km) north of Kursi. Nearby is the remains of a Late-Roman / Byzantine fishing village, with later Islamic and Ottoman occupation. More than likely the village did not exist during the Second Temple period. The breakwater for the harbor curved north for 82 yards (75 m).[27]

CONNECTIONS BETWEEN THE HARBORS AND GOSPEL EVENTS

A handful of these harbors bear direct connections to key events recorded in the Gospels. Five specifically will be discussed below:

1. the location of the calling of the disciples at Tabgha, the fishing suburbs of Capernaum (Matt 4:18–22; Mark 1:16–20; John 21:1–17)

2. the location of the casting of the demons into the swine at the harbor of Gadara, modern day Kibbutz Ha'on harbor (Matt 8:28–34; Mark 5:1–20; Luke 8:26–40)

3. the location of the feeding of the five thousand near the Aish Harbor, the probable fishing suburbs of Bethsaida-in-Galilee (Matt 14:15–21; Mark 6:32–44; Luke 9:12–17; John 6:1–14)

---

24. Nun, Sea of Galilee: Newly Discovered Harbours, 3rd ed., 38–39; DeLuca and Lena, "Harbor of the City," 117.

25. Nun, Sea of Galilee: Newly Discovered Harbours, 3rd ed., 40–42; Nun, "Ports of Galilee," 24–25; DeLuca and Lena, "Harbor of the City," 117.

26. Nun, Sea of Galilee: Newly Discovered Harbours, 3rd ed., 42; DeLuca and Lena, "Harbor of the City," 117; Stepansky et. al., "'Path Circling around the Kinneret,' Survey." Hadashot Arkheologiyot: Excavations and Surveys in Israel 123 (2011): n.p., http://www.hadashot-esi.org.il/report_detail_eng.aspx?id=1715&mag_id=118.

27. Nun, Sea of Galilee: Newly Discovered Harbours, 3rd ed., 12–13; DeLuca and Lena, "Harbor of the City," 117–18.

Church of Saint Peter's Primacy

4. the location of the feeding of the four thousand, which I believe is at Kursi (Matt 15:32–39; Mark 8:1–9)

5. the location of Magdala / Dalmanutha (Matt 15:38; Mark 8:10)

THE CALLING OF THE DISCIPLES

The location of the calling of the first disciples of the Lord Jesus was most likely at the "harbor of St. Peter." Tabgha, the corrupted Arabic form of the Greek name Heptategon, means "seven springs." It is the winter fishing ground for fishermen from Capernaum.[28] During the winter months its seven warm springs attract musht, commonly called "St. Peter's fish," to its shores. This would be the logical place for Peter and Andrew to have been throwing their cast nets during, in all probability, the winter of AD 28 when Jesus called them to become fishers of men (Matt 4:19; Mark 1:17), more than a year after putting their trust in the Lord Jesus as Savior (John 2:11).

Several months later, after the Sermon on the Mount, the Lord had to "recall" Peter while he was washing his

---

28. Bargil Pixner, "The Miracle Church of Tabgha on the Sea of Galilee," *BA* 48 (1985): 196–206.

nets along the shore in the morning after a long, unproductive night of fishing. The springs would be an ideal place for this activity. Jesus got Peter's attention by a miraculous draw of fish. This was indeed a miracle because the net Jesus commanded Peter to let down was a trammel net. This type of net is used only at night and close to shore (Luke 5:1–11).[29] [30] The goodness of God led Peter to repentance. He confessed, "Depart from me, for I am a sinful man, O Lord." Following this experience, the disciples "left all to follow Him" (Luke 5:11).[31]

An early church tradition places Jesus' post-resurrection appearance to the disciples here at Tabgha (John 21).[32] Here, by the "coals of fire" the Lord Jesus asked Peter three times if he loved the Lord. Peter answered in the affirmative each time. Interestingly, the only other time the phrase "coals of fire" is used in the Gospels is in John 18:18 where Peter denied the Lord three times by the coals of fire! From this point on (John 21), Peter does not go back fishing for fish, but fishing for the hearts and souls of men and women.

CASTING THE DEMONS INTO THE SWINE

In Matthew 8, Mark 5, and Luke 8 we have the account of Jesus exorcising demons from a man, or two men (compare Matt 8:28) who lived in a cemetery near the Sea of Galilee. The location of this event has been uncertain.[33] There is disagreement as to whether the text should read "Gergesa," "Gerasa," or "Gadara." The proper reading of the text should be the region of the "Gergesenes" in Matthew's Gospel (8:28) and the region of the "Gadarenes" in Mark's (5:1) and Luke's (8:26) Gospels. Matthew, a former tax collector from Capernaum on the northern shore of the Sea of Galilee, is writing primarily to a Jewish audience, most likely in the land of Israel. Mark appears to be addressing a Jewish audience in the Diaspora, possibly Rome. Luke is writing to a Gentile audience somewhere in the Roman world.

If the reading in Matthew's Gospel is "Gergasenes," then there are two possible interpretations of the name.[34] The first is it stands for an "old Gergashite family." Unfortunately, of the seven references to the nation of the Girgashites that were in the land of Canaan when the Israelites entered, none of them give any geographical hints as to where the nation was located (Gen 10:16; 15:21; Deut 7:1; Josh 3:10; 24:11; 1 Chr 1:14; Neh 9:8). Matthew, writing to a Jewish audience, would refer to the region by its old Semitic name. This phenomenon can be illustrated by the city of Beth-Shean, another Decapolis city. During the Hellenistic period, the name of the city was changed to Scythopolis, yet "the Jews there continued to call the place by its old name. A bilingual ossuary inscrip-

---

29. See J. Carl Laney, "Fishing the Sea of Galilee" on pg. 165.

30. Mendel Nun, *The Sea of Galilee and Its Fishermen in the New Testament* (Kibbutz Ein-Gev: Kinnereth Sailing, 1989), 28–40.

31. Gordon Franz, "The Greatest Fish Stories Ever Told," *Bible and Spade* 6.3 (1993): 92–96. Unless otherwise indicated, Scripture quotations in this article are from the NKJV.

32. Nun, *Sea of Galilee and Its Fishermen*, 41–44.

33. Nun, *Gergesa (Kursi)*.

34. John Lightfoot, *A Commentary on the New Testament from the Talmud and Hebraica*, 4 vols. (1859; repr., Peabody, MA: Hendrickson, 1989), 2:166, 409–10.

Shore of the Sea of Galilee at Tabgha

tion found in Jerusalem has the Semitic inscription "Ammyiah ha-Beshanit" and "Hanin ha-Beshani," which corresponds in the Greek part of the inscription to "Ammia Skuthopolitissa" and "Anin Skuthpoleites." Josephus makes a point of saying that the "Greeks" called the place Scythopolis (*Ant* 12:348; 13:188), and the Talmudic sources always call the place by the shortened form "Beishan" (which is preserved in the Arabic "Beisan").[35] There is another bilingual ossuary from Jerusalem with the name "Papias, / the Be(t)shanite" in Hebrew and "Papias and Salomich (!) / the Scythopolitans" in Greek.[36] Mark and Luke, writing to audiences that might not be acquainted with the geography of the region, refer to the place by its Greek name, Gadara, one of the Decapolis cities.

Some have objected to these readings because Gadara, located at Umm Qeis about six miles southeast of the Sea of Galilee, is too far away to have a harbor on the lake. In 1985, as a result of the low water level, a harbor was discovered south of Tel Samra, now the campground of Kibbutz Ha'on. It is the closest point along the lake shore relative to Umm Qeis. What is more, the Kibbutz Ha'on harbor is the largest on the east side of the lake. Its outer breakwater is about 273 yards (250 m), with a 5.5 yard (5 m) wide base. The quay, or landing area, is approximately 219 yards (200 m) long. There is also a 547 yard (500 m) pier along the shore.[37] Nun surmises:

One can only assume that a splendid harbor such as this did not

---

35. Anson F. Rainey, Unpublished notes for Sources for Historical Geography (Jerusalem: Institute of Holy Land Studies, 1973).

36. Levi Rahmani, *A Catalogue of Jewish Ossuaries in the Collections of the State of Israel*, (Jerusalem: Israel Antiquities Authorities and the Israel Academy of Sciences and Humanities), 112, no. 139.

37. Nun, *Sea of Galilee: Newly Discovered Harbours*, 16–18.

serve a small population. It is much more likely that it once had been the harbor of Gadara, located on the heights of Gilead above the Yarmuk River—the largest and most magnificent of the Hellenistic towns that encircled the Sea of Galilee.[38]

Coins from Gadara depict boats commemorating the "Naumachia," or naval battles reenacted by the people of Gadara. Several scholars have suggested that these battles took place on the Yarmuk River.[39] A more plausible setting is the Kibbutz Ha'on harbor. Here, there is sufficient room for maneuvering and the long pier would provide seating for spectators.

Recently, a Byzantine church was discovered at Tel Samra adjacent to the harbor.[40] To whom or what was this church dedicated? Did it commemorate the demoniac event?

Assuming that the demoniac event took place at the harbor of Gadara, how does the geography fit the biblical text? Jesus and his disciples landed at the harbor and were met by a demon possessed man who lived in tombs (Mark 5:2; Luke 8:27; Matt 8:28 says there were two demoniacs). That there were tombs here is attested by the discovery of three sarcophagi in the area. The demons requested that they be thrown into a herd of swine which were "a good way off," "on / near the mountain(s)" i.e., perhaps the Golan Heights (Matt 8:30; Mark 5:11; Luke 8:32). The swine then ran down a "steep place into the sea and drowned" (Matt 8:32; Mark 5:13; Luke 8:33).

There are two possibilities as to where this event took place. The first is just behind Kibbutz Ha'on where a ridge coming down from the Golan Heights fits the description. The second is on the grounds of Kibbutz Ma'agan, about a mile to the southwest. Located here is the only cliff which drops directly into the sea.[41]

After the demise of the swine, the predominantly Gentile population of the Decapolis pleaded with Jesus to leave their territory. One scholar has suggested that killing the pigs could have been an attack on the cultic practices of the Decapolis cities.[42] Jesus departed, but he left the delivered demoniac to proclaim the great things Jesus had done for him (Mark 5:20; Luke 8:39). The fruit of his labors is seen by the Gentile multitude that showed up for the feeding of the four thousand.

FEEDING THE FIVE THOUSAND

Just before Passover (John 6:4), Jesus performed the miracle of feeding five thousand men, plus women and children, with five barley loaves and two small sardines. At Tabgha there is a mosaic commemorating this miracle. In addition, an early church tradition places the event

---

38. Nun, *Sea of Galilee: Newly Discovered Harbours*, 17.

39. Gustaf Dalman, *Sacred Sites and Ways* (London: Society for Promoting Christian Knowledge, 1935), 178–79; Mendel Nun, *The Land of the Gadarenes: New Light on an Old Sea of Galilee Puzzle* (Kibbutz Ein-Gev: Kinneret Sailing, 1996), 16–18.

40. Nun, *Sea of Galilee: Newly Discovered Harbours*, 16.

41. See Todd Bolen, "Where Did the Possessed-Pigs Drown?" on pg. 196.

42. Earl S. Johnson, "Mark 5:1–20: The Other Side," *Irish Biblical Studies* 20 (1998): 49–50.

at Tabgha.[43] But, does Tabgha fit the geographical data in the Gospels?

The twelve disciples were sent out to preach the gospel to the "lost sheep of the house of Israel." Upon their return (probably to Capernaum), Jesus took them by boat to a deserted place (Matt 14:13; Mark 6:32) which "belonged to the city of Bethsaida" (Luke 9:10). The problem here is that there are two towns named Bethsaida. I believe this text refers to Bethsaida-in-Galilee, located at Tel el-Araj on the north shore of the lake.[44] The other Bethsaida is Bethsaida Julias, one of the capitals of Gaulanitis, which I believe to be located at el-Mes'adiyeh, to the southeast of Tel el-Araj.[45]

The multitude ran before the boat and arrived at the site of the feeding before Jesus and his disciples. There is no indication that they crossed the Jordan River, which would have been high due to the spring rains. Thus, the feeding of the five thousand should be placed in Galilee, to the west of the Jordan River. I suggest this feeding of the multitude took place in the area of Moshav Almagor, between Capernaum and Bethsaida-in-Galilee, within the district of Bethsaida.

After feeding the multitudes, Jesus sent his disciples by boat to Bethsaida (probably Julias). Just below Moshav Almagor, to the east of Ammun Bay, which is rich in sweet water springs, is an anchorage at Aish, also known as Khirbet Osheh. It is located about one mile northeast of Capernaum and a little over one mile west of Bethsaida-in-Galilee. It had a 109 yard (100 m) long promenade built of large stones and two parallel breakwaters, 22 yards (20 m) apart, extending into the lake.[46] It is likely that this was where the disciples' boat was moored during the feeding of the five thousand and where they departed to the "other side." Possibly Jesus was concerned for their safety. Herod Antipas would not have been pleased with the idea of making Jesus "King of Israel" (John 6:15).

The area of Moshav Almagor and the Aish anchorage nicely fits the Gospel descriptions of the feeding of the five thousand. Placing the miracle at Tabgha was no doubt for the convenience of early pilgrims.[47]

As the disciples were crossing the lake, a violent winter wind storm swept down from the Golan Heights. It was on this occasion that Jesus walked upon the sea and calmed the wind (Matt 14:25-32; Mark 6:48-51; John 6:19-21).[48] Eventually they landed on the west side of the lake at the "land of Gennesaret," where they anchored in the harbor of Gennesar.[49]

43. J. Shenhav, "Loaves and Fishes Mosaic Near Sea of Galilee Restored," BAR 9.6 (1983): 24-31; Pixner, "Miracle Church of Tabgha," 196-206.

44. J. Carl Laney, "Geographical Aspects of the Gospels," in Essays in Honor of J. Dwight Pentecost, ed. Stanley D. Toussaint and Charles H. Dyer (Chicago: Moody, 1986), 81-82.

45. See also Benjamin A. Foreman, "Jesus Heals a Blind Man Near Bethsaida" on pg. 270.

46. Nun, Sea of Galilee: Newly Discovered Harbours, 23.

47. For more details on the argument for Moshav Almagor as the feeding location, see Gordon Franz, "The Feedings of the Multitudes" on pg. 237, especially the section "Locating Bethsaida."

48. See also Gordon Franz, "What Type of Storms Did Jesus Calm: Wind or Rain?" on pg. 175.

49. Nun, Sea of Galilee: Newly Discovered Harbours, 23.

The next day Jesus went to the synagogue of Capernaum about 3 miles (4.8 km) away and gave his discourse on the "Bread of Life" (John 6:22-71).

FEEDING THE FOUR THOUSAND

The focus of Jesus' ministry changed after the feeding of the five thousand. Now, he wanted to spend time alone with his disciples. They traveled to Tyre and Sidon where they spent much time together. After ministering to the Syro-Phoenician woman, they departed from the region and came to the Sea of Galilee in the region of the Decapolis (Mark 7:31). There Jesus healed many, primarily Gentiles, for three days. As a result, they "glorified the God of Israel" (Matt 15:29-31; Mark 7:31-37). Toward the end of the third day the multitudes were fed with seven loaves of bread and a few small fish. Although we can be certain that the event took place on the east side of the lake, exactly where is another matter.

Father Bargil Pixner places the event at Tel Hadar on the northeast shore of the lake.[50] Tel Hadar, however, is in the region of Gaulanitis, north of the area of the Decapolis. The border between the Decapolis and Gaulanitis apparently was the Wadi Samak.[51] I suggest that the feeding of the four thousand took place at the Kursi Church, excavated in the 1970s, just south of the Wadi Samak. In fact, I believe the church was built to commemorate the feeding of the four thousand, rather than the casting of the demons into the swine as the excavators propose.[52]

There are several reasons for this suggestion. First, as discussed earlier, I believe the demoniac event took place at Gadara eight miles to the south. Second, there is no indication from the mosaics on the floor of the church that it commemorated the demoniac event. Third, early church sources and pilgrim accounts, while stating that the demoniac event took place on the east side of the lake, do not give a specific location. Fourth, the mosaic floors in the Kursi church provide a hint that this is where Jesus fed the four thousand.

The church was built in the late fifth, or early sixth, century AD and lasted until the Persian invasion of AD 614 when it was destroyed. Approximately sixty percent of the mosaic floor survived the destruction. The central nave suffered the most. Except for some bird and animal medallions which were destroyed during an Islamic iconoclastic movement, the two side aisles are relatively intact. The side aisles were made up of 296 medallions containing various depictions. Vassilios Tzaferis, the excavcator, describes them as follows:

> [They] contained a variety of exotic and common birds, different types of fish, stylized flowers, plants, vegetables, harvest symbols and ceremonial objects. Within the row each motif was repeated four times. For the most part, the arrangement of the motifs alternated between rows of

---

50. Bargil Pixner, *Paths of the Messiah and Sites of the Early Church from Galilee to Jerusalem*, trans. Keith Myrick, Sam Randall, and Miriam Randall, ed. R. Riesner (San Francisco, CA: Ignatius, 2010), 71-72.

51. Dalman, *Sacred Sites and Ways*, 170.

52. Tzaferis, *Excavations of Kersi-Gergesa*, 43-48; idem, "A Pilgrimage to the Site of the Swine Miracle," *BAR* 15.2 (1989): 44-51; Nun, *Gergesa (Kursi)*.

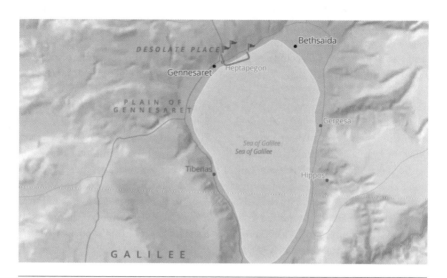

images such as birds, fish, every-day objects, or plant motifs.[53]

What interests me the most are the fish.[54] Although they have been partially destroyed, Nun has identified them as barbel fish.[55] The Gospel narratives state that the fish involved in this miracle were "small fish," possibly the sardines for which the Wadi Samak is noted. There are also baskets in the mosaics.[56] They have handles, as did those in the Gospel account. One basket is similar to the one on the mosaic floor at Tabgha.

To the southeast of the church, on the slopes of Wadi Samak, is an ancient tower. According to the excavator, this is the "chapel of the miracle of the swine."[57] Some have suggested it was built over the tombs in which the demoniac(s) lived. Nothing in the chapel, however, indi-cates to whom or what it was dedicated. It could just as well have been dedicated to the healing events which took place prior to the feeding of the 4,000. Matthew tells us that Jesus "went up on the mountain and sat down there" (15:29). Kursi, inter-estingly enough, means "chair," a place for sitting down. Most likely, for the convenience of pilgrims, the chapel was placed only a little ways up the slope of the mountain.

After feeding the four thousand, Jesus and his disciples went to Dalmanutha / Magdala on the west side of the lake. Some 328 yards (300 m) to the west of the church is a small, 2.5 acre, site named Tel Kursi. North of Tel Kursi are the remains of an ancient harbor. Its breakwater curves for 164 yards (150 m), and it has a holding tank for fish, with an

---

53. Tzaferis, *Excavations of Kersi-Gergesa*, 24.

54. Tzaferis, *Excavations of Kersi-Gergesa*, Plate 11.1.

55. Nun, *Sea of Galilee and Its Fishermen*, 24.

56. Tzaferis, *Excavations of Kersi-Gergesa*, Plate 10.5.

57. Tzaferis, *Excavations of Kersi-Gergesa*, 49–51.

Remains of a Mosaic at Kursi

aqueduct for bringing fresh water from the Wadi Samak.[58] This would have been the harbor from which Jesus left to go to Magdala.

LOCATION OF MAGDALA (DALMANUTHA)

Magdala is located about 3 miles (4.8 m) northwest of modern Tiberias. Remains of a harbor have surfaced here.[59] It consisted of two parts: an open dock for loading and unloading during the summer, and a basin, within a 77 yard (70 m)

breakwater to protect the ships from the winter storms. Mark's Gospel calls the area the "region of Dalmanutha." How is this to be understood?

It has been suggested that Dalmanutha is a transliteration of the Syriac word for "harbor."[60] Magdala, also known as Taricheae, was noted as a place for salting fish. Possibly it got its nickname, "the harbor," because fishermen brought their sardines here for salting. Josephus records that there were many ships at Magdala, 230 or 330, depending on which

---

58. Nun, *Sea of Galilee: Newly Discovered Harbours*, 3rd ed., 8–11.

59. Nun, *Sea of Galilee: Newly Discovered Harbours*, 3rd ed., 34–35.

60. Laney, "Geographical Aspects," 85.

Magdala, at the foot of Mount Arbel

account you read (*War* 2:635–637), during the battle of the First Jewish Revolt. He also hints that one of the other industries in the area was shipbuilding. The nickname could also derive from this activity.

In the recent past, two important discoveries have been made at Magdala. In February 1986, the now famous first century AD boat was found in the harbor. The boat has been variously called "The Jesus Boat," the "Disciples' Boat," or the "Josephus Boat." It is now on display at Kibbutz Ginossar.[61] Second, a first century AD synagogue has been excavated by the Franciscans near the town square.[62] Another synagogue was found in 2009 when the Christian Pilgrim Center of Magdala was being built. Perhaps this is the place where the Pharisees and Sadducees came to seek a "sign from heaven" from Jesus (Matt 16:1–4; Mark 8:11–13).

CONCLUSIONS

Jesus and his disciples traveled the Sea of Galilee by boat, going from one harbor to another. Recent climatic conditions have resulted in the exposure of many ancient harbors around the lake. This has given scholars fresh data with which to resolve old problems.

The harbor at Tabgha confirms that fishermen from Capernaum fished there during the winter months, lending evidence to the fact that this is where Jesus called his first disciples. The harbor at Gadara (Kibbutz Ha'on) adds credibility to the reading of "Gadara" in the Gospel narratives, specifically with respect to where the demoniac was healed and the swine entered the lake. Light is shed on the term "Dalmanutha" ("harbor") as a result of new finds at Magdala. Finally, I have proposed that the feeding of the five thousand took place near Moshav

---

61. Shelley Wachsman, "Galilee Boat: 2,000 Year Old Hull Recovered Intact," *BAR* 14.5 (1988): 18–33; idem, *The Excavations of an Ancient Boat in the Sea of Galilee (Lake Kinneret)*, 'Atiqot 19 (Jerusalem: Israel Antiquities Authority, 1990).

62. V. Corbo, "La citta romana di Magdala," *Studia Hierosolymitana in onore del P. Bellarmino Bagatti*, eds. I. Mancini and M. Piccirillo (Jerusalem: Francisca, 1976), 355–78; James Strange and Hershel Shanks, "Synagogue Where Jesus Preached Found in Capernaum," *BAR* 9.6 (1983): 29.

Almagor with the disciples departing from the Aish harbor and that the Kursi church has been misidentified. Rather than being the place where Jesus cast the demons into the swine, it is likely the place where Jesus fed the four thousand.

For the last two thousand years, pilgrims and tourists have been attracted to the Sea of Galilee to worship, understand, and appreciate the person and work of the Lord Jesus Christ. I trust these ideas will serve to draw us closer to him, encourage us to walk in his footsteps and be more like him, day by day.

BIBLIOGRAPHY

Corbo, V. "La citta romana di Magdala." Pages 365-68 in *Studia Hierosolymitana in onore del P. Bellarmino Bagatti*. Edited by I. Mancini and M. Piccirillo. Jerusalem: Franciscan Printing Press, 1976.

Dalman, Gustaf. *Sacred Sites and Ways: Studies in the Topography of the Gospels*. Translated by Paul P. Levertoff. London: Society for Promoting Christian Knowledge, 1935.

DeLuca, Stefano, and Anna Lena. "The Harbour of the City of Magdala/Taricheae on the Shores of the Sea of Galilee, from the Hellenistic to the Byzantine Times: New Discoveries and Preliminary Results." Pages 113-63 in vol. 1 of *Harbors and Harbor Cities in the Eastern Mediterranean from Antiquity to the Byzantine Period: Recent Discoveries and Current Approaches*. Edited by S. Sabine Ladstätter, Felix Pirson, and Thomas Schmidts. Istanbul: Österreichisches Archäologisches Institut, 2014.

Franz, Gordon. "The Greatest Fish Stories Ever Told." *Bible and Spade* 6.3 (1993): 92-96.

Johnson, Earl S. "Mark 5:1-20: The Other Side." *Irish Biblical Studies* 20 (1998): 57-74.

Laney, J. Carl. "Geographical Aspects of the Gospel." Pages 75-88 in *Essays in Honor of J. Dwight Pentecost*. Edited by Stanley D. Toussaint and Charles H. Dyer. Chicago: Moody, 1986.

Lightfoot, John. *A Commentary on the New Testament from the Talmud and Hebraica*. 4 vols. 1859. Reprint, Peabody, MA: Hendrickson, 1989.

Nun, Mendel. *Gergesa (Kursi): Site of a Miracle, Church and Fishing Village*. Kibbutz Ein Gev: Kinnereth Sailing Co., 1989.

———. *The Land of the Gadarenes: New Light on an Old Sea of Galilee Puzzle*. Kibbutz Ein Gev: Sea of Galilee Fishing Museum, 1996.

———. "Ports of Galilee. Modern Drought Reveals Harbors from Jesus' Time. *BAR* 25.4 (1999): 18-31.

———. *The Sea of Galilee and Its Fishermen in the New Testament*. Kibbutz Ein Gev: Kinnereth Sailing Co., 1989.

———. *Sea of Galilee: Newly Discovered Harbours from New Testament Days*. 3rd ed. Kibbutz Ein Gev: Kinnereth Sailing Co., 1992.

———. *Sea of Galilee: Newly Discovered Harbours from New Testament Days*. Kibbutz Ein Gev: Kinnereth Sailing Co., 1989.

———. *The Sea of Galilee: Water Levels, Past and Present*. Kibbutz Ein Gev: Kinnereth Sailing Co., 1991.

Pixner, Bargil. "The Miracle Church of Tabgha on the Sea of Galilee." *BA* 48 (1985): 196-206.

————. *Paths of the Messiah and Sites of the Early Church from Galilee to Jerusalem*. Translated by Keith Myrick, Sam Randall, and Miriam Randall. Edited by R. Riesner. San Francisco, CA: Ignatius, 2010.

Rahmani, Levi. *A Catalogue of Jewish Ossuaries in the Collections of the State of Israel*. Jerusalem: Israel Antiquities Authority, 1994.

Rainey, Anson F. Unpublished notes for Sources for Historical Geography. Jerusalem: American Institute of Holy Land Studies, 1973.

Shenhav, J. "Loaves and Fishes Mosaic Near Sea of Galilee Restored." *BAR* 10.3 (1984): 22–31.

Stepansky, Yosef, Oren Zingboym, and Anastasia Shapiro. "'Path Circling around the Kinneret,' Survey." *Hadashot Arkheologiyot: Excavations and Surveys in Israel* 123 (2011): n.p. http://www.hadashot-esi.org.il/report_detail_eng.aspx?id=1715&mag_id=118.

Strange, James, and Hershel Shanks. "Synagogue Where Jesus Preached Found in Capernaum." *BAR* 9.6 (1983): 24–31.

Tzaferis, Vassilios. *The Excavations of Kersi-Gergesa*. 'Atiqot 16. Jerusalem: Israel Department of Antiquities and Museums, 1983.

————. "A Pilgrimage to the Site of the Swine Miracle." *BAR* 15.2 (1989): 44–51.

Wachsmann, Shelley. "The Galilee Boat: 2,000 Year Old Hull Recovered Intact." *BAR* 14.5 (1988): 18–33.

————. *The Excavations of an Ancient Boat in the Sea of Galilee (Lake Kinneret)*. 'Atiqot 19. Jerusalem: Israel Antiquities Authority, 1990.

CHAPTER 23

THE FEEDINGS OF THE MULTITUDES: WHEN, WHERE, AND WHY?

Matt 14:13-21; 15:29-39; Mark 6:31-44;
8:1-10; Luke 9:11-17; John 6:1-13

Gordon Franz

KEY POINTS

- The Gospels record two events where Jesus fed a multitude of people by multiplying fish and loaves of bread.

- Before answering "why" Jesus performed two similar miracles it is necessary to answer "when" and "where" each miracle occured.

- With these ancillary questions resolved, it becomes clear that Jesus uses both feeding miracles to communicate that he is the "bread of life" for Jews and Gentiles alike.

All four Gospels record the miracle of the feeding of the five thousand (Matt 14:13-21; Mark 6:31-44; Luke 9:11-17; John 6:1-13), but only Matthew (15:29-39) and Mark (8:1-10) record the feeding of the four thousand. Are these feedings actually the same event, as some critical scholars suggest, or are they two separate events?[1] When did they take place

and why does the Lord Jesus perform the same miracle twice? Who are the recipients of Jesus' miracles? What actually took place on the hillside of Galilee and elsewhere?

The early pilgrims to the Holy Land commemorated both feedings (they assumed there were two feedings) at the site of Heptapegon (Greek for "seven

---

1. Bargil Pixner, "Was there One Multiplication Miracle or Two?" *BA* 48.4 (1985): 199. Unless otherwise indicated, Scripture quotations in this article are from the NKJV.

The Mosaic at the Church of the Multiplication

springs").[2] A pilgrim, tourist, or student of the Bible lands visiting Israel today might recognize the Greek name in the Arabic name Tabgha where the Benedictine monastery and church are situated.[3] Is this tradition accurate? The visitor to the site would view the mosaic floor from the Byzantine church that depicts a basket containing four loaves marked with crosses and two fish on each side.[4]

Ironically, the artisan who made this mosaic floor did not read his Bible or eat in any of the local fish restaurants while he was employed at the church. First, the Bible says there were five loaves of bread, not four. Second, the fish depicted on the floor has two dorsal fins. These are not indigenous to the Sea of Galilee! The musht fish (Arabic for "comb"), better known as the "Saint Peter's Fish," has only one dorsal fin.[5] Does this site square with the information given to us in the Bible? If not, how and why did the tradition move there? Is it possible to identify the site where Jesus performed both miracles?

THE FEEDING OF THE FIVE THOUSAND

WHEN DID THIS EVENT TAKE PLACE?

This is probably the easiest question to answer because the Gospels are quite clear on the matter. John 6:4 says, "Now the Passover, a feast of the Jews, was near."

---

2. Bargil Pixner, "The Miracle Church at Tabgha on the Sea of Galilee." *BA* 48.4 (1985): 196–206.

3. Bargil Pixner, *Paths of the Messiah and Sites of the Early Church from Galilee to Jerusalem*, trans. Keith Myrick, Sam Randall, and Miriam Randall, ed. R. Riesner (San Francisco, CA: Ignatius, 2010), 81.

4. Pixner, "Miracle Church at Tabgha," 196.

5. See J. Carl Laney, "Fishing the Sea of Galilee" on pg. 165.

Assuming an AD 30 crucifixion and resurrection for the Lord Jesus, the event took place in the spring of AD 29, right before Passover. Another time indicator in the Gospel accounts has to do with the grass. Matthew states that Jesus commands the multitudes to "sit down on the grass" (14:19). Mark says the grass is green (6:39), and John informs us there "was much grass in the place" (6:10). There is always lush vegetation in Galilee during the springtime, especially right before Passover. However, soon after Passover, the *hamsin* winds from the Arabian Desert blow, and the heat kills off all the flowers and grass (see Ps 103:15, 16; Isa 40:6–8; see infographic "Agricultural Cycle of the Levant/Palestine" on pg. 530). If the Synoptic Gospels are in chronological order at this point, then the feeding of the five thousand follows immediately after Jesus is informed of the beheading of John the Baptizer (Matt 14:22). It also took place after the Twelve who had been sent out two-by-two to the "lost sheep of the House of Israel" returned for their "debriefing." Jesus wanted to spend time alone with his disciples.

WHERE DID THIS EVENT TAKE PLACE?

This is the most difficult question to answer, and scholars continue to disagree on the answer. The Gospels give several clues that need to be reconciled. First, the Synoptic Gospel writers say it was a "deserted place" (Matt 14:13, 15; Mark 6:31, 32, 35; Luke 9:10, 12). Luke adds that this deserted place belonged to the city of Bethsaida (9:10). Second, John informs us that it was up on a mountain (6:3) and that after the feeding of the multitudes, the disciples "went down to the sea" (6:16). Third, Jesus and his disciples went out by boat to this place (Matt 14:13; Mark 6:32), and after the feeding of the multitude, Jesus immediately made his disciples get into their boat and head for the "other side" (Matt 14:22; Mark 6:45; John 6:16–17). The phrase "other side" generally refers to the eastern side of the Sea of Galilee, either Gaulanitis or the Decapolis, territory which is predominately populated by Gentiles.[6]

Mendel Nun, a retired fisherman from Kibbutz Ein Gev, has done an extensive survey of the ancient harbors and anchorages around the Sea of Galilee.[7] Due to abnormally low water levels at times, he located and documented sixteen ancient harbors and anchorages. It would make sense that Jesus and his fisherman-disciples would anchor their boat in one of these harbors. Fourth, the multitudes came from the surrounding cities on foot. It would be impossible for such a large number of people to cross the Jordan River in such a short time, especially during the spring flood stage. Thus the multitudes would have to be either from the east side of the Jordan River or the west. Fifth, after the disciples got into the boat to head for Bethsaida and the "other side" (Mark 6:45), a strong east wind that was "contrary," or "against them" (Matt 14:24; Mark 6:48), blew them off course to the land of the Gennessaret and Capernaum (Matt 14:34; Mark 6:53; John 6:17, 21). This

---

6. See Cyndi Parker, "Crossing to 'The Other Side' of the Sea of Galilee" on pg. 157.

7. Mendel Nun, *Sea of Galilee. Newly Discovered Harbours from New Testament Days*, 3rd ed. (Kibbutz Ein Gev: Kinnereth Sailing Co., 1992).

eastern wind storm, called a *sharkia*, suddenly blew off the Golan Heights.[8] This storm could not have been the westerly winter storm that brought rain because the disciples (most of whom were fishermen) were well aware of how to interpret the appearance of the sky (Matt 16:1–3): "When it is evening, you say, 'It will be fair weather; for the sky is red.' And in the morning, 'It will be stormy today, for the sky is red and threatening.'" The fisherman-disciples would not have, then, ventured out on the lake if they knew a westerly or northerly rain storm was coming (compare Prov 25:23). However, the easterly windstorms arise suddenly, unexpectedly, when the sky is clear. This is the storm the fishermen of the lake fear most.[9] These are the biblical requirements for the location of the feeding of the five thousand.

Gustaf Dalman,[10] the first director of the German Protestant Institute of Archaeology in Jerusalem (1900–1914), places the miraculous feeding at Mika' 'Edlo, between Kursi and Ein Gev, on the east side of the lake.[11] The late Father Bargil Pixner, a biblical geographer who lived at Tabgha, follows the traditional identification of this event and places it at Tabgha.[12] One of the earliest pilgrim's accounts for this event is by Egeria, a Spanish noblewoman (AD 383). She states,

Not far away from there [Capernaum] are some *steps* where the Lord stood. And in the same place by the sea is a grassy field with plenty of hay and many palm trees. By them are *seven springs*, each flowing strongly. And this is the field where the Lord fed the people with five loaves and the two fishes. In fact the stone on which the Lord placed the bread has now been made into an altar. People who go there take away small pieces of the stone to bring them prosperity, and they are very effective. Past the walls of this church goes the public highway on which the Apostle Matthew has his *place of custom*. Near there on a mountain is the cave to which the Savior climbed and spoke the Beatitudes.[13]

There are three geographical features that are known today. The "stone steps" are clearly visible today on the lake side of the Church of the Primacy. The "seven fountains" is a clear reference to Heptapegon. The "stone" is the altar area of the Church of the Multiplication of the Fish and the Loaves. Egeria points out that the "seat of custom" was next to the church; however, geographically Matthew would have had his custom house either in Capernaum or east

---

8. Mendel Nun, *The Sea of Galilee and Its Fishermen in the New Testament* (Kibbutz Ein Gev: Kinnereth Sailing Co., 1989), 54.

9. See Gordon Franz, "What Type of Storms Did Jesus Calm: Wind or Rain?" on pg. 175.

10. Marcel Serr, "Understanding the Land of the Bible," *Near Eastern Archaeology* 79.1 (2016): 27–35.

11. Gustaf Dalman, *Sacred Sites and Ways: Studies in the Topography of the Gospels*, trans. Paul P. Levertoff (London: Society for Promoting Christian Knowledge, 1935), 173.

12. Pixner, "Miracle Church at Tabgha."

13. John Wilkinson, *Egeria's Travels to the Holy Land* (Jerusalem: Ariel, 1981), 196–200.

of Capernaum toward Gaulanitis. The Sermon on the Mount is localized here as well. Even as early as the fourth century, several events from the Gospels were localized in one area. More than likely, this was done for the convenience of the pilgrims. The site was chosen because it was near the main highway, the seven springs would draw visitors because of its natural beauty and the abundance of drinking water, and the area was sanctified by the memory of Christ and the Twelve.[14] But was it the real site? The biggest drawback to this site, as well as for Dalman's suggested location, is that it does not belong to the territory of Bethsaida.

Locating Bethsaida

A short digression should be made to discuss the identification of Bethsaida. Geographers of the Bible have hotly debated the identification of this site and whether there was one Bethsaida or two.[15] Josephus describes Bethsaida Julias as the southern capital of Gaulanitis under the rule of Philip the Tetrarch (4 BC to AD 34).[16] The Gospel of John states that Bethsaida, the meaning of which is "house of the fisherman," was the home (apo, ἀπό) of Philip, one of the Twelve, and the birthplace (ek, ἐκ) of Andrew and Peter (1:44). He also states that Philip, the disciple, came from (apo, ἀπό) "Bethsaida in Galilee" (12:21). Is Bethsaida Julias the same city as Bethsaida in Galilee?

More than likely, Bethsaida Julias is located at el-Mesadiyye, just southeast of Tel el-Araj. According to Josephus, the border between Galilee (to the west) and Gaulanitis (to the east) is the Jordan River. Bethsaida in Galilee should be located at Khirbet el-'Araj, named after a sacred zizyphus tree, and is also east of the present day Jordan River. However, several scholars have suggested that the Jordan River ran east of the Khirbet el-'Araj during the Second Temple period, thus putting the site in Galilee. If this is the case, it has far reaching implications for the identification of the location for the feeding of the five thousand. Luke places the event in a deserted place belonging to Bethsaida. Assuming Bethsaida in Galilee is being referred to, then the event took place on one of the hills *west* of the Jordan River, rather than on the Plains of Bethsaida east of the river. I propose that the feeding of the five thousand took place in the vicinity of present day Moshav Almagor (6.5 kilometers northeast of Capernaum; 2.5 kilometers northwest of Tel el-Araj). (See "Ancient Harbors of the Sea of Galilee" map on pg. 221.)

The three major Jewish cities on the northwest shore of the Sea of Galilee are Capernaum, Chorizin, and Bethsaida of Galilee—called the "Evangelical Triangle" by Father Pixner.[17] These are the three cities that the Lord Jesus pronounces woes against (Matt 11:21–22; Luke 10:13).

---

14. Clemens Kopp, *The Holy Places of the Gospels* (New York: Herder and Herder, 1963), 218.

15. Gordon Franz, "Text and Tell: The Excavations of Bethsaida," *Archaeology in the Biblical World* 3.1 (1995): 6–11; R. Steven Notley, "Et-Tell Is *Not* Bethsaida," *Near Eastern Archaeology* 70.4 (2007): 220–30; Mendel Nun, "Has Bethsaida Finally Been Found?" *Jerusalem Perspective* 54 (1998): 12–31; Bargil Pixner, "Searching for the New Testament Site of Bethsaida," *BA* 48.4 (1985): 207–16.

16. Josephus, *Jewish Antiquities* 18.28 (LCL).

17. Pixner, *Paths of the Messiah*, 54–55.

A careful examination of a topographical map reveals some very interesting data to help understand these cities and the territories under their control. Between Capernaum and Bethsaida there are three wadis (dry river beds) that drain into the Sea of Galilee. Moving from west to east is Wadi Korazeh that turns into Wadi el-Wabdah as it drains into the lake. The middle wadi is Wadi en-Nashef (Nahal Cah), and finally west of Bethsaida is Wadi Zukluk (Nahal Or). The fishing grounds for Capernaum is Tabgha to the west of the city. The fishing grounds for Bethsaida of Galilee would be Khirbet 'Oshsheh (Aish) to the west. Both sites have ancient anchorages. The territory controlled by Capernaum would be everything west of Wadi Korazeh, including Tabgha. Chorazin would probably control the land between Wadi Korazeh and Wadi en-Nashef. Bethsaida would control the land from Wadi en-Nashef to the Jordan River. The elevated location of Moshav Almagor would be within the control of Bethsaida in Galilee and thus the "desert place."[18][19]

The biblical accounts have Jesus going up a mountain and there feeding the multitudes. The site of Moshav Almagor has a commanding view of the entire area and a clear view down to Bethsaida in Galilee. When Jesus saw the multitudes, he turned to Philip and asked him where one could buy bread. Philip, who was from Bethsaida of Galilee, would have known where all the bakeries were in the city just down the hill. Jesus probably met his disciples in Capernaum in order to take them by boat to this deserted place. Wherever the deserted place was, they would have landed in one of the harbors or anchorages along the shore. The Khirbet 'Oshsheh (Aish) anchorage would fit the topography well.[20] One could visualize the disciples walking down the hill to get to their boat that was left in the anchorage and head across the lake in an eastward direction.

Most of the people in the crowd that Jesus preached to and fed were Galilean Jews. For them to travel on foot to Almagor would not have been that difficult. If the multitude had to cross the Jordan River at flood stage in order to get to the east side, this would have been more difficult. Dalman did not think this was a difficulty. He recalled, "On Oct. 10, 1921, I saw that it was almost possible to cross over the Jordan dry-shod, just where it enters the lake. An absolutely dry bar lay before the mouth." It should be pointed out that the river would be low in October because the former rains had not begun, thus causing the river to overflow its banks (compare Matt 7:27; Luke 6:48, 49). Finally, Jesus commanded his disciples to get in the boat and head for Bethsaida, probably el-Mesadiyya, in an eastward direction to the "other side." The indication seems to be that they are headed eastward toward Gaulanitis, or southeastward toward the Decapolis area. This withdrawal would make good political sense. The crowd wanted to make Jesus king because of the miracle that he had performed (John 6:15). If word got back to Herod Antipas in Tiberias, he would send out a detachment of soldiers to arrest Jesus and his

---

18. See also Benjamin A. Foreman, "Jesus Heals a Blind Man Near Bethsaida" on pg. 270.

19. Mendel Nun, "The 'Desert' Place of Bethsaida," *Jerusalem Perspective* 53 (1997): 16–17, 37.

20. Nun, *Sea of Galilee. Newly Discovered Harbors*, 42.

disciples for insurrection. Only a few weeks before, Herod had John the Baptist beheaded because he did not like what he heard from him. The Lord Jesus, knowing his time was not yet come, wanted to avoid trouble and withdraw from Galilee. True, he was in Capernaum the next day (a Galilean city), but soon after, he takes off for Tyre and Sidon. The disciples headed in an eastward direction but were met with strong east winds off the Golan Heights. This wind blows them in the direction of the land of Gennesaret, of which Capernaum is the easternmost part.

THE FEEDING OF THE
FOUR THOUSAND

In order to answer the question "why" Jesus fed this multitude of five thousand, the "when" and "where" of the feeding of the four thousand should be addressed. The focus of the ministry of the Lord Jesus toward his disciples changed after the feeding of the five thousand. He wanted to spend time alone with his disciples in order to instruct them more fully and also to avoid the crowds. They traveled to Tyre and Sidon to escape the arm of Herod Antipas, but also to spend time together (Matt 15:21; Mark 7:24). After ministering to the Syro-Phoenician woman, they departed from the region and "came through the midst

of the region of the Decapolis to the Sea of Galilee" (Mark 7:31). There, the Lord Jesus performed a number of healing miracles for three days, primarily to a Gentile audience,[21] and they "glorified the God of Israel" (Matt 15:29-31; Mark 7:31-37). Toward the end of the third day the multitudes are fed with seven loaves of bread and a few small fish. This event takes place on the east side of the lake, but where?

Father Bargil Pixner places the feeding of the four thousand at Tel Hadar and has even put up a marker to commemorate the site.[22] This site, however, is north of the area of the Decapolis. The border between the Decapolis and Gaulanitis apparently was the Wadi Samak.[23] I propose that the feeding of the four thousand took place at the Kursi church and, in fact, that it is the event that the church commemorates, rather than the casting of the demons into the swine.[24]

There are several reasons for this suggestion. First, I have already suggested elsewhere that the demoniac event took place near the harbor of Gadara in the southeastern corner of the Sea of Galilee.[25][26] The ancient harbor is located near Tel Samra on the property of Kibbutz Ha'on.[27] Second, there is no indication from the inscriptions or the mosaics on the floor of the Kursi church that

---

21. More than likely these Gentiles had heard about the miracles that the Lord Jesus had done from the demoniac of Gadara. The Lord Jesus had commanded him to tell his family and friends what great things the Lord / God had done for him (Mark 5:19; Luke 8:39).

22. Pixner, *Paths of the Messiah*, 68.

23. Dalman, *Sacred Sites and Ways*, 170.

24. Vassilios Tzaferis, *The Excavations of Kursi-Gergesa*, 'Atiqot 16 (Jerusalem: Israel Department of Antiquities and Museums, 1983), 1–65.

25. See also Todd Bolen, "Where Did the Possessed-Pigs Drown?" on pg. 196.

26. Gordon Franz, "Ancient Harbors of the Sea of Galilee," *Archaeology and Biblical Research* 4.4 (1991): 114–16.

27. Nun, *Sea of Galilee: Newly Discovered Harbours*, 20–23.

it commemorates the demoniac event.[28] Third, the early church sources and pilgrim accounts just state that the demoniac event took place on the east side of the lake, but are not specific as to where it was. Fourth, the mosaics at the Kursi church seem to hint that this is where Jesus fed the four thousand.

The mosaic floor is partially intact. Still visible are some of the plants and animals. Most of the animals were destroyed during an Islamic iconoclastic craze yet some can still be discerned. The fish that were partially destroyed interested me the most.[29] Mendel Nun identified them as barbell fish, yet the Gospel narrative states they were "small fish," most likely the sardines that Wadi Samak is noted for. The other thing that interested me was the baskets.[30] They contained handles which were mentioned in the Gospel narratives of the feeding of the four thousand (Matt 15:37; 16:10; Mark 8:8, 20). One basket is similar to the basket on the mosaic floor at Tabgha.[31] Unfortunately this floor was vandalized a few years ago. If this proposal is accepted, then the church commemorates the feeding of the four thousand rather than the demoniac event.

To the southeast of the basilica, on the slopes of the Wadi Samak, is an ancient tower. According to the excavator, this is the "chapel of the miracle of the swine."[32] Some have suggested this was built over the tombs that the demoniacs lived in. Nothing in the chapel indicates to whom or what it was dedicated. If my suggestion is accepted, it could possibly be dedicated to the healing events that took place just prior to the feeding of the multitudes. The text states that Jesus "went up on the mountain and sat down there." For the convenience of the pilgrims, this chapel was placed just above on the slopes of the mountain. Kursi, interestingly enough, means "armchair, chair," a place for sitting down.

THE PURPOSE OF THE FEEDING OF THE FIVE THOUSAND

There are at least three reasons why Jesus performed this miracle. The primary reason was to teach the disciples a lesson in faith. Several months before this event, the Lord Jesus had sent out his disciples on their own for the first time to preach the gospel to the "lost sheep of the House of Israel." He gave them authority over unclean spirits, the power to heal diseases, and to raise the dead (Matt 10:8). Now they were returning from their preaching tour and Jesus wanted to hear what they did and the response they received to the gospel message. This time was sort of a "debriefing" session. As the Master Teacher, the Lord Jesus wanted to reinforce the lessons taught and learned. He challenged the disciples to continue using the power he gave them. Here was a teaching moment. The multitudes that were gathered needed to be fed. Yet it seems the disciples had a "laid back" attitude (i.e., "Well Lord, we're with you now; we'll let *you* do the miracles!"). Jesus wanted them to get involved. After the

---

28. Tzaferis, *Excavations of Kursi*, 23–29.

29. Tzaferis, *Excavations of Kursi*, Plate 11.1.

30. Tzaferis, *Excavations of Kursi*, Plate 10.5.

31. Tzaferis, *Excavations of Kursi*, Plate 11.4.

32. Tzaferis, *Excavations of Kursi*, 49–51.

supper, there were twelve baskets of left-over bread picked up, one basket by each disciple. The Lord Jesus may have done this to convict each of the disciples of their lack of faith and to show them his power and provision.

The second reason was to provide a setting for the gospel to be preached the next day in the synagogue in Capernaum. John informs us that he wrote his Gospel for the specific purpose of setting forth seven (or eight, depending on how you count them) "signs" (miracles) to demonstrate that "Jesus is the Christ, the Son of God, and that by believing you might have life through His name" (John 20:30–31). The crowd wanted to make Jesus king because He provided for their physical needs. The next day in the Shabbat service at the synagogue in Capernaum the Lord Jesus expounded the real meaning of the miracle: he was the "Bread of life" (John 6:35, 48).

The final reason was to enhance the understanding of the disciples (Mark 8:21). Jesus appears to be trying to teach "kosher" disciples, who were always reluctant to have any association with Gentiles, that salvation was for all, both Jews and Gentiles. Origen may have had a point when he allegorized the two accounts in this manner. He suggested that the feeding of the five thousand was to a Jewish audience, and the twelve baskets taken up represented the twelve tribes of Israel. Origen would be geographically correct if the feeding of the five thousand took place at Moshav Almagor. The feeding of the four thousand took place in the Decapolis area (assuming Kursi is the proper location). The seven baskets that were taken up would represent, according to Origen, the seven Gentile nations in the land when Joshua entered it (Deut 7:1; Acts 13:19).[33]

If Origen is correct, the lesson is clear: the offer of salvation is for all, both Jews and Gentiles. The disciples of the Lord Jesus should remove the prejudices they have toward those who are not like themselves and share the gospel with all. The gospel was then, and is now, the good news of salvation for any and all who put their trust in the Lord Jesus Christ as their Savior, because he was the one who died for all their sins and rose from the dead three days later to show sin had been paid for in full. God offers his righteousness to any and all who trust the Lord Jesus, and him alone, and not their own works of righteousness (1 Cor 15:1–4; Eph 2:8–9; Phil 3:9).[34]

BIBLIOGRAPHY

Dalman, Gustaf. *Sacred Sites and Ways: Studies in the Topography of the Gospels.* Translated by Paul P. Levertoff. London: Society for Promoting Christian Knowledge, 1935.

Franz, Gordon. "Ancient Harbors of the Sea of Galilee." *Archaeology and Biblical Research* 4.4 (1991): 111–21.

———. "Text and Tell: The Excavations at Bethsaida." *Archaeology in the Biblical World* 3.1 (1995): 6–11.

Josephus. *Jewish Antiquities, Books 18–19.* Translated by Louis H. Feldman. LCL. Cambridge, MA: Harvard University, 1965.

---

33. Pixner, *Paths of the Messiah*, 69.

34. See John A. Beck, "The Geography of Forgiveness" on pg. 258.

Kopp, Clemens. *The Holy Places of the Gospels.* New York: Herder and Herder, 1963.

Notley, R. Steve. "Et-Tell Is Not Bethsaida," *Near Eastern Archaeology* 70.4 (2007) 220–30.

Nun, Mendel. "The 'Desert' of Bethsaida." *Jerusalem Perspective* 53 (Oct–Dec 1997): 16–17, 37.

———. "Has Bethsaida Finally Been Found?" *Jerusalem Perspective* 54 (1998): 12–31.

———. *The Sea of Galilee and Its Fishermen in the New Testament.* Kibbutz Ein Gev: Kinnereth Sailing Co., 1989.

———. *Sea of Galilee: Newly Discovered Harbours From New Testament Days.* 3rd ed. Kibbutz Ein Gev: Kinnereth Sailing Co., 1992.

———. "Ports of Galilee: Modern Drought Reveals Harbors from Jesus' Time." *BAR* 25.4 (1999): 18–34, 64.

Pixner, Bargil. "The Miracle Church of Tabgha on the Sea of Galilee." *BA* 48.4 (1985): 196–206.

———. *Paths of the Messiah and Sites of the Early Church from Galilee to Jerusalem.* Translated by Keith Myrick, Sam Randall, and Miriam Randall. Edited by R. Riesner. San Francisco: Ignatius, 2010.

———. "Searching for the New Testament Site of Bethsaida." *BA* 48.4 (1985): 207–16.

———. "Was There One Multiplication Miracle or Two?" *BA* 48.4 (1985): 199.

Serr, Marcel. "Understanding the Land of the Bible: Gustaf Dalman and the Emergence of the German Exploration of Palestine." *Near Eastern Archaeology* 79.1 (2016): 27–35.

Tzaferis, Vassilios. *The Excavations of Kursi-Gergesa.* 'Atiqot 16. Jerusalem: Israel Department of Antiquities and Museums, 1983.

Wilkinson, John. *Egeria's Travel to the Holy Land.* Rev. ed. Jerusalem: Ariel Publishing, 1981.

CHAPTER 24

JESUS' JOURNEY INTO GENTILE TERRITORIES

Mark 7:24-31; Matt 15:21-29[1]

Emily J. Thomassen

KEY POINTS

- Some question the accuracy of Mark's records of Jesus' journey from Tyre to the Sea of Galilee: (1) it is far from the most direct route, and (2) it puts Jesus in an area where Jews and Gentiles had a historically strained relationship.

- However, Mark's use of geographic references does more than point to a place; it demonstrates that Jesus' kingdom message and miracles were not just for the Jews, but for the Gentiles too.

- Although the majority of Jesus' ministry took place within the traditional borders of Israel, among a predominately Jewish population, Jesus' journeys to Gentile territory were meant to prepare the disciples to take the gospel to the ends of the earth.

MARK'S STRATEGIC USE OF GEOGRAPHY IN NARRATIVE

Both Matthew and Mark record Jesus' journey to the region of Tyre, his encoun-

ter with a Gentile woman there, and his return to the Sea of Galilee (Matt 15:21-29; Mark 7:24-31).[2] The itinerary in Mark 7:31 describes Jesus returning from the

---

1. While both Matthew and Mark record the account of Jesus' journey to the region of Tyre, this essay is focused on the itinerary described by Mark, including a discussion of places mentioned in 7:24-31: the region of Tyre (*ta horia Tyrou*, τὰ ὅρια Τύρου), Sidon (*Sidōnos*, Σιδῶνος), the Sea of Galilee (*tēn thalassan tēs Galilaias*, τὴν θάλασσαν τῆς Γαλιλαίας), and the Decapolis (*horiōn Dekapoleōs*, ὁρίων Δεκαπόλεως), while making reference to significant points of comparison with the account in Matthew.

2. Matthew reports that Jesus went to the district of Tyre and Sidon (*ta merē Tyrou kai Sidōnos*, τὰ μέρη Τύρου καὶ Σιδῶνος; Matt 15:21) while Mark specifies the region of Tyre (*ta horia*

region of Tyre by "going through Sidon" (ēlthen dia Sidōnos, ἦλθεν διὰ Σιδῶνος) to the Sea of Galilee, then "into the midst of the region of the Decapolis" (ana meson tōn horiōn Dekapoleōs, ἀνὰ μέσον τῶν ὁρίων Δεκαπόλεως). This route raises interpretive questions. Since this is not the most direct route from Tyre to the Sea, some have suggested Mark's geography is confused, hypothetical, or impossible to reconstruct.[3] The problematic nature of the itinerary has led some interpreters to suggest Mark was not a native of Palestine.[4] However, before jumping to conclusions about Mark's knowledge and use of geography, one must examine the significance of place names within a narrative context to understand the significance of Jesus' journey through multiple Gentile regions.

Mark's mention of place names is purposeful and intended to illicit a response from the reader. In biblical narrative, authors often mention place names in order to communicate a message of theological importance.[5] Therefore, one must be careful with arguments that suggest Mark was confused or not purposeful in his writing. Instead, one should determine the possible geographical and literary significance of the description of

the route. It is of vital importance that a reader of the Gospels pays attention to how geographic references are utilized by the author. As Shimon Bar-Efrat states, "places in the narrative are not merely geographical facts, but are to be regarded as literary elements in which fundamental significance is embodied."[6] In the ancient world, authors strategically used, reused, and nuanced geographic references in order to impact the reader.[7] The Gospel authors were able to use geography as a narrative tool to inform their readers.[8]

Mark is deeply aware of the practice of symbolic use of geography in narrative and in the genre of rewritten Scripture. Mark's use of geographic references demonstrates that Jesus' kingdom message and miracles were not just for the Jews, but for the Gentiles as well. Jesus' decision to travel out of the comfortable corridors of Judaism and into Gentile territory may have been regarded by his followers as strange or unconventional. Furthermore, Jesus' movement beyond the boundaries of Israel parallels the ministry of the ninth century BC prophet Elijah. During a famine in Israel, Elijah performed a miracle for a Phoenician woman at Zarephath in the region of Tyre and Sidon (1 Kgs 17:8–16; compare

---

Tyrou, τὰ ὅρια Τύρου; Mark 7:24). Mark calls the woman a Greek Syrophoenician (Hellēnis, Syrophoinikissa, Ἑλληνίς, Συροφοινίκισσα; 7:26), but Matthew identifies her using the Old Testament term Canaanite (Matt 15:22).

3. C. S. Mann, Mark: A New Translation with Introduction and Commentary, AB 27 (Garden City, NY: Doubleday, 1986), 322.

4. Joel Marcus, Mark 1–8, AB 27 (New York: Doubleday, 2000), 472.

5. Anson F. Rainey and R. Steven Notley, The Sacred Bridge (Jerusalem: Carta, 2006), 361.

6. Shimon Bar-Efrat, Narrative Art in the Bible (Sheffield: Almond, 1989), 194.

7. Tremper Longman III, "Biblical Narrative," in A Complete Literary Guide to the Bible, eds. Leland Ryken and Tremper Longman III (Grand Rapids: Zondervan, 1993), 75.

8. When comparing miracle accounts and the reaction of the crowds present, one will notice that often people's reaction to a miracle or their interaction with Jesus will vary depending on the setting of the pericope.

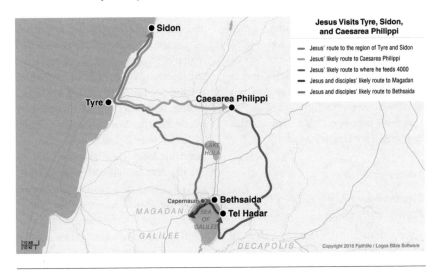

Luke 4:25-26). Jesus' miracle in the region of Tyre sends a similar, and perhaps controversial, message: the salvation of God is not only for the Israelites but also for Gentiles.

JESUS' JOURNEY TO TYRE AND RETURN TO THE SEA OF GALILEE

CONTEXT: CONFLICT IN GALILEE PRIOR TO JESUS' JOURNEY INTO GENTILE TERRITORY

Prior to his journey into the region of Tyre, Jesus faced opposition in Galilee from the Pharisees and scribes who had come from Jerusalem (Mark 7:1). These religious leaders had heard about Jesus' controversial teaching and had come from Jerusalem to question Jesus' interpretation of the law.[9] The specific topic of their concern was the issue of ritual cleaning before a meal (Mark 7:1-5). Jesus' statement—"There is nothing outside the man which can defile him if it goes into him, but the things which proceed out of

the man are what defile the man" (Mark 7:15 NASB)—brought great opposition from the religious leaders (Mark 7:5, 18). Perhaps the leaders' opposition and their failure to understand compelled Jesus to decide to journey deep into Gentile territory: first to the region of Tyre, then to Sidon, and finally to the region of the Decapolis before returning to the Sea of Galilee. Jesus' intention was to drive his lesson home for the disciples by taking them on an extensive trip through Gentile territory rather than bringing them back to their Galilean home base by the shortest and most direct route. A longer trip through threatening or unfamiliar Gentile regions outside of the Jewish homeland would give the disciples more time to think about the implications of Jesus' miracles and teachings.

THE PLAIN OF GENNASARET

Before Jesus traveled to the region of Tyre, the last place Mark mentions is Gennesaret (Mark 6:53). The plain of

---

9. Paul Wright, *Rose Then and Now Bible Map Atlas with Biblical Background and Culture* (Torrance, CA: Rose Publishing, 2012), 198.

Gennesaret is a fertile plain 3.5 miles (5.6 km) long and 1.5 miles (2.4 km) wide on the northwest shore of the Sea of Galilee between Capernaum and Tiberias. Presumably, it was from this plain on the northwestern shores of the Sea of Galilee that Jesus set out on his journey to the region of Tyre (Mark 7:24).

THE REGION OF TYRE

Tyre and Sidon in the Manuscript Tradition

Some manuscripts of Mark 7:24 contain the addition of the word Sidon, describing the place Jesus went to as "the region of Tyre *and Sidon*" rather than simply the region of Tyre.[10] There are two possible explanations for this textual addition. The longer reading can be explained by haplography if *kai Sidōnos* (καὶ Σιδῶνος) was inadvertently omitted due to the repetition of another *kai* (καί) that immediately follows (*Tyrou kai Sidōnos. Kai eiselthōn*, Τύρου καὶ Σιδῶνος. Καὶ εἰσελθὼν; Mark 7:24). However, as Bruce Metzger suggests, it is more probable that the longer reading came about by virtue of assimilation to Matt 15:21 and Mark 7:31, which both mention Tyre and Sidon.[11]

Arrival to the Region of Tyre

When Jesus arrived in the region of Tyre, Mark does not specify whether Jesus entered the city limits of Tyre or remained outside of the city. Both Tyre and Sidon had extensive territories during the New Testament period. The region of Tyre went as far inland as the city Cadasa in the hills of Upper Galilee overlooking the Huleh valley. Sidon had a common border with Damascus, far inland from the Mediterranean coast.[12]

Jesus' journey to Tyre is not the first time Mark records Jesus entering Gentile territory. Prior to his journey to Tyre, Jesus had been in the region of the Decapolis, where he was asked to leave after casting the demon out of the Gerasene demoniac (Mark 5:1–20). Perhaps his desire to remain unnoticed in the region of Tyre was based on the prior negative response in the Decapolis.

Upon arriving in the region of Tyre, attempting to remain unnoticed, Jesus entered a house (Mark 7:24). Mark does not specify whether its occupants were Jewish or Gentile. Josephus' writings indicate that there may have been a substantial Jewish population in Tyre. When the Jewish revolt against Rome broke out in AD 66, Josephus records that the people of Tyre put a great number of Jews in their city to death and kept a great number in prison (*War* 2.478). This would indicate there may have been Jews living in Tyre during the New Testament period. Mark does not specify whether Jesus entered the house of a Jewish family who had chosen to live in Gentile territory, outside the comforts of Jewish Galilee.

---

10. Marcus, *Mark 1–8*, 462.

11. Bruce M. Metzger, *A Textual Commentary on the Greek New Testament* (New York: United Bible Societies, 1971), 85; Marcus, *Mark 1–8*, 462. See note 2 above. Perhaps Sidon was added to help make sense of the geographical peculiarity of the return trip from Tyre to Sidon to the Sea of Galilee, which will be discussed below.

12. Yohanan Aharoni, Michael Avi-Yonah, Anson F. Rainey, Ze'ev Safrai, and R. Steven Notley, *The Carta Bible Atlas*, 5th ed. (Jerusalem: Carta, 2011), 178.

*Socio-economic Relationship
between Tyre and Galilee*

The inhabitants of Tyre had a historically rocky relationship with the Jews of
Galilee and Judea.[13] The Jewish historian
Flavius Josephus records that in 40 BC
Marion of Tyre marched into Galilee and
established three strongholds with garri-
sons there, but he was ousted by Herod
the Great soon after (*Ant.* 14.298–99; *War*
1.238).

A number of sources suggest tension
between the Phoenician coast and Galilee
during the period prior to the New
Testament. The prophet Joel condemns
Tyre and Sidon for selling the people of
Judah and Jerusalem to the Greeks (HB
livne hayyewanim; LXX *tois huiois tōn
Hellēnōn*; Joel 4:4–6 [Engl. Joel 3:4–6]). The
notion that Phoenicians played a role in
the buying and selling of Jewish slaves
is supported by 2 Macc 8:11, which indicates that the Phoenicians played a role as
intermediaries in the slave trade during
the Hellenistic period. Furthermore,
during the Ptolemaic period, slaves
bought in Palestine were sold in Tyre
in what Martin Hengel suggests was a
highly profitable business.[14]

Tyre's economic development
impacted Jews living in Galilee. Gerd
Theissen suggests that the Tyrians put
an economic strain on the Galileans and
that there was bad blood between them.[15]

Large quantities of minted coins from
Tyre have been found in settlements in
Galilee and throughout Palestine. Tyre
played a significant role in the political
and economic situation in Palestine, but
the degree of Tyrian involvement in the
Galilean economy remains uncertain.[16]
According to Acts 12:20, Herod Agrippa
I supplied food to Tyre and Sidon. Much
of the produce of Jewish Galilee may
have ended up in Gentile Tyre, the main
urban area near Galilee. This may have
left Jewish Galilean peasants to go hungry.

These sources highlight the tension
between inhabitants of Tyre and inhabitants of Galilee and provide important
context for the discussion Jesus had with
the Syro-Phoenician woman. Perhaps
Jesus' statement about the unfairness of
taking bread from the mouths of (Jewish)
children and giving it to (Gentile) dogs
reflected the socio-economic tension
between Tyre and Galilee.[17]

THE "SEA OF GALILEE"

The name "Sea of Galilee" in English
refers to a fresh water lake in the region
of northern Israel that was known by
several names in ancient sources. Just as
English speakers must decide whether to
call a large body of water a sea or a lake,
New Testament authors writing in Greek
had to choose whether to refer to the body
of water as a *thalassa* (θάλασσα, "sea") or

---

13. Douglas R. Edwards, "Tyre," *ABD* 6:690–92. See section D, "Tyre in the Greco-Roman Period."

14. Martin Hengel, *Judaism and Hellenism: Studies in their Encounter in Palestine during the Early Hellenistic Period*, vol. 1 (London: SCM Press, 1974), 34, 41–42.

15. Gerd Theissen, *The Gospels in Context: Social and Political History in the Synoptic Tradition* (Minneapolis: Fortress, 1992), 72–80.

16. Richard A. Hanson, *Tyrian Influence in Upper Galilee*, Meiron Excavation Project 2 (Cambridge, MA: American Schools of Oriental Research, 1980).

17. Marcus, *Mark 1–8*, 462.

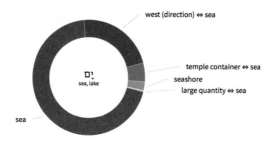

Bible Word Study: Biblical Hebrew *yam*

a *limnē* (λίμνη, "lake").[18] Matthew, Mark, and John all use the phrase *hē thalassa tēs Galilaias* (ἡ θάλασσα τῆς Γαλιλαίας; Matt 4:18; 15:29; Mark 1:16; 3:7; 7:31) for the Sea of Galilee. John adds further specification that the sea was also known as the Sea of Tiberias (*tēs thalassēs tēs Galilaias tēs Tiberiados*, τῆς θαλάσσης τῆς Γαλιλαίας τῆς Τιβεριάδος; John 6:1), identifying it in reference to the city of Tiberias, a town built by Herod Antipas on the western shore of the Sea of Galilee. Near the end of the Gospel, John refers to the Sea of Galilee as simply the Sea of Tiberius (*tēs thalassēs tēs Tiberiados*, τῆς θαλάσσης τῆς Τιβεριάδος; John 21:1). Luke is the only Gospel to use the toponym *limnē Gennēsaret* (λίμνη Γεννησαρέτ, "the Lake of Gennesaret", Luke 5:1-2; 8:23, 33).

The decision of Matthew, Mark, and John to use *thalassa* (θάλασσα) instead of *limnē* (λίμνη) may reflect their knowledge of the Septuagint and their preference to use the terminology employed by the Septuagint translator. In the Hebrew Bible, the "Sea of Galilee" is known as the Sea of Kinnereth (*yam-kinnereth*; Num 34:11; Josh 13:27; also spelled *yam kinroth*; Josh 12:3). In Hebrew there is only one word for a large body of water: *yam*, used both for bodies of saltwater and bodies of freshwater. The Septuagint translators could have used either *thalassa* or *limnē*, but they went with *thalassa* or "sea" (*thalassa Chenara* [θαλάσσα Χεναρα] in Num 34:11 and *thalassa Chenereth* [θαλάσσα Χενερεθ] in Josh 12:3; 13:27).

The Greek name *Gennēsaret* (Γεννησαρέτ, "Gennesaret") preserves the Hebrew name Kinnereth and is likely the oldest name for the Sea of Galilee.[19] Luke's use of *limnē Gennēsaret* closely parallels the name used by Josephus, who also referred to the body of water as *limnē* rather than *thalassa*. Josephus called it the Lake of Gennesaret (*War* 2.573; *Ant.* 5.84; 18:28) and noted that was also the name used by the local population (*War* 3.463). Josephus also used the name known from the Gospel of John, Tiberias, but with the descriptor

---

18. In Greek, *thalassa*, θάλασσα typically refers to a sea of salt water, frequently the Mediterranean Sea (Acts 10:6; 32; 17:14; 27:30, 38, 40) or the Red Sea (Acts 7:36; Heb 11:29; 1 Cor 10:1). On the other hand, *limnē* (λίμνη) often refers to an inland body of water, either a lake, (Luke 5:1-2; 8:23, 33), or a stagnant pool or marsh. See LSJ, s.v. λιμναγενής for a more thorough description. In addition to Luke, *limnē* is used in Revelation to refer to the apocalyptic lake of fire (Rev 19:20; 20:10, 14-15; 21:8).

19. Seán Freyne, "Galilee, Sea of," *ABD* 2:900.

lake (*Tiberiada limnēs*, Τιβεριάδα λίμνης; *War* 3.57; 4.456) rather than *thalassa* (John 6:1; 21:1). The Sea of Galilee is also known by the name Gennesar in 1 Macc 11:67 (*to hydōr tou Gennēsar*, τὸ ὕδωρ τοῦ Γεννησαρ) and in the writings of Pliny, who notes that some call it lake of Taricheae (*Natural History* 5.71). It is likely that Luke, Josephus, Pliny, and the author of 1 Macc all preserve the older name of the sea and that Mark's use of the term Sea of Galilee attempts to preserve the Hebrew word *yam* alongside an updated toponym, Galilee.[20]

THE DECAPOLIS

The term Decapolis, which means "Ten Cities" in Greek, refers to a group of Hellenistic towns on the east and southeast side of the Sea of Galilee. The cities were all located east of the Rift Valley except for Scythopolis (Beth Shean). The Decapolis cities consisted of a group of cities from Damascus in the north to Philadelphia in the south. During the New Testament era, the Decapolis cities were under Roman control and were inhabited by a predominately Gentile population.

The creation of the Decapolis is often attributed to the conquest of Alexander the Great in 332 BC and the arrival of Greek Hellenistic influence. Elsewhere the origin of the Decapolis is ascribed to Pompey in 63 BC as part of his annexation of the region of Syria-Palestine on behalf of Rome.[21] Prior to Pompey, this region had been fought over by the Ptolemies, Seleucids, Jews, and Nabateans. The Roman intervention led by Pompey may have brought relief for the troubled Decapolis cities, ending the anarchy in

the region that resulted from local power struggles (see map "Kingdom of Herod the Great" on pg. 531).

The oldest known usage of the term Decapolis is found in the Synoptic Gospels, once in Matthew (2:25) and twice in Mark (5:20, 7:31). Matthew specifies that crowds from the Decapolis followed Jesus, noting that the followers came "from Galilee and the Decapolis and Jerusalem and Judea and from beyond the Jordan" (Matt 4:25 NASB). Mark mentions Jesus' journey into the Decapolis on two occasions. First, Jesus was on the other side of the lake, in the country of the Gerasenes (Mark 5:1) when he healed a possessed man, who went and proclaimed in the Decapolis what Jesus had done for him (Mark 5:20). Second, on Jesus' return trip from Tyre, he went through the middle of the region of the Decapolis on his way to the Sea of Galilee (Mark 7:31).

The term Decapolis, "ten cities," is also known in extra-biblical sources. Pliny the Elder's *Natural History* contains the longest known passage about the Decapolis:

Adjoining Judaea on the side of Syria is the region of the Decapolis, so called from the number of its towns, though not all writers keep to the same list; most however include Damascus, with its fertile water-meadows that drain the river Chrysorrhoe, Philadelphia, Raphana (all these three withdrawn towards Arabia), Scythopolis (formerly Nysa, after Father Liber's nurse, whom he buried there) where a colony of Scythians are settled; Gadara, past

---

20. Rainey and Notley, *Sacred Bridge*, 352–53.

21. For further discussion on this topic, see Jean-Paul Rey-Coquais, "Decapolis," trans. by Stephen Rosoff, *ABD* 2:116–21.

which flows the river Yarmuk; Hippo mentioned already, Dion, Pella rich with its waters, Galasa, Canatha.[22]

Pliny mentions that in his day there was some uncertainty about the exact number and list of cities in the Decapolis, but he gives what he believes to be the most correct list.

Ptolemy, a source from the second-century AD, provides a list of eighteen Decapolis towns consisting of nine of the ten towns mentioned by Pliny with the addition of nine new towns.[23] It is therefore difficult to establish an exact list of ten cities of the Decapolis.

Josephus mentions the Decapolis four times in his writings, three times in *Life* and once in *Jewish War*.[24] In *Life*, Josephus describes the situation in Galilee during the first Jewish Revolt, writing that a segment of the Galilean Jewish population made war against the Decapolis and ordered their villages to be burnt. Residents of the Decapolis in turn complained to Vespasian for protection against Jewish rioting in their villages.[25]

Archaeological excavations carried out in a number of Decapolis cities shed considerable light on individual towns of the region, which are distinguished from neighboring towns by their Hellenistic character.[26] The Decapolis cities were home to Greek cults and divinities, sanctuaries, monuments, porticoed streets, and theaters. Although the shared architectural features may have given the cities a feeling of shared culture, there is little evidence that they were a unified league of cities.[27]

In the Gospels, Jesus is only described as being in the region of the Decapolis, never in a specific city of the Decapolis. Perhaps there were real or perceived hostilities between the Galilean Jews and the Gentiles of the Decapolis already during the period when Jesus and the disciples visited the region.

JESUS' RETURN ITINERARY FROM TYRE TO GALILEE (MARK 7:31)

As noted above, Mark's description of Jesus' return from Tyre to the shores of the Sea of Galilee raises interpretive questions because it is not the most direct route from Tyre to the Sea of Galilee. Mark describes that Jesus and the disciples' initial route took them from Tyre north through Sidon, the opposite direction of the Sea of Galilee from Tyre. Then they went into the midst of the Decapolis, which meant they went east, past the Sea of Galilee and across the Rift Valley. One author suggests Mark's itinerary "is like

---

22. Pliny, *Natural History* 5.74 (Rackham, LCL).

23. Ptolemy, *Geography* 5.14, 22. The nine additional cities listed by Ptolemy that are not listed by Pliny are Heliopolis, Abila, Saana, Hina, Abila Lysanius, Capitolias, Edrei, Gadora, and Samulis. Of the ten cities listed by Pliny, only Raphana is missing from Ptolemy's list. However, some consider Raphana to be identical with Capitolias. For further discussion, see S. Thomas Parker, "The Decapolis Reviewed," *JBL* 94 (1975): 439n11.

24. Josephus specified that Scythopolis, on the west side of the Jordan River, was the largest of the Decapolis cities (*War* 3.446).

25. Josephus, *Life* 341–42.

26. Rey-Coquais, "Decapolis," 119; Parker, "Decapolis Reviewed," 437–41.

27. Parker, "Decapolis Reviewed," 440.

going from Chicago to New York by way of Minneapolis and Toronto."[28]

A more direct route from Tyre to the Sea of Galilee would have been south from Tyre to Ptolemais and east to Magdala (Taricheae) through the finger of the Beth Netofa Valley. Another direct route from Tyre to the Sea of Galilee runs southeast from Tyre through the hills of Upper Galilee directly to the Sea. Neither of these direct options includes Sidon or the Decapolis.

In an attempt to understand Mark's supposed mix-up, some suggest that this point of geographic confusion may stem from Mark's awareness of the usual ordering of the city names as found in other texts: first Tyre followed by Sidon (LXX Jer 47:4; Joel 3:4; Zech 9:2; Matt 11:21; Acts 12:20). This conventional ordering may have led Mark to incorrectly list Sidon after Tyre, wrongly suggesting that Jesus traveled through Sidon after being in the region of Tyre on his way back to the Sea.[29] If this is the case, then Mark did not intend to describe Jesus as heading north, the opposite direction of the Sea of Galilee, after his visit with the Greek Syro-Phoenician woman in the region of Tyre. However, there are other considerations to keep in mind when analyzing the logic behind the itinerary. Did Jesus decide to journey back through Gentile territory in order to emphasize to his followers that his ministry was also directed towards Gentile populations?

Some have noted that Mark's itinerary put Jesus in the neighborhood of Markan Christianity. Acts 21:3–7 describes the Christian community in the region of Tyre and Sidon. Damascus, which Pliny lists among the cities of the Decapolis (*Natural History* 5.16.74), was known as an important Christian center.[30] Gerd Theissen has argued Mark may have deliberately constructed an itinerary for Jesus through Gentile areas surrounding Galilee based on the locations of Christian communities known to Mark in his own day.[31] Jesus' visit to the Gentile region of Tyre and Sidon may function as a foreshadowing of the movement of the gospel from Jerusalem to Judea, Samaria, and the ends of the earth (Acts 1:8).

The itinerary in Mark 7:31 may represent Mark's attempt to do justice to all the information known to him while depicting Jesus' inclusion of all people. Mark's use of geography emphasizes Jesus' mission to the Gentiles. While on earth, Jesus' journeys to Gentile territory was meant to prepare the disciples to take the gospel to the ends of the earth.

JESUS' TRAVELS IN GALILEE AS PREPARATION FOR THE SPREAD OF THE GOSPEL

"But you will receive power when the Holy Spirit comes on you; and you will be my witnesses in Jerusalem, and in all Judea and Samaria, and to the ends of the earth" (Acts 1:8 NIV). In Jesus' last recorded words to his disciples before his ascension, he outlined the progression of the gospel, which would spread from Jerusalem to the surrounding region of Judea, north to Samaria, and onward to the ends of the earth. Upon hearing these

28. C. C. McCown, "Gospel Geography: Fiction, Fact, and Truth," *JBL* 60.1 (1941): 5.

29. Rainey and Notley, *Sacred Bridge*, 361. Although one should also note Judith 2:28 ("Sidon and Tyre"), which strays from the usual order.

30. Joel Marcus, *Mark 1–8*, 472.

31. Theissen, *The Gospels in Context*, 243–45.

words, the disciples' initial reaction may have been to question what Jesus meant by "ends of the earth." For a Jew living in Galilee during the first century, where did the "ends of the earth" begin? Jesus' itinerant ministry within the wider Galilee region, particularly into Gentile territory, gave the disciples an idea of what it would mean for them to take the gospel to the ends of the earth.

The majority of Jesus' ministry took place within the traditional borders of Israel, among a predominately Jewish population. Matthew and Mark record that Jesus' hometown was Capernaum (Matt 9:1; Mark 2:1), and that Jesus taught and performed miracles in a number of towns throughout Galilee (Matt 11:1; Mark 1:39). Matthew suggests that most of Jesus' miracles were performed in a relatively small area defined by the cities Chorazin, Bethsaida, and Capernaum (Matt 11:20–23). In accordance with the Jewish pilgrimage festivals, Jesus also traveled to Jerusalem where he taught and performed miracles (Luke 2:22–38, 41; John 2:13; 5:1; 10:22–23).

On a few occasions, Jesus journeyed with his disciples into Gentile territory (Matt 15:21–29; 16:13–28; Mark 5:1–20; 7:24–31; 8:27–30; Luke 9:52–56; 17:11). Jesus encountered a wide array of people in his itinerant ministry: a Syro-Phoenician woman, Roman commanders and soldiers, Samaritans, Jews, and Gentiles. Jesus' movements in the region reflect his objective to spread the message of the kingdom of God to people of all ethnicities and backgrounds.

Jesus' ministry base in Galilee prepared his disciples to take the gospel into all the earth. The training ground Jesus chose for his disciples was a politically, culturally, and economically diverse region. A wide array of people lived in Galilee, not to mention those passing through along the international highway that traversed the region. Jesus' travels and encounters with various population groups prepared the disciples to be sent out into the world to share the gospel with all nations. By choosing Galilee as the base of his ministry, Jesus placed himself in a region where he could easily influence a large and diverse population and equip his disciples to effectively spread the gospel.

BIBLIOGRAPHY

Aharoni, Yohanan, Michael Avi-Yonah, Anson F. Rainey, Ze'ev Safrai, and R. Steven Notley. *The Carta Bible Atlas.* 5th ed. Jerusalem: Carta, 2011.

Bar-Efrat, Shimon. *Narrative Art in the Bible.* Sheffield: Almond, 1989.

Edwards, Douglas R. "Tyre." *ABD* 6:690–92.

Freyne, Seán. "Galilee, Sea of." *ABD* 2:900.

Hanson, Richard A. *Tyrian Influence in Upper Galilee.* Meiron Excavation Project 2. Cambridge, MA: American Schools of Oriental Research, 1980.

Hengel, Martin. *Judaism and Hellenism: Studies in their Encounter in Palestine during the Early Hellenistic Period.* Vol. 1. London: SCM Press, 1974.

Longman, Tremper, III. "Biblical Narrative." Pages 69–107 in *A Complete Literary Guide to the Bible.* Edited by Leland Ryken and Tremper Longman III. Grand Rapids: Zondervan, 1993.

Mann, C. S. *Mark: A New Translation with Introduction and Commentary.* AB 27. Garden City, NY: Doubleday, 1986.

Marcus, Joel. *Mark 1–8.* AB 27. New York: Doubleday, 2000.

McCown, C. C. "Gospel Geography: Fiction, Fact, and Truth." *JBL* 60.1 (1941): 1–25.

Metzger, Bruce M. *A Textual Commentary on the Greek New Testament.* New York: United Bible Societies, 1971.

Rainey, Anson F., and R. Steven Notley. *The Sacred Bridge.* Jerusalem: Carta, 2006.

Rey-Coquais, Jean-Paul. "Decapolis." Trans. by Stephen Rosoff. *ABD* 2:116–21.

Parker, S. Thomas. "The Decapolis Reviewed." *JBL* 94 (1975): 437–41.

Theissen, Gerd. *The Gospels in Context: Social and Political History in the Synoptic Tradition.* Minneapolis: Fortress, 1991.

Wright, Paul. *Rose Then and Now Bible Map Atlas with Biblical Background and Culture.* Torrance, CA: Rose Publishing, 2012.

CHAPTER 25

THE GEOGRAPHY OF FORGIVENESS

Matt 14:13-21; 15:29-39; 16:5-12

John A. Beck

KEY POINTS

- The geographical significance of the two feeding miracles brings fresh understanding to Jesus' warning about the "yeast" of the Pharisees and Sadducees.

- Each miracle was performed in a different political region for two different crowds: first for the Jews in Galilee, then for the Gentiles in the Decapolis.

- With both sites in view from their boat, Jesus implicitly affirms his love and forgiveness for all people as he verbally warns them of the worldview that seeks to fence in God's mercy.

The words and actions of Jesus speak to our deepest need, the need to know that we are forgiven. Each sinner who feels the looming shadow of divine displeasure longs to know that this vital message of hope applies to them, to people who live where they do. So the Bible speaks to the geographical scope of forgiveness more than once and in more than one way. John declares it in these familiar words: "For God so loved *the world* that he gave his one and only Son, that whoever believes in him shall not perish but have eternal life" (John 3:16 NIV, emphasis added). What John clearly declared, Jesus demonstrated with two feeding miracles performed in two different places for two different ethnic groups to illustrate that the kingdom of God was meant for people on all shores of the Sea of Galilee.[1] After the second miracle, Jesus raised the topic once again to confirm the matter in Matt 16:5-12.

---

1. This is an expansion of a segment from a prior publication. The content has been adapted from pages 257-60 of the *Discovery House Bible Atlas*, © 2015 by John A. Beck, and used by permission of Discovery House, Grand Rapids, Michigan 49501. All rights reserved.

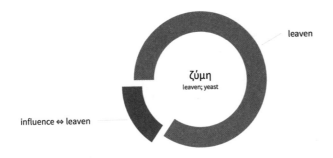

Bible Word Study: ζύμη, *zymē*

WHAT IS THE "YEAST OF THE PHARISEES AND THE SADDUCEES"?

But there was a problem. The disciples had missed the larger point of the two feeding miracles and left themselves open to a dangerous way of thinking that would bring serious harm to the kingdom of God. Jesus addresses the magnitude of their failure with sharp and critical language. They were not remembering. They were not thinking carefully. And this had to stop. But before he speaks to the problem, he recasts the problem using the image of yeast. He employs a phrase which he repeats three times in eight verses. He urges them to be on their guard against "the yeast of the Pharisees and the Sadducees" (Matt 16:6, 11, 12).

Yeast was and is an important ingredient used when making bread. And if there is one thing we meet frequently in this and the preceding chapters, it is bread. It is mentioned three times in the feeding of the five thousand (Matt 14:17, 19), once in the exchange with the Canaanite woman from the region of Tyre and Sidon (Matt 15:26), and three times in the feeding of the four thousand (Matt 15:33, 34, 36). In each case, the NIV translates the Greek term for bread (*artos*, ἄρτος) with either "bread" or "loaf." This

same word appears no less than seven times in Matt 16:5–12. With all this bread strewn throughout these verses, we may fall into the same careless pattern of thinking that plagued the disciples. They assumed that Jesus was still talking about literal bread when they got into the boat. In fact, they assumed Jesus' sharp words were meant to criticize their failure to secure the bread needed for the extended trip they were starting as they pushed off from shore.

But the sharp language of Jesus and his repeated mention of "yeast" addressed something much more problematic than a lack of bread in the boat. Let's start with the simple fact that the lack of bread was not a problem. The disciples should have known this given the two feeding miracles they had just witnessed. Jesus could have miraculously supplied the bread which they had forgotten to bring. The lack of bread was not the problem; the problem was a form of "yeast."

This was as common a product as you could find within the culture of Jesus' day, but it looked much different from the yeast we might purchase for baking. It did not come in a small packet purchased from the local grocery store. The yeast of Bible times was a piece of fermented bread dough which had been saved from the previous session of bread making.[2] When a small amount of this yeast is mixed into the new batch of bread dough, it produces carbon dioxide which causes the larger mass of dough to rise and enhance the taste of the bread.

The Bible invites us to think positively about it. Yeast is an ingredient used to prepare temple sacrifices (Lev 7:13; 23:17) and is used by no less than Jesus to speak metaphorically about the growth of the kingdom of God (Matt 13:33). But yeast can also carry a strong negative connotation. It was removed from the Israelite home during Passover and the Feast of Unleavened Bread (Exod 12:15, 18–20). The negative connotation associated with yeast persists into 1 Cor 5:6–8. Here it becomes a metaphor for how something small can have a dramatic yet harmful effect. It is this kind of "yeast" Jesus has in mind in these verses. He likens a notion championed by the Jewish religious leaders to a small amount of yeast. Many had adopted the notion and considered it a helpful way of thinking. By contrast Jesus knew it would have a far-reaching and devastating impact on the kingdom of God if left unchecked.

What is this teaching? Some have concluded that Jesus was warning against adopting the Sadducees' rejection of the resurrection (Matt 22:23) or the Pharisees' misuse of human tradition (Matt 15:2–3).[3] A stronger case could be made from the nearer context in which the Pharisees and Sadducees demand a sign from Jesus

(Matt 16:1–4).[4] What is missing from both explanations is interaction with the geography of this story, the geography of the two feeding miracles, and the way in which the feeding miracles are meant to defeat the errant thinking Jesus refers to as the "yeast of the Pharisees and the Sadducees."

THE GEOGRAPHICAL SIGNIFICANCE OF THE TWO FEEDING MIRACLES

So let's start again, but this time we will begin with the geography that sets up this strong warning of Jesus. The feeding of the five thousand comes first. Matthew summarizes the event in Matt 14:13–21. This miracle is set in a "solitary" or "remote" place with seating available on green grass and with enough physical space for thousands to gather in view of one another. The other Gospel writers tell us that it was close to the shore of the Sea of Galilee on a mountainside (John 6:1, 3), near Bethsaida (Luke 9:10). Given the mention of Passover (John 6:4), we can infer that the site was near a road used by pilgrims on the way to Jerusalem for this festival.[5] When we put all this data together, we can locate the feeding of the five thousand on the north side of the Sea of Galilee, in Galilee, just west of Bethsaida Julius.

Matthew also tells the story of the feeding of the four thousand (Matt 15:29–39), but it has a different location. Matthew tells us that Jesus was near the

---

2. Philip J. King and Lawrence E. Stager, *Life in Biblical Israel* (Louisville, KY: Westminster John Knox Press, 2001), 65.

3. Craig S. Keener, *The IVP Bible Background Commentary: New Testament* (Downers Grove, IL: InterVarsity Press, 1993), 89.

4. D. A. Carson, "Matthew," in *The Expositor's Bible Commentary*, ed. Frank E. Gaebelein (Grand Rapids: Zondervan, 1984), 8:362.

5. See A. D. Riddle, "The Passover Pilgrimage from Jericho to Jerusalem" on pg. 395.

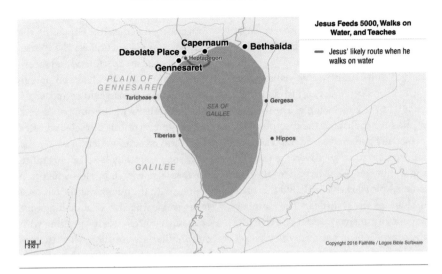

Sea of Galilee on a mountainside which was also a "remote place." It also could accommodate thousands but was on the opposite side of the lake from Magadan (Magdala). To this we can add that Mark has Jesus traveling through the region of the Decapolis just before he reports on this miracle (Mark 7:31). This data allows us to place the feeding of the four thousand on the northeast or east side of the Sea of Galilee in the region of the Decapolis controlled by the city of Hippos.

With these two events on the map, we can return to our story to see how it relates to this geography of the two feeding miracles. The last report of Jesus' position by Matthew puts him on the west side of the Sea of Galilee at Magdala (Matt 15:39). After a brief exchange with the Pharisees and Sadducees, Jesus sets out across the lake once again (Matt 16:5). The boat they board is headed for the north side of the lake with plans to disembark near Bethsaida (Mark 8:22). From there, Jesus and the disciples will continue on foot in the direction of Caesarea Philippi (Matt 16:13). This means that as Jesus and the disciples were crossing the

Sea of Galilee from west to north, and as the topic of yeast and the two feeding miracles was surfacing in their conversation, they were sailing within sight of the locations that had hosted both feeding miracles.

This gave Jesus the opportunity to reinforce the key differences between the feeding of the five thousand and the feeding of the four thousand, which each benefited different ethnic groups. The first miracle was performed for the benefit of Jews; the second was performed for the benefit of Gentiles. This ethnic distinction is communicated in a couple of different ways. The first is the one Jesus formally mentions in his words of warning.

Do you still not understand? Don't you remember the five loaves for the five thousand, and how many basketfuls you gathered? Or the seven loaves for the four thousand, and how many basketfuls you gathered? (Matt 16:9–10 NIV)

At the conclusion of the feeding of the five thousand, the disciples gathered twelve basketfuls of leftovers (Matt 14:20). This number is an ethnic marker for the descendants of Abraham who were divided into twelve tribes (Gen 49:28; Exod 24:4; Num 17:6; Josh 3:12; Matt 19:28). At the conclusion of the feeding of the four thousand, the disciples had personally gathered seven basketfuls of leftovers (Matt 15:37). Given the parallel use of numbers, it seems best to take this as an ethnic marker as well. But this time it signifies the Gentiles.[6] The number appears in this way when referring to the seven Gentile nations which Israel would displace from the promised land (Deut 7:1; Acts 13:19).

The geography of the two feeding miracles clearly supports this ethnic distinction as well. Human nature causes us to associate and live with those who are most like us. The shoreline of the Sea of Galilee in Jesus' day reflected this propensity. Observant Jewish folks who loved the Lord, ate kosher, and observed the Sabbath were inclined to live on the northwest shore of the Sea of Galilee. This is where we find Jesus speaking to the lost sheep of the house of Israel in communities like Capernaum, Chorazin, and Bethsaida, the towns in which the Galilean ministry of Jesus was focused (Matt 11:20–24).[7] When we combine the number twelve with the geographical setting for the feeding of the five thousand, it is clear that the beneficiaries of this miracle of provision were Jewish.

By contrast, the feeding of the four thousand took place in the Decapolis. The Decapolis was composed of a chain of Graeco-Roman cities like Hippos on the east side of the Sea of Galilee. These cities were designed to superintend and secure important routes as well as compel the locals to adopt Roman culture and worldview.[8] Together with the number "seven," the geography of this miracle indicates that it was directed to Gentiles.

If the geography is so important to the message, why didn't Jesus mention it along with the number of the baskets? Jesus was using the kind of language economy we often use in speaking with one another. He mentions the disciples' experience of collecting the baskets, something which they cannot see. And he leaves unmentioned what is important but already communicated by the view from the boat. Remember they are sailing within sight of the two locations where Jesus performed the feeding miracles; those locations, combined with the number of baskets collected, define the ethnic composition of the two groups served by the miracles.

THE PROVISION OF FOOD AND FORGIVENESS TO EVERY SHORELINE

Each of the two feeding miracles considered on its own merits is powerful. The multiplication of food in unthinkable fashion demonstrates the incredible power of Jesus. The way in which Jesus addresses the hunger of thousands of families gives evidence of the compassion he has for those in need. And both combine to certify that he is the promised messiah. But only when we bring

---

6. Donald A. Hagner, *Matthew 14–28* (Dallas: Word Books, 1995), 452, 460.

7. See Chris McKinny, "The Words and Teachings of Jesus in the Context of Galilee" on pg. 134.

8. For a discussion of the Decapolis cities, see Anson F. Rainey and R. Steven Notley, *The Sacred Bridge* (Jerusalem: Carta, 2006), 362.

them together and consider the geography of these two miracles does it become clear that they are not just about food but also about forgiveness. And that brings us back to the question about the "yeast of the Pharisees and the Sadducees" that both miracles address.

"Yeast" was a symbol for an idea that had become widely promoted within Judaism regarding the composition of the kingdom of God. Earlier in Matthew's Gospel and well before the two feeding miracles are recorded, Jesus spoke about many coming "from the east and the west" who would take part in the "feast with Abraham, Isaac and Jacob in the kingdom of heaven" (Matt 8:11 NIV). For many Jews and particularly the Jewish leaders, this wonderful meal had a limited guest list. Those who could be invited is debated. Some presumed the guest list was limited to Jewish scholars, others limited it to the descendants of Abraham, and a few included a small number of Gentiles in the mix.[9] The general exclusion of Gentiles from the "feast" shows up in various ways and places in the New Testament.

When Jesus went to his hometown of Nazareth, he filled the synagogue with those anxious to hear him. But the warm welcome quickly gave way to menacing actions when Jesus touched on this very topic of who was welcomed in the kingdom. As soon as he mentioned Elijah's care for a Gentile widow in the region of Sidon and Elisha's healing of the Gentile Naaman, the room erupted. They seized Jesus and marched him to the brow of the hill near the village, fully intending to end his life (Luke 4:24-30).[10] After

Jesus had called for the evangelizing of all nations (Matt 28:19-20), Peter struggled with the notion. He seemed content to witness in the Jewish seaport of Joppa. But it took the repetition of a vision to get Peter to a Gentile's home in the seaport of Caesarea Maritima. And once there, he seems hardly convinced by the vision: "You are well aware that it is against our law for a Jew to associate with or visit a Gentile. But God has shown me that I should not call anyone impure or unclean" (Acts 10:28 NIV). Nevertheless the piety and humility of the Gentiles in that home won him to a new perspective: "Then Peter began to speak: 'I now realize how true it is that God does not show favoritism but accepts from every nation the one who fears him and does what is right'" (Acts 10:34-35 NIV). Peter carried this new perspective back to the Jewish church in Jerusalem. We see the same surprise in them which we saw in Peter: "So then even to Gentiles God has granted repentance that leads to life" (Acts 11:18 NIV). In our Gentile laden church, we may presume this was always the perspective. But if we are going to understand the message of the two feeding miracles, we need to see that this was not standard-issue thinking within first-century Judaism.

This was the yeast that needed to be removed. And Jesus did two feeding miracles to address this very matter. He met with two different groups each numbering in the thousands, one on the north side of the Sea of Galilee and one on the east side; one was Jewish and one was Gentile. Matthew's telling of the stories makes it clear that Jesus responded to the needs of both groups in exactly the

---

9. See b. Baba Bathra 75 and Craig S. Keener, *A Commentary on the Gospel of Matthew* (Grand Rapids: Eerdmans, 1999), 269-70.

10. See Elaine A. Phillips, "On the Brow of the Hill at Nazareth" on pg. 263.

same way, treating Jews and Gentiles alike. This is the lesson from the two feeding miracles which was meant to disable the yeast of the Pharisees and the Sadducees. While there were those who wished to limit the "feast" and the kingdom of heaven to just one side of the lake, Jesus was intent on removing that boundary line. The geography of forgiveness extended to every shoreline.

This is a lesson we still need to engage. All of us are prone to think of the church as most naturally composed of the kind of people we see in the mirror every morning. This becomes a subtle, but ever so harmful, replaying of the yeast that will devastate the growth of the kingdom of heaven. In response Jesus puts us back in the boat with him and turns our eyes to the shoreline of the Sea of Galilee. He urges us to note the location of these two miracles and to count the baskets. When we do, we see Jesus treated all people on the lakeshore in the same way. Forgiveness extends to both sides of the lake, to Jews and to Gentiles, to those like us and to those who are very different. We see that the two feeding miracles are not just about food but also about the geography of forgiveness.[11]

BIBLIOGRAPHY

Beck, John A. *Discovery House Bible Atlas*. Grand Rapids: Discovery House, 2015.

Carson, D. A. "Matthew." Pages 1–599 in *The Expositor's Bible Commentary*. Edited by Frank E. Gaebelein. Vol. 8. Grand Rapids: Zondervan, 1984.

Hagner, Donald A. *Matthew 14–28*. WBC 33B. Dallas: Word Books, 1995.

Keener, Craig S. *A Commentary on the Gospel of Matthew*. Grand Rapids: Eerdmans, 1999.

———. *The IVP Bible Background Commentary: New Testament*. Downers Grove, IL: InterVarsity Press, 1993.

King, Philip J., and Lawrence E. Stager. *Life in Biblical Israel*. Louisville: Westminster John Knox Press, 2001.

Rainey, Anson F., and R. Steven Notley. *The Sacred Bridge*. Jerusalem: Carta, 2006.

---

11. See Gordon Franz, "The Feedings of the Multitudes: When, Where, and Why?" on pg. 237.

CHAPTER 26

NATURAL AMPHITHEATERS ALONG THE SEA OF GALILEE

Matt 14:13-21; 15:29-39; Mark 6:30-44;
8:1-10; Luke 9:10-17; John 6:1-14

Perry G. Phillips

KEY POINTS

- How was Jesus heard by thousands of people without modern sound equipment or even a Greek or Roman theater?

- Three factors govern the crowd's ability to hear Jesus: 1) voice strength, 2) ambient noise, and 3) the surrounding terrain.

- Jesus used the natural amphitheaters existing all along the shores of the Sea of Galilee as "public address systems" to teach the crowds.

THE ACOUSTIC QUERY

For many, delivering an intelligible talk to a room filled with just forty or fifty persons is a daunting task—even more so without a public address system. Yet Jesus spoke outdoors to crowds ten times that number. On one occasion, five thousand men—not including women and children—heard him speak. He so captivated them that they didn't think about eating (Matt 14:13-21; Mark 6:30-44; Luke 9.10-17; John 6:1-14). Shortly thereafter, four thousand men, besides women and children, heard his teachings and wit-

nessed his healings, again foregoing food (Matt 15:29-39; Mark 8:1-10).

Five thousand? Four thousand? How in the world could so many individuals hear and understand the man from Galilee clearly enough to hang on his words for hours? He had no public address system, nor did he pull his crowds into Greek or Roman theaters to take advantage of their acoustics. Nothing of the sort—yet thousands flocked to listen to his message.

But how could he communicate to so many at once? As the Son of God, did he imprint his message directly on his listeners' ears, a sonic miracle perhaps? Hardly. One need not look to heavenly interventions; earthly explanations suffice.

THE PHYSICS OF SOUND AND THE PHYSIOLOGY OF THE BRAIN

Sounds surround us: pleasant music, shouts at a ballgame, incessant traffic, the annoying hum of a mosquito. All these sounds have one thing in common: they consist of vibrations (technically, pressure waves)[1] that propagate through the air, impinge on our eardrums, and set off a chain of events by which our brains convert the vibrations into intelligible information.

Two basic factors govern the clarity by which one hears and understands a speaker: the strength of the speaker's voice and the level of interference from ambient noise. Outdoor settings are intrinsically noisy, which demands that the speaker have a loud voice. How loud? Probably seventy-five decibels (db)[2] and above, or about as loud as being in the same room with a vacuum cleaner. (Normal conversation registers sixty db.)

George Whitefield, the well-known early American evangelist, spoke to crowds estimated to number in the tens of thousands. His voice level could reach ninety db.[3] Jesus spoke to many crowds, and like many outdoor speakers, he surely possessed a very sturdy voice.

A robust voice, however, does not suffice. The listener must also filter the speech from the ambient noise—winnowing, as it were, intelligible wheat from cacophonous chaff. No doubt the crowds were noisy: people coming and going, internal chatting, fussy children, the wind rustling the grass, goats and sheep bleating in the background. The human brain, however, possesses an uncanny ability to focus on intelligible sounds in the midst of competing din. At the same time, the brain interpolates the message and fills in words or short phrases lost to surrounding commotion.[4] The brain makes partial speech whole.

The above picture, however, is incomplete. One other very important factor remains: the surrounding terrain. But how does *that* help?

---

1. Further explanation exceeds the scope of this article. For additional information, see Chris Woodford, "Sound," last updated February 29, 2016, accessed May 3, 2016. http://www.explainthatstuff.com/sound.html.

2. The measure of sound intensity is the decibel (db). This is a logarithmic measurement: A change in ten db corresponds to a factor of two in perceived sound intensity. That is, every change in ten db doubles the perceived intensity from the previous level (e.g., fifty db seems two times louder than forty db, four times louder than thirty db, and eight times louder than twenty db.) For comparisons between the db scale and common sounds, see "Comparitive [sic] Examples of Noise Levels," IAC Acoustics, accessed May 6, 2016, http://www.industrialnoisecontrol.com/comparative-noise-examples.htm.

3. Joel Shurkin, "Orators Unplugged," *Inside Science*, December 10, 2013, accessed May 6, 2016, https://www.insidescience.org/content/orators-unplugged/1510.

4. Known formally as the "Phonemic Restoration Effect" (see Makio Kashino, "Phonemic Restoration: The Brain Creates Missing Speech Sounds," *Acoustical Science and Technology* 27.6 [2006]: 318–21, https://www.jstage.jst.go.jp/article/ast/27/6/27_6_318/_pdf). Less formally, the phenomenon is known as the "Cocktail Party Effect" (see Boston University, "Picking Out Specific Sounds in A Complex Scene: Researchers Study 'Cocktail Party Effect', Measure Auditory Dynamics of Selective Attention." *Science Daily*, ScienceDaily, 25 August 2008, accessed May 3, 2016, https://www.sciencedaily.com/releases/2008/08/080821164607.htm).

Traditional Site of the Feeding of the 5,000

HOW TERRAIN AFFECTS OUTDOOR SPEECH

Jesus gave numerous speeches around the Sea of Galilee,[5] and the region's combination of hills, vales, and land ascending away from the shore provided natural amphitheaters for addressing large crowds.

This point was sufficiently proved by an experiment in the 1970s by lay archaeologist B. Cobbey Crisler and professional sound engineer Mark Miles.[6] Crisler and Miles set up equipment at a cove on the shore of the Sea of Galilee near Tabgha, also near Capernaum. They chose this specific location to reproduce the event of Mark 4:1 where Jesus, pressed by the crowd, retreated to a boat from where he presented the parable of the Sower.[7] Crisler and Miles did not use a boat, but a large rock protruding out of the water a little more than thirty feet (ten meters) off the shore served the purpose.

To begin, Miles set up his sound generator on the rock. The device emitted a "shrill, sustained tone" whose signal strength Miles measured while walking away from the shore along a couple lines centered on the rock and radiating outwards at roughly a thirty degree angle. (Think of a thin slice of pie with its point at the rock and the rim on the shore.) The signal was clear all the way to a road about three hundred feet (one

---

5. For all the occasions of Jesus' speaking to crowds, see "Crowds around Jesus," http://bible.knowing-jesus.com/topics/Crowds-Around-Jesus.

6. B. Cobbey Crisler, "The Acoustics and Crowd Capacity of Natural Theaters in Palestine." *The Biblical Archaeologist* 39.4 (1976): 128–41, doi: 10.2307/3209424.

7. Matthew 13:1 states that Jesus came out of the house, and in v. 36 he went back into the house. Mark implies the house was that of Simon and Andrew, located in Capernaum (Mark 1:21, 29).

hundred meters) distant that runs east-west between Tabgha and Capernaum.

The second experiment involved Crisler's standing on the rock and breaking balloons while Miles stood at various distances from the shore. Miles clearly detected the bursting balloons—as did everyone else passing along the road during the experiment.

Crisler and Miles initially embarked on investigating whether the natural terrain served as an auditorium with Jesus at the "stage" (the boat) and the crowd in the "seats" (the slopes). But Crisler and Miles unexpectedly found that the reverse also occurred: speech from the "seats" was clearly heard at the "stage." Crisler explains:[8]

> For example, two cases, involving U.N. cars, are worthy of particular mention. The first car was on its way *to* Capernaum. The passenger's window was down. Suddenly and quite visibly to me on the rock, the car slowed. I couldn't make out the faces from one hundred meters, but the voices were unmistakable. One said, 'What's he doing down there?' The other answered, 'I don't know! He's just standing there holding some balloons.'
>
> The second car was on its way *from* Capernaum. The car did not slow perceptibly and it looked to me like there was only a driver.

But there must have been a passenger as well or the outburst I heard would have been even more remarkable. It was in German, a language I do not speak. But, what I heard sounded completely comprehensible. It was *"Ist ein Baloonist!"*[9]

Their experiments demonstrated that natural terrain can act as an outdoor auditorium. No doubt Jesus was aware of this and took advantage of natural features around the Sea of Galilee to speak to large crowds. For example, the miracle of the feeding of the five thousand took place somewhere around the city of Bethsaida (Luke 9:10). The feeding of the four thousand occurred in the Decapolis (Mark 8:1–9; see 7:31).[10] Both locations have excellent acoustical topography. In short, natural amphitheaters exist all along the shores of the Sea of Galilee, and Jesus used them as "public address systems" to teach the crowds.

Yes, the crowds had no problem hearing what Jesus said. But Jesus knew that hearing was not enough. One has to hear with the heart, not just with the ears.[11] Note Jesus' insistence on *hearing* in the parable of the sower: He begins the parable with "Listen; behold" (Mark 4:3 NASB) and ends with "If anyone has ears to hear, let him hear," and "take care what you listen to" (4:23–24 NASB). How interest

---

8. Crisler, *Acoustics and Crowd Capacity*, 135.

9. The reverse acoustics—that is, the speaker at a higher vantage point than the listeners—particularly comes into play for the Sermon on the Mount where Jesus goes up a mountain to speak to the crowd below (Matt 5:1). And the crowds clearly heard him, for they were amazed at this teaching (7:28).

10. For the implications of the different locations of these similar miracles see John A. Beck, "The Geography of Forgiveness" on pg. 258.

11. What follows is a theological point made by Crisler, *Acoustics and Crowd Capacity*, 138.

ing that Jesus used the surrounding terrain both for acoustic enhancement and as an illustration of the receptivity of the human heart to his message.

BIBLIOGRAPHY

Boston University. "Picking Out Specific Sounds in A Complex Scene: Researchers Study 'Cocktail Party Effect', Measure Auditory Dynamics of Selective Attention." *ScienceDaily*. ScienceDaily, 25 August 2008. Accessed May 3, 2016. https://www.sciencedaily.com/releases/2008/08/080821164607.htm.

Crisler, B. Cobbey. "The Acoustics and Crowd Capacity of Natural Theaters in Palestine." *The Biblical Archaeologist* 39.4 (1976): 128–41. doi: 10.2307/3209424.

IAC Acoustics. "Comparitive [sic] Examples of Noise Levels." Accessed May 6, 2016. http://www.industrialnoisecontrol.com/comparative-noise-examples.htm.

Kashino, Makio. "Phonemic Restoration: The Brain Creates Missing Speech Sounds." *Acoustical Science and Technology*. 27.6 (2006): 318–21. https://www.jstage.jst.go.jp/article/ast/27/6/27_6_318/_pdf.

Knowing-Jesus.com. "Crowds around Jesus." Accessed May 6, 2016. http://bible.knowing-jesus.com/topics/Crowds-Around-Jesus.

Shurkin, Joel. "Orators Unplugged." *Inside Science*, December 10, 2013. Accessed May 6, 2016. https://www.insidescience.org/content/orators-unplugged/1510.

Woodford, Chris. "Sound." 2009/2014. Last updated February 29, 2016. Accessed May 3, 2016. http://www.explainthatstuff.com/sound.html.

CHAPTER 27

JESUS HEALS A BLIND MAN NEAR BETHSAIDA

Mark 8:22-26

Benjamin A. Foreman

KEY POINTS

- The healing of the blind man near Bethsaida took place at a time when Jesus was attempting to avoid attention from Jewish crowds and authorities.

- The location of Bethsaida is yet to be determined conclusively, though the general area is more or less agreed upon.

- The miracle itself is unique in the New Testament as it occurs in two stages and at multiple locations.

THE TIMING OF THE EVENT

Bethsaida played an important role in Jesus' Galilean ministry.[1] It was the hometown of Philip, Andrew, and Peter (John 1:44),[2] and Matthew notes that it was one of the cities in which "most of his mighty works had been done" (Matt 11:20 ESV). Jesus healed a number of people in Bethsaida just prior to the feeding of the five thousand (Luke 9:11), and several months after this miraculous feeding he returned to Bethsaida and performed the miracle recorded in our pericope. This account is best understood within the wider context of Jesus' Galilean ministry; thus a brief review of when this event took place is necessary.

---

1. The city is mentioned seven times: Matt 11:21; Mark 6:45; 8:22; Luke 9:10; 10:13; John 1:44; 12:21.

2. Since Andrew and Peter were business partners with James and John (Luke 5:10) some suggest that the latter two were also from Bethsaida, though this is uncertain. See M. J. Wilkins, "Disciples" in *Dictionary of Jesus and the Gospels*, ed. Joel B. Green and Scot McKnight (Downers Grove, IL: InterVarsity Press, 1992), 179.

The feeding of the five thousand was a turning point in Jesus' Galilean ministry. After eating their fill, the overzealous crowd attempted to take Jesus by force and make him king (John 6:15). This fanaticism was anything but flattering to the Jewish leadership, and an execution order for Jesus was quickly issued (John 7:1). The crowd's feverish enthusiasm undoubtedly struck a chord of disfavor with Herod Antipas as well, who mistakenly believed Jesus was the recently executed John the Baptist, revivified (Mark 6:14). Given this religious and political opposition, Jesus kept a low profile for the next several months (from Passover to the Feast of Tabernacles). Throughout this time he generally stayed away from large Jewish crowds and was more reserved in the miracles he performed. Mark, in particular, highlights this change in strategy (see Mark 7:24, 33, 36; 8:12, 23, 26, 30; 9:9, 25, 31).

During this six-month period of time Jesus took two major trips, mainly into Gentile regions. On the first of these he journeyed north to the Gentile region of Tyre and Sidon (Mark 7:24–30), through the Decapolis (Mark 7:31–8:9), then across the lake to the district of Dalmanutha (perhaps the Plain of Magdala; Mark 8:10). His second journey took him north through the Huleh Valley to the region of Caesarea Philippi (Mark 7:27), then down through Upper Galilee to Capernaum (Mark 9:30, 33). It is on this trip, just before his nearly thousand-foot ascent

to the Huleh Valley, that Jesus came to Bethsaida.

THE LOCATION OF BETHSAIDA

The location of the city of Bethsaida has been the subject of much scholarly debate. Josephus gives us some valuable information on its whereabouts and thus is a good starting point. He states that Bethsaida was located "in lower Gaulanitis" (War 2.168), "close to the river Jordan" (Life 399; see also War 3.515). He also notes that,

> Philip ... raised the village of Bethsaida on Lake Gennesaritis to the status of city by adding residents and strengthening the fortifications. He named it after Julia, the emperor's daughter (Ant. 18.28).

This text gives us two additional geographical details: (1) the city was located in Philip's territory (east of the Jordan River), and (2) it sat on the shore of the Sea of Galilee.[3] According to Josephus, therefore, Bethsaida was located on the northern shore of the lake, just east of the Jordan River, close to where the river flows into the sea.

John 12:21, however, tells us that Philip "was from Bethsaida in Galilee" (emphasis added). Since the eastern border of Galilee was the Jordan River (War 3.37), if Bethsaida is located east of the Jordan River, it would not technically be in Galilee.[4] Some scholars, therefore, believe that there were two Bethsaidas

---

3. Josephus confirms this in his autobiography, where he relates that after being wounded near Julias, reinforcements were sent by ships to the city to rescue him (Life 406).

4. Those who place the feeding of the five thousand on the Plain of Bethsaida might also take Mark 6:45, which states that Bethsaida is on "the other side" of the lake, as evidence that there were two Bethsaidas. This does not need to be the case, however. See Gordon Franz, "The Feedings of the Multitudes" on pg. 237.

in Jesus' day: one in Galilee (west of the Jordan River), and one in Philip's territory (east of the Jordan River).[5] But this is unlikely since neither the Gospels nor any other ancient historical texts clearly indicate that there were two cities with this name.[6] It is more likely that in John 12:21 the evangelist simply uses "Galilee" to designate the region in a non-technical sense. Bethsaida sat right on the political boundary of Galilee, so it is understandable why John, having a Jewish audience in mind, would mention Galilee (which was predominantly Jewish) as a point of reference rather than Trachonitis or Gaulonitis (which were predominantly Gentile).

The primary site identified with Bethsaida is a large ruin to the north of the Sea of Galilee called et-Tell. This identification was first proposed by Edward Robinson in 1838, and according to Rami Arav, the archaeologist who has excavated the site for nearly thirty years, "The finds at et-Tell support Robinson's proposal that Bethsaida should be identified with it."[7] Elsewhere, Arav conclusively reports that although the village was lost to history sometime after the first century AD, "Bethsaida has been found once again [at et-Tell]."[8] This identification has won the day, so much so that even the sign on the main road leading to the site today reads "Bethsaida."

There are several difficulties, however, with this identification. The first is that et-Tell sits about 1.85 miles north of the shore of the Sea of Galilee, and about .4 miles east of the Jordan River. This is problematic because Josephus says that Bethsaida was accessible by boat (*Life* 406). Even the name Bethsaida means "house of fishing."[9] Responding to the problem of distance, Arav maintains that the Sea of Galilee reached the southern slopes of the mound in Jesus' day. Over time, he argues, the shore of the Sea of Galilee has moved further away from et-Tell through the accumulation of silt carried down by the Jordan River.[10] Thus, in antiquity: "The Sea of Galilee covered much of the Bethsaida Plain and reached the slopes of the mound."[11]

Although it is likely that some sedimentation has occurred over the centuries near the mouth of the Jordan River, the Sea of Galilee could not have reached up to the slopes of et-Tell as Arav claims. According to the archaeological expedition's own geological research, the base

---

5. E. Robinson and E. Smith, *Biblical Researches in Palestine, Mount Sinai and Arabia Petraea: A Journal of Travels in the Year 1838*, vol. 3 (Boston: Crocker & Brewster, 1841), 290, 294; Bargil Pixner, "Searching for the New Testament Site of Bethsaida" *BA* 48.4 (1985): 207–16.

6. Pliny the Elder (ca. AD 77) also states that the city was east of the Jordan (*Natural History* 5.15).

7. Rami Arav, "Bethsaida (Et-Tell)," *NEAEHL* 5:1612.

8. Rami Arav, Richard A. Freund, and John F. Shroder, Jr., "Bethsaida Rediscovered," *BAR* 26.1 (Jan/Feb 2000): 45.

9. The Hebrew word for net is related to the word Bethsaida: *metsodah*.

10. Arav, Freund, and Shroder, "Bethsaida Rediscovered," 48.

11. Rami Arav, "Bethsaida—A Response to Steven Notley," *NEA* 74.2 (2011): 97. This same claim is made in his earlier *BAR* article ("Bethsaida [Et-Tell]," 48): "Up against the base of the et-Tell mound, we found lake clays containing crustacean microorganisms. At one time, Bethsaida was right on the water!"

of the tell is 669 feet below sea level (-201 meters).[12] The city of Capernaum, however, sits at approximately 686 feet below sea level (or -209.25 meters). Thus, if the Sea of Galilee had reached up to the base of et-Tell in Jesus' day, Capernaum would have been approximately 17 feet underwater![13] Even the black mud lower down from the tell (which they believe is evidence that the lake reached up to the site) is approximately 13 feet higher in elevation (-672.5 feet) than Capernaum. In other words, if the Sea of Galilee had extended up to et-Tell in Jesus' day: "The lake would have inundated the shoreline promenade at Capernaum (-686.5 feet / -209.25 meters), the ports of Tiberias (-686.4 feet / -208.3 meters) and Kursi (-686.5 feet / -209.25 meters), and every other known first-century settlement around the lake."[14]

Another difficulty in equating Bethsaida with et-Tell is that the results of nearly thirty years of excavation suggest that et-Tell was fairly modest in size during the first century AD. This is a problem because Josephus implies that Bethsaida was a sizeable city in the first century AD. He notes that Philip increased its population, strengthened its fortifications, and elevated it to the status of "city" (polis, πόλις; Ant. 18.28).[15] The dearth of first-century remains is reflected in the architectural remains uncovered at et-Tell: aside from a private residential building, the only other structure found by the archaeologists that was built in the Roman period was a Roman temple—which Arav believes served a cult to Julia Augusta.[16] No evidence of Philip's fortification of the city has been found, and none of the other expected structures of a city granted the status of polis have been uncovered at et-Tell. The material evidence also seems to imply that the city was in decline during the early Roman period.[17]

Arav, on the other hand, claims, "The amount of Roman material surpasses that found in Capernaum, Chorazin, Nazareth, and Khirbet Kana combined."[18] But, as Notley rightly counters: "Where is it? Voluminous finds exceeding these four sites certainly were not published

---

12. John Shroder, Jr., and Moshe Inbar, "Geologic and Geographic Background to the Bethsaida Excavations," in vol. 1 of Bethsaida: A City by the North Shore of the Sea of Galilee, ed. Rami Arav and Richard Freund (Kirksville: Thomas Jefferson University Press, 1995), 86.

13. Postulating that seismic activity uplifted the land near Bethsaida will not solve the problem since the geologists of the et-Tell excavation team state that an uplift of five meters in about two thousand years "seems about two or three times too rapid for the region and therefore probably should not be used to account for the observed difference in altitude of lake muds above present water level. We can hypothesize reasonably that only one-quarter to one-third of the difference in levels to be uplift related" (Shroder and Inbar, "Geologic and Geographic Background," 90).

14. Anson F. Rainey and R. Steven Notley, The Sacred Bridge (Jerusalem: Carta, 2006), 358.

15. This seems to have occurred toward the end of Philip's reign (ca. AD 30); see R. Steven Notley, "Et-Tell is Not Bethsaida," NEA 70.4 (2007): 224-25.

16. Arav, "Bethsaida—A Response to Steven Notley," 97.

17. For example, the excavators found 105 coins from the Hellenistic period, 9 from the early Roman period, and 16 from the Middle to Late Roman period (Notley, "Et-Tell is Not Bethsaida," 226).

18. Arav, "Bethsaida—A Response to Steven Notley," 93.

Location of et-Tell

in the volumes of the BEP [Bethsaida Excavation Project] excavation reports (1995–2009)."[19] These two central challenges have led some scholars to question the conclusion that et-Tell is the ancient city of Bethsaida.

The best alternative to et-Tell is a site 1.3 miles (2.1 km) to the south called el-Araj. Since the ancient sources say that Bethsaida was a fishing village accessible by boat, el-Araj is a better fit geographically—it is only about .5 miles (.8 km) from the northern shore. Based on the expected amounts of silt accumulation from the Jordan, this distance from the water can be accounted for with much less difficulty than the nearly 2 miles (3.2 km) of accumulation necessary at et-Tell. More significantly, its highest point is only 679 feet (201 m) below sea level, which means that it would have been on the shore of the sea even if the water level in the first century AD was the same as its average today (about -690 feet / -210 meters).

Unfortunately, el-Araj has not been systematically excavated. In 1987 Arav conducted a limited excavation and survey of the site but found no remains from the first century AD. According to his findings, el-Araj was not inhabited until the Byzantine period (fourth century AD).[20] If Arav is correct in this assertion, then it cannot be Bethsaida. But the evidence is not as conclusive as Arav insinuates. Several members of the Israel Antiquities Authority surveyed the site in 1990 and found pottery from the early Roman period (first century AD) as well as the foundations of

19. R. Steven Notley, "Reply to Arav," NEA 74.2 (2011): 101.

20. Arav, Freund, and Shroder, "Bethsaida Rediscovered," 48; Arav, "Bethsaida (Et-Tell)," 1612; idem, "Bethsaida—A Response to Steven Notley," 92; idem, "A Response to Notley's Reply," NEA 74.2 (2011): 104.

several buildings.[21] Some of these finds (which include a column base, capital, and basalt frieze) are on display at Kibbutz En Gev nearby. Most recently (2014), Mordechai Aviam, along with a team from the Center for Holy Lands Studies, conducted a five-day shovel-testing survey of el-Araj. The results of the survey have not yet been officially published, but Aviam has reported in an interview that their expedition found pottery from the Late Hellenistic (second century BC), Early Roman (first century AD), Middle and Late Roman (fourth century AD), Byzantine (sixth century AD), Mameluke (14/15th century AD), and Ottoman (16th century AD) periods. To date, nearly ten architectural fragments from large public buildings have been recovered at the site.[22] None of this is conclusive evidence that el-Araj is ancient Bethsaida, but it certainly means that it is a viable candidate. And given the difficulties associated with et-Tell, el-Araj is at present perhaps the best candidate. Further excavations may settle the issue definitively.[23][24]

THE MIRACLE

Several passages in the Old Testament suggest that one of the signs of the messianic age is that the blind will regain their sight (Isa 29:18; 35:5; 42:7). Therefore, one of the ways that Jesus proved he was the messiah was by opening the eyes of the blind.[25] There are five specific healings of blindness recorded in the New Testament, and Matt 15:30 and 21:14 suggest that Jesus healed many more. These healings, according to the Gospels, occurred in Capernaum, Bethsaida, the region of the Decapolis, Jericho, and Jerusalem. His ministry of healing the blind was not limited to a particular geographical region, nor to the Jews only.

The healing of the blind man at Bethsaida, however, is unique in two ways. First, this is the only miracle in the New Testament that occurred in two stages. As Mark records, Jesus spat on the man's eyes and partially healed his vision, then fully restored his eyesight by placing his hands on the man's eyes again (Mark 8:23). Many scholars believe that these two stages are symbolic of the disciples' process of coming to faith.[26] Like the healing of the blind man, the enlightenment of the disciples came gradually and in stages.[27] One difficulty with this interpretation is that the Gospel of Mark does not clearly portray the disciples' coming to faith as a two-

21. Yosef Stepansky, "Kefar Nahum Map, Survey," in *Excavations and Surveys in Israel 1991*, eds. Ayala Sussmann, Dafnah Strauss, and Rafi Greenberg (Jerusalem: Israel Antiquities Authority, 1992), 87.

22. The interview is available online at: https://www.youtube.com/watch?v=e4oiudXfCrA&index=2&list=PLGG_otCZ87fqsoGuCCCMD81oar5Q3dMJv.

23. See also Gordon Franz, "The Feedings of the Multitudes" on pg. 237.

24. El-Araj is scheduled to be excavated in the summer of 2016.

25. When John the Baptist sent messengers to ask Jesus if he was the "one who is to come," Jesus responded affirmatively by pointing in part to his healing of the blind (Matt 11:5). It is also interesting to note that there are no recorded instances in the New Testament of the apostles healing the blind (though Paul strikes the Cypriot magician with blindness in Acts 13:11).

26. Blindness is often symbolic of ignorance (see Mark 8:18; Matt 15:14; 23:16–26).

27. See, for example, James Edwards, *The Gospel According to Mark* (Grand Rapids: Eerdmans, 2002), 244.

stage process.[28] In the end, it may be that this abnormal process of healing is more trivial than many scholars assume. Jesus did not always heal the needy in the same way. Sometimes he healed by speaking (John 5:8), by touching (Mark 1:31), or even embracing (Luke 14:4). He healed the deaf man in Mark 7:33 by spitting and touching the man's tongue. In other instances people were healed when *they* touched him (Mark 5:28–29; 6:56). Even his healings of the blind displayed variety. When two blind men were brought to him in Capernaum, he healed them by touching their eyes and speaking to them (Matt 9:29).[29] In Jerusalem, Jesus spat on the ground, made mud with his spittle, anointed the man's eyes with the mud, and then sent him to wash in the pool of Siloam. Only once the man went and washed was his vision restored (John 9:7). Given the variety of methods Jesus used to heal the sick, it may be prudent not to read too much into the two-stage healing process in our narrative. He healed in a variety of ways, and rarely are we able to answer why he chose any particular method.

Second, this is one of only two times in the Gospels where Jesus personally took someone to a different location to heal him.[30] Jesus did not heal the man in Bethsaida; rather, "He took the blind man by the hand and led him out of the village" (Mark 8:23). In Mark 7:33 Jesus acted in a similar manner. Taking the deaf man away from the crowd that had gathered in the Decapolis, Jesus healed him privately. It is important to notice that both of these healings occurred during the "private"

phase of Jesus' Galilean ministry. As mentioned above, Jesus deliberately avoided large Jewish gatherings during this phase of his ministry in order not to prick the attention of the religious and political authorities. For these few months he generally stayed out of the public spotlight and focused predominantly on training his disciples. Since healing the man in Bethsaida had the potential of attracting too much attention, Jesus led him out of the city and healed him somewhere away from the crowds. Apparently the man was not from Bethsaida, since after healing him Jesus sent him home and forbade him from entering the village (Mark 8:26). His vision restored, the man presumably returned home, and Jesus, unhindered by a large following of spectators, journeyed with his disciples to yet another predominantly Gentile region—the district of Caesarea Philippi in the far north.

BIBLIOGRAPHY

Arav, Rami. "Bethsaida—A Response to Steven Notley." *Near Eastern Archaeology* 74.2 (2011): 92–100.

———. "Bethsaida (Et-Tell)." *NEAEHL* 5:1612.

———. "A Response to Notley's Reply." *Near Eastern Archaeology* 74.2 (2011): 103–4.

Arav, Rami, Richard A. Freund, and John F. Shroder, Jr. "Bethsaida Rediscovered." *BAR* 26.1 (Jan/Feb 2000): 44–56.

Edwards, James. *The Gospel According to Mark*. PNTC. Grand Rapids: Eerdmans, 2002.

---

28. For further critique, see Robert Stein, *Mark* (Grand Rapids: Baker, 2008), 392–93.

29. Jesus used the same method in Jericho (Matt 20; 29–34; Mark 10:46; Luke 18:35–43).

30. In John 9:7 Jesus sends the blind man to the pool to be healed, but he does not personally take him there.

Notley, Steven. "Et-Tell is *Not* Bethsaida." *Near Eastern Archaeology* 70.4 (2007): 220–30.

———. "Reply to Arav." *Near Eastern Archaeology* 74.2 (2011): 101–3.

Pixner, Bargil. "Searching for the New Testament Site of Bethsaida." *BA* 48.4 (1985): 207–16.

Rainey, Anson F., and R. Steven Notley. *The Sacred Bridge*. Jerusalem: Carta, 2006.

Robinson, Edward, and Eli Smith. *Biblical Researches in Palestine, Mount Sinai and Arabia Petraea: A Journal of Travels in the Year 1838*. Vol. 3. Boston: Crocker & Brewster, 1841.

Shroder, John, Jr., and Moshe Inbar. "Geologic and Geographic Background to the Bethsaida Excavations." Pages 65–98 in vol. 1 of *Bethsaida: A City by the North Shore of the Sea of Galilee*. Edited by Rami Arav and Richard Freund. Kirksville, MO: Thomas Jefferson University Press, 1995.

Stein, Robert. *Mark*. BECNT. Grand Rapids: Baker, 2008.

Stepansky, Yosef. "Kefar Nahum Map, Survey." *Excavations and Surveys in Israel 1991*. Edited by Ayala Sussmann, Dafnah Strauss, and Rafi Greenberg. Jerusalem: Israel Antiquities Authority, 1992.

Wilkins, M. J. "Disciples." Pages 176–81 in *Dictionary of Jesus and the Gospels*. Edited by Joel B. Green and Scot McKnight. Downers Grove, IL: InterVarsity Press, 1992.

CHAPTER 28

JESUS' INTERPRETATION OF WEATHER PATTERNS

Matt 16:1-4; Luke 12:44-55

Elaine A. Phillips

KEY POINTS

- Jesus relies on his audience's familiarity with their physical surroundings to ground his teachings and increase their impact.

- On two occasions Jesus uses their knowledge of weather patterns to rebuke them.

- Jesus demonstrates his power by calming the stormy Sea of Galilee and by walking across the surface of its water.

THE PERENNIAL IMPACT OF WEATHER PATTERNS

Jesus, the consummate teacher, directed the attention of his audiences to their immediate surroundings on multiple occasions. He drew on their daily lived experiences in the land. At the same time, he tapped into the centuries-old biblical narratives and traditions that likewise grew out of life in this challenging land. We want to stitch together observations about the immediate physical geography with the rich biblical heritage in which there were already deeply embedded lessons. As we read the Gospel narratives, we often wear such heavy stained-glass lenses that we forget this is an encounter with real people. They contended with stark realities of discomfort, fear, and despair prompted by their surroundings. They also rested and were refreshed in moments of provision and safety.

Jesus offered trenchant observations about the weather patterns that he and his disciples experienced day after day. They would have walked numerous times between the cities in the Galilee, where they would have felt weather changes through the course of each day and from week to week. Along with farmers and shepherds, they would have kept a close eye on wind, clouds, and the intensity of the heat. They knew intimately the importance of rain, the dread of drought and famine, and other aspects of the sometimes harsh climate. They knew what different kinds of clouds meant in terms of approaching weather.

The seasonal weather changes would also have been significant, indicating the arrival of planting and harvest. Green grass would be a spring time phenomenon. As they journeyed to Jerusalem for Passover, there would also have been weather events during the spring time of the year. In other words, the land vividly shaped the daily lives of God's people during the first centuries BC and AD.

In addition to directing his audience's attention to their physical surroundings, Jesus repeatedly pointed to the text of the Old Testament. As we explore the transformative power of Jesus' words in his day to those disciples and crowds gathered around, we would be remiss if we did not also search the Scriptures that infused his life and teachings and that were likewise filled with allusions to life in the land. With that in mind, we investigate what we know about weather and climate, both as they shaped Jesus' teachings and as they are embedded in the words of the Old Testament. Then we can begin to unpack the lessons bound up in the Jews' experience of daily weather patterns.

OBSERVABLE WEATHER PATTERNS AS SIGNS

On two recorded occasions, Jesus spoke of daily weather observations. He knew his audience watched the weather forecast in the same way that we do in order to determine how our days will unfold. There were signs they knew were indicative of what was to come; they were predictable. Identifying these signs and understanding their implications for the next hours and days was second nature. At the same time, however, it seems Jesus' audience was missing whole additional levels of meaning latent in these ecolog-

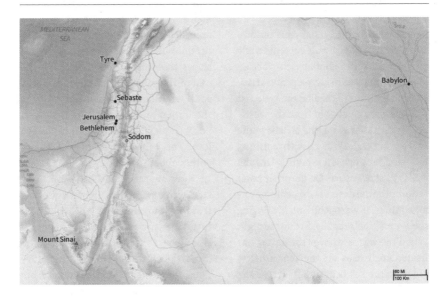

Atlas: The Levant

ical realities, which garnered for them rather sober rebukes from Jesus.

REGULAR WEATHER PATTERNS

We need to visit the geographical regions at the eastern end of the Mediterranean Sea in order to appreciate the force of Jesus's declarations. This large area is commonly called the Levant, and we will use that term here, even though the land in which most of the Bible events unfolded is considerably smaller. Knowing climate, seasonal changes, and regular weather patterns in the Levant will help us hear Jesus with a more sensitive set of ears. The weather of this land is particularly affected by four interrelated factors: (1) air currents, (2) elevation, (3) seasons, and (4) hot winds.

AIR CURRENTS

First, the juxtaposition of the Mediterranean Sea to the west with the great desert to the east means ongoing movements of air on a major scale. The larger meteorological picture is worth noting. Particularly in the summer, a low pressure area settles over the Persian Gulf and also over Cyprus. Extensive air currents circle all the way from the Indian Ocean across Mesopotamia, around Cyprus, and arrive back on the eastern Mediterranean coast. Note they are coming in from the west.

On a smaller scale, the air above the vast body of water is laden with moisture; it is humid and dense and both warms and cools at a slower pace. On the other hand, the air over the desert is exceedingly dry and lighter. It warms up quickly during the day and cools rapidly during the night. When the warm air over the desert has heated up, it rises and the denser heavy air from the sea is drawn in across the land. This happens with clocklike regularity. Generally, by about noon to 1:00 PM,

these breezes have made their way into the land as far as Jerusalem. In antiquity and well into the twentieth century, these strong breezes served the local farmers as they counted upon them to help thresh the grain in the afternoon. After the sun sets and the land cools, the winds blow more gently from land to sea.

This pattern is most notable during summer months. In the winter there is more variability because low pressure areas form and reform during winter, mostly over the Mediterranean Sea. As the prevailing westerly and southwesterly winds pass over the Levant, they draw in continental air from both north and south. In the summer, they switch somewhat to the northwest and bring cooling breezes across the land.

ELEVATION

A second factor is significant at this point. In spite of its relatively small area, this land enjoys a significant range of elevation, from sea level to higher hills that at points come close to 2700 feet (823 m) above sea level. These higher elevations are called a "mountain" spine, but we must not think of snow-covered, treeless rugged slopes; these hills are tree-covered. To the east of this spine, which runs primarily south-southwest to north-northeast, is the immense Rift Valley—at its lowest point some 1300 feet (396 m) below sea level. These elevation changes take place within about 50 miles (80 km).

Now, merge that formidable barrier with our regular movement of air from west to east. As the heavier moisture-laden air moves eastward, it must rise up over these hills and, in doing so, it cools. As it cools, it loses its moisture. Thus, the western slopes enjoy rain, but once we cross the watershed, the eastern side of the hill country spine is in a rain shadow. The Jordan Valley is especially in that shadow and the southernmost part of it near Jericho and the Dead Sea average only two to four inches of rainfall per year. To summarize the meteorological implications: as we travel from west to east, the rainfall decreases; as we move from north to south rainfall decreases; as we reach higher elevations, rainfall increases. This small strip of land was on the margins of the Fertile Crescent, and it was the stage for understanding the implications of water rights in a land so easily prone to famine.

SEASONS

There are additional influences that come into play. There are essentially two seasons: a rainy and a dry season, with transitional periods in between. The rainy season is at its peak in December and January. If it is a good year, the land enjoys what are called the early (autumn) rains and the latter (spring) rains. In a particularly good year, rainfall may start as early as late September, and there will be extra rains into April. Both of these periods are especially important for softening up the land for sowing in autumn and extending the growing season in the spring. Rainfall varies considerably between the southern part of the country (the biblical Negev) where eight to twelve inches per year is the average, to the central hill country around Jerusalem (approximately twenty-five inches per year) to the slopes of Mount Carmel (more than thirty-two inches) to the northern Mount Hermon (approximately fifty inches per year). While the summer is the dry season, dew forms as the moist air cools overnight. This brings sufficient moisture to carry crops through until the harvests of vineyards and orchards (see infographic "Agricultural Cycle of the Levant/Palestine" on pg. 530).

HOT WINDS

One other phenomenon is most evident during the transitional periods when the weather is characteristically less stable. The prevailing westerly wind pattern is reversed and fierce hot winds sweep across the land from the east, southeast, south, or even southwest, bringing very hot dry air that is often laden with fine dust particles. There are three different terms that are used to refer to this weather event. In popular parlance these terms are often interchanged. The Arabic word *khamsin* describes the witheringly hot winds that sweep dust along with them. These occur when air from Africa and Arabia is drawn north and eastward across Israel. The phenomenon may also be called a *sirocco*. The term *sharav* technically refers to a barometric high over the land itself where air is compressed and heated. It is not necessarily accompanied by the scorching winds.[1]

Occasionally, the same very parched conditions will affect the land during the hottest summer months as well. The *khamsin* dries everything in its path. In addition, it may be that those tiny dust particles in the atmosphere naturally "seed" the clouds so that, when the wind swings back around, it can come in with storm force— either heavy rain or, as I have seen on one occasion (March of 1998), snow.

---

1. Efraim Orni and Elisha Efrat, *Geography of Israel*, 3rd rev. ed. (Jerusalem: Keter Publishing House, 1971), 141–42. See also D. Kelly Ogden, "Sirocco and Sharav in the Bible" in *Geography of the Holy Land: Perspectives*, eds. William A. Dando, Caroline Z. Dando, and Jonathan J. Lu (Taiwan: Holy Light Theological Seminary Press, 2005), 67.

JESUS' OBSERVATIONS OF SIGNS (MATT 16:1–4; LUKE 12:44–55)

With these factors in mind, let us probe more deeply several specific responses of Jesus to his audiences. When the Pharisees and Sadducees asked Jesus to give them a "sign from heaven" (Matt 16:1–4), they were being provocative. After all, they had already seen a formidable number of demonstrations of Jesus' power by this time in his ministry. His response to their demand drew their attention to the weather, of all things. It was a pun: *ouranos* (οὐρανός) means both "heaven" and "sky." Matthew is the only one to record this detail. Looking to the signs of the sky was clearly under their radar-screens, and they may have scoffed a bit. No doubt they were looking for something much more spectacular. Instead, Jesus simply noted the implications of the color of the sky: an evening red sky meant good weather was coming; a morning red sky augured storms forthcoming. In the former case, it was appropriate that there would be moisture in the air to the west over the sea. Breezes would be bringing those clouds inland, causing the beauty of a red sunset from the perspective of someone in the hills.

When the sun shone in the morning, however, if there were clouds of dust or other particles in the atmosphere to the east, the hue would be reddish and the sunlight somewhat dimmed. That meant the kinds of weather unrest we have noted above. They knew these phenomena well. And then came the punchline. Observing the weather and drawing conclusions was parallel to understanding the times. Instead of asking for some sort of miraculous sign, they should have been attentive to the implications of Jesus' presence and activities in their midst. They should have had their cov-

enant in mind and the importance of obedience to the Torah. All of those were entirely sufficient signs; but the Pharisees and Sadducees, self-styled as Israel's brightest and best teachers and leaders, had missed them entirely. Jesus instead called them a "wicked and adulterous generation" and said the only sign would be that of Jonah. The message was clear: apart from repentant hearts, judgment was forthcoming.

Luke offers us the second of Jesus' weather observations. This one is embedded in a series of challenges to the gathered crowds. Jesus had just challenged them to sacrificial actions that would result from deep trust in their heavenly Father (Luke 12:22–34), to be ready for action (Luke 12:35–48), and to be prepared for the inevitable divisiveness at the claims of Jesus on their lives (Luke 12:49–53). And then Jesus said, "When you see a cloud rising in the west, you know it is going to rain, and it does." They all knew the winds brought clouds from the sea in the manner that we have described. It was predictable. Likewise, when the south wind blows (the *khamsin*), it is going to be hotter than blazes. Again, it was entirely predictable (Luke 12:44–55).

The lessons from both of these incidents were the same. They could see enough to keep their physical lives in order. Like us, they planned accordingly after seeing the "weather report." But they missed the deeper implications of what was going on. In the former case reported by Matthew, Jesus' audience asked for a "sign"; they received a verbal rebuke. Luke reports Jesus' admonition as the culmination of a series of one-two punches. Here he called them "hypocrites," which suggests they were maintaining a façade of interest in what Jesus was doing but were undermining

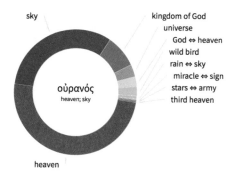

sky

kingdom of God
universe
God ⟷ heaven
wild bird
rain ⟷ sky
miracle ⟷ sign
stars ⟷ army
third heaven

οὐρανός
heaven; sky

heaven

Bible Word Study: οὐρανός, *ouranos*

it with utter disregard for the long-term implications. The rebuke follows directly on the need for preparation for difficult times. It was not a happy message; in fact, they may have wanted to kick it down the line a decade or two.

OBSERVING SIGNS FROM
THE OLD TESTAMENT

Although these are the only two specific references to weather patterns in the Gospels, we remember that Jesus also knew the Hebrew Bible well. The wider range of weather-related Old Testament allusions, especially in the Torah and the Prophets, were the textual backdrop for much of his teaching. Here are a few. The climate of the land compelled the people of God to be dependent on God's bounty from the heavens. This was crystal clear in the covenant. In fact, their lives were to be quite different from their prior experience in Egypt (Deut 11:10–17). The land promised to them in the covenant was designed to foster obedience and trust. Deuteronomy 11 mentions the early and latter rains as particular blessings. In Moses' final blessing on Israel, he notes the gift of dew from heaven above as part of Joseph's blessing (Deut 33:13). Jesus would have grown up with

this same framework in mind, and it no doubt informed the challenges he issued to his audiences.

In addition to these deep covenantal connections, the prophets also observed the weather and drew the same kinds of lessons. Jesus was following in a long prophetic tradition and would have been fully aware of these references—and we want to be as well. Dew was a centerpiece of the prophet Haggai's opening salvo against the people. When they disregarded their responsibility to care for the temple, God's dwelling place, God himself would withhold the dew from *their* dwelling place in the land. Instead, there would be drought (Hag 1:10–11). Likewise, the top of Mount Carmel withered when rain and dew were withheld in the face of disobedience of God's people (Amos 1:2; Nah 1:4). The fierce desert wind made the most sober impression. It is noted by Jeremiah as a severe judgment, not to winnow or to cleanse (Jer 4:11–12). Likewise an east wind scattered God's people (Jer 18:17), dried up the fruit of the allegorical vine in Ezek 19:12, and wrecked Tyre in the heart of the sea (Ezek 27:26). This was the textual backdrop for Jesus' allusions to what the Jews of his day should have known.

WEATHER PATTERNS IN THE GALILEE AS EVEN RICHER SIGNS (MATT 14:22–36; MARK 6:45–53)

With those rudimentary weather patterns as foundational, several additional incidents in the Galilean ministry of Jesus warrant sharper focus. The narratives are familiar. In the first, at evening the master and his band of disciples set out across the Sea of Galilee, traveling from Capernaum to the east side of the lake. A squall (called a "great windstorm" in both Matthew and Mark) threatened their small boat. They woke Jesus and he stilled the waves, followed by an inquiry about their present fear and absent faith. They in turn noted in astonishment that the winds and waves obeyed him.[2] All of this was a lesson in identity; they no doubt had in their hearts the truths about the Lord of Hosts in Ps 89:9: "You rule the raging of the sea; when its waves rise, you still them."

In the second incident, the drama was higher. After feeding five thousand men, in addition to women and children (Matt 14:21), the crowd wanted to make Jesus king by force, but he slipped away into the hills (John 6:15). Again, it was night when the disciples headed across the water toward Capernaum or other points north and west. They were facing a strong adverse wind, and in that context, Jesus both came walking on the water to them and stilled the waves. In the face of their abject terror, his declaration "It is I" was again a statement of his identity. This time there was not only the allusion to the power of the Lord of heaven but also Jesus' use of the Name—"It is I." Matthew recorded their response after Jesus rescued Peter and the wind ceased: "Surely, you are the Son of God" (Matt 14:22–36; Mark 6:45–53). Thus, the sign of controlling the sea, a place associated with chaos and evil, communicated profoundly to the disciples Jesus' identity.[3]

With that theological lesson firmly in mind, let us explore the context that shaped these two events. In other parts of the country, the prevailing winds from the west are blocked by the generally north-south range of hills and thus the western slopes enjoy rainfall. In Lower Galilee, however, due to faults in the hill country, the topography changes. There are east-west ridges and valleys and those prevailing winds from the west funnel right through those valleys from the Mediterranean Sea to the Sea of Galilee. The intensity of the wind increases as the day goes on. In addition, the Sea of Galilee itself is about 600 feet below (183 m) sea level and the air above it is warm, moist, and heavy. The intersection of the cool rush of air from the west with this air pocket creates extraordinary turbulence in the evening hours. The disciples would have known this well and probably were accustomed to fighting those waves. In this case, however, they experienced the power of God incarnate stilling the tumult.

BIBLIOGRAPHY

Baly, Denis. *The Geography of the Bible.* Rev. ed. New York: Harper and Row, 1974.

Beck, John A. *The Land of Milk and Honey: An Introduction to the Geography of Israel.* Saint Louis, MO: Concordia Publishing House, 2006.

---

2. Matthew 8:23–27; Mark 4:35–41; Luke 8:22–25.
3. See Gordon Franz, "What Type of Storms Did Jesus Calm: Wind or Rain?" on pg. 175.

Mather, John R. "The Winds of Galilee."
    Pages 54-60 in *Geography of the Holy
    Land: Perspectives*. Edited by William
    A. Dando, Caroline Z. Dando, and
    Jonathan J. Lu. Taiwan: Holy Light
    Theological Seminary Press, 2005.
Ogden, D. Kelly. "Sirocco and Sharav in
    the Bible." Pages 67-70 in *Geography
    of the Holy Land: Perspectives*. Edited
    by William A. Dando, Caroline Z.

Dando, and Jonathan J. Lu. Taiwan:
    Holy Light Theological Seminary
    Press, 2005.
Orni, Efraim, and Elisha Ephrat.
    Geography of Israel. 3rd rev. ed.
    Jerusalem: Keter Publishing House,
    1971.
Wright, Paul H. *Greatness Grace & Glory:
    Carta's Atlas of Biblical Biography*.
    Jerusalem: Carta, 2008.

CHAPTER 29

PETER'S DECLARATION AT CAESAREA PHILIPPI

Matt 16:13-23; Mark 8:27-30; Luke 9:18-20

Elaine A. Phillips

KEY POINTS

- Peter's declaration took place in Caesarea Philippi, at the base of Mount Hermon in front of the Temple of Pan at the Banias Spring—all these locations share a long history with pagan deities.

- When Jesus owned the titles "Son of the living God" and "Son of Man" in Caesarea Philippi, he upended all the pagan notions associated with this location.

"Who do people say that I am?" Jesus posed this question to his disciples at a significant place and at a critical time. Their responses started with John the Baptist and extended back to Elijah or another one of the prophets. Jesus pressed them a second time—"Who do *you* say that I am?"—to which Peter responded, "You are the Christ, the Son of the living God" (Matt 16:16). The location, Caesarea Philippi, was the perfect backdrop for Peter's dramatic declaration, as the setting was rich with symbolic possibilities due to the layers of religious and historical structures that were in place by the first centuries BC and AD. Together these contributed compelling imagery as the exchange between Jesus and his disciples unfolded. We need to explore the background in order to appreciate the rich implications of the question and the answers Jesus posed and the disciples gave.

THE NATURAL SETTING

Caesarea Philippi was located at the southern base of the majestic Mount Hermon, a massive block of hard limestone deposited during the Cenomanian geological period. Mount Hermon is the southern extension of the Anti-Lebanon range of peaks. The slopes of Mount Hermon are shared by modern Israel, Syria, and Lebanon. A huge fault separates two major sections of the southern block. The eastern flank where Caesarea Philippi was located has a more mixed geological composition, with marls, shale, and an abundance of basalt.[1] The elevation of Mount Hermon exceeds nine thousand feet. This, in combination with its more northerly location, means that it receives a significant amount of precipitation.[2] In the winter season and well into April and May, the expansive slopes glisten brilliantly with snow and are visible from far to the south on clear days.

Because limestone interacts chemically with water, this massive mountain is interlaced with underground fissures and caverns called karsts. Much of the precipitation percolates through the porous layers of bedrock, creating vast underground reservoirs. The direction of the underground flow of water is affected by fault lines and less permeable layers that cause it to issue forth in karstic springs. Three particularly large springs at the western and southern limits of Mount Hermon are the headwaters of what eventually becomes the Jordan River. These are at Hasbani in modern Lebanon (becomes the Senir River), Dan (Dan River), and Banias (Hermon River).

Banias is the contemporary name of the site, and it preserves the original Paneas (also Panias). (The letter "p" does not exist in Arabic; its substitute is "b.") We will address below the reason the location was initially named Paneas during the Second Temple period. Paneas was renamed Caesarea Philippi during the reign of Herod Philip the tetrarch (4 BC–AD 34). For our purposes of elucidating the biblical text, the springs at Dan and Banias are the most significant. In fact, the karstic spring at Dan is the largest in the Middle East. Just about three miles to the east, the city of Caesarea Philippi expanded near the Banias spring at the base of an immense scarp, thirty meters high and eighty meters long.[3] In the first century, the water apparently gushed from just below the huge cave, still evident in the rock face. In the words of Josephus:

> [The place is called] *Paneion*. At this spot a mountain rears its summit to an immense height aloft; at the base of the cliff is an opening into an overgrown cavern; within this, plunging down to an immeasurable depth, is a yawning chasm, enclosing a volume of still water, the bottom of which no sounding line has been found long enough to reach. Outside and from beneath the cavern well up the springs from which, as some think, the Jordan takes its rise.[4]

In the succeeding two millennia, seismic activity has shifted the terrain sufficiently so today the water bubbles from the ground farther down the stream bed.

---

1. These and following data on geology are drawn from Andreas Hartmann, "Process-based modelling of karst springs in Mt. Hermon, Israel" (Diplomarbeit [Master's thesis], Albert-Ludwigs-Universität Freiburg im Breisgau, 2008, http://www.hydrology.uni-freiburg.de/abschluss/Hartmann_A_2008_DA.pdf), 8–9.

2. The meteorological principle may be summarized as follows: there is more precipitation the farther west, the farther north, and the higher the elevation. Add to this the expanse of the vast mountain range and the potential for abundant water is high. Rainfall can reach as much as 60 inches per year.

3. Tvi Uri Ma'oz, "Banias," *NEAEHL* 1:140.

4. Josephus, *War* 1.404–406 [LCL].

THE HISTORY OF THE SITE

DURING OLD TESTAMENT TIMES

With this abundance of water, it is no wonder that Dan and Caesarea Philippi attracted significant communities. Already in the book of Judges, we read of the migration of at least part of the tribe of Dan from their initial tribal allotment west of Judah and Benjamin to this well-watered and attractive location. At that time, the city was called Laish, but after the Danites conquered it, they changed its name to Dan (Judg 18:29), settled in, and established a worship site complete with the trappings they had stolen en route from an Ephraimite named Micah (Judg 18:1–31). Thus, the stage was set for the more formal worship center where Jeroboam son of Nebat set up one of the two golden calves (1 Kgs 12:25–33). The other calf was positioned at Bethel. Between the two of them, the Israelites in the northern kingdom had easy access to a religious installation that looked legitimate on the surface, even though it was false at its core.[5]

It seems that the location the Danites chose was already considered sacred ground by the Canaanites in the land. The name Hermon is related to the Hebrew word ḥerem, which means some thing or place that was sacred. We have evidence from both the biblical text and extra-biblical sources that this vast mountain traditionally was considered holy ground. Both its formidable height and the abundance of water would contribute to that sense of sanctity.

At the time of the conquest and settlement, Mount Hermon was called Baal Hermon, suggesting the association of the known Baal figure with the mountain range (Judg 3:3; 1 Chr 5:23; see also Josh 11:17). That association is not surprising as Baal was presumed to be the god of storm, rain, and thus agricultural productivity. The abundant precipitation on the slopes of Mount Hermon made this a perfect "residence" for Baal. In addition, the Amorites called the mountain Senir, while it was Sirion to the Sidonians (Deut 3:9).[6] These two biblical names surface in Egyptian Execration texts from the nineteenthth century BC and in a treaty from the fourteenth century BC between Hittites and Amorites. In the latter, both sides swear by the "gods of Mt. Shariyanu."[7] The entire vast mountain had an aura of transcendence that would extend well beyond the small location of Dan.

As the Danites relocated, what they did not know was that their descendants would be on the invasion route from the north for every enemy force coming from the north and east. The biblical text indicates that when Ben-Hadad from neighboring Syria (Aram) attacked the northern kingdom in response to Asa's plea for help, Dan was among the first cities to fall (1 Kgs 15:16–22; see 2 Chr 16:1–10 for the prophetic critique of Asa's choice). Likewise, Tiglath-pileser III of Assyria ravaged the whole of northern

5. Archaeological finds indicate that the altar and high place at Dan continued to thrive well into the Hellenistic period (Avraham Biran, "Dan," *NEAEHL* 1:331–32).

6. We find an external corroboration of this in an Ugaritic text about building a house (palace) for mighty Baal. It sets the cedars of Sirion in parallel with trees of Lebanon (*ANET*, 134).

7. Michael Avi-Yonah and Efraim Orni, "Hermon, Mount," *EJ* 9:30–31.

Israel and Transjordan. Although Dan is not named, it was on the front-line of attack as Ijon, Abel-beth-Maacah, Janoah, Kedesh, Hazor, Gilead, Galilee, and all the land of Naphtali fell (2 Kgs 15:29).

UNDER PTOLEMAIC INFLUENCE

The military might and cultural conquest of Alexander the Great swept across the Levant in 333 BC. After Alexander's death and several decades of political turmoil, the eastern Mediterranean was parceled out between Ptolemy and Seleucus, two of Alexander's generals. Ptolemy took control of Egypt, and Seleucus established his mandate over Syria and geographically proximate regions. For the next century, their successors vied for control of what had been Israel. During the third century BC, the Ptolemies held the land. The balance of power changed in 198 BC when Antiochus III (a Seleucid) defeated the Egyptian general, Scopas, at Paneas (so named after the god Pan).

Along with the waves of military conquest came the accompanying cultural conquest. Greek gods and goddesses in profusion were added to the sacred locations that were already well-established. The most prominent in this location was Pan, an Arcadian god of flocks, represented as part goat and part human. The name "Pan" comes from Old Arcadian and means "to pasture."[8] Pan was a rustic figure, inhabiting high hills and caves and worshiped in outdoor contexts, particularly where abundant water sources pointed to fertility. Pan was often portrayed dancing, a euphemistic representation of sexual fertility rites. In addition, Greek sources in antiquity associated Pan with victory in battle as his elusive presence legendarily instilled panic in enemy armies.[9] Crossing cultural boundaries into the east, the figure of Pan often joined that of Dionysius in depictions of processions. All these motifs may have influenced the naming of this site. The walls of the cave dedicated to Pan had marble plaques, evidenced by remnants of the plaster that held them. Coins indicate that statues of Pan were put into the niches in the huge rock face. In time, shrines and worship niches for other gods and goddesses appeared as well. Among them were Zeus, Hermes, and Nemesis.[10]

In this context, it is important to visit briefly the realm of Hades as it interfaces with elements of the pagan worship practices we have already described. Our tour takes us first to Homer's description of the three-fold division of all things among the three sons of Cronos: Zeus, Poseidon, and Hades. Whereas Poseidon was granted the sea and Zeus the heavens, Hades received the "murky darkness" of the dead below[11] and was utterly ruthless and unyielding of all gods, the one most hateful to humans.[12] In time, the name Hades came to refer to the place of the dead as well as the god of the dead.

In one of Homer's oft-quoted lines, Achilles says: "For hateful to me, even as the gates of Hades, is that man who hides one thing in his mind and says

---

8. Michael Eisenberg, "Pan at Hippos," *BAR* 41.6 (2015): 42–45, 72.
9. "Pan," at *Theoi Greek Mythology* (website), accessed May 1, 2016, http://www.theoi.com/Georgikos/Pan.html.
10. Ma'os, "Banias," 140.
11. Homer, *Illiad* 15.187–93.
12. Homer, *Illiad* 9.157–58.

another."[13] The dark images of the house and gates of Hades recur throughout the *Illiad* and *Odyssey* and are lodged well beyond classical Greece. They represent the wide swath of human dread for death. This same ominous imagery of "gates of death" and "gates of deep darkness" appears already in Job 38:17. It was a place only God knew.[14] The web of related metaphors expands to include the "bars of *sheol*" (Job 17:16) and the "gates of *sheol*" (Isa 38:10). Sheol, representing the numinous and fearsome aspects of death and the grave, was beyond the limits of human experience. Likewise, beyond the mouth of the cave of Pan at Paneas were the dreaded shadows; at the entrance was the threshold into death. In sum, with the developing array of ritual sites and pagan figures, Paneas became the Hellenistic counterpart and rival to the traditional quasi-Jewish worship at Dan.

UNDER SELEUCID INFLUENCE

Coming under Seleucid political and religious control meant a radical change for the Jewish population. Whereas the Ptolemies had been relatively tolerant, the Seleucids were actively hostile to the Jews and their religious practices. As a result, the mid-second century BC saw the Maccabean revolt, the establishment of the Jewish Hasmonean dynasty, and a semi-independent state for almost a century, all amidst a swirl of political intrigue and complications.

UNDER ROMAN INFLUENCE

In the first century BC, this land was under the shadow of the growing presence of Rome. The names of Julius Caesar and Octavian (Caesar Augustus) were high profile. Amidst internal and external crises, Antipater II, the father of Herod the Great, managed to stay on top of the turbulence and acquired for his son the governorship of the Galilee. Herod did not come easily to his ultimate position as "king of the Jews." When he was appointed by the Roman Senate in 40 BC, he first consolidated his power by brutal suppression of all the Jewish opposition. Then he burnished his honor by building monumental structures around the country. This was a political balancing act: he rebuilt the Jerusalem temple, ostensibly for the Jews, but he also built numerous temples in honor of Rome's gods and emperors.

When Herod was given the city of Paneas in 20 BC, Josephus tells us he proceeded to build a temple of white marble and to dedicate it to Augustus:

> And when he returned home after escorting Caesar to the sea, he erected to him a very beautiful temple of white stone in the territory of Zenodorus, near the place called Paneion. ... It was this most celebrated place that Herod further adorned with the temple which he consecrated to Caesar.[15]

This contributed to the fundamental transition toward the imperial cult.

This structure was directly in front of the cave of Pan from which the spring waters issued forth. It supplanted the worship of Pan that had been centered at the cave. When Herod's son, Philip

---

13. Homer, *Illiad* 9.312–13.

14. See also Pss 9:13; 107:18.

15. Josephus, *Ant.* 15.363–64 [LCL].

the tetrarch, was appointed ruler of the Greek-speaking territories to the north and east of the Sea of Galilee, he enlarged the temple dedicated to Augustus, rebuilt and beautified the town, and re-named the city Caesarea.[16] Philip issued coins to indicate that he had founded the city, and his own name was attached to the place that became the center of his rule.[17]

To the east of the monumental temple built for Augustus lies another temple foundation. Although that temple is not identified directly, the goddess Nemesis is associated with it. Nemesis was worshiped in other places in the land as a hypostasis of Tyche, whose temple does appear on the city coins.[18]

Unlike the Galilee under Herod Antipas' control, the population in Gaulanitis, Trachonitis, and Iturea remained primarily Gentile. Caesarea Philippi was a center of Hellenistic pagan worship along with the exaltation of the Roman emperor. During Jesus' day, references to "the district of Caesarea Philippi" (Matt 16:13) and "the villages of Caesarea Philippi" (Mark 8:27) reflect the city's status as the power center of Philip's territory. Thus, this part of Jesus' ministry took place in a major pagan city.

The changing winds of power affected the city. When Agrippa II (AD 50–95) received it as a gift from Nero, he rebuilt it and renamed it Neronias in Nero's honor.[19] During the Galilean phase of the First Jewish Revolt, Vespasian camped in the vicinity of the city prior to the slaughter of Jews on the Sea of Gennesaret. In his description of these events, Josephus refers to the city as Caesarea Philippi to distinguish it from Caesarea on the sea.[20] Even though Caesarea Philippi was an important Christian site, the name did not hold, and by the time of the Arab conquest, it had become Banias, echoing the earlier name of Paneas.

JESUS' MINISTRY OUTSIDE OF JEWISH TERRITORY

It is important to review the development of Jesus' itinerant ministry leading up to this crucial exchange with Peter regarding his identity. When Jesus fed the five thousand, it was almost Passover (John 6:4); both Mark and John make a note of the spring green grass (Mark 6:39; John 6:10). This was a critical turning point for Jesus in the Galilee; all four Gospels record the event.[21] John expands on the aftermath of this miracle story. Jesus refused to allow the crowds to make him king, i.e., the kind of messiah they wanted (John 6:15). Their demands for a sign became more strident (John 6:30–59). They deemed his teaching difficult and many left him (John 6:60–66).

---

16. Josephus, *Ant.* 17.189; 18.28.

17. Ma'oz, "Banias," 138.

18. Ma'oz, "Banias," 140–41. Nemesis was viewed as the goddess of righteous indignation against false pride and therefore a moving force behind events that brought equilibrium in the arena of divine justice. Those who were too happy were visited by Nemesis ("Nemesis," at *Theoi Greek Mythology* [website], accessed May 1, 2016, http://www.theoi.com/Daimon/Nemesis.html).

19. Josephus, *Ant.* 20.211.

20. Josephus, *War* 3.443–44.

21. Matt 14:13–21; Mark 6:30–44; Luke 9:10–17; John 6:1–15. This four-fold attestation is true only of one other narrative in the Gospels, and that is the resurrection.

Between that incident and about six months later at the Feast of Tabernacles (John 7), Jewish leaders from Jerusalem dogged Jesus' footsteps (Matt 15:1; Mark 7:1). Matthew and Mark report that Jesus was on Herod Antipas' radar (Matt 14:1-2; Mark 6:14-16); Herod wondered if this person about whom he was hearing was John the Baptist come back to life. The prospect of Herod's closer attention may have prompted Jesus' journey into Phoenician territory (Matt 15:21-28; Mark 7:24-30), back across Galilee, east into the Decapolis region (Mark 7:31-8:26), and finally north to Caesarea Philippi (Matt 16:13; Mark 8:27). At the base of Mount Hermon, this last stop was well outside Antipas' territory (see map "Kingdom of Herod the Great" on pg. 531).

THE EXCHANGE BETWEEN JESUS AND PETER

THE SIGNIFICANCE OF PETER'S DECLARATION

Matthew gives us the fullest account of the conversation between Jesus and Peter (Matt 16:13-20; see the compressed versions in Mark 8:27-29; Luke 9:18-20). All three Synoptic Gospels have the question from Jesus: "Who do people say the Son of Man is?" (This is Matthew's report; both Mark and Luke have simply "Who do people/the crowds say that I am?"). Jesus had chosen long before to identify himself as "Son of Man," a title full of meaning from the prophetic traditions of Ezekiel and Daniel. God repeatedly addressed the prophet Ezekiel as "son of man," emphasizing that he was a human being chosen by God to give God's word. "Son of Man" in Daniel is radically different. Daniel saw the throne of the Ancient of Days and "one like a Son of Man" coming into the presence of the Ancient

of Days. When he did, he was given all the attributes of divinity—"dominion and glory and a kingdom ... all peoples, nations and languages should serve him; his dominion is an everlasting dominion, which shall not pass away and his kingdom is one that shall not be destroyed" (Dan 7:13-14). Thus, Jesus' intentional choice of this title was a declaration that as "Son of Man," he was fully human and fully divine. He now demanded them to come to grips with the profound implications of that title.

Their initial responses reported the popular gossip. Some said John the Baptist; a related possibility was Elijah since John had come "in the spirit and power of Elijah" (Luke 1:17; echoing Mal 4:5-6). Matthew tells us that Jeremiah was in the mix, and all say the speculation ranged through other ancient unnamed prophets as well. Jesus pressed them: "What do *you* say?" Peter then declared Jesus to be the Messiah ("Anointed One"), already a significant variation from the popular perception of Jesus as prophet. Luke has it as "Messiah of God." Matthew, however, reports a full and remarkable affirmation—"You are the Messiah, the Son of the living God." Jesus answered in turn that this announcement from Peter was laden with theological significance. Only revelation from God the Father would enable Peter to speak truth of this magnitude.

At this point, we need to reflect briefly on the implications of Jesus' questions and Peter's reply in the immediate spatial and cultural context. In the heart of this thriving Hellenistic city, encompassed by stone images to Syrian and Greek gods and an imposing temple devoted to the imperial cult, Jesus asked his disciples to identify him. He was compelling them to buck the consensus—and not just of the foreign culture into which they had come for a reprieve. That was difficult enough. He was also asking them to declare his uniqueness from everything that had preceded him in their own venerable tradition. Peter's response addressed both of these contextual problems. Amidst the stone dead images that surrounded them in Caesarea Philippi, he declared Jesus to be the Son of the *living* God, challenging both the dead gods and those who were foolish enough to worship them as if they really existed. In addition, instead of simply identifying Jesus as a prophet—a comfortable assertion—he announced that Jesus was indeed the "Anointed One" and the "Son of God." That meant Jesus was the fulfillment of all their hopes, ill-shaped as those hopes might have been at the time.

JESUS HAD MORE TO SAY

Jesus affirmed Peter's words, saying that this could only have been revealed by "my Father in heaven." What he said next is rich with symbolism at a number of levels. "You are Peter (*Petros*, Πέτρος) and on this rock (*petra*, πέτρα) I will build my church" (16:18 NRSV, ESV, NIV). He went on to declare that the "gates of Hades" would not overcome or prevail against the church. As Jesus was standing with his disciples in front of the sheer cliff at Caesarea Philippi, his use of the metaphor "rock" was vivid. To be sure, there is considerable difference of opinion as to the size of rock indicated by *petros* (πέτρος) and whether *petros* and *petra* are, in fact, interchangeable. In addition, sorting through the related implications of Peter, Cephas, and Simon son of Jonah, as Jesus doled out those names, is complicated. Nevertheless, it seems that Jesus affirmed Peter as having potential for a kind of rock-like stability, a hope-filled

statement in light of the mercurial character that Simon Peter often demonstrated. At the same time, *petra* was the appropriate term to describe the massive precipice in front of which this dialogue unfolded. (Note its use in Matt 7:24, 25: "who built his house upon the rock [*petra*].")

INTERPRETIVE ISSUES

There has been a centuries-old discussion regarding Peter's traditional role vis-a-vis the church: What did Jesus mean when he said "on this rock (*petra*) I will build my church"? Was it intended to present Peter as the primary leader of the church? There are certainly hints in the Gospels of Peter's prominent role from the very beginning. "Simon, whom he named Peter," is first in the lists of apostles (Matt 10:2; Mark 3:16; Luke 6:14; see also Acts 1:13). His name is also first of the three in the inner circle. When Jesus healed the daughter of the synagogue ruler, Peter, James, and John were the only disciples to witness it (Mark 5:35–43; Luke 8:49–56). Peter, James, and John were with Jesus as he was transfigured before them (Matt 17:1; Mark 9:2; Luke 9:28). Mark notes the inquiry of "Peter, James and John" that launched Jesus into the Olivet Discourse (Mark 13:3). In the Garden of Gethsemane, not only does Peter's name appear first but Jesus addressed him directly after coming back from prayer (Matt 26:36–46; Mark 14:32–43). On more than one occasion, Peter served as the spokesman for the other disciples (Matt 18:21; 19:27; Mark 8:27; Luke 12:41; 18:28) and was recognized as a leader even by those outside the circle of disciples (Matt 17:24).

On the other hand, there are those who interpret Jesus' announcement as affirming the very foundation of the church. It would be built on the rock-solid truth of Peter's confession that Jesus was the Christ, Son of the Living God. Neither of these possibilities should be discounted lightly. It may be possible, however, to elucidate the matter further with a heightened awareness of the geographical surroundings, along with a venture into literary contexts, and some help from the Greek language.

GEOGRAPHY AND WORLDVIEWS

In light of the massive rock scarp against which Caesarea Philippi was built and into which were hewn images of dead gods and goddesses, Jesus may have been using *petra* to refer to the worldviews represented in that rock face. They appeared to be insurmountable, but, here, Jesus was declared to be *the* living God. In other words, this encounter represented a stinging condemnation of all forms of pagan worship. This is even more dramatic in light of the layers of religious history that had accumulated here.

As we noted earlier, Mount Hermon was called both Baal Hermon and Senir (Judg 3:3; 1 Chr 5:23), and the latter name along with Sirion was attested outside the immediate geo-political culture. Biblical Mount Hermon may also be associated with Zaphon, which appears in Ugaritic texts as the dwelling place of Baal.[22] According to Canaanite myth, Baal died for the summer dry months and rose again with the winter rains that resuscitated the land.[23] Worship of Baal not only celebrated this seasonal dying and rising but also centered on rituals to

bring fertility into every realm of human existence. Thus, there was already a rich backdrop here for a tangle of religious worldviews that had to do with life and death.

Add on the veneer of Hellenistic worship of Pan, Zeus, and Nemesis with the same overtones of life and death activities. Finally, lodge the "gates of Hades" at the dark entrance to the cave of Pan, and the place was teeming with the shadowy and unpredictable gods that brought numinous terror and dismay. One popular tradition from Late Antiquity may augment this picture. There is a rabbinic discussion as to the wide range of conditions that will (or will not) prevail when the Messiah (Son of David) comes. The final contribution reads as follows:

> The disciples of R. Jose b. Kisma asked him, 'When will the Messiah come?'—He answered, 'I fear lest ye demand a sign of me [that my answer is correct].' They assured him, 'We will demand no sign of you.' So he answered them, 'When this gate falls down, is rebuilt, falls again, and is again rebuilt, and then falls a third time, before it can be rebuilt the son of David will come.' They said to him, 'Master, give us a sign.' He protested, 'Did ye not assure me that ye would not demand a sign?' They replied, 'Even so, [we desire one].' He said to them, 'if so, let the waters of the grotto of Paneas turn into blood;' and they turned into blood. When

---

22. The name Zaphon that appears in these Ugaritic texts is related to the Hebrew *tsafon*, meaning "north," and could refer to the massive mountain in the north of the country. See John Day, *Yahweh and the Gods and Goddesses of Canaan* (Sheffield: Sheffield Academic Press, 2000), 107–14.

23. Day, *Yahweh and the Gods*, 91–92; 117–22.

he lay dying he said to them, 'place my coffin deep [in the earth].' (b. Sanhedrin 98a)

While the rabbinic traditions were written significantly later and include some likely fanciful elements, the connection between "this gate" and "the waters of the grotto of Paneas" establishes the location and indicates that the numinous world beyond that rock face terrified people. For Jesus to own in Caesarea Philippi the titles "Son of the living God" as well as "Son of Man" would upend all of the pagan notions associated with the location. Further, Jesus soon commenced teaching them about a radically different death and resurrection from the myth that enshrouded the Baal narratives (Matt 16:21).

AN ALTERNATIVE TRANSLATION AND INTERPRETATION

We bring one further lens through which to view this scene. As is true with any language, there are multiple possibilities for translating Greek prepositions. In this case, instead of translating the preposition epi (ἐπί) as "upon," perhaps it should be translated and interpreted as "against." It is one of the translation options, even though it is much less frequent. In other words, perhaps Jesus declared that he would build his church *against* this rock face with all its etchings and niches devoted to gods and goddesses, all of which represented crushing falsehood. The church was to be on the offensive against the destructive world views

that rob people of life and hope. The gates of death would collapse as the church and the Son of the Living God moved forward with power.[24]

This would turn upside down everything that his disciples knew and experienced. Jesus' teaching incessantly compelled them to think in terms of reversals and this was no different. Immediately following this declaration, Jesus told them not to reveal his identity as the Messiah. After such a radical revelation, how were they expected to keep quiet? Then he spoke of his impending death, followed by his resurrection. Peter likely heard the ominous words about suffering and death but was not able to process rising again. Thus, just sentences after exalting Peter, Jesus turns and calls him "Satan"—adversary. That led to the admonition to take up the cross, to lose life in order to save it. No wonder their heads were left spinning!

THE AFTERMATH

Just about a week later, Jesus took Peter, James, and John up to a high mountain by themselves.[25] While it is not named, the proximity of Mount Hermon makes it a likely candidate for this event. The other traditional suggestion is Mount Tabor, between the south end of the Sea of Galilee and Nazareth. That may be unlikely simply from a political standpoint. In the previous months, Jesus avoided Jewish territory and likely continued to do so until he "set his face to go to Jerusalem" (Luke 9:51) following the transfiguration.

24. This passage is one of only two places where Matthew uses the word *ekklēsia* (ἐκκλησία) for "church"; the other is in 18:17.

25. Matt 17:1–8; Mark 9:2–8; Luke 9:28–36. While Matthew and Mark have six days, Luke tells us it was about eight days later. It may be that Luke accommodated the time it would take to ascend the mountain. No doubt that was close to a day.

Jesus' appearance was changed and his clothing became brilliant and radiantly white. Moses and Elijah joined Jesus and they spoke of his "departure" (exodos, ἔξοδος Luke 9:31) that he was about to accomplish in Jerusalem. Peter, James, and John saw the manifest glory of Jesus; the overwhelming brilliance almost defies each Gospel writer's ability to put it into words. Matthew said his face was like the sun and his clothes were "dazzling white." Mark adds that no one on earth could bleach them to that degree of whiteness.

Peter blurted out a suggestion about building booths, probably because it was near the Feast of Tabernacles, and according to tradition the messiah would return at that festival.[26] As the cloud of glory enveloped them, they heard the voice commanding them to "listen." That would mean truly hearing the things that Jesus said that were difficult to hear. He would return to the theme of his impending betrayal and death.

Mount Hermon was set apart from the teeming world below it. Luke indicates it was the "next day" (9:37) that they rejoined the throngs of people. That too fits well with the extent of the mountain slopes and the time it would take to ascend and descend. The descent was ominous; it was back into the darkness of demon affliction and arguments among the disciples (Matt 17:14–19; Mark 9:14–29; Luke 9:37–50). Nevertheless, Jesus continued to challenge them to greater faith, and even that exhortation drew on the image of this massive, immovable mountain: "If you had faith you could move this mountain" (Matt 17:20). From there, the evangelists tell us that Jesus and his disciples went through Galilee to Capernaum (Matt 17:22–24; Mark 9:30–33).

BIBLIOGRAPHY

Avi-Yonah, Michael, and Efraim Orni. "Hermon, Mount." EJ 9:30–31.

Bailey, Kenneth E. Jesus Through Middle Eastern Eyes: Cultural Studies in the Gospels. Downers Grove, IL: InterVarsity Press, 2008.

Baly, Denis. The Geography of the Bible. Rev. ed. New York: Harper and Row, 1974.

Beck, John A. The Land of Milk and Honey: An Introduction to the Geography of Israel. Saint Louis, MO: Concordia Publishing House, 2006.

Biran, Avraham. "Dan." NEAEHL 1:331–32.

Day, John. Yahweh and the Gods and Goddesses of Canaan. Sheffield: Sheffield Academic Press, 2000.

Eisenberg, Michael. "Pan at Hippos." BAR 41.6 (2015): 42–45, 72.

Epstein, Isador. The Hebrew-English Edition of the Babylonian Talmud. London: The Soncino Press, 1994.

Hartmann, Andreas. "Process-based modelling of karst springs in Mt. Hermon, Israel." Diplomarbeit [Master's thesis], Albert-Ludwigs-Universität Freiburg im Breisgau, 2008. http://www.hydrology.uni-freiburg.de/abschluss/Hartmann_A_2008_DA.pdf.

Josephus. Translated by Henry St. J. Thackeray et al. 10 vols. LCL. Cambridge, MA: Harvard University Press, 1926–1965.

Mao'z, Zvi Uri. "Banias." NEAEHL 1:136–43.

---

26. This would be based on the association between the return of Yahweh as King and the Feast of Tabernacles (Zech 14:16–19).

"Nemesis." *Theoi Greek Mythology* (website). Accessed May 1, 2016. http://www.theoi.com/Daimon/ Nemesis.html.

Orni, Efraim, and Elisha Ephrat. *Geography of Israel*. 3rd rev. ed. Jerusalem: Keter Publishing House, 1971.

"Pan." *Theoi Greek Mythology* (website). Accessed April 26, 2016. http://www. theoi.com/Georgikos/Pan.html.

Wright, Paul H. *Greatness Grace & Glory: Carta's Atlas of Biblical Biography*. Jerusalem: Carta, 2008.

CHAPTER 30

THE GEOGRAPHICAL SIGNIFICANCE OF THE TRANSFIGURATION

Matt 17:1-13; Mark 9:2-13; Luke 9:28-36

Benjamin A. Foreman

KEY POINTS

- Four primary mountains have been posited as the location of the transfiguration: the Mount of Olives, Mount Tabor, Mount Meron, and Mount Hermon.

- In light of tradition, textual evidence, and geographical constraints, the most likely candidate is Mount Hermon.

- Paying attention to those present at the transfiguration (Moses and Elijah), as well the common ground shared among them (Mount Sinai), is evidence God is moving in ways as he did in Israel's past.

It is clear from all four of the Gospels that Jesus was more than just a provocative Galilean rabbi. His claims went well beyond those of any teacher of his day.[1] Not only did he identify himself as the messiah the Old Testament predicted (e.g., Luke 24:44) but he also brazenly claimed to be *God* (e.g., John 10:30). Yet these bold assertions were more than just hollow hubris. Time and time again he authenticated this claim to deity by per-forming miracles, acts which no mere man could ever do (see John 20:30-31). The transfiguration, however, was more than just another display of Jesus' miraculous abilities. Rather than revealing his power, it laid bare his divine *essence*. As Gathercole correctly notes, "The purpose of God's action in transforming Jesus in this way is to show the disciples what is actually the case, namely Jesus' divine sonship."[2]

---

1. For a stimulating discussion of Jesus' claims, see John Stott, *Basic Christianity* (Leicester: Inter-Varsity, 1958), 21-34.
2. Simon J. Gathercole, *The Preexistent Son: Recovering the Christologies of Matthew, Mark, and Luke* (Grand Rapids: Eerdmans, 2006), 50.

The event is mentioned in the three Synoptics, but none of them divulge where it happened.[3] Since the setting of the transfiguration receives no interpretation in the Gospels, its venue does not appear to be theologically significant (like, for example, the ascension on the Mount of Olives). Nevertheless, its location is certainly of historical interest, and this article will focus primarily on exploring the possibilities of where this unique event may have occurred.

POSSIBLE LOCATIONS OF THE EVENT

As noted elsewhere, the six months following the feeding of the five thousand was a time of relative seclusion for Jesus.[4] Over the course of that time Jesus took two major trips, and it was on the second of these that he was transfigured before Peter, James, and John. Although the transfiguration was crucially important christologically, it was a private event, witnessed only by his three closest disciples.

Three general indications of where it occurred can be gleaned from the narrative. First, all three of the Gospels give a time reference. Matthew and Mark say the event took place "after six days" (Matt 17:1; Mark 9:2); Luke maintains it happened "about eight days after these sayings" (Luke 9:28). The different number

(six versus eight) can be easily explained: Luke's reference is simply more general than that of Matthew and Mark. More important, the time reference points back to Peter's confession in the district of Caesarea Philippi since this is the preceding event in all three of the Gospels.[5] The mount of transfiguration, therefore, was no further than a six day journey from Caesarea Philippi. Second, all three of the Gospels state that Jesus was transfigured on a "high" mountain (Matt 17:1; Mark 9:2; Luke 9:28). Although the adjective "high" (hypsēlos, ὑψηλός) is a relative term, the point is that Jesus was transfigured on a mountain that is noticeably tall, not just any hill. Third, the event transpired in a secluded location. Matthew and Mark indicate that Jesus took the three disciples up a mountain "by themselves" (Matt 17:1) to be "alone" (Mark 9:2). The mountain, therefore, was in an isolated place.

THE MOUNT OF OLIVES

One early Byzantine source locates the transfiguration on the Mount of Olives. In an *itinerarium* dating to AD 333, an anonymous pilgrim to the land of Israel (known as "the Pilgrim of Bordeaux") states, "Not far from thence [the Mount of Olives] is the little hill which the Lord ascended to pray when he took Peter and John with Him, and Moses and Elias were beheld."[6]

---

3. Although one of John's main purposes is to show that Jesus is God (John 20:31), he does not mention the transfiguration.

4. See Benjamin A. Foreman, "Jesus Heals a Blind Man Near Bethsaida" on pg. 270.

5. It is true that between the confession at Caesarea Philippi and the transfiguration all three of the Synoptics include a section in which Jesus predicts his death and resurrection and exhorts his disciples to pick up their cross and follow him. However, the Gospels record no geographical movement after Peter's confession; the natural assumption is to connect the dialogue to the event at Caesarea Philippi.

6. Pilgrim of Bordeaux, *Itinerary from Bordeaux to Jerusalem*, xii. Translation from Aubrey Stewart, trans., *Itinerary from Bordeaux to Jerusalem: 'The Bordeaux Pilgrim' (333 A.D.)* (London: Palestine Pilgrims' Text Society, 1887), 25.

The Mount of Olives is approximately 120 miles from Caesarea Philippi (travelling through the Jordan Valley). If the transfiguration occurred on the Mount of Olives, Jesus and his disciples would have had to travel an average of twenty miles a day to make it there in six days. This would have been physically possible for itinerants like Jesus and his disciples who travelled everywhere on foot, but it still is quite far. Moreover, Matthew (17:22, 24) and Mark (9:30, 33) state that Jesus travelled through Galilee to Capernaum after the transfiguration. From the Mount of Olives, most of the journey to Capernaum would not be through Galilee, but either through Judea and Samaria or the Jordan Rift. Also, it would be odd to refer to the Mount of Olives as a "high" mountain, since it rises only about 150 feet above the Temple Mount (the Pilgrim of Bordeaux even seems to contradict the Gospels when he says that it was a "little hill").[7] Finally, the Mount of Olives is not in a secluded area and thus the event would have been anything but private. In short, although the suggestion can be traced back to the Byzantine period, it is highly unlikely that Jesus was transfigured on the Mount of Olives.

MOUNT TABOR

For pilgrims visiting the land of Israel today, it is a foregone conclusion that the transfiguration occurred on Mount Tabor. The mountain is roughly forty-seven miles from Caesarea Philippi, a reasonable distance to travel in six days. Also, although it reaches an elevation of only about 1800 feet above sea level, it stands out prominently in the Jezreel Valley and therefore from the perspective of the valley floor, one could conceivably call it a "high mountain."[8] The strongest argument for Mount Tabor, however, is its lengthy tradition, which may go all the way back to the second century AD. Commenting on John 2:12, Origen (ca. AD 184–253) quotes from an apocryphal gospel called the *Gospel According to the Hebrews*, which scholars date to the late first or early second century AD. This gospel has unfortunately not been preserved, but the text he cites mentions "the great Mount Tabor."[9] The transfiguration is not explicitly referred to in that passage, but the reference to Mount Tabor "the great" may imply that this identification had already been made back then.[10] At the very latest, the tradition can be traced back to the early fourth century.

---

7. In Matt 4:8 Jesus is taken to a "very high mountain" and tempted by the devil to bow down to him. If this scene is attached to the second temptation (where Jesus is taken to the pinnacle of the temple), an argument might be made that Matthew refers to the Mount of Olives (or a mountain nearby) as being "very high." It is unclear, however, where this third temptation occurred, or even whether it took place in the physical realm at all. See Carson's cautious comments in D. A. Carson, "Matthew," in *Expositor's Bible Commentary*, ed. Frank E. Gæbelein (Grand Rapids: Zondervan, 1984), 111.

8. It rises about 1450 feet above the Jezreel Valley floor.

9. See the text in J. K. Elliott, *The Apocryphal New Testament: A Collection of Apocryphal Christian Literature in an English Translation* (Oxford: Clarendon Press, 1993), 9.

10. Notley and Safrai go slightly beyond the evidence in categorically saying, "Origen relates that this gospel reports that the miracle of the Transfiguration occurred on Mount Tabor" (R. Steven Notley and Ze'ev Safrai, *Eusebius, Onomasticon: The Place Names of Divine Scripture Including the Latin Edition of Jerome Translated into English and with Topographical Commentary* [Leiden: Brill, 2005], 95n500).

In AD 326 Constantine's mother Helena built a church on top of the mountain, and Cyril of Jerusalem (ca. AD 313-386) unambiguously noted that the transfiguration occurred "on Mount Tabor" (*Catechetical Lectures* 12.16). Around the same time, Ephrem the Syrian (early fourth century AD) also positively located the transfiguration on Mount Tabor in a Syriac hymn.[11] Eusebius (ca. AD 260-340) was familiar with the tradition, but was less certain about its accuracy. Although he mentions the mountain thirteen times in the *Onomasticon*, and frequently discusses the transfiguration, he only once links the two, and even then in a veiled manner. Commenting on the Greek Ps 88:13 [89:12], he suggests that the references to Mount Tabor and Mount Hermon in that verse might be a prophecy of Jesus' "marvelous transfigurations" (pl.) on these mountains.[12] A little over a century later, Jerome (ca. AD 346-420)— probably following Cyril of Jerusalem— also definitively identified Mount Tabor as the mount of transfiguration (*Epistles* 46.12; 108:13). For the next six hundred years the site continued to be venerated by Christian pilgrims. In AD 1099 the Crusaders built a church on the summit, but it was destroyed by Saladin's forces

in 1187. Franciscan monks nevertheless continued to commemorate the transfiguration at the site for the next seven centuries, and in 1921-1924 they built a basilica over the crusader and Byzantine foundations.[13]

Although 1700 years (nearly) of tradition is weighty evidence and is an important factor to consider, it is also prudent to remember that tradition is not usually founded on rigorous scholarly research. Popular conceptions, rather, frequently give rise to tradition. The tradition of Mount Tabor could be such an instance and its popularity might be accounted for linguistically, aesthetically, and geographically. According to Luke's account, Jesus took his three disciples up to *the* mountain to pray (Luke 9:28). Given the definite article, a popular understanding of this might lead one to search for a large independent mountain, like Mount Tabor.[14] Aesthetically, the mountain is visually appealing. This is significant because in the popular mind such an incredible event as the transfiguration appropriately requires an awe-inspiring location. Unlike almost any other mountain in Israel, Mount Tabor is nearly perfectly hemispherical, and as Murphy-O'Connor puts it, "It excites awe and

---

11. Hymns on the Virginity and on the Symbols of the Lord, Hymn 21: "Simon, going up to Mt. Tabor, lovely and undisturbed by the crucifiers, persuaded the Lord, 'It is good, my Lord, for us to be here, without disturbers; it is fitting for us with righteous men in tents; it is peaceful for us with Moses and Elijah rather than in the Temple full of the confusion and bitterness of the Jews" (Kathleen E. McVey, *Ephrem the Syrian Hymns* [New York: Paulist Press, 1989], 352).

12. See P. W. L. Walker, *Holy City, Holy Places? Christian Attitudes to Jerusalem and the Holy Land in the Fourth Century* (Oxford: Clarendon Press, 1990), 146.

13. K. G. Jung, "Tabor, Mount" *ISBE* 4:714.

14. Although linguistically impossible from the perspective of the Greek, Matt 17:1 might also be misunderstood to mean that Jesus took his three disciples to a mountain that stood apart "by itself" (compare KJV: "and bringeth them up into a high mountain apart"). Again, Mount Tabor is a perfect match!

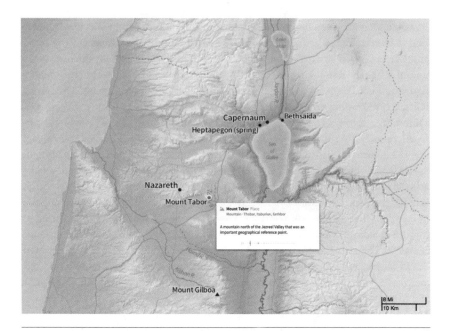

wonder; it has the aura of a sacred mountain."[15] Geographically, Mount Tabor is conveniently located. Near Nazareth, and sitting on the main branch of the international highway leading up to Tiberias and the Sea of Galilee, it is easily accessible to Christian pilgrims. In short, Mount Tabor fits the bill perfectly. It meets all of the expectations of Christian pilgrims and thus the rise of the tradition can easily be explained.[16]

On the negative side of the argument, there are several factors that point away from locating the transfiguration on Mount Tabor. First, ancient sources imply that there was a city on top of the mountain in Jesus' day. According to Polybius, Antiochus the Great captured the *city* on Mount Tabor in 218 BC (*Histories* 5.70). Josephus states that

Mount Tabor was one of the "cities" that the Jews held under the rule of Alexander Jannaeus (ca. 106–73 BC; *Ant.* 13.396). In his day he claims to have fortified the settlement (*War* 2.573; *Life* 1.87–88), eventually even building a wall around it (*War* 4.54–56). These passages suggest that there was continuous occupation on Mount Tabor from the third century BC through the first century AD. If this was the case, then Mount Tabor is an unlikely candidate for the transfiguration, which was a private event.

Not only was the transfiguration itself a hidden incident, but Jesus in general stayed out of the Jewish public spotlight during this entire phase of his ministry. Mark tells us that Jesus passed through Galilee and "did not want anyone to know where they were, because he was teach-

---

15. Jerome Murphy-O'Connor, *The Holy Land: An Oxford Archaeological Guide from Earliest Times to 1700*, 4th ed. (Oxford: Oxford University Press, 1998), 366.

16. See the excellent discussion in Walker, *Holy City, Holy Places*, 151–55.

ing his disciples" (Mark 9:30–31 NIV). Mount Tabor is in lower Galilee—which was much more populated than upper Galilee—and would be an odd region for him to pass through if he were looking for seclusion.

Finally, Matthew 17:24 and Mark 9:33 specify that Jesus and his disciples made their way back to Capernaum after the transfiguration. Mount Tabor is not on the way from Caesarea Philippi to Capernaum. Locating the transfiguration at Mount Tabor, therefore, makes Jesus' journey quite circuitous.[17]

MOUNT MERON

One suggestion that has gained the support of some recent commentators is Mount Meron in Upper Galilee.[18] This identification is promising for some since: (1) it is a "high" mountain (3900 feet, the second tallest in all of Israel), (2) it is a reasonable distance from Caesarea Philippi (twenty-seven miles following the most likely route of travel), (3) it is relatively secluded in upper Galilee, and (4) there are several Jewish villages in the area (more on this below). Although this identification has no ancient adherents, it is usually offered as the best alternative to Mount Hermon, which for various reasons is thought to be an unlikely candidate. Mount Meron, however, is in Galilee, and a close reading of Mark insinuates that the transfig-

uration did not occur in this region (see below). As will be shown in the next section, not only can the objections to Mount Hermon be countered, but several indications in the text suggest that it is more probable.

MOUNT HERMON

Mount Hermon is the tallest mountain in the land of Israel. It is not a single peak but is a large block of folds pushed up by the Syro-African rift, whose tallest crest rises to 9232 feet. The entire range, with Caesarea Philippi on its lower slopes, was part of the (mostly Gentile) territory known as Gaulanitis and was governed by Herod's son Philip. Mount Hermon not only fits the three general criteria mentioned above, but seems to have been recognized as a possible candidate already in the Byzantine period.[19]

This identification has been challenged for two main reasons. First, Mark 9:14 says that when Jesus, Peter, James, and John came down from the mountain, they saw a large crowd—which included scribes—arguing with the rest of the disciples. Since Mount Hermon is in a predominantly Gentile territory, the presence of teachers of the law there is in the estimation of some "almost inconceivable."[20] Second, Luke 9:37 indicates that Jesus and his three disciples came down from the mountain the next day. The summit of Mount Hermon, it is argued, is so high

---

17. Walter L. Liefeld, "Theological Motifs in the Transfiguration Narrative," in *New Dimensions in New Testament Study*, ed. Richard N. Longenecker (Grand Rapids: Zondervan, 1974), 167n27.

18. W. Ewing, "The Mount of Transfiguration," *Expository Times* 18.7 (1907): 333–34; Liefeld, "Transfiguration Narrative," 167n27; followed by R. T. France, *The Gospel of Matthew* (Grand Rapids: Eerdmans, 2007), 646–47; Craig Blomberg, *Matthew* (Nashville, TN: Broadman, 1992), 263; Carson, "Matthew," 384.

19. E.g., Eusebius (see above).

20. Carson, "Matthew," 384.

Mount Hermon

and so cold that it would be an unusual place to spend the night.[21]

Neither of these objections is convincing. First, it is gratuitous to argue that the teachers of the law would never enter Gentile territory. Paul, who described himself as more zealous for Judaism than many of his countrymen (Gal 1:14; Phil 3:6), traveled all the way to Damascus to persecute the early believers (Acts 9:1-8). When he was later arrested and brought to Caesarea, the high priest Ananias and some of the elders came down to the city—which was very Roman—to testify against him (Acts 24:1-9). If this was the case in Paul's day, why should we expect the teachers of the law to be any less ambitious in their desire to silence Jesus? Second, the claim that the ascent to the top of Mount Hermon is too strenuous of a climb for the

disciples not only fails to take into account the fact that people walked everywhere and thus were much more fit than they are today, but also goes beyond what the text says. None of the Gospels explicitly say that the four hiked to the top of the summit, nor that they spent the night on top. We simply do not know how far up the mountain they climbed, nor where on the mountain they passed the night. As for the cold temperature, it is important to remember that the event occurred several weeks (we are not told exactly how long) before the Feast of Booths (see Matt 17:4 and parallels; also John 7:1-2). This places the transfiguration sometime in early- to mid-September, which is still one of the hottest times of the year.

As for positive evidence pointing to Mount Hermon, the flow of the narra-

---

21. Edersheim, for example, writes, "Now, to climb the top of Hermon is, even from the nearest point, an Alpine ascent, trying and fatiguing, which would occupy a whole day (six hours in the ascent and four in the descent), and require provisions of food and water; while, from the keenness of the air, it would be impossible to spend the night on the top" (Alfred Edersheim, *The Life and Times of Jesus the Messiah*, 2 vols. [New York: E.R. Herrick & Co.], 2:94).

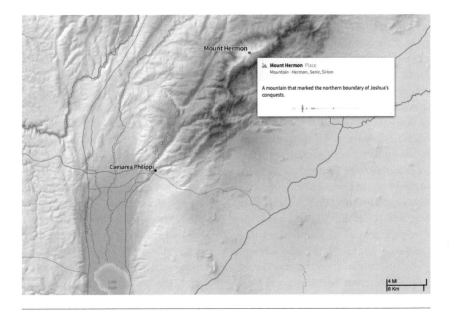

tive in Matthew and Mark suggests this. Both of them state that Peter confessed Jesus as the Messiah in the district of Caesarea Philippi (Matt 16:13–20; Mark 8:27–30), but neither imply that Jesus travelled anywhere between Peter's confession and the transfiguration.[22] The natural conclusion of the reader, therefore, is that the "high mountain" is in the region of Caesarea Philippi—the last named locale. This suspicion seems to be confirmed in the subsequent narrative, particularly in Mark. After coming down from the mountain, the four find the rest of the disciples arguing with the scribes. Seeing Jesus, the crowd swarms toward him, bringing him a boy with a demon. Because an even larger crowd was beginning to form, Jesus then quickly heals the boy and enters into a house. It is only *after* this scene, however, that Mark tells us that "they went on from

there and passed through Galilee" (Mark 9:30a; compare Matt 17:22). If Jesus was transfigured in Galilee (at either Mount Meron or Mount Tabor), then why does Mark write that they passed through Galilee only at this point in his narrative? Mark 9:30a makes much more sense before Mark 9:2 if they had crossed over into Galilee six days earlier, as would be the case with a setting at either Mount Meron or Mount Tabor.

An examination of Mark's Gospel reveals that he was very interested in recording Jesus' movements. Comparing Mark with Matthew and Luke reveals that there are no instances where Jesus' movements are recorded in Matt and/or Luke but not in Mark. Put differently: Mark always records Jesus' movements when Matt and/or Luke do; Matthew and/or Luke do not always mention them when Mark does. A few examples

---

22. Luke does not state the whereabouts of Peter's confession.

will suffice to illustrate this. In Luke 5:17–26 Jesus heals a paralytic, but it is unclear where the miracle occurred. Mark 2:1 (also Matt 9:1) clarifies that it occurred in Capernaum. Thus, Luke fails to record that Jesus returned from "one of those cities" in Galilee (Luke 5:12) to his hometown to perform the miracle. In Luke 9:18–20, Luke does not state that Jesus moved from Bethsaida (Luke 9:10) to the district of Caesarea Philippi. Again, Mark explains this (Mark 8:22), as does Matthew (Matt 16:13). Luke records the disciples' argument about who is the greatest in the kingdom (Luke 9:46–48), but gives no indication that it occurred near Capernaum. Mark 9:33 and Matt 17:24, however, provide this information. Matthew is generally more interested in recording Jesus' movements than Luke, but he also fails to record some of his relocations. In Matthew 12:22 a demon-possessed man is brought to Jesus, but the narrative gives no indication that this happened after Jesus had returned home to Capernaum. Only Mark 3:20 supplies us with this detail. Finally, Matthew's narrative implies that Jesus cleansed the temple immediately after the triumphal entry (Matt 21:12–17). Mark again traces Jesus' steps more specifically: Jesus entered Jerusalem after the triumphal entry, but because it was late, he went back to Bethany that evening and cleansed the temple only on the following day (Mark 11:11–19).

In short, Mark's Gospel stands out in its sensitivity to the geographical locations of the events of Jesus' ministry.[23] With this in mind, it would seem odd for him in particular to fail to mention that the transfiguration occurred twenty-seven miles (Mount Meron) or forty-seven miles (Mount Tabor) away from the last site he named, and then state that Jesus and his disciples "passed through Galilee" six days after they have already been there. Taking all of these factors together, the best conclusion is that the transfiguration occurred somewhere on Mount Hermon.

THE GEOGRAPHICAL SIGNIFICANCE OF THE EVENT

The theological significance of the transfiguration has been considered from many angles. One approach that might provide an interesting perspective on the event is to look at it through a geographical lens. This is the only place in the Bible where Moses and Elijah are explicitly named together.[24] Since Moses was forbidden from entering the promised land (Num 11:10–13), the two did not minister in the same region.[25] But there was one geographical intersection between both their ministries—another mountain, Mount Sinai (Exod 19; 1 Kgs 19:8–18).

---

23. Some may wish to argue that the feeding of the five thousand is an exception. Luke mentions Bethsaida explicitly (9:10); Mark only says that he went to a lonely place (Mark 6:31–32). But even in this narrative, Mark does not fail to record Jesus' movement. He may not reference the city on the outbound journey (though he does on the return; Mark 6:45), but he still makes it clear to the reader that the miraculous feeding occurred in a different location than the previous event.

24. Some associate Moses and Elijah with the two witnesses in Rev 11:6, but they are not there named.

25. Elijah was active primarily in the northern kingdom of Israel, Moses ministered in Egypt and in the wilderness.

Aside from Moses (and Joshua his helper), Elijah is the only other person in all of Israel's history who went up Mount Sinai.[26] And significantly, both Moses and Elijah witnessed a theophany on top of the mountain. If this connection is made, then the transfiguration, like many of the other narratives of Jesus' life, is evidence that God is once again working in a way similar to how he had in the past. Once again Moses and Elijah are the spectators of the transcendent manifestation of God, only this time on the mount of transfiguration. For the disciples, and subsequent readers familiar with Israel's Scriptures, this was a powerful witness to the divine nature of their Galilean rabbi.

BIBLIOGRAPHY

Blomberg, Craig. *Matthew*. New American Commentary. Nashville, TN: Broadman, 1992.

Carson, D. A. "Matthew." Pages 1–599 in vol. 8 of *Expositor's Bible Commentary*. Edited by Frank E. Gæbelein. Grand Rapids: Zondervan, 1984.

Edersheim, Alfred. *The Life and Times of Jesus the Messiah*. 2 vols. New American edition. New York: E.R. Herrick & Co., 1886.

Elliott, J. K. *The Apocryphal New Testament: A Collection of Apocryphal Christian Literature in an English Translation*. Oxford: Clarendon Press, 1993.

Ewing, W. "The Mount of Transfiguration." *Expository Times* 18.7 (1907): 333–34.

France, R. T. *The Gospel of Matthew*. NICNT. Grand Rapids: Eerdmands, 2007.

Gathercole, Simon J. *The Preexistent Son: Recovering the Christologies of Matthew, Mark, and Luke*. Grand Rapids: Eerdmans, 2006.

Jung, K. G. "Tabor, Mount." *ISBE* 4:713–14.

Liefeld, Walter L. "Theological Motifs in the Transfiguration Narrative." Pages 162–79 in *New Dimensions in New Testament Study*. Edited by Richard N. Longenecker. Grand Rapids: Zondervan, 1974.

Murphy-O'Connor, Jerome. *The Holy Land: An Oxford Archaeological Guide from Earliest Times to 1700*. 4th ed. Oxford: Oxford University Press, 1998.

Notley, R. Steven, and Ze'ev Safrai. *Eusebius, Onomasticon: The Place Names of Divine Scripture Including the Latin Edition of Jerome Translated into English and with Topographical Commentary*. Leiden: Brill, 2005.

McVey, Kathleen E. *Ephrem the Syrian Hymns*. New York: Paulist Press, 1989.

Pilgrim of Bordeaux. *Itinerary from Bordeaux to Jerusalem: 'The Bordeaux Pilgrim' (333 A.D.)*. Translated by Aubrey Stewart. London: Palestine Pilgrims' Text Society, 1887.

Stott, John. *Basic Christianity*. Leicester: Inter-Varsity, 1958.

Walker, P. W. L. *Holy City, Holy Places? Christian Attitudes to Jerusalem and the Holy Land in the Fourth Century*. Oxford: Clarendon Press, 1990.

---

26. Mount Sinai is also called Mount Horeb.

CHAPTER 31

MILLSTONES IN CAPERNAUM

Matt 17:24-18:14; Mark 9:33-49; Luke 17:1-2

Cyndi Parker

KEY POINTS

- Capernaum had a diverse population due to its proximity to international roads, its fishing shoreline, and its rich soil.

- The imagery of a millstone tied around one's neck was more powerful due to Capernaum's millstone industry and close proximity to the sea.

- God's care for each individual is evidenced by his judgment on those who would make another sin.

I n Matthew 18, Jesus and the disciples are in Capernaum. The disciples question Jesus about who will be the greatest in the kingdom of heaven. He draws their attention to a child and replies, "Unless you change and become like little children, you will never enter the kingdom of heaven" (Matt 18:3).[1] Jesus tells the disciples that the one who assumes a humble position like a child will be the greatest in the kingdom (Matt 18:4), and that receiving such a child in his name is receiving him (Matt 18:5). However, for the one who causes a "little one" to sin, it would be better "to have a large millstone hung around their neck and to be drowned in depths of the sea" (Matt 18:6; compare Mark 9:42; Luke 17:2). The same teaching recorded in the Gospel of Mark is also set in Capernaum (Mark 9:33), but the Gospel of Luke does not specify Jesus' location. Jesus' example of a millstone is not a random reference for the residents of Capernaum. Therefore, becoming familiar with the characteristics of Capernaum and its local environs helps the reader better understand Jesus' teachings.

---

1. Unless otherwise indicated, Scripture quotations are from the NIV.

308

THE GEOGRAPHY OF CAPERNAUM

Capernaum sits on the wide, northern shoreline of the Sea of Galilee and at the southern base of the Rosh Pina Sill—a large pile of basalt rock, courtesy of the now-extinct volcanic cones dotting the high plateau to the east (the modern day Golan Heights). The Rosh Pina Sill pushes the Jordan River to the east where the river cuts a channel between the eastern edge of the Rosh Pina Sill and the foothills of the Golan Heights and flows south into the Sea of Galilee.

The location of Capernaum was advantageous for several reasons.[2] The town is located to the west of the Jordan River, placing it near the border between two first century political areas. The Jordan River was the boundary between the political district of Galilee, ruled by Herod Antipas, and the political district of Gaulanitis, ruled by Herod Philip. Located to the west of the Jordan River, Capernaum is in Herod Antipas' territory. In fact, it is the only significant town on the northern shore of the Sea of Galilee in Galilee.

Additionally, the abundance of basalt from the Rosh Pina Sill had a positive influence on the life of the local residents. The hard and durable basalt is a good building material, and it erodes into a nutrient-dense soil perfect for agriculture. Although Capernaum was not a large city, it was carefully designed and was full of modest houses with a synagogue in the center of town, all built with local basalt. In the outer environs of Capernaum, the black, nutrient rich basalt soil, along with the warm winters and hot summers, creates an ideal agricultural environment, contributing to the region's reputation for producing high quality grain.

The residents of the town also used the basalt to create durable agricultural tools. Such tools included olive presses, mortars, household grinding stones, and large industrial millstones. The small grinding stones used in the house had a slightly concave stone base on which grain was ground with a hand-held stone. Also used in the house were hand mills consisting of two circular stones resting on each other. Grain was placed between the stones, and the top stone was rotated to create the milling action.[3] The industrial millstones are significantly larger and heavier. They have a bottom piece that is cone-shaped and is placed on the ground with the pointed end up. It is topped with a cylindrical stone that looks like it has been cinched in the middle with a belt to make it hour-glass shaped. A large log fit into the middle "belt" and became a lever to which a donkey was attached. The grain would be poured into the top and milled into flour as the donkey turned the heavy top stone. Due to the multiple unfinished tools found in Capernaum, too many for the town's population, one can conclude the fabrication of such tools created an important aspect of the local economy.[4]

---

2. See Jonathan Reed, *Archaeology and the Galilean Jesus: A Re-examination of the Evidence* (Harrisburg, PA: Trinity Press International, 2000), 144–48; Stanislao Loffreda, *Recovering Capharnaum*, 2nd ed. (Jerusalem: Franciscan Printing Press, 1993), 18.

3. One of these household millstones is likely what is referred to in Matt 24:41 and Rev 18:42 (compare Deut 24:6; Judg 9:53; 2 Sam 11:21; Jer 25:10).

4. Loffreda, *Recovering Capharnaum*, 20.

House made from basalt in Chorazin, about two miles north of Capernaum

Daily life in Capernaum also revolved around the sea. Capernaum controlled five miles of shoreline between the Jordan River and several fresh water springs west of the town. The remains of at least eight large stone piers indicate that Capernaum was one of the largest fishing towns around the perimeter of the sea.[5]

The fishing, farming, and manufacturing industries of Capernaum were served well by the presence of an important imperial north-south trade route that runs along the flat Mediterranean coastline before turning inland to connect with the northwestern shoreline of the Sea of Galilee. The road continues along the northern perimeter of Capernaum, crosses the Jordan River, and turns north towards Damascus. The coins and imported vessels found during the excavations of Capernaum suggest the modest town was connected by trade to Syria, Phoenicia, and Cypress.[6]

Since Capernaum was located near an artery road and was close to the political border between Galilee and Gaulanitus, the town was also home to traders, tax collectors, and Roman soldiers.[7] These groups of people combined with the local fishermen, farmers, and synagogue officials created a diverse population group in Capernaum.

MATTHEW 18

The first few verses of Matthew 18 build on a conversation that is introduced in Matthew 16. When Jesus visits the district of Caesarea Philippi (Matt 16:13), he declares his messianic role, a role that

---

5. Loffreda, *Recovering Capharnaum*, 19–20.

6. Loffreda, *Recovering Capharnaum*, 19.

7. Vassilios Tzaferis, *Excavations at Capernaum: Vol. 1, 1978–1982* (Winona Lake, IN: Eisenbrauns, 1989), 202.

includes returning to Jerusalem to suffer and to be killed (Matt 16:21). The difficulty of understanding Jesus' portrayal of the humble role of the Messiah is evident not only in Peter's protest against Jesus' announcement of his coming death (Matt 16:22) but also in the continued conversation among the disciples regarding who would be appointed to positions of power in the new kingdom (Matt 20:20–24). Jesus emphasizes that those who are considered great in the kingdom of heaven must be willing to follow his example and take on a humble position (Matt 16:24; 20:25–28). The conversation discussed below from Matt 18 follows the same theme. Jesus presents a picture to his disciples of an upside-down power structure of the kingdom in which the greatest are not those who assume the most power and authority but those who humble themselves. Jesus begins his teaching emphasizing the necessity of exercising child-like humility, but then he warns the disciples of the severe punishment of causing others to stumble. To underscore this teaching, Jesus uses a millstone, which was an object familiar to his Capernaum-based audience.

MATTHEW 18:1–4

Jesus and the disciples are in the political region of Galilee, having returned to Capernaum from their travels (Matt 17:22, 24). The disciples ask Jesus a question, "Who, then, is the greatest in the kingdom of heaven?" (Matt 18:1).[8] The inquiry reflects the disciples' anticipated view of a human kingdom, betraying their misunderstanding of the kingdom of heaven. Jesus brings a child into their

midst and says that unless one becomes like such a child, one cannot enter the kingdom. Given the diverse population of Capernaum, which included fishermen, farmers, tax collectors, synagogue offi-

Millstone found at Capernaum

cials, and Roman soldiers, Jesus' choice of a small child is striking because it opposes the common understanding of those who occupy influential positions of power.

However, Jesus' point is similar to his previous teaching at Caesarea Philippi. The kingdom of heaven has an upside-down power structure, exemplified by the Messiah who humbly goes to Jerusalem to die. With his reply, Jesus shifts the focus from who will occupy positions of greatness to who will be willing to follow his example and take a lowly position.[9] Those

---

8. Compare Matt 20:20–28 and Mark 10:34–45.

9. Compare Matt 20:27; 23:12.

who take the humble position of a child will be the greatest in the kingdom of heaven (Matt 18:4).

MATTHEW 18:5-9

The one who welcomes "one such child"—not just the child in their midst at that moment—welcomes Jesus (Matt 18:5). If the person assuming a child-like position is the greatest in the kingdom of heaven, and if welcoming such a person in the name of Jesus means welcoming Jesus himself, then respect should be given to those in such a humble position. Indeed, anyone who causes a "little one"—or one who believes in Jesus—to sin[10] will suffer severe punishment. With the use of the phrase "little one," the reader might question if Jesus is still talking about children, like the one in their midst in the previous verses. However, the parenthetical phrase "one who believes in me" emphasizes that it is faith in Jesus that is in question. Jesus warns his listeners that it would be better for anyone who causes another to sin to take a large millstone and hang it around their neck and be drowned in the sea (Matt 18:6).

The two Greek words *mylos onikos* (μύλος ὀνικὸς) translated as "large millstone" (NIV, TNIV, NLT), "great millstone" (RSV, NRSV, ESV, ASV), or "heavy millstone" (NASB) specify the industrial kind of millstones produced and exported

from Capernaum. The adjective *onikos* (ὀνικὸς), meaning "heavy" or "pertaining to a donkey," refers to upper millstones turned by donkeys in the milling process.[11] Jesus uses both a familiar object like a millstone and also the proximity to the Sea of Galilee to create a striking visual image for the audience. Indeed, cutting off parts of the body and yet still entering the kingdom is better than causing one who believes to stumble and being guaranteed death (Matt 18:8-9).[12]

MATTHEW 18:10-14

The reader may question why the punishment of causing a "little one" to stumble is so severe. Jesus explains by saying, just as a shepherd leaves ninety-nine sheep on a hill to search for the one that wandered off,[13] and who then rejoices when the lost sheep is found, so too, God is not willing to have a "little one" perish (Matt 18:12-14). Therefore, the one who "despises" (*kataphroneō*, καταφρονέω) one of these little ones is in direct contrast to the persistent love and attention God gives to each of his children.

CONCLUSION

The location of Capernaum is advantageous for its proximity to international roads, its extensive shoreline for fishing, and the rich soil for agriculture. Due to these advantages, Capernaum

---

10. Morris notes the verb used here suggests entrapment. The specific sin need not be mentioned because Jesus is communicating a larger idea. Anyone deceiving another into committing sin will be punished. Leon Morris, *The Gospel According to Matthew* (Grand Rapids: Eerdmans, 1992), 461n16. Compare R. T. France, *The Gospel of Matthew* (Grand Rapids: Eerdmans, 2007), 205-6; Craig S. Keener, *A Commentary on the Gospel of Matthew* (Grand Rapids: Eerdmans, 1999), 449.

11. See Keener, *A Commentary on the Gospel of Matthew*, 449; Donald Hagner, *Matthew 14-28* (Dallas: Word Books, 1995), 522.

12. Compare 1 Cor 8:12.

13. Compare Luke 15:3-7.

had a diverse population base, making Jesus' response to the disciples' question about those who are considered great in the kingdom of heaven poignant. Jesus' message goes against normal human hierarchies of power. He emphasizes the humility and the willingness to follow his own example that are the qualities of greatness in the kingdom of heaven. A child is chosen instead of a more visible person of power or higher economic status. The importance of not taking advantage of one who has taken such a humble position is underscored by Jesus' dramatic example of the millstone imagery and his proximity to the lake. To think a person could lift the upper portion of an industrial millstone on their own, much less tie it around their neck, walk to the edge of the water, and jump in, is extreme—but the exaggerated visual image emphasizes the impossibility of escaping judgment. The image also underscores the contrast between the one who causes another to sin and God's character. God is like a shepherd who goes out of his way to search for the one who wandered away. Great rejoicing occurs for every lost one who is brought home. If God cares deeply for every single individual, then woe to the one who causes even one of them to wander from God.

BIBLIOGRAPHY

France, R. T. *The Gospel of Matthew.* NICNT. Grand Rapids: Eerdmans, 2007.

Hagner, Donald. *Matthew 14–28.* WBC 33b. Dallas: Word Books, 1995.

Keener, Craig S. *A Commentary on the Gospel of Matthew.* Grand Rapids: Eerdmans, 1999.

Loffreda, Stanislao. *Recovering Capharnaum.* 2nd ed. Jerusalem: Franciscan Printing Press, 1993.

Morris, Leon. *The Gospel According to Matthew.* PNTC. Grand Rapids: Eerdmans, 1992.

Reed, Jonathan. *Archaeology and the Galilean Jesus: A Re-examination of the Evidence.* Harrisburg, PA: Trinity Press International, 2000.

Tzaferis, Vassilios. *Excavations at Capernaum: Vol. 1, 1978–1982.* Winona Lake, IN: Eisenbrauns, 1989.

CHAPTER 32

GEHENNA: JERUSALEM'S GARBAGE DUMP OR PLACE OF ESCHATOLOGICAL JUDGMENT?[1]

Mark 9:42-50

Gordon Franz

KEY POINTS

- Some believe Gehenna was a dump located outside the walls of Jerusalem that was dedicated to the burning of garbage and criminal bodies.

- However, neither history, archaeology, nor literary evidence supports this view.

- Criminals and waste were not burned during the Second Temple period, and even if they were the prevailing westerly winds would have blown foul smells over the city discouraging this practice.

- The actual dumping ground was located in the Kidron Valley.

- Despite popular misconceptions, Gehenna is not a burning dump but a location of eschatological judgment.

POPULAR BELIEF

There is a popular belief among some evangelicals that Gehenna was a gar-bage dump in the Hinnom Valley near Jerusalem where they burned criminals' bodies and rubbish. Recently, this point

---

1. This is a revised and expanded version of my paper "Gehenna: Garbage Dump or Place of Eternal Punishment," presented at the Evangelical Theological Society, 39th National Conference, Dec 3–5, 1987, South Hamilton, MA. Unless otherwise indicated, Scripture quotations in this article are from the NKJV.

of view has been espoused by John Noe,[2] and the idea is also the cornerstone of Jehovah's Witnesses' theology.[3]

This view is most graphically described by Sharon Baker in her book, *Razing Hell*, when she writes about the garbage dump in the Hinnom Valley:[4]

Well before the time of Jesus, the valley was also used as a refuse heap. The people in the surrounding areas dumped their trash in Gehenna, where it burned day and night. The fire never went out. It smoldered there beneath the surface, incinerating the rotten, smelly garbage. New garbage was piled on top of the old decaying garbage: rotting fish, slimy vegetation, decaying human refuse of every imaginable sort. And as you know from experience, a dump without flies is a dump without garbage. The flies laid eggs on the surface of the dump. So just imagine the hundreds of thousands of squirmy, wormy maggots living there, eating the rotting refuse. All the while, under the surface, the fire still burned, devouring the putrid garbage from days and weeks past.

It was a fire that burned forever, where the worm did not die and where people went to throw their trash, grimacing from the stench, gritting their teeth in revulsion, never venturing too close for fear of falling into the abhorrent abyss. In times of war, decaying human flesh mingled with the rotting garbage—imagine the vile vision. When Jesus spoke of Gehenna, his hearers would think of the valley of rotting, worm-infested garbage, where the fire always burned, smoke always lingered, and if the wind blew just right, a smell that sickened the senses wafted in the air. The word "Gehenna" called to mind total horror and disgust.[5]

Peter M. Head, New Testament tutor at Wycliffe Hall in the University of Oxford, observed that: "There is no convincing evidence in the primary sources for the existence of a fiery rubbish dump in this [the Hinnom Valley] location (in any case, a thorough investigation would be appreciated)."[6] This essay is a brief, but thorough, investigation of the subject, examining the history, archaeology, and geography of "Gehenna." The study shows that there was no garbage dump in the Hinnom Valley—ever!

There are at least five reasons why there is no historical, archaeological, or geographical basis for the claim that

---

2. John Noe, *Hell Yes / Hell No. What Really is the Extent of God's Grace ... and Wrath?* (Indianapolis, IN: East2West, 2011).

3. Watchtower Bible and Tract Society, *Make Sure of All Things, Hold Fast to What is Fine* (Brooklyn, NY: Watchtower Bible and Tract Society, 1965), 209–10, 230.

4. Sharon Baker, *Razing Hell: Rethinking Everything You've Been Taught about God's Wrath and Judgment* (Louisville, KY: Westminster John Knox, 2010).

5. Baker, *Razing Hell*, 129–30.

6. Peter M. Head, "The Duration of Divine Judgment in the New Testament," in *'The Reader Must Understand': Eschatology in Bible and Theology*, ed. K. Brower and M. Elliott (Eugene, OR: Wipf and Stock, 1997), 223. Brackets added by author.

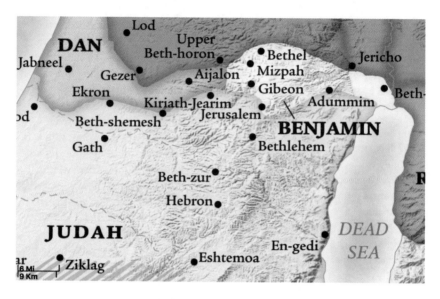

Tribal Distribution of Palestine

there was a garbage dump in the Hinnom Valley where criminals' bodies and rubbish were burned. But first, we need to discuss the Hinnom Valley itself.

THE GEOGRAPHY OF THE HINNOM VALLEY

The Hinnom Valley has been identified with Wadi er-Rababi which is located on the west and south side of the Old City of Jerusalem and modern-day Mount Zion. The Hebrew word *gay'* ("valley") denotes a sharp valley with slopes on its sides, an excellent description of the Hinnom Valley. On the eastern end, the Hinnom Valley meets the Kidron Valley. In the Bible it is called the "Valley of Hinnom" (Josh 15:8; 18:16; Neh 11:30); the "Valley of the son of Hinnom" (Josh 15:8; 18:16; 2 Kgs 23:10; 2 Chr 28:3; 33:6; Jer 7:31–32; 19:2, 6; 32:35); and a variant reading has the "Valley of the sons of Hinnom" (2 Kgs 23:10). Once it is called simply "the valley" (Jer 2:23). The fact that it is called *bēn*

("son") of Hinnom suggests that Hinnom was a personal name, either of a human being or a Jebusite deity.

The Hinnom Valley was the border between the tribal territory of Benjamin to the north, and Judah to the south and west (Josh 15:8; 18:16; Neh 11:30). It was also notorious during the Judean monarchy as a place of Baal worship (Jer 2:23; 32:35). Outside the "Potsherd Gate," located near the Pool of Siloam, was a place for potters to make pottery (Jer 19:2), but the infamous Tophet where people sacrificed their children to the god Molech was also there. King Ahaz offered his children to this god (2 Chr 28:3), as did King Manasseh (2 Chr 33:6). King Josiah, however, defiled the Tophet (2 Kgs 23:10). Apparently after his death, the kings of Judah rebuilt the high places of Tophet and reinstituted the practice of sacrificing children to the god Molech (Jer 7:31). Yet the Lord said he would change the name of the valley

The Babylonian Chronicles

Babylon, 6th century BC

500 years of Babylonian history

Jehoiakim refuses to pay tribute
(2 Kings 24:11)

Nebuchadnezzar's Jerusalem seige
(2 Kings 24:10–11)

Jehoiachin's capture
(2 Kings 24:12)

from Hinnom to the Valley of Slaughter because that is where the Babylonians slaughtered the Jerusalemites as they fled the city in 586 BC. The Babylonians came into Jerusalem by the "front door" (the Middle Gate)[7] as the Jerusalemites, including King Zedekiah, fled out the "back door" (the "Gate between two walls" and the "Potsherd Gate" down by the Pool of Siloam; 2 Kgs 25:4; Jer 39:3–4). Apparently there were Babylonian forces waiting to slaughter the Jerusalemites as they fled the city and place their bodies in the Tophet, so they could be eaten by the birds and beasts (Jer 7:32–34; 19:6). It is important to note that there is no mention of burning the bodies of the dead Jerusalemites; they were left for the birds and the beasts to eat.

John Noe made a mistake when he tried to tie three passages together from the book of Jeremiah (7:32–34; 19:1–15; 31:38–40) and say they referred to the destruction of Jerusalem in AD 70. The first two passages are clearly talking about the Tophet in the Hinnom Valley

and the near-fulfillment of the burial of Jerusalemites in the valley by the Babylonians in 586 BC. The third passage, Jeremiah 31:38–40, however, is almost certainly not talking about the Hinnom Valley. The phrase in question in Jer 31:40 is "and the whole valley of the dead bodies and of the ashes." The valley referred to in this passage is not the Hinnom Valley. In this verse the word *'ēmeq* is used for valley, not *gay'* ("valley") as in the case of the Hinnom Valley. A *gay'* is a sharp valley with steep slopes in it, but an *'ēmeq* is a broad valley. Gabriel Barkay conducted a careful study of locations in this passage, and he shows that this area is in the northern suburbs of Iron Age Jerusalem.[8] The memory of the "dead bodies" or corpses goes back to the visitation of the angel of the Lord to the Assyrian army that was encircling Jerusalem in 701 BC. The same Hebrew word for "dead bodies" or corpses used in Jeremiah 31 is used specifically elsewhere for this event: *peger* (2 Kgs 19:35; Isa 34:3; 37:36). The camp of the Assyrians

---

7. Nahman Avigad, *Discovering Jerusalem* (Nashville, TN: Thomas Nelson, 1980), 50, 59.

8. Gabriel Barkay, "Northern and Western Expansion of Jerusalem in the End of the Iron Age" (Hebrew; PhD thesis, Tel Aviv University, 1985), 1:49–50; 2:ii, 67.

was in the area of the Damascus Gate and the ʿēmeq would have been the broad valley just to the north of the gate.

During the Persian period, the "Potsherd Gate" was known as the "Dung, or Refuse Gate" (Neh 2:13; 3:13–14; 12:31).[9]

#1 – BURIAL PRACTICES FOR CRIMINALS

The first reason the Hinnom Valley was not a garbage dump where they burned criminals is that criminals' bodies were never burned during the Second Temple period. It is true that certain people were burned to death in the earlier Old Testament period, for example, Achan (Josh 7:15, 25) and a priest's daughter who committed adultery (Lev 21:9), but during the Second Temple period this practice was abandoned with only one known exception.

The Mishnah says that the Sanhedrin had the power to inflict four kinds of executions: stoning, burning, beheading, and strangling (m. Sanhedrin 7:1). The tractate goes on to describe how a person is to be burned. That person is restrained, and a strip of molten lead is thrown down the throat, burning the stomach and entrails (m. Sanhedrin 7:2). There was, however, one example during the Second Temple period where a person was burned at the stake:

> Rabbi Eliezer ben Zadok said: "It happened once that a priest's daughter committed adultery and they encompassed her with bundles of branches and burnt her." They said to him: "Because the court at that time had not right

knowledge." (m. Sanhedrin 7:2 [Danby])

Elsewhere it is explained that this court was made up of Sadducees in about AD 62. Ironically, this is precisely what the Mosaic Law required for the daughter of a priest who committed adultery! The Mishnah describes one burial practice for criminals:

> They used not to bury him in the burying place of his fathers, but two burying-places were kept in readiness by the court, one for them that were beheaded or strangled, and one for them that were stoned or burnt. When the flesh had wasted away they gathered together the bones and buried them in their own place. (m. Sanhedrin 6:5–6)

In other words, the body of an executed criminal was placed in a court grave until the flesh had rotted away. After a year, the family came and gathered up the bones and took them to the family tomb for reburial.

Another burial custom for criminals was used when the corpse was buried directly in the family tomb and not the court tomb; in such cases a stone was placed over the criminal. Mishnah Semaḥot ("Mourning") 5:13 states:

> One who died while under a ban should be stoned. It is not that a great heap of stones should be raised over him as in the case of Achan, rather a court messenger takes a stone and puts it on a coffin

9. Leen Ritmeyer and Kathleen Ritmeyer, *Jerusalem in the Time of Nehemiah* (Jerusalem: Carta, 2005), 39–41.

so that the law of stoning might be carried out.[10]

A confirmation of this rabbinic passage was observed during the excavation of a burial cave in Ramot, one of the northern suburbs of Jerusalem. The skeletal remains of a young man, between the ages of 18–21, were found with a heavy stone on top of him.[11] In both cases regarding the burial practices for criminals, the body was never burned and taken outside the city of Jerusalem and placed in a garbage dump in the Hinnom Valley.

#2 – WASTE DISPOSAL PRACTICES

Second, the disposal of garbage via burning is a relatively modern invention. There was very little garbage to burn during the Second Temple period. In a salvage excavation in the City of David, Yigal Shiloh discovered in Area A, a "heap containing dozens of whole vessels of the 1st century AD, discarded together with thousands of broken vessels, indicates that the area north of the thick wall was a rubbish dump and hints at its proximity to the original 'Dung Gate,' which stood here during the Second Temple period."[12] Elsewhere, Shiloh gives a more detailed description of this dump and says that

"no ashes" were found.[13] This indicates that the garbage dump was for broken pottery but not for burning the content of the broken vessels.

#3 – THE REAL GARBAGE DUMP

Third, the Second Temple garbage dump for Jerusalem was located in the Kidron Valley and not the Hinnom Valley. This subject was studied by Ronny Reich and Eli Shukron, the recent excavators of the City of David.[14] They described the city dump on the eastern slopes of the City of David in these terms:

In almost every excavated area, an extremely thick layer of loose debris just under surface [was encountered]. This layer is made of earth, loose rubble, small stones and a large amount of broken artifacts (mainly pottery shards with fragments of stone and glass vessels, coins, etc.), as well as broken animal bones. It seems to be ordinary household garbage, which was dumped down the slope, as is characterized by the slanting bedding lines of the debris. These bedding lines have a constant gradient of approximately 32 degrees, and they show occasional sorting

10. Dov Zlotnik, *The Tractate "Mourning" (Regulations Relating to Death, Burial, and Mourning)* (New Haven, CT: Yale University, 1966), 47.

11. Joe Zias, "A Rock-Cut Tomb in Jerusalem," *BASOR* 245 (1982): 53–56.

12. Yigal Shiloh, "City of David, Excavation 1978," *BA* 42.3 (1979): 168.

13. Yigal Shiloh, "Jerusalem: The City of David, 1978," *IEJ* 28.4 (1978): 275.

14. Ronny Reich and Eli Shukron, "The Jerusalem City-Dump in the Late Second Temple Period," *Zeitschrift des Deutschen Palastina-Vereins* 119.1 (2003): 12–18; Ronny Reich and Guy Bar-Oz, "The Jerusalem City Dump in the Late Second Temple Period: A Quantitative Study," *New Studies on Jerusalem*, vol. 12, eds. E. Baruch and A. Faust (Ramat-Gan: Bar-Ilan University, 2006), 83–98, 14–15; Ronny Reich, *Excavating the City of David. Where Jerusalem's History Began* (Jerusalem: Israel Exploration Society, 2011), 219–25.

Kidron Valley (looking south)

of the components according to mass and size.[15]

They describe the average depth of the layer of debris as between twenty to twenty-six feet thick (six to eight meters), and in some places up to thirty feet thick (ten meters). They also observed that "such a phenomenon [i.e., layers of debris], dated to the late Second Temple period, *is not present on any other side of the immediate outskirts of the city*" (emphasis added).[16] In other words, there was not a garbage dump in the Hinnom Valley in Jerusalem during the Second Temple period (see infographic "Ancient Jerusalem" on pg. 528).

Reich and Shukron summarized the size and date of this dump by saying:

The mantle of debris covers the entire eastern slope of the south western hill (the City of David). This area of debris is at least 400 meters long on the North-South axis (i.e., the length of the hill), and 50–70 meters wide on the West-East axis (i.e., the length of the slope). A modest estimate will show that we deal here with a huge deposit which measures, at least, 400 x 50 x 10 m = 200,000 cubic meters. According to a preliminary reading of the artifacts retrieved from the debris, the greater part of this amount was accumulated during a period of time that extends approximately from the middle of the 1st century

---

15. Reich and Shukron, "Jerusalem City-Dump," 12.
16. Reich and Shukron, "Jerusalem City-Dump," 12.

Kidron Valley (looking west)

B.C.E. to the year 70 C.E., i.e., over approximately 100–120 years.[17]

There were new excavations (2013–2014) by Yuval Gadot of Tel Aviv University on the slopes of the City of David. He observed that the "landfill located on the eastern slopes of the city is not just impressive for its size: its alternating layers of ancient trash and soil suggest there was a deliberate attempt to systematically cover the garbage to prevent smells and deter scavengers."[18] There apparently was some sort of a department of sanitation for the city of Jerusalem that organized the disposal of the garbage for the city. Gadot commented on his research:

Most of the garbage in the landfill is leftovers from a typical middle-class lunch or dinner at the time, including animal bones, charred remains of grains, olive pits and wood from household ovens. The picture that emerges is of a fairly wealthy city, with plenty of meat to go around and even fish brought in from distant locations like the Mediterranean and the Sea of Galilee.[19]

He also observed that there were very few bronze or iron metal objects in the dump, indicating that the people recycled these metals. Also, a previous excavation near the Temple Mount found a

---

17. Reich and Shukron, "Jerusalem City-Dump," 14.

18. Ariel David, "Ancient Romans, Jews Invented Trash Collection, Archaeology of Jerusalem Hints," *Haaretz*, June 29, 2016, http://www.haaretz.com/jewish/archaeology/. premium-1.727585.

19. David, "Ancient Romans."

large number of pigeon bones, bones that were not found elsewhere in other dumps. Pigeons were used for sacrifices in the temple, thus making this "holy garbage."

All of this information is indicative that the garbage dump for Jerusalem was in the Kidron Valley and not the Hinnom Valley. The archaeologists concluded that the dump was "a dry dump, with minimal content of decaying organic material, which probably create[d] less environmental influence than modern dumps."[20]

#4 – SECOND TEMPLE CEMETERIES

Fourth, it would be inconceivable to have a garbage dump in the section of the valley south of the ancient city of Jerusalem because it was occupied by at least sixty-nine Jewish tombs, or more, of the Second Temple period.[21] Some of the tombs at the eastern end of the Hinnom Valley, in the area of Akeldama, are very elaborate tombs, and one may even be of the high priest Annas.[22] Three others were found, intact, and full of rich burial goods.[23] It would be unimaginable for the Jerusalemites to take a body of the deceased, especially a high priest, to a tomb for their final resting place in the Hinnom Valley through the smoke and

putrid smell of a burning garbage dump. The Jewish people, having respect for the dead, would not have located a garbage dump in a cemetery and burned rubbish there.

#5 – PREVAILING WESTERLY WINDS

Finally, a garbage dump could not be located in the section of the valley to the west of the ancient city of Jerusalem because the smoke and putrid smell from the burning dump would have blown up and over the city wall into the upper city where the aristocracy lived. The wealthy and influential people would have been complaining about the stink and poor city-planning. But the most important aristocrat was Herod the Great. In 25 BC, he built a palace on the western edge of the upper city, just south of the present day Jaffa Gate. He placed it there to get the cool breeze from the prevailing westerly winds, especially during the summer months. Josephus gives a description of this lavish and ornate palace (*War* 5.176–181; 1.402; *Ant* 15.318).[24] Knowing Herod the Great's personality and temperament, if the alleged burning garbage dump was in existence during the last twenty years of the reign of Herod the Great, he would have had the officials

---

20. E. Weiss, R. Bouchnik, G. Bar-Oz, and R. Reich, "A Dump Near the Temple? Two Difficulties Regarding the City Dump Adjacent to the Second Temple," in *New Studies on Jerusalem*, vol. 12, eds. E. Baruch and A. Faust (Ramat-Gan: Bar-Ilan University, 2006), 15.

21. Amos Kloner, "The Necropolis of Jerusalem in the Second Temple Period" (PhD dissertation, The Hebrew University, Jerusalem, 1980 [Hebrew, with English abstract]), 60–66, 275–76; idem, *Survey of Jerusalem: The Northeastern Sector* (Jerusalem: Israel Antiquities Authority, 2001).

22. Leen Ritmeyer and Kathleen Ritmeyer, "Akeldama: Potter's Field or High Priest's Tomb?" *BAR* 20.6 (1994): 22–35, 76, 78.

23. Gideon Avni and Zvi Greenhut, "Akeldama: Resting Place of the Rich and Famous," *BAR* 20.6 (1994): 36–46.

24. Ehud Netzer, *The Palaces of the Hasmoneans and Herod the Great* (Jerusalem: Yad Ben-Zvi and Israel Exploration Society, 2001), 125–28.

Akeldama (within the Hinnom Valley)

responsible for allowing a garbage dump in that area executed!

I mentioned the prevailing westerly wind to someone who supports locating the garbage dump in the Hinnom Valley, and he wanted to know what Scripture support I had for asserting that the wind blows from the west. I replied I did not have any Scripture for the prevailing westerly winds, but I lived on the edge of the Hinnom Valley at the Institute of Holy Land Studies for fifteen months. During that time, I observed the wind direction of the flag over the St. Andrews Scottish Presbyterian Church. After that conversation, I wanted to have a more factual, documented reply, rather than my own personal experience. I checked the daily weather patterns that were recorded in the weather charts of the *Palestine Exploration Quarterly* for a thirty-two year period from 1882 to 1913. The prevailing westerly winds, coming from the south-west, west, and northwest—which would have blown the smoke and smell over the city walls—blew sixty-five percent of the year! The other directions were: north seven percent of the year, east twenty-six percent of the year, and south two percent of the year. This data makes it inconceivable that a burning garbage dump would be in the Hinnom Valley.

THE REAL NATURE OF GEHENNA

The first mention of a garbage dump in the Hinnom Valley does not appear in the literature until about AD 1200. Rabbi David Kimhi, in his commentary on Psalm 27, states: "Gehenna is a repugnant place, into which filth and cadavers are thrown, and in which fires perpetually burn in order to consume the filth and bones; on which account, by analogy, the judgment of the wicked is called 'Gehenna.'"[25] But as shown above, there is no historical, archaeological, or literary

25. Cited in Lloyd Bailey, "Gehenna: The Topography of Hell," *BA* 49.3 (1986): 188.

1. Herod's Palace
2. Upper City

Herodian Towers
3. Mariamne
4. Phasael
5. Hippicus

Herod's Palace in Jerusalem

evidence from the Second Temple period to support this claim. So, if Gehenna is not a garbage dump in Jerusalem where they burn criminals' bodies and refuse, then what is it?

The word "Gehenna" is used twelve times in the New Testament, eleven of those times it comes from the lips of the Lord Jesus (Matt 5:22, 29, 30; 10:28; 18:9; 23:15, 33; Mark 9:43, 45, 47; Luke 12:5); the other time it is found in the Epistle of James (3:6).

Hans Scharen divides these verses into three groups: "(a) warnings addressed to the disciples concerning stumbling blocks (Matt 5:29-30; 18:8-9; Mark 9:43-48); (b) warnings addressed to the disciples in relation to their personal destiny (Matt 5:22; 10:28; Luke 12:4-5); and (c) condemnation of the scribes and Pharisees (Matt 23:15, 33)."[26]

Gehenna is a place where the "worm dies not and the fire is not quenched" (Mark 9:44, 46, 48). Elsewhere the Lord Jesus describes Gehenna—without naming it—as a place of "everlasting fire, prepared for the devil and his angels" (Matt 25:41; compare Rev 20:10). Yet the "goats" that are separated from the "sheep" are also sent to everlasting fire and punishment in Gehenna (Matt 25:31-46). Duane Watson has observed:

With the possible exception of Luke 12:5, the NT distinguishes Gehenna and Hades. Whereas Hades is the provisional place of the ungodly between death, resurrection, and final judgment (cf. Rev 20:13-14 where Hades yields up its dead for judgment and is thrown into the lake of fire at the last judgment), Gehenna is the eternal place of the wicked after final judgment. Hades receives the soul only (Acts 2:27, 31), Gehenna receives both body and soul (Matt 10:28; cf. Luke 12:5). The NT does not describe the tor-

---

26. Hans Scharen, "Gehenna in the Synoptics, Part 1," *Bibliotheca Sacra* 149.595 (1992): 330.

ment of Gehenna or portray Satan as the lord of Gehenna.[27]

Mark 9 states that Gehenna is a place where the "worm dies not and the fire is not quenched" (9:44, 46, 48). Critics who deny the existence of hell are quick to point out that Mark 9:44 and 9:46 have been omitted in some manuscripts. Be that as it may, 9:48 is in all of them. If one takes this passage literally, and they should, they could walk the whole length of the Hinnom Valley today and not find a burning garbage dump. If there was one, the fire has been quenched.

Peter Head has pointed out that the image of the worms and unquenchable fire is found in the last verse in the book of Isaiah:

> And they shall go forth and look upon the corpses of men who have transgressed against Me. For their worm does not die, and their fire is not quenched. They shall be an abhorrence to all flesh. (Isa 66:24)

Head notes: "The point of this language seems to be to stress the permanence of the experience of judgment. The worm and the fire relate to the bodies of rebellious men: their destructive, distasteful activity continues eternally as an abhorrence to 'all flesh' (that is, those saved at the end)."[28]

Some have said that the reference to hell, or Gehenna, in Mark 9:42–50 is a parable or an earthly illustration. If it is only a parable or illustration, what is it a picture of? The thing being illustrated must have been far worse! Gehenna is not a garbage dump in Jerusalem, but rather, a place of eschatological judgment.

BIBLIOGRAPHY

Avigad, Nahman. *Discovering Jerusalem.* Nashville, TN: Thomas Nelson, 1980.

Avni, Gideon, and Zvi Greenhut. "Akeldama: Resting Place of the Rich and Famous." *BAR* 20.6 (1994): 36–46.

Bailey, Lloyd. "Gehenna: The Topography of Hell." *BA* 49.3 (1986): 187–91.

Baker, Sharon. *Razing Hell: Rethinking Everything You've Been Taught about God's Wrath and Judgment.* Louisville, KY: Westminster John Knox, 2010.

Barkay, Gabriel. "Northern and Western Jerusalem in the End of the Iron Age." PhD thesis, Tel Aviv University, 1985. Hebrew.

Bouchnik, Ram, Guy Bar-Oz, and Ronny Reich. "Animal Bone Remains from the City Dump of Jerusalem from the Late Second Temple Period." Pages 50–80 in vol. 10 of *New Studies on Jerusalem.* Edited by E. Baruch and A. Faust. Ramat-Gan: Bar-Ilan University, 2004. Hebrew.

Danby, Herbert. *The Mishnah: Translated from the Hebrew with Introduction and Brief Explanatory Notes.* Oxford: Oxford University Press, 1933.

David, Ariel. "Ancient Romans, Jews Invented Trash Collection, Archaeology of Jerusalem Hints." *Haaretz,* June 29, 2016. http://www.haaretz.com/jewish/archaeology/.premium-1.727585.

Head, Peter M. "The Duration of Divine Judgment in the New Testament." Pages 221–27 in *'The Reader Must*

---

27. Duane Watson, "Gehenna," *ABD* 2:927.

28. Head, "Duration of Divine Judgment," 223.

Understand': Eschatology in Bible and Theology. Edited by K. Brower and M. Elliot. Eugene, OR: Wipf & Stock, 1997.

Kloner, Amos. "The Necropolis of Jerusalem in the Second Temple Period." PhD dissertation, Hebrew University of Jerusalem, 1980. Hebrew with English abstract.

———. *Survey of Jerusalem: The Northeastern Sector*. Jerusalem: Israel Antiquities Authority, 2001.

Netzer, Ehud. *The Palaces of the Hasmoneans and Herod the Great*. Jerusalem: Yad Ben-Zvi and Israel Exploration Society, 2001.

Noe, John. *Hell Yes / Hell No*. Indianapolis, IN: East2West, 2011.

Reich, Ronny. *Excavating the City of David. Where Jerusalem's History Began*. Jerusalem: Israel Exploration Society, 2011.

Reich, Ronny, and Eli Shukron. "The Jerusalem City-Dump in the Late Second Temple Period." *Zeitschrift des Deutschen Palastina Vereins* 119.1 (2003): 120–18.

Reich, Ronny, and Guy Bar-Oz. "The Jerusalem City Dump in the Late Second Temple Period: A Quantitative Study." Pages 83–98 in vol. 12 of *New Studies on Jerusalem*. Edited by E. Baruch and A. Faust. Ramat-Gan: Bar-Ilan University, 2006. Hebrew with English abstract on pp. 14–15.

Ritmeyer, Leen, and Kathleen Ritmeyer. *Jerusalem in the Time of Nehemiah*. Jerusalem: Carta, 2005.

———. "Akeldama: Potter's Field or High Priest's Tomb?" *BAR* 20.6 (1994): 22–35, 76, 78.

Scharen, Hans. "Gehenna in the Synoptics, Part 1." *Bibliotheca Sacra* 149.595 (July–September 1992): 324–37.

Shiloh, Yigal. "City of David, Excavation 1978." *BA* 42.3 (1979): 165–71.

———. "Jerusalem: City of David." *IEJ* 28 (1978): 274–76.

Watchtower Bible and Tract Society. *Make Sure of All Things, Hold Fast to What is Fine*. Brooklyn, NY: Watchtower Bible and Tract Society, 1965.

Watson, Duane. "Gehenna." *ABD* 2:926–28.

Weiss, E., R. Bouchnik, G. Bar-Oz, and R. Reich. "A Dump Near the Temple? Two Difficulties Regarding the City Dump Adjacent to the Second Temple." In *New Studies on Jerusalem*, vol. 12. Edited by E. Baruch and A. Faust. Ramat-Gan: Bar-Ilan University, 2006. Hebrew with English abstract on pg. 15.

Zias, Joe. "A Rock-Cut Tomb in Jerusalem." *BASOR* 245 (1982): 53–56.

Zlotnick, Dov. *The Tractate "Mourning" (Regulations Relating to Death, Burial, and Mourning)*. New Haven, CT: Yale University Press, 1966.

CHAPTER 33

GRAIN, WINE, AND OIL: THE ESSENTIALS OF LIFE

Matt 6:11, 25–33

Gordon Franz

KEY POINTS

- Those living in the land of the Bible depended on a small variety of foods but three were staples: grain, wine, and oil.

- God's children prayed to him for the right types of wind and rain to come at the right time, so that they might receive their "daily bread."

- The Last Supper would have included all three elements, though olive oil is implied since the meal would have taken place after dark.

- When Jesus turned water to wine on the spot this was partly a polemic against Dionysus, the Greek god of vegetation, who invariably made his worshipers wait an entire agricultural cycle and another year of fermentation before they could drink the grapes' vintage.

- The olive oil extracted from the first press of the olives belonged to God; the subsequent presses were dedicated to increasingly more mundane uses.

STAPLE FOODS

Four foods—wheat, barley, wine, and olive oil—should draw the Bible student's attention to a phrase used throughout the Hebrew Scriptures for the essential foods of daily life for all people. This phrase, "grain, wine, and oil", is used at least eighteen times in the Hebrew Scriptures (Deut 7:13; 11:14; 12:17; 14:23; 18:4; 28:51; 32:14; 1 Chr 9:29; 2 Chr 2:15; 31:5; 32:28; Neh 5:11; Ps 104:15; Jer 31:12; Hos 2:8, 22; Joel 2:19; Hag 1:11). These four foods were the most important foods of the "seven varieties" (Deut 8:7–10). The figs, pomegranates, and (date) honey make up the other three. These seven foods all share a common fate that is determined by a

327

very delicate weather balance between Passover and Pentecost (Shavuot).[1]

THE THEOLOGY OF GRAIN, WINE, AND OIL

In Deuteronomy 11, Moses gives a description of the Promised Land that the tribes of Israel were about to enter (11:8–12). He then challenges the nation by saying:

> And it shall be that if you earnestly obey My commandments which I command you today, to love the LORD your God and serve Him with all your heart and with all your soul, then I will give you the rain for your land [of Israel] in its season, the early rain [October–November] and the latter rain [March–April], that you may gather in your grain [April–May], your new wine [June–September], and your oil [September–November]. And I will send grass in your fields for your livestock, that you may eat and be filled. Take heed to yourselves, lest your heart be deceived, and you turn aside and serve other gods and worship them, lest the LORD's anger be aroused against you, and He shut up the heavens so that there be no rain, and the land yield no produce, and you perish quickly from the good land

which the LORD is giving you (Deut 11:13–17).[2]

There was a tall commercial grain silo in Beersheva, at the center of the biblical Negev, which had a quote from Rabbi Eleazar ben Azariah painted on the side: "Without bread [literally "flour"] there is no Torah; without Torah there is no bread!" (m. Avot 3:18). This seems like a "Catch-22". If you do not have bread, you will die of starvation and not be able to study Torah. On the other hand, if you do not read and obey the Torah then God will not send the rain in its season and you will not have grain to make bread! The bottom line is this: If you want bread, study and obey the Word of God (in rabbinic writings, Torah often refers to Scripture in general, not just the books of law). The book of James says that Christians are to be "doers of the word, and not hearers only" (Jas 1:22), a paraphrase of the main point of the parable of the two builders at the end of the Sermon on the Mount (Matt 7:24–27),[3] as well as the parable of the two foundations in the Sermon on the Plain (Luke 6:46–49).

An observant Jewish farmer, rich or poor, living in the land of Israel in the Second Temple period would remember the phrase, "grain, wine, and oil," every time he recited Deut 11 at the Shabbat meal. On Friday night the Shabbat dinner table would be set with *hallah* bread made

---

1. Nogah Hareuveni, *Nature in Our Biblical Heritage* (Kiryat Ono, Israel: Neot Kedumim, 1980), 30–45.

2. Compare Matt 22:37; Mark 12:30. Deut 11:13–17 is one of four passages that are in the two phylacteries (*tefillin*) that are worn by Jewish men on their foreheads and left arms (Exod 13:9, 16; Deut 6:8; 11:18; compare Matt. 23:5). Brackets added by author. The months of the rains and harvest are found at: Oded Borowski, *Agriculture in Iron Age Israel* (Winona Lake, IN: Eisenbrauns, 1987), 33, 37. Unless otherwise indicated, Scripture quotations in this article are from the NKJV.

3. Gordon Franz, "The Parable of the Two Builders," *Archaeology in the Biblical World* 3.1 (1995): 6–11.

from grains, wine from grapes, and the oil lamp filled with olive oil, which gave light for the meal.[4] Each was a reminder that their "daily bread"—the essentials for life—came from the hand of the Lord and that they were dependent upon the Lord for their daily existence.

A farmer would also pray for the right wind to blow at the appropriate time during the seven weeks, or fifty days, between *Pesach* (Passover) and Shavuot (Pentecost / Feast of Weeks). The rabbis say,

> The northern wind is beneficial to wheat when it has reached a third of its ripening and is damaging to olive trees when they have blossomed. The southern wind is damaging to wheat when it has reached a third of its ripening and is beneficial to olives when they have blossomed. This is symbolized for you by [placing] the table to the north [side of the tabernacle and the temple] and the menorah in the south [side of the tabernacle and temple]. (b. Bava Batra 147a).[5]

The north wind during the winter months usually brings rains (Prov 25:23) and is beneficial in the first third of the ripening of the wheat and barley. Yet this same rain would ruin the buds of the olive trees or grape vines if the buds were already opened. In the case of open buds, the rain would wash away the pollen so the tree or vine would not be pollinated and fertilized. The southern wind is good for the pollination process of the olives and grapes if they come later in the fifty days. If the southern wind comes early, the grain will not fill with starch and the crop will be decimated (compare Gen 41:6). The farmer prays to the Lord that the winds would come at the right time (see infographic "Agricultural Cycle of the Levant/Palestine" on pg. 530). If, however, the winds come at the right time, but the rain comes after "its season" the grain crop will still be ruined (Lev 26:4; Deut 11:14; 28:12; compare 1 Sam 12:13-25).

GRAIN, WINE, AND OIL IN THE GOSPELS

There are no passages in the Gospels that mention grain, wine, and oil as a unit. At the Last Supper bread and wine are mentioned, but oil is not explicitly mentioned, although it is implied. There is only one passage in the New Testament where all three are mentioned by name together and that is found in Rev 6:5-6.[6] This essay will examine the use of each of the foods individually and demonstrate how they are part of the everyday life in the world of Jesus in the Second Temple period.[7]

---

4. At the modern Shabbat dinner the oil lamp is replaced with a candle. For Shabbat in the 1st century AD, see Robert Smith, "The Household Lamps of Palestine in New Testament Times," *BA* 29.1 (1966): 7-9.

5. As cited in Nogah Hareuveni, *The Emblem of the State of Israel* (Kiryat Ono: Israel, Neot Kedumim, 1988), 21.

6. Gordon Franz, "The King and I: Opening the Third Seal," *Bible and Spade* 13.1 (2000): 9-11.

7. For the food of the Second Temple period, see Douglas Neel and Joel Pugh, *The Food and Feasts of Jesus: The Original Mediterranean Diet* (Lanham, MD: Rowman and Littlefield, 2012); Nathan MacDonald, *What Did the Ancient Israelites Eat? Diet in Biblical Times* (Grand Rapids: Eerdmans, 2008). For the archaeology of the "seven species," see Joan Westenholz, ed., *Sacred Bounty Sacred Land: The Seven Species of the Land of Israel* (Jerusalem: Bible Lands Museum Jerusalem, 1998).

Wheat Field in Upper Galilee

GRAINS

For the Jewish farmer, Shavuot (Pentecost) was the beginning of the wheat harvest (Exod 23:16; Num 28:26). Helen Frenkley, the director of Neot Kedumim (a biblical nature reserve in Israel), points out: "The Hebrew for Feast of Harvest is *Hag Ha-Katzir*. *Katzir* means harvest of grain and since the barley harvest begins on Passover, *Shavuot* is the start of the wheat harvest."[8]

Wheat and barley are the stuff of life and are both mentioned in the Gospels for making bread on a daily basis. The Lord Jesus taught his disciples to pray, "Give us this day our daily bread" (Matt 6:11; Luke 11:3). The Lord Jesus was a good rabbi. Not only did he teach his disciples *what*

to pray (Matt 6:9–13) but he also taught them *why* they are to pray that way (Matt 6:16–7:6). Finally, he taught them *how* to pray (Matt 7:7–8): keep on asking, seeking, and knocking. The commentary on "give us this day our daily bread" is found in Matt 6:25–33. The Lord Jesus comments, not to worry like the Gentiles about what you will eat (your daily bread), what you will drink (wine), or what you will wear. These are the essentials of everyday life. He gives two illustrations from nature about the birds of the air and the grass of the fields, but he concludes this section, "But seek first the kingdom of God and his righteousness, and all these things [food, clothing, and drink] shall be added to you" (Matt 6:33). The point of this commentary

---

8. Personal correspondence, August 24, 1997.

A Threshing Floor

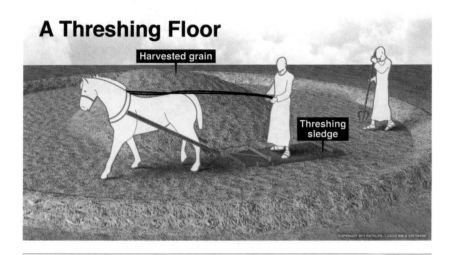

Harvested grain

Threshing sledge

is that the disciples were to be "on praying grounds" in order for God to answer their prayer for daily bread. The Lord promises to provide their daily needs if they are seeking his kingdom and his righteousness.

At the Last Supper, the Lord Jesus instituted the Lord's Supper when he took unleavened bread and wine and gave them to his disciples and said: "This is my body ... this is my blood." (Matt 26:26–29; Mark 14:22–25; Luke 22:19–20; 1 Cor 11:23–26). Since it was a Passover meal,[9] it would have taken place after dark and the oil lamps, with olive oil in them, would have been burning. Thus, the grain, wine, and oil are together at the Passover meal.

In Luke 5, the Lord Jesus preformed a miracle by providing a large number of fish to his disciples when it was not the right time to catch these fish with the

trammel net.[10] Peter recognized that and said, "Lord, depart from me, I am a sinful man." After this fishing expedition they returned to the harbor of Capernaum and Luke records, "So when they had brought their boats to land. They forsook all to follow him" (5:11). The disciples sold their boats, their nets, and changed their business from fishing for fish to fishing for human beings. Their economic status changed from middle class to poor.

In Luke 6:1–5 the disciples were embroiled in a controversy with some Pharisees. It took place on the second Sabbath of the counting of the omer after Passover.[11] The disciples had plucked barley grain from the field and rubbed it together with their hands and ate it. The Pharisees did not accuse them of stealing grain because they were poor now, and it was permissible to glean from the field (Deut 23:25). But some Pharisees would

9. Barry D. Smith, "The Chronology of the Last Supper," *Westminster Theological Journal* 53.1 (1991): 29–45.

10. See J. Carl Laney, "Fishing the Sea of Galilee" on pg. 165; Gordon Franz, "The Greatest Fist Stories Ever Told," *Bible and Spade* 6.3 (1993): 93–94.

11. Shmuel Safrai, "Sabbath Breakers?" *Jerusalem Perspective* 3.4 (1990): 3.

Grain-mill

accuse them of working on the Sabbath, but others would not.[12] The Lord Jesus mentions David going into the tabernacle and taking bread from the table when he was hungry (1 Sam 21:6). Mark records the words of the Lord Jesus: "The Sabbath was made for man, and not man for the Sabbath. Therefore the Son of Man is also Lord of the Sabbath" (2:27–28).

The day after the Lord Jesus fed five thousand men, plus women and children, with five barley loaves and two sardines, he spoke in the synagogue of Capernaum (John 6:22–59). The people wanted another handout of food, just like the day before, but the Lord Jesus said, "You seek me, not because you saw the signs, but because you ate of the loaves and were filled" (6:26). When the crowd mentioned that God fed their forefathers in the wilderness and gave them manna from heaven (Exod 15:16;

Ps 78:24), Jesus responded: "Most assuredly, I say to you, Moses did not give you bread from heaven, but my Father gives you the true bread from heaven. For the bread of God is he who comes down from heaven and gives life to the world" (John 6:32–33). The crowd wanted this bread from heaven, so the Lord Jesus identifies himself as that bread: "I am the bread of life. He who comes to me shall never hunger. And he who believes in me shall never thirst" (John 6:35). The Lord Jesus took a common, daily object and used it to demonstrate who he was—the bread of life.

The Lord Jesus used a grain of wheat to illustrate the importance of his disciples unselfishly serving him:

Unless a grain of wheat falls into the ground and dies, it remains

---

12. Safrai, "Sabbath Breakers," 4–5. I would disagree with Safrai on this point: the disciples' economic status had changed and they would be considered poor so they were permitted to glean in the field.

alone; but if it dies, it produces much grain. He who loves this life will lose it, and he who hates this life in this world will keep it for eternal life. (John 12:24–25)

When Peter took six of his fellow disciples fishing after the resurrection of the Lord Jesus, the Lord Jesus manifested himself to his disciples and asked, "Did you catch any fish?" Peter recognized it was the Lord Jesus. He put on his cloth and dragged his net with 153 large fish to shore. The Lord Jesus had sardines and bread waiting for him by the fire of coals (John 21:1–9). Most likely the Lord Jesus got the flour for the bread from the mills that were located by the springs at Heptatagon, known as Tabgha today. More than likely the grain was barley because the wheat harvest had not begun yet.

WINE

The first recorded miracle that the Lord Jesus preformed was turning water into wine at a wedding in Cana of Galilee (John 2:1–11).[13] This is when his disciples (students) put their trust in the Lord Jesus as Savior. The purpose of the "signs" (miracles) in John's Gospel is to demonstrate that Jesus is the Christ, the Son of God (John 20:31).

Across the Beth Netofa Valley from Cana was the Roman city of Sepphoris (Zippori). In the third century AD there was a palatial mansion built with beautiful mosaics on the floor. The center of one of the mosaics depicted a drinking contest between Hercules and Dionysius, the god of wine and merrymaking. Dionysius is depicted with his hand

raised and his drinking cup turned over showing it was empty, indicating that he won the drinking contest. Hercules, on the other hand, is drunk. This mosaic seems to indicate that Dionysius was venerated in Galilee in the third century AD, and more than likely the Romans worshiped him as a god in the first century AD, although there is no archaeological or literary evidence to prove this point. Assuming he was venerated, John includes this account to demonstrate that the Lord Jesus is infinitely superior to Dionysius. People prayed to Dionysius for a good harvest, and then good fermentation after the grapes were pressed, and they then had to wait for at least a year for the wine to age and be drinkable. On the other hand, the Lord Jesus spoke, and the water was instantaneously turned to wine. The master of the feast described the wine as "good wine" (John 2:10).

As mentioned above, wine was used at the Last Supper when the Lord Jesus instituted the Lord's Supper and took unleavened bread and wine and gave them to his disciples and said: "This is my body ... this is my blood" (Matt 26:26–29; Mark 14:22–25; Luke 22:19–20; 1 Cor 11:23–26).

After the Last Supper was instituted, the Lord Jesus and his disciples went to the Mount of Olives. In the moonlit night of Passover, they could see the golden grapevine over the façade of the temple. Flavius Josephus, the first-century Jewish historian, described this grapevine: "Above these [the entrance doors], under the cornice, spread a golden vine with grape-clusters hanging from it, a marvel of size and artistry to all who saw

13. See Emily J. Thomassen, "Jesus' Ministry at Cana in Galilee" on pg. 74.

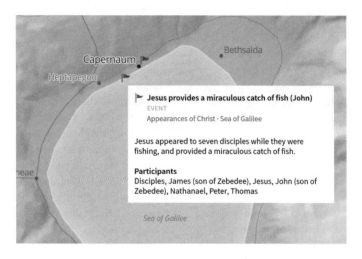

Jesus provides a miraculous catch of fish (John)
EVENT
Appearances of Christ · Sea of Galilee

Jesus appeared to seven disciples while they were fishing, and provided a miraculous catch of fish.

Participants
Disciples, James (son of Zebedee), Jesus, John (son of Zebedee), Nathanael, Peter, Thomas

with what costliness of material it had been constructed" (*Ant.* 15.394–95 [LCL]). Elsewhere he said: "It had, moreover, above it [the door] those golden vines, from which depended grape-clusters as tall as a man" (*War* 5.210 [LCL]). The Mishnah recorded: "A golden vine stood over the entrance to the Sanctuary, trained over posts; and whosoever gave a leaf, or a berry, or a cluster as a free-will offering, he brought it and [the priest] hung it thereon" (m. Middot 3:8 [Danby]). The grapevine represented Israel (Ps 80:7–19; Isa 5:1–7; 27:2–6; Jer 2:21; Hos 10:1–2; Ezek 15:1–5; 17:1–21; 19:10–15). At midnight of Passover the full moon would have been due south of the Temple Mount. With a bright moon-lit night, the golden grapes would have reflected the light and left a deep impression on the disciples. Jesus said he was the true vine and he wanted his disciples to bear much fruit for God's glory. This was the word-picture from the golden grapes.

OLIVE OIL

The oil mentioned in the Bible is olive oil and not petroleum oil. This oil comes from the olive tree. At the time of harvest, the branches of the tree were hit with sticks so the olives would fall to the ground, then the olives were gathered into baskets and taken to the olive press. First, the olives were crushed in an olive crusher and then the olives were placed in baskets and placed on the olive press. The first oil that was collected was the one hundred percent pure virgin olive oil. This was devoted to the Lord for use in the temple and was also for eating. Then a beam was put on top to extract more oil. This "grade B" olive oil was used for cooking. Stone weights were hung from the beam and "grade C" oil was extracted and this was used as fuel in the oil lamps. More weights were added and more oil extracted, but not of the best quality. Olive oil had a multi-faceted use, including as a base for cosmetics and making

Ancient Methods of Vine Training

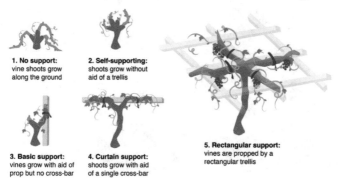

1. No support: vine shoots grow along the ground

2. Self-supporting: shoots grow without aid of a trellis

3. Basic support: vines grow with aid of prop but no cross-bar

4. Curtain support: shoots grow with aid of a single cross-bar

5. Rectangular support: vines are propped by a rectangular trellis

soap. The leftovers of the olives were used for kindling and fuel for baking bread.[14]

Olive oil was used in oil lamps to give light. The Lord Jesus refers to oil lamps on a number of occasions. For example, in the Sermon on the Mount, he talks about lighting a lamp and putting it on a lampstand in order to light the whole room (Matt 5:15). In the parable of the lamp Jesus talked about putting the lamp where all can see, just like their lives are not to be hidden, but open for all to see (Luke 8:16–18; Mark 4:21–23). He gives another parable of the lighted lamp and makes the analogy that the lamp is the eye; his disciples should have good eyes so their bodies are full of light (Luke 11:33–36). In the parable of the lost coin, a woman lit a lamp to search for the missing coin (Luke 15:8). In the parable of the unjust steward (Luke 16:1–9), wheat and oil are mentioned. John the Baptizer is called a "burning and shining lamp" (John

5:35). Finally, the Lord Jesus gave a parable of ten virgins; five were wise and five were foolish (Matt 25:1–13). The foolish virgins only had their oil lamps, but the wise virgins had their oil lamps plus a vessel containing extra olive oil just in case they needed it. They did need it since the bridegroom was delayed and the oil lamps were beginning to fade. When he came at midnight, the wise virgins were ready to meet him because they had the extra olive oil. When the Lord Jesus gave a parable he often illustrated it with everyday household objects such as oil lamps that were fueled by olive oil.

Olive oil is used for medicinal purposes as well. Sometimes healing ointments have an olive oil base to them (Isa 1:6). The Lord Jesus acknowledged the healing power of olive oil when he gave the parable of the good Samaritan (Luke 10:29–37). The man had fallen among robbers and was beaten up. The Samaritan bandaged him after he poured oil and

---

14. For a survey of the use of olive oil in the Iron Age, see Borowski, *Agriculture*, 117–26.

Wine Press

wine on the wounds (Luke 10:34; compare James 5:14).

The Lord Jesus visited Jerusalem for the Feast of Dedication, also known as Hanukkah in John 10:22–39. It was also called the Festival of Lights because the rabbis recounted the miracle of Hanukkah which commenced on the 25th of Kislev and lasted for eight days. The rabbinic writings record:

> When the Greeks entered the Temple, they defiled all the oils therein, and when the Hasmonean dynasty prevailed against, and defeated them, they made search and found only one cruse of oil which lay with the seal of the High Priest, but which contained sufficient for one day's lighting only; yet a miracle was wrought therein and they lit [the lamp] therewith for eight days. The following year these days were appointed a

Festival with the recital of *Hallel* and thanksgiving (b. Shabbat 21b).

The centerpiece of the celebration is a nine-branch candelabrum. The first candle is called the "servant" candle and is used to light one additional candle each night to commemorate the eight days of the miracle.

After the Passover meal was over, the Lord Jesus and eleven of his disciples crossed over the brook Kidron to the Mount of Olives (John 18:1). Perhaps it was cold that night, so they stayed in Gethsemane, a place meaning olive press. There is a cave near the Church of All Nations that has an olive oil press in it and is the traditional cave of Gethsemane. Since olives were harvested and pressed from September to November, the cave stood empty for the rest of the year. The owner of the cave let pilgrims visiting Jerusalem stay in the cave at night. It was here that the Lord Jesus prayed three times before he went to the garden and was arrested by the Temple guards.[15][16]

BIBLIOGRAPHY

Borowski, Oded. *Agriculture in Iron Age Israel*. Winona Lake, IN: Eisenbrauns, 1987.

Danby, Herbert. *The Mishnah: Translated from the Hebrew with Introduction and Brief Explanatory Notes*. Oxford: Oxford University Press, 1933.

Franz, Gordon. "The Greatest Fish Stories Ever Told." *Bible and Spade* 6.3 (1993): 92-96.

———. "The King and I: Opening the Third Seal." *Bible and Spade* 13.1 (2000): 9-11.

———. "The Parable of the Two Builders." *Archaeology in the Biblical World* 3.1 (1995): 6-11.

Hareuveni, Nogah. *The Emblem of the State of Israel*. Translated by Helen Frenkley. Kiryat Ono, Israel: Neot Kedumim, 1988.

———. *Nature in Our Biblical Heritage*. Translated by Helen Frenkley. Kiryat Ono, Israel: Neot Kedumim, 1980.

Josephus. Translated by Henry St. J. Thackeray, et al. 10 vols. LCL. Cambridge, MA: Harvard University Press, 1926-1965.

MacDonald, Nathan. *What Did the Ancient Israelites Eat? Diet in Biblical Times*. Grand Rapids: Eerdmans, 2008.

Neel, Douglas, and Joel Pugh. *The Food and Feasts of Jesus: The Original Mediterranean Diet*. Lanham, MD: Rowman and Littlefield, 2012.

Safrai, Shmuel. "Sabbath Breakers?" *Jerusalem Perspective* 3.4 (1990): 3-5.

Smith, Barry D. "The Chronology of the Last Supper." *Westminster Theological Journal* 53.1 (1991): 29-45.

Smith, Robert. "The Household Lamps of Palestine in New Testament Times." *BA* 29.1 (1966): 1-26.

Taylor, Joan. "The Garden of Gethsemane: Not the Place of Jesus' Arrest." *BAR* 21.4 (1995): 26-35, 62.

Westenholz, Joan, ed. *Sacred Bounty Sacred Land: The Seven Species of the Land of Israel*. Jerusalem: Bible Lands Museum Jerusalem, 1988.

---

15. See Aubrey L. Taylor, "In the Garden of Gethsemane: Jesus' Choice to Remain or Run from His Father's Will" on pg. 476.

16. Joan Taylor, "The Garden of Gethsemane: Not the Place of Jesus' Arrest," *BAR* 21.4 (1995): 26-35, 62.

CHAPTER 34

THE WORDS AND TEACHINGS OF JESUS IN THE CONTEXT OF JUDEA

Luke 10:29-37; 19:11-27; 24:13-35; John 2:18-22; 3:22-4:3; 5:2-17; 7:37-38; 9:1-12; 10:22-39

Chris McKinny

KEY POINTS

- Jesus often used his immediate geographical backdrop to shape the way he delivered his message for those who listened.

- The bulk of Jesus' Judean ministry took place in and around Jerusalem.

- Knowledge of the main road from Jerusalem to Jericho provides a backdrop for the parable of the good Samaritan and clues for understanding the parable of the unjust nobleman.

- The appearances of Jesus in Jerusalem were all connected to Jewish rites and festivals, and references to "living water" are related to temple scenes.

INTRODUCTION

The ministry of Jesus occurred almost entirely within the historic boundaries of the land of Israel. Specifically, the Gospel writers relay that over the course of his short ministry Jesus visited and taught in:

- the regions of Galilee (numerous)

- the district of Caesarea Philippi (Matt 16:13; Mark 8:27)

- the Decapolis (Matt 8:28; Mark 5:1, 20; 7:31; Luke 8:26; cf. Matt 4:25)

- Phoenicia (Matt 15:21-28; Mark 7:24-31; cf. Mark 3:8; Luke 6:17)

- Samaria (Luke 9:52-56; 17:11; John 4:1-42; cf. Luke 10:33; 17:16)

- Perea (Mark 10:1; John 1:28; 3:26; 10:40; cf. Matt 4:15, 25; Mark 3:8; Luke 6:17)

- Judea (numerous)

In a parallel article in this volume, Vernon Alexander has demonstrated the particular geographical language that Jesus used during his ministry in Galilee where he spent the bulk of his ministry.[1] This paper will examine the geographically specific language used by Jesus in Judea and Jerusalem.

GEOGRAPHIC PARTICULARITIES OUTSIDE OF GALILEE AND JUDEA

Before we begin our Judea-specific analysis, it is worth briefly examining the geographical particularities of the language Jesus used in the regions outlined above (besides Galilee and Judea).[2] In general, many of Jesus' actions and teachings bear a particular geographical distinctiveness that is often rooted in earlier biblical accounts, contemporary realities within the region, and topographic considerations. This brief discussion is not meant to be an exhaustive list of this dynamic in the regions mentioned, but rather to illustrate the types of geographical particularities that were highlighted by the Gospel writers.

In Caesarea Philippi, it seems to be no coincidence that Jesus chose to reveal his true identity (Son of Man) and purpose (death) to his disciples in a predominantly Gentile territory (Matt 16:13–28). These events likely prefigured the inclusion of the Gentiles in the kingdom.

In Samaria, James and John suggested to Jesus that they should call down "fire from heaven to consume them," because the Samaritan village had refused to receive him, on account of the fact that Jesus' "face was set toward Jerusalem" (Luke 9:52–54). While the name of the Samaritan village is not given, it brings to mind similar events in the ministries of Elijah (2 Kgs 1:10–12) and Elisha (2 Kgs 2:23–25) where judgment was brought upon the inhabitants of Samaria (in the national sense, i.e., Israel), because of their rejection of Yahweh's chosen messenger (Elijah/Elisha) and place (Jerusalem versus Bethel).[3] In John 4, Jesus interacted with a Samaritan woman at the traditional well of Jacob (John 4:5–6; cf. Gen 33:18–20), and beneath the "mountain" (John 4:19–24) that included a large Samaritan temple on top of Gerizim.[4] These contemporary realties are reflected in the language Jesus used with the Samaritan woman. Besides numerous other passages related to supernatural water (e.g., Ezek 47:1–12, see also below), Jesus' metaphor for drinking "living waters" seems to be strongly alluding to Jacob's interaction with Rachel "at the well" (Gen 29:1–14). Also, Jesus' denunciation of the Samaritan religious system and its central location on Mount Gerizim (John 4:19–24) can only be understood against the backdrop of

---

1. See Vernon H. Alexander, "The Words and Teachings of Jesus in the Context of Galilee" on pg. 134.

2. See Chris McKinny, "Pig Husbandry in Israel during the New Testament" on pg. 183 for a discussion of this dynamic relating to the Decapolis.

3. Interestingly, the intertextuality between the Elijah-Elisha cycle seems to continue in Luke 9:59–62, which clearly hearkens back to Elisha's call to the ministry (1 Kgs 19:19–21).

4. Ephraim Stern and Yitzhak Magen, "Archaeological Evidence for the First Stage of the Samaritan Temple on Mount Gerizim," *IEJ* 52.1 (2002): 49–57; Yitzhak Magen, "The Temple of YHWH at Mt. Gerizim," *Eretz-Israel* 29 (2009): 277–97, http://www.jstor.org/stable/23631331. See also Perry Phillips, "At the Well of Sychar" on pg. 192.

Jewish-Samaritan relations during the late 6th-1st centuries BC.[5]

Likewise, in Phoenicia (Matt 15:21-28; Mark 7:24-30), the Gospel writers once again drew from the intertextual parallels from the Elijah-Elisha cycle (1 Kgs 17:8-24) to show Jesus' typological relationship as a prophet (and a "son of David"; see Matt 15:21-22) who ministered to Phoenicians beyond Israel's borders (see Luke 4:25-26).

GEOGRAPHICAL PARTICULARITIES IN JUDEA AND JERUSALEM

THE GEOGRAPHY OF THE ROMAN PROVINCE OF JUDEA

Judea became part of the Roman Empire following Pompey's conquest (without a fight) in 63 BC.[6] The boundaries of Roman Judea were largely identical to Judea/Yehud during the preceding Hellenistic and Persian periods, and to a lesser extent the kingdom of Judah from the First Temple period (see map "Kingdom of Herod the Great" on pg. 531). Each of these entities included the regions of Benjamin, the western and northwestern shores of the Dead Sea (see Josephus, *Ant.* 14.55; 15.96-99; 15.253-58 for disputes between Herod and Cleopatra over territory including the region of Jericho), the northern portion of the Judean Hill country (north of

Beth-zur; see 1 Macc 1:46; 2 Macc 11:5), and the northern valleys of the Judean Shephelah including the Aijalon, Sorek, and Elah valleys (the area south of these valleys was in the territory of Idumea; see map "Kingdom of Herod the Great" on pg. 531).[7]

As we shall demonstrate, most of Jesus' activity in Judea was in Jerusalem with the bulk of events and teachings occurring in and around the Temple Mount. Outside of Jerusalem and its immediate vicinity, there is no record of Jesus traveling further south than Bethlehem, or any indication that he visited the Negeb or the Shephelah during his ministry. However, there are a few accounts that deal with Jesus in Jerusalem's periphery. We will address these texts separately.

JESUS IN JUDEA

Baptizing in the Judean Countryside (John 3:22-4:3)

The first instance of Jesus in Judea comes from John, who records that Jesus was baptizing in the "Judean countryside" (John 3:22-4:3) following the Passover festival (John 2:13, 23) and before John had been "put in prison" (John 3:24). While none of Jesus' "words" are recorded in this account, it is worth noting that Jesus was baptizing at a different location than John the Baptist,[8] and that a discussion arose concern-

---

5. See e.g., Gary N. Knoppers, *Jews and Samaritans: The Origins and History of Their Early Relations* (Oxford: Oxford University Press, 2013).

6. Anson F. Rainey and R. Steven Notley, *The Sacred Bridge* (Jerusalem: Carta, 2006), 335.

7. U. Hübner, "Idumea," *ABD* 3:382-83.

8. "Aenon near Salim" (John 3:23), which literally means "springs" near Salim, is most likely located near Tell Sheikh Selim in the Jordan Valley - for alternate suggestions see Jerry A. Pattengale, "Aenon," *ABD* 1:87; Y. Tsafrir, L.D. Segni, and J. Green, *Tabula Imperii Romani Iudaea-Palestina: Eretz Israel in the Hellenistic, Roman and Byzantine Periods; Maps and*

ing Jewish ritual purification among John's disciples. Given the critical role water purification (via a ritual bath) played in Jewish religious practice,[9] it is interesting that Jesus practiced baptism (through his disciples; John 4:2) in the same manner as John. Clearly, from the "baptism of John" (e.g., Matt 21:25) the practice of baptism developed into a critical part of the Gospel movement (e.g., Matt 28:19; Mark 16:16), so this "early" reference to Jesus' participation in this practice demonstrates the significance of baptism to the entire kingdom movement. While no specific location is given for Jesus' baptism, there are many springs in the vicinity of Jerusalem, particularly in the south and west (e.g., Moza, Sataf, Tzuba, etc.), that could have served as a baptism site.[10] Even until today, visitors to these springs will often find Jewish men using the springs as a ritual bath.[11]

The Parable of the Good Samaritan (Luke 10:29-37)

In the famous parable of the good Samaritan (Luke 10:29-37), Jesus used the real physical setting of the road from Jerusalem to Jericho (i.e., the Ascent of Adummim; Josh 15:7; 18:17; compare Josephus, War 4.474; 5.69-70;[12] Eusebius, Onomasticon 24.5) as the background of a parable illustrating actions that represent being a true "neighbor" (Luke 10:37). The ascent of Adummim is a well-known route that connects Jerusalem to Jericho. The ascent is marked by a continuous ridge that descends down from the eastern side of the Mount of Olives just south of the Augusta Victoria Hospital and continues past modern Ma'ale Adummim toward Jericho above Wadi Qelt.[13]

The biblical references[14] refer to the ridge route and not a specific place along the route. Yet, the most notable part of the route is marked by a series of later

---

Gazetteer (Jerusalem: The Israel Academy of Sciences and Humanities, 1994), 58. Eusebius located Aenon "eight milestones south of Scythopolis near Salim and the Jordan" (Onomasticon 40.1).

9. Jodi Magness, Stone and Dung, Oil and Spit: Jewish Daily Life in the Time of Jesus (Grand Rapids: Eerdmans, 2011), 16-17; compare R. Reich, "Miqwa'ot (Jewish Ritual Baths) in Eretz-Israel, in the Second Temple, Mishnah and Talmud Periods" [Hebrew] (PhD thesis, Hebrew University, 1990); J. D. Lawrence, Washing in Water: Trajectories of Ritual Bathing in the Hebrew Bible and Second Temple Literature (Atlanta: Society of Biblical Literature, 2006).

10. See m. Miqwa'ot 1:1-8 for the "six grades among pools of water, more excellent than the other."

11. See Aubrey L. Taylor, "Wilderness Events: The Baptism and Temptation of Jesus" on pg. 53.

12. According to Josephus, this route was eighteen Roman miles (150 stadia), and the Tenth Roman Legion used this route in order to lay siege to Jerusalem (Henry O. Thompson, "Adummim," ABD 1:86).

13. D. A. Dorsey, The Roads and Highways of Ancient Israel (Baltimore and London: The Johns Hopkins University, 1991), J32, 204-6; Yohanan Aharoni, The Land of the Bible: A Historical Geography, trans. Anson F. Rainey (Philadelphia: Westminster Press, 1979), 44, 60; E. E. Voigt, "Bahurim," The Annual of the American Schools of Oriental Research 5 (January 1, 1923): 70-71.

14. The Arabic name of Tal'at ed-damm preserves the ancient name in the same way that Jerome understood the name to mean "ascent of blood" (Eusebius, Onomasticon 25.10).

buildings built on top of a highpoint where the rock is especially marked by red streaks in the Senonian limestone, which seem to have given the name to the route. [15] During the Late Roman period, a road was built along the natural route,[16] and fortresses were constructed during the Late Roman and Crusader periods on the hill opposite the Byzantine church where excavations revealed remains from the Second Temple period beneath the fortress.[17] The Ascent of Adummim connected Jerusalem and Judea with the Jewish communities in Perea and Galilee, which would have made it a logical place for robberies (Luke 10:29), a main thoroughfare for Levites and priests (Luke 10:30-31), and perhaps an unlikely route for a Samaritan (Luke 10:32). With regards to robbers, Jerome relays that St. Paula "went through the place of the Adummim, which means 'blood' because a great deal of blood was spilled there as a result of frequent attacks by robbers."[18] Given all of the surrounding evidence, it seems that Jesus aptly used the geographical and socio-political setting of his day to illustrate a powerful rhetorical statement about being a true "neighbor."[19]

The Parable of the Nobleman (Luke 19:11-27)

Following the salvation of Zacchaeus (Luke 19:1-10), Jesus told a parable to those at Zacchaeus' house who were partaking in a meal together. Significantly, this parable was told "because he was near to Jerusalem, and because they supposed that the kingdom of God was to appear immediately" (Luke 19:11). This indicates that Jesus had travelled along the main road through Perea[20] before entering the region of Jericho. In the chronology of the Gospels, this parable seems to have been told the night before Jesus' journey to Jerusalem via the Ascent of Adummim. Since it seems that Jesus shared a Shabbat meal on Friday night with Mary, Martha, and Lazarus before the triumphal entry on Sunday of passion week (John 12:1), then this parable would have been told the Thursday before the approaching Shabbat.

---

15. The Byzantine so-called "Inn of the Good Samaritan" (Khan el-Ahmar), which commemorates the parable of the good Samaritan (Luke 10:34, although the passage is a parable and indicates that the inn was actually in Jericho) and the Crusader Tour Maledoin or Chastel/ Citerne Rouge (Thompson, "Adummim," 86).

16. Michael Avi-Yonah, "The Development of the Roman Road System in Palestine," *IEJ* 1.1 (1950): 54-60; idem, "A New Dating of the Roman Road From Scythopolis to Neapolis," *IEJ* 16.1 (1966): 75-76; S. Applebaum, "Betthar and the Roman Road System," *Zeitschrift Des Deutschen Palästina-Vereins (1953-)* 103 (1987): 137-40; M. Fischer, B. H. Isaac, and I. Roll, *Roman Roads in Judaea 2: The Jaffa-Jerusalem Roads* (Oxford: Tempus Reparatum, 1996).

17. Thompson, "Adummim," 1.86; Tsafrir, Segni, and Green, *Tabula Imperii Romani Iudaea-Palestina*, 176; Bellarmino Bagatti, *Ancient Christian Villages of Samaria* (Jerusalem: Franciscan Printing Press, 2002), 90-94; A. Sussmann, ed., *Excavations and Surveys in Israel* (Jerusalem: Israel Antiquities Authority, 1984), 55.

18. A. Cain, ed., *Jerome's Epitaph on Paula: A Commentary on the Epitaphium Sanctae Paulae with an Introduction, Text, and Translation* (Oxford: Oxford University Press, 2013), 58-59.

19. See A. D. Riddle, "The Passover Pilgrimage from Jericho to Jerusalem" on pg. 395.

20. For a discussion of the boundaries and texts associated with Perea, see Diane I. Treacy-Cole, "Perea," *ABD* 5:224.

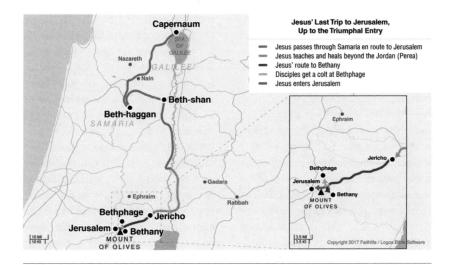

In light of the close proximity of the Herodian residence of Herod Archelaus (Archelais – Khirbet el-Beiyudat) to Jericho, many scholars have pointed to Archelaus' "journey" to Rome (Josephus, *Ant.* 17.342–343; *War* 2.111–113) as the background for Jesus' parable of the nobleman who went to a far country to receive himself a kingdom and then return (Luke 19:12).[21] The palatial compound at Jericho that was greatly enlarged by Herod the Great (located beneath Cypros and along Wadi Qelt) is well-known, and discussed in several accounts by Josephus.[22]

Herod's building at Jericho is one of numerous complex, monumental building projects that were undertaken by Herod the Great. Conversely, Archelais is the only known building project attributed to Archelaus. According to Josephus, Archelais was founded in Archelaus' first year, which is usually dated to 4 BC (*Ant.* 17.340;[23] 18.31; see also Pliny, *Natural History* 13.44, who states that the village was between Jericho and Phasaelis).[24]

Excavations at the site have revealed "an agricultural estate (date groves) with

---

21. See e.g., Walter L. Liefeld, "Luke," in vol. 8 of *Expositor's Bible Commentary*, ed. Frank E. Gæbelein (Grand Rapids: Zondervan, 1984), 1009; Darrell L. Bock, *Luke 1:1–9:50* (Grand Rapids: Baker, 1994), 308; Rainey and Notley, *The Sacred Bridge*, 363. This account seems to have been widely known as it occurs twice in Josephus as well as other Roman sources (e.g., *Ant.* 17.342–43; *War* 2.111–13).

22. See e.g., Ehud Netzer, *The Architecture of Herod, the Great Builder* (Grand Rapids: Baker Academic, 2008), 42–80.

23. "He also magnificently rebuilt the royal palace that had been at Jericho, and he diverted half the water with which the village of Neara used to be watered, and drew off that water into the plain, to water those palm trees which he had there planted: he also built a village, and put his own name upon it, and called it Archelaus" (Josephus, *Ant.* 17.340).

24. H. Hizmi, "Beiyudat, Khirbet El- (Archelais)," *NEAEHL* 1:181. In the Tabula Peutingeriana, Archelais was located twelve Roman milestones north of Jericho and twenty-four Roman

a tower and an aqueduct that brought water from the el-'Auja spring (located 8.5 km to the west)."[25] As noted by Hizmi, in addition to its purpose as an agricultural estate for dates (and perhaps balsam), Archelais seems to have also been used as a waystation for collecting taxes of travelers.[26] The residence remained active throughout the Early Roman period, and a "monumental ashlar tower" was added during the time of the Roman procurators, as demonstrated by the discover of coins relating to Valerius Gratus, Pontius Pilate, and Antonius Felix.[27] These details provide an additional background layer to the character and employment (i.e., tax-collector) of Zacchaeus (Luke 19:2), as well as providing a physical element of Rome's presence along the main Jewish pilgrim route to Jerusalem from Perea and Galilee.

Archelaus was recalled by Caesar "in the tenth year of his government" (AD 6), because he had "broken the commands of Caesar" (*Ant.* 17.342–343). Caesar called "Archelaus' steward" who informed his master of his decision, and, after sailing for Rome, Archelaus was banished to Vienna (in Gaul), and his money was taken away from him (*Ant.* 17.343–344).

Many of these details have parallels in Jesus' parable including the departure of the nobleman (Archelaus), the calling of a steward, and the hatred of citizens who sent a delegation to the king. Of course, the outcome of the events in the parable are reversed from reality, as Jesus imagined a situation in which the nobleman returned, and dealt harshly with those who had spoken ill of him and not acted faithfully with his wealth (Luke 19:13–26), whereas Archelaus never did return. Conversely, and given the severe actions of Archelaus before his banishment, as well the well-known jealousy-driven cruelty of his father (Herod the Great), Jesus' warnings in his revisionist parable offered a realistic depiction of the consequences for disobedience had Archelaus been allowed to return. Jesus' parable seems to be a clear example of him using his contemporary setting to illustrate a larger theological point. [28]

The Walk to Emmaus (Luke 24:13–35)

Moving to the western side of Judea, Luke records that Jesus travelled with "two disciples" to the village of Emmaus following his resurrection (Luke 24:13–35). Regarding this account, several geographical comments can be made that help illustrate this dramatic discussion between Jesus and two of his dejected followers (one was named Cleopas, Luke 24:18). Emmaus was located west of Jerusalem at a distance of either thirty, sixty or one hundred sixty[29] stadia along the main Roman road from Jerusalem to

---

milestones of Scythpolis, but it actually is located fifteen Roman miles from Jericho (Hizmi, "Beiyudat," 181).

25. H. Hizmi, "Beiyudat, Khirbet El- (Archelais)," *NEAEHL* 5:1601–2; see also Hizmi, "Beiyudat, Khirbet El- (Archelais)," *NEAEHL* 1:181–82.

26. Hizmi, "Beiyudat, Khirbet El- (Archelais)," *NEAEHL* 5:1602.

27. Hizmi, "Beiyudat, Khirbet El- (Archelais)," *NEAEHL* 5:1600.

28. See Aubrey L. Taylor, "The Historical Basis of the Parable of the Pounds" on pg. 385.

29. The majority of the textual tradition has σταδίους ἑξήκοντα, and it appears that the reading "160 stadia" (e.g., Codex Siniaticus) arose in connection with the "patristic identifications of Emmaus with Amwas-Nicpolis" (James Strange, "Emmaus," *ABD* 2:497). While

Herod's Winter Palace in Jericho

the Aijalon Valley and the coastal plain. This road is sometimes referred to as the "Kiriath-jearim ridge route," and it is largely identical to the modern Jerusalem-Tel Aviv highway.[30]

Regardless of the precise identification of New Testament Emmaus (perhaps Qaloniyeh/Moza), the direction of their journey indicates that these fol-lowers of Jesus actually resided in Judea, as opposed to the majority of his follow-ers, who would have been from Galilee. In fact, besides Joseph of Arimithea (Matt 27:57; Mark 15:43; Luke 23:50; John 19:38),[31] these two are the only known of Jesus' followers who were from Judea and lived outside of Jerusalem. It is also interesting to note that the conversation

Emmaus-Nicopolis has the patristic tradition, it does not fit the textual data, and it is hard to imagine that the two disciples could have made the return uphill, 17-mile journey to Jerusalem following their evening meal (see Luke 24:28–35). On account of this, several candidates have been offered as alternate sites for Emmaus. These include the following: el-Qubeibeh, Abu Ghosh, and Qaloniah/Moza. For Qaloniah/Moza to be identified with Emmaus, one must assume that the "60 stadia" refers to the "roundtrip" distance from Jerusalem to Emmaus, as Josephus states that this Emmaus was thirty stadia from Jerusalem (*War* 7.217). See Strange, "Emmaus," for a discussion of each of these possibilities; see also Josephus, *War* 2.497–98.

30. See Perry G. Phillips, "The Post-Resurrection Appearances of Christ" on pg: 518.

31. And also possibly Judas Iscariot (e.g., Matt 26:14). Iscariot is sometimes understood to be a reference to the city of Kerioth in the Negeb of Judah (Josh 15:25; see discussion in e.g., W. Klassen, "Judas Iscariot," *ABD* 3:1091). But this is unlikely, as Kerioth-hezron in Josh 15:24 is probably a modifier to the preceding town that defines the type of settlements (i.e., cities of agricultural enclosures), as opposed to a specific town name (see Chris McKinny, "A Historical Geography of the Administrative Division of Judah: The Town Lists of Judah and Benjamin in Joshua 15:21–62 and 18:21–28" [PhD diss., Bar Ilan University, 2016], 126).

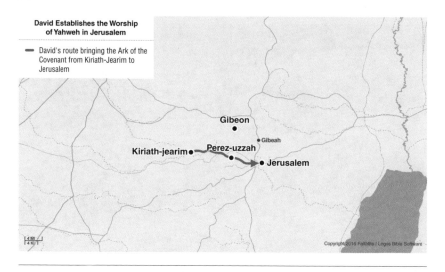

between Jesus and his two unsuspecting followers occurred along the same route that was taken by David when he brought the ark of the covenant from Kiriath-jearim to Jerusalem (2 Sam 6). Perhaps Jesus mentioned this fact to the two when he began with "Moses and then all the prophets interpreting to them in all the Scriptures the things concerning himself" (Luke 24:26).

JESUS IN JERUSALEM – RITUALS AND FEASTS

With our discussion of the narratives associated with Judea complete, we can now turn our attention to Jesus' numerous statements in Jerusalem. All of the Gospel narratives of Jesus in Jerusalem are related to a particular Jewish rite or festival. In several instances during his ministry, Jesus made a declaration of intent to go to Jerusalem. These visitations to Jerusalem and accompanying declarations include the following:

- Joseph and Mary present Jesus to the Lord at the temple on the eighth day after his birth (Luke 2:22).

- Jesus travelled to Jerusalem with his parents for Passover at the age of twelve (Luke 2:41–51).

- The first Passover of Jesus' ministry (John 2:13, 23).

- Jesus travelled to Jerusalem for "a feast of the Jews," which was possibly the Feast of Tabernacles (John 5:1).

- The second Passover of Jesus' ministry (John 6:4), but with no record of Jesus travelling to Jerusalem.

- Private journey to Jerusalem for the Feast of Tabernacles with public ministry during the middle of the feast (John 7:2, 10, 14, 37).

- Hanukkah (Feast of Dedication) in Jerusalem (John 10:22).[32]

---

32. In addition, Jesus visited Bethany (near Jerusalem) in the weeks before Passover, at which time, he raised Lazarus from the dead (John 11:1–44). Following Lazarus' resurrection

• Death and resurrection prediction before final Passover in Jerusalem (Matt 20:17–19; Mark 10:32–34; Luke 18:31–33; cf. Luke 9:31, 51–55; 13:22, 31–35; John 11:55; 12:1).

These eight instances illustrate the significance of Jerusalem in the ministry of Jesus. Luke's account provides the early record of Jesus' circumcision[33] and presentation as a son of the covenant as a youth (see Luke 2:22–28) Besides the final Passover that is mentioned in all four Gospels, John includes four additional journeys to Jerusalem by Jesus (see above). Due to limitations of space, I am limiting the discussion of Jesus in Jerusalem to the timeframe before his entrance into the city during the final Passover/passion week.[34] In this final section, we will discuss each of the four earlier visits Jesus made to Jerusalem according to the Gospel of John.

Destroy "This" Temple (John 2:18–22)

During Jesus' initial visit to Jerusalem to celebrate the Passover, John records that Jesus cleansed the temple from the money-changers and sacrifice-sellers (John 2:14–17).[35] In the aftermath of this action, the following interchange took place

between Jesus and the Jews who were present at the temple.

> So the Jews said to him, 'What sign do you show us for doing these things?' Jesus answered them, 'Destroy this temple [τὸν ναὸν τοῦτον], and in three days I will raise it up.' The Jews then said, 'It has taken forty-six years to build this temple [ho naos houtos, ὁ ναὸς οὗτος], and will you raise it up in three days?' But he was speaking about the temple of his body. When therefore he was raised from the dead, his disciples remembered that he had said this, and they believed the Scripture and the word that Jesus had spoken. (John 2:18–22 ESV)

John's theological explanation is clear. Jesus was referring to the temple as a metaphor for his own body that would be crucified and raised with power after three days (see also Matt 26:61; 27:40; Mark 14:58; 15:29). On the other hand, scholars have been divided over the meaning of the Jews' confused response to Jesus, which makes reference to a duration of forty-six years in connection with the construction of the temple. As noted by Hoehner, Josephus made a distinction between

---

and in light of the danger from the Jewish religious establishment, Jesus and his disciples did not enter Jerusalem, but withdrew to "the region near the wilderness, to a town called Ephraim" (John 11:54).

33. In a later context, and while on the Temple Mount, Jesus used circumcision on Shabbat as an example of a greater law overriding Shabbat (John 7:22–24).

34. Regarding Jesus' geographical language during passion week, there are a number of clear examples that are worth further study: e.g., the usage of the Mount of Olives and its Old Testament parallels in the triumphal entry (Matt 21:1–9; Mark 11:1–10; Luke 19:29–38; John 12:12–15; compare 2 Sam 15:30–16:4), the cursing of the fig tree (Matt 21:18–22; Mark 11:12–14, 20–24; compare Jer 24; Hos 9:10), the Olivet discourse (Matt 24:1–51; Mark 13:1–37; Luke 21:5–36; compare Zech 14:1–5), the judgment (Matt 25:31–46; compare Joel 3:1–3, 14 including the Kidron Valley), the ascension (Luke 24:50–53; Acts 1:6–11; compare Ezek 11:22–24; Zech 14:1–5).

35. See further discussion of this in Chris McKinny, "Southern Temple Mount Excavations: Archaeological Discoveries" on pg. 442.

the temple itself (ναὸς) and the entire Temple Mount complex (ἱερός).[36] This distinction was also used in the Gospels (e.g., Luke 21:5). Therefore, in this context Jesus and the Jews were referring to the temple building itself (naos, ναός), which had commenced in the eighteenth year of Herod the Great (20/19 BC; Josephus, Ant. 15.380; also War 1.401, which dates this event to the fifteenth year of Herod the Great; see discussion in Hoehner) and finished a year-and-a-half later in 18/17 BC (Ant. 15.421). Therefore, the Jews' statement that the temple (naos, ναός) had been standing for "forty-six years" (i.e., in the year AD 29/30) indicates that the building that had been standing most, if not all, of their lifetimes.[37] They understood the monumental effort undertaken in constructing the temple, and it was unimaginable that such a majestic structure could be destroyed and re-built in a mere three days.[38]

Chronological issues aside, Jesus' use of the temple as a metaphor for his body is even more shocking than the Jews' understanding of his statement as a prophecy/threat. The temple was the most important part of Jewish life. It was the house of Yahweh, where his Spirit dwelled (e.g., 1 Kgs 8:4–11), and the focal point of all religious expression and life in Jerusalem. In this metaphor, Jesus was pointing to the parallels between the temple and himself. Both the temple and Jesus were indwelt with God's Spirit. Both the temple and Jesus were the culmina-

tion of a long process in God's redemptive plan. Shockingly, both the temple and Jesus would be unexpectedly destroyed and, yet, raised again.

From a hermeneutical perspective, it is important for readers to realize that the Jews of that day did not understand Jesus' theological metaphor, and, in fact, even his disciples did not understand the metaphor until after his death (John 2:22). They had a clear understanding of the image that Jesus was using (i.e., the temple building). While modern readers have the benefit of John describing the purpose of the metaphor (John 2:22), we can easily struggle in imagining the visuals that Jesus was drawing on to illustrate his point, because we were simply not there. However, in order to fully understand the implications of Jesus' prophetic metaphor we need to see through the eyes of those who had witnessed the building and lived with the colossal Herodian temple. Only then can we possibly grasp their incredulousness at Jesus' statement. Conversely, only we (those living this side of the cross and the empty tomb) can fully understand the true shock of the rejection and death of the true living temple, which is only surpassed by the outright astonishment of the true temple's resurrection in three days.

The Blind and the Lame (John 5:2–17; 9:1–12)

John's "six miracles"[39] are considered by many to be the main literary structure

---

36. See references in Harold W. Hoehner, *Chronological Aspects of the Life of Christ*, Kindle ed. (Grand Rapids: Zondervan, 2010), n.p.

37. Hoehner, *Chronological Aspects*, n.p.

38. See Todd Bolen, "Magnificent Stones and Wonderful Buildings of the Temple Complex" on pg. 462.

39. 1) Water into wine (John 2:1–11); 2) healing the paralytic (John 5:2–17); 3) feeding the 5,000 (John 6:1–14); 4) walking on the sea (John 6:16–20); 5) healing the blind man (John

of his Gospel. Two of these miracles occurred in Jerusalem. First, Jesus healed the man who had been paralyzed for thirty-eight years (John 5:2-17) at the pools of Bethesda during the unnamed Jewish feast of John 5:1.[40] Second, Jesus healed the man born blind in the Lower City and the pool of Siloam (John 9:1-12) during the Feast of Tabernacles (see John 7:2).[41] From a geographical perspective, these two events occurred at the northern and southern ends of the eastern hill of Jerusalem, respectively. During the Gospel era, the pools of Bethesda were located north of the Herodian Temple Mount and outside of the fortifications of the second wall,[42] whereas the pool of Siloam (Luke 13:4; John 9:7, 11; see also 2 Kgs 20:20; 2 Chr 32:30; Neh 3:5; Isa 8:6) was located at the southern end of the Lower City within the Central Valley,

and near the confluence of the Kidron, Hinnom, and Central Valleys (see infographic "Ancient Jerusalem" on pg. 528).[43]

While these narratives clearly serve multiple literary purposes in the context of John's Gospel (e.g., as a narrative device for showing the hypocrisy of the Jewish religious establishment), it is interesting to note that the physical misfortunes (i.e., being lame and blind) of these two men have a very clear intertextual parallel with the "blind and lame" inhabitants of the city when David conquered it.[44] According to 2 Samuel 5:6-9, the "blind and the lame" of Jebus could not enter the house of David, because the Jebusites used them to taunt David on account of his presumed inability to conquer the city.[45] Despite the Jebusite claim, David (via Joab; compare 1 Chr 11:6) conquered the city using the water

---

9:1-12); and 6) raising Lazarus from the dead (John 11:1-44).

40. See Gordon Franz, "Jesus at the Pool of Bethesda" on pg. 125.

41. See Elaine A. Phillips, "Healing by Living Water at the Pool of Siloam" on pg. 365.

42. According to Strange, the pools of Bethesda (or Beth-zatha) may also be mentioned in the Copper Scroll with the dual ending of "*Beteshdathaim*" (3Q15.xi.12), which may reflect the fact that Bethesda was a double pool. See J. Strange, "Beth-Zatha," *ABD* 1:700-1. The complex was excavated in the late nineteenth century and again in the late 1950s, revealing the two massive pools and the accompanying five porches, which matched the descriptions in John 5:2 and Origen (*Commentary on John* 5.2-4.532; see Strange, "Beth-Zatha," 1:701).

43. Excavations at the pool of Siloam have revealed the northern portion of a massive Herodian pool connected to a series of monumental steps and a street leading up through the Lower City to the Temple Mount. See R. Reich, E. Shukron, and O. Lernau, "Recent Discoveries in the City of David, Jerusalem," *Israel Exploration Journal* 57, no. 2 (January 1, 2007): 153-69, http://www.jstor.org/stable/27927171. See also Chris McKinny, "Southern Temple Mount Excavations: Archaeological Discoveries" on pg. 442.

44. In another context, Jesus answered what amounted to John's deathbed question of "are you the one who is to come, or shall we look for another?" with the statement "the blind receive their sight and the lame walk" (Matt 11:3-5, cf. Isa 35:5-6). For a discussion of the connection between David and Jesus with regards to the blind and the lame, see also Ronald F. Youngblood, "1 and 2 Samuel," in vol. 3 of *Expositor's Bible Commentary*, ed. Frank E. Gæbelein (Grand Rapids: Zondervan, 1992), 853-56.

45. While acknowledging the problematic Hebrew text of 2 Samuel 5:6-9 (compare 1 Chr 11:4-6), this interpretation, which is reflected in many modern English translations (e.g., ESV), makes good sense of a difficult passage. See discussion in Youngblood, "1 and 2 Samuel", 854-55.

system,[46] after which he made his pronouncement concerning the blind and the lame. Besides the clear similarity between the blind and the lame in the narratives, it is also interesting that a Jerusalem water system is the method of salvation in all three accounts. Finally, as is often the case with Gospel intertextual parallels, the main point of the allusion is to demonstrate the superiority of Jesus over his predecessor. In this instance, David refused to let the blind and the lame into his palace, whereas Jesus healed the blind and the lame so that they might enter into his house (i.e., the temple; see also Isa 35:5–6; Jer 31:8; Matt 11:5).

Living Waters from the Temple (John 7:37–38)

On the last day of the Feast of Tabernacles (John 7:2),[47] Jesus "stood up in the temple" and stated, "if anyone thirsts, let him come to me and drink. Whoever believes in me, as the Scripture has said, 'Out of his heart will flow rivers of living water'" (John 7:37–38). Within the context of the Feast of Tabernacles (Lev 23:34–39; Num 29:12–34), this statement has clear allusions to the Israelites' wilderness wandering experience in which they were hungry and thirsty (e.g., Deut 8:5). On the other hand, there are several prophetic statements that refer to a future "living" fountain or river that would flow from the temple to both the Mediterranean Sea and the Dead Sea (Ezek 47:1–12; Joel 3:18; Zech 14:8).[48] The prophets used the image of a flowing fountain from the temple that would flow through the Kidron Valley and into the Judean Wilderness, causing the land around, and even the Dead Sea itself, to flourish and bring forth life. Against this prophetic and geographical background, Jesus stood in the very place where the prophets had stated that these things would occur "on that day" (i.e., the Day of Yahweh; see Joel 3:14) and claimed to be the very fountain that had been promised by the prophets.[49]

In Solomon's Portico (John 10:22–39)

Solomon's Portico (stoa, στοά), which is referenced in John 10:22 and Acts 3:11, is usually identified with the eastern colonnade or porch of the Temple Mount.[50] According to Josephus, this section had been previously built by Solomon; he wrote, "this was the work of king Solomon, who first of all built the entire temple" (Ant. 17.221). These passages indicate that the Jews of the Second Temple

---

46. The exact interpretation and location of this event remain uncertain.

47. The last day of the Feast of Tabernacles.

48. In both Joel 3:18 and Ezekiel, the fountain seems to have flown to the east via the Kidron Valley. In Ezekiel, the water flows to the Dead Sea and makes it fresh. In Joel, the water flows to the "Canyon of Shittim" (i.e., the canyon of Acacia trees). The exact canyon (nahal) relating to Shittim is difficult to determine. It is possible that Shittim is a wordplay for Siddim (i.e., the Salt Sea – see Gen 14:3, 8, 1), and/or connected to Abel-shittim, which is located on the northeastern banks of the Dead Sea (Num 25:1; 33:49; Josh 2:1; 3:1; Mic 6:5). It could also be simply related to the acacia trees that are often found in or near the canyons as they enter the Dead Sea.

49. See Cyndi Parker, "The People's Thirst at the Feast of Tabernacles" on pg. 356.

50. See e.g., Leen Ritmeyer, The Quest: Revealing the Temple Mount in Jerusalem (Jerusalem: Carta, 2006), 113. The interior of the Temple Mount had a colonnaded porch on the north, west, and east sides, with the Royal Stoa serving the same purpose in the south.

period believed that the eastern side of the Temple Mount was the most ancient section of the structure. In fact, Ritmeyer has conclusively demonstrated that this portion of the eastern wall was initially constructed during the First Temple period (i.e., Iron Age II; see infographic "Solomon's Portico" on pg. 533).[51]

During Hanukkah in the winter before the final Passover of his ministry, Jesus taught in Solomon's Portico (John 10:22). From a practical perspective, the weather was likely the cause for Jesus teaching in the relative shelter of Solomon's Portico, as opposed to the open "Court of the Gentiles," which surrounded the temple. On the other hand, and given the fact that shade in Israel is always preferable to standing in the hot Mediterranean sun (as many can attest!), it is possible that the mention of Solomon's Portico is meant to draw the reader's attention to parallels between Solomon and the substance of Jesus' teaching.

The reign of Solomon (c. 971–931 BC) was the unquestioned golden age of ancient Israel. From a literary perspective, this is highlighted in a number of ways in the book of Kings. Following David, his messianic father (see 1 Sam 16; 2 Sam 7), Solomon was the "christ" (mšḥ; see 1 Kgs 33–40) who oversaw a period of prosperity when "Judah and Israel were as many as the sand by the sea" (1 Kgs 4:20). This summary statement closely matches the promises of the Abrahamic covenant (Gen 22:17), and indicates a partial fulfillment of that covenant. Moreover, Solomon had built his palace just south of the temple (see 1 Kgs 6–7) and presided over the indwelling of

Yahweh's temple (1 Kgs 8) — both of these structures had been located in the immediate proximity of Solomon's Portico.

These are important background details for understanding Jesus' response to the questions regarding whether or not he claimed to be the messiah (John 10:25). The preceding "Good Shepherd" sermon and the confusion of Jesus' audience (John 10:1–21) are also worth considering. In this sermon, which apparently occurred some months earlier during or just after the Feast of Tabernacles, Jesus used the familiar shepherd image to illustrate his covenantal claim to the role of the Davidic messiah (see 2 Sam 5:2; Ezek 34:23–24; 37:24). In John 10:22–31, Jesus reiterated the Davidic shepherd metaphor (10:25–27); claimed that his authority was derived from "his Father," with whom he was equal (10:25, 29), like Solomon had been with David; and offered eternal life to his followers (10:28 - compare to the kingdom conditions during the reign of Solomon; see above). While it would be an overstatement to point to a direct intertextual link between this passage and 1 Kings, the lasting memory of Israel's golden age under Solomon and the expectation that even that era would be surpassed as a result of Solomon's coming successor should be taken into account when considering the crowd's questions and Jesus' response.

Moreover, and besides the possible parallels with Solomon, the fact that this interchange occurred during Hanukkah should also cause us to examine the events connected with the development of the Feast of Hanukkah for potential textual ramifications. Hanukkah (or the Feast of Dedication) was a Jewish

---

51. Ritmeyer, *The Quest*, 101–5.

festival that was observed in the winter months (November–December) in celebration of the Hasmonean/Maccabean re-dedication of the temple and the altar (1 Macc 4:36–61; 2 Macc 1:18; 2:!6, 19; 10:3, 5, 7) in late 165 or 164 BC following its desecration by the Seleucid monarch Antiochus IV.[52] In Jesus' day, the festival was widely observed by Jews. During the brief period of Hasmonean rule (c. 165–63 BC), Judea was independent, and even expansionistic, ultimately attaining a kingdom roughly the size of the kingdom under David and Solomon.[53]

Significantly, the rise of the Hasmonean dynasty coupled with the re-dedication of the temple meant that this brief period was the only time in which daily sacrifices were not offered in honor of an imperial power who controlled Yehud/Judea (see Ezra 6:10).[54] This practice began following the return to Judah under Cyrus I after 539 BC, and was presumably resumed following the Roman annexation of Judea by Pompey in 63 BC.[55] It is worth noting that the Jews of Jerusalem received special privileges from Rome in that they were not required to offer sacrifices to the emperor *as a deity*, but, instead, they offered sacrifices in his honor and for his well-being and the

well-being of his family (see Josephus, *Ag. Ap.* 2.77–78).[56] However, it appears that even this practice was abhorrent to many Jews, as made evident by Josephus' statement that refers to the cessation of the imperial sacrifice as the "true beginning of our war with the Romans, for they rejected the sacrifice of Caesar" (*War* 2.409–410).

Against this historical backdrop, Jesus' strongly implied claim to be the messiah in the Davidic/Solomonic line (in addition to being "one with the father" and the "I am" – John 10:25–38) would have had multiple layers of meaning. Theology was the primary layer highlighted by John based on Jesus' claim to divinity and the spectators' hostile response. However, it seems there would have also been contemporary political undertones in Jesus' claim. In fact, following the feeding of the 5,000, John made an explicit reference to Jesus' awareness of the crowd's desire to "take him by force to make him king" (John 6:15). In this regard, it can be safely stated that Jesus was aware of the historical background of the imperial sacrifice, the Hasmonean re-dedication of the altar and the temple, and the deep-seated Jewish animosity of Rome's renewal of this practice. Subsequently, and given

52. See discussion in James C. VanderKam, "The Feast of Dedication," *ABD* 2:123–25.

53. Rainey and Notley, *The Sacred Bridge*, 308–33.

54. Additional support for prayers and sacrifices made in honor of the emperor can be found in the Cyrus Cylinder (COS 2.315–16), Herodotus (*Histories* 1.131), and the Elephantine texts (see especially C 30/31). Bezalel Porten, ed., *The Elephantine Papyri in English: Three Millennia of Cross-Cultural Continuity and Change*, 2nd ed. (Atlanta: SBL, 2011), 355–61; compare Bezalel Porten, *Archives from Elephantine: The Life of an Ancient Jewish Military Colony* (Los Angeles: University of California Press, 1968), 290–91.

55. See references in M. P. Ben Zeev, "From Toleration to Destruction: Roman Policy and the Jewish Temple," in *The Temple of Jerusalem: From Moses to the Messiah: In Honor of Professor Louis H. Feldman*, ed. S. Fine (Leiden: Brill, 2011), 65.

56. See e.g., M. P. Ben Zeev, *Jewish Rights in the Roman World: The Greek and Roman Documents Quoted by Josephus Flavius* (Tübingen: Mohr Siebeck, 1998), 474; M. Niehoff, *Philo on Jewish Identity and Culture* (Tübingen: Mohr Siebeck, 2001), 82.

The Cyrus Cylinder

Dates to sixth century BC

1st section: Cyrus' greatness/mercy

2nd section: Cyrus returned captive peoples and their gods to their native lands.

Description of Cyrus' mercy and efforts supports Ezra 1.

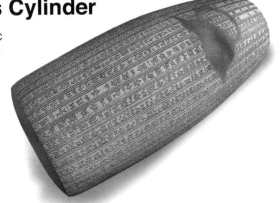

the above-mentioned examples of geographically and politically driven themes in Jesus' teaching, it seems that Jesus was using the existing political environment to demonstrate his true and Rome-surpassing authority as the Son of God and the true messianic King of Israel.[57]

CONCLUSION

In this essay, we have looked at several different examples of Jesus using language that was distinctive to the geographical and political setting of Judea and Jerusalem during the Gospel era. Despite the fact that Jesus grew up and spent most of his ministry outside of Jerusalem, it is quite clear from the examples discussed that Jesus had an intimate knowledge of the landscape and political realities of Judea. This reality can be observed in the ways in which Jesus used his Judean surroundings as a way of illustrating his teachings and his interpretation of Old Testament prophecies and allusions concerning himself.

BIBLIOGRAPHY

Aharoni, Yohanan. *The Land of the Bible: A Historical Geography.* Translated by Anson F. Rainey. Philadelphia: Westminster Press, 1979.

Applebaum, S. "Betthar and the Roman Road System." *Zeitschrift Des Deutschen Palästina-Vereins (1953-)* 103 (1987): 137–40. http://www.jstor.org/stable/27931310.

Avi-Yonah, Michael. "A New Dating of the Roman Road From Scythopolis to Neapolis." *IEJ* 16.1 (1966): 75–76. http://www.jstor.org/stable/27925043.

———. "The Development of the Roman Road System in Palestine." *IEJ* 1.1 (1950): 54–60. http://www.jstor.org/stable/27924424.

Bagatti, Bellarmino. *Ancient Christian Villages of Samaria.* Jerusalem: Franciscan Printing Press, 2002.

Ben Zeev, M. P. "From Toleration to Destruction: Roman Policy and the Jewish Temple." Pages 57–68 in *The*

---

57. Of course, the spiritual element of the kingdom seems to have been lost on the audience (see Jesus' statement to Pontius Pilate; John 10:36).

Temple of Jerusalem: From Moses to the Messiah: In Honor of Professor Louis H. Feldman. Edited by S. Fine. Leiden: Brill, 2011.

———. *Jewish Rights in the Roman World: The Greek and Roman Documents Quoted by Josephus Flavius*. Tübingen: Mohr Siebeck, 1998.

Bock, Darrell L. *Luke 1:1–9:50*. BECNT. Grand Rapids: Baker, 1994.

Cain, A., ed. *Jerome's Epitaph on Paul: A Commentary on the Epitaphium Sanctae Paulae with an Introduction, Text, and Translation*. Oxford: Oxford University Press, 2013.

Dorsey, D. A. *The Roads and Highways of Ancient Israel*. Baltimore, MD: The Johns Hopkins University Press, 1991.

Fischer, M., B. H. Isaac, and I. Roll. *Roman Roads in Judaea 2: The Jaffa-Jerusalem Roads*. Oxford: Tempus Reparatum, 1996.

Hizmi, H. "Beiyudat, Khirbet El-(Archelais)." *NEAEHL* 1:181–82

———. "Beiyudat, Khirbet El-(Archelais)." *NEAEHL* 5:1600–1602.

Hoehner, Harold W. *Chronological Aspects of the Life of Christ*. Grand Rapids: Zondervan, 2010. Kindle edition.

Hübner, U. "Idumea." *ABD* 3:382–83.

Klassen, W. "Judas Iscariot." *ABD* 3:1091–96.

Knoppers, Gary N. *Jews and Samaritans: The Origins and History of Their Early Relations*. Oxford: Oxford University Press, 2013.

Lawrence, J. D. *Washing in Water: Trajectories of Ritual Bathing in the Hebrew Bible and Second Temple Literature*. Atlanta: Society of Biblical Literature, 2006.

Liefeld, Walter L. "Luke." Pages 795–1059 in vol. 8 of *Expositor's Bible Commentary*. Edited by Frank E.

Gaebelein. Grand Rapids: Zondervan, 1984.

Magen, Yitzhak. "The Temple of YHWH at Mt. Gerizim." *Eretz-Israel* 29 (2009): 277–97. http://www.jstor.org/stable/23631331.

Magness, Jodi *Stone and Dung, Oil and Spit: Jewish Daily Life in the Time of Jesus*. Grand Rapids and Cambridge: Wm. B. Eerdmans Publishing, 2011.

McKinny, Chris. "A Historical Geography of the Administrative Division of Judah: The Town Lists of Judah and Benjamin in Joshua 15:21–62 and 18:21–28." PhD diss., Bar Ilan University, 2016.

Netzer, Ehud. *The Architecture of Herod, the Great Builder*. Grand Rapids, MI: Baker Academic, 2008.

Niehoff, M. *Philo on Jewish Identity and Culture*. Mohr Siebeck, 2001.

Pattengale, Jerry A. "Aenon." *ABD* 1:87.

Porten, Bezalel. *Archives from Elephantine: The Life of an Ancient Jewish Military Colony*. Los Angeles: University of California Press, 1968.

———, ed. *The Elephantine Papyri in English: Three Millennia of Cross-Cultural Continuity and Change*. 2nd ed. Atlanta: Society of Biblical Literature, 2011.

Rainey, Anson F., and R. Steven Notley. *The Sacred Bridge*. Jerusalem: Carta, 2006.

Reich, R. "Miqwa'ot (Jewish Ritual Baths) in Eretz-Israel, in the Second Temple, Mishnah and Talmud Periods." PhD thesis, Hebrew University, 1990. Hebrew.

Reich, R., E. Shukron, and O. Lernau. "Recent Discoveries in the City of David, Jerusalem." *IEJ* 57.2 (2007): 153–69. http://www.jstor.org/stable/27927171.

Ritmeyer, Leen. *The Quest: Revealing the Temple Mount in Jerusalem.* Jerusalem: Carta, 2006.

Stern, Ephraim, and Yitzhak Magen. "Archaeological Evidence for the First Stage of the Samaritan Temple on Mount Gerizim." *IEJ* 52.1 (2002): 49–57. http://www.jstor.org/stable/27926987.

Strange, James. "Beth-Zatha." *ABD* 1:700–1.

———. "Emmaus." *ABD* 2:497–98.

Sussmann, A., ed. *Excavations and Surveys in Israel.* Jerusalem: Israel Antiquities Authority, 1984.

Thompson, Henry O. "Adummim." *ABD* 1:86–87.

Treacy-Cole, Diane I. "Perea." *ABD* 1:86–87.

Tsafrir, Y., L. D. Segni, and J. Green. *Tabula Imperii Romani Iudaea-Palestina: Eretz Israel in the Hellenistic, Roman and Byzantine Periods; Maps and Gazetteer.* Jerusalem: The Israel Academy of Sciences and Humanities, 1994.

VanderKam, James C. "The Feast of Dedication." *ABD* 2:124–25.

Voigt, E. E. "Bahurim." *The Annual of the American Schools of Oriental Research* 5 (January 1, 1923): 67–76. doi:10.2307/3768520.

Youngblood, Ronald F. "1 and 2 Samuel." Pages 551–1104 in vol. 3 of *Expositor's Bible Commentary.* Edited by Frank E. Gæbelein. Grand Rapids: Zondervan, 1992.

CHAPTER 35

THE PEOPLE'S THIRST AT THE FEAST OF TABERNACLES

John 7:37-39

Cyndi Parker

KEY POINTS

- Water was a highly valued resource in the ancient world, and the best kind was "living water" (moving water from a stream or spring).

- The agricultural season consists of only two seasons: the rainy season and the dry season.

- The water ceremony during the Feast of Tabernacles symbolized God's provision of living water, his Holy Spirit, at a time when physical thirst was prevalent.

- Jesus' message at the Feast of Tabernacles could not have been more timely: the agricultural cycle was over, and the people were thirsty and anticipating God's provision of water for the coming year's crops.

- Jesus' call to "come to me and drink" puts himself in the position of God, the supplier of living water.

The significance of Jesus' teaching on the last day of the Feast of Tabernacles in John 7:37-39 is best understood within the greater geographical and religious context, because Jesus uses the physical and cultural context of the first century to make bold claims about his divinity.

THE SIGNIFICANCE OF WATER

Residents of Palestine did not depend on large rivers for water like the people living in Mesopotamia and Egypt; instead, they lived in a land that drank its "water from heaven, a land the Lord cares for" (Deut 11:11-12). It was a thirsty land where the required amount of annual water

Cistern at Qumran

to support the agricultural life was not guaranteed. In this region, where both farmers and shepherds lived off the land, people became sensitized to the quality and source of their fresh water. They described the best kind of water as living water, because it was naturally filtered, clean, and flowing from a stream or spring. The volume of water was less significant than the quality of the water, for even a small spring could support a local community with fresh water filtered through rocks.

Sometimes water filtered through the hills was not accessible from a spring, but the water table was high enough for people to dig a well to retrieve water. Although a well provided fresh water, it required more work and maintenance from the community to keep the water clean and without contaminants.

However, as populations grew and communities developed in areas with limited access to springs and wells,

necessity drove the people to develop additional water management systems. With rain as the primary source of water, families were driven to collect and store rain through the rainy season to support them through the dry season. People created cisterns by digging holes into rock and plastering the inside to prevent the water from seeping out. Cisterns had long narrow necks and a large bulbous bottom. Water channels helped direct runoff rainwater into the cistern's narrow opening; the opening was, then, covered by a large stone to prevent sunlight from interacting with stagnate water and creating bad bacteria (i.e., pathogens). Any sediments that were drug into the cistern by the flow of water eventually sunk to the bottom. By necessity, families had to manage their water collection for the duration of the dry season, until the fresh water of the following rainy season could replenish the cistern. With only a rainy and a dry season, it was mandatory that the residents of the land be careful with how they used this precious resource.

THE AGRICULTURAL SEASON

The annual cycle of rainfall affected the agricultural season as well as those religious holidays that were connected to a pattern of life determined by the agricultural calendar. In contrast to a modern western view of the calendar as a linear progression of time, communities living in the land of the Bible approached the calendar according to the land's repetitive cycle.

The land has only two seasons: the rainy season (from October to early May) and the dry season (from May to early October). The agricultural season begins when the "early rains" usher in the beginning of the rainy season. These initial rains are gentle and sporadic but effectively soften the surface of the land that was baked hard under the hot summer sun. They make plowing through the hard ground possible. Farmers loosen the soil in preparation for the more substantial rains to follow. They scatter seed in the fields, plow the fields again to turn the seeds into the soil, and then wait for the heavy winter showers to provide the necessary water for a viable crop. The showers replenish the ground water, support the crops, and refill the family cisterns. Therefore, both the early rains and the heavy winter rains are critical for agrarian families.

As the winter rains taper off, the season's "later rains" conclude the rainy season. Like the "early rains," the "later rains" are sporadic but essential for saturating the soil and providing the mois-

ture needed for the summer fruits. The first crop of the harvest season is barley. Farmers begin to harvest this crop in March and April, and then harvest wheat in April and May. The dry season begins in May and which is mitigated only by the heavy dew in June. The heat of the summer sun helps the summer fruit ripen. Typically at the end of the dry season, farmers move into their fields and stay in tents or watchtowers to protect their harvest from being ravaged. The olive harvest concludes the growing season and marks the transition into the next agricultural cycle (in October). As farmers bring the olives in from the fields, they are aware of the necessity of the early rains coming again to soften the ground and to allow the land's cycle to begin anew (see infographic "Agricultural Cycle of the Levant/Palestine" on pg. 530).

THE RELIGIOUS CALENDAR

The religious calendar is connected to the agricultural cycle of the land. An important symbolic activity for Israel is feasting from the produce gathered from the land. The communal act of eating connects past memories—told within the context of the festivals—with the generosity and provision from God in the present. Each festival is an inclusive activity for all people in Israelite society, allowing the whole community to rejoice over the provisions of the land that sustains them. Each of the three pilgrimage festivals has strong agricultural ties.

Mosaic law instructs the Israelites to make a pilgrimage to the temple for three separate festivals: (1) the Feast of Unleavened Bread/Passover,[1] (2) the Feast

---

1. Exod 12:15–20; 23:15; 34:18; Lev 23:6–8; Num 28:17–25; Deut 16:1–8. The Passover meal is celebrated the night before the seven day Feast of Unleavened Bread. Deut 16:1–8 combines Passover and the Feast of Unleavened Bread as one pilgrimage festival. Elsewhere in the

Jewish Calendar of Feasts

of Weeks/Pentecost,[2] and (3) the Feast of Tabernacles.[3] The first two religious festivals frame the barley and wheat harvests in April-May while the third festival follows the olive harvest in October.[4] Israel celebrated Passover during the time of the barley harvest[5] in order to commemorate the night before the exodus when the angel of death passed over the Israelite homes. Passover blended directly into the seven day celebration of the Feast of Unleavened Bread which celebrated the exodus from Egypt. Seven weeks (or fifty days) later at the conclusion of the

---

Pentateuch these holidays are addressed as two independent festivals with the Feast of Unleavened Bread beginning the day after the Passover. Tigay suggests that because the Passover commemorates the sacrifices made by the Israelites on the night before the exodus, and the Feast of Unleavened Bread commemorates the next day when the people left Egypt, and because unleavened bread was eaten during the Passover meal, to consider the Passover meal as part of the Feast of Unleavened Bread is not unreasonable. Jeffrey Tigay, *The JPS Torah Commentary: Deuteronomy* (Philadelphia: The Jewish Publication Society, 1996), 152.

2. Exod 34:22; Num 28:26–31; Deut 16:9–12. The Feast of Weeks is called the Feast of Harvest in Exod 23:16 and is unnamed in Lev 23:15–22. The Feast of Weeks was celebrated seven weeks after Passover; therefore, the fifty day gap between the two holidays led to the term Pentecost (meaning "fifty").

3. Exod 23:14–17; 34:18–23; Deut 16:16–17.

4. See Shemuel Safrai, "The Temple," in *The Jewish People in the First Century: Historical Geography, Political History, Social, Cultural and Religious Life and Institutions*, eds. S. Safrai and M. Stern in co-operation with D. Flusser and W. C. van Unnik., vol. 2 (Philadelphia: Fortress Press, 1987), 885–87; 891–95.

5. Note that in Exod 9:31 the barley in the Egyptian fields was destroyed by the hailstorm, but the wheat was not destroyed because it had not yet come to fruition.

grain harvest, the Israelites celebrated the Feast of Weeks (or Pentecost, a name taken from the fifty day gap between holidays). This festival helped the people be mindful to celebrate the firstfruits of what they had sowed in the fields. The final pilgrimage festival—the Feast of Tabernacles[6]—took place at the conclusion of the agricultural harvest when the farmers finished gathering the last of the summer fruit—grapes, figs, pomegranates, and olives. During this festival the people constructed temporary living structures. Spending a week living in these booths helped the population identify with the Israelite experience of the exodus as well as God's provisions for the people during their wilderness wanderings (Lev 23:34, 42–43). Such provisions were associated with the people's present reality of the annual agricultural yield made possible by God provision of the early and later rains. By combining the agricultural cycle and the religious calendar, the land's annual cycle pulls its observers through a memory of who they are and what their identity is as God's people.[7]

The Feast of Tabernacles, which takes place in October, is also a time of year the people are more mindful of the benefits provided by the early rains, which set the stage for a successful agricultural season for the following year. The feast facilitates the Israelites' joy over the harvest

and their awareness that God's provision of the early and later rains produced the bountiful blessing from the land. The timing of the Feast of Tabernacles weaves the awareness of God's past provisions of rain into the awareness of the people's continued dependence on God's provision of rain in the following year. In addition, the feast is at the end of the dry season when the water in cisterns throughout the country are getting low. Thus, during the Feast of Tabernacles, the people are aware of their desperate need for water.

THE WATER CEREMONY DURING THE FEAST OF TABERNACLES

In the first century, the city of Jerusalem was draped over two small hills. At the southernmost end of the city and nestled between the two hills, the pool of Siloam collected rain, runoff water, and fresh water from the Gihon Spring. A steep, stone-paved road connected the pool to the retaining wall of the Temple Mount where one could access the temple. Although there is no Mosaic law requiring water libations during the Feast of Tabernacles, by the Second Temple period[8] a water ceremony was incorporated as a significant component of the festal celebrations. This ceremony helped people be mindful of their dependence on the rainfall in the coming year, and the ceremony was accompanied

---

6. Lev 23:34–43; Deut 16:13–15. The Feast of Tabernacles is called the Feast of Ingathering in Exod 23:16 and 34:22, and is unnamed in Num 29:12–35.

7. For reviews of critical scholarship on the issue of the annual festivals see Bernard Levinson, *Deuteronomy and the Hermeneutics of Legal Innovation* (Oxford: Oxford University Press, 1997), 53–97; Nathan MacDonald, *Not Bread Alone: The Uses of Food in the Old Testament* (Oxford: Oxford University Press, 2008), 80–83; Gordon McConville, *Law and Theology in Deuteronomy* (Sheffield: JSOT Press, 1984), 99–110.

8. The Second Temple period began when Jews, under the rule of Persia, were permitted to return to Jerusalem to rebuilt the temple. The period continues for almost six hundred years and ends when the Romans destroyed the Jerusalem temple in AD 70.

1. Upper City
2. Lower City
3. City of David
4. Kidron Valley
5. Mount of Olives
6. Temple Mount
7. Siloam Reservoir
8. Dam
9. Pool of Siloam

Overview of Jerusalem

by prayers for agricultural blessings. Crowds watched as a priest drew water from the pool of Siloam and proceeded up the road to the temple and to the ramp of the sacrificial altar. The joyful celebration included music from trumpets and flutes that accompanied the crowds as they sang songs and as the priest poured the water he had collected on the altar.[9] Prayers that God would provide the early and later rains accompanied the water ceremony.

The water ceremony had spiritual symbolism. A link between water and the Holy Spirit is implied in the parallel structure of Isaiah 44:3, "For I will pour water on the thirsty land, and streams on the dry ground; I will pour out my Spirit on your offspring, and my blessing on your descendants" (NIV). Spiritual thirst is described in terms of physical thirst. Isaiah 55:1a states, "Come, all you who are thirsty, come to the waters; and you who have no money, come, buy and eat!" God promises to provide the water that will satisfy the needs of the people. Similarly, Isa 58:11 states that God will satisfy the people's needs "in a sun-scorched land," and the people will be "like a well-watered garden, like a spring whose waters never fail." Their needs are met with the best possible kind of water—living water.[10] Therefore, as the people prayed for rain during the Feast of Tabernacles,

---

9. These joyous festivities were associated with Isa 12:3: "With joy you will draw water from the wells of salvation." The Babylonian Talmud records that "he who has not seen the rejoicing at the place of the Water-Drawing has not seen rejoicing in his life" (b. Sukkah 51 a–b). See also the explanation of the water ceremony in Leon Morris, *The Gospel According to John*, rev. ed. (Grand Rapids: Eerdmans, 1995), 372; Safrai, "The Temple," 894–95.

10. Some writings record a Jewish belief—although it is uncertain when the belief developed—that the water ceremony symbolized a foretaste of the rivers of living water from Ezekiel (47:1–9) and Zechariah (13:1); compare D. A. Carson, *The Gospel According to John* (Grand Rapids: Eerdmans, 1991), 322.

they also were praying for God's provision of spiritual rain and for the outpouring of the Holy Spirit as prophesied in Joel 2:28–29.

JOHN 7

JOHN 7:2–13

The historical context of this chapter is provided when John records that the Feast of Tabernacles was near (John 7:2). From this comment, the reader can infer that the following events occurred in the month of October. The farmers have finished harvesting the olives, and with the olive harvest, the entire agricultural cycle comes to a conclusion. October is also the end of the dry season, so water sources are diminishing and the water in the family cistern is becoming murky.

Jesus' brothers want him to leave Galilee to go to Jerusalem for the feast, and not just to be a pilgrim, but to assertively demonstrate "to the world" who he was (John 7:3-4)—an easy thing to do during a festival when Jews from all over the country and the diaspora have gathered. Their suggestion implies that if Jesus were to go to Jerusalem for the Feast of Tabernacles, huge crowds would hear his message. Jesus could use the feast to his advantage.[11] Jesus does not go to Jerusalem with his brothers, but instead sends them to the festival without him (John 7:8-9). Jesus does not permit them to influence how or when he delivers his message. When he does go to Jerusalem to celebrate the Feast of Tabernacles, he goes in private, distancing himself from

those trying to influence the timing of his message (John 7:10).[12]

JOHN 7:14–36

In the middle of the festival, Jesus goes to the temple to teach (John 7:14). His words amaze the crowds (John 7:15) and stir up questions about the source of his message, the purpose of his teachings, and the authority behind his actions. Jesus proclaims a message from God, a message that does not serve his own purposes but instead brings glory to God (John 7:16-18). He claims an authority that does not originate from an earthly source or teacher but from God (John 7:28-29). He has a divine message to bring to the people. John's description of these events comes to a dramatic climax on the final day of the feast when Jesus stands up and proclaims who he is.

JOHN 7:37–39

The timing of Jesus' proclamation is significant. As mentioned above, pilgrims go to Jerusalem for the Feast of Tabernacles to remember God's provisions for their forefathers in the wilderness, but also to look towards the future and to the next agricultural cycle when the people need God to provide the early rains again for another viable harvest.[13] The community feasts and rejoices over the harvest even as they crave the early rains for the next year.

Additionally, the people are engaged in celebrating the water ceremony—a ceremony that reminds the people of their dependence on God to provide not

---

11. Carson, *John*, 306; Morris, *John*, 350.

12. Morris, *John*, 354.

13. See A. D. Riddle, "The Passover Pilgrimage from Jericho to Jerusalem" on pg. 395.

only the season's early and later rains but also the living water of the Holy Spirit. Within this context, on the last day of the feast,[14] when the people start to focus their attention on their immediate need for the next season's early rains, Jesus gets up to teach (John 7:37).

Jesus' initial statement, "If anyone is thirsty ..." (John 7:37b), would have resonated with people on multiple levels. Physically, the whole community is thirsty. The dry season is almost over, the cisterns are drying up, fields have been baked dry by the sun, and the people need rain for the viability of the next agricultural season. So who in Jesus' audience was thirsty? The majority of his listeners would have been. Also, the people have been engaged in the water ceremony in which the dual significance of water—the physical rain for life and the spiritual provision from God—is at the forefront of their thoughts.

The conclusion of Jesus' sentence, "let him come to me and drink" (John 7:37c), is provocative due to the distinct echo of Isa 55:1 wherein God is the one claiming to satisfy the thirst of those in a sun-scorched land. Cistern water is getting thin, and people are aware that God is the one who looks upon the land and is the provider of early and later rains (Deut 11:11–12). God is the only true source of living water, which, as mentioned above, is the best, most refreshing, and filtered water—and yet, Jesus is calling those who believe to himself. Jesus continues by claiming, "He

who believes in me, as the Scripture said, 'From his innermost being will flow rivers of living water'" (John 7:38). Again, echoes of Isaiah and of God's promises to provide the living water capable of turning a scorched land into a well-watered garden make Jesus' claims extraordinary in the ears of the audience who are attuned to the quality and source of their fresh water. Jesus claims that all who are thirsty and all who believe in him will be satisfied as with the best kind of water. He puts himself in the position of God who is the supplier of living water.[15]

Jesus turns the physical context of the people—the end of the dry season, the celebration of God's past and present provisions, the water ceremony, and the people's prayers for rain—into a teachable context. The feast drew the people's attention to their need for rain and for the spiritual refreshment from the living waters of the Holy Spirit, and Jesus says that belief in who he is will provide such water. Just as living water is refreshing and ever-flowing, Jesus affirms that the needs of the people will not just be moderately satiated (as with cistern water) but will be provided for in abundance and in the most satisfying way (as with living water). Jesus turns the Old Testament references exemplifying God's provision in terms of living water onto himself by taking the symbolism of water from the Feast of Tabernacles and equating it to the living water he will provide for the people.[16]

---

14. The timing of Jesus' proclamation could be either on the seventh day of the week-long festival (Lev 23:36a, 39a) or on the eighth day, the day of the solemn assembly (Lev 23:36b, 39b; Num 29:35). Even if the feast had been extended to the eighth day, there is no evidence that the water ceremony extended beyond the seven days. See Carson, *John*, 321; Morris, *John*, 349n5; 373n79.

15. Morris, *John*, 374.

16. Morris, *John*, 373.

BIBLIOGRAPHY

Carson, D. A. *The Gospel According to John.* PNTC. Grand Rapids: Eerdmans, 1991.

Levinson, Bernard. *Deuteronomy and the Hermeneutics of Legal Innovation.* Oxford: Oxford University Press, 1997.

MacDonald, Nathan. *Not Bread Alone: The Uses of Food in the Old Testament.* Oxford: Oxford University Press, 2008.

McConville, Gordon. *Law and Theology in Deuteronomy.* Sheffield: JSOT Press, 1984.

Morris, Leon. *The Gospel According to John.* Rev. ed. NICNT. Grand Rapids: Eerdmans, 1995.

Safrai, Shemuel. "The Temple." Pages 865–907 in *The Jewish People in the First Century: Historical Geography, Political History, Social, Cultural and Religious Life and Institutions.* Edited by S. Safrai and M. Stern in co-operation with D. Flusser and W. C. van Unnik. Vol. 2. Philadelphia: Fortress Press, 1987.

Tigay, Jeffrey H. *The JPS Torah Commentary: Deuteronomy.* Philadelphia: The Jewish Publication Society, 1996.

CHAPTER 36

HEALING BY LIVING WATER AT THE POOL OF SILOAM[1]

John 9:1–41

Elaine A. Phillips

KEY POINTS

- The Pool of Siloam is a natural water source in Jerusalem with a rich history extending back to Hezekiah's tunnel.

- Jesus instructed a blind man to wander a half-mile from the Temple Mount to the Pool of Siloam to wash the spit and mud from his eyes with that water—and the man was healed.

- The Hebrew name that provides the basis for "Siloam" means "to send," which amplifies the overall healing event given Jesus' recent claims to be sent from God and having sent the blind to the living water.

The miracle recorded in John 9 occurred at a compelling location, one that was rich with layers of history. In addition, in the trajectory of Jesus' ministry, the timing of this miracle was significant. To appreciate the rich theological implications of this event, we probe a wide range of interrelated geographical, archaeological, textual, and historical data.

THE GEOGRAPHICAL SETTING OF THE POOL OF SILOAM

The centuries of habitation that are reflected in the archaeology of Jerusalem were defined by its water source, the Gihon Spring. The spring is located on the eastern flank of the lower spur that extends south of the massive platform that supported Herod's Temple in Jesus' day. More than a millennium before, this

---

1. Unless otherwise indicated, Scripture quotations in this article are from the NRSV.

was the water source for the Canaanite Jebusite city, and later the city of David, Zion. The Kidron Valley defines the eastern side of the Temple Mount and this lower city; the Gihon Spring flowed into the Kidron Valley (see infographic "Ancient Jerusalem" on pg. 528).

"Gihon" (gihon) means "gusher" and the name is appropriate. The spring has an irregular flow and yields a considerable amount of water at intermittent intervals. Long before David and the Israelites conquered the city (see below), there were channels to direct some of the spring waters toward the southern part of the city and the excess farther down the Kidron Valley for irrigation purposes. The network of rock-hewn channels and pools near the source of the water is still evident.

Directly west of David's Jerusalem was a less pronounced valley, which Josephus called the Tyropoeon ("cheesemakers'") Valley. This is also known as the Central Valley. Josephus noted that this valley distinguished the hill of the upper city from that of the lower and "extends down to Siloam (mechri Silōas, μεχρι Σιλωας); for so we called that fountain" (War 5.140 [LCL]). In the first century AD context of Josephus, the source of water for the pool located at the southern end of the Central Valley was thought to be near the pool itself.[2]

West of the Central or Tyropoeon Valley is a higher and much more formidable crest that is known as the Western Hill. Beyond that, the Hinnom Valley defines both the western and southern sides as it swings around to meet the Kidron Valley.[3] Where the Central Valley meets the Kidron Valley was the general location of the pool of Siloam. For the sake of perspective, the pool was just about half a mile south of the Temple Mount where Jesus first encountered the blind man, and the route to the pool would have involved a descent of about three hundred fifty feet over the course of that half mile. How the pool came to be located at this point is the focus of our historical investigation.

TEXTUAL AND ARCHAEOLOGICAL EVIDENCE OF THE POOL OF SILOAM

The city's water source at the Gihon Spring had to be protected. Already in the Canaanite period (Middle Bronze, approximately 2000–1550 BC), monumental towers guarded the spring and gate area, and this continued to be the case. David's capture of the Jebusite city (2 Sam 5:6–9) required a strategic operation that apparently took advantage of an already existing underground water system. The unusual Hebrew word tsinnor ("water course") is used also in Ps 42:8 (Heb) in the context of torrents of water, waves, and breakers. When David said "whoever would strike the Jebusite, let him approach in the tsinnor" (2 Sam 5:8), he was describing an unusual means

2. This was also the conclusion of the nineteenth century explorer Edward G. Robinson (E. Robinson and E. Smith, Biblical Researches in Palestine, and in the Adjacent Regions: Journal of Travels in the Year 1838, 3 vols., 11th ed. [Boston: Crocker and Brewster, 1874], 1:333–43. Robinson was a careful student of the land, the oral reports of local populations, and the centuries of written records from Jerome in the late fourth century up to the nineteenth century.

3. Robinson erroneously concluded that the Gihon Spring was on the west side of the city in the Hinnom Valley and, after it was stopped up by Hezekiah, had since dried up. Following the local custom, he called the spring feeding the channel leading to the pool of Siloam the Virgin's Fountain (Robinson and Smith, Biblical Researches, 1:346–47).

Inscripton from Hezekiah's Tunnel

Jerusalem, 800–700 BC

Hezekiah fortified city before invasion

Tunnel brought water into Jerusalem
(2 Kings 20:20)

Stone marks where tunnel was completed

of access to the city through water that apparently was moving. Implicit in this could be the gushing spring and the complex of channels and pools.

Following David's conquest and his increasingly tumultuous reign over Israel, Solomon was anointed king at the Gihon Spring. This was in the face of Adonijah's attempt to take the throne from the aging David. It seems to have been a symbolic gesture to arrange for anointing at a water source. Adonijah himself prepared his own celebration at the Spring of Rogel, apparently somewhat south of the Gihon (1 Kgs 1) although the exact location is uncertain. Once Solomon consolidated his kingdom (970 BC), he expanded the city to the north by constructing the temple on Mount Moriah.

During the reign of Hezekiah in the late eighth and early seventh centuries (715-686 BC), the higher Western Hill was extensively settled. Excavations in the Jewish Quarter of the Old City of Jerusalem indicate evidence of this expansion and the eventual construction of a wall to protect the citizenry there (see Isa 22:9–11; 2 Chr 32:5). A part of this expansion may have been due to the influx of religious refugees from the northern kingdom after the fall of the north to Assyria (2 Kgs 17), coupled with Hezekiah's invitation to the northern tribes to come and celebrate the second Passover (2 Chr 30). Because the primary source of water for both the lower and upper cities was the Gihon Spring and its outflow, protecting that water was critical.

Toward that end, Hezekiah's engineers hewed a tunnel through the bedrock to transport water from the Gihon Spring on the east side of the hill of Zion to a south pool that would have been inside the city walls and more easily accessed by those who lived on the Western Hill. These residents would no longer have to descend to the Central Valley and climb back over the ridge of the lower city to the entrance of the water system. Instead, they could head down the Central Valley to the pool. The underground tunnel itself is S-shaped and approximately one-third of a mile in length. The remarkable nature of its construction was preserved in the "Siloam Inscription," discovered in the 1880s. The inscription describes workers cutting the stone from both ends, hearing as each group approached the other, and finally breaking through.

As a result, the water flowed from the Gihon Spring to the safely enclosed water reservoir. This would become the pool of Siloam. The inscription describes this as the waters going from the "source"

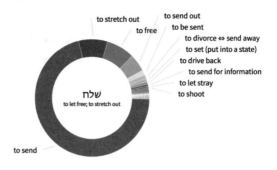

to stretch out

to free

to send out

to be sent

to divorce ⟷ send away

to set (put into a state)

to drive back

to send for information

to let stray

to shoot

שלח
to let free; to stretch out

to send

Bible Word Study: *shalah*

to the "pool." Given the impending threat of Sennacherib's siege of Jerusalem (701 BC), this was a matter of survival. The biblical text remembers Hezekiah's efforts toward that end (2 Kgs 20:20; 2 Chr 32:3–4; Isa 22:9–11). The Chronicler indicates that Hezekiah "closed the upper outlet of the waters of Gihon and directed them to the west side of the City of David" (2 Chr 32:30). Hezekiah's son, Manasseh, would likewise fortify Jerusalem after his repentance and restoration to the city: "he built an outer wall for the city of David west of Gihon in the valley … he carried it around Ophel" (2 Chr 33:14).

Isaiah's reference to the "old pool" (Isa 22:11) suggests that perhaps there was already a pool in this general location that had been fed by seepage through fissures in the bedrock from the spring. That might be bolstered by another Isaiah reference: "Because this people has refused the waters of Shiloah that go slowly … therefore, the LORD will raise up against them the waters of the River, powerful and mighty, the king of Assyria … (Isa 8:6–7). In Nehemiah's description of the wall repairs, he mentions that Shallum strengthened the Spring Gate and the wall of the "pool of Shelah" to the king's garden and the steps that go down from the city of David

(Neh 3:15). These references are important because the Hebrew verb *shalah* means "to send."

We do not know how long Hezekiah's tunnel actively functioned. Over the centuries it apparently filled with silt so that by the first century AD, references to the pool suggest that its water source was nearby and not one-third of a mile north. In addition to Josephus' indication (above), the Jewish ritual that took place at the Feast of Tabernacles (Sukkot) involved filling a golden vessel with water "from the *Shiloah*" (m. Sukkah 4:9 [Neusner]), carrying it up to the altar, and pouring it out in worship. Even though the Mishnah was put into writing around AD 220, it purports to reflect the activities in conjunction with the festival when the temple was standing.

Although references to the spring in conjunction with events during the united monarchy use the term Gihon ("gusher"), subsequent allusions employ some form of *shiloah*, which, as we have already noted, is related to the Hebrew verb *shalah* ("to send"). This is significant in the narrative in the Gospel of John, but there is merit in exploring the possibly earlier layer of meaning as well. Perhaps early on, Israelites came to think of the waters as "sent" from the source at the gushing (Gihon) spring to provide precious irrigation to the southern part of the Kidron Valley and Jerusalem. That would be why we encounter the name Shiloah in Isaiah as well as the post-exilic reflections of Nehemiah. This name continued into rabbinic Hebrew usage as evidenced in the text of the Mishnah (m. Sukkah 4:9). This symbolic "sending" of waters from their source could be the basis of the exquisite parallel that John develops through this section of his Gospel. Jesus repeatedly emphasized that he had been *sent* by the Father.

We need to investigate one additional language factor. Here is the question: Why does the Greek represent this as *Silōam* (*Siloas* in the *Jewish Wars* reference) rather than *Shiloah*? Both John and Luke read *Silōam* in reference to this location (John 9:7,11; Luke 13:4). So does the Septuagint in Isa 8:6; the name does not appear in the Greek version of Neh 3:15 [Ezra 13:15]. This seems, however, to lose the direct meaning of "sent" even though that is the steady drumbeat theme of these chapters of John's Gospel.

Since there does not seem to be a linguistic pattern of shifting from the Hebrew guttural *het* to the *mu* in Greek, we might explore other possible explanations. It may be that case endings in Greek demanded something other than a guttural letter at the end of a word. Additional references to Siloam in Josephus employ dative and accusative forms and each has dropped the final *het*.[4] But here is one more possibility: perhaps in the Second Temple period, as some Jewish population centers both in the land of Israel and in the diaspora were

shifting toward use of the Greek language, they incorporated into this highly significant place another equally venerable name that referred to Jerusalem, that being Salem (Gen 14:18; compare Ps 76:2). Both Salem and Shiloah defined early strata of Jerusalem's history. Why might they do this? The name Shiloah was little known because it was not used apart from the references noted above. It continued into the rabbinic Hebrew texts as the Mishnah cited above demonstrates. The archaic and poetic name Salem (*Shalem*), however, would evoke the long history of this place, going back to the kingly figure of Melchizedek. It would also tie it to the wider implications of the word group sh-l-m, meaning "to set right" and restore wholeness. With those possibilities in mind, let us investigate the timing of this miracle at the Pool of Siloam.

JESUS' MINISTRY AT THE POOL OF SILOAM

Jesus spent a good part of his last half year of ministry in Jerusalem. He arrived part way through the Feast of Tabernacles (John 7) in late September or early October. The exchanges in John 8–9 seem to follow directly his declarations in conjunction with this festival. He was there again in December for the Feast of Dedication (Hanukkah; John 10).

The tension had been escalating ever since Jesus fed the five thousand about six months earlier at the time of Passover (John 6 and parallels in the Synoptic Gospels).[5] In between that Passover and Tabernacles, Jesus and his disciples retreated outside Jewish

---

4. Examples include *yper tēn Silōan* (υπερ την Σιλωαν) (*War* 5.145); *ypo tē Silōa* (υπο τη Σιλωα) (*War* 6.401). But see also *Kata tēn Silōam* (Κατα την Σιλωαμ) (*War* 5.505).

5. See Gordon Franz, "The Feedings of the Multitudes" on pg. 237.

Galilee, first to Phoenician territories, then back across to the Decapolis, and finally north to Caesarea Philippi at the foot of Mount Hermon.[6] Following Peter's declaration that Jesus was the Christ, the Son of the Living God (Matt 16:16), Jesus began to speak directly to his disciples of his future suffering, death, and resurrection.[7] This would have generated an ominous foreboding. Intertwined with these announcements was his continued ministry of healing, his constant travel, and the growing messianic fervor on the part of expectant audiences. In addition, some were looking for an opportunity to get rid of him (John 7:1). All of these circumstances likely explain why Jesus decided to go up to Jerusalem quietly and only partway through the Feast of Tabernacles (John 7:10): Given the fever pitch of ill-directed messianic ideas, he would not want to fan that flame at the outset of the feast, which was already traditionally associated with messianic expectations.

Once Jesus arrived in Jerusalem and was teaching in the temple (John 7:14), he began to emphasize the "One who *sent* me." That One is true; Jesus was from him and was going to him (John 7:28–29,33; 8:26,29). Because Jesus was "sent" by the Father, he did not come on his own; this was in the Father's true plan (John 8:43). On the last great day of the feast, Jesus was teaching in the temple, inviting those who were thirsty to come to him and promising that "rivers of living water" would flow from within them (John 7:38). Jesus joined the invitation in Isa 55:1 and its promises of cleansing water and the spirit (Ezek 36) with the drama of that

Jewish ritual of pouring living water over the altar. All of this took place with the backdrop of the "sent" waters—the waters of Shiloah.

The time interval between that declaration and the high-tension altercations in John 8 is not clear. But we do know that Jesus left the temple after his opponents were ready to stone him for blasphemy. At that point, he and his disciples encountered a man who had been blind from birth (John 8:59–9:1). The disciples asked where the culpability lay in this tragedy—with the man or his parents. Jesus' response indicated again his mission. He had been sent to do the work of God, particularly as God's power would be revealed in this blind man. Declaring that he was the light of the world, Jesus spit on the ground, mixed up some mud, spread it on the man's eyes, and then told him to make his way to the pool of Siloam (John 9:5–7). John adds in the note that the name means "sent," referencing the clear Hebrew background of the location's name.

The waters of Shiloah were "sent," Jesus was sent by his Father to do the works that would manifest God's glory, and Jesus sent the man—who acted in faithful obedience and was healed. It is important to pause and imagine this blind man slowly and painstakingly working his way the half mile through crowded and twisting byways until he reached the pool. Even the journey was a walk of faith, especially as he was a known figure in those parts and people would ask him why the curious wads of mud were on his face and where he was headed. Even more significant was that

---

6. Matt 15; Mark 7–8; Luke 9.
7. See Elaine A. Phillips, "Peter's Declaration at Caesarea Philippi" on pg. 286.

restoring sight to the blind was a miracle that was prophesied in conjunction with the eschatological hope of the coming kingdom of God (Isa 29:18; 35:5). While there were dramatic healings recorded in the Old Testament, even restoration of life (1 Kgs 17; 2 Kgs 4), no one received sight back. In this way as well, Jesus declared his messianic identity.

The man doggedly stuck by his story, even though the Pharisees were exceedingly exercised about the fact that Jesus had broken the Sabbath and likewise caused the man to break the Sabbath. They also terrified the man's parents with threats of expulsion from the synagogue. When the Pharisees indeed drove the man out, Jesus found him. Asked by Jesus if he believed in the Son of Man, the man declared his readiness to believe, and Jesus told him that he had now seen him (John 9:37) — an added gift for the man who was formerly blind.

ADDITIONAL ARCHAEOLOGICAL CONFIRMATIONS

The rediscovery of Hezekiah's tunnel helps us further understand the network of watercourses that existed throughout the history of Jerusalem. The tunnel ended at a pool presumed to be the New Testament pool of Siloam. After the empire transitioned from pagan Roman to Christian in the fourth century AD, a church was built where the water exited from the tunnel. From Jerome onward, there are references in pilgrim itineraries and records from Crusade period

historians that indicate a pool in this location. In the seventeenth century, Quaeresmius described the connection between the spring and the pool.[8] Robinson describes his own examination and measurement of the entire passage on two separate days in April 1838.[9]

The presence of Christian structures is important. After the resurrection of Jesus, Jewish Christians continued their presence in Jerusalem in spite of the persecution that drove many of them out for a time (Acts 8:1). The church would have been determined to preserve its memories of significant places in the ministry of Jesus. Not only would the hill of Golgotha and the tomb be important; so would locations of healings, particularly those at pools such as Bethesda (John 5) and Siloam.[10]

An unexpected discovery in 2004 contributes to our greater understanding of the pool's location, structure, and relationship to the city and temple. In the process of digging to refurbish a sewer line between the end of the rock scarp at the southern end of the City of David and a fertile garden area, a set of steps was uncovered. Further excavation revealed three sets of descending steps with wider landings between the sets, perhaps to accommodate the fluctuation in water level. The entire north side of the pool is exposed (225 ft / 69 m) but the rest remains under a cultivated orchard. It is evident that the pool was not strictly a rectangle since the angles of the exposed corners are more than 90

---

8. Robinson and Smith, *Biblical Researches*, 1:334–38.

9. Robinson and Smith, *Biblical Researches*, 1:338–41. It was Charles Warren who first linked it with the reign of Hezekiah following the discovery of the Siloam inscription.

10. See Benjamin A. Foreman, "Locating Jesus' Crucifixion and Burial" on pg. 504.

Remains of the Pool of Siloam

degrees.[11] This last detail is fascinating in light of a datum recorded by Robinson. At the mouth of the Tyropoeon Valley the ground was lower,

> forming a sort of basin, which is now tilled as a garden. Here, according to reports of travelers near the close of the sixteenth century, was formerly another larger reservoir, in the form of a parallelogram rounded off at the western end. It was dry in that age, and was probably not long after broken up.[12]

Coins of Alexander Jannaeus (103–76 BC) were plastered into the second set of steps indicating that the pool was likely initially constructed in the late Hasmonean or early Herodian period, at least one generation prior to Jesus' advent. Near a corner of the pool, excavators found coins dated to years two, three, and four of the First Jewish Revolt. Apparently, the pool was used until the end of the revolt and then likely abandoned. This means it would have flourished in Jesus' day, perhaps used for ritual cleansing. The presence of flowing water would qualify it for that purpose. After the Roman destruction, erosion during the rainy season would soon fill in and cover the pool.[13]

---

11. Hershel Shanks, "The Siloam Pool: Where Jesus Cured the Blind Man," in *Ten Top Biblical Archaeology Discoveries* (Washington, D.C.: Biblical Archaeology Society, 2011), 88–90; Paul H. Wright, *Greatness Grace & Glory: Carta's Atlas of Biblical Biography* (Jerusalem: Carta, 2008), 190.

12. Robinson and Smith, *Biblical Researches*, 1:336.

13. Shanks, "The Siloam Pool," 90–91.

CONCLUDING OBSERVATIONS

The biblical account of this restoration of sight is already dramatic, and it comes even more alive in the context of "the waters of Shiloah" and the power of the One who sent and who was sent to bring healing as the messiah of Israel.

BIBLIOGRAPHY

Josephus, Flavius. *Josephus II: The Jewish War, Books I-III*. Translated by H. St. J. Thackeray. LCL. Cambridge, MA: Harvard University Press, 1927.

Neusner, Jacob. *The Mishnah: A New Translation*. New Haven, CT: Yale University Press, 1988.

Robinson, Edward G. *Biblical Researches in Palestine, and in the Adjacent Regions: Journal of Travels in the Year 1838*. 3 vols. 11th ed. Boston: Crocker and Brewster, 1874.

Shanks, Hershel. "The Siloam Pool: Where Jesus Cured the Blind Man." Pages 86–93 in *Ten Top Biblical Archaeology Discoveries*. Washington, D.C.: Biblical Archaeology Society, 2011.

Wright, Paul H. *Greatness Grace & Glory: Carta's Atlas of Biblical Biography*. Jerusalem: Carta, 2008.

CHAPTER 37

THE "GOOD SHEPHERD" AND OTHER METAPHORS OF PASTORALISM

Matt 18:10–14; 25:31–46; Luke 15:1–7;
John 10:1–15; Acts 8:26–35

Vernon H. Alexander

KEY POINTS

- Those familiar with Jesus may have been surprised with his identification as a shepherd, since he was a carpenter by profession and spent much time around the Sea of Galilee with fishermen.

- The shepherd metaphor was a prudent choice by Jesus on multiple levels: history, geography, politics, theology, and the widespread experience of the occupation.

- Multiple parables and sayings of Jesus are enriched with a deeper understanding of pastoralism—for instance, the value of livestock, the responsibilities of a shepherd, and the differences between sheep and goats.

THE GOOD SHEPHERD

Jesus made one of his most famous statements of self-revelation in John 10:11: "I am the Good Shepherd." This description is notable for several reasons: 1) Jesus himself was a *tektōn* (τέκτων), a master-builder by trade, 2) in Galilee, the vast majority of laborers worked in agriculture, not animal husbandry, and 3) given his primary ministry region around the Sea of Galilee, one would not err to have expected him to describe himself as a fisherman. Yet, he chose "shepherd" as his metaphor of choice.[1] Jesus' decision

---

1. A metaphor works by taking one tangible concept, the *source*, and applying it to another tangible concept, the *target*. In this case, the source is the shepherd and all the vast images and

Remains of Jericho

was strategic on multiple levels: it is historic, geographic, tangible, political, and theological. Pastoralism was part and parcel of ancient Jewish culture and society. By appropriating "shepherd" as a metaphor for his identity and task, Jesus was reaching deeply into the ancient Jewish psyche, drawing on its very cultural DNA to better present himself as Israel's messiah.

A HISTORY OF PASTORALISM

The origin of pastoralism in ancient Israel is very clear: the patriarchs.

Abraham, Isaac, and Jacob were all pastoralists. Upon his arrival in the land of Canaan, Abraham commenced a pastoral pattern of what is best described as transhumance pastoralism.[2] Isaac and Jacob both continued the family vocation, alternating between Hebron and Beer Sheva as their grazing loci.

Pastoralism continued into Israel's time in Egypt. Joseph enlisted his family to become the royal herdsmen, settling them in the land of Goshen, in the eastern Nile Delta.[3] As Israel grew from one man and his twelve sons into clans and tribes,

---

meanings that define "shepherd", and apply those meanings to the target, in this case, Jesus himself (see Ed Greenstein, "Some Metaphors in the Poetry of Job," in *Built by Wisdom, Established by Understanding. Essays on Biblical and near Eastern Literature in Honor of Adele Berlin*, ed. Maxine L. Grossman [Bethesda, MD: University Press of Maryland, 2013], 181–83). For more on metaphors, see *Lexham Figurative Language of the Bible Glossary*, Section 2: "Figurative Language Categories."

2. I.e., having semi-permanent bases from which to graze his flocks. More on how transhumance pastoralism functions will follow. See Oded Borowski, *Every Living Thing: Daily Use of Animals in Ancient Israel* (Walnut Creek, CA: AltaMira Press, 1998), 40–45; Victor H. Matthews and Don C. Benjamin, *Social World of Ancient Israel: 1250–587 B.C.E.* (Peabody, MA: Hendrickson, 1993), 53–54.

3. Anson F. Rainey and R. Steven Notley, *The Sacred Bridge* (Jerusalem: Carta, 2006), 119.

more of the population worked in other professions (e.g., farming and construction), although pastoralism continued to form a primary aspect of Israel's identity (Exod 1:11, 10:9). According to the biblical tradition, Israel shifted back into a nearly exclusive pastoral society after leaving Egypt behind, sometimes embracing a more nomadic style of pastoralism,[4] particularly as they migrated along the territorial fringes of Edom, Moab, and Ammon. After crossing the Jordan and the conquest of Canaan, Israel transitioned into primarily a settled, agrarian society, while still maintaining a substantial pastoral component to its economy/ society. This social structure became the norm for ancient Israel, from the period of the judges, through the monarchies and subsequent exile, to the Persian, Hellenistic, and Herodian eras.

THE GEOGRAPHICAL BASIS
OF PASTORALISM

The preservation of this pastoral culture can be attributed directly to the geographic character of the land of Israel. The land of Israel can be classified by four geographic regions:

1. the coastal plain

2. the central hill country

3. a portion of the Rift Valley

4. the Transjordanian plateau

The coastal plain lies along the Mediterranean Sea. It is broad and open, though in many places it is covered by sand dunes, kurkar (fossilized sand), and marshy areas. The central hill country is a long, hard limestone spine (Cenomanian) that runs from upper Galilee south over eighty miles (129 km) approaching Beer Sheva, with average elevations of between 2500–3000 feet (762–914 m) above sea level. The hard limestone erodes into very sharp, narrow V-shaped valleys, which make agriculture, travel, and animal husbandry very difficult. The third region is a portion of the Rift Valley, which alternates between lying above and below sea level through its length through the land of Israel—approximately +280 feet (85 m) in the Huleh Basin below Dan; -690 feet (210 m) at the Sea of Galilee; -1300 feet (396 m) near Jericho along the northern shore of the Dead Sea.[5] Finally, the Transjordanian plateau is a region that encompasses the entirety of the biblical lands east of the Rift Valley: the Golan Heights (Bashan), lower and upper Gilead, Ammon, the Medeba plateau, Moab, and Edom. The Transjordanian plateau rises up rapidly from the Rift Valley, reaching heights of over four thousand feet (1219 m) in upper Gilead, and averaging around three thousand feet (914 m) in elevation along the north-south length of the plateau. The plateau then flattens out and merges with the great Arabian desert.

The most important geographic contribution to the preservation of a pastoralist culture is a distinct feature of the central hills—their eastern slopes, often referred to as the "wilderness,"

---

4. Israel is depicted as spending a substantial amount of time at the oasis of Kadesh Barnea, which seems to have functioned as a semipermanent base, akin to transhumant pastoralism.

5. Yohanan Aharoni, *The Land of the Bible: A Historical Geography*, trans. Anson F. Rainey (London: Burns & Oates, 1979), 31–35; Paul H. Wright, "The Illustrated Guide to Biblical Geography," (Jerusalem: Jerusalem University College, 2012), 141, 288, 301.

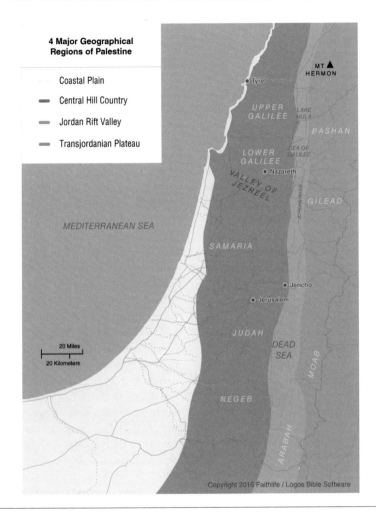

drop down four thousand feet (1219 m) in elevation down into the Rift Valley.[6] These slopes lie in a rain shadow and are comprised of a soft, chalky limestone (Senonian), which will support a limited amount of grasses and flowers during the rainy winter. During the warmer months, this flora withers and dies off, but the

---

6. The best known portion of this sub-region is the Wilderness of Judah, which extends from roughly due east of Jerusalem south to the eastern basin of the biblical Negev, centered on the ancient and modern town of Arad. "Wilderness" is used to translate the Hebrew word *midbar*. *Midbar* refers to an arid/semi-arid region that can sustain minimal life (this can include the region of the Negev centered around Beer-sheba, Gerar, and Arad). While *midbar* is often translated as "wilderness," e.g., the Wilderness (*midbar*) of Judah, it can generally refer to a regional grazing area. See Nogah Hareuveni, *Desert and Shepherd in Our Biblical Heritage* (Lod, Israel: Neot Kedumim, 2007), 26–27.

dried plants can still proffer sustenance for animals.[7]

Like all societies, ancient Israel needed access to meat and dairy products, as well as raw material for woven materials. The Central Hill Country's geography does not lend itself to supporting large animals, specifically cattle. While families or clans could have maintained a few head of cattle (e.g., the fatted calf; Gen. 18:7), large herds of cattle cannot be supported by the landscape and its flora. However, the central hills can easily support flocks of sheep and goats. These animals provide needed dairy and meat. They also supply wool and hair, important renewable resources. These animals can live with ease off of simple grasses and flowers, like those that grow during Israel's cold, wet, rainy season. Sheep and goats can also derive sustenance off of dead grasses, flowers, and thorns and thistles. This hardiness made their ongoing inclusion in ancient Israelite society a foregone conclusion.

THE TANGIBLE ASPECT OF PASTORALISM

Pastoralism in ancient Israel seems to have fallen along several different lines: semi-nomadic, and two types of sedentary herders.[8] Semi-nomadic herders were integrally connected with a village, or set of villages, and helped to create a dimorphic economy, working in tandem with the farmers of the village. On the other hand, sedentary part-time herders were actual members of the village, and participated in the farming of the local village during certain seasons, while herding during the non-agricultural seasons. By and large, they remained in the immediate vicinity of their village. Similarly, sedentary full-time herders were "transhumance," meaning they were permanently established at one city or village, but would move out from the home base, often for weeks at a time, finding forage for the flocks.[9] Their grazing patterns were dictated by the seasons: during the hot, dry summer months, they would graze up in the Hill Country, where temperatures were comparatively mild and there was plenty of stubble in the recently harvested grain fields. During the cold, wet winter, the herders would drive their flocks either (1) east towards the eastern slopes lying in the rain shadow (e.g., the Judean wilderness), or (2) south into the region of the Negev, near Arad, Beer-sheba, and Gerar. Temperatures there were warmer than in the hill country, and these semi-arid zones were alive with marginal grasses, flowers, and thistles, which provided ample forage for the sheep and goats (see infographic "Agricultural Cycle of the Levant/Palestine" on pg. 530). In either case, these grazing zones are in close proximity to the cultivated areas of the central hill country.

Shepherds were responsible to maintain the health and safety of the flock. They were to insure a minimum survival

---

7. Wright, "Illustrated Guide," 141.

8. Matthews and Benjamin, *Social World of Ancient Israel*, 53–54.

9. A prime biblical example is Jacob's sons in Gen 37. While Jacob's main camp was in Hebron, his sons were in the vicinity of Dothan, some eighty miles (129 km) to the north. Jacob's family had undoubtedly secured grazing and water rights with the villagers, not only of Dothan but of towns and villages along the main north-south road through the Hill Country (Borowski, *Every Living Thing*, 42–43).

Negev: Makhtesh Ramon

rate of eighty percent of all new births in the flock. It was assumed that fifteen percent of the adult sheep and fourteen percent of the adult goats would die during a normal grazing season. Anything above these percentages, and the hired herdsman was required to recompense the owner of the flocks.[10]

All of this meant that pastoralism was a common and tangible metaphor to Jesus' audience. They likely had either participated directly in tending flocks of sheep and goats, or had frequent dealings with those who did. They would have understood immediately all the possible applications of the shepherd-metaphor to Jesus' self-revelation. Indeed, today in modern Israel and the Palestinian territories, visuals of flocks of sheep and goats are ubiquitous. These flocks are common both in the sparsely populated area of the Judean wilderness as well as around more heavily urbanized areas.[11]

THE POLITICAL POINTS OF PASTORALISM

The pastoral image of a shepherd was also deeply ingrained politically. Over a dozen references depict ancient Israel's leaders as shepherds. Moses requested that YHWH appoint a leader over Israel after he was to die, so that Israel would not become like "sheep without a shepherd" (Num 27:17). In 2 Samuel 7:7, YHWH referred to the leaders of the tribes as shepherds. Occasionally, "shepherd" was used for a specific person, e.g., David (Ps 78:70–72), Cyrus (Isa. 44:28), or Jeremiah (e.g. Jer. 17:16). The typical usage was that of the king or Israel's political caste: the bureaucracy and professional religious functionaries (Ezek 34).

THEOLOGICAL MOTIFS OF PASTORALISM

Likewise, the pastoral image of shepherd was powerfully theological. Nine times in the Old Testament, YHWH is directly

---

10. Matthews and Benjamin, *Social World of Ancient Israel*, 54–58.

11. The author has seen flocks being moved through grocery store parking lots in central Jerusalem.

depicted as a shepherd. The most famous of these depictions is Psalm 23, where the psalmist illustrates how YHWH provides pasturage, water, and protection. YHWH is not only a skilled shepherd, he is also sheikh-like: he provides lavish hospitality and protection.

By describing both YHWH and ancient Israel's leadership as shepherds, the Old Testament authors were making not only a comprehensible metaphor for their audience but they were making a major social statement as well. Even though herdsmen and farmers needed to work together and depended on one another's goods and resources, there was a distinct social tension between the two groups. Foreign herdsmen were a threat, as they could arrive unannounced prior to the grain harvest and unleash their flocks in the fields, causing major economic damage. Local villagers viewed foreign herdsmen (i.e., those not from the village or in covenantal relationship with the village) with deep suspicion: they were "spies or tricksters" who would exploit and desolate water and land resources.[12] Even though shepherds had a rather divergent reputation, they were still the source for a major metaphor to describe Israel's leadership class and, more incredibly, YHWH himself.[13]

SUMMARY

It is this polyphonic metaphor that Jesus draws upon in one of his most powerful self-revelations. A Jewish listener would have been thoroughly saturated by a culture steeped in the historic, vocational, practical, political, and theological aspects of pastoralism, and thus instantly and viscerally connecting to Jesus' statement. His self-revelation is both abundantly clear, yet shrewdly veiled as well. Jesus' self-appropriation of the vocation "shepherd" would have had an immediate cultural resonance.[14]

OTHER METAPHORS OF PASTORALISM

THE GOOD SHEPHERD DISCOURSE (JOHN 10:1–15)

Jesus begins the Good Shepherd discourse (John 10:1–15) by referencing a common shepherding apparatus: the sheepfold. In ancient (and still modern) times, a sheepfold was often a cave with a rock fence enclosure surrounding the opening of the cave. Or, it could simply be a free-standing, circular rock fence enclosure. In either case, a small gap was left in the walk to allow the flock to enter and exit the sheepfold to find pasturage or security. The shepherd, or other trusted individual, would then station themselves in the opening of the enclosure, acting as the door, and thus protecting the flock from any predators who might attempt to attack the flocks. Any attempted entry into the sheepfold over or through the fence at a different location was agressively seeking to harm either the animals or the owner of the animals.

Further, Jesus referred to well-known shepherding techniques: calling to the sheep to lead and guide them, as well

---

12. Matthews and Benjamin, *Social World of Ancient Israel*, 54–55.

13. Greenstein, "Some Metaphors in the Poetry of Job", 181–83.

14. A parallel American concept would be that of a pioneer: pioneers spanned multiple eras in US history; they came from a variety of ethnic and racial backgrounds; they are part of the national DNA of exploration and settlement of the frontier.

as defending them. Today, one can hear shepherds making very distinct sounds akin to whistling, chirping, purring, or other guttural sounds. These sounds are unique to each shepherd and the flocks respond and follow upon hearing the shepherd's voice. Jesus makes a sharp distinction between a hired herdsman and the one who owns the sheep. According to Jesus, the hired herdsman, if his life is truly in danger, will abandon the flock. The wolf will attack and kill one of the weaker animals, while the other flock animals scatter across the hillsides, also becoming instantly vulnerable to death, by attack, or perhaps to a lack of water and pasturage. By contrast, the owner of the flock will go so far as to "lay down his life" in order to defend the flock and rescue any lost members. It is this very action that David presents to King Saul as his combat experience resume: fighting the lion and bear, and at extreme risk given that David avers that he was able to grab the wild animal by its "beard" (1 Sam 17:34–35). Like David before him, Jesus is proclaiming that he will do what is necessary to defend and rescue his flock, up to and including the loss of his own life in the battle against the forces that would kill and destroy the sheep.

THE PARABLE OF THE LOST SHEEP (MATT 18:10–14; LUKE 15:1–7)

Sheep (and goats) are valuable animals. In the ancient city of Larsa, one animal was worth the equivalent of three months' wages.[15] The magnitude of a lost sheep is reflected in repeated Old Testament references to the people of Israel and Judah as being sheep that are "lost" or "scattered." They have wandered away from the flock on their own, cut off from the safety and security of the flock and the shepherd, vulnerable to wild animals, bandits, or death due to lack of water. These circumstances are made even worse by the shepherds of Israel (kings, prophets, priest, etc.), who have purposefully led the flock to bad pasturage or abandoned them to the hillside.[16]

In this parable of the lost sheep, the owner rejoices not only because the animal has been found, but because something of extreme monetary value that went missing was restored.[17] If there is rejoicing over a sheep, how much more so when a human life is saved (see Matt 6:25–33)?

THE JUDGMENT OF SHEEP AND GOATS (MATT 25:31–46)

Understanding the composition of an ancient flock of sheep and goats provides a simple understanding of Jesus' metaphor for the eschaton. Sheep and goats were mixed in order to help curb each animal's poorer qualities. Sheep are notorious for consuming not only the blades of grass, but the roots as well. In this fashion, they will denude a pasturage, leaving it devastated. Goats, on the other hand, continually graze, eating only the blades and leaving the stem and roots. The sheep will follow after the goats, thus nullifying their more destructive habits.[18] On the

---

15. Larsa was situated in southern Mesopotamia, about 200 miles (322 km) south of modern Baghdad, reaching its zenith between 2030–1763 BC (Matthews and Benjamin, *Social World of Ancient Israel*, 56–57).

16. Isa 53:6; Jer 23:1; 50:6, 17; Ezek 34; Zech 10:2.

17. Jesus taught a nearly identical parable in Matt 18:10–14.

18. Matthews and Benjamin, *Social World of Ancient Israel*, 57.

other hand, goats are known for consuming not only the grass, but also the leaves and fruits of shrubs and trees, thus causing damage to valuable orchards.[19]

While these character traits may be a useful tool in determining why Jesus calls the righteous "sheep" and the unrighteous "goats," it is better to see that both animals comprise one flock. They are easily distinguished from one another and thus easily separated. Like the parable of the wheat and the tares, the animals are to be left together until the time of separation has arrived, thus not harming the righteous, who may not have yet fully developed.[20]

THE LAMB OF GOD (JOHN 1:29, 36)

In both John 1:29 and 1:36 Jesus is referred to as a sacrificial lamb. Ancient Israel, as well as New Testament era Judaism, practiced animal sacrifice in order to atone for sins against YHWH (Isa 53:7).[21] Different animals were permitted for different sacrifices. In the atonement sacrifices— burnt (olah), guilt (asham), and sin/purification (chattath) offerings—lambs were among the permissible ruminant animals.[22] Further, an ancient Jewish listener would have been drawn to make comparisons with the Passover lamb, whose blood demarcated between Israelites and

Egyptians, sparing the Israelites from YHWH's judgment (Exod 12:3, 13).

LIKE A LAMB TO THE SLAUGHTER (ACTS 8:26-35)

In Acts 8:26-35, Luke describes the encounter of Philip with an Ethiopian eunuch, who was reading from Isaiah 53:7. Philip interpreted this passage as having its fulfillment in the recently crucified and resurrected Jesus. The imagery in Isaiah is that of a silent, passive animal on its way to its end (or less violently, to be sheared). This silence is dramatic in a scenario where the victim is innocent: like the lamb, Jesus offers no resistance or cries of distress. It is a stark contrast with his culture, where passivity is not common.[23] This image of the lamb to slaughter gives great weight to the reality of a kingdom that does not expand by force or violence, one that confounds the rulers of this earth (John 18:28–19:12).

CONCLUSION

By utilizing the metaphor of a shepherd, Jesus presented his credentials as the Messiah of Israel. First, he made the historic connection with the ancient progenitors of Israel: Abraham, Isaac, and Jacob, herdsmen all. This placed him in the line of Israel's source, the cultural fount

---

19. Hareuveni, *Desert and Shepherd*, 41. Contra Matthews and Benjamin, Hareuveni states that it is the goat who grazes the grasses too tightly, in addition to damaging trees.

20. Hareuveni, *Desert and Shepherd*, 41-42. Compare Matt 13:24-30.

21. Not all sacrifices were for atonement; for example, the peace offering which could simply be used to give thanks (*toda*), or to complete a vow (*neder*). Ancient Israel also made a grain offering (*minhah*). See Gary A. Anderson, "Sacrifice and Sacrificial Offerings: Old Testament," *ABD* 5:870-86; Matthews and Benjamin, *Social World of Ancient Israel*, 192.

22. Borowski, *Every Living Thing*, 214.

23. The modern resonances of this culture are visible in the daily interactions of the denizens and workers in the Old City of Jerusalem.

from which they sprang. Next, he was making the cultural connection: "I am a son of Israel, because I am a shepherd."[24] This is the cultural identity that Jesus embraced: wandering Arameans and shepherds.[25] Further, by identifying with shepherding, he was identifying with a very common profession and experience of the Jewish people. In effect, he was saying, "I understand. I too, am a shepherd, caring for that which is mine. I live the same struggle, and share the same fears, doubts, and hopes that you do."

In a deft move, by claiming the title of shepherd, Jesus was, first, appropriating the office of king/ruler of Israel. In particular, Jesus was revealing himself as the fulfillment of Ezekiel's prophecies that YHWH would raise up his servant David to shepherd Israel (Ezek 34:23; 37:24). It was a claim to Israel's throne. Jews of Jesus' day knew that ancient Israel's leaders and kings were referred to as shepherds. By tending to the practical needs of his audience—feeding, healing, caring, expounding upon and living out the Torah—Jesus was doing what Israel's leaders were tasked with doing but failed to do (Ezek 34:2, 5, 7–10).

Finally, Jesus was doing something extraordinarily subversive: he was placing himself within the role and identity of YHWH himself. "YHWH is my shepherd" the author of Ps 23 confidently states. Ezekiel proclaimed that YHWH *himself* would shepherd Israel in lieu of the failed and false shepherds of Israel's leadership class (Ezek 34:15). When Jesus calmed the storm on the Sea of Galilee, he was doing what only YHWH had done: calm the raging seas, bring sailors to their destination, and bring order from chaos (Job 26:12; Pss 65:7, 77:16–19, 89:9, 107:23–29, Prov 8:27–29). He was establishing his equality with YHWH: "The Father and I are One" (John 10:30). Similarly, by appropriating the divine title of "Shepherd," Jesus was standing in the place and position of YHWH, the Shepherd of Israel, hinting not so subtly at his divine identity (Gen 49:24).

BIBLIOGRAPHY

Aharoni, Yohanan. *The Land of the Bible: A Historical Geography*. Translated by Anson F. Rainey. London: Burns & Oates, 1979.

Anderson, Gary A. "Sacrifice and Sacrificial Offerings: Old Testament." *ABD* 5:870–86.

Borowski, Oded *Every Living Thing: Daily Use of Animals in Ancient Israel*. Walnut Creek, CA: AltaMira Press, 1998.

Greenstein, Ed. "Some Metaphors in the Poetry of Job." Pages 179–85 in *Built by Wisdom, Established by Understanding: Essays on Biblical and Near Eastern Literature in Honor of Adele Berlin*. Edited by Maxine L. Grossman. Bethesda, MD: University Press of Maryland, 2013.

Hareuveni, Nogah. *Desert and Shepherd in Our Biblical Heritage*. Lod, Israel: Neot Kedumim, 2007.

Matthews, Victor H., and Don C. Benjamin. *Social World of Ancient Israel: 1250–587 B.C.E.* Peabody, MA: Hendrickson, 1993.

---

24. The authors of Hebrews, 1 Peter, and Revelation also utilized Jesus' self-identity as a shepherd in communicating with their audiences, even though the latter two books directly address audiences outside the land of ancient Israel (Heb 13:20; 1 Pet 2:25, 5:4; Rev 7:17).

25. Deut 26:5.

Rainey, Anson F., and R. Steven Notley.
     The Sacred Bridge. Jerusalem: Carta,
     2006.
Wright, Paul H. "The Illustrated Guide
     to Biblical Geography." Jerusalem:
     Jerusalem University College, 2012.

CHAPTER 38

THE HISTORICAL BASIS OF THE PARABLE OF THE POUNDS

Luke 19:11–27

Aubrey L. Taylor

KEY POINTS

- Although the parable of the pounds and the parable of the talents share many similarities, there are important differences that require distinct models of interpretation.

- When the setting of the parable of the pounds is accounted for, it becomes clear Jesus is delivering a critique of exploitative power structures—not celebrating them as a model of discipleship.

- A few decades before Jesus delivered this parable, Herod Archelaus (a previous ruler of Judea) murdered three thousand Jews at the temple in Jerusalem during the Passover.

- With Jerusalem and the Passover at the forefront of the disciples' minds, Herod Archelaus was a likely target for Jesus' portrayal of the unjust nobleman in the parable.

- Unlike those who ruled the Jews through violence and oppression, Jesus subsequently indicated that his kingdom would come through peace by entering Jerusalem during the Passover on a donkey.

PUTTING THE PARABLE(S) IN CONTEXT

The parable of the pounds (also called the parable of the ten minas) has posed an interpretive puzzle for Bible readers. Notably, it shares much in common with the parable of the talents in Matt 25:14–30, so these two passages are often treated together. Both tell of a master entrusting money to his slaves prior to a journey. Then, upon returning, he settles accounts with them. Two of the slaves have increased their master's money, but a third slave hid the sum entrusted to him and returns it without profit, stating that he acted out of fear because the master is a "harsh man" who profits from other people's labor. The master rewards the two entrepreneurial slaves and denounces the third who did not generate a profit. Although there are minor differences between the two versions up to this point, the primary divergence lies in the additional material found in Luke, known as the "throne claimant" theme.[1] In it, the master is of noble birth and the purpose of his journey is to gain a kingdom. Opposed by a delegation of his citizens, he still succeeds in being named king, and, upon returning, he executes those who attempted to thwart his bid for power. Though there have been many discussions regarding the authenticity of this additional material and what

might represent Lucan or Matthean editorial work as opposed to the authentic words of Jesus, for our purposes, we will approach this passage independent of its Matthean counterpart.[2] This is in part to limit the scope of the discussion, but also out of respect for the apparent intentionality which has delivered the story as it now stands within the broader context of the Lucan travel narrative.[3]

As with many parables, this passage is typically approached allegorically. The nobleman is identified as a Christ-figure, and the story is taken as both an example of the desirable traits of a disciple and a warning regarding the delay of the *parousia* ($\pi\alpha\rho o \upsilon \sigma i\alpha$).[4] However, given the characterization of the nobleman as violent and rapacious, some scholars have cautioned against equating this character with Christ and linking his rule with the kingdom of God.[5] One often-overlooked

---

1. The theme is sometimes treated as a separate parable that was combined with the parable of the pounds (Joseph A. Fitzmyer, *The Gospel According to Luke (X–XXIV)* [New York: Doubleday, 1985], 1231).

2. There is good reason to suggest that the account preserved in Luke represents the original context for the telling of the parable and thus most accurately records the original words of Jesus. In particular, the implicit references to Archelaus and his palace found in this parable would have had little meaning a generation after Jesus. See Brian Schultz, "Jesus as Archelaus in the Parable of the Pounds (Lk. 19:11–27)," *NovT* 49 (2007): 105–27.

3. Luke's so-called travel narrative spans Luke 9:51–19:45. Adam F. Braun makes a good argument for approaching these texts independently in "Reframing the Parable of the Pounds in Lukan Narrative and Ecomonic Context: Luke 19:11–28," *CurTM* 39 (2012): 442–48.

4. Fitzmyer sees an exhortation toward vigilance and productivity in expectation of Jesus' return (*The Gospel According to Luke (X–XXIV)* [New York: Doubleday, 1985], 1229). Green, though hesitant to call the master Jesus, still equates his rule with the kingdom of God and the servants with disciples whose faithfulness is tested as they wait for the "full realization" of the kingdom (*The Gospel of Luke* [Grand Rapids: Eerdmans, 1997]). See also C.H. Dodd, *The Parables of the Kingdom* (Glasgow: William Collins Sons & Co. Ltd., 1961), 108–13; Joachim Jeremias, *The Parables of Jesus* (London: SCM Press, 1963), 48–63, esp. 61–2; Jack T. Sanders, "The Parable of the Pounds and Lucan Anti-Semitism," *TS* 42 (1981): 666–67; Ben Chenoweth, "The Vulnerability of the Literalist: A Critique of William R. Herzog II's Interpretation of the Parable of the Talents," *Pacifica* 21 (2008): 175–91.

5. Richard L. Rohrbaugh, "A Peasant Reading of the Parable of the Talents/Pounds: A Text of Terror?" *BTB* 23 (1993): 32–39; William R. Herzog, *Parables as Subversive Speech: Jesus as Pedagogue of the Oppressed* (Louisville, KY: Westminster, 1994), 150–70; Ernest van Eck, "Do Not Question My Honor: A Social-Scientific Reading of the Parable of the Minas (Lk 19:12b–24, 27),"

clue in navigating this question is *place*. When this parable's setting is taken into account, it lends credence to a theory that it was meant to deliver a critique of exploitative power structures, not celebrate them as a model of discipleship. Rather, it suggests another way forward for Jesus' followers, warning his audience against perpetuating violence and injustice in their own bid for freedom.

"BECAUSE HE WAS NEAR JERUSALEM"

In Luke's Gospel, the parable of the pounds is recounted near the end of Jesus' final journey to Jerusalem in the vicinity of Jericho, just prior to the triumphal entry: "he proceeded to tell a parable, because he was near to Jerusalem" (19:11 ESV). A day's walk from Jerusalem and governing the capital city's eastern access, the city would have been a hub of activity in the first century.[6] From Jericho, one might cross the Jordan River with relative ease and travel eastward into Transjordan via the Medeba Plateau in order to gain access to the King's Highway, which connected travelers and traders at this time with Nabatea in the south all the way north to the trade-hub of Damascus. Livias, capital of the Roman political district of Perea, lay immediately east of this crossing. Overlooking the border with Judea, it operated as an administrative

and taxation center in much the same way that Jericho would have served for the Roman Empire on the west side of this border.

As Jesus enters Jericho, he is already traveling in a crowd.[7] Surely some, including the disciples, had been following him from Galilee to Jerusalem for the Passover festival. Yet, this was a busy artery, and Jesus' notoriety would have attracted attention. Others on the road, many likely also making the pilgrimage, may have joined the group en route and could have represented a broad social spectrum. However, common across social strata were the messianic hopes prevalent within first century Judaism. Often referenced in short-hand as "the kingdom of God" or "the kingdom of heaven," there was an expectation developed from the Hebrew Scriptures that the God of Israel would act on his people's behalf to rescue them from oppressive empires and restore them to independent rule with YHWH himself returning to inhabit the temple in Jerusalem.[8] Passages such as Zechariah 12:3–9 couched this restoration in militaristic terms, and many in the first century expected the kingdom of God to appear via violent rebellion against Rome, reminiscent of the Maccabean revolt, with a charismatic leader at the fore.[9] Around the time of Passover, these hopes were

---

HTS Teologiese Studies/Theological Studies 67.3 (2011), Article 977; Richard B. Vinson, *Luke* (Macon, GA: Smyth & Helwys, 2008), 593–99; Braun, "Reframing the Parable of the Pounds," 442–48; Luise Schottroff, *The Parables of Jesus* (Minneapolis: Augsburg Fortress, 2006), 181–87.

6. See A. D. Riddle, "The Passover Pilgrimage from Jericho to Jerusalem" on pg. 395.

7. Luke 18:35–36, 19:3.

8. Zech 14:9; Isa 31:1–6; Zeph 3:11–20; Ezek 43:1–5. See N. T. Wright, *The New Testament and the People of God* (Minneapolis: Fortress Press, 1992), 280–86.

9. Other examples include Jer 25:33; 46:10; Isa 34:8; 63:4; Ps 11:5–6. See Richard Horsley, *The Prophet Jesus and the Renewal of Israel: Moving Beyond a Diversionary Debate* (Grand Rapids: Eerdmans, 2012), 79–94.

especially high because the festival recalled YHWH's past intervention to liberate his people from Egypt, and many insurrections in the first century are recorded during this time of year.[10] Those who knew of Jesus' ministry would have likely seen his journey to Jerusalem for the festival as the culmination of their expectations that God would finally act to liberate them, and the shouts of the crowds in the triumphal entry bear witness to the atmosphere.[11]

In light of this, Jesus' interactions with the tax collector Zacchaeus, recorded in Luke 19:1–10, must have seemed strange to those following him. Tax collectors were, in essence, traitors. They had collaborated with Rome in enforcing imperial taxation, which many nationalists opposed on account of the support it provided a foreign, pagan ruler.[12] Moreover, the system of taxation used by the Roman Empire encouraged corruption. Known as tax-farming, a wealthy individual bid for rights to tax a given region. The highest bidder paid the sum in advance to the Roman government and then went about extracting what he could from the local population with little or no oversight from Rome. Anything he might collect above the original sum was his to keep. Not surprisingly, this led to numerous abuses, and an unscrupulous man could make himself very rich. Zacchaeus' position in the border town of Jericho presented great opportunities, and when he says "if I have defrauded anyone of anything" (Luke 19:8 ESV), we should probably read it as "if, and I certainly have." This is not the sort of person most Jews of the day would expect to take part in the coming restoration of Israel—this was the enemy the messiah was supposed to overthrow. And yet, in response to Zacchaeus' repentance, Jesus declares this man a "son of Abraham." Note that, like John the Baptist, Jesus does not counsel Zacchaeus to cease collecting taxes.[13] Despite being an anti-social profession, it was not illegal.[14] Rather, the sin for which he repents is exploitative gain. His repudiation of this accepted practice may have disrupted the imperial economic system, but it earned him inclusion in the community of Israel, about to be redeemed, irrespective of his profession. The parable of the pounds is told following directly on the heels of this interaction.

---

10. For an overview of significant first century insurrections, see Marinus de Jonge, "Messiah," ABD 4:784; Richard A. Horsley, "Messianic Movements in Judaism," ABD 4:791–97.

11. In all four Gospels, Jesus is declared king. All but Luke record the crowds shouting "Hosanna!"—the Hebrew imperative "Save!" or "Help!" Although it is easy for a modern audience to spiritualize this plea for salvation, from a first-century perspective, it references the intolerable political and social circumstances of the Jewish people under Roman imperial rule.

12. T. E. Schmidt, "Taxes," Dictionary of Jesus and the Gospels, ed. Joel B. Green and Scot McKnight (Downers Grove, IL: InterVarsity Press, 1992), 804–6; Horsley, The Prophet Jesus and the Renewal of Israel, 86. Compare Matt 22:17.

13. Luke 3:12–13; 20:20–25; Matt 17:24–27; 22:20–21.

14. Though tax collectors are called sinners throughout the Gospels, the term "sinner" was often applied to those outside of the social in-group. It does not necessarily reference moral failing or law breaking (e.g., Matt 9:10–11; Luke 7:34; 15:1; see also M. J. Wilkins, "Sinner," Dictionary of Jesus and the Gospels, ed. Joel B. Green and Scot McKnight [Downers Grove, IL: InterVarsity Press, 1992], 757).

WHO IS THE UNJUST
NOBLEMAN?

As Jesus leaves Zacchaeus to continue his journey to Jerusalem, he delivers the parable of the pounds. It is generally recognized that elements of this parable, specifically those stemming from what is known as the "throne claimant" theme, probably reference events in the life of Archelaus, son of Herod the Great and ruler of Judea, Samaria, and Idumaea from 4 BC to AD 6.[15] Josephus recounts how, following Herod's death, Archelaus faced political instability and struggled to contain the growing unrest. In one particularly brutal incident, fearing insurrection, he killed approximately three thousand Jews in the temple in Jerusalem during the Passover festival. Directly after this, he went to Rome to lay claim to the title of king in his father's place, but a delegation from the Jews followed him to Rome to petition against his appointment in light of his great cruelty and economic oppression. The Passover incident served as a notable example. However, Archelaus succeeded in being named ethnarch, though not king, and returned to take revenge, continuing to exercise power in just those ways against which the delegation had protested.[16] In the year AD 6, he was finally dismissed from his position by Caesar Augustus as reports of his cruelty offended even Roman sensibili-

ties. From that time forward, Judea came under direct Roman rule.

The similarity between these events and the parable in Luke 19 is uncanny. Having taken place just a generation prior and during the same time of year, the mention of just a few of these details would have been enough to awaken the sober memory of the events of Archelaus' reign in the minds of Jesus' audience. To further solidify the connection, Luke records Jesus telling this parable along the road to Jerusalem, as he was leaving Jericho. Jerusalem, where Archelaus' infamous slaughter took place, was growing near, and every Passover presented the possibility of a similar tragedy. Even more evocative, however, would have been the imposing specter of the Herodian palaces along this path on the west edge of town as one begins the ascent to Jerusalem. Last remodeled during Archelaus' day, the lavish palaces were a monument to the Herodian family and all they represented: collaboration with Rome, oppression, and exploitation of the poor for unbridled power and economic gain.[17] Given these clues, the crowds with Jesus could not have failed to make the connection between the cruel ruler in the parable and the one memorialized in stone before their eyes. However, with this clear connection drawn between the master in the parable

---

15. Jeremias, *The Parables of Jesus*, 59; Green, *The Gospel of Luke*, 676; Ernest van Eck, "Social Memory and Identity: Luke 19:12b–24 and 27," *BTB* 41.4 (2011): 201–12, esp. 205; Schultz, "Jesus as Archelaus," 109–10.

16. Josephus, *War* 2.80–100, 111; *Ant.* 17.206–49, 299–314, 339–44. See also David C. Braund, "Archelaus," *ABD* 1:367–68.

17. Josephus, *Ant.* 17:340; Ehud Netzer, *Hasmonean and Herodian Palaces at Jericho I: Stratigraphy and Architecture (Final Reports of the 1973–1987 Excavations)* (Jerusalem: Israel Exploration Society and the Institute of Archaeology of the Hebrew University of Jerusalem, 2001), 1–10; Schultz, "Jesus as Archelaus," 114–15.

and the historical Archelaus, it becomes increasingly difficult to suggest that the ruler in the parable is meant to represent Jesus, and his rule, the kingdom of God. How then should we understand this strange story? Additional background information provides a way forward.

AN ALTERNATIVE INTERPRETATION

A significant obstacle to interpreting this passage stems from our distance from first-century society, especially their worldview and economic structures. We live in a world that champions economic gain. In the ancient world, market economies and capitalism were viewed with deep suspicion.[18] This is partly because resources were viewed differently as well. The concept of "limited good" describes a worldview in which resources are viewed as fixed and finite.[19] These resources must then be distributed and shared amongst a population. From this perspective, if one member of society increases their share, it can only be at the expense of others. Thus, the qualities of greed, dishonesty, and injustice become automat-

ically associated with the wealthy and with the merchant class.[20] Aristotle, writing in the fourth century BC, declared exchange for profit unnatural, and usury, or "the breeding of money," the most censure-worthy of all.[21] The Hebrew Bible is replete with admonitions against money-lending, and Josephus, commenting on this in the late first century AD, states that "what is not by any one intrusted to another, ought not to be required back again."[22] Jesus himself teaches against seeking repayment of a loan entirely.[23]

However, for the wealthy, money-lending was one of the primary means of acquiring further wealth.[24] Poor peasants, whose tax burden already placed them in a precarious situation, could easily find themselves incapable of both meeting their financial obligations and feeding their families, especially in a drought year.[25] In order to cover the shortfall or to purchase seed for the next year, they could seek a loan from a money lender who acted as a broker for a wealthy landowner. The rates were often exorbitant, but the true profit was made possible by the terms of the loan: if the

---

18. Samuel L. Adams, *Social and Ecomonic Life in Second Temple Judea* (Louisville, KY: Westminster John Knox, 2014), 99–100; Rohrbaugh, "A Peasant Reading of the Parable of the Talents," 33–35.

19. Rohrbaugh, "A Peasant Reading of the Parable of the Talents," 33, citing George Foster, "Peasant Society and the Image of Limited Good," *Archäologischer Anzeiger* 67 (1965): 296.

20. For example, Sir 13:18–20; 26:29; Ps 73; Prov 22:7; 28:6.

21. Aristotle, *Politics* I, 9; 10, 4–5.

22. Exod 22:25; Lev 25:37; Deut 23:19; Neh 5:10; Josephus, *Ag. Ap.* 2.208 [Whiston].

23. Matt 6:12; 18:23–35; Luke 6:34–35.

24. Schmidt, "Taxes," 806.

25. The evidence for tax rates is spotty, but Judea seems to have suffered under an extraordinarily high rate for a subsistence economy due to the three different collecting hierarchies: the Roman empire, the Herodian rulers, and the temple leaders. Tribute to Rome, which can set a baseline, was likely 12.5% of yield annually, with additional levies for local building projects, temple tax, etc. on top of that, not to mention the additional burden placed on them by local tax farmers (see above). See Schmidt, "Taxes," 804–5; Adams, *Social and Ecomonic Life in Second Temple Judea*, 172–79; Van Eck, "Do Not Question My Honor," 7.

borrower defaulted, his lands and perhaps his person would be taken in payment of the debt.[26] In this way, those who already had much continued to acquire more, but those who had little could not even hold on to what they had. This is the economic system to which the nobleman in our parable adheres and that which he intends to implement in his kingdom (Luke 19:26).[27]

Without question, the nobleman would have infuriated a first-century audience. In a culture in which the very act of doing business for profit was considered immoral, the profit margins presented by the first two slaves (one thousand percent and five hundred percent respectively) were downright evil. The rate of return was either a preposterous exaggeration or evidence of extraordinarily unscrupulous dealings. To have generated anywhere near these amounts, they would have most likely had to either participate in the aforementioned foreclosure and indenturement system, aimed at exploiting the peasantry, or have harassed and terrified the population as outright robbers.[28] This is the behavior our nobleman rewards.

What then of the third slave—the one who hid his master's deposit and returned it without interest? William Herzog has suggested that in him we find the true hero of our story, for he refused to participate in the exploitation of others.[29] He acted honorably, resisting the immoral system in which he found himself otherwise powerless. This conclusion seems the likely judgment of a first century audience, and, interestingly, in the fourth century, Eusebius evidences a similar perspective. Commenting on a version of this parable found in the Gospel of the Nazorean, he assumes that the third slave is the one rewarded.[30]

Notably, the master in the story does not condemn the third slave as he does those who openly rejected his rule.[31] The delegation who opposed him he has slaughtered before his eyes, but he merely calls the third slave wicked and gives his deposit to another. Though uncooperative, the third slave never directly defies the master's authority. That, in addition to returning the deposit intact, secures him legally.[32] He has upheld traditional Jewish values, yet by wisely playing by the rules, he has also positioned him-

---

26. Though the Roman Empire set the legal rate of interest at 12%, records from Elephantine indicate predatory rates of 60% and 75% were at times applied. Van Eck suggests rates up to 20%; however, the true goal of lending remained the seizure of land and the enslavement of the farmer upon default (see Bruce W. Frier, "Interest and Usury in the Greco-Roman Period," *ABD* 3:424; Adams, *Social and Ecomonic Life in Second Temple Judea*, 79–80, 111; Van Eck, "Do Not Question My Honor," 7; Herzog, *Parables as Subversive Speech*, 206).

27. Vinson, *Luke*, 598.

28. Vinson, *Luke*, 597.

29. Herzog, *Parables as Subversive Speech*, 155–68.

30. Eusebius, *Theophania* 22, commenting on *Nazorean* 18, a variant to Matt 25:14–30 (see Rohrbaugh, "A Peasant Reading of the Parable of the Talents," 37).

31. Van Eck, "Do Not Question My Honor," 8.

32. Rabbinic law suggests there should be no liability regarding loss of an entrusted sum if it is purposefully hidden. Also, though lacking the rights of a *persona*, slaves were protected in cases where their master required them to perform illegal tasks, and liability regarding a deposit had limits, especially if the whole was returned (see Rohrbaugh, "A Peasant

self above reproach. So too, Jesus often walks this tightrope in his ministry. Though clearly critical of the prevailing economic system, he frequently urges non-violent resistance and respect for those in power.[33] Jesus' interaction with Zacchaeus illustrates this because he both censures Zacchaeus' prior abuses and celebrates his repentance, which is ultimately a strategy of resistance within the existing system.

But more than a commentary on survival within an oppressive system, this parable is delivered to answer expectations regarding the coming kingdom. Luke 19:11 states that, as Jesus sat out on the road to Jerusalem, those with him "supposed that the kingdom of God was to appear immediately" (ESV). In response, Jesus recounts the tale of a morally corrupt leader and contrasts him with the powerless slave who yet finds power to resist. In what way does this depict the kingdom of God? Richard Vinson suggests that this parable presents an antitype of Jesus, and its purpose was to draw attention to the folly of a nationalistic ideology that perpetuates violence, seeking to establish the kingdom of God on the model of Rome.[34]

A KINGDOM COME OF PEACE

Jesus' ministry was, among other things, intent on humanizing and accept-

ing Gentiles and sinners in a way that broadened the scope of God's redemptive work beyond nationalistic aspirations.[35] But even among his own disciples, let alone those who fomented opposition to Archelaus's reign in 4 BC or the overwhelming number of Jews that would ultimately side with the Zealots against Rome in AD 66, this was inconceivable. Surely the coming kingdom was to be, if nothing else, a reversal of fortunes.[36] Those once ruled shall rule, the day of vengeance will come (Isa 61:2), and "the house of Israel will possess the nations as male and female slaves in the LORD's land; they will take captive those who were their captors, and rule over those who oppressed them (Isa 14:2 NRSV)."

As an oppressed people, it would have been irresistible to envision this reversal in terms of the empire under which they already lived, with Jesus as the new Caesar. However, merely changing the players serves to perpetuate the cycle of violence and injustice, reestablishing the very conditions that led to the exile.[37] Thus, perhaps Jesus' caricature of this sort of kingdom was intended to highlight how wrong it would be to suppose that the kingdom of God would look anything like an earthly empire, and Archelaus served as a handy foil. Rather, Jesus indicated that the kingdom would come about through small but steady

---

Reading of the Parable of the Talents," 36; W. W. Buckland, *The Roman Law of Slavery: The Slave in Private Law from Augustus to Justinian* [New York: AMS Press, 1969], 94, 176–78; see also Josephus, *Ant.* 4.285–87).

33. Other examples of Jesus' teaching in regard to the economics of his day: Matt 5:42; 6:24; 19:21; 20:24–28; 25:31–46; Mark 10:45; Luke 6:27–31; 12:32–33; 14:12–14; 21:1–4. Examples of non-violence: Matt 5:3–12, 38–42; 23:1–3; 25:15–22; 26:52; Luke 12:11–12; Mark 13:9–11.

34. Vinson, *Luke*, 598–99.

35. Luke 4:16–30; 5:29–32; 7:1–10; 8:26–39; Mark 11:17.

36. Consider also Luke 1:51–53; 2:71, 74; 22:24–27.

37. Vinson, *Luke*, 598–99 (e.g., Isa 5:1–10; Jer 5:26–29; Amos 5:10–15; Mic 3:1–3, 9–12).

acts of honorable resistance, in which God's people represented him within an unjust and corrupt world. And those who favored violent confrontation had only to look to the recent past to see where that path would lead.

Therefore, following this parable, Jesus enters Jerusalem on a donkey—a symbol drawn from Zech 9:9, intended to indicate the type of messiah he was: not a warrior on a war horse, but one come to make peace. But, in the midst of the crowds calling out for a king and a rescuer, he must have realized that his message was falling on deaf ears. He looked out over the city and, seeing where this violent trajectory would carry them, wept, saying "If you, even you, had only recognized on this day the things that make for peace! But now they are hidden from your eyes" (Luke 19:42 NRSV).

BIBLIOGRAPHY

Adams, Samuel L. *Social and Ecomonic Life in Second Temple Judea.* Louisville, KY: Westminster John Knox, 2014.

Braun, Adam F. "Reframing the Parable of the Pounds in Lukan Narrative and Ecomonic Context: Luke 19:11-28." *CurTM* 39 (2012): 442-48.

Braund, David C. "Archelaus." *ABD* 1:367-68.

Buckland, W. W. *The Roman Law of Slavery: The Slave in Private Law from Augustus to Justinian.* 1908. Reprint, New York: AMS Press, 1969.

Chenoweth, Ben. "The Vulnerability of the Literalist: A Critique of William R. Herzog II's Interpretation of the Parable of the Talents." *Pacifica* 21 (2008): 175-91.

Dodd, C.H. *The Parables of the Kingdom.* Glasgow: William Collins Sons & Co. Ltd., 1961.

Fitzmyer, Joseph A. *The Gospel According to Luke (X-XXIV).* AB 28A. New York: Doubleday, 1985.

Foster, George. "Peasant Society and the Image of Limited Good." *American Anthropologist* 67 (1965): 293-315.

Frier, Bruce W. "Interest and Usury in the Greco-Roman Period." *ABD* 3:423-24.

Green, Joel B. *The Gospel of Luke.* NICNT. Grand Rapids: Eerdmans, 1997.

Herzog, William R. *Parables as Subversive Speech: Jesus as Pedagogue of the Oppressed.* Louisville, KY: Westminster, 1994.

Horsley, Richard. *The Prophet Jesus and the Renewal of Israel: Moving Beyond a Diversionary Debate.* Grand Rapids: Eerdmans, 2012.

Horsley, Richard A. "Messianic Movements in Judaism." *ABD* 4:791-97.

Jeremias, Joachim. *The Parables of Jesus.* Rev. ed. London: SCM Press Ltd., 1963.

Jonge, Marinus de. "Messiah." *ABD* 4:777-88.

Netzer, Ehud. *Hasmonean and Herodian Palaces at Jericho I: Stratigraphy and Architecture (Final Reports of the 1973-1987 Excavations).* Jerusalem: Israel Exploration Society and the Institute of Archaeology of the Hebrew University of Jerusalem, 2001.

Rohrbaugh, Richard L. "A Peasant Reading of the Parable of the Talents/Pounds: A Text of Terror?" *BTB* 23 (1993): 32-39.

Sanders, Jack T. "The Parable of the Pounds and Lucan Anti-Semitism." *TS* 42 (1981): 660-68.

Schmidt, T. E. "Taxes." Pages 804-7 in *Dictionary of Jesus and the Gospels.* Edited by Joel B. Green and Scot

McKnight. Downers Grove, IL: InterVarsity Press, 1992.

Schottroff, Luise. *The Parables of Jesus.* Minneapolis: Fortress, 2006.

Schultz, Brian. "Jesus as Archelaus in the Parable of the Pounds (Lk. 19:11–27)." *NovT* 49 (2007): 105–27.

Van Eck, Ernest. "Do Not Question My Honor: A Social-Scientific Reading of the Parable of the Minas (Lk 19:12b–24, 27)." *HTS Teologiese Studies/Theological Studies* 67.3 (2011): Article 977, 1–11. doi:10.4102/hts. v67i3.977.

———. "Social Memory and Identity: Luke 19:12b–24 and 27." *BTB* 41.4 (2011): 201–12.

Vinson, Richard B. *Luke.* SHBC. Macon, GA: Smyth & Helwys, 2008.

Wilkins, M. J. "Sinner." Pages 757–60 in *Dictionary of Jesus and the Gospels.* Edited by Joel B. Green and Scot McKnight. Downers Grove, IL: InterVarsity Press, 1992.

Wright, N. T. *The New Testament and the People of God.* Minneapolis: Fortress Press, 1992.

CHAPTER 39

THE PASSOVER PILGRIMAGE FROM JERICHO TO JERUSALEM
JESUS' TRIUMPHAL ENTRY

Matt 21:1–9; Mark 11:1–10;
Luke 19:28–40; John 12:12–19

A.D. Riddle

KEY POINTS

- The road from Jericho to Jerusalem was loaded with thousands of pilgrims once a year as a means of passage to celebrate the Passover.

- These pilgrims would face an elevation change of around 3,370 feet (1025 m) over the course of approximately 14.5 miles (23.3 km).

- When Jesus made his final trek into Jerusalem along this route, he stopped in Bethany and then Bethphage, where he secured a colt, before proceeding down the Mount of Olives into Jerusalem for his triumphal entry.

THE GOSPEL ACCOUNTS

Each spring the week before Easter, Christian churches assemble to celebrate Palm Sunday. On this day believers commemorate Jesus' triumphal entry into Jerusalem, just days before his crucifixion. This phase of Jesus' final journey began in Jericho, down in the Jordan River Valley. Making the ascent into the central mountains, Jesus reached the Mount of Olives which overlooks Jerusalem from the east. Just like thousands of other pilgrims, Jesus had made this very same journey for the annual festivals, especially Passover. But this time Jesus' arrival at the Mount of Olives promised something different.

For Matthew and Mark, the triumphal entry marked the moment when Jesus began publicly to reveal himself as the Jewish messiah. Prior to this, he had instructed people to keep it secret (e.g., Matt 8:4; Mark 7:36), but now he was about to show himself to be king, not the conquering hero that many expected, but a humble and suffering servant. Indeed, Matthew interprets this event as the fulfillment of Zech 9. For Luke, Jesus' entry marked the climax of a journey that began in Luke 9:51 when he "made the determination to go to Jerusalem." This time, Jesus is not coming to the Holy City as "just another pilgrim"—he is coming as king.[1]

In Matthew's account of the journey, Jesus departs Jericho along with his disciples and a company of others (20:29, 34). As they draw near to Jerusalem, they approach the village of Bethphage (21:1). Matthew gives the impression that Bethphage is the first village one would encounter on the Mount of Olives. Both Mark and Luke mention that Jesus approached Bethphage *and Bethany*. If these are to be read in geographical order, i.e., as an itinerary, it would suggest that Bethphage is further east, because it comes first, and then Bethany must lie between Bethphage and Jerusalem. Jesus dispatches two disciples to an unnamed village which is *before them* to retrieve a colt that he will ride into Jerusalem for his triumphal entry. If they are at Bethphage, then perhaps Jesus is sending the disciples into Bethany. On the other hand, if Jesus is just arriving at Bethphage,[2] then perhaps he sends the disciples into that same village.

John 12:1 states that Jesus came to Bethany six days before Passover, and the following day made his entrance into Jerusalem (John 12:12). Yet Matthew does not mention Bethany until Matt 21:17, and the events which take place in Bethany are not narrated until Matt 26. It seems that in placing Bethphage first, Matthew has telescoped events and displaced Bethany for thematic reasons.[3]

This essay will explore the geographic dimensions of Jesus' journey from Jericho to the Mount of Olives and Jerusalem, as described in the Synoptic Gospels. The main road between Jericho and Jerusalem can be traced with a high degree of accuracy for much of its length, thanks to the topography of this region and to the preservation of physical remains from the Roman road. A survey of historical references attests to the existence of this same road even prior to Roman construction. Finally, because Jesus traveled first to the villages of Bethany and Bethphage, the locations of these sites will be discussed along with any auxiliary roads which would have connected these villages to Jerusalem and to the Jerusalem-Jericho road. An understanding of the Roman road and the geography of this area will elucidate Jesus' final journey to Jerusalem.

PILGRIMAGE AND THE ROMAN ROAD

According to Josephus, the population of Jerusalem during the Passover would swell many times its ordinary size, with incredible numbers like 2,700,200 (*War*

---

1. Craig Evans, *Luke* (Peabody, MA: Hendrickson, 1990), 289.

2. This use of the aorist verb *ēlthon*, ἦλθον is understood then to denote an ingressive action. This seems to be Carson's point in "Matthew," 493.

3. Osborne suggests that chronologically Matt 26:6–13 occurred prior to Jesus' triumphal entry, but that it is placed later to offer a contrast between the woman's anointing and Judas' betrayal (Grant R. Osborne, *Matthew* [Grand Rapids: Zondervan, 2010], 948n1).

6.425) and 3 million (*War* 2.280).[4] Susan Haber believed that these numbers are exaggerated, but that it is clear Jerusalem's population would double, triple, or even quadruple during the feasts.[5] Jerusalem and its villages would have needed provisions to feed and shelter pilgrims,[6] as well as navigable roads to receive them. One passage in rabbinic literature states:

> On the fifteenth day of [Adar] agents of the court go out and repair the paths and roads which were ruined in the rainy season, a month before the festival [of Passover], toward the time [in which] the festival pilgrims come up, so that they should be repaired for the three festivals" (t. Sheqalim 1:1).[7]

In addition to roads, the Gospels give hints that Jericho was an important waypoint for pilgrimage to Jerusalem. This is confirmed by Josephus who reports that, among Herod's building accomplishments, "the king erected *other places at Jericho* also, between the citadel Cypros and the former palace, such as *were better and more useful* than the former *for travelers*" (*War* 1.407).

Among the various perils faced by travelers, bandits posed the most serious threat.[8] Along the Roman road, guard posts were established in order to alleviate this danger. Moreover, pilgrims traveled in numbers for safety. It will be recalled that Jesus' parents were part of a pilgrim caravan when they left Jerusalem, and that they had assumed young Jesus was among the travelers (Luke 2:44). Naturally, in the final journey to Jerusalem, Jesus was in a company that included his disciples and many others.

Virtually the entire extent of the Jerusalem-Jericho road lies on the leeward side of the central mountains. Moisture coming from the Mediterranean is blocked by the Mount of Olives ridge, creating a rain shadow effect to the east. Thus, most of the road's length resides in an arid environment: There are no trees beyond the east slopes of the Mount of Olives, and desert conditions prevail. The road from Jericho to Jerusalem generally runs northeast-southwest. From the palaces of Herod the Great in Jericho, where the Wadi Qelt discharges from the Judean mountains, to the northeast corner of Jerusalem's city wall, the entire Roman road measures approximately

---

4. Susan Haber, "Going Up to Jerusalem: Pilgrimage, Purity, and the Historical Jesus," in *"They Shall Purify Themselves": Essays on Purity in Early Judaism*, ed. S. Haber (Atlanta: Society of Biblical Literature, 2008), 185. Haber also mentions a rabbinic source (t. Pesaḥim 4:15) which she said gives a total of twelve million in Jerusalem for Passover, but this reading does not appear to be correct. Jacob Neusner's translation of this passage says there were only 600,000 Passover sacrifices. See Jacob Neusner, *The Tosefta Translated from the Hebrew: Second Division, Moed: The Order of Appointed Times* (Atlanta: Scholars Press, 1981), 137–38.

5. Haber, "Going Up," 185–86.

6. Josephus refers to one Passover during which an "innumerable multitude" gathered from all over, with some sleeping in tents outside the temple (*Ant.* 17.214, 217).

7. Neusner, *Tosefta*, 167. This reference is given in Israel Roll, "The Roman Road System in Judaea," in *The Jerusalem Cathedra: Studies in the History, Archaeology, Geography and Ethnography of the Land of the Bible*, ed. L. I. Levine (Jerusalem: Yad Izkah Ben-Zvi, 1983), 140.

8. Haber lists various accounts of dangers encountered by pilgrims ("Going Up," 188–91).

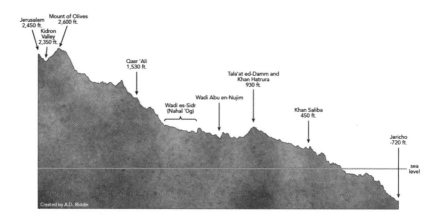

Elevation Profile of Jerusalem to Jericho

14.5 miles (23.3 km).[9] The route is uphill most of the way, for over its course the traveler must overcome a vertical displacement of some 3,370 feet (1025 m). The Temple Mount in Jerusalem sits at an elevation of about 2,450 feet (745 m) above sea level, whereas the summits of the Mount of Olives are between 2,640 and 2,710 feet in elevation (805–825 m). Jericho, on the other hand, lies about 720 feet *below* sea level (-220 m) in the Jordan Rift Valley. Various travelers have reported that the trip from Jericho to Jerusalem takes between eight and nine hours, and thus could have been completed in a single day.

The Romans developed sophisticated methods for constructing roads which, when preserved, leave identifiable traces in the archaeological record. Although the construction of the Jerusalem-Jericho road was not as developed as that of other Roman roads,[10] the Roman engineers employed their distinctive techniques. Roman road construction in general involved two basic steps. First, the road bed was prepared by building up thin layers of materials (e.g., cement, crushed bricks, clay), or by leveling exposed bedrock. Second, the surface was paved with flat stones. Roman roadworks primarily served a military purpose: the straightening of existing roads, paving, drainage, and maintenance were necessary for the movement of mass forces, siege machines, communications, and supplies.

In the 1950s, Robert Beauvéry provided the most detailed study of the

----

9. This measurement was calculated using GIS tools. It is equivalent to 15.8 *mille passuum*. Early reports, however, give a distance of 18 *mille passuum*, which is equivalent to 16.5 miles. See the Bordeaux Pilgrim (ca. AD 333) in John Wilkinson, *Egeria's Travels*, 3rd ed. (Oxford: Aris & Phillips, 1999), 32; and Theodosius (ca. AD 518) in Wilkinson, *Jerusalem Pilgrims before the Crusades*. 2nd ed. Warminster: Aris & Phillips, 2002), 103.

10. Robert Beauvéry, "La route romaine de Jérusalem a Jéricho [The Roman Road from Jerusalem to Jericho]," *Revue Biblique* 64 (1957): 101.

Wadi Qelt

Roman road between Jericho and Jerusalem.[11] About twenty years later, the road was examined again by John Wilkinson,[12] but some remains which had been noted by Beauvéry did not survive the intervening decades. The evidence for the Jericho-Jerusalem road in particular, adduced by Beauvéry and Wilkinson, include: (1) rock cuttings and construction of embankments and retaining walls to widen the road, (2) quarrying of steps into bedrock and raising of ramps to reduce steep gradients, (3) erection of milestones, and (4) installation of ancillary features such as cisterns, sta-

tions, and guard posts. The earliest datable Roman roads in Israel belong to the reign of Claudius (AD 41-54).[13] Beauvéry believed the Roman roadworks on the Jerusalem-Jericho road commenced during the reign of Vespasian (AD 69-79), in order to facilitate troop movements during the First Jewish Revolt.[14]

The Roman road begins near Herod the Great's palaces in Jericho by ascending the south bank of Wadi Qelt. For the first half of the road's length, the road follows a ridge confined by Wadi Tala'at ed-Damm on the south and Wadi Qelt on the north. Beauvéry identified

11. Beauvéry, "La route romaine." Kuhl and Meinhold published earlier studies in 1928 and 1929, but these were inaccessible at the time of writing.

12. John Wilkinson, "The Way from Jerusalem to Jericho." BA 38 (1975): 10-24.

13. David F. Graf, Benjamin Isaac, and Israel Roll, "Roads and Highways: Roman Roads," ABD 5:785.

14. Beauvéry, "La route romaine," 100.

four ruin sites along this stretch, some of which may have been Roman guard posts.[15] At about the midway point, the road reaches a crest. This height is occupied by remains of a Crusader castle named Talaʿat ed-Damm. The castle was built on Roman-period foundations, as observed by Beauvéry.[16] Excavations have revealed two other sites in the vicinity of the castle, neither of which were noted by Beauvéry or by Wilkinson. In a shallow ravine southwest of Talaʿat ed-Damm lies Khan Hatrura, known as the Good Samaritan Inn. Yitzhak Magan began excavating Khan Hatrura in 1999. Beneath the Crusader and Byzantine remains, he exposed a few wall segments dating to the Second Temple period.[17] In addition, Magen discovered a palace of Herod the Great about 900 feet (275 m) north of the castle.[18] Remains included a bathhouse, frescoes, stucco, and mosaics. At this location, the palace probably functioned as a rest-house for royal travel between Jerusalem and Jericho.

Continuing on, the Roman road descends into a depression formed by the Wadi es-Sidr (modern N. ʾOg).[19] Along the bank of Wadi es-Sidr, Beauvéry explored the remains of a Roman road station and possible stables.[20] The road then climbs the south bank of Wadi es-Sidr and proceeds to Qasr ʿAli, another Roman station. From here until the vicinity of Ras et-Tmim (biblical Bahurim) the road runs just below the crest of a ridge parallel to Wadi Umm esh-Shid. Finally, the road climbs the eastern slope of the Mount of Olives, crossing a saddle south of Augusta Victoria Hospital, and descends to the Kidron Valley and over to Jerusalem.

Four mile-stations, with fragments of twelve milestones, have been recorded for the Jerusalem-Jericho road. They were found at the first, third, seventh, and fourteenth miles from Jerusalem. None of the milestones bear engraved inscriptions, and today, only the fragments of three milestones remain *in situ* at the third mile-station.[21] Roman paving was observed in only one location where modern road construction on the Mount of Olives cut through the ancient road

---

15. Beauvéry, "La route romaine," 94–98.

16. Beauvéry, "La route romaine," 95. Magen observed no Roman architectural remains, but noted there were Second Temple finds all over the site (Yitzhak Magen, "The Inn of the Good Samaritan at Maʿale Adummim," in *The Samaritans and the Good Samaritan* [Jerusalem: Israel Antiquities Authority, 2008], 283).

17. Magen, "Inn of the Good Samaritan," 287.

18. Magen, "Inn of the Good Samaritan," 281, 283.

19. Gustaf Dalman refers to this wadi as Wadi Debr in 1930 (*Jerusalem und sein Gelände* [1930; repr., Hildesheim: Georg Olms, 1972], 249), and as Wadi es-Sidr in 1935 (*Sacred Sites and Ways: Studies in the Topography of the Gospels* [London: Society for the Promoting of Christian Knowledge, 1935], 245).

20. Beauvéry, "La route romaine," 86–94.

21. Chaim Ben David, "All Roads Lead to Jerusalem: Aeila Capitolina and the Roman Imperial Road Network (Hebrew)," in *New Studies in the Archaeology of Jerusalem and Its Region: Collected Papers VII*, eds. G. D. Stiebel, O. Peleg-Barkat, D. Ben-Ami, S. Weksler-Bdolah, and Y. Gadot (Jerusalem: Tel Aviv University Institute of Archaeology, 2013), 210, and personal communication. When Wilkinson traveled the road, he reported remains of four milestones (Wilkinson, "Way from Jerusalem," 22).

revealing its profile, and there are a few stretches of the Roman road which exhibit no traces at all.

HISTORICAL REFERENCES TO THE JERUSALEM-JERICHO ROAD

Assuming Roman road construction postdates the time of Jesus, there is plenty of historical evidence to demonstrate the Jerusalem-Jericho road was a well-known and well-utilized route prior to the Roman engineers carrying out their roadworks. It is possible that in a few locations, the more ancient road followed an easier course along wadi beds rather than the course of the Roman road, or so Beauvéry believed.[22] The Romans adhered to higher elevations whenever possible for strategic reasons, even if this was not always the easiest course for travel.[23] Nevertheless, in most cases, the Romans simply took advantage of an existing route and improved upon it.

When David fled Jerusalem as a result of Absalom's usurpation, he crossed the Kidron Valley, east of the city, and ascended the slope of the Mount of Olives (2 Sam 15:23, 30). The royal household and servants who accompanied David passed by on the *road leading to the desert* (2 Sam 15:23). As David crested the Mount of Olives, "where he used to worship God," David dispatched his trusted advisor Hushai back into the city to disrupt the counsel of Absalom's advisor (2 Sam 15:32–34). Then David crossed over the summit, at which point he was supplied with provisions (2 Sam 16:1), and then proceeded to Bahurim (Ras et-Tmim), a village on the eastern slope of the Mount of Olives (2 Sam 16:5). Shimei, a relative of King Saul, appeared, and as David and his company traveled down the road, Shimei pursued them, casting curses, stones, and dirt upon David and his men from the *ridge above the road* (2 Sam 16:13). His flight led David and those with him to ford the Jordan River and move on to Mahanaim where they found relief (2 Sam 17:22, 26; see map "Absalom Attempts a Coup, David Flees" on pg. 527).

When the Babylonian army broke through the walls of Jerusalem, the last king of Judah, Zedekiah, would also flee the city down *the road to the Jordan Valley* (*Aravah*). By the time he reached the plains of Jericho, the Babylonians had caught up to him and captured him (2 Kgs 25:4–5; Jer 39:4–5).

In the New Testament, Luke reports that Jesus' parents made annual pilgrimage to Jerusalem for the Passover festival (Luke 2:41). Many of these journeys, if not all of them, must have brought the family to Jericho and then up the ascent to Jerusalem. On one occasion, after visiting Jerusalem for the Hannukah feast (John 10:22), Jesus descended down the road towards Jericho in order to cross over to the district of Perea on the other side of the Jordan River (John 10:40). While beyond the Jordan, Jesus received word that Lazarus had become sick, and thus he returned on the same road to Bethany, a village situated near Jerusalem on a ridge extending from the Mount of Olives (John 11:1, 6–7, 17–18). On another occasion, Jesus is said to have visited the home of Mary and Martha (Luke 10:38), elsewhere revealed to be in Bethany (John 11:1). In Jesus' parable of the good Samaritan, the man who was attacked

---

22. Beauvéry, "La route romaine," 79.
23. Roll, "Roman Road System," 148–50.

had set out from Jerusalem on the road to Jericho (Luke 10:30).

Josephus likewise records events which involved use of the Jerusalem-Jericho road. The son-in-law of Simon Maccabee, Ptolemy, when he was denied entrance to Jerusalem, removed to the fortress Dagon in Jericho. Hyrcanus mounted an armed expedition in pursuit and laid siege to the fortress (*Ant.* 13.229–230; *War* 1.55–60). Later, in an attempt to settle claims to the throne, Hyrcanus and Aristobulus waged battle at Jericho. Hyrcanus' troops defected to Aristobulus, forcing Hyrcanus to flee up the road to Jerusalem where he found shelter in the citadel (*Ant.* 14.5–6; *War* 1.120–122). When the Roman general Pompey the Great marched past Beth Shan down the Jordan valley, Aristobulus came from the fortress at Alexandrium/Sartaba (about 17 miles [27 km] north of Jericho) to plead his case before the general. Aristobulus, in an act of treachery, agreed to hand over control of his cities to Pompey, but in fact he retreated to Jerusalem to make preparations for war. Pompey continued to Jericho where he bivouacked for one night, and then proceeded up the road to Jerusalem. Aristobulus welcomed Pompey to the city and offered tribute which he did not pay, thereby prompting Pompey to lay siege to Jerusalem (*Ant.* 14.54–63; *War* 1.134–151). Herod the Great, after being installed as king by the Romans, set about establishing control of his territory. His siege against Jerusalem was repelled by Antigonus, so Herod, in order to thwart his opponent, ordered the collection of all provisions throughout Samaria and had them sent to Jericho. Antigonus sent armed men down to Jericho to ambush the collectors, but Herod responded

by sending his own army and seizing control of the city (*Ant.* 14.407–411; *War* 1.299–302).

At one point during his reign, Herod appointed Aristobulus, the brother of his wife Mariamne, to be high priest, but thought better of it when Aristobulus' popularity appeared to threaten his own. After the Feast of Tabernacles that same year, Aristobulus was sent at night from Jerusalem to Jericho. There Herod had the young high priest murdered by drowning (*Ant.* 15.50–56; *War* 1.437). Shortly before Herod's death, Judas and Matthias incited a rebellion in Jerusalem. The rebellion was put down and forty of the participants were bound and taken to Jericho (*Ant.* 17.160). Finally, when Titus organized the movement of troops for the siege of Jerusalem, he ordered the Tenth Legion stationed at Jericho to march on Jerusalem. The legions camped on the Mount of Olives, and the Tenth Legion had orders to secure the pass which led over the ridge into the city (*War* 5.42, 69).

AUXILIARY ROADS TO BETHANY AND BETHPHAGE

The Roman road crosses the Mount of Olives about one-half mile (0.8 km) north of the traditional sites of Bethany and Bethphage. According to the Gospels, Bethany is located near to (*pros*, πρός) the Mount of Olives (Mark 11:1; Luke 19:29), about 15 *stadia*, or 1.7 miles (2.8 km), from Jerusalem (John 11:18). The location of the village al-'Azariya conforms well to this description, and in the village today one can still visit what is traditionally identified as the tomb of Lazarus. In the early fourth century AD, Eusebius records in his *Onomasticon* that Bethany is "a village at the second mile from Jerusalem, on the slope of the Mount of Olives.

Christ raised Lazarus there. Until today the place of Lazarus is shown."[24] The pilgrim from Bordeaux gave a similar report in AD 333, namely that Bethany is located on the east side of the Mount of Olives one and one-half miles from Jerusalem, and in the village is the crypt of Lazarus. The female pilgrim Egeria (AD 381) documented the name Lazarium for the tomb, a name which later came to be used for the entire village. The modern name al-ʿAzariya is thought to derive from Lazarium.[25] By the time of Jerome, ca. AD 390, a church had been built in the village to mark the tomb of Lazarus.

Sylvester Saller and Bellarmino Bagatti conducted excavations at al-ʿAzariya from 1949 to 1952.[26] They exposed remains from the ancient village south and west of Lazarus' tomb. The finds indicated that the village had been continuously occupied since the Persian period. There is no reason to doubt al-ʿAzariya is the site of ancient Bethany.

As with Bethany, the Gospels describe Bethphage as being near to (or on) the Mount of Olives, but no distance is given. Eusebius provides no additional information, perhaps suggesting that he was not familiar with the site. Modern interpreters tend to follow one of four views: (1) the location of Bethphage is unknown,[27] (2) Bethphage is identified with the village of Abu Dis, southeast of Bethany,[28] (3) Bethphage is identified with the village of (Kefr) et-Tur on a summit of the Mount of Olives,[29] or (4) Bethphage occupied an area which included both the eastern brow of a hill east of et-Tur and the saddle joining et-Tur to the Bethany ridge.[30] The latter is the traditional site of Bethphage, home to modern Franciscan and Greek Orthodox churches.

24. R. Steven Notley and Ze'ev Safrai, *Eusebius, Onomasticon: The Place Names of Divine Scripture Including the Latin Edition of Jerome* (Leiden: Brill, 2005), 59.

25. Thus Edward Robinson and Eli Smith, *Biblical Researches in Palestine, Mount Sinai and Arabia Petræa. A Journal of Travels in the Year 1838*, vol. 2 (Boston: Crocker & Brewster, 1841), 102. According to Dalman, the village also went by the name el-ʿEzaryah, which he explained, "The Moslem inhabitants call it after Elʿezer (el-ʿuzer), who is supposed to have been a brother of Lazarus" (see *Sacred Sites*, 249n3).

26. Sylvester J. Saller, *Excavations at Bethany (1949–1953)*. (Jerusalem: Franciscan Press, 1957).

27. Osborne writes, "Bethany and Bethphage (unknown but placed within a mile of the Holy City in rabbinic writings) were on the southeast side of the Mount of Olives" (*Matthew*, 753). John Nolland says, "The precise location of Bethphage is not known, but its pairing with Bethany in Mark 11:1 suggests that it was not far from Bethany" (*The Gospel of Matthew: A Commentary on the Greek Text* [Grand Rapids: Eerdmans, 2005], 832).

28. Bock writes, "The exact location of Bethphage is not known … Most place it on the southeast side of the Mount of Olives, southeast of Bethany, at a place known today as Abu Dis; others suggest higher up the Mount of Olives, northwest of Bethany, near what is known as Kefr eṭ-Ṭur. If the order of the cities reflects the order of travel from Jericho, then Abu Dis is more likely" (Darrell L. Bock, *Luke 9:51–24:35* [Grand Rapids: Baker, 1996], 1552).

29. Charles Clermont-Ganneau, "The Stone of Bethphage I," *Palestine Exploration Fund – Quarterly Statement* 10.2 (1878): 60.

30. Conrad Schick, "The Mount of Olives," *Palestine Exploration Fund – Quarterly Statement* 21.3 (1889): 177.

An important clue to the location of Bethphage is provided by Rabbinic literature. These sources make several mentions of Bethphage[31] in connection with two laws in particular, namely (1) the preparation of the shew-bread and two loaves, and (2) the presentation of a sacrifice *together with* its bread offering. If the bread offering or any steps in bread preparation are located "outside the walls" of Bethphage, then they are deemed not valid (m. Menaḥahot 11:2; b. Pesaḥim 63b). This description establishes Bethphage as the outer limit of Jerusalem, and would place it between the temple and Bethany. Such a position conforms to the location on the east slope of the Mount of Olives and north of Bethany, while at the same time it rules out the identification with Abu Dis.

In the 1850s, Conrad Schick explored the traditional site of Bethphage, including a ruin site immediately to the north named Kh. en-Kashe, and there he recognized the vestiges of an ancient village which had been abandoned.[32] In 1877, at the site of the modern Franciscan church, Charles Clermont-Ganneau discovered a cube-shaped monolith attached to bedrock which was dated to the Crusader period by the Latin inscriptions upon it.

The inscriptions mentioned Bethphagus, and three sides of the monolith were painted with scenes depicting the resurrection of Lazarus and the two disciples receiving the donkey and colt from their master.[33] Excavations around the monolith revealed foundations of an earlier Byzantine church.[34] While conducting excavations at Bethany in the 1950s, Saller conducted his own survey of traditional Bethphage, both the ruins on the Franciscan property and adjacent Khirbet en-Kashe, and substantiated Schick's earlier claim that this was indeed the site of an ancient village.[35] There is much to commend, therefore, the traditional site of Bethphage as the location of the biblical place.

The Roman road reached Jerusalem from the northeast, whereas the main gates to the temple were approached from the south. Omri Abadi, drawing on recent research by Tepper and Tepper,[36] notes that Jerusalem pilgrimage routes did not necessarily follow the Roman roads. Because pilgrimage fulfills a ritual function, the route chosen may not necessarily be the easiest one for travel.[37] In addition, the villages of Bethany and Bethphage are situated about one-half mile south of the saddle where the Roman road crosses the

---

31. Gottfried Reeg, *Die Ortsnamen Israels nach der rabbinischen Literatur* (Wiesbaden: Dr. Ludwig Reichert, 1989), 120–21.

32. Schick, "Mount of Olives," 177. Robinson and Smith (*Biblical Researches*, 103) and Dalman (*Sacred Sites*, 251) were unable to locate remains of a village.

33. Clermont-Ganneau, "Stone of Bethphage."

34. Clermont-Ganneau, "Stone of Bethphage," 56–57.

35. Sylvester J. Saller and Emmanuele Testa, *The Archaeological Setting of the Shrine of Bethphage* (Jerusalem: Franciscan Press, 1961).

36. Yigal Tepper and Yotam Tepper, *The Roads That Bear the People: Pilgrimage Roads to Jerusalem in the Second Temple Period* [Hebrew] (Tel Aviv: Hakibbutz Hameuchad, 2013).

37. Omri Abadi, "Ancient and more ancient roads: Do the routes of Roman roads necessarily follow even more ancient routes? The ceremonial route from Jericho to Jerusalem during the Second Temple as a case study" (Hebrew), *Negev, Dead Sea and Arava Studies* 8 (2016): 23.

Mount of Olives, so it seems apparent that Jesus and his disciples must have turned off the Roman road at some point prior to reaching the Mount of Olives. Gustaf Dalman described a southern road which branched off from the main road where the latter crossed the Wadi es-Sidr (N. 'Og).[38] This southern road would have utilized the Wadi el-Hod to reach Bethany.[39] No vestiges of an ancient road have yet been discovered, but its existence is a sure inference. Topography makes it a natural choice,[40] and, in fact, roads from later periods used this route to travel between Bethany and Jericho. The terrain through which the southern road passes is more difficult to travel and places pilgrims in a more vulnerable position for bandits.

A second alternative is suggested by the Piacenza Pilgrim (ca. AD 570). He described the ascent from Jericho thus: "We arrived at Bahurim [Ras et-Tmim or neighboring site], and from there we went left [south] to the towns on the Mount of Olives, and at Bethany to Lazarus' Tomb."[41] In this scenario, the pilgrim traveled further on the Roman road to the foot of the Mount of Olives before turning south to reach Bethany.[42] From Bethany, several paths crossed the Mount of Olives, linking the village with Bethphage and Jerusalem (see map on pg. 343 for details).

CONCLUSION

Jesus' final journey to Jerusalem and his triumphal entry, as recounted in Matt 21, Mark 11, and Luke 19, mark a critical juncture in his Messianic mission. This essay has considered aspects of pilgrimage from Jericho to Jerusalem, paying particular attention to geographical features of the route that Jesus and his disciples would have traveled. The main road coming from Jericho is well-attested, both in archaeological finds and in historical sources. From the Gospel of John, it is learned that Jesus reached Bethany first, perhaps by taking the southern route through Wadi el-Hod or perhaps by turning south at Bahurim (Ras et-Tmim). From Bethany, Jesus took the path up the ridge towards Bethphage and, reaching the village, sent two disciples into it to fetch a donkey and its colt. Mounting the colt, Jesus proceeded to the crest of the Mount of Olives, overlooking the city of Jerusalem and its Temple Mount. As he drew close to the descent down the western slope of the mountain (Luke 19:37), the crowd of pilgrims around him erupted in praise and declared him the messianic king.

BIBLIOGRAPHY

Abadi, Omri. "Ancient and more ancient roads: Do the routes of Roman

---

38. Dalman, *Jerusalem*, 249–64. Dalman suggests this is the route Jesus would have taken (*Sacred Sites and Ways*, 245).

39. Dalman refers to the lowers reaches of this wadi as Wadi es-Sikkoh (*Sacred Sites*, 245) or Wadi es-Sikke (*Jerusalem*, 259; *Hundert deutsche Fliegerbilder aus Palästina* [Gütersloh: C. Bertelsmann, 1925], 8, 26).

40. So Dalman, *Jerusalem*, 253.

41. Wilkinson, *Jerusalem Pilgrims*, 138.

42. Schick suggests this is the route Jesus would have taken (Conrad Schick, "Reports and Papers by Dr. Conrad Schick [1822–1901]," *Palestine Exploration Fund – Quarterly Statement* 29.2 [1897]: 117).

roads necessarily follow even more ancient routes? The ceremonial route from Jericho to Jerusalem during the Second Temple as a case study (Hebrew)." *Negev, Dead Sea and Arava Studies* 8 (2016): 17–24.

Beauvéry, Robert. "La route romaine de Jérusalem a Jéricho [The Roman Road from Jerusalem to Jericho]." *Revue Biblique* 64 (1957): 72–101, pl. I–III.

Ben David, Chaim. "All Roads Lead to Jerusalem: Aeila Capitolina and the Roman Imperial Road Network (Hebrew)." Pages 207–18 in *New Studies in the Archaeology of Jerusalem and Its Region: Collected Papers VII*. Edited by G. D. Stiebel, O. Peleg-Barkat, D. Ben-Ami, S. Weksler-Bdolah, and Y. Gadot. Jerusalem: Tel Aviv University Institute of Archaeology, 2013.

Bock, Darrell L. *Luke, Volume 2: 9:51–24:35*. BECNT. Grand Rapids: Baker, 1996.

Carson, D. A. "Matthew." Pages 23–670 in vol. 9 of *The Expositor's Bible Commentary*. Rev. ed. Edited by Tremper Longman III and David E. Garland. Grand Rapids: Zondervan, 2010.

Clermont-Ganneau, Charles. "The Stone of Bethphage I." *Palestine Exploration Fund - Quarterly Statement* 10.2 (1878): 51–60.

Dalman, Gustaf. *Hundert deutsche Fliegerbilder aus Palästina*. Gütersloh: C. Bertelsmann, 1925.

——. *Jerusalem und sein Gelände*. Gütersloh: C. Bertelsmann, 1930. Repr., Hildesheim: Georg Olms, 1972.

——. *Sacred Sites and Ways: Studies in the Topography of the Gospels*. London: Society for the Promoting of Christian Knowledge, 1935.

Evans, Craig A. *Luke*. New International Biblical Commentary. Peabody, MA: Hendrickson, 1990.

Graf, David F., Benjamin Isaac, and Israel Roll. "Roads and Highways: Roman Roads." *ABD* 5:782–87.

Haber, Susan. "Going Up to Jerusalem: Pilgrimage, Purity, and the Historical Jesus." Pages 181–206 in *"They Shall Purify Themselves": Essays on Purity in Early Judaism*. Edited by S. Haber. Atlanta: Society of Biblical Literature, 2008.

Kuhl, C. "Römische Straßen und Straßenstationen in der Umgebung von Jerusalem, I. Entstehung und Technik des Straßennetzes." *Palästinajahrbuch* 24 (1928): 113–40.

Kuhl, C., and W. Meinhold. "Römische Straßen und Straßenstationen in der Umgebung von Jerusalem, II. Die Straßenstationen." *Palästinajahrbuch* 25 (1929): 95–124.

Magen, Yitzhak. "The Inn of the Good Samaritan at Maʿale Adummim." Pages 281–313 in *The Samaritans and the Good Samaritan*. Jerusalem: Israel Antiquities Authority, 2008.

Neusner, Jacob. *The Tosefta Translated from the Hebrew: Second Division, Moed: The Order of Appointed Times*. Atlanta: Scholars Press, 1981.

Nolland, John. *The Gospel of Matthew: A Commentary on the Greek Text*. NIGTC. Grand Rapids: Eerdmans, 2005.

Notley, R. Steven, and Zeʾev Safrai. *Eusebius, Onomasticon: The Place Names of Divine Scripture Including the Latin Edition of Jerome*. Leiden: Brill, 2005.

Osborne, Grant R. *Matthew*. Zondervan Exegetical Commentary on the New Testament 1. Grand Rapids: Zondervan, 2010.

Reeg, Gottfried. *Die Ortsnamen Israels nach der rabbinischen Literatur.* Wiesbaden: Dr. Ludwig Reichert, 1989.

Robinson, Edward, and Eli Smith. *Biblical Researches in Palestine, Mount Sinai and Arabia Petræa. A Journal of Travels in the Year 1838.* Vol. 2. Boston: Crocker & Brewster, 1841.

Roll, Israel. "The Roman Road System in Judaea." Pages 136–61 in *The Jerusalem Cathedra: Studies in the History, Archaeology, Geography and Ethnography of the Land of the Bible.* Edited by L. I. Levine. Jerusalem: Yad Izkah Ben-Zvi, 1983.

Saller, Sylvester J. *Excavations at Bethany (1949–1953).* Jerusalem: Franciscan Press, 1957.

Saller, Sylvester J., and Emmanuele Testa. *The Archaeological Setting of the Shrine of Bethphage.* Jerusalem: Franciscan Press, 1961.

Schick, Conrad. "Reports and Papers by Dr. Conrad Schick [1822–1901]." *Palestine Exploration Fund – Quarterly Statement* 29.2 (1897): 103–22.

———. "The Mount of Olives." *Palestine Exploration Fund – Quarterly Statement* 21.3 (1889): 174–84.

Tepper, Yigal, and Yotam Tepper. *The Roads That Bear the People: Pilgrimage Roads to Jerusalem in the Second Temple Period* (Hebrew). Tel Aviv: Hakibbutz Hameuchad, 2013.

Wilkinson, John. *Egeria's Travels.* 3rd ed. Oxford: Aris & Phillips, 1999.

———. *Jerusalem Pilgrims before the Crusades.* 2nd ed. Warminster: Aris & Phillips, 2002.

———. "The Way from Jerusalem to Jericho." *BA* 38 (1975): 10–24.

CHAPTER 40

A LESSON ON PRAYER
FROM THE LANDSCAPE

Matt 21:18–22

John A. Beck

KEY POINTS

- The illustration of casting a mountain into the sea was not an abstract or far-fetched saying: Jesus was referring to a specific mountain and a specific sea—and the disciples knew it.

- The Herodium was a man-made mountain fortress that symbolized the Roman occupation of the promised land, and it even had a history of being moved.

- The Dead Sea was the designated Jewish dump for pagan idols and icons.

- Through prayer, Jesus affirmed that his disciples could upend and set right all that was wrong in their world.

"The prayer of a righteous person is powerful and effective" (James 5:16b NIV). James' bold assertion is meant to shape how we think about prayer and how we conduct our prayer life. But all too often, our time in prayer fails to reflect this kind of confidence. We horribly underestimate what we might accomplish with prayer. The same was true of Jesus' disciples. They did not yet have the language of James to shape their attitude towards prayer, but Jesus had personally encouraged them to pray and taught them how they ought to (Matt 6:5–13). Yet in the last week of Jesus' life, as the divine curriculum was coming to a close, Jesus observed an attitude towards prayer in the disciples that would not do. The lesson on prayer that followed was provoked by the disciples' response to a miracle. Crossing from Bethany to Jerusalem, Jesus had cursed a fruitless fig

Bethany

tree to teach a lesson about the failure of the Jerusalem religious establishment.[1] But the lesson was nearly lost on his disciples who were consumed by the rapid and unexpected withering of the fig tree.[2] They were "amazed." Their wonder left the larger lesson about the failed temple leadership unclaimed, and it laid bare a weakness in their perspective on prayer. In response, Jesus lifts their eyes from the fig tree to the horizon for a lesson on prayer drawn from the landscape. We have that lesson in Matt 21:18–22.

THE GEOGRAPHY OF THE TEXT

Three elements of geography play a role in delivering his lesson on prayer: (1) Jesus' route of travel, (2) the mountain that the disciples could move, and (3) the sea they could move it to. Like many of Jesus' lessons, this one occurs while traveling. The itinerary of Jesus during passion week included two daily trips between Bethany and Jerusalem. In the evening, he would walk from Jerusalem to Bethany where he stayed at the home of Mary, Martha, and Lazarus. In the morning, he would leave Bethany and walk to Jerusalem where he spent the day teaching in the city.

Jesus' daily commute meant that he walked the well-worn path that climbed over the Mount of Olives. We know the most likely location of that path because we know something about ancient travel and route preferences. People in Bible times walked when traveling. This meant that they selected routes that avoided the more rigorous elevation changes since those caused their thighs to burn with

---

1. R. T. France, *The Gospel of Matthew* (Grand Rapids: Eerdmans, 2007), 792.

2. For information on the lifecycle of the fig tree of Israel and its multiple sets of fruit, see John A. Beck, "Fig," in *Zondervan Dictionary of Biblical Imagery* (Grand Rapids: Zondervan, 2011), 85–87.

each step of the climb. In this case, the route of choice between Bethany and Jerusalem would have gone through the saddle in this extended ridge of the Mount of Olives. Here the legs were spared the burden of greater elevation gain. It is important to start here. Because if we know the route Jesus took, we will know what was in view along that route. This will help us define both the mountain and the sea that became part of Jesus' lesson on prayer the morning he crossed from Bethany to Jerusalem.

IDENTIFYING THE MOUNTAIN

Although Jesus could have built the lesson on a more generic reference to "a mountain," he elects instead to base the lesson on moving "this mountain" (Matt 21:21), a specific mountain in view along the route. Given their location in the mountainous terrain of Judea, there were many mountains in view. But Jesus has one particular mountain in mind and uses a demonstrative adjective to designate it: "this mountain." Had we been there, this would have been enough language to know the mountain to which he pointed. But neither Jesus nor Matthew go the next step and provide a specific name. This is rather typical of Matthew. He regularly makes reference to specific mountains without using their proper names. He references rising terrain with phrases like: a "high mountain" (Matt 4:8; 17:1), a "mountainside" (Matt 5:1), "this mountain" (Matt 17:20), and "the mountain" where Jesus directed the disciples to meet him (Matt 28:16). With a little interpretive

digging, we can come to a reasonable identification for all of these mountain references including the one before us in this text.

Some have linked the mountain with Mount Zion under the assumption that the withering of the fig tree prefigures the destruction of the temple by the Romans in AD 70.[3] Others have identified the mountain with the Mount of Olives, linking it to the end times prophecy of Zech 14:4.[4] But we prefer the mountain fortress constructed by Herod the Great, known as the Herodium, for three reasons. First, the Herodium is in view from the slopes of the Mount of Olives. This desert fortress is 7.5 miles (12 km) from Jerusalem, but due to its imposing stature, it remains in view from the Mount of Olives even today. Second, the mountain is distinctive in appearance. Many mountains are in view from the slopes of the Mount of Olives, but none of them has the distinctive round shape, exalted architecture, and elegant symmetry of the Herodium. These qualities are intentional. Herod refashioned the natural appearance of the terrain in order to make it stand out, resembling a volcanic cinder cone rather than the typical mountain of Judea. He built a monumental palace complex on top of this mountain which included a multi-story, circular hall (207 ft / 63 meters in diameter) that encircled the perimeter of the mountain, rising above the cone by five stories. On the eastern side of the complex, he built a massive tower that rose another three stories above the circular

3. J. Daniel Hays and J. Scott Duvall, ed., *The Baker Illustrated Bible Handbook* (Grand Rapids: Baker Books, 2011), 535.

4. Craig S. Keener, *A Commentary on Matthew* (Grand Rapids: William B. Eerdmans, 1999), 505; France, *Matthew*, 795. But see the refutation by D. A. Carson, "Matthew," in *The Expositor's Bible Commentary*, ed. Frank E. Gaebelein (Grand Rapids: Zondervan, 1984), 8:446.

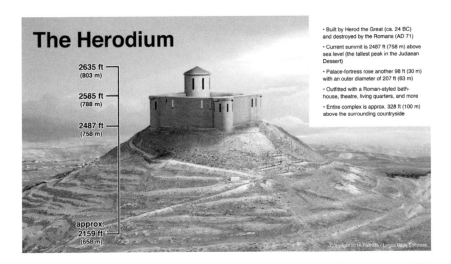

The Herodium

2635 ft
(803 m)

2585 ft
(788 m)

2487 ft
(758 m)

approx.
2159 ft
(658 m)

• Built by Herod the Great (ca. 24 BC)
and destroyed by the Romans (AD 71)

• Current summit is 2487 ft (758 m) above
sea level (the tallest peak in the Judaean
Dessert)

• Palace-fortress rose another 98 ft (30 m)
with an outer diameter of 207 ft (63 m)

• Outfitted with a Roman-styled bathhouse, theatre, living quarters, and more

• Entire complex is approx. 328 ft (100 m)
above the surrounding countryside

Copyright 2016 Faithlife / Logos Bible Software.

hall.[5] Looking south from the Mount of Olives the Herodium stands out on the landscape to this day, even though its superstructure is long gone. If we restored the structures it held in Jesus' day, it would stand out even more.

Third, the Herodium is the only mountain in view that had a history of being moved, a fact that Jesus alludes to in his lesson from the landscape. Herod directed his builders to remove the material from the mountain adjacent to the Herodium in order to have the material needed to create an artificial slope, which flowed from the circular hall down to the base of the Herodium. Pitched at thirty-two degrees, it gave the Herodium a symmetry not found in the natural world and created a structure unique to the Hellenistic-Roman world, much less the region of first-century Judea.[6] Thus, the Herodium with its high elevation, unique shape, distinctive architecture, and history of being moved is the most likely

referent of "this mountain" which Jesus includes in his lesson on prayer.

IDENTIFYING THE SEA

With "this mountain" identified, that leaves the sea into which the disciples were to move the Herodium yet to be identified. When Matthew makes reference to a "sea" or "lake," it almost always is a reference to the Sea of Galilee (Matt 4:18; 8:24, 32; 13:1, 47; 14:25–26; 15:29; 17:27). But this connection would not make sense in this case as Jesus was delivering his lesson from the Mount of Olives in Judea, far from the Sea of Galilee. The one inland lake that is in view from his teaching location was the Dead Sea, a body of water located just east of the Herodium. The high chemical content of the Dead Sea meant that the aquatic life we typically associate with an inland lake is nonexistent. This lifeless quality of the lake may have played a role in a recommendation offered in the Mishnah (tra-

---

5. Ehud Netzer, *The Architecture of Herod, the Great Builder* (Grand Rapids: Baker Academic, 2008), 183–86.

6. Netzer, *Architecture of Herod*, 188–89.

Location of the Herodium

ditional Jewish writings) for those living in the promised land who happened upon an unholy object in the Holy Land: The rabbis directed that utensils with pagan figures on them or wood which had been associated with pagan worship should be discarded by throwing them into the Dead Sea (m. Avodah Zarah 3:3, 9).

THE LESSON ON PRAYER

This is the geography Jesus integrates into his lesson on the effectiveness of prayer. He picked the Herodium not only because it was easily seen from the Mount of Olives but also because of what it symbolized for the disciples. Places have connotations. It is what we think about when we visit a place and how it makes us feel when we hear it mentioned. Some public buildings, like the White House of the United States, create very positive and respect-filled thoughts and feelings. For the disciples, the Herodium generated the opposite. They, along with other working class folks of the land, paid taxes that were used to create opu-

lent structures such as the Herodium. But they could only watch as the privileged few swam in its large swimming pool, sauntered through is lower palace gardens, and walked the two hundred marble stairs to the upper palace complex. They paid for it but would never enjoy its formal dining room, Roman bathhouse, or colonnaded gardens. Built by the Roman-backed king, Herod the Great, it represented the Roman occupation of the promised land and was the poster child of pagan corruption. From the disciples' perspective, the Herodium represented everything that was wrong in their society. But what could they do? They were little more than peasants caught up in the large and menacing machinery of the Roman world.

As these men marveled at the sudden withering of a fig tree, Jesus calls for them to lift their eyes from the tree to the horizon, to the mountain that symbolized what needed fixing in the world. If they would pray in faith they could accomplish so much more than causing

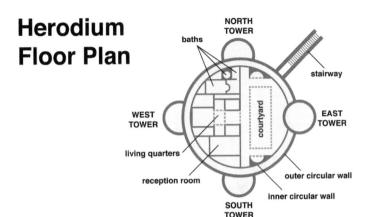

Herodium Floor Plan

a fig tree to wither. They could ask that the Herodium and all it symbolized be thrown into the place where all pagan objects belong—the Dead Sea—and it would happen.

And that brings this lesson from the landscape to the block on which we live. It is easy to focus at ground level and marvel over the accomplishments of an organization or person greater in stature than us. We get caught up with the "withered fig tree," feeling that accomplishments like this are beyond us. Perhaps these words come to our lips, "If only I could ..." And that is when Jesus taps us on the shoulder and lifts our eyes from the fig tree to the horizon. He points to the real challenge out there, our Herodium, and invites us to think differently about prayer than we have before. Perhaps the biggest obstacle standing in the path of the church and the advance of God's kingdom is not what is out there on the horizon but what is within us. When we underestimate the power of faith-filled prayer, we leave Herodiums standing in our culture which need to be retired to the Dead Sea. Jesus' words are meant for us as well.

Truly I tell you, if you have faith and do not doubt, not only can you do what was done to the fig tree but also you can say to this mountain, "Go, throw yourself into the sea," and it will be done. If you believe, you will receive whatever you ask for in prayer. (Matt 21:21-22 NIV)

BIBLIOGRAPHY

Beck, John A. *Zondervan Dictionary of Biblical Imagery*. Grand Rapids: Zondervan, 2011.

Carson, D. A. "Matthew." Pages 1-599 in *The Expositor's Bible Commentary*. Edited by Frank E. Gaebelein. Vol. 8. Grand Rapids: Zondervan, 1984.

France, R. T. *The Gospel of Matthew*. Grand Rapids: Eerdmans, 2007.

Hays, J. Daniel and J. Scott Duvall, eds. *The Baker Illustrated Bible Handbook*. Grand Rapids: Baker Books, 2011.

Keener, Craig S. *A Commentary on Matthew*. Grand Rapids: Eerdmans, 1999.

Netzer, Ehud. *The Architecture of Herod, the Great Builder*. Grand Rapids: Baker Academic, 2008.

CHAPTER 41

INDICTING HYPOCRISY
WITH IMAGERY FROM
THE TEMPLE MOUNT

Matt 23:1–36; Luke 11:37–42

Paul H. Wright

KEY POINTS

- When Jesus visited the temple in Jerusalem, he likely followed the custom of other rabbis and taught from the large stairway at the southern entrance.

- The area around the southern steps of the Temple Mount was filled with real-life places and things Jesus used to illustrate his teachings.

- The seat of Moses, whitewashed tombs, Gehenna, and the gates to the temple are just a few of the nearby objects Jesus coopted for these purposes.

THE GEOGRAPHICAL AND ARCHAEOLOGICAL CONTEXT

Matthew 23:1–36 records a lengthy discourse in which Jesus indicted the Pharisees of Jerusalem for hypocrisy. To illustrate what hypocrisy was, he cleverly compared the Pharisees to activities or things that would have been familiar to people living in Jerusalem. Earlier, Jesus had made similar statements while dining with a Pharisee (Luke 11:37–42). The time and place of that account is unknown, but it had to have been weeks or months prior to his last journey to Jerusalem for the Passover (compare Luke 13:22). Each of the items that Jesus used to illustrate the Pharisees' hypocrisy could stand alone as a pithy saying, and he likely said many of them individually as situations arose now and again, here or there, throughout his ministry. Indeed, in a time when information was transferred by word of mouth, itinerant rabbis like Jesus must have repeated things often, and in many different places, as they traveled from village to village encoun-

414

tering people who had not heard them before.[1] In this way Jesus' indictments of the Pharisees are similar to the way that rabbis used parables, stories that were shaped to specific situations yet could easily be tooled to new audiences down the road.[2]

THE SOUTHERN STEPS OF THE TEMPLE MOUNT

The southern steps of the Temple Mount are the likely geographical context for Jesus' discourse against the Pharisees as it is recorded in Matt 23. Many of the specific objects or situations in life to which Jesus compared the Pharisees are things that were in close proximity to the grand stairway on the southern wall of the temple complex, the way by which most visitors ascended to and descended from the temple. Several of them could actually be seen by someone standing on these stairs. Most were things common to ancient Israel (marketplaces and tombs, for instance). However, because all were present in combination in this part of Jerusalem, the grand entryway to the temple compound would have been a particularly useful place for Jesus' audience to see and understand the images he used.

But why here? The Babylonian Talmud preserves a memory that rabbis would sit on the steps of the temple compound to address their disciples:

It once happened that Rabban Gamaliel was sitting on a step on the temple hill and the well known scribe Johanan was standing before him while three cut sheets were lying before him. "Take one sheet," he said, "and write an epistle to our brethren in Upper Galilee and to those in Lower Galilee ... Take another sheet and write to our brethren of the South ... And take the third and write to our brethren the Exiles in Babylon and to those in Media, and to all the other exiled [sons] of Israel, saying: 'May your peace be great for ever!'" (b. Sanhedrin 11b, Soncino translation)

A number of things are interesting about this passage. One is the location: "a step on the temple hill." Likely the reference is to the grand staircase by which the Temple Mount was approached from the south, rather than a step within the temple complex itself since the reference is to the temple hill rather than the temple per se. In the first century AD this grand staircase was a very busy place, with much coming and going, and, as such, it was a place where persons with something to say could gain a quick audience. Note as well that Rabbi Gamaliel was sitting on the step, the normal posture for rabbis as they taught (see Matt 5:1; Mark 4:1). It seems that the area functioned as a kind of outdoor synagogue, a situation not unknown in first century Judaism (see Acts 16:13). In this connection Matthew was quite specific in opening his account with the words "Jesus spoke to the crowds and to his disciples" (Matt 23:1 NIV). The setting suggests a place in Jerusalem that was large enough to hold a large number of people,

---

1. Note for instance the "do not hide your light in a basket" sayings in Matt 5:14–16 and Luke 11:33–36, and the "do not be anxious" sayings in Matt 6:25–34 and Luke 12:22–31.

2. R. Steven Notley and Ze'ev Safrai, Parables of the Sages: Jewish Wisdom from Jesus to Rav Ashi (Jerusalem: Carta, 2011), 58–66.

as well as a place where crowds of people naturally *would* gather and where they might have expected to hear something. The broad, busy staircase by which most people entered and exited the temple compound easily fits both criteria.

It is also interesting to note, though as a sidelight here, that the rabbi the Talmud tells us taught on these stairs was most likely Gamaliel the Elder, grandson of Hillel and the same Gamaliel under whom Saul of Tarsus (later the apostle Paul) learned "the law of our fathers" (Acts 22:3 NIV).[3] It was from these stairs that Gamaliel dictated letters to Jews living in the diaspora, a means of communication that his zealous disciple likely noticed. The Mishnah mentions that Gamaliel was known in particular for his devotion to Torah, purity, and abstinence (m. Sotah 9:15), all things about which the apostle Paul would later write at length.

THE TOPOGRAPHY OF THE
SOUTHERN STEPS

The topographical setting of this stairway is also important. First, the larger context. The retaining walls of the Temple Mount (the *Haram esh-Sharif*, or "Noble Sanctuary") dominate the site today. They enclose an area that comprises twenty percent of the area of the modern Old City of Jerusalem. This enclosure is situated at the northern end of a narrow ridge or elongated hill. The high point of this ridge, where bedrock is exposed within the Dome of the Rock, is 2438 feet (743 m) above sea level. This was most likely the location of the Holy of Holies of the Herodian-era temple of Jesus' day, as well as that of

the temple built by Solomon. From this point, the ridge slopes gradually but dramatically downward to the south, ending at the Pool of Siloam (John 9:11), 450 feet (137 m) lower and just over one-half mile (.8 km) away. This narrow, sloping ridge, popularly known as Jerusalem's eastern hill, is marked along its long eastern edge by the Kidron Valley and along its western edge by the Tyropoean ("Cheesemaker's") Valley (*War* 5.140). This latter valley was called the *Makhtesh* ("crater" or "mortar") in the time of the Old Testament (Zeph 1:11). Because the Tyropoean Valley largely has been filled in by the rubble of the centuries, the natural topography of the southern end of the Temple Mount is not readily noticed by visitors to the site today. To the west rises a higher, broader and flatter western hill, the area of the modern Jewish and Armenian Quarters of the Old City of Jerusalem. Josephus called this western hill the "upper city," while the eastern hill he designated the "lower city" of Jerusalem (*War* 5.140). The southern end of the eastern hill, today lying completely outside of the walls of Jerusalem, is the location of the city that was conquered by David (the City of David; 2 Sam 5:6–9). David purchased the threshing floor of Araunah (Ornan) the Jebusite (2 Sam 24:18–25; 1 Chr 21:18–30), which was located at the highest, northern end of the eastern hill, outside the walls of David's City, as a place for Solomon to build the temple. This Solomon did, likely walling in the sacred compound at the same time (see map "New Testament Jerusalem" on pg. 532).

Details as to how and to what extent the area of the Temple Mount was walled

---

3. Everett Ferguson, *Backgrounds of Early Christianity*, 2nd ed. (Grand Rapids: Eerdmans, 1993), 461.

during the centuries following Solomon are unclear in the archaeological and textual record. A slight bend near the southern end of the line of the eastern wall seems to indicate that the walled compound was expanded southward by the Hasmoneans (Maccabees) in the late second or early first century BC. What is more relevant for the time of the Gospels is that Herod the Great initiated a lengthy, expensive, and very elaborate building project by which the platform of the Temple Mount was extended even further south as well as to the west and the north. To do so, his workmen built out over the drop of the Tyropoean Valley westward, and southward over the eastern hill's dramatic slope toward the City of David. In order to keep the platform level, his workmen constructed huge supporting walls of enormous Herodian margin-and-boss stones which enclosed vaulted supporting arches and masses of rubble-fill within. The temple compound, defined by these massive walls still today, was connected to the rest of the city of Jerusalem by a network of gates, bridges, and stairways. Herod never lived to see the completion of this work, as he died in 4 BC. A coin found under the southwest corner foundation of the retaining wall stone dates to AD 17.[4] This indicates that the entire project, including the Royal Stoa which sat on the expanded platform above and where Jesus likely over-

turned the moneychangers' tables, as well as the grand stairway by which people ascended to the platform from the south, was very newly completed when Jesus was in Jerusalem for his final Passover (c. AD 30).[5]

The area south of the southern wall of the Temple Mount was excavated from 1968 to 1978 by Benjamin Mazar of Hebrew University's Institute of Archaeology.[6] Mazar uncovered a large portion of the grand stairway, allowing us to understand the size and character of the area in the time of Jesus. The stairway was located on the rounded crest of the eastern hill as it rose naturally toward the Temple Mount. It was constructed partially out of cut bedrock and partially from large stones, thereby enabling a constant angle for the steps. The stairs are not of a uniform tread but alternate with the sequence of one broad step (35 inches), then one narrow (12 inches). This worked to break the stride of persons ascending to the temple, ensuring that they would approach holy ground with a slow, reverential gait. Altogether Mazar's team uncovered space for thirty steps, fifteen broad and fifteen narrow in tread. This number corresponds nicely to the number of Songs of Ascent found in the book of Psalms (120–134), and it is possible that these songs were sung in their entirety, each one progressively on each successive broad step, by the Levitical

4. Ronny Reich and Eli Shukron, "Excavations at Robinson's Arch: From Paved Street to Natural Rock," in *New Studies on Jerusalem*, vol. 17 (eds. Eyal Baruch, Ayelet Levy-Reifer, and Avraham Faust; Ramat Gan: Rennert Center Publications, 2011), 219–38. Hebrew with English abstract.

5. Note that John 2:20 mentions that it had taken forty-six years to build the temple—so far.

6. B. Mazar, "The Archaeological Excavations Near the Temple Mount," in *Jerusalem Revealed: Archaeology in the Holy City, 1968–1974*, ed. Yigael Yadin (Jerusalem: Israel Exploration Society, 1976), 25–40. Note also the discussion, with illustrations, in Leen Ritmeyer, *The Quest: Revealing the Temple Mount in Jerusalem* (Jerusalem: Carta, 2006), 60–101.

choir as it entered the temple compound. Mazar uncovered the stairs to a width of 105 feet (32 m), half of the original width. The full size of the original stairway would have provided plenty of room not only for masses of pilgrims to enter the temple compound, but for groups of persons to stop and interact with each other, or for rabbis to gather up a crowd.

To the east of the grand stairway Mazar found the remains of a building that enclosed large *mikva'ot*, Jewish ritual baths. Here pilgrims—Jews as well as Gentiles—purified themselves by full body immersion into the ritual waters before entering the temple compound (*Ant.* 12.145–46; m. Kelim 1:8). It is important to note that ritual purity was not due to sin but by coming into contact with a dead body or through certain bodily discharges (Lev 15:1–33). Just beyond, Mazar found the remains of a large Herodian building that may have been one of three structures where the Sanhedrin met in council session (m. Sanhedrin 11:2). Adjacent to the east was another staircase of the same type as the grand stairway, though narrower in dimensions. A wide street ran the width of this stair complex between the top of the stairs and the base of the Temple Mount wall. This, too, was a place where crowds could gather. The eastern, more narrow stairway led directly to a triple gate in the retaining wall of the Temple Mount, while the larger grand stairway to its west ascended to a double gate of the same type. These gates allowed worshipers to process along ornate, stepped passageways beneath the platform of the Temple Mount, eventually surfacing at a point between the temple and the Royal Stoa (m. Middot 1:3). Pilgrims generally entered through the right hand, triple gate and exited through the double gate,

moving in a counterclockwise motion in their visit to the temple courtyard (m. Middot 2:2). An entrance more grand, or better equipped to handle large crowds and liturgical processions, can scarcely be imagined.

In Jesus' day the view from these stairs took in a large sweep of urban Jerusalem: the area of David's City in the lower city to the south, the rise of the upper city replete with Herod's palace and a number of priestly mansions to the west, and a busy area of commercial activity in the folds of the Tyropoean Valley between. Above the top of the city wall to the east, it would have been possible to see across the Kidron Valley to the Mount of Olives, and to the south, the rise of the Judean hills beyond the lowest point of the city at the Pool of Siloam and the Hinnom Valley. Today, the view to the west, toward the upper city (the modern Jewish and Armenian quarters), is blocked by a large portion of a city wall that dates to the time of the Crusades. With a little imagination, visitors to the grand stairway are able to breathe in the aura that a pilgrim to Jerusalem at the time of Jesus may have felt; certainly most of the horizon line remains the same.

This, then, is the likely geographical context of Jesus' indictment of the Pharisees as recorded in Matt 23. While not all of the visuals to which Jesus unfavorably compared the Pharisees are in close proximity to these stairs, many are, and several can actually be seen by someone looking outward, or up to the temple complex above. This allowed Jesus to not only make reference to objects that were well known to his listeners, but to actually call them to visual attention. By doing so, Jesus reinforced the reality of his message. If Jesus were sitting on these stairs as Rabbi Gamaliel was wont to do, then his back was probably toward the entrance gates of the temple compound, with the crowds and his disciples standing more or less at eye level on lower steps below. This is exactly opposite of how groups visiting the stairs gather before their (standing) guides today. Jesus' hearers would have been able to take in the full sweep of his view, object by object, by easily shifting position as he spoke.

THE SPECIFIC SITUATION OF JESUS' INDICTMENT OF THE PHARISEES

SITTING IN MOSES' SEAT

The teachers of the law and the Pharisees sit in Moses' seat. (Matt 23:2 NIV)

This is the earliest reference to "Moses' seat" in ancient literature. More striking is that the term "Moses' seat" appears only *once* in all of rabbinic literature, and there in reference not to a synagogue seat but to a description of Solomon's throne, saying that "it resembled the seat of Moses" (Pesiqta de Rav Kahana 7b). There are a number of references to seats for dignitaries at banquets and in synagogues generally, both in the Gospels and in early Jewish literature (e.g., Matt 23:6; Luke 14:7-11; t. Sukkah 51b), but the seat of Moses seems to be something set apart and more special even than these. Archaeologists have found special

chairs in synagogues at Chorazin (north of Capernaum), Hammat Tiberias (on the western shore of the Sea of Galilee) and En Gedi (at the Dead Sea) dating to the third and fourth centuries AD, but none from the time of the New Testament. Rahmani has suggested that because these chairs were found near the place of the Torah Ark (where the Torah scroll was kept) and some distance from the benches where congregants sat, they were "empty thrones," not for a deity as was the custom in pagan temples but where the scroll was "enthroned" during synagogue services.[7] This custom is still practiced by Samaritan priests today who place the scroll of the Samaritan Pentateuch on a special wooden chair in their synagogue during prayer services. Jesus' referent for "Moses' seat" seems to be something else, however. Because he said that "*Pharisees sit* in Moses' seat," this seat perhaps was the chair of honor in the synagogue on which the rabbi sat to expound the Torah, a place near the repository of the Torah scroll and in view of the congregants. In this context the name "Moses' seat" also embodies the idea that the person who taught in the synagogue did so with the authority of Moses himself (m. Pirqe Avot 1.1).[8]

While the entire city of Jerusalem in Jesus' day was imbued with the aura of Mosaic authority, due to the the presence of the temple there, it is clear that there were also synagogues in the city that must have had "Moses' seats."[9] The gen-

---

7. L. Y. Rahmani, "Stone Synagogue Chairs: Their Identification, Use and Significance," *IEJ* 40 (1990): 192-214. Note the reference to Solomon's throne in Pesiqta de Rav Kahana 7b mentioned previously.

8. John J. Rousseau and Rami Arav, "Moses' seat," in *Jesus and His World: An Archaeological and Cultural Dictionary* (Minneapolis: Fortress Press, 1995), 205.

9. The Palestinian Talmud says that Titus destroyed 480 synagogues when he conquered Jerusalem in AD 70 (y. Megillah 73d). The Babylonian Talmud mentions 394 synagogues in

Robinson's Arch

eral location of at least one of these, the so-called "Theodotus synagogue,"[10] was visible from the stairway at the southern end of the temple precinct. This synagogue is known from a Greek inscription found in the southern part of Jerusalem's lower city that dates to the first century AD, mentioning a Theodotus, who was head of a synagogue and the one responsible for its construction. Acts 6:9 mentions another synagogue in Jerusalem, the Synagogue of the Freedmen, although without reference to its specific location. In any case, Jesus' reference to "Moses' seat" would have been immediately familiar to an audience in Jerusalem.

HAULING HEAVY LOADS

> They tie up heavy loads and put them on men's shoulders (Matt 23:4 NIV)

Two major urban thoroughfares ran the length of the Tyropoean Valley, one on either side of the valley. Remains of both have been uncovered at the southernmost part of the city of Jerusalem near the Pool of Siloam. Evidence of the street

---

Jerusalem (b. Ketubbot 105a). These numbers are clearly exaggerations, but do suggest that synagogues were present in the city even while the temple was still standing.

10. Stanley A. Cook, "The Synagogue of Theodotos at Jerusalem," *PEFQS* (1921): 22–23; and Gerald M. FitzGerald, "Notes on Recent Discoveries: The Theodotus Inscription," *PEFQS* (1921): 175–81. The idea that the Synagogue of the Freedmen and the so-called Theodotus synagogue were the same building cannot be proven; see Lester L. Grabbe, "Synagogues in Pre-70 Palestine: A Re-Assessment," *JTS* 39:2 (1989): 406.

following the western side of the valley can also be seen in the area of Robinson's Arch at the southwestern corner of the Temple Mount, as well as in various places along the entire western side of the Temple Mount enclosure wall.[11] Both streets were stepped to conform to the gradual rise of the Tyropoean Valley, and at least some of their paving stones have the same type of margin-and-boss design on their upper surfaces, in shallow relief, that the Herodian building stones of the Temple Mount enclosure wall have on their exposed sides.

These streets were lined with shops which seem to have been part of a busy market district in Jesus' day (see notes on Matt 23:6–7 below). Anyone trudging upward would climb nearly 300 feet (91.4 m) over the course of just under half a mile (.8 km)—a stiff walk especially for someone carrying a heavy burden. From these streets other streets angled even higher to the upper city to the west. The sight of people struggling up these long, stepped inclines with bags of wares over their shoulders or on their backs must have been a familiar one in Jesus' Jerusalem, and it remained one up to the introduction of motored vehicles in modern times. These streets, and those navigating them, would have been in easy sight of anyone on the southern stairway of the Temple Mount.

PLACES OF THE HAUGHTY ELITE

They love the place of honor at banquets and the most important seats in the synagogues; they love to be greeted in the market places (Matt 23:6–7 NIV)

The Jerusalem of Jesus' day was a true world-class city. Herod the Great, client king of Rome, had established policies of building, administration, and finance that pushed Jerusalem to the forefront of Roman imperial interests in the region, and this even though the city lay off the major natural through-routes of the province of Judea. Herod's attention to Jerusalem only served to strengthen the local power structures centered on Jewish religious and social life in the temple. The city's geographical position, with a tight horizon line high in the hills of Judea, served to focus the grandeur of the city inward, to its exquisite architecture and grand living spaces. Jesus' mention of banquet halls, synagogues, and marketplaces—places representing social, religious, and economic institutions that could be found throughout Judea and Galilee—here, in Jerusalem, conjures up images that were the best of the best. From the grand stairway rising to the Temple Mount complex from the south, Jesus and his disciples had full view of the basin of Jerusalem and its westward rise to the Herodian Quarter in the upper city. The view would have taken in mansions, synagogues, and market places.

The slope of Jerusalem's upper city that faced the temple was a popular place for the elite of the city to build elaborate homes and palaces (see infographic "Ancient Jerusalem" on pg. 528). One palace in particular, now preserved in the Wohl Museum in Jerusalem's Jewish Quarter, contains the remains of a large banquet or reception hall, replete with stucco ornamentation on the walls and ceiling typical to that of mansions in

Pompeii.[12] It was, moreover, a room with an unobstructed view of the Temple Mount. Tableware of finely worked pottery and glass was found in connection with this and other mansions in the area. Clearly a banquet held in rooms like these was an event to be noted, especially by those seated in "places of honor" around the table.

As noted with reference to Matt 23:2 above, a number of synagogues stood in Jerusalem at the time of Jesus, before the temple was destroyed. Each served a congregation that included persons worthy to sit in the more important seats of the building. Such seats likely were either those closest to the Torah Ark, or ones in an elevated spot where their occupants had the best view of the Torah scroll and would be able to rest their backs against the wall.

For centuries, one of the main market districts in Jerusalem was at the upper part of the Tyropoean Valley, in the area outside the southern and western walls of the Temple Mount.[13] One might expect as much simply by the name of the valley in the time of the New Testament: Tyropoean or "Cheesemakers," a likely reference to processes of manufacture and distribution within. Note as well the description of this part of Jerusalem by the prophet Zephaniah in the late seventh century BC:

> Wail, you who live in the market district (*makhtesh*; "mortar" or "crater," a reference to this valley);

> all your merchants will be wiped out,
>
> all who trade with silver will be ruined. (Zeph 1:11 NIV)

Much of the business activity in the Tyropoean Valley was temple related (the temple was the largest economic institution in the city) and so quite naturally was located in close proximity to the temple compound. Nehemiah spoke of goldsmiths and perfume-makers in the area (Neh 3:8), persons likely in the employment of the temple but who would have also sold their wares to a waiting public. Archaeological evidence shows that the streets around the temple compound, especially those that led to its gates, were lined with shops. A host of fine specialty items—including imported wares—must have been sold in these shops, and archaeologists have found many such items in the remains of the Jerusalem of Jesus' day. To these we must add the money-changers whose tables Jesus overturned (Matt 21:12–13) and who ran a market in currency and sacrificial animals; their transactions seem to have been conducted in the Royal Stoa on the Temple Mount platform directly above the main access gates in the southern wall of the compound. All evidence thus suggests that Jerusalem was a particularly lively market town in the first century AD, one that offered goods that attracted the city's elite and allowed them to strut in style. This Jesus surely noticed.

---

12. Nahman Avigad, *Discovering Jerusalem* (Nashville, TN: Thomas Nelson, 1983), 81–138.

13. Michael Avi-Yonah, "Jerusalem in the Hellenistic and Roman Periods," in *The Herodian Period*, vol. 7 of *The World History of the Jewish People*, ed. Michael Avi-Yonah (New Brunswick, NJ: Rutgers University Press, 1975), 240.

Southern Entrance to the Temple Mount

GATEKEEPERS OF THE KINGDOM OF HEAVEN

You shut the kingdom of heaven in people's faces. You yourselves do not enter, nor will you let those enter who are trying to (Matt 23:13 NIV)

While it was possible to enter the temple through any of several gates at the time of Jesus, most of the pilgrims who approached the compound did so from the south. To do so, a pilgrim would first take a ritual immersion bath (*Ant.* 15.419), either in a *miqveh* ("ritual bath") at home or in the public *mikva'ot* (pl.) adjacent to the grand stairway along the southern wall of the temple compound. Then, he or she would ascend to the entrance of the temple compound via the triple gate above the eastern section of the grand stairway (m. Middot 2:2). In doing so, pilgrims would pass by the large public building that seems to have been one of the three sites where the Sanhedrin, or ruling Jewish body, convened for business:

One [Council] used to sit at the gate of the Temple Mount, one used to sit at the gate of the Temple court, and one used to sit in the Chamber of Hewn Stone (m. Sanhedrin 11:2).

The gate of the temple court and the Chamber of Hewn Stone were both located within the walls of the Temple Mount itself, while "the gate of the Temple Mount" referenced here was most likely the busy, southern entrance to the compound above the grand stairway.

In this regard it is helpful to note the theological concept of holy space.

Rabbinic Judaism conceived of the world as a set of ten concentric rings, or degrees, of holiness, whereby the level of holiness increased as one proceeded from the outer rings inward toward the center (m. Kelim 1:6–9). In this view, passage from one circle into the next brought the pilgrim ever closer to the kingdom of heaven. Heaven on earth, so to speak, was the temple compound, and the gates to that compound were controlled, quite literally, by Jewish authorities answerable to the Sanhedrin which met just outside this main entrance to the Temple Mount. One wonders if Jesus might have raised his voice at this point in his indictment against the Pharisees since he may well have been within earshot of the Sanhedrin chambers at the time.

SWEARING BY GOLD

> If anyone swears by the temple, it means nothing; but if anyone swears by the gold of the temple, he is bound by his oath (Matt 23:16 NIV)

Scholars typically suggest that Jesus was referring either to the temple treasury or to the gold of the altar and cultic vessels in the temple in this saying. They link his statement to persons who would consider oaths made in reference to this gold to be *korban* (κορβᾶν), meaning dedicated to God, and hence more inviolable than were oaths made otherwise.[14] The idea may well be correct, but the gold of the temple was much more extensive than just that of the objects housed in its inner chambers. In his lofty descrip-

tion of the Jerusalem temple, Flavius Josephus mentioned that several parts of the temple compound were overlaid with gleaming gold (*War* 5.201, 208–224). Although Josephus was typically prone to exaggeration, the gold of the temple must have been plentiful enough to have been readily visible to worshippers and known by reputation to everyone else. This makes it an easy referent for Jesus and the crowds gathered outside of the Temple Mount's main entrance gateways.

WHITEWASHED TOMBS

> For you are like whitewashed tombs, which look beautiful on the outside but on the inside are full of dead men's bones and everything unclean (Matt 23:27 NIV)

Jesus most pointedly compared the Pharisees to whitewashed tombs, reserving the term "hypocrisy" (*hypokrisis*, ὑπόκρισις) for this image in particular (Matt 23:28). Corpses could not be buried within walled cities, especially Jerusalem, in deference to the conviction that anyone who touched or came near a dead body became ritually unclean (Num 6:6; 19:11–13; m. Kelim 1:1, 7–8; m. Ohalot 1:7–8). For this reason, it is often possible to estimate the size of an ancient city by the location of tombs on its perimeter. Indeed, the necropolis of ancient Jerusalem expanded over the centuries to correspond with the growth of the city's walls. In the time of the New Testament, the arc demarcated by cemeteries around Jerusalem extended 3.5 miles (5.6 km) north-south and 2.5 miles

---

14. For instance, W. D. Davies and Dale C. Allison, *A Critical and Exegetical Commentary on The Gospel According to Saint Matthew* (Edinburgh: T & T Clark, 1997), 290–91.

(4 km) east-west.[15] These cemeteries were not located right next to the city walls as the Muslim cemetery along the eastern wall of the Temple Mount is today, but at a bit of a distance, on the opposite slopes of the Kidron and Hinnom valleys for instance, facing the city.

Over eight hundred rock-cut tombs dating to the Second Temple (Early Roman) period have been found around Jerusalem. Many thousands more will never be found due to natural deterioration or ongoing construction activities in the area. Most people were too poor to be able to afford much of a tomb anyway, and for them a simple hole scratched into the ground had to suffice; these grave sites are gone forever. The tombs that have been found, even the ones of relatively simple construction, must have belonged to the more wealthy strata of Jerusalem society.[16]

The largest concentration of tombs from the time of the New Testament was on the Mount of Olives, just across the Kidron Valley from Jerusalem to the east. There are three reasons for this. First, the whitish bedrock found on the Mount of Olives, a local type of limestone called *mizzi hilu*, or "sweet rock," is easily carved into caves or tombs but is generally too soft to be used as building blocks for houses. Second, this was an area easily accessible to persons living in Jerusalem and hence convenient for burials. That it is also visible from many parts of the city strengthened the tie between those still alive and those dearly departed. And third, the theological conviction that associates "east" with the appearance of God (Ezek 43:1–5; Hab 3:3–4; Zech 14:1–5) prompted people to want to be buried in the direction of his coming.

Bodies were typically placed in tombs after having been wrapped in cloth, though not placed in coffins (Matt 27:59). If the family was able to afford a formal rock cut tomb (as was Joseph of Arimathea; Matt 27:60), the body was laid in a *kokh*, a tube-shaped compartment that projected into the bedrock from a room within the tomb. The *kokh* (most tombs had several and some had many) and the outer entrance to the tomb each were covered with stone slabs, sometimes round but usually squared, as plug-stones. These stones protected the corpse from wild animals and those still living from the stench of the grave. One year after burial, after the flesh had decayed and only the bones were left, the bones were gathered together and placed into small limestone boxes called ossuaries, which were then left in the tomb. Archaeologists are sometimes able to identify the interred inhabitants of a tomb from names inscribed on ossuaries found therein.[17]

Jesus compared the actions of the Pharisees specifically to tombs that had been whitewashed (*kekoniamenois*, the passive participle of *koniaō*, κονιάω, "to whitewash"). In Acts 23:3 the apostle Paul defended himself before the Sanhedrin by calling the high priest Ananias a "whitewashed wall" (*toiche kekoniamene*), also to illustrate hypocrisy. The prophet Ezekiel used a similar image in likening lying prophets to a wall plastered with whitewash (Ezek 13:8–16).

---

15. John J. Rousseau and Rami Arav, "Jerusalem, Tombs," in *Jesus and His World: An Archaeological and Cultural Dictionary* (Minneapolis: Fortress Press, 1995): 168.

16. Rousseau and Arav, "Jerusalem, Tombs," 167.

17. Rousseau and Arav, "Jerusalem, Tombs," 165.

Cemetery on Mount of Olives

In the ancient world, whitewash was derived from lime: a white, chalky residue of burned limestone. Mixed with water, it provided a thin covering quickly applied to structures such as houses, walls, or tombs to hide discoloration or defects. When mixed with lesser amounts of water and fortified with binding agents such as crushed seashells, crushed pottery, or plant fibers, the lime mixture became plaster and was used to provide a smooth, flawless covering over stone construction. How "whitewashed" the material appeared to be depended on the type and ratio of its ingredients. We might assume that the richer the person, the finer and brighter his home and tomb would have been. Unfortunately, whitewash does not stand up well to decades, let alone centuries, of weathering, and so archaeological evidence of tombs from the time of Jesus that might have been whitewashed is essentially nonexistent.

Today the southern end of the Mount of Olives, a place easily visible from the stairway south of the Temple Mount, is filled with thousands of graves. Most of these have been constructed out of limestone blocks white enough to give the impression of having been whitewashed. Together, they provide an immediate and visible reminder of the reality of whitewashed tombs as an image of personal hypocrisy.

MISLEADING MONUMENTS

> You build tombs for the prophets and decorate the graves of the righteous (Matt 23:29 NIV)

Among the many tombs surrounding Jerusalem known from the time of the New Testament are several that were clearly meant to be seen. Most of these are known to us by traditional names that are speculative at best and misno-

Tombs of Hezir and Zechariah

mers in fact. Among the better known are the "Tomb of the Kings" north of today's walled city of Jerusalem, the "Tomb of the Sanhedrin" to the northwest, "Herod's Family Tomb" on the watershed ridge opposite the Hinnom Valley west of the city, and three tombs forming a neat row on the lower slopes of the Mount of Olives opposite the southeastern corner of the Temple Mount: the "Tomb of Zechariah," the Bene-Hezir (sons of Hezir) Tomb, and the "Tomb of Jehoshaphat" behind "Absalom's Pillar."[18] Of these, only the Bene-Hezir Tomb has been correctly identified: Hezir is a known priestly family from the time of the Old Testament (1 Chr 24:15; Neh 10:20) that continued to thrive into the time of the New Testament. While each of these monumental tombs is unique in detail, they tend to share common characteristics: palatial dimensions with multiple spots in which to lay the mortal remains of the deceased, ornately decorated facades, and a structure outside that served as a monument to the person or persons buried inside. "Absalom's Pillar" is perhaps the best preserved monument of this type, although for whom it was constructed is unknown. Standing 65 feet (19.8 m) high, it combines Egyptian and Hellenistic architectural forms (both Doric and Ionic) in a creative, majestic, and highly unusual way. All of these monumental tombs date to the Second Temple period generally, from the time of the Hasmonean Kingdom (late second century BC) through the first century AD, although the specific date and identification of each is debated.

18. L. Y. Rahmani, "Ancient Jerusalem's Funerary Customs and Tombs: Part Three," *BA* 45.1 (1981): 43–53.

What is clear is that such tombs, with their fronting monuments, belonged to the highest aristocratic elements of Jerusalem. Their intent was to remind later generations of Jerusalemites of the person or persons interred. Whether those persons were actually "prophets" or "righteous" is beside the point; this is how the tomb owners themselves wanted to be remembered. The Greek word for monument, mnēmeion (μνημεῖον, "sign of remembrance"), is used especially for funerary monuments in front of graves, though by extension it sometimes is used for the grave or tomb itself (hence the NIV translation "graves of the righteous" here). The Hebrew term for the same is nephesh, "self" or "soul." As these tombs were made for Jews, not Greeks, the Hebrew term must better reflect the cultural or theological idea behind the monument. That is, the monument in stone was meant to portray permanently something about the actual identity of the person for whom the tomb was built. In reality, more often than not what was intended to be remembered was something more majestic than what the person was in real life (a tombstone, supersized). Jesus used the reality of tombs like these, some of which were very near to the grand stairway south of the Temple Mount, to warn of dangers inherent in the natural tendency toward self-aggrandizement while at the same time being blind to actions that denigrate others. Another way of saying the same is found in the Jerusalem Talmud: "We do not build monuments over the graves of the righteous, for their words are their memorial" (y. Shekalim 47a).

ESCAPING GEHENNA

How will you escape being condemned to hell [Gehenna]? (Matt 23:33 NIV)

Jesus' condemnation of the hypocrisy of the Pharisees reached its climax with a reference to Gehenna, which in many English translations of the New Testament (including the NIV) is rendered "hell." Gehenna (geenna, γέεννα) is a Greek form of the Aramaic word Gehinnam, itself a form of the Hebrew place name ge hinnom ("Valley of Hinnom"), a shortened form of ge ven-hinnom ("Valley of the Son of Hinnom") (Josh 15:8; 18:16; 1 Chr 28:3) or ge bene-hinnom ("Valley of the Sons of Hinnom") (2 Kgs 23:10). The Hinnom Valley joins the Kidron Valley in a broad, flat juncture just south of the City of David, a little beyond the location of the Pool of Siloam. This lower end of the Hinnom Valley, where the sides are steepest, is the portion of the valley most closely associated with the ancient city of Jerusalem and, as a result, most likely the part of the valley that originally carried the name Hinnom or "sons of Hinnom" (likely the Hinnom clan owned land or lived in this part of the valley). By the time of the New Testament, this portion of the valley had gained a rather nasty reputation, in large measure due to the pagan practice of Ahaz and Manasseh, father and son of Hezekiah, by which they "made [their] son[s] pass through fire" (2 Kgs 16:3; 21:6; 23:10).[19] Jeremiah (19:6) and writers in the Second Temple period (1 En 27:1–5; 54:1–6; 90:25–27; 2 Esd 7:36; 2 Bar 85:13; m. Pirqe

---

19. This may or may not have been child sacrifice. See George C. Heider, The Cult of Molek: A Reassessment (Sheffield: JSOT Press, 1985), 66–81, 223–383.

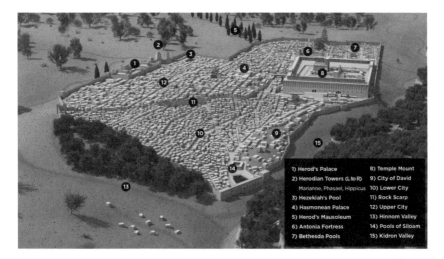

1) Herod's Palace
2) Herodian Towers (L to R)
   Marianne, Phasael, Hippicus
3) Hezekiah's Pool
4) Hasmonean Palace
5) Herod's Mausoleum
6) Antonia Fortress
7) Bethesda Pools
8) Temple Mount
9) City of David
10) Lower City
11) Rock Scarp
12) Upper City
13) Hinnom Valley
14) Pools of Siloam
15) Kidron Valley

Hinnom Valley and the Temple Mount

Avot 1:5) came to speak of the place in terms of eschatological judgment. This area of the Hinnom Valley is the lowest point visible from Jesus' position on the southern steps to the Temple Mount; indeed, topographically the entire city is angled that direction, giving dramatic, visible significance to his last referent, Gehenna.

CONCLUSION

Based on the topographical shape of Jerusalem, on what is known of the city's architecture and infrastructure from the time of Jesus, and on its role as the social, religious, and economic center of Judaism in the first century AD, the grand stairway leading to the main gates of the temple complex from the south was a natural setting for Jesus' denunciation of the hypocrisy of the Pharisees as described in Matt 23. The visible proximity of many of the items to which Jesus compared the Pharisees in this passage not only provided immediate and relevant imagery for his audience, but shows Jesus to have

been an engaging teacher of "the more important matters of the law" (Matt 23:23 NIV).

BIBLIOGRAPHY

Avigad, Nahman. *Discovering Jerusalem*. Nashville: Thomas Nelson, 1983.

Avi-Yonah, Michael. "Jerusalem in the Hellenistic and Roman Periods." Pages 207–49 in *The Herodian Period*. Vol. 7 of *The World History of the Jewish People*. Edited by Michael Avi-Yonah. New Brunswick, NJ: Rutgers University Press, 1975.

Cook, Stanley A. "The Synagogue of Theodotos at Jerusalem." *PEFQS* (1921): 22–23.

Danby, Herbert. *The Mishnah: Translated from the Hebrew with Introduction and Brief Explanatory Notes*. Oxford: Oxford University Press, 1933.

Davies, W. D., and Dale C. Allison. *A Critical and Exegetical Commentary on the Gospel According to Saint Matthew*. Vol. 3. Edinburgh: T & T Clark, 1997.

Ferguson, Everett. *Backgrounds of Early Christianity*. 2nd ed. Grand Rapids: Eerdmans, 1993.

FitzGerald, Gerald M. "Notes on Recent Discoveries: The Theodotus Inscription." *PEFQS* (1921): 175–81.

Grabbe, Lester L. "Synagogues in Pre-70 Palestine: A Reassessment." *JTS* 39:2 (1989): 406.

Heider, George C. *The Cult of Molek: A Reassessment*. Sheffield: JSOT Press, 1985.

Mazar, Benjamin. "The Archaeological Excavations Near the Temple Mount." Pages 25–40 in *Jerusalem Revealed: Archaeology of the Holy City, 1968–1974*. Edited by Yigael Yadin. Jerusalem: Israel Exploration Society, 1976.

Notley, R. Steven, and Ze'ev Safrai. *Parables of the Sages: Jewish Wisdom from Jesus to Rav Ashi*. Jerusalem: Carta, 2011.

Rahmani, L. Y. "Ancient Jerusalem's Funerary Customs and Tombs: Part Three." *BA* 45.1 (1981): 43–53.

———. "Stone Synagogue Chairs: Their Identification, Use and Significance." *IEJ* 40 (1990): 192–214.

Reich, Ronny, and Eli Shukron. "Excavations at Robinson's Arch: From Paved Street to Natural Rock." Pages 219–38 in *New Studies on Jerusalem*, vol. 17. Edited by Eyal Baruch, Ayelet Levy-Reifer, and Avraham Faust. Ramat Gan: Rennert Center Publications, 2011.

Ritmeyer, Leen. *The Quest: Revealing the Temple Mount in Jerusalem*. Jerusalem: Carta, 2006.

Rousseau, John J., and Rami Arav. *Jesus and His World: An Archaeological and Cultural Dictionary*. Minneapolis: Fortress Press, 1995.

CHAPTER 42

THE VINE, THE BRANCHES, AND WHAT IT MEANS TO ABIDE[1]

John 15:1–11

Carl J. Laney

KEY POINTS

- The location of the upper room is somewhere in Jerusalem west of the Kidron Valley (the exact location remains unknown).

- Jesus used an old metaphor with a new twist to illustrate the type of relationship he (the vine) and God (the vinedresser) have with disciples (the branches).

- To abide is to believe in Jesus as the Messiah and Son of God.

THE LOCATION OF THE DISCOURSE

John 15:1–11 is set in the context of Jesus' final message to his disciples which was given in the upper room of a house in Jerusalem on the night before his crucifixion and death. It is speculated that this upper room may have been in the house of Mary, the mother of John Mark, which appears to have been a gathering place for Jesus' followers (Acts 12:12). Only Mark and Luke identify this gathering place as a "large upper room" (ESV; Mark 14:15; Luke 22:12). The disciples were led to the house where this room was located by "a man carrying a jar of water" (Mark 14:13; Luke 22:10), possibly John Mark. It was there they prepared to celebrate Jesus' last Passover with his disciples.

THE GEOGRAPHICAL CONTEXT

The exact location of the upper room is not identified in Scripture. Mark indicates that the disciples "went into the city"

---

1. Parts of this article have been adapted from my journal article "Abiding Is Believing: The Analogy of the Vine in John 15:1–6," *Bibliotheca Sacra* 146 (1989): 55–66. Unless otherwise indicated, Scripture quotations are from the NIV.

[of Jerusalem] to prepare the Passover meal (Mark 14:16). After Jesus finished his final discourse and prayer, the disciples left the upper room, "crossed the Kidron Valley" (John 18:1), and proceeded to an olive grove called Gethsemane at the foot of the Mount of Olives (Matt 26:36; John 18:1). This indicates that the house with the upper room where the disciples celebrated their last Passover with Jesus was somewhere in Jerusalem west of the Kidron Valley.

The traditional room of the Last Supper is located on Jerusalem's western hill, known since the Crusades as "Mount Zion." It is situated on the second floor of a twelfth century building directly above the traditional tomb of King David. Beneath this building archaeologists have discovered pavements that go back to the Roman and Byzantine periods. This may have been the location of a church that existed on Mount Zion mentioned by Epiphanius of Salamis (AD 130). The upper room that Christian visitors see today was built in the twelfth century by the crusaders as part of the Church of Saint Mary of Zion. That structure fell into disrepair after the defeat of the crusaders but was revived and restored by the Franciscans in the fourteenth century. Under Ottoman rule the building was transformed into a mosque featuring the traditional Tomb of David on the lower level. The room above, identified in Christian tradition as the room of the Last Supper, retains evidence of its use as a mosque, including stained glass windows with Arabic inscriptions and a small alcove (*mihrab*) indicating the direction of Mecca. An exterior stairway leads up to a minaret on the roof which provides splendid views of Jerusalem and the Mount of Olives.[2]

THE LITERARY CONTEXT

In John 13–17 Jesus prepares his apostles for his death and for the ministry they will have after his ascension. The Passover evening begins with Jesus washing the disciples' feet and is followed by the dismissal of Judas (John 13:37) from the upper room. Jesus then announces his departure and prepares the Eleven for their future ministry by promising them the indwelling ministry of the Holy Spirit (John 14:17). The discourse continues in John 15 as Jesus speaks of his relationship with the disciples and their relationship with the unbelieving world. In John 16 he gives them a word of encouragement, promising that while they will have temporary sorrow at his departure, they will have full and permanent joy because of his resurrection (John 16:22). Having concluded his final discourse, Jesus prays for himself, his disciples, and the spiritual unity of future believers (John 17).

John 15:1–11 is central to the upper room discourse in emphasizing the relationship between Jesus and his disciples. But in order to understand this relationship, we must first understand the agricultural analogy Jesus develops in this teaching. The important lesson presented by Jesus in this text is that fruitfulness in the Christian life results from abiding in Christ.

THE CULTURAL CONTEXT

Vineyards were a common sight in the Mediterranean world during the biblical period. Moses told the Israelites in the wilderness that God was bringing them

---

2. For further description of the traditional room of the Last Supper, including photographs, go to www.sacred-destinations.com/israel/jerusalem-last-supper-room.

grapevine

ἄμπελος
vine; grapevine

wine ↔ product of grapevine

Bible Word Study: ἄμπελος, ampelos

into a good land, "a land with wheat and barley, vines" (Deut 8:8). The Hebrew word for "vine" (*gefen*) is used fifty-five times in the Old Testament, and the corresponding Greek word (*ampelos*, ἄμπελος) is used nine times.

The vine was a common figure used to represent Israel in the Old Testament. Isaiah describes Israel as a "vineyard" which God planted, tended, and allowed to be destroyed because the people had broken God's covenant (Isa 5:1–7). Jeremiah declares how God planted the people of Israel as "a choice vine" (Jer 2:21). Ezekiel, Hosea, and the psalmist use the same imagery (Ezek 15:1–8, 17:6–9; Hos 10:1; Ps 80:8–16). In each illustration, the vine disappoints the vineyard keeper and the fruitless vine is judged. We find the words "trampled" (Isa 5:5), "destroy," "strip off" (Jer 5:10), "thrown on the fire" (Ezek 15:4), "withers" (Ezek 17:9), "cut down" and "burned with fire" (Ps 80:16) used to describe the destiny of a worthless, fruitless vine.

The vine was such a familiar image that the Jews featured a vine branch and leaf on the coins they minted during the Jewish war (AD 66–70).[3] And Josephus

reports that a huge gold sculpture of a vine was fixed over the entrance of the door of the Second Temple (*War* 5.210).

It was customary in ancient times to grow grapes in the loose, rich soil of terraced hillsides. The more level ground of the broad valleys was reserved for grain. Vineyards were often located at the junction of *wadis* or small valleys where the soil received plenty of moisture during Israel's season of winter rain. In the first century, Galilee had the reputation of being the best region for growing grapes. Even today the wine produced in Galilee is highly regarded.

A hedge or stone wall was usually placed around the vineyard to protect the crop from animals and thieves (Ps 80:12–13; Song 2:15; Isa 5:2). The stones removed from the field were used to build the wall and a watchtower. Isaiah records how God cared for his vineyard: "He dug it up and cleared it of stones" (Isa 5:2).

THE ANALOGY OF THE VINE (JOHN 15:1-2)

Beginning the analogy, Jesus introduces himself as the vine. The definite article ("the") with the adjective *alēthi-*

---

3. Arthur L. Friedberg, *Coins of the Bible* (Atlanta: Whitman Publishing, 2004), 73.

nos (ἀληθινός) indicates that Jesus is the "true" or "genuine" vine. Although Israel was viewed as the vine in numerous Old Testament texts, Jesus is the "true vine" who fulfills God's expectation for his people. A growing vine needs care and so Jesus identifies God the Father as the farmer or gardener. God is the one who does the planting, watering, and pruning of the vine. As in Isa 5:1–6, the vineyard is under God's care and sovereign authority.

Jesus goes on in John 15:2 to describe the work of the gardener or vinedresser in relationship to the branches (klēma, κλῆμα) which are attached to the vine. Jesus doesn't identify the branches with a particular group of his followers, but he does identify two kinds of branches: the fruit bearing and the fruitless.

It is obvious in this analogy that Jesus is speaking about people, not plants. The context suggests Jesus is referring to his disciples, broadly defined as "interested listeners." A disciple (mathētēs, μαθητής) is one who listens and learns, "a learner." A disciple would follow his teacher, learning from what he did as well as from what he said.

Jesus is teaching that there are two kinds of disciples—those who "bear fruit" and those who do not. Crucial to an understanding of this text is the fact that not all disciples continue with Jesus. John records that some of Jesus' disciples turned away from Jesus' hard teaching in the synagogue at Capernaum: "After this many of his disciples turned back and no longer walked with him" (John 6:66 ESV). John's point is clear: Not all "disciples" are believers. Some listen and learn for a

time, but then turn away, rejecting Jesus and his teaching.

Continuing his application of the analogy, Jesus describes two actions that are taken with regard to the branches. The vinedresser "takes away" (airō, αἴρω) the fruitless branches and "prunes" (kathairō, καθαίρω) the fruit bearing branches. The latter verb can also be translated "to cleanse," "to purge," or "to purify." While it was commonly used in contexts of ceremonial cleansing,[4] kathairō is not the normal word for pruning. Its use here can be attributed to the fact that Jesus is talking about people rather than vines.

Regular pruning is absolutely necessary to maximize the fruit production of a vine. The Mishnah refers to the thinning of the grape vines and the removal of branches that have defective clusters (m. Peah 7:4–5). Robin Murto, a grape grower in Yamhill County, Oregon, says, "Pruning is the single most important job you can do in a vineyard. What eventually ends up in a bottle of wine starts right here." It is a job that must be done carefully to avoid injury to the vine. She adds, "All it takes is one wrong clip to reduce any given vine's productivity by half." Dick Shea, another grape grower in Oregon, notes, "Pruning isn't something that seems to intrigue people, but it is just absolutely critical. It's integral to the quality of the grapes."[5]

Drawing insight from a publication by the California Agricultural Extension Service, Rosscup describes several different kinds of pruning. First, there is the pinching with the thumb and finger

---

4. J. H. Moulton and G. Milligan, *The Vocabulary of the Greek Testament* (Grand Rapids: Eerdmans, 1930), 310.

5. *The Oregonian/Oregon Live* (February 18, 2011).

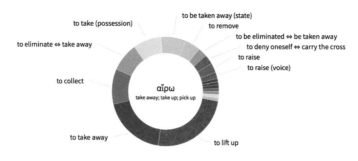

Bible Word Study: αἴρω, airō

to remove the growing tip of a vigor-ous shoot, so that it will not grow too quickly and be broken or damaged by a gust of wine. Second, there is topping, the removal of one or two feet from the end of a growing shoot to prevent a later loss of the entire shoot, which might be snapped off by the wind. Third, thin-ning involves the removal of grape flow-ers or clusters, which enables the rest of a branch to bear more and better qual-ity fruit. Fourth, there is the pruning or cutting away of suckers, which rise from below the ground or from the trunk and main branches of the vine.[6] Some of the pruning takes place during the growing season, but the main pruning takes place in the fall or winter when the grower prunes the vine severely to prepare it for the next growing season.

What is the spiritual lesson Jesus is revealing by this analogy? Jesus is teach-ing the Eleven in the upper room that as the vinedresser cuts away and removes that which would hinder the productiv-ity of the vine, so God the Father, through loving discipline, removes things from the lives of believers that hinder their spiritual fruitfulness. While the Greek word (kathairō) is translated "to prune,"

it could just as well be translated "to cleanse." And in the next verse Jesus uses the nominal form of this word to say that the Eleven are "clean" (katharos, καθαρός) by virtue of their response to the teach-ings of Jesus (John 15:3).

As pruning is absolutely critical to growing grapes, so it is in developing spiritual maturity and fruitfulness. And while spiritual pruning in the lives of believers is productive, it is a painful process! The most productive and fruit-ful Christian leaders are those whom God has pruned. God's pruning takes place in different ways and often through humbling experiences. But it is always intended to prepare a disciple for a more fruitful and God-glorifying ministry.

While God "prunes" the fruit bear-ing branches, "he takes away" (airō) the fruitless branches. The Greek word airō is used twenty-three times in John's Gospel. In eight places it could be translated "to take" or "to lift up" (John 5:8, 9, 10, 12; 10:18, 24). In thirteen places it must be translated "to take away" or "to remove" (John 11:39, 41, 48, 16:22; 17:15; 19:15, 31, 38; 20:1, 2, 13, 15). How is Jesus using airō in this context? Can the first century cul-tural background provide a clue?

---

6. James A. Rosscup, *Abiding in Christ: Studies in John 15* (Grand Rapids: Zondervan, 1973), 50.

Ancient Methods of Vine Training

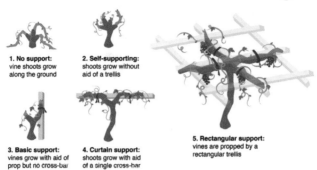

1. **No support:** vine shoots grow along the ground

2. **Self-supporting:** shoots grow without aid of a trellis

3. **Basic support:** vines grow with aid of prop but no cross-bar

4. **Curtain support:** shoots grow with aid of a single cross-bar

5. **Rectangular support:** vines are propped by a rectangular trellis

Dillow argues that the fruitless branches are lifted up and encouraged: "A fruitless branch is lifted up to put it into a position of fruit-bearing."[7] He appeals to R. K. Harrison who writes that fallen vines were lifted "with meticulous care" and allowed to heal.[8] It has been suggested that the vines were allowed to lie on the ground during winter and then "lifted" so they could be productive during the growing season. Dillow adds: "If after this encouragement, they do not remain in fellowship with Him and bear fruit, they are then cast out."[9]

Radmacher reports seeing vineyards in Israel with the stalks of the grape vines down on the ground.[10] He explains that during the growing season the vine-tenders would place a rock under the vine to raise it up. Several days later they would do this again, repeating the process until the vine is raised up and properly positioned for fruit bearing.

While this interpretation has gained interest in recent years, it does not appear to be supported by the practices of vine growing in antiquity. Pliny the Elder (AD 23–79), a naturalist and a Roman official, explains five methods for arranging vines in ancient vineyards:[11] (1) vines spread over the ground, a method referred to in Ezek 17:6; (2) self-supporting vines; (3) vines with a prop but no cross-bar; (4) a vine propped up by a single cross-bar; (5) a vine trellised on a rectangular frame. Pliny says that vines which are propped or trellised are better for wine grapes since this provides more sunshine, better airflow for getting rid of dew, and easier access for pruning. They were also easier to harvest since the grapes hung down and were more accessible.

Nowhere does Pliny describe a process of "lifting up" the fruitless branches of the vine. In fact, the Mishnah indicates that the wine presented with the

---

7. Joseph C. Dillow, "Abiding Is Remaining in Fellowship: Another Look at John 15:1–6," *Bibliotheca Sacra* 147 (1990): 44–53.

8. R. K. Harrison, "Vine," *ISBE* 4:986.

9. Dillow, "Abiding Is Remaining in Fellowship," 51.

10. Earl D. Radmacher, "The Word As Truth: Its Authority" in *Celebrating the Word* (Portland, OR: Multnomah Press, 1987), 22–23.

11. Pliny the Elder, *Natural History* 17.35.164–66.

offerings in the temple had to be produced from vines that were *not* trellised, "but only from vines growing from the ground" (m. Menahot 8:6). Dayagi-Mendels explains that vines that spread along the ground are preferred since they produce "a large quantity of fruit" and are "easy to protect from the summer winds."[12] He adds: "Such vines ripened early in the land of Israel because of the warm ground temperature; this was seen as an advantage. However, the disadvantage for ground spreading vines was that they were easier prey for mice and foxes."

One could wonder whether the methods of growing grapes have changed in Israel since the biblical period. James S. Snyder, director of the Israel Museum in Jerusalem, answers: "Methods for cultivating grapes and producing wine have not changed significantly over the centuries."[13]

Contrary to the views of some interpreters, the normal meaning of the Greek word *airō* is "to take away" or "remove." This understanding has the support of a leading Greek lexicon which cites John 15:2 and says that this word is used of branches that are "cut off."[14]

POSSIBLE INTERPRETATIONS

If the fruitless branches are "cut off," what does this suggest about their spiritual condition and destiny? Some would argue that the fruitless branches represent Christians who lose their salvation. They may have believed for a time, but their fruitlessness indicates they have lost their faith and forfeited their salvation. This interpretation, however, appears

contrary to the clear teaching of Jesus in John 10:28–29, that those who are given eternal life are safe in the hands of the Father and Son and "shall never perish."

Others have suggested that the fruitless branches represent true Christians who are removed to heaven by physical death as God's final step of divine discipline. They lose their lives, but not their salvation. The difficulty with this interpretation is John 15:6 where the removal of the fruitless branch is a prelude to judgment, not blessed fellowship with Christ in heaven. A judgment by fire is the destiny of unbelievers only (Matt 3:12; 5:22; 18:8–9; 25:41; 2 Thess 1:7–8; Rev 20:15). Although Paul mentions fire in connection with the judgment seat of Christ, it is a person's "work" that is burned, not the person (1 Cor 3:13, 15). There is no text in the New Testament suggesting believers undergo a judgment by fire where they themselves are burned.

A view that commends itself by the context and the agricultural background is that the fruitless branches represent disciples who are severed from a superficial connection with Christ, the vine. The fruitless branch represents one who has made an external profession of faith that is not matched by a corresponding internal union with Christ.

At first glance, the phrase "in me" (*en emoi*) appears to be a problem for this interpretation. How can the fruitless branches be "in Christ" if they represent unbelievers? The words "in me" can be understood in either an adjectival or adverbial sense, meaning they can be used to describe a noun or a verb. These

---

12. Michal Dayagi-Mendels, *Drink and Be Merry: Wine and Beer in Ancient Times* (Jerusalem: The Israel Museum, 1999), 18.

13. Dayagi-Mendels, *Drink and Be Merry*, 6.

14. BDAG, s.v. "αἴρω."

words are often read in an adjectival sense in John 15:2: "*Every branch in me that does not bear fruit he takes away*" (ESV). However, every other time the words "in me" are used in John's Gospel they are used adverbially. This pattern of usage suggests the words should be read adverbially here, too, giving the sense, "Every branch that does not *bear fruit in me* he takes away." Bearing fruit is a process that happens only in and through Christ. A branch cannot bear fruit apart from a life-giving connection with Christ, the vine.

THE APPLICATION OF THE ANALOGY (JOHN 15:3–11)

Jesus addresses his disciples in John 15:3 saying, "You are already clean" (*katharoi*). This is the noun form of the verb *kathairō* translated in John 15:2 as "he prunes." Here, the noun form is translated "clean" because of the pruning analogy. The vines are *cleaned* through the pruning process. Judas has already left the upper room (John 13:27–30), so Jesus is telling the Eleven that they have already been pruned ("you are clean") and can be expected to produce fruit.

Jesus explains further that the disciples are already "clean" (or pruned) "because of the word" he has spoken to them. This indicates that the Father's pruning of Jesus' disciples is not necessarily physical. It can take place through teaching, exhortation, or rebuke (2 Tim 4:2).

Jesus goes on to reveal the secret of bearing fruit (John 15:4–5). As a branch cannot bear fruit unless it is connected with the vine, so Jesus' disciples will not

bear fruit unless they abide in him. There is no fruit bearing apart from abiding in Jesus! Two questions must be answered: (1) What does it mean "to abide"? (2) What does it mean "to bear fruit"?

WHAT IT MEANS TO "ABIDE"

The word "abide" (*menō*, μένω) literally means "to remain" or "to stay." The implication of the word is that of a continual, permanent connection or relationship (1 John 3:15). There is a clear relationship in John's Gospel between believing and abiding. The one who believes in Jesus—that is, who "eats my flesh and drinks my blood" (a concept exegetically parallel to "believes in him"; John 6:54)—abides in Jesus. Everyone who genuinely believes in Jesus does not abide in "darkness" (John 12:46), a Johannine symbol of unbelief (John 12:35–36). John equates confessing Jesus as the Son of God with abiding in God (1 John 4:15). He equates the commandment to "believe" with abiding (*menō*) in him (1 John 3:23–24). One who allows the gospel message to "abide" in his heart "will abide in the Son and in the Father" (1 John 2:24 ESV). Kent comments, "These passages show that confessing Jesus as the Son of God (i.e., believing in Jesus) establishes the relation of abiding. Thus to abide in Christ is equivalent to believing on Christ."[15] S. T. James concludes: "In his Gospel, John consistently uses *menō* to indicate the permanent nature of relationships."[16] This assessment seems to be especially true in John 15:1–6, which helps explain the rather strange absence of "believe" in this passage.[17]

15. Homer A. Kent, *Light in the Darkness* (Grand Rapids: Baker, 1974), 183.

16. Sujaya T. James, *Salvation and Discipleship Continuum in Johannine Literature* (Lewiston, NY: The Edwin Mellen Press, 1914), 197.

17. Leon Morris, *The Gospel of John* (Grand Rapids: Eerdmans, 1971), 336.

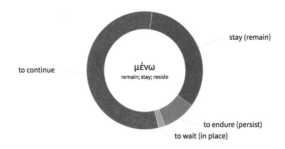

Bible Word Study: μένω, menō

To "abide" is to maintain a vital (life-giving) contact with the vine, the source of life. Belief is the connection which unites the vine and branches. The lack of fruit indicates that one is not abiding (believing) in Christ. The absence of abiding indicates deficient belief, as seen in John 2:23–25; 7:31; 8:31, 40, 45, 46; 12:11, 37. Tenney refers to this "belief" which falls short of genuine faith as "superficial."[18] Morris calls it "transitory belief," which is not saving faith.[19] It appears to be based merely on an outward profession which is not an inward spiritual reality coupled with regeneration.

The problem with this "belief" is its content. Such belief is based on something other than a clear understanding of Jesus the Messiah and Son of God. Many people are inclined to believe something about Jesus, but are unwilling to yield him their allegiance, trusting him as their personal sin-bearer. Paul's comment about the Cretans is a case in point: "They claim to know God, but by their actions they deny him. They are detestable, disobedient and unfit for doing anything good" (Titus 1:16). If there

is no fruit, there is no faith, regardless of one's verbal profession.

If "abiding" means "believing," what is the result of not abiding? This is the question addressed in John 15:6 where Jesus explains the destiny of the branch that bears no fruit and is removed. The branch that does not have a life-giving connection with Christ the vine (i.e., "does not abide") is "thrown away, "withers," and is "burned." This corresponds to the tares in Matt 13:40–42 that are gathered, bound in bundles, and burned. In a phone conversation with Nogah Hareuveni, founder of Neot Kedummim (the Biblical Landscape Reserve in Israel) and an expert in ancient agriculture, I asked what was done with the trimmings that were pruned from the vine. He answered: "When the branches dry, they make good kindling."

Only unbelievers are destined for a judgment by fire (Matt 3:12; 25:41). When believers are judged, only their "work" is burned (1 Cor 3:13, 15). The fruitless branches which do not abide are "cast out" (*eblethe exo*), something Jesus promised he would not do to believers (John 15:6; 6:37). This conclusion may be supported

---

18. Merrill C. Tenney, "Topics from the Gospel of John, Part IV: The Growth of Belief," *Bibliotheca Sacra* 132 (1975): 351.

19. Morris, *The Gospel of John*, 603.

by Jeremiah's use of the vine imagery to describe God's judgment of Judah where he writes: "Strip off her branches, for these people do not belong to the Lord" (Jer 5:10).

Some have found it troubling that people who have had some sort of connection with Jesus as professing believers are eventually severed from Christ. But this teaching is not unique to this text. John the Baptist instructed the religious leaders who approached him for baptism to "produce fruit in keeping with repentance" (Matt 3:8). He added, "Every tree that does not produce good fruit will be cut down and thrown into the fire" (Matt 3:10). Jesus warned of the same consequences and added, "Thus, by their fruits you will recognize them" (Matt 7:19–20). James wrote that a faith which is not accompanied by actions is "dead" (Jas 2:17).

THE RESULT OF ABIDING

What, then, is the result of abiding? What kind of fruit might be expected of those who have a life-giving connection with Christ the vine? It is often thought that Jesus is suggesting that true believers will be fruitful as they participate in the harvest of souls for the kingdom (John 4:35–38). Others recall the words of Paul to the Galatians where he identifies nine fruits of the Spirit (Gal 5:22–23). But sound principles of exegesis require that we consider the immediate context first.

There are six results of abiding that Jesus mentions specifically in the verses following the analogy of the vine and branches: (1) effectual prayer (John 15:7), (2) glorifying the Father (John 15:8a), (3) authenticating oneself as a genuine disciple (John 15:8b), (4) a continued confidence in Jesus' love (John 15:9), (5) obedience to Jesus' commandments

(John 15:10), and (6) fullness of joy (John 15:11). Other fruit that result from abiding in Christ are not excluded from this list, but these appear from the immediate context and are the focus here.

Jesus' teaching on the vine and the branches is not intended to undermine a sense of assurance for true believers, those "branches" that have a life-giving connection with Christ, the vine. Nevertheless, self-evaluation is good. Paul does so himself (2 Cor 13:15). Are there people who have merely professed to be Christians without having experienced the regenerating work of the Holy Spirit in their lives? If so, this text calls us to recognize the need to trust Jesus alone for our salvation and to enter into the blessings of the New Covenant.

Why did Jesus give this teaching to the Eleven who were true believers? Remember Judas? He had spent three years as an apostle, traveling with Jesus, seeing his miracles and listening to his words. Yet in the end, Judas died in unbelief (John 17:12). On the night of his betrayal of Jesus he left the upper room where the disciples had gathered. John's words, "And it was night" (John 13:30), reflect the spiritual condition of the heart of one who had cut himself off from Jesus, the light of the world. Jesus gave the analogy of the vine and the branches so that his disciples would be able to distinguish true belief from a mere profession of faith and be able to minister to "professing" believers appropriately.

Fruit bearing inevitably results from abiding (believing) in Christ. If there is no life-giving connection with Christ, the vine, there will be no fruit. Although God alone knows for sure who are his own, the test of fruitfulness will help believers to discern whether or not a professing Christian's faith is genuine. This spiritual insight is not designed to give us some basis for spiritual pride, but to enable us to minister to those whose baptism or church membership might lead them to think they are believers when in fact they have no vital, life-giving relationship with Jesus, the vine.

BIBLIOGRAPHY

Dayagi-Mendels, Michael. *Drink and Be Merry: Wine and Beer in Ancient Times.* Jerusalem: The Israel Museum, 1999.

Dillow, Joseph C. "Abiding Is Remaining in Fellowship: Another Look At John 15:1-6." *Bibliotheca Sacra* 147 (1990): 44-53.

Friedberg, Arthur L. *Coins of the Bible.* Atlanta: Whitman Publishing, 2004.

Harrison, R. K. "Vine." *ISBE* 4:986-87.

James, Sujaya T. *Salvation and Discipleship Continuum in Johannine Literature.* Lewiston, NY: The Edwin Mellen Press, 2014.

Kent, Homer A. *Light in the Darkness.* Grand Rapids: Baker, 1974.

Laney, J. Carl. "Abiding is Believing: The Analogy of the Vine in John 15:1-6." *Bibliotheca Sacra* 146 (1989): 55-66

Moulton, J. H., and G. Milligan. *The Vocabulary of the Greek Testament.* Grand Rapids: Eerdmans, 1930.

Morris, Leon. *The Gospel of John.* NICNT. Grand Rapids: Eerdmans, 1971.

Radmacher, Earl D. "The Word as Truth: Its Authority." Pages 22-23 in *Celebrating the Word.* Portland, OR: Multnomah Press, 1987.

Rosscup, James A. *Abiding in Christ: Studies in John 15.* Grand Rapids: Zondervan, 1973.

Smith, Charles R. "The Unfruitful Branches in John 15. *Grace Journal* 9 (1968): 3-22.

Tenney, Merrill C. "Topics from the Gospel of John, Part IV: The Growth of Belief." *Bibliotheca Sacra* 132 (1975): 343-57.

CHAPTER 43

SOUTHERN TEMPLE MOUNT EXCAVATIONS
ARCHAELOGICAL DISCOVERIES

Matt 21:1–11; 23:13–39; Mark 11:1–11;
Luke 19:28–40; John 9:1–7; 12:12–19

Chris McKinny

KEY POINTS

- The Jerusalem Archaeological Park is less a park in the traditional sense and more a dedicated zone of ongoing excavations with respect to specific locations around the Temple Mount.

- Many of the sites of the park provide significant archaelogical context for a more sensitive reading of the Gospels.

- Remains of the southwest corner and southern wall of the Temple Mount point to a bustling place of city and temple commerce, as worshipers purchased offerings or took ritual baths before entering the temple via Robinson's Arch or the Guldah Gates.

- The Guldah Gates located at the southern wall marked the busiest entry and exit points to the temple, and the stairs leading up to these gates are probably where Jesus taught from on multiple occasions, using landmarks and objects in the vincinity as teaching aids.

INTRODUCTION

The Jerusalem Archaeological Park and Davidson Center[1] is among the most-vis-ited locations in Jerusalem. The park, which is also known as the "southern archaeological park" or the "south-

---

1. The Davidson Center is a museum near the entrance of the park that displays some of the objects found during the excavation, two films, and several other exhibits.

ern Temple Mount excavations," is the site of one of the largest archaeological projects ever undertaken in the State of Israel. From a geographical perspective, the park is situated on a portion of the eastern hill of Jerusalem and the central or Tyropoeon Valley (Josephus, *War* 5.140). This valley separates the eastern (Temple Mount, Jebus, City of David, etc.) and western hills (encompassing most of the present-day Jewish, Armenian, and Christian Quarters) of Jerusalem, and served as the western boundary of the city at various times in Jerusalem's history.[2]

The Jerusalem Archaeological Park is limited on the north by the southern wall of the Temple Mount (Haram esh-Sharif), which includes the Herodian double and triple gates (i.e., the "Huldah Gates") and the north-south running fortification wall from the Ottoman period that divides the park in half. The road from modern Mount Zion to the Kidron Valley limited the extent of excavations in these directions on the south and east. Finally, the rise of the western hill (i.e., present-day Jewish Quarter) along with the large courtyard of the Western Wall

limited archaeological work on the west and northwest. The ancient structures and finds found near and within the Jerusalem Archaeological Park are some of the most impressive and monumental building remains ever found in Jerusalem. Although some of these structures either pre-date[3] or post-date our period of interest (i.e., the Early Roman period—from the conquest of Pompey until the destruction of the Jewish temple by Titus, 63 BC–AD 70). Accordingly, this essay will attempt to describe the geographical and archaeological details related to the Early Roman period within and near the Jerusalem Archaeological Park. This will be accomplished by discussing the history of excavations, the historical development of Jerusalem in relation to the park, the main Herodian architectural remains, and several events in the Gospels that relate to the structures within the park.

HISTORY OF EXCAVATIONS

Following the Six-Day War and the unification of Jerusalem in 1967, Israel ceded control of the Temple Mount to the *Waqf* (the Islamic religious authority of

---

2. The Jerusalem Second Temple Model (located at the Israel Museum), which was created by Michael Avi-Yonah in the 1970s, provides a unique view into the topographical and archaeological layout of first century (AD) Jerusalem that incorporates and illustrates details from the New Testament (primarily the Gospels and the book of Acts), Josephus, the Mishnah/Talmud, and other ancient Jewish writings.

3. Two areas produced important archaeological strata that can be associated with the Kingdom of Judah during the Iron Age II. The first of these areas relates to Iron II fortifications and surrounding structures located in the Ophel north of the City of David. See Eilat Mazar and Benjamin Mazar, *Excavations in the South of the Temple Mount: The Ophel of Biblical Jerusalem*, Qedem 29 (Jerusalem: Hebrew University, 1989); Eilat Mazar, ed., *The Ophel Excavations to the South of the Temple Mount*, Final Reports Volume 1 (Jerusalem: Shoham and Old City Press, 2015). In addition, a large Iron II water cistern was discovered beneath the Herodian street near the southwestern corner of the Herodian Temple Mount and the large Iron II water (see "A Public Water Reservoir Dating to the First Temple Period Has Been Exposed for the First Time Next to the Western Wall," IAA Press Release, September 2012.) Structures from the early Second Temple period (Persian, Hellenistic, and Hasmonean) were also found within and just outside the park.

Jordan), but annexed the rest of the Old City of Jerusalem. From 1968 until 1978, Benjamin Mazar carried out a massive archaeological project in the area south and southwest of the Temple Mount in what later would become the Jerusalem Archaeological Park.[4] Beginning in 2009 and continuing until 2013, Eilat Mazar (B. Mazar's granddaughter) renewed excavations in the Ophel, focusing primarily on the eastern and southern areas of the park.[5] Besides these two major projects, several other smaller projects have been carried out in the park since B. Mazar's excavations that shed light on the nature of the settlement in this area during the Early Roman period. In 1994-1996, R. Reich and Y. Billig excavated in the vicinity of Robinson's Arch and the Umayyad palace and found the remains of two stones seats of a Roman period theater.[6] From 2011-2012, E. Shukron and R. Reich excavated a portion of the drainage canal located beneath the Herodian street in the vicinity of Robinson's arch.[7] This excavation was resumed in 2013-2014 by J. Uziel, who continued to expose the area of the drainage channel as well as the southwestern foundations of the Temple Mount that had previously been exposed by C. Warren in the 1860s.[8] As a result of these recent excavations, it is now possible for visitors to walk the entire length of the Herodian street from the vicinity of the Herodian Siloam Pool (partially on the street and partially in the drainage canal) until the Jerusalem Archaeological Park near Robinson's Arch.[9]

---

4. Benjamin Mazar, "Herodian Jerusalem in the Light of the Excavations South and South-West of the Temple Mount," *IEJ* 28.4 (1978): 230-37; Mazar and Mazar, *Excavations in the South of the Temple Mount*; Eilat Mazar, *The Temple Mount Excavations in Jerusalem 1968-1978 Directed by Benjamin Mazar Final Reports Vol. II: The Byzantine and Early Islamic Periods*, Qedem 43 (Jerusalem: Hebrew University, 2003); idem, *The Temple Mount Excavations in Jerusalem 1968-1978 Directed by Benjamin Mazar, Final Reports Vol. III: The Byzantine Period*, Qedem 46 (Jerusalem: Hebrew University, 2007); idem, *The Temple Mount Excavations in Jerusalem 1968-1978 Directed by Benjamin Mazar, Final Reports Volume IV: The Tenth Legion in Aelia Capitolina*, Qedem 52 (Jerusalem: Hebrew University, 2011); Mazar, *The Ophel Excavations to the South of the Temple Mount*; see also Eilat Mazar, *The Complete Guide to the Temple Mount Excavations* (Jerusalem: Shoham - Academic Research & Publication, 2002).

5. Her excavations focused primarily on the Iron II fortifications and accompanying structures and the Byzantine structures (which included the golden "treasure"); Mazar, *The Ophel Excavations to the South of the Temple Mount*.

6. R. Reich and Y. Billig, "A Group of Theatre Seats Discovered near the South-Western Corner of the Temple Mount," *IEJ* 50.3/4 (2000): 175-84. It is difficult to determine whether these seats should be related to the Herodian or Hadrianic theaters. For a discussion of these issues see J. Patrich, "Herod's Theatre in Jerusalem: A New Proposal," *IEJ* 52.2 (2002): 231-39.

7. E. Shukron and R. Reich, "Jerusalem, Robinson's Arch," *Hadashot Arkheologiot* 123 (2011); R. Reich and E. Shukron, "Excavations Next to Robinson's Arch 2011 - from the Level of the Paved Street to Bedrock," in *New Studies on Jerusalem*, ed. E. Baruch, A. Levy-Reifer, and A. Faust, vol. 17 (Ramat Gan: Ingeborg Rennert Center for Jerusalem Studies, 2012), 219-38.

8. M. Hagbi and J. Uziel, "Jerusalem, The Old City, The Western Wall Foundations," *Hadashot Arkheologiot* 127 (2015).

9. See N. Hasson, "Underground Jerusalem: An Interactive Journey," *Haaretz*, May 24, 2016, http://www.haaretz.com/st/c/prod/eng/2016/05/jeruz/01/. Hasson discusses the archaeological background of these excavations and provides several videos taken from within the tunnels.

Herod's Temple on the Temple Mount
Circa AD 62–64

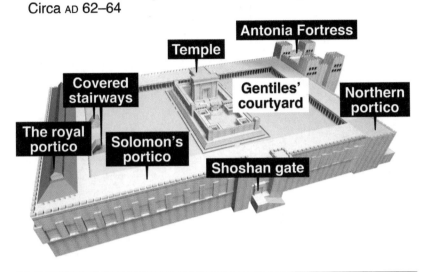

THE HISTORICAL
DEVELOPMENT OF JERUSALEM
IN RELATION TO THE PARK

Mazar's excavations revealed a wide range of archaeological periods from the Chalcolithic until modern times, but the remains from the Early Roman period were particularly well-represented as they were uncovered beneath the massive debris from the collapse of large sections of the Herodian Temple Mount and adjoining structures (e.g., Robinson's arch). In many places, this debris covered street levels and buildings that date to the AD 70 destruction of Titus. In general, the Herodian construction of the Temple Mount and its environs completely covered, and, in most cases, destroyed earlier remains since most of the Roman structures and streets were founded directly on bedrock. Following the destruction of Jerusalem in AD 70, the area of the

western street and southern stairs (i.e., the Jerusalem Archaeological Park) laid in a massive heap of ruins on account of the Roman destruction of much of the Temple Mount's western retaining wall. Many of the collapsed Herodian ashlars of the Temple Mount were re-used in subsequent building projects in Jerusalem in the Late Roman, Byzantine, Early Arab,[10] Crusader, and Late Arab (including Ottoman) periods. In order to comprehend the significance of the area of the Jerusalem Archaeological Park in the Herodian period, it is important to understand the development of this area of Jerusalem in the periods preceding the Early Roman period.

The southern end of the eastern hill was first established as a permanent settlement during the Early Bronze Age (c. 3300–2500 BC) and became a fortified town during the Middle Bronze Age

---

10. Including the Umayyad period (c. 660–750 AD) buildings that are located in the central part of the Jerusalem Archaeological Park.

Remains of the Western Wall

(c. 2000–1550 BC). This fortified town was known as Jebus and Salem in the Bible (Gen 14:18; Ps 76:2), which according to 2 Samuel 5:6–10 (compare 1 Chr 11:4–8) was conquered by David and renamed the "City of David" (also Jerusalem). The fortifications of Jebus/Davidic Jerusalem only included the southeastern portion of the eastern hill with the Kidron, Hinnom, and Central (i.e., Tyropoeon) Valleys demarcating the eastern, southern, and western sides of the city's fortifications, respectively. The northern side was presumably fortified in the area just south of the Ophel; however, no fortifications from these periods have been found in archaeological excavation, nor are they specifically mentioned in the biblical text.

From the time of David (tenth century BC) until the destruction by the Romans

(AD 70), the eastern hill was continuously inhabited by Judahites/Judeans (although it was destroyed several times) and affiliated with the kingdoms of (united) Israel and (divided) Judah and the imperial province of Yehud/Judea (Persian-Roman periods). The city expanded throughout the Iron Age II (c. 980–586 BC), but particularly during the reigns of Solomon, who built his palace and Yahweh's temple on the northern end of the eastern hill (i.e., the area of the Temple Mount; see 1 Kgs 6), and Hezekiah, who built a large fortification wall that encompassed the entire western hill from the northwestern side of the eastern hill until the southwestern end of the eastern hill (see Isa 22:9–11). Solomon's expansion[11] caused the northern half of the eastern hill (i.e., including the major-

---

11. See note 3 above for a discussion of the possible archaeological evidence associated with this expansion towards the "Ophel."

Solomon's Temple
Circa 957–587 BC

ity of the Jerusalem Archaeological Park) to become a permanent element of the inhabited and walled area of Jerusalem while the central valley (i.e., the western side of the Jerusalem Archaeological Park) continued to serve as the western boundary of the city. Hezekiah's fortification of the western hill of Jerusalem caused the central valley to become the center of the city.[12]

Following the return from exile in the Persian period and during the time of Ezra and Nehemiah (see Neh 1:3), only the eastern hill was fortified, and the central valley once again served as the western boundary of Jerusalem. However, after the Hasmoneans defeated the Seleucids (see 1-2 Macc; Josephus, *Ant.* 12), they built a fortification wall (late second and early first century BC) along the previous topographic line as Hezekiah's wall that had enclosed the western hill and incorporated the central valley into the fortified area of Jerusalem (e.g., 1 Macc 13:10). This wall was later rebuilt and expanded by Herod the Great (late 1st century BC) along the lines of the "first wall" of Jerusalem (see *War* 5.136-83). In sum, during periods of relative weakness, the central valley served as the western boundary of Jerusalem. Conversely, the fortification of the western hill marked the peaks of habitation in Jerusalem during the First and Second Temple periods at which times the central valley was incorporated into the city of Jerusalem.[13]

Besides the historical importance of the development of Jerusalem in relation to these topographic features, the area of the Jerusalem Archaeological Park served

---

12. Perhaps this was the rationale behind the creation of the Iron IIB large water cistern that was found below the Herodian street (see above).

13. For maps and a discussion of the development of Jerusalem in these periods see: Barry J. Beitzel, *The New Moody Atlas of the Bible* (Chicago: Moody, 2009), 220-31; W. Schlegel, *Satellite Bible Atlas: Historical Geography of the Bible* (Santa Clarita, CA: Master's College, 2013), Map 11-2; Dan Bahat, *Carta's Historical Atlas of Jerusalem* (Jerusalem: Carta, 2015); see also Josephus, *Josephus Carta's Illustrated the Jewish War*, ed. R. Steven Notley (Jerusalem: Carta, 2016); R. Steven Notley, *Jerusalem: City of the Great King* (Jerusalem: Carta, 2016).

as the main business and public center of Jerusalem during the Early Roman period. Broadly speaking, Jerusalem at the time of Jesus had been planned within the "first and second walls," around the Herodian Temple Mount, and along the north-south Herodian street, which ran from the northwestern end of the Temple Mount in the north until the pool of Siloam in the south and divided Josephus' "upper and lower cities" of Jerusalem (see *War* 5.136–141). Significantly, the Herodian street and its accompanying structures were clearly part of a larger city plan that also included a large system of city dumps along the eastern slopes of the eastern hill above the Kidron Valley (see infographic "Ancient Jerusalem" on pg. 528).[14]

THE HERODIAN REMAINS OF THE PARK IN CONTEXT OF THE GOSPELS

Herod's Temple Mount is a massive rectangular platform that completely encapsulated the northern half of the eastern hill and supported the Antonia Fortress (northwest corner), the temple (center), and the Royal Stoa (southern end). Beginning in 20 BC, Herod built this platform over the remains of an earlier Temple Mount that seems to date to the Iron Age II with perhaps a southern extension during the time of the Hasmoneans.[15] According to Josephus, the western wall of the Temple Mount included four gates leading to the temple and another large entrance on the southern wall that he described in the passage cited below.

Now, in the western quarter of the enclosures of the temple there were four gates; (1) the first led to the king's palace, and went to a passage over the intermediate valley [Wilson's Arch[16]]; (2–3) two more led to the suburbs of the city [i.e., Warren's Gate and Barclay's Gate[17]]; (4) and the last led to the other city, where the road descended down into the valley by a great number of steps, and thence up again by the ascent [i.e., Robinson's Arch, see below]; for the city lay over against the temple in the manner of a theatre, and was encompassed with a deep valley along the entire south quarter, but the fourth front of the temple, which was southward, had indeed itself gates in its middle [i.e., the Huldah Gates

---

14. R. Reich and E. Shukron, "The Jerusalem City-Dump in the Late Second Temple Period," *Zeitschrift Des Deutschen Palästina-Vereins* 119 (2003): 12–18; G. Bar-Oz et al., "'Holy Garbage': A Quantitative Study of the City-Dump of Early Roman Jerusalem," *Levant* 39.1 (2007): 1–12; Y. Gadot, "Preliminary Report on the Excavations at Jerusalem's Southeastern Hill, Area D3," *Hebrew Bible and Ancient Israel* 3.2 (2014): 282; Y. Gadot and Y. Adler, "A Quantitative Analysis of Jewish Chalk Vessel Frequencies in Early Roman Jerusalem: A View from the City's Garbage Dump," *IEJ* 66.2 (2016): 202–19.

15. Evidence for these two earlier structures can be seen on the eastern wall of the Temple Mount at the so-called "bend" and "seam"; see Leen Ritmeyer, *The Quest: Revealing the Temple Mount in Jerusalem* (Jerusalem: Carta, 2006), 102–5, 178–80; see also Leen Ritmeyer and Kathleen Ritmeyer, *Jerusalem: The Temple Mount* (Jerusalem: Carta, 2015).

16. For a discussion of Wilson's Arch, see Ritmeyer, *The Quest*, 30–34.

17. For a discussion of Warren's Gate and Barclay's Gate, see Ritmeyer, *The Quest*, 25–30; 34–38.

and Southern Stairs, see below] (*Ant.* 15.410–411).[18]

With regards to these entrances, we will now discuss the building remains that are within the Jerusalem Archaeological Park and their relationship to the cultural and religious background of the Gospels.

ROBINSON'S ARCH AND THE
HERODIAN NORTH-SOUTH
UPPER AND LOWER STREET

As we have shown above, excavations have exposed sections of the Herodian north-south street from the northwestern corner of the Temple Mount until the Siloam pool at the southern end of Herodian Jerusalem. Within the Jerusalem Archaeological Park, a long section of this street along with an upper eastern street was exposed. Above this street and directly north of the southwestern corner of the Temple Mount are the remains of a massive arched staircase that were initially identified by E. Robinson (in 1838) as the bridge

mentioned by Josephus (*Ant.* 15.410) that spanned the central valley and connected the western and eastern hills.[19] However, C. Warren's explorations (1867–1870) in the immediate vicinity demonstrated that Robinson's "bridge" did not continue to the western hill, and correctly suggested that Wilson's Arch (see above) should be connected with the bridge mentioned by Josephus.[20] Slightly later (in 1896), C. Watson correctly suggested that Robinson's arch was the fourth western gate that led up to the Temple Mount.[21]

B. Mazar's excavations (and later Reich and Billig's excavation) of the north-south street near Robinson's Arch revealed the collapse of the staircase, which lay on top of the paved street, a lower street, and a pier that received the staircase arch.[22] With regards to events associated with Jesus in Jerusalem, several finds in the excavation of this area bear special mention[23] as they relate to the cultural and religious background of first-century Jewish purity, sacrifice, and other religious expressions. These finds include the following: an inscribed

18. All translations of Josephus taken from Josephus, *The Works of Josephus: Complete and Unabridged, New Updated Edition*, trans. W. Whiston, Updated edition (Peabody, MA: Hendrickson, 1987).

19. Edward Robinson and Eli Smith, *Biblical Researches in Palestine and the Adjacent Regions: A Journal of Travels in the Years 1838 & 1852 by Edward Robinson, Eli Smith and Others*, 3rd ed. (London: John Murray, 1867), 3.356–64; see also Ritmeyer, *The Quest*, 44–45.

20. Charles Warren, *Underground Jerusalem: An Account of Some of the Principal Difficulties Encountered in Its Exploration and the Results Obtained. With a Narrative of an Expedition Through the Jordan Valley and a Visit to the Samaritans* (London: R. Bentley and Son, 1876), 316; Ritmeyer, *The Quest*, 45.

21. C. M. Watson, "The Site of the Temple," *Palestine Exploration Fund Quarterly Statement* 28.1 (1896): 59; see Ritmeyer, *The Quest*, 45–50 for a further discussion.

22. Reich and Billig, "A Group of Theatre Seats Discovered near the South-Western Corner of the Temple Mount," 340–50; Ritmeyer, *The Quest*, 47–48.

23. For a discussion of the relationship between the Herodian ashlar masonry on the Temple Mount and the disciples' statement about the "magnificent stones and wonderful buildings" (e.g., Mark 13:1), see Todd Bolen, "Magnificent Stones and Wonderful Buildings of the Temple Complex" on pg. 462.

Remains of Robinson's Arch

(top) cornerstone,[24] several ritual baths,[25] shops, stone vessels,[26] and coins of different denominations.[27]

Inside the foundations of the staircase pier (that received the arched staircase from the western wall) and the upper street were found smaller arches that seem to have been used as shops that lined the main street on the west (near the staircase) and east.[28] The close proximity of these shops to the entrance to the temple and Royal Stoa, as well as the presence of several ritual baths in close proximity, suggests that these shops would have serviced worshippers on their way to the Temple Mount. Animals for sacrifice, stone vessels, access to public ritual baths, and other temple-related wares and services may have been sold within these shops. In this vein, these shops (or others nearby) could have serviced Mary, Joseph, and Jesus.

---

24. Aaron Demsky, "The Trumpeter's Inscription from The Temple Mount," *Eretz Israel* 18 (1985): 40-42; Ritmeyer, *The Quest*, 57-60.

25. Jodi Magness, *Stone and Dung, Oil and Spit: Jewish Daily Life in the Time of Jesus* (Grand Rapids: Eerdmans, 2011), 16-17; see also R. Reich, "Miqwa'ot (Jewish Ritual Baths) in Eretz-Israel, in the Second Temple, Mishnah and Talmud Periods" (PhD diss., Hebrew University, 1990); J. D. Lawrence, *Washing in Water: Trajectories of Ritual Bathing in the Hebrew Bible and Second Temple Literature* (Atlanta: Society of Biblical Literature, 2006).

26. Magness, *Stone and Dung, Oil and Spit*, 70-74.

27. Including especially the "Tyrian shekel" (i.e., tetradrachmas), see Magness, *Stone and Dung, Oil and Spit*, 97-106.

28. The full extent of this upper street is unknown, as it has been excavated only up until the area of the Mughrabi Gate (i.e., the temporary ramp leading to the Temple Mount). The upper street also continues along the southern face of the Temple Mount (see below).

3D Model of Southwestern Corner of the Temple Mount

When the time came for their purification according to the Law of Moses they brought him up to Jerusalem to present him to the Lord (as it is written in the Law of the Lord, 'every male who first opens the womb shall be called holy to the Lord') and to offer a sacrifice according to what is said in the Law of the Lord, a pair of turtledove, or two young pigeons (Luke 2:22–24; compare Lev 12:15[29]).

On their way to the temple where they would meet Simeon and Anna (Luke 2:25–38), perhaps Mary and Joseph also paid to use ritual baths in the vicinity[30] before ascending to the temple courtyard (see also Luke 2:41–51). It seems likely that Jesus and the disciples would have also used this area for similar purposes during their numerous visits to Jerusalem and the temple.

This commercial/cultic backdrop in the area just outside of the temple precinct should also be remembered when reading the numerous Gospel passages related to Jesus' denouncement of the religious establishment in Jerusalem (e.g., the devouring of widows' households by the Jewish religious elite; Luke 20:45–21:4). Perhaps the most well-known of these episodes is Jesus turning over the money-changers' tables inside the temple. This event (or events) most likely took place in or near the Royal Stoa (the main public space on top of the Temple

---

29. These passages might indicate that Mary and Joseph could not afford a lamb for the required sacrifice.

30. But see E. Regev, "The Ritual Baths Near the Temple Mount and Extra-Purification Before Entering the Temple Courts," *Israel Exploration Journal* 55, no. 2 (January 1, 2005): 194–204, http://www.jstor.org/stable/27927107; with a reply from Y. Adler, "The Ritual Baths Near the Temple Mount and Extra-Purification Before Entering the Temple Courts: A Reply to Eyal Regev," *IEJ* 55.2 (2006): 209–15.

Mount), which would have been directly reached by passing through Robinson's Arch. With regards to this event, one can vividly imagine the commotion Jesus caused when he drove out the moneychangers, along with the "oxen, sheep, and pigeons," who must have run down either Robinson's Arch or the Huldah Gates on their way out of the Temple Mount (see Matt 21:12–16; Mark 11:15–19; Luke 19:45–46; John 2:14–15; Ps 69:9; Isa 56:7; Jer 7:11). Given that this area was the focal point of Herodian Jerusalem, news of Jesus' actions against the religious establishment would have certainly spread quickly throughout the city, which was overflowing with Passover pilgrims. In the context of the Synoptics (Matt 21:12–16; Mark 11:15–19; Luke 19:45–46), this event set the stage for Jesus' total control over the Temple Mount during the first several days of the Passover Feast/passion week (see especially Mark 11:16; Luke 19:47–48).

Much of the Gospels are devoted to Jesus' ministry in Jerusalem during different Jewish festivals (e.g., Passover), and focused on healings that Jesus purposefully accomplished on the Sabbath

in order to demonstrate the hypocrisy of the "scribes and Pharisees" and his authority over the Sabbath (e.g., John 5, John 9). Interestingly, among the debris from the collapse of Robinson's Arch and the western retaining wall of the Temple Mount, B. Mazar found the upper-most cornerstone from the top of the structure[31] with the following broken Hebrew inscription, "to the place of trumpeting to ..."[32] This inscription probably marked the location where priests were supposed to sound a trumpet at the beginning of the Sabbath and other festivals (see *War* 4.582; Num 10:2; m. Sukkah 5:5[33]). Therefore, it is most probable that Mary, Joseph, Jesus, and his disciples would have regularly heard the trumpet sound from this cornerstone at various points during their travels to Jerusalem.[34]

THE SOUTHERN STAIRS AND THE DOUBLE AND TRIPLE GATES

B. Mazar's excavation revealed a massive set of stairs descending from the southern wall of the Temple Mount towards the south and the Lower City. These stairs are connected to the upper street that continued along the southern wall

---

31. In my opinion, there is no basis for the suggestion that the "pinnacle of the Temple" (*pterygion tou hierou*, πτερύγιον τοῦ ἱεροῦ) where Jesus was tempted by Satan (Matt 4:5; Luke 4:9) should be located at the top of the southwestern corner above the Herodian street. See e.g., J. McRay, *Archaeology and the New Testament*, 2nd ed. (Grand Rapids: Baker Academic, 2008), 102–4. It seems more likely that the Temple itself is the building being referred to despite the fact that *naos*, ναός is not used in these passages.

32. Ritmeyer, *The Quest*, 58–61; see also S. Rozenberg, ed., *Herod the Great: The King's Final Journey* (Jerusalem: Israel Museum, 2013), 42–43. See image of the "Trumpeting Stone" on pg. 61.

33. Regarding this passage, Ritmeyer states the following, "Every day during the Temple services trumpets were blown at different places, according to Mishnah Sukkah 5.5. There were never less than 21 blasts per day, but not more than 48 altogether. Some of these would have been blown above the southwest corner, as the Mishnah notes: 'On the eve of the Sabbath they used to blow six more blasts, three to cause the people to cease from work and three to mark the break between the sacred and the profane'" (Ritmeyer, *The Quest*, 59).

34. See Aubrey L. Taylor, "Wilderness Events: The Baptism and Temptation of Jesus" on pg. 53.

of the Temple Mount and across the two sets of stairs (near the "master course" of Herodian stones). From the south, the two stairs led to two large sets of entrances that are known as the "double and triple gates" or the "Huldah Gates."[35] Today, the double and triple gates are blocked, but the inside of the passageways are still intact and continue to be used by Muslim worshippers beneath Al-Aqsa Mosque.[36] Between the two stairs, B. Mazar found the remains of a large public ritual bath and another public building.[37] In addition, evidence of a large plaza was found at the base of the stairs extending towards the area of the Ophel, which together with the monumental character of the stairs and the entrances indicates that this area was the main pilgrim entrance into the Temple Mount.

The southern entrances into the Temple Mount and accompanying structures are connected to the same commercial and religious center as the western entrances and the Herodian north-south street. In fact, these southern entrances should probably be considered the busiest and most important section of the public space beneath the Temple Mount. While it is impossible to point to any specific event or sermon in the life of Jesus that occurred in or near the southern steps/entrances, it seems very probable that Jesus and the disciples would have used this entrance to access the temple, and perhaps even ministered on the

steps and plaza. Beyond general travel from the lower city to the Temple Mount, this large public space would have been used for many different activities including praise/worship (see the Psalms of Ascent; Ps 120–134), ritual purification, public speaking and gathering, tithing, ceremonial processions, and others. In this section, we will discuss the connection between the southern entrances into the Temple Mount and the healing of the man born blind (John 9), the triumphal entry (Matt 21:2–9; Mark 11:1–11; Luke 19:29–38; John 12:12–15), and the discourse of the "seven woes" (Matt 23).

Healing a Blindman

In the Gospel of John, Jesus healed a man "blind from birth" by coating his eyes with mud and sending him to "wash in the pool of Siloam (which means Sent)" (John 9:1–7). Jesus' initial meeting with the blind man could have occurred at many different places in Jerusalem, but the southern stairs should be considered a prime candidate due to the public nature of these structures. Interestingly, portions of both the Pool of Siloam and the north-south stepped street[38] leading to the pool have been uncovered in recent years, which allows modern readers to visualize the blind man's journey to and from the Pool of Siloam.[39] After being healed, the blind man "came back seeing" (John 9:7), and then had a lengthy discussion with the Pharisees concerning

35. "There were five gates to the Temple Mount: the two Huldah Gates on the south, that served for coming in and for going out" (m. Middot 1:3 [Danby, 590]).

36. For a lengthy discussion of the southern stairs, the double and triple gates, and their continuation beneath the Temple Mount see Ritmeyer, *The Quest*, 63–90.

37. Ritmeyer, *The Quest*, 75.

38. R. Reich, E. Shukron, and O. Lernau, "Recent Discoveries in the City of David, Jerusalem," *IEJ* 57.2 (2007): 153–69.

39. See Elaine A. Phillips, "Healing by Living Water at the Pool of Siloam" on pg. 365.

Southern Wall of the Temple Mount

Jesus, his healing, and the Sabbath (John 9:13–34). The location of this "hearing" is not given; however, the Royal Stoa, which seems to have been the main meeting area of the Sanhedrin,[40] is the most likely candidate. If this analysis is correct, then the blind man would have travelled to and from the Temple Mount by means of the stepped street and the southern stairs. Following his meeting with the Pharisees,

the blind man met Jesus somewhere in the city, and "believed" (John 9:35–37).

The Triumphal Entry

All of the Gospels include the triumphal entry of Jesus into Jerusalem at the beginning of the Passover. The parallels between the triumphal entry and other Old Testament passages[41] are numerous and have been discussed at length by commentators.[42] On the other hand,

---

40. Ritmeyer, *The Quest*, 88.

41. See especially 1 Kings 1:33–38 (Solomon's coronation while riding David's royal mule), 2 Kings 9:13 (the coronation of Jehu with men casting down their garments and proclaiming Jehu king), Zechariah 9:9 (cited prophecy of the king coming to Jerusalem on a donkey), and Psalm 118 ("Save us [Hossana]" and "Blessed is he who comes in the name of the Lord"; see particularly Ps 118:12–29).

42. See e.g., B. Kinman, *Jesus' Entry Into Jerusalem: In the Context of Lukan Theology and the Politics of His Days* (Leiden: Brill, 1995); compare references above in G. K. Beale and D. A. Carson, eds., *Commentary on the New Testament Use of the Old Testament* (Grand Rapids: Baker Books, 2007).

The Triple Gate

the exact route of Jesus' entry into the temple has not been definitively determined. With regards to the route, several details can be extracted from the Gospel accounts. The entire procession seems to have lasted for most of the day (see Mark 11:11) and included a journey from the area of Bethany, Bethphage, and the Mount of Olives (Mark 11:1) to the temple. Visitors to modern Jerusalem and traditional sites associated with passion week (e.g., Dominus Flevit, Garden of Gethsemane) may be inclined to conclude that the triumphal entry followed the modern pilgrim route. This route begins at the eastern slopes of the Mount of Olives (i.e., the vicinity of Bethany),[43] ascends to the summit of the ridge and then past Dominus Flevit[44] and the Garden of Gethsemane, and would have (theoretically) gone into the Temple Mount through the Golden Gate.[45] [46]

---

43. Herodium and the tomb of Herod, the so-called "King of the Jews" and Jesus' attempted murderer (see Matt 2:1–12), can be clearly seen to the south while walking along this route. See also Luke 19:38b, which hearkens back to the language of the angels at the birth announcement of Jesus (Luke 2:14).

44. The traditional location of Luke 19:41–44.

45. See A. D. Riddle, "The Passover Pilgrimage from Jericho to Jerusalem" on pg. 395.

46. There appears to have been two eastern entrances into the Temple Mount along the eastern wall, including the famous Golden Gate (which includes Herodian remains beneath the Ottoman-era gate) and a large staircase with a double entry near the southeastern corner of the Temple Mount that appears to have been identical to Robinson's Arch. With regards to these entrances and access to the Temple Mount from the Mount of Olives, some have suggested that there was a bridge that spanned the Kidron Valley and connected the Mount of

This route is logistically possible, but not necessarily preferable given the purposes behind Jesus' processional entry to the temple. The actual route may have followed the pilgrim route until the Kidron Valley, but instead of using one of the eastern entrances to ascend into the Temple Mount, perhaps the procession continued along the Kidron Valley[47] and entered into the lower city (i.e., the City of David) near the Siloam Pool.[48] From the southern end of the city, Jesus could have slowly ascended to the Temple Mount along the main north-south street via the southern stairs and the Huldah Gates.

At this point, and with much of the surrounding archaeology and geography described, we can visualize the conclusion of Jesus' entry into the temple. As the procession concluded inside the temple and the last "songs of salvation" (Ps 118:15), shouts of "Hosanna" (Mark 12:10-11; Ps 118:25) and "Blessed is the King who comes in the name of the Lord!" (Ps 118:26) rang out, perhaps the participants were aware of the fact that their king was the "light shone upon them" (Ps 118:27), who had walked through "gates of righteousness" and the "gate of the Lord" (Ps 118:19-20), and that this day was, in fact, "the day that the Lord had made" (Ps 118:24). However, despite their obvious joy at the coming of the king, it seems that they were not aware of the fact that their king was also the "stone that the builders rejected" (Ps 118:22; Matt 21:42; Mark 12:10; Luke 20:17),[49] or the "festal sacrifice" that would be bound and offered on "the horns of the altar" (Ps 118:27), or, most importantly, the one whom the Lord would "discipline ... severely but not be given over to death" and who would "not die, but live" (Ps 118:17-18).

The Seven Woes

Matthew's account of Jesus' last public appearance before his crucifixion (Matt 23) returns to the language of the triumphal entry in Jesus' discourse of the "seven woes" aimed at the "scribes and Pharisees" (see Matt 23:13-39). This event occurred a few days following the triumphal entry. Interestingly, this discourse includes many details that reference "sights and sounds" that could have been observed from the southern stairs or within the Temple Mount.[50] Besides clear references to the temple and events that occurred within the temple precinct (e.g., swearing by the temple/gold of the temple and the altar/sacrifice on the altar; Matt 23:16-21), several contemporary elements bear mentioning and are listed with a discussion below.

- **Moses' seat** (Matt 23:2) — The seat of Moses was an actual,

---

Olives to the Temple Mount (citing m. Parah 3:6). However, Ritmeyer demonstrates the difficulties with this interpretation. See Ritmeyer, *The Quest*, 105-13.

47. Although we should also remember that archaeologists have demonstrated that much of the western slope of the Kidron Valley was used for garbage collection during this period; see above.

48. Interestingly, this route goes right past the site of Solomon's coronation and near Adonijah's failed coronation (1 Kgs 1:9, 33-53).

49. Compare Acts 4:11; 1 Pet 2:7.

50. See Paul H. Wright, "Indicting Hypocrisy with Imagery from the Temple Mount" on pg. 414.

physical seat of honor in a Jewish synagogue as made clear by the discovery of one such seat in a fifth century AD synagogue at Chorazin.[51]

- **Broad phylacteries and long fringes** (Matt 23:5) — From the Second Temple until modern times, phylacteries[52] (i.e., prayer boxes worn on the arms and forehead) and fringes (i.e., the tassels of the prayer shawl) continue to be used by Jews in religious contexts particularly within the Western Wall plaza.

- **Places of honor at feasts** (Matt 23:6) — In the context of the days preceding the *seder* and the Passover sacrifices, Jesus' statement against those who sought the "place of honor at feasts" was an indictment of the Jewish religious establishment that condoned this type of outward righteousness.

- **Greetings in the marketplace and tithing of mint, dill, and cumin** (Matt 23:7, 23) — These references to the marketplace and the "tithing of mint, dill, and cumin,"[53] could apply to the shops

in and around the upper and lower streets within the Jerusalem Archaeological Park.

- **Gehenna** (Matt 23:15, 33) — The New Testament word for "hell" is Gehenna (*geenna*, γέεννα), which is actually the Hellenization of the Hebrew *gê hinnōm* (see Josh 15:8). Scholars have debated whether or not the term Gehenna retained its locative connotation during the late Second Temple period.[54] However, in my opinion, its inclusion in the context of Matt 23 beside possible references to funerary structures and burial practices in the nearby Kidron Valley and Mount of Olives (see below) would seem to suggest that the term has a locative connotation in Matt 23:15, 33. If so, Jesus' use of Gehenna may be an allusion to Jeremiah's apocalyptic prediction of the demise of Jerusalem's inhabitants and the Molech cult[55] with its Topheth in the Hinnom Valley (Jer 7:31–34; 19:6).

- **Ritual purity of (stone?) vessels** (Matt 23:25–26) — The Jewish ritual purity of consumption vessels (along with the purification

---

51. Other seats of this type have been found at Hammath Tiberias and Delos. For a discussion of these seats, see: Anson F. Rainey and R. Steven Notley, *The Sacred Bridge* (Jerusalem: Carta, 2006), 356; see also J. Ory, "An Inscription Newly Found in the Synagogue of Kerazeh," *PEQ* 59.1 (1927): 51–52.

52. See Geza Vermes, "Pre-Mishnaic Jewish Worship and the Phylacteries from the Dead Sea," *Vetus Testamentum* 9.1 (1959): 65–72.

53. Magness, *Stone and Dung, Oil and Spit*, 190.

54. See especially the Enochic literature (1 Enoch 26–27; 54:1–6; 56:1–4; 90:24–27), which seems to associate Gehenna with the Hinnom Valley. For a discussion of this issue and references to Gehenna in early rabbinic literature, see L. R. Bailey, "Gehenna: The Topography of Hell," *BA* 49.3 (1986): 187–91; and Duane Watson, "Gehenna," *ABD* 2:926–28.

55. See Lev 18:21; 20:1–5; Deut 19:9–13; 2 Kgs 16:3–4; 23:10; 2 Chr 28:1–4; 33:6; Isa 30:31–33; Jer 32:35; Ezek 20:25–26.

of the body and hands) is one of the defining characteristics of late Second Temple Judaism.[56] With regards to this, the usage of stone vessels was especially popular due to the belief that the vessel could be cleansed if it became impure. In addition, a large public ritual bath designated for the immersion of stone vessels was found south of the Triple Gate below the stairs.[57] The high quantities of stone vessels found in the various excavations of the Jerusalem Archaeological Park and the adjoining Early Roman-era garbage dump (see above) provides important background information for understanding Jesus' metaphor.

- **White-washed tombs and the tombs of the righteous** (Matt 23:27–31) — Many Second Temple period burial monuments and "white-washed" tombs have been found along the slopes of the Mount of Olives, the Kidron Valley (e.g., Absalom's Pillar/Tomb of Jehoshaphat, Tomb of Zechariah, and Tomb of Benei Hezir), and the Hinnom Valley (e.g., the "tomb

of Annas"[58]). As Jesus delivered his sixth and seventh "woe!" to the scribes and Pharisees (Matt 23:27–31), it seems clear that he was using visible funerary structures in the surrounding geography of Jerusalem to vividly illustrate the hypocrisy of the Jewish religious establishment.

After severely criticizing the hypocrisy of the scribes and Pharisees, Jesus concluded his sermon with a prophetic pronouncement of the coming destruction of Jerusalem (Matt 23:37–39). This prophecy was clearly fulfilled in the AD 70 destruction of the city by the Romans, as evidenced by the massive destruction of much of the Temple Mount.[59] In the area of the southern stairs, this destruction included everything above the "master course" of stones that are located directly above the stairs and the upper stepped street. Finally, in referencing his entry as king a few days prior, Jesus accused the scribes and Pharisees of stoning "those who were sent to" Jerusalem and stated that they would not see him again until they said, "blessed is he who comes in the name of the Lord" (Matt 23:38). This is a clear repetition of the quotations of Psalm 118:26 in the tri-

---

56. Magness, *Stone and Dung, Oil and Spit*, 54–76; Y. Adler, "Religion, Judaism: Purity in the Roman Period," in *The Oxford Encyclopedia of the Bible and Archaeology*, ed. Daniel M. Master (Oxford: Oxford University Press, 2013), 240–49.

57. R. Reich, G. Avni, and T. Winter, *The Jerusalem Archaeological Park* (Jerusalem: Israel Antiquities Authority, 1999), 41. Another example of this type of ritual bath was found near Wilson's Arch in the "Western Wall Tunnels" in an area excavated near the Herodian Street.

58. Ritmeyer, *The Quest*, 80–86.

59. Above the Herodian street near Robinson's Arch, a Hebrew graffiti inscription was found that seems to be a variant of Isaiah 66:14 that reads as follows, "you shall see, and your heart shall rejoice; your bones shall flourish like the grass." Some scholars have suggested that it was written during the reign of Julian the Apostate (362–363 AD) when Jews were given the order to restore the temple. Todd Bolen, *Pictorial Library of Bible Lands* (Grand Rapids: Kregel, 2004), "Southern Temple Mount Excavations."

umphal entry and demonstrates that the true coming "day that the Lord had made" could only occur when the king "did not die, but lived" (Ps 118:17).

CONCLUSION

In this paper, we have examined the archaeology and the geography of the area of the Jerusalem Archaeological Park, which coincides with the central valley and a portion of the eastern hill of Jerusalem. I have attempted to demonstrate the importance of this area throughout Jerusalem's history, but specifically during the time of Jesus. During the Early Roman period, this area served vast amounts of Jewish pilgrims from Jerusalem, Judea, Galilee, and the diaspora, who worshiped in the Herodian Temple. Many of the details related to the massive structures in and around the Temple Mount that we have discussed provide crucial background information for understanding Jerusalem as it appeared during the Gospel era.

BIBLIOGRAPHY

Adler, Y. "Religion, Judaism: Purity in the Roman Period." Pages 240–49 in *The Oxford Encyclopedia of the Bible and Archaeology*. Edited by Daniel M. Master. Oxford: Oxford University Press, 2013.

———. "The Ritual Baths Near the Temple Mount and Extra-Purification Before Entering the Temple Courts: A Reply to Eyal Regev." *IEJ* 56.2 (2006): 209–15. http://www.jstor.org/stable/27927145.

"A Public Water Reservoir Dating to the First Temple Period Has Been Exposed for the First Time next to the Western Wall." IAA Press Release, September 2012.

Bahat, Dan. *Carta's Historical Atlas of Jerusalem*. Jerusalem: Carta, 2015.

Bailey, L. R. "Gehenna: The Topography of Hell." *BA* 49.3 (1986): 187–91.

Bar-Oz, G., R. Bouchnik, E. Weiss, L. Weissbrod, D. E. Bar-Yosef Mayer, and R. Reich. "'Holy Garbage': A Quantitative Study of the City-Dump of Early Roman Jerusalem." *Levant* 39.1 (2007): 1–12. doi:10.1179/lev.2007.39.1.1.

Beale, G. K., and D. A. Carson, eds. *Commentary on the New Testament Use of the Old Testament*. Grand Rapids: Baker Books, 2007.

Beitzel, Barry J. *The New Moody Atlas of the Bible*. Chicago: Moody, 2009.

Bolen, Todd. *Pictorial Library of Bible Lands*. Grand Rapids: Kregel, 2004. Digital ed.

Danby, Herbert. *The Mishnah: Translated from the Hebrew with Introduction and Brief Explanatory Notes*. Oxford: Oxford University Press, 1933.

Demsky, Aaron. "The Trumpeter's Inscription from The Temple Mount." *Eretz Israel* 18 (1985): 40–42.

Gadot, Yuval. "Preliminary Report on the Excavations at Jerusalem's Southeastern Hill, Area D3." *Hebrew Bible and Ancient Israel* 3.2 (2014): 279–92. doi:10.1628/2192227 14X14067042117656.

Gadot, Yuval, and Yonatan Adler. "A Quantitative Analysis of Jewish Chalk Vessel Frequencies in Early Roman Jerusalem: A View from the City's Garbage Dump." *IEJ* 66.2 (2016): 202–19.

Hagbi, M., and J. Uziel. "Jerusalem, The Old City, The Western Wall Foundations." *Hadashot Arkheologiot* 127 (2015). http://www.hadashot-esi.org.il/report_detail_eng.aspx?id=15729&mag_id=122.

Hasson, N. "Underground Jerusalem: An Interactive Journey." *Haaretz,* May 24, 2016. http://www.haaretz.com/st/c/prod/eng/2016/05/jeruz/01/.

Josephus. *Josephus Carta's Illustrated the Jewish War.* Edited by R. Steven Notley. Jerusalem: Carta, 2016.

———. *The Works of Josephus: Complete and Unabridged, New Updated Edition.* Translated by William Whiston. Updated edition. Peabody, MA: Hendrickson, 1987.

Kinman, B. *Jesus' Entry Into Jerusalem: In the Context of Lukan Theology and the Politics of His Days.* Leiden: Brill, 1995.

Lawrence, J. D. *Washing in Water: Trajectories of Ritual Bathing in the Hebrew Bible and Second Temple Literature.* Atlanta: Society of Biblical Literature, 2006.

Magness, Jodi. *Stone and Dung, Oil and Spit: Jewish Daily Life in the Time of Jesus.* Grand Rapids: Eerdmans, 2011.

Mazar, Benjamin. "Herodian Jerusalem in the Light of the Excavations South and South-West of the Temple Mount." *IEJ* 28.4 (1978): 230–37. http://www.jstor.org/stable/27925680.

Mazar, Eilat, ed. *The Ophel Excavations to the South of the Temple Mount.* Final Reports Volume 1. Jerusalem: Shoham and Old City Press, 2015.

———. *The Temple Mount Excavations in Jerusalem 1968–1978 Directed by Benjamin Mazar, Final Reports Vol. III: The Byzantine Period.* Qedem 46. Jerusalem: Hebrew University, 2007.

———. *The Temple Mount Excavations in Jerusalem 1968–1978 Directed by Benjamin Mazar Final Reports Vol. II: The Byzantine and Early Islamic Periods.* Qedem 43. Jerusalem: Hebrew University, 2003.

———. *The Temple Mount Excavations in Jerusalem 1968–1978 Directed by Benjamin Mazar, Final Reports Volume IV: The Tenth Legion in Aelia Capitolina.* Qedem 52. Jerusalem: Hebrew University, 2011.

Mazar, Eilat. *The Complete Guide to the Temple Mount Excavations.* Jerusalem: Shoham – Academic Research & Publication, 2002.

Mazar, Eilat, and Benjamin Mazar. *Excavations in the South of the Temple Mount: The Ophel of Biblical Jerusalem.* Qedem 29. Jerusalem: Hebrew University, 1989.

McRay, J. *Archaeology and the New Testament.* 2nd ed. Grand Rapids: Baker Academic, 2008.

Notley, R. Steven. *Jerusalem: City of the Great King.* Jerusalem: Carta, 2016.

Ory, J. "An Inscription Newly Found in the Synagogue of Kerazeh." *PEQ* 59.1 (1927): 51–52. doi:10.1179/peq.1927.59.1.51.

Patrich, J. "Herod's Theatre in Jerusalem: A New Proposal." *IEJ* 52.2 (2002): 231–39. http://www.jstor.org/stable/27927010.

Rainey, Anson F., and R. Steven Notley. *The Sacred Bridge.* Jerusalem: Carta, 2006.

Regev, E. "The Ritual Baths Near the Temple Mount and Extra-Purification Before Entering the Temple Courts." *IEJ* 55.2 (2005): 194–204. http://www.jstor.org/stable/27927107.

Reich, R. "Miqwa'ot (Jewish Ritual Baths) in Eretz-Israel, in the Second Temple, Mishnah and Talmud Periods." PhD diss., Hebrew University, 1990. Hebrew.

Reich, R., G. Avni, and T. Winter. *The Jerusalem Archaeological Park.*

Jerusalem: Israel Antiquities
Authority, 1999.

Reich, R., and Y. Billig. "A Group of
Theatre Seats Discovered near
the South-Western Corner of the
Temple Mount." *IEJ* 50.3/4 (2000):
175–84. http://www.jstor.org/
stable/27926936.

Reich, R., and E. Shukron. "Excavations
Next to Robinson's Arch 2011 – from
the Level of the Paved Street to
Bedrock." Pages 219–38 in vol. 17 of
New Studies on Jerusalem. Edited by
E. Baruch, A. Levy-Reifer, and A.
Faust. Ramat Gan: Ingeborg Rennert
Center for Jerusalem Studies, 2012.

———. "The Jerusalem City-Dump in
the Late Second Temple Period."
*Zeitschrift Des Deutschen Palästina-
Vereins* 119 (2003): 12–18. http://www.
jstor.org/stable/27931709.

Reich, R., E. Shukron, and O. Lernau.
"Recent Discoveries in the City of
David, Jerusalem." *IEJ* 57.2 (2007):
153–69. http://www.jstor.org/
stable/27927171.

Ritmeyer, Leen. *The Quest: Revealing
the Temple Mount in Jerusalem*.
Jerusalem: Carta, 2006.

Ritmeyer, Leen, and Kathleen Ritmeyer.
Jerusalem: The Temple Mount.
Jerusalem: Carta, 2015.

Robinson, Edward, and Eli Smith.
*Biblical Researches in Palestine and the
Adjacent Regions: A Journal of Travels
in the Years 1838 & 1852*. 3rd ed. 3 vols.
London: John Murray, 1867.

Rozenberg, S., ed. *Herod the Great: The
King's Final Journey*. Jerusalem: Israel
Museum, 2013.

Schlegel, W. *Satellite Bible Atlas:
Historical Geography of the Bible*.
Santa Clarita, CA: Master's College,
2013.

Shukron, E., and R. Reich. "Jerusalem,
Robinson's Arch." *Hadashot
Arkheologiot* 123 (2011). http://www.
hadashot-esi.org.il/report_detail_
eng.aspx?id=1884&mag_id=118.

Vermes, Geza. "Pre-Mishnaic Jewish
Worship and the Phylacteries
From the Dead Sea." *Vetus
Testamentum* 9.1 (1959): 65–72.
doi:10.1163/156853359X00078.

Warren, Charles. *Underground Jerusalem:
An Account of Some of the Principal
Difficulties Encountered in Its
Exploration and the Results Obtained.
With a Narrative of an Expedition
Through the Jordan Valley and a Visit
to the Samaritans*. London: R. Bentley
and Son, 1876.

Watson, C. M. "The Site of the Temple."
*Palestine Exploration Fund Quarterly
Statement* 28.1 (1896): 47–60.
doi:10.1179/peq.1896.28.1.47.

Watson, Duane. "Gehenna." *ABD*
2:926–28.

CHAPTER 44

MAGNIFICENT STONES AND WONDERFUL BUILDINGS OF THE TEMPLE COMPLEX

Matt 24:1-2; Mark 13:1-2; Luke 21:5-6

Todd Bolen

KEY POINTS

- The construction of the Temple Mount is a modern marvel to both the common observer and civil engineer.

- Among the 36 acres (14.6 hectares) of architecture that comprise the Temple Mount are massive limestone ashlars, carefully carved and stacked.

- Multiple gates allowed access to the Temple Mount but along the southern wall were two sets of gates at the top of a huge stairway that had the most foot traffic and likely was the location where Jesus taught on multiple occasions.

- Aside from the temple itself, the Royal Stoa was the largest and most ornate structure on top of the Temple Mount, complete with 162 columns that were 47 feet (14.3 m) tall and roughly 4.8 feet (1.5 m) in diameter.

- With such a recent and marvelously built temple, it was no doubt hard for the disciples to imagine that it would be destroyed as Jesus proclaimed in the Olivet Discourse.

The glory of Herod's temple complex amazed Jesus' disciples. For several days they had been with their master as he taught in the temple courts and overturned the tables of the moneychangers. Now, as Jesus departed for the last time, they called his attention to the buildings (Matt 24:1). Luke observes that some of the disciples were discussing "how the temple was adorned with beautiful stones and with gifts dedicated to God" (Luke 21:5). Mark records the very words of one: "Look, Teacher! What massive stones! What magnificent buildings!" (Mark 13:1). In all of the ancient world, everyone appears to have agreed with the disciples' assessment. Today, visitors to Jerusalem's Temple Mount are no less impressed with the visible remains. Jesus, however, knew that as great as these structures were, their destruction was certain. Such a possibility, even while construction on the temple complex was ongoing (John 2:20), must have boggled their minds. The temple was not only the chosen dwelling place for the true God, but the Temple Mount constituted one of the greatest feats of human engineering and construction ever known to man.

Even Herod's enemies could not restrain their praise for the temple buildings. The rabbis declared that whoever had not seen Herod's building "has never seen a beautiful building in his life" (b. Bava Batra 4a). The Talmud remembers the Jewish teachers who observed that "it is very beautiful to behold, for it is like the waves of the sea" (b. Sukkah 51b). When Roman historians mentioned Jerusalem, their praise went first to the temple. Tacitus (AD 56–ca. 120) spoke of the "temple of immense wealth" (Hist. 5.8), and Pliny the Elder (AD 23–79) considered Jerusalem to be "by far the most famous city, not of Judea only, but of the East," no doubt because of the presence of Herod's Temple (Natural History 5.15.70). Philo (ca. 15 BC–ca. AD 50) reports

on the visit of Marcus Agrippa, son-in-law of Emperor Augustus, who was so "delighted with the spectacle of the building" that "he could talk of nothing else to his companions but the magnificence of the temple and everything connected with it" (Embassy 294–96).

Scholars who study the Temple Mount today confirm the words of the ancient historians. Ehud Netzer, an archaeologist who excavated at most of Herod's building projects in Israel, considers the temple to be "one of Herod's greatest building feats."[1] Steven Notley observes that the Herod's temenos (sacred precinct) was the largest known in the world at that time.[2] The Jerusalem temple was "far larger and even more magnificent" than the temple of Artemis in Ephesus, one of the seven wonders of the ancient world.[3] What Herod accomplished was more than an engineering masterpiece: he "brilliantly used every architectural device to create a heightened feeling of religious community and invest the worshippers' religious experience with a sense of grandeur and focused intensity."[4]

THE WALLS OF THE TEMPLE MOUNT

The sense of awe began before the visitor even ascended one of the monumental staircases onto the temple courts. The podium that Herod constructed around the ancient Mount Moriah doubled the

---

1. Ehud Netzer, The Architecture of Herod, the Great Builder (Tübingen: Mohr Siebeck, 2006), 137.

2. R. Steven Notley, Jerusalem: City of the Great King (Jerusalem: Carta Jerusalem, 2015), 79.

3. Craig S. Keener, The IVP Bible Background Commentary: New Testament, 2nd ed. (Downers Grove, IL: IVP Academic, 2014), 106. Keener suggests that the Jerusalem temple could have qualified as one of the seven wonders except for anti-Jewish prejudice (162).

4. Simon Goldhill, The Temple of Jerusalem, Wonders of the World (Cambridge, MA: Harvard University Press, 2005), 61.

Herod's "Second" Temple

size of the temple courts and required all-new construction on three sides of the mountain. The western wall—which includes the famous place of prayer today—was 1,574 feet (492 m) long, more than the length of five football fields.[5] The northern wall measures 1,005 feet (314 m) and the southern 902 feet (282 m). Because of the steep drop-off into the Kidron Valley, Herod preserved the position of the eastern wall and extended it to the north and south for a total of 1,504 feet (470 m). In sum, the four walls stretched 4,985 feet (1,558 m), nearly a mile in length and encompassed an area of 36 acres (14.6 hectares), more than 25 football fields. Herod's podium was thus twice the size of Trajan's later forum in Rome and triple the size of the temples of Jupiter and Astarte-Venus in Baalbek.[6]

All of this construction was more challenging because of the topography. In order to expand the complex, Herod's design required filling a fosse north of the temple and spanning part of the Central Valley to the west and the Kidron Valley to the south.[7] This required an immense amount of fill dirt that probably served the builders working from the inside[8] as well as providing the foundation for

---

5. The dimensions for the retaining walls come from Peretz Reuven, "A Comparison of the Temple Mount Compound with Other Sacred Precincts from the Classical Period," in *The Walls of the Temple Mount*, ed. Eilat Mazar (Jerusalem: Shoham Academic Research and Publication, 2011), 289.

6. Carol Meyers, "Temple, Jerusalem," *ABD* 6:365.

7. Daniel M. Gurtner and Nicholas Perrin, "Temple," *DJG* 940.

8. Leen Ritmeyer, *The Quest: Revealing the Temple Mount in Jerusalem* (Jerusalem: Carta, 2006), 136.

The Golden Gate

streets and shops built along the exterior of the wall.[9]

The height of the walls varied, because they were laid on bedrock that decreased in elevation to the south. The highest point of the southern retaining wall was 130 feet (40 m), and the highest point on the eastern wall was 160 feet (48 m) above bedrock.[10] The walls were 15 feet wide.[11]

All the walls were constructed with local Jerusalem limestone.[12] Herod's engineers knew the different types of limestone and utilized them strategically. The hardest type of stone is *mizzi yahudi*, and because it was difficult to quarry, its use was reserved for places like thresholds and door sockets.[13] *Mizzi hilu* is a softer stone that was ideal for use in decorative elements. The most common stone

9. Dan Bahat, "The Second Temple in Jerusalem," in *Jesus and Temple: Textual and Archaeological Explorations*, ed. James H. Charlesworth (Minneapolis: Fortress Press, 2014), 69.

10. Ritmeyer, *The Quest*, 136. At the southeastern corner today, 148 feet are still standing (Notley, *Jerusalem*, 79).

11. Leen Ritmeyer, "Imagining the Temple Known to Jesus and to Early Jews," in *Jesus and Temple: Textual and Archaeological Explorations*, ed. James H. Charlesworth (Minneapolis: Fortress Press, 2014), 36.

12. Both Josephus and the Talmud claim that the temple was built with marble (*War* 5.190; b. Sukkah 51b), but as no traces of marble have been found in any of Herod's construction works (with the exception of some flooring materials used late in his reign), this cannot be true. References to marble must be understood either as white limestone, white plaster, or stuccowork (Netzer, *Architecture*, 310).

13. Ritmeyer, *The Quest*, 133.

Large Stones from the Western Wall

in use in the walls was *meleke*, a suitable material because it is softer when underground but then hardens when exposed to the air. Josephus says that a thousand wagons and ten thousand skilled workmen were employed in the project, many no doubt involved in extracting and transporting the stones from the quarries to the site (*Ant.* 15.390).

How Herod moved the stones into their precise location is a marvel for civil engineers even today. Max Schwartz has written a book to try to explain how they did it, and he notes that "even with modern computers and technology, it would take great expertise to carve and fit these stone blocks so accurately."[14] Of the largest stones, Netzer writes, "I wonder if any reasonable explanation can be given for this phenomenon, as well as how such stones were quarried and transported."[15]

THE MASSIVE STONES OF THE TEMPLE MOUNT

While we may not understand it, we can hardly deny that Herod's engineers were capable of placing in perfect alignment the smallest stones that weighed several tons, the larger stones placed at the corners that weighed up to 100 short tons, as well as the most enormous stones that were part of the Master Course. The placement was precise indeed, and study today reveals that the courses were intentionally offset by about 1 inch (2.5 cm) as the wall ascended, apparently to counter the optical effect that the wall was toppling over the viewer below.[16] Similar

---

14. Max Schwartz, *The Biblical Engineer: How the Temple in Jerusalem Was Built* (Hoboken, NJ: Ktav, 2002), xvii.

15. Netzer, *Architecture*, 162.

16. Dan Bahat, "The Western Wall Tunnels," in *Ancient Jerusalem Revealed*, ed. Hillel Geva (Jerusalem: Israel Exploration Society, 1994), 183.

Master Course along the Southern Wall

precision is present in the southern wall where the courses "were laid at an incline of half a degree toward the center of the wall" in order to overcome optical distortion.[17] Eilat Mazar affirms that "the builders of the wall utilized astoundingly deft planning in erecting this uniform structural unit."[18]

In some cases, the average bystander would not be aware of the engineering skills required to create the effects of the massive walls, but in other cases, they are hard to miss. The "Master Course" constitutes the most impressive of all of the "massive stones" in the wall. At the top of the monumental staircase in front of the Double Gate, a series of stones measuring up to 6.4 feet (2.0 m) high runs to the southeastern corner.[19] These stones are one and a half times the height of the standard courses (3.2–3.8 feet; 1.0–1.2 m), and measure up to 21 feet (6.6 m) long. While these stones were at eye-level for all those entering through the most popular gates of the Temple Mount, the Master Course was intended not only to impress but to provide a leveling effect between the western and eastern sides of

17. Eilat Mazar, *The Walls of the Temple Mount* (Jerusalem: Shoham Academic Research and Publication, 2011), 16.

18. Mazar, *Walls*, 16.

19. Mazar believes, but could not confirm, that the Master Course continues a bit to the west of the Double Gate as well. These stones differ in height because of variance in the height of the bedrock and courses below (Mazar, *Walls*, 17, 202, 222).

Largest Stone in the Temple Mount

the southern wall where the bedrock of Mount Moriah had separated the lowest courses.[20]

The longest stone in the Temple Mount has long been admired by visitors who did not realize what they were seeing. For more than a century, visitors and archaeologists gazing upon Robinson's Arch have been unaware that its second course is a single stone.[21] This 45.6 foot (14.27 m) stone is even longer than the massive monolith near Warren's Gate that measures 43.4 feet (13.55 m). The latter stone is far larger, however, for it is 10.2 feet (3.2 m) tall, an estimated 13.4–15.7 feet (4.2–4.9 m) deep, and weighs up to 570 short tons.[22] Another stone nearby is as tall and almost as long, measuring 38.7 feet (12.1 m) long. Located next to Warren's Gate, this course surely drew the eye of all who passed through.[23]

THE BEAUTIFUL DESIGN OF THE TEMPLE MOUNT

It was not size alone that left the ancient peoples astonished, but the beautiful

20. Mazar, *Walls*, 222–23.

21. Mazar, *Walls*, 16–17.

22. The depth estimate comes from ground-penetrating radar tests reported in Bahat, "The Western Wall Tunnels," 180. The other figures are from Mazar, *Walls*, 90.

23. Bahat suggests that the purpose of the Western Master Course was to strengthen the wall where it was opposite a large interior vault structure that supported the Temple Mount platform above (Bahat, "The Western Wall Tunnels," 181).

Margins and Bosses on the Temple Mount Walls

design of the stones as well. Because of Herod's commitment to dry masonry, the massive stones were held together purely by their weight and precise cut. Even today, visitors are unable to wedge a razor blade between two courses—so tightly do they fit together. The visible sides of the stones were finely chiseled with margins on all four sides to surround a central protruding boss. The upper margin was slightly wider than the others "in order to achieve a more regular optical effect when viewed from below."[24] The high quality craftsmanship of Herod's workers can be compared today with the earlier Hasmonean construction at the "seam" on the eastern wall. The play of light and shadow, especially in the early morning and late afternoon hours, must have been particularly pleasing.[25]

The upper courses of the Temple Mount were adorned with pilasters, or engaged columns. This is not easy to visualize today because no pilasters remain in place.[26] Their presence must have contributed immensely to the beauty of the walls, as can be seen from smaller, contemporary examples preserved at the

24. Andreas J. M. Kropp and Daniel Lohmann, "'Master, Look at the Size of Those Stones! Look at the Size of Those Buildings': Analogies in Construction Techniques Between the Temples at Hierapolis (Baalbek) and Jerusalem," *Levant* 43.1 (2011): 45.

25. Hershel Shanks, *Jerusalem's Temple Mount: From Solomon to the Golden Dome* (New York: Continuum, 2007), 72–73.

26. One pilaster has been preserved, but it is not accessible today. Conder discovered this pilaster in 1873, but even Mazar in her recent survey was unable to view or study this section (Mazar, *Walls*, 113–18).

Machpelah in Hebron and the nearby Mamre.[27]

THE ENTRANCES TO THE TEMPLE MOUNT

Visitors to the temple entered through one of at least seven gates. Josephus mentions four on the western wall, all of which have been identified today and are named after modern explorers. The northernmost one, Warren's Gate, as well as the third, Barclay's Gate, opened into subterranean passageways that led up to the temple courts. The second gate is no longer preserved but passed over Wilson's Arch, providing direct access from the upper city both for people and for an aqueduct. The southernmost gate was entered via a monumental staircase 49 feet (15.3 m) wide that was supported by Robinson's Arch and rose from the valley street below. One gate, the Tadi Gate, was located on the northern wall, but it apparently was little used. There was also one gate on the eastern side, but the presence of a Muslim cemetery along this wall today prevents more than speculation about the location and design of the Susa Gate.[28]

Most pilgrims entered the temple complex from the south, the traditional route since the time that David inhabited the hill below. A massive 208 foot (65 m) wide staircase led up to the Double Gate, and a narrower staircase provided access to the Triple Gate. Most of the western

Double Gate Lintel and Relieving Arch

staircase is preserved today, and a unique short-step, long-step pattern may have encouraged a reverential approach to the holy site. At the top of the 30 steps, a 21 foot (6.4 m) wide street was built with enormous paving stones, one of which is 16.7 feet (5.1 m) long and 7.9 feet (2.4 m) wide.[29] Crossing over this street, the worshiper entered into the Double Gate, nearly all of which stands today, though it is inaccessible to non-Muslims.[30] Photographs and drawings inside the Double Gate reveal four beautifully decorated domes supported by Herodian columns. The domes are each 15 feet (4.7 m) in diameter and are carved with floral and geometric designs, with strict adherence to the prohibition against depicting images of people or animals.[31] The primary floral design is a grapevine, recalling the golden vine that decorated

---

27. Netzer, *Architecture*, 163.

28. Bahat argues that because the Mishnah reserved this gate for taking out the red heifer, it was never used by Jesus or any other pilgrims ("The Second Temple in Jerusalem," 69). This proposal may be supported by the fact that Josephus never mentions this gate but speaks only of the western and southern gates.

29. Ritmeyer, *The Quest*, 66.

30. The function of the Triple Gate is unclear, but some believe that it was used only by priests (Ritmeyer, *The Quest*, 87–88).

31. Shanks, *Jerusalem's Temple Mount*, 82.

Reconstruction of the Royal Stoa

the temple.[32] These decorations are the closest we have to what must once have adorned the temple itself.[33]

THE BUILDINGS ON THE TEMPLE MOUNT

Continuing from the Double Gate, one passed through a tunnel upwards to the level of the temple courts. The visitor emerged from the passageway in the shadow of the Royal Stoa, a massive basilica on the southern side of the Temple Mount that Josephus termed as "more noteworthy than any other [structure] under the sun" (*Ant.* 15.412). While Herod chose to surround the other three sides with double colonnades, the southern colonnade consisted of four rows of Corinthian columns reaching 47 feet high with a central aisle that was double that height.[34] To judge from Josephus' observation that only three men with arms outstretched could encircle a column, it is estimated that each of the 162 columns was about 4.8 feet (1.5 m) in diameter (*Ant.* 15.413). While nothing remains today of the Royal Stoa, a study of hundreds of fragments found in the excavations near the Double Gate has identified pieces of column bases, column drums, capitals, cornices, ceiling decorations, and doorframes.[35] Peleg-Barkat has summarized

---

32. Josephus, *War* 5.210; *Ant.* 5.395; m. Middot 3:8.

33. Ritmeyer notes that some believe that this was the Beautiful Gate, given its lavish decoration and its function as the primary entrance onto the Temple Mount (Ritmeyer, "Imagining the Temple," 41).

34. These dimensions follow Netzer, who deems Josephus's height of 27 feet inaccurate (*Architecture*, 167).

35. Aryeh Shimron and Orit Peleg-Barkat, "New Evidence of the Royal Stoa and Roman Flames," *BAR* 36.2 (2010): 56–62.

the craftsmanship as "fine and delicate," providing "an enormous variety of floral and geometrical motifs."[36] Netzer, whose life was devoted to investigating all of the Herod's archaeological remains, believes that the Royal Stoa "was probably the most magnificent secular building ever erected by Herod."[37]

Less is known about the other buildings on the Temple Mount itself because the Roman destruction was apparently so thorough, and the Muslim presence today precludes archaeological work. Thus from this point on, we are entirely dependent upon written sources, especially the tractate on measurements ("Middot") in the Mishnah. The Court of the Gentiles was the outermost court, and though it may be supposed that this was the place of Jesus' earlier overturning of the tables, little can be said about its ancient features.[38] Gentiles were barred from passing beyond the partition wall which had engraved notices warning trespassers of death.[39] Beyond this, the Court of the Women was open to all Jews in a state of ritual purity. Separate chambers were provided for Nazirites completing their vows and cleansed lepers seeking purification, and there were storage areas for wood, oil, and wine to be used in temple ceremonies. A staircase with 15 steps led up to the Nicanor Gate which separated the Court of the Women from the Court of the Israelites and was renowned for its beauty. With a large central opening and two side gates, the enormous doors were about 35 feet (10.9 m) high and made of Corinthian bronze, which Josephus declared superior to those covered only with silver and gold (War 5.201).[40]

THE TEMPLE BUILDING

Behind the altar rose the temple building itself. All sources agree that the porch was 100 cubits (172 feet; 53.8 m) high (War 5.207; m. Middot 4:6), the equivalent of an 18-story building today and one that would dwarf the present Dome of the Rock.[41] Josephus describes the powerful effect that the temple façade had upon visitors, particularly at sunrise when its golden plates "reflected back a very fiery splendor, and made those who forced themselves to look upon it to turn their eyes away, just as they would have done at the sun's own rays. But this temple appeared to strangers, when they were at a distance, like a mountain covered with snow; for, as to those parts of it that were not gilt, they were exceeding white" (War 5.222–23). The top was crowned with golden spikes to prevent birds from polluting the temple. The largest stones of

---

36. Shimron and Peleg-Barkat, "New Evidence of the Royal Stoa and Roman Flames," 58.

37. Netzer, Architecture, 170.

38. Jesus' quotation of Isaiah that the temple should be a house of prayer "for all nations" suggests that the merchandising activity had overspilled the bounds of the Royal Stoa and was interfering with the area provided for Gentiles to worship the Lord (Mark 11:17).

39. One complete copy of this inscription was discovered in 1871 north of the Temple Mount and is now on display in the Istanbul Archaeological Museum. A fragmentary copy was discovered in 1935 near St. Stephen's Gate and is exhibited at the Israel Museum. Shanks, Jerusalem's Temple Mount, 68; P. Kyle McCarter, Jr., Ancient Inscriptions: Voices from the Biblical World (Washington, DC: Biblical Archaeology Society, 1996), 129–30.

40. Ritmeyer, The Quest, 356.

41. Ritmeyer, "Imagining the Temple," 55; Netzer, Architecture, 143.

Herod's Temple

the temple, according to Josephus, were 76 feet (23.8 m) long, 8.5 feet (2.7 m) high, and 10.2 feet (3.2 m) deep (*War* 5.224). While these dimensions may be exaggerated,[42] there can be no doubt that the temple was of surpassing beauty.

JESUS' RESPONSE

All of this, however, did not impress Jesus. These magnificent buildings were nothing more than the glory of man to him, soon to pass away like the flowers of the field (Isa 40:6-8). Had Jesus spoken of the destruction of any other building, it would not have carried the shock of his pronouncement of judgment upon one of the most physically outstanding structures in the world. The failure, of course, was not in the buildings themselves, nor even particularly in their builder. The

destruction of the temple was explained by Jesus only moments before, when he condemned the Jewish leaders for undermining the law, misleading the nation, and murdering the prophets (Matt 23:1-39). The "house is left to you desolate" because the nation had violated their covenant with God and was soon to crucify the Messiah that God sent (Matt 23:38; compare 21:33-22:14).

Matthew and Mark both explicitly note Jesus' departure from the temple, likely an echo of the Lord's departure from the first temple shortly before its destruction (Matt 24:1; Mark 13:1; Ezek 10:18). These marvelous buildings would not protect the nation from God's judgment any more than Solomon's Temple protected Israel in the days of Jeremiah (Jer 7:3-15). The Lord would not tolerate

---

42. When archaeologists are able to compare Josephus's dimensions with discovered remains, they often find that he is inaccurate (see Ritmeyer, "Imagining the Temple," 31). In this case, Josephus contradicts himself, giving significantly reduced numbers in *Ant.* 15.392.

his people using his house as a shield so they could persist in their wicked ways. Jesus certainly knew this from the prayer of Solomon (1 Kgs 8:46) and the principle established in Jeremiah, but he also knew Daniel's prophecy that spoke of the destruction of this temple (Dan 9:24–27). That this was foremost in his mind is likely given the following discourse from the Mount of Olives in which Jesus answered his disciples' questions by expositing Daniel 9:24–27 (see Matt 24:4–24). Once the Messiah was cut off, "the people of the ruler who will come will destroy the city and the sanctuary" (Dan 9:26). This the disciples had failed to grasp, believing along with many in their nation that the temple was too new, too beautiful, and too marvelous to fall. But though the effort required the full power of the Roman legions in the year AD 70, the temple was destroyed, such that not one stone was left upon another.[43]

BIBLIOGRAPHY

Bahat, Dan. "The Second Temple in Jerusalem." Pages 59–74 in *Jesus and Temple: Textual and Archaeological Explorations*. Edited by James H. Charlesworth. Minneapolis: Fortress Press, 2014.

———. "The Western Wall Tunnels." Pages 177–90 in *Ancient Jerusalem Revealed*. Edited by Hillel Geva. Jerusalem: Israel Exploration Society, 1994.

Goldhill, Simon. *The Temple of Jerusalem*. Wonders of the World. Cambridge, MA: Harvard University Press, 2005.

Gurtner, Daniel M., and Nicholas Perrin. "Temple." *DJG* 939–47.

Keener, Craig S. *The IVP Bible Background Commentary: New Testament*. 2nd ed. Downers Grove, IL: IVP Academic, 2014.

Kropp, Andreas J. M., and Daniel Lohmann. "'Master, Look at the Size of Those Stones! Look at the Size of Those Buildings': Analogies in Construction Techniques Between the Temples at Hierapolis (Baalbek) and Jerusalem." *Levant* 43.1 (2011): 38–50.

Mazar, Eilat. *The Walls of the Temple Mount*. Jerusalem: Shoham Academic Research and Publication, 2011.

McCarter, P. Kyle, Jr. *Ancient Inscriptions: Voices from the Biblical World*. Washington, DC: Biblical Archaeology Society, 1996.

Meyers, Carol. "Temple, Jerusalem." *ABD* 6:350–69.

Netzer, Ehud. *The Architecture of Herod, the Great Builder*. Tübingen: Mohr Siebeck, 2006.

Notley, R. Steven. *Jerusalem: City of the Great King*. Jerusalem: Carta Jerusalem, 2015.

Reuven, Peretz. "A Comparison of the Temple Mount Compound with Other Sacred Precincts from the Classical Period." Pages 289–91 in *The Walls of the Temple Mount*. Edited by Eilat Mazar. Jerusalem: Shoham Academic Research and Publication, 2011.

Ritmeyer, Leen. "Imagining the Temple Known to Jesus and to

---

43. Jesus' prophecy seems directed to the temple building and not the broader temple complex. If the latter is taken as his reference, one must assume either that his statement was figurative, referring to the defiling and abandonment of the entire complex, or that a future destruction was in view.

Early Jews." Pages 19-57 in *Jesus and Temple: Textual and Archaeological Explorations*. Edited by James H. Charlesworth. Minneapolis: Fortress Press, 2014.

Ritmeyer, Leen. *The Quest: Revealing the Temple Mount in Jerusalem*. Jerusalem: Carta, 2006.

Schwartz, Max. *The Biblical Engineer: How the Temple in Jerusalem Was Built*. Hoboken, NJ: Ktav, 2002.

Shanks, Hershel. *Jerusalem's Temple Mount: From Solomon to the Golden Dome*. New York: Continuum, 2007.

Shimron, Aryeh, and Orit Peleg-Barkat. "New Evidence of the Royal Stoa and Roman Flames." *BAR* 36.2 (2010): 56–62.

CHAPTER 45

IN THE GARDEN OF GETHSEMANE
JESUS' CHOICE TO REMAIN OR RUN
FROM HIS FATHER'S WILL

Matt 26:36–46; Mark 14:32–42; Luke 22:39–46

Aubrey L. Taylor

KEY POINTS

- The Garden of Gethsemane is located somewhere on the Mount of Olives, east of Jerusalem and across the Kidron Valley (the exact location remains unknown).

- Jesus frequented the garden, often as a retreat from the bustling city, especially during Jewish festivals when pilgrims would flood the city and temple.

- The Mount of Olives is situated along the main road connecting Jerusalem and Jericho, with the Judean Wilderness between.

- This route was often used by God's people for pilgrimage purposes or even to escape from enemies by fleeing deep into the wilderness.

- When Jesus retired to the garden the night of his arrest, he had two options: recommit himself to his Father's will, or escape his accusers by fleeing over the ridge and into the wilderness.

Jesus' prayer in the Garden of Gethsemane prior to his arrest presents an archetypal image of the humanity of Christ. Countless devotionals have been written on his agonized request that the "cup" might pass from him, and yet his faithful obedience to the Father's will led him to remain and allow events to unfold. Augmenting these observations with an awareness of the geographical context of this passage allows us to enrich our interpretation, highlighting both the character of Christ and the critical nature of the moment.

Mount of Olives (looking southeast)

IMMEDIATE RELATIONS TO JERUSALEM

The exact location of Gethsemane is unknown. The name appears only in Matt 26:36 and Mark 14:32, though from the context it is undoubtedly on the Mount of Olives (Matt 26:30, Mark 14:26). Several other passages indicate that Jesus had a customary spot on the mountain, likely this same location. From these references, we can infer a general location: along the western slope, facing the city.[1] Today there are several sites in this area that claim to preserve at least a portion of the ancient plot of land.[2]

The name Gethsemane (*Gethsēmani*, Γεθσημανί in Greek) comes from the Hebrew *gat šĕmānê*, meaning oil press.[3] Presses for olive oil were often conveniently located within olive groves so that the harvest could be processed on site. Situated on the Mount of Olives, which takes its name from the olive orchards planted there in antiquity, this association with olive oil production is fitting. From the Gospel of John we receive the additional information that Gethsemane was likely an enclosed garden (John 18:1). In English, the word "garden" tends to conjure up images of flower beds and peaceful pathways. However, in Greek *kēpos* (κῆπος) simply indicates an agricultural space, and we would be better off imagining a cultivated stretch of hillside,

---

1. For example, Mark 13:3; Luke 22:39; John 18:2.

2. The most commonly visited site is the Church of All Nations at the base of the hill. It is run by the Roman Catholic Church and maintains an attractive garden with some very old olive trees. Often touted as the original trees under which Jesus prayed, they date most probably to the 12th century AD. See Mauro Bernabei, "The Age of the Olive Trees in the Garden of Gethsemane," *JAS* 53 (2015): 43–48.

3. BDAG, s.v. "Γεθσημανί."

Olive Trees in the Garden of Gethsemane

with terracing, olive trees, and industrial installations such as oil presses carved into the exposed bedrock, enclosed with a rough stone wall, not unlike Palestinian orchards today.

Overlooking Jerusalem, the Mount of Olives is one of several peaks within a mountain range that rims the city on its eastern side. Standing at 2660 feet (811 m) above sea level—over one hundred feet (thirty m) higher than the hills upon which Jerusalem is built—it provides dramatic views westward down into the city and screens off a view of the wilderness, which begins immediately on its eastern slope. The Kidron Valley, which separates this range from the city of Jerusalem, is nearly seven hundred feet (213 m) lower in elevation, and those entering the city from the east must, upon cresting the summit of the Mount of Olives opposite the Temple Mount, descend into the dry stream bed of the Kidron before ascending on the other side to climb up into the city (See infographic "Ancient Jerusalem" on pg. 528).

REMOTE RELATIONS TO JERICHO AND THE WILDERNESS

In its larger context, the Mount of Olives stands at the crest of the arduous climb up from Jericho, which is located in the Rift Valley. Traversing the Judean Wilderness, this road climbs approximately four thousand feet (1219 m) in elevation over thirteen miles (twenty-one km), tracing treeless ridge tops in the glaring sun and overlooking dramatic canyons. However, this was Jerusalem's only direct corridor to the east, aligning with a significant fording point along the Jordan River and with the Medeba Plateau and King's Highway in Transjordan beyond.[4]

---

4. Paul H. Wright, *Greatness Grace & Glory: Carta's Atlas of Biblical Biography* (Jerusalem: Carta, 2008), 202.

Because of these critical connections, the road from Jericho has played a significant role in the history of Jerusalem and in biblical imagery (see below). Certainly essential for trade traffic in and out of the capital city, it would have also been a necessary part of the administrative network of the nation. However, due to the immediate access it provides out of Jerusalem and into the Judean Wilderness, this road also became the road for escape from Jerusalem in times of crisis.

Once on the eastern side of the Mount of Olives, the wilderness takes over quickly and the harsh environment, plus the innumerable natural hideouts, becomes a deterrent to anyone who would give chase. Exiles, refugees, and rebels were all at times forced to strike out across this wasteland of chalk hills and deep ravines, and those with special survival skills, like shepherds, had a good chance of eluding their pursuers and disappearing into the barren void.

David flees from Absalom along this route, eventually taking up position in Upper Gilead to stage his return to power (2 Sam 15:32). So too, Zedekiah, the last king of Judah, flees from the Babylonian invaders along the Kidron Valley, eastward, finding his way to the plains of Jericho, before being caught (2 Kgs 25:1–7). In a general sense, eastward is the path of those exiled after the Babylonian conquest, and Ezekiel draws upon this to picture the Spirit of God leaving the temple

and hovering above the Mount of Olives, before heading eastward in a corresponding exile. Likewise, he envisions YHWH's return from this same direction.[5] In this, he may have taken inspiration from Isa 40:3–5, in which a road through the wilderness is prepared for YHWH's return, or Zech 14:1–11, which speaks of YHWH's return to Zion from the east, specifically envisioning a climactic moment when YHWH would stand on the Mount of Olives, overlooking the city (see map "Absalom Attempts a Coup, David Flees" on pg. 527).[6]

Jesus himself travels this road many times. As a child he came with his family to Jerusalem for the yearly Passover pilgrimage, and he seems to have continued this practice into adulthood (Luke 2:41). Coming from Galilee, the road through Samaria was the most direct; however, the alternative road through Perea, on the eastern side of the Jordan River, was also commonly used by Jewish pilgrims. On this route, travelers would cross the Jordan across from Jericho before beginning the final ascent to Jerusalem.[7] Jesus' baptism likely occurred at this point along the Jordan, and subsequently, the Gospels record a period of forty days in which he was tempted in the wilderness, presumably the Judean Wilderness between Jericho and Jerusalem.[8][9]

Bethany, the home of Mary, Martha, and Lazarus, lay just east of the crest of the Mount of Olives, overlooking the wil-

5. Ezek 9:3, 10:18–19, 11:22–23, 43:1–5.

6. And this, echoed by John the Baptist (Matt 3:3; Mark 1:2–3; Luke 3:4–6; John 1:23).

7. At times, the road through Samaria was considered dangerous and may have been avoided. See Warren J. Heard, Jr., "Olives, Mount Of," *ABD* 5:14; Josephus, *Ant.* 20.118–24, *War* 2.232–46.

8. See Aubrey L. Taylor, "Wilderness Events: The Baptism and Temptation of Jesus" on pg. 53.

9. Matt 3:13–4:11; Luke 3:21–4:15.

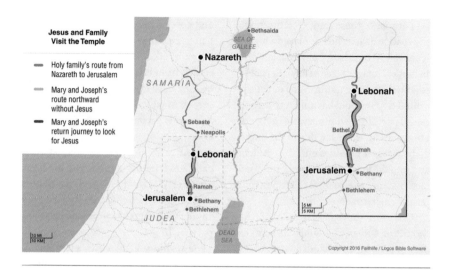

derness. Jesus seems to have stayed with them whenever he visited Jerusalem.[10] Each day he would have entered Jerusalem, less than an hour's walk down the Mount of Olives, to worship and teach in the temple courtyards; and each night he would have returned along the same path to spend the night with his friends. On the Sunday prior to Passover, the Gospels record Jesus' triumphal entry, in which he makes this very journey into Jerusalem.[11] [12] Throughout passion week, Jesus continues to lodge in Bethany; however, on the day of the festival, Jesus sends his disciples to prepare a location within the city for their Passover meal.[13] Following the meal, he and the disciples leave the city and, beginning the walk up the Mount of Olives, turn off the road and into an olive grove along the slope.

JESUS' CHOICE TO RUN AWAY OR REMAIN

As previously noted, Jesus seems to have made a habit of visiting this site. It surely provided beautiful views of the city, as well as refuge from what would have been an overcrowded and chaotic city. During the first century, pilgrimage to Jerusalem was an important aspect of Jewish religious life. During the holiday, the city of Jerusalem would become heavily burdened by the influx of pilgrims, and the religious fervor and excitement, coupled with the press of the crowds, would certainly be enough to drive some-

---

10. Matt 21:17; Mark 11:11-12; Luke 10:38-42; John 11:1-44; 12:1-8. The residents of Jerusalem and the surrounding villages would house pilgrims as an act of hospitality. See Douglas E. Neel and Joel A. Pugh, *The Food and Feasts of Jesus: Inside the World of First-Century Fare, with Menus and Recipes* (Lanham, MD: Rowman & Littlefield, 2012), 144-45.

11. See A. D. Riddle, "The Passover Pilgrimage from Jericho to Jerusalem" on pg. 395.

12. Matt 21:1-11; Mark 11:1-10; Luke 19:28-46.

13. Matt 26:17-19; Mark 14:12-16; Luke 22:7-13.

Bethany

one out to the surrounding hills for a little peace and quiet.[14]

The image of Jesus' prayer here in the garden is one of a man overwrought. Christian tradition has generally interpreted the strong emotion depicted in this passage and Jesus' request that the "cup" pass from him as a reference to Jesus' fears regarding his upcoming torture and execution, revealing a desire to avoid this if at all possible. However, it is also possible to understand the depicted struggle as a time of temptation. His prayer was not a perfunctory one—he had the power to act. In Gethsemane, Jesus was kneeling in prayer alongside the very road his people had always used for escape. Within a few more minutes' walk, he could crest the hill and disappear into the wilderness. Furthermore, he knew how to survive in the wilderness, having spent forty days there during his period of testing at the outset of his ministry. His mind could have easily flown back to that time, remembering the vast expanse of undulating hills and the ease with which he could elude his accusers. However, his previous temptation experience benefited him in a different way. Rather than using his knowledge and skills to escape, he let the former temptations strengthen his resolve. Jesus had surrendered his fears and desires to the Father before. Therefore, unlike those that came before him on the road that led to exile, he chose to remain.

---

14. Based on the available evidence, it is difficult to know how many pilgrims would have attended the festival. A common estimate is between 300,000 and 500,000. Josephus' estimate, at nearly three million, is wildly improbable (*War* 6.422-27; Richard B. Vinson, *Luke* [Macon, GA: Smyth & Helwys, 2008]), 667.

BIBLIOGRAPHY

Bernabei, Mauro. "The Age of the Olive Trees in the Garden of Gethsemane." *JAS* 53 (2015): 43–48.

Heard, Warren J., Jr. "Olives, Mount Of." *ABD* 5:13–15.

Neel, Douglas E., and Joel A. Pugh. *The Food and Feasts of Jesus: Inside the World of First-Century Fare, with Menus and Recipes*. Lanham, MD: Rowman & Littlefield, 2012.

Vinson, Richard B. *Luke*. SHBC. Macon, GA: Smyth & Helwys, 2008.

Wright, Paul H. *Greatness Grace & Glory: Carta's Atlas of Biblical Biography*. Jerusalem: Carta, 2008.

CHAPTER 46

FROM THE UPPER ROOM TO THE JUDGMENT SEAT
RETRACING THE STEPS OF JESUS

Matt 26:47-27:1, 11-26; Mark 14:43-15:15;
Luke 22:47-23:25; John 18:2-19:16

Benjamin A. Foreman

KEY POINTS

- The Garden of Gethsemane was a strategic location to apprehend a well-known figure like Jesus quietly (as opposed to the upper room).

- Although the location of Annas' and Caiaphas' residence where Jesus was examined is unknown, it was most likely located somewhere on the top of the Western Hill with a good view of the Temple Mount.

- When Jesus appeared before the Sanhedrin he was taken from the high priests' residence to the "Chamber of Hewn Stone" within the temple compound itself.

- Following the Sandhedrin examination, Jesus was taken across town due west to Herod's palace where he was questioned a number of times by Pilate, who looked for ways to let Jesus go free in spite of the Jews' death wish.

- Sandwiched between Pilate's questioning, Jesus was sent to Herod Antipas who was likely residing at the Hasmonean palace.

- The clandestine events preceding the crucifixion are riddled with irony and mystery, much like Jesus' ministry.

Most of the residents of Jerusalem were probably shocked to see Jesus hanging on a cross on the morning of the "day of preparation" (Mark 15:42; Luke 23:54; John 19:14). Their bellies still full after a long Passover meal, many had no idea of what Jesus had experienced throughout the night. As they gazed upon the crucified rabbi they surely wondered how such a popular figure could now be crucified between two criminals. What happened? What events led to this tragic end? Where in Jerusalem did all of this take place?

These questions are not new. The waters of historical accuracy, however, have been muddied by centuries of tradition and Christian speculation. This essay deals with the arrest, trials, and conviction of Jesus, and will focus primarily on where these incidents occurred in the Holy City.

THE ARREST (MATT 26:47–56; MARK 14:43–52; LUKE 22:47–53; JOHN 18:2–12)

Slipping out of the upper room virtually unnoticed, Judas swiftly wove his way through the dark alleyways of the Western Hill to his contact among the chief priests (see Matt 26:14). If the last supper was eaten in the area near the traditional site of the upper room (just south of today's Zion Gate), the trip took no more than a few minutes. Welcoming the possibility of arresting Jesus, the chief priests immediately began to alert the proper Jewish authorities. Matters of civil disorder were under the jurisdiction of the captain of the temple (see Acts 4:1), whom the Mishnah says was also in charge of guarding the temple at night

(m. Middot 1:1–2), and thus the chief priests probably notified him first and he in turn summoned the rest of his temple police force. Since none of this appears to have been preplanned,[1] assembling the chief arresting officers must have taken some time.

But this was no ordinary arrest. Jesus was incredibly popular, and the Jewish police rightly recognized the need to involve the Roman authorities. Once assembled, therefore, Judas, the chief priests, and the temple police snaked through the streets of the Western Hill and down the Transversal Valley to the Antonia Fortress on the northwest corner of the Temple Mount, where the Roman forces were stationed (War 5.238–47; see infographic "Ancient Jerusalem" on pg. 528). Rightly recognizing the potential for a riot, the Roman chiliarch (the commander of a thousand) quickly dispatched his cohort, and soon Judas found himself at the head of a band of several hundred men.[2]

At some point during all of this, the Passover meal came to a close in the upper room. Since the temple was closed at night, Jesus and his disciples probably made their way to the Mount of Olives by walking around the southern end of the Temple Mount. After crossing the Kidron Valley, they arrived at a place called Gethsemane, where there was a garden (John 18:1; Matt 26:36).

---

1. The Synoptics all say Judas *was seeking* an opportunity to betray Jesus (Matt 26:16; Mark 14:11; Luke 22:4–6).

2. A full Roman cohort consisted of one thousand men, but usually numbered only six hundred. The Greek word *speira* (σπεῖρα; John 18:3) can refer to a maniple (i.e., subdivision) of two hundred men, and some argue John is not trying to say the full maniple was sent (e.g., Leon Morris, *The Gospel According to John*, rev. ed. [Grand Rapids: Eerdmans, 1995], 656). It is hard to know how many Roman soldiers were dispatched. The Romans sometimes sent out a large number of forces (e.g., 470 soldiers protected Paul in Acts 23:23), and given the high profile of the case, that it was the night of the Passover, and the presence of the temple police, it is possible the Romans took no chances and sent out a large contingency of forces.

Clearly a quiet arrest was in the best interest of all the parties involved. Detaining Jesus in the heart of the upper city had the potential of drawing too much attention, and so it is possible Judas never intended on having him seized in the upper room. The guest room was prepared as the place where Jesus and his disciples would "eat" the Passover (Mark 14:12), and since Bethany was beyond the distance permitted to travel on a holy day,[3] Judas may have led the Roman cohort and temple police (John 18:3) directly to the Garden of Gethsemane (Matt 26:36–46; Mark 14:32–42; Luke 22:40–46; John 18:1; note Luke 22:39 maintains this was a customary place for Jesus to meet). Since Jesus was well-known to the public officials, Judas' role was not primarily to identify Jesus, "but to locate Jesus' entourage and to distinguish them from others who were likely encamped on the hillside."[4] In an incredible act of treachery, Judas led Jesus' captors to Gethsemane and exposed the band of Galileans with whom he had spent the past three years. A struggle ensued, and after convincing his arrestors to let the disciples go free, Jesus was seized and taken to Annas, the high priest emeritus.[5]

JESUS IS EXAMINED BY ANNAS (JOHN 18:12–24)

It is surprising that Jesus was first taken to the house of Annas since he was not the ruling high priest that year. Pixner believes this was a "delaying tactic" meant to buy time for the Sanhedrin to convene.[6] But this is unlikely. Annas was a prominent religious figure. He himself served as high priest from AD 6–15, and five of his sons also held the office (Josephus, *Ant.* 20.198). Although Caiaphas was the ruling high priest at the time, Annas clearly continued to have a powerful influence on the high priesthood. John notes the Jews continued to refer to him as "high priest" (John 18:15, 16, 19, 22), and according to Luke 3:2, John the Baptist began his ministry during the high priesthood of Annas and Caiaphas (note Annas is listed first).[7] In Acts 4:5 Caiaphas is not even credited with the title high priest, but Annas is. These are not historical blunders (John correctly credits Caiaphas with the high priesthood in John 18:24) but indications of the influential role Annas played in the religious leadership.[8] In bringing Jesus to Annas, therefore, the Jews were probably seeking the wise counsel of the most influential religious figure of the day.[9]

---

3. Anson F. Rainey and R. Steven Notley, *The Sacred Bridge* (Jerusalem: Carta, 2006), 365.

4. Rainey and Notley, *Sacred Bridge*, 365.

5. See Aubrey L. Taylor, "In the Garden of Gethsemane: Jesus' Choice to Remain or Run from His Father's Will" on pg. 476.

6. Bargil Pixner, "Mount Zion, Jesus, and Archaeology," in *Jesus and Archaeology*, ed. James H. Charlesworth (Grand Rapids: Eerdmans, 2006), 320.

7. A modern parallel is found in the United States presidency. Former presidents retain their title and usually continue to be an influential voice even after they leave office.

8. Bruce Chilton, "Caiaphas," *ABD* 1:804.

9. Since the high priesthood was originally retained for life (see Num 35:25, 28), some argue the Jews believed Annas was still the rightful high priest. This explanation, however, overlooks the fact that other high priests were deposed prior to their death as well.

Many scholars believe Annas and Caiaphas shared the same residence.[10] This appears to be a correct deduction since John says Peter followed Jesus into the courtyard and began warming himself by the fire when Jesus was brought to Annas (John 18:18); he then notes Peter was still warming himself by the fire when Jesus was taken to Caiaphas (John 18:25).[11]

The Gospels do not say where this dwelling was located. Josephus mentions the house of Annas and implies it was near the palaces of Agrippa and Bernice in the upper city (the Western Hill; *War* 2.426). But this reference is very general, and there are two traditions for where on the Western Hill Caiaphas' (and Annas') house was located. The oldest goes back at least as far as the Pilgrim of Bordeaux (AD 333), who writes, "There [i.e., at the house of Caiaphas] still stands a column against which Christ was beaten with rods."[12] Theodosius (AD 530) also mentions the house of Caiaphas and states, "From holy Sion to the house of Caiaphas, now the Church of S. Peter,

it is 50 paces more or less."[13] Traces of the ancient Holy Zion church were found by Heinrich Renard in 1899 in the area of the Dormition Church, just before it was built.[14] It is clear Theodosius is describing the same building as the Pilgrim of Bordeaux because Theodosius later writes, "The pillar formerly in the house of Caiaphas, at which the Lord Christ was scourged, is now in holy Sion."[15] Early tradition, therefore, locates the residence of Caiaphas on the top of the Western Hill in the Armenian garden, just outside of today's Zion Gate. Magen Broshi excavated the area in 1971–1972 and found it was densely populated in the first century AD. Many of the buildings had two or three stories, and some were decorated with frescoes with animal motifs. He concluded the top of the Western Hill was a wealthy private residential area.[16] Although this fits what we know about the priests from historical sources (namely that they were wealthy), nothing definitively connecting the site to Caiaphas' house has been found.

---

10. Shimon Gibson, *The Final Days of Jesus: The Archaeological Evidence* (New York: HarperCollins, 2009), 82; D. A. Carson, *The Gospel According to John* (Grand Rapids: Eerdmans, 1991), 582.

11. Dalman cites, however, a fifteenth-century tradition placing the house of Annas at a different location from that of Caiaphas, namely just north of the Church of St. Zion, inside the present Old City walls (Gustaf Dalman, *Sacred Sites and Ways: Studies in the Topography of the Gospels*, trans. Paul P. Levertoff [London: Society for the Promoting of Christian Knowledge, 1935], 330).

12. See translation in *Itinerary from Bordeaux to Jerusalem: 'The Bordeaux Pilgrim' (333 A.D.)*, trans. Aubrey Stewart (London: Palestine Pilgrims' Text Society, 1887), 23.

13. Theodosius, *On the Topography of the Holy Land*, 45. Translation from J. H. Bernard, *Theodosius (A.D. 530)*, Palestine Pilgrims' Text Society (London: Hanover Square, 1893), 10.

14. See M. Broshi, "Excavations in the House of Caiaphas, Mount Zion," in *Jerusalem Revealed: Archaeology in the Holy City 1968–1974*, ed. Yigael Yadin (Jerusalem: Israel Exploration Society, 1975), 58–59; Bargil Pixner, "Church of the Apostles Found on Mt. Zion," *BAR* 16.3 (May/June 1990): 16–35.

15. Theodosius, *Topography*, 11.

16. Broshi, "Excavations in the House of Caiaphas, Mount Zion," 57–58.

Church of Peter in Gallicantu

Another tradition locates Caiaphas' residence on the southeastern corner of the Western Hill, where the Church of Peter in Gallicantu now stands. This site was first excavated in 1889 and the remains of a Byzantine church and monastery dating to the fifth century were found. Below the ancient church is a Second Temple period structure identified by Christian tradition as the house of Caiaphas.[17] It contains a series of rock-cut cellars, cisterns, and stables dating to the Herodian period.[18] One of these crypts is traditionally identified as the prison where Jesus was held before he was tried by Caiaphas. A large church was built there in the Crusader period

as well.[19] The modern church was built in 1931 by the Augustinians and named after the ancient Church of Saint Peter mentioned by Theodosius (see above).[20]

It is unlikely the fifth century structure under the Gallicantu Church is the Church of Saint Peter mentioned by Theodosius. The Byzantine building under the Gallicantu Church is about three hundred yards (274 m) from the Holy Zion Church (if it has been correctly identified as the building under the Dormition Church). Theodosius, however, states the Church of Saint Peter is about fifty paces from the Holy Zion Church. The Gallicantu Church, therefore, is too far away. Although recent excavations have

17. Hillel Geva, "Jerusalem: The Byzantine Period," *NEAEHL* 2:778.

18. Jerome Murphy-O'Connor, *The Holy Land: An Oxford Archaeological Guide from Earliest Times to 1700*, 4th ed. (Oxford: Oxford University Press, 1998), 107.

19. Dan Bahat, "Jerusalem: Churches," *NEAEHL* 2:799.

20. The phrase *in Gallicantu* is Latin for "the cock crowed" and was added because it was believed this was where Peter denied Jesus.

uncovered several other large homes from the Second Temple period in the area,[21] nothing has been found identifying any of the buildings as the house of Caiaphas. Certainty is not possible, but it is more likely the high priest would have resided further up the hill near the top, where there is a better view of the temple.[22]

Annas and his family were consistently opposed to Jesus and his followers. In Acts 4 Annas again presided over a hearing, there against Peter and John.[23] As in Acts, however, his prosecutorial skills produced no results with Jesus. Unable to extricate any blasphemous or seditious statements, he sent Jesus, still bound, to his son-in-law Caiaphas the presiding high priest.

JESUS IS QUESTIONED BY CAIAPHAS
(MATT 26:57-75; MARK 14:53-72; LUKE 22:54-65; JOHN 18:25-27)

In AD 18, Caiaphas was made high priest by the Judean prefect Valerius Gratus, the same Roman ruler who deposed Annas. That same year Pilate replaced Valerius Gratus as prefect of Judea and Samaria. The three high priests preceding Caiaphas retained the office for only one year each, and so Caiaphas' rule of eighteen years, double that of his father-in-law, was significant (Josephus, *Ant.*

18.33–34). He clearly was liked by Pilate, whose rule overlapped almost entirely with Caiaphas' (see below).

His family tomb may have been found several kilometers south of the ancient city of Jerusalem. In 1990 a tractor accidentally uncovered a rock-hewn tomb containing twelve ossuaries (bone boxes), two of them inscribed with the name "Caiaphas." The most beautifully decorated ossuary had the name "Joseph son of Caiaphas" etched on it and contained the bones of a man who was approximately sixty years old. Since Josephus identifies the high priest as "Joseph who is called Caiaphas" (*Ant.* 18.34) these are most likely the very bones of the high priest who tried Jesus on that cold night in Jerusalem.[24] Archaeologists have probably found the tomb of his father-in-law Annas as well, just south of the Hinnom Valley at the site traditionally known as Akeldama, the field of blood.[25]

Although it is impossible at the moment to definitively pinpoint the house of Caiaphas, excavations led by Nahman Avigad in the Jewish Quarter after the Six-Day War help to illustrate the kind of residence Annas and Caiaphas probably shared. All four Gospels mention Peter warming himself by a fire in the courtyard of the compound. In an exciting discovery, Avigad uncovered a

---

21. Hillel Geva, "Jerusalem: The Church of St. Peter in Gallicantu," *NEAEHL* 5:1814–15.

22. Murphy-O'Connor, *Holy Land*, 107. A helpful summary of this discussion is also found in John McRay, *Archaeology and the New Testament* (Grand Rapids: Baker, 1991), 199–202.

23. Bruce Chilton, "Annas," *ABD* 1:257.

24. For an analysis of the inscriptions and bibliography, see Craig Evans, "Excavating Caiaphas, Pilate, and Simon of Cyrene: Assessing the Literary and Archaeological Evidence," in *Jesus and Archaeology*, ed. James H. Charlesworth (Grand Rapids: Eerdmans, 2006), 323–39. For pictures, see Hershel Shanks, *Jerusalem: An Archaeological Biography* (New York: Random House, 1995), 187–91.

25. See Leen and Kathleen Ritmeyer, "Akeldama: Potter's Field or High Priest's Tomb?" *BAR* 20.6 (Nov/Dec 1994): 20–35.

The "Burnt House"

first century AD palatial mansion that occupied an area of six hundred square meters (nearly 6500 square feet) near the top of the Western Hill. The mansion had two levels and a basement containing private pools, baths, and cisterns. It was built around a square courtyard paved with flagstones and provided access to a large reception hall, guest chambers, and other wings of the building. Some of the rooms were beautifully paneled with painted frescoes, displaying typical Hellenistic-Roman decorations. Very close to the same spot, another building, called the "Burnt House," was discovered. It contained a large number of stone vessels, some furniture, and other domestic finds, but perhaps the most important find was a stone weight with an inscription reading "Son of Kathros." This is an

important discovery because the Kathros family is known from rabbinical sources to have been one of the families of the high priests (b. Pesahim 57a).[26] The entire neighborhood, therefore, was the priestly quarter of Jerusalem, and Avigad even speculates that given the large number of mikvehs and the wealth displayed in the compound, the palatial mansion may have belonged to a family of high priests.[27] Although it is possible this was the very residence of Annas and Caiaphas, nothing was found that makes this certain.

Jesus knocked heads with the religious authorities on several levels. Theologically, his claims to forgive sins (Mark 2:10), to be one with the Father (John 10:30), and to be the resurrection and the life (John 11:25)—just to name a few—were deeply offensive to

---

26. See Nahman Avigad, *Discovering Jerusalem* (Nashville, TN: Thomas Nelson, 1983), 95-139.

27. Nahman Avigad, "Jerusalem: Herodian Period," *NEAEHL* 2:733

the Sadducees and Pharisees. Beyond the theological, his popularity was also alarming to the religious leaders (John 11:48), and many of his actions were viewed as a direct affront to their authority. His cleansing of the temple is one such example. The Babylonian Talmud states the house of Annas and several other priestly families were in charge of the temple finances (b. Pesahim 57a).[28] If Chilton is correct in arguing Caiaphas personally installed the money vendors in the temple, he may have taken Jesus' cleansing of the temple more personally than is often recognized.[29]

Caiaphas realized, however, that personal and religious disagreements were not enough to secure a death warrant from Pilate.[30] Insurrection would be a much more alarming and compelling indictment, and so Caiaphas attempted to extract from Jesus a statement with seditious overtones. Jesus' confusing words about destroying the temple—which would have been a matter of concern for the Romans—were recalled (and slightly twisted), but to no avail. Exasperated by Jesus' reticence, Caiaphas bluntly asked Jesus: "Are you the messiah, the son of God?" (Matt 26:63). Such an admission would also be cause for concern to Pilate since "messiah" had overtones of insurrection in the first century AD. In the end, however, Caiaphas' religious nature got the best of him. Although Jesus admit-

ted to being the messiah (Mark 14:62), Caiaphas found his claim to be the "son of man" unbearable and thus indicted Jesus with the charge of blasphemy.[31]

An interesting detail is recorded in Luke 22:61. After Peter denied Jesus three times, Luke states, "The Lord turned and looked at Peter." The chronological relationship between Peter's denials and Jesus' appearance before Annas and Caiaphas is difficult to establish. It is possible, however, that Jesus and Peter made eye contact as Jesus was led through the courtyard from Caiaphas' quarters to be examined by the Sanhedrin.

JESUS IS TRIED BY THE SANHEDRIN (MATT 27:1; MARK 15:1; LUKE 22:66–71)

Although Jesus' appearance before the Sanhedrin is mentioned in the three Synoptics, only Luke says this occurred in a different location from the house of Annas and Caiaphas (Luke 22:66). One of the difficulties in harmonizing the accounts is that Matthew (26:59) and Mark (14:55) say "the whole council" was present at the high priestly residence. But since both books also affirm that a further consultation was held at daybreak, it is clear the formal convention of the Sanhedrin did not take place until after Caiaphas examined Jesus.

In the New Testament, the term "Sanhedrin" most frequently refers to the

---

28. Rainey and Notley, *Sacred Bridge*, 365.

29. Chilton, "Caiaphas," 805–6.

30. "It is probable that Pilate occupied himself with major projects, such as the renovation of the harbor at Caesarea Maritima, and left Jewish matters in the hands of Caiaphas and his priestly colleagues" (Evans, "Excavating Caiaphas," 337).

31. "To claim to be Messiah was hardly in itself blasphemous ... But to claim to be God's anointed in such an improbable situation ... might well be seen as 'taking God's name in vain', especially when the title 'Son of God' has been included in the claim" (R. T. France, *Matthew: An Introduction and Commentary* [Downers Grove: IVP, 1985], 387).

supreme Jewish council in Jerusalem that made rulings on religious, political, and legal matters. (It can also refer to local judicial courts in the non-technical sense; e.g., Matt 10:17; *War* 1.537.) The leader of the Sanhedrin was the high priest (1 Macc 14:44; Matt 26:57; *Ant.* 20.200), and according to the Mishnah it was comprised of 71 members (m. Sanhedrin 1:6).[32] Some scholars believe the membership was limited to the Sadducaic party,[33] but John (11:47) and Luke (Acts 23:6) explicitly state it had Pharisaic representation as well. Since the high priest was a Sadducee, the Pharisees were probably a small minority.

According to the Mishnah, "The court had power to inflict four kinds of death-penalty: stoning, burning, beheading, and strangling" (m. Sanhedrin 7:1).[34] Whether or not the Sanhedrin had the power to execute in the first century AD, however, is a question scholars have hotly debated.[35] The matter is complicated, but in the final analysis it would be difficult to explain why the Sanhedrin involved Pilate in the case if they *did* have jurisdiction over capital punishment, especially given their heavy disdain for Jesus.[36] Their assertion that "it is not lawful for us

to put anyone to death" (John 18:31) is best taken at face value, and the Sanhedrin's examination of Jesus was probably meant to prepare the charge-sheet that would be given to Pilate.[37]

Where the Sanhedrin convened for this early morning pre-trial is not a question that has taken center stage throughout history. As Dalman bluntly expresses, "Christian tradition has never troubled itself about this place."[38] It is important to note, however, that the three Synoptics state the council was convened "when day came" (Matt 27:1; Mark 15:1; Luke 22:66). Since the Mishnah says trials for capital cases could not be held during the night (m. Sanhedrin 4.1), the assembling of the Sanhedrin at daybreak appears to have been a formal convention, not an *ad hoc* meeting at an indiscriminate location. This being the case, Jesus almost certainly was led to the Temple Mount, several hundred yards to the east.

At one point, the Sanhedrin met in the Chamber of Hewn Stone (called *Lishkath ha-Gazith*), which according to the Mishnah was one of three chambers in the building lining the southern rim of the temple court (m. Middot 5:4).[39] More specifically, it seems to have been

---

32. The Mishnah also maintains there was another "lesser" Sanhedrin with a membership of twenty-three. Scholars generally agree there were two Sanhedrins (a "greater" and "lesser") only after AD 70 (see G. H. Twelftree, "Sanhedrin," *DNTB* 1062).

33. E.g., Anthony Saldarini, "Sanhedrin," *ABD* 5:976.

34. Translation from Herbert Danby, *The Mishnah* (London: Oxford University Press, 1933).

35. See Twelftree, "Sanhedrin," 1064.

36. Gibson believes the Sanhedrin did not have jurisdiction on matters of sedition and insurrection. He posits the council was unable to find Jesus guilty of blasphemy and therefore the case had to be dealt with by the Roman governor. The problem with this theory, however, is the Gospels *do* imply the council found him guilty of blasphemy (compare Luke 22:69 with Matt 26:64–65; *The Final Days of Jesus*, 84–85).

37. Paul Winter, *On the Trial of Jesus* (Berlin: de Gruyter, 1974), 43.

38. Dalman, *Sacred Sites*, 330.

39. Josephus (*War* 5.144), however, seems to imply it was in the western wall of the Temple Mount (so Twelftree, "Sanhedrin," 1064).

The Sanhedrin

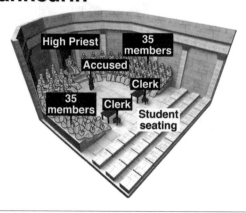

located in the southeastern corner of the temple court, just south of the Nicanor Gate.[40] The Jewish sources, however, state that 40 years prior to the destruction of the temple (AD 30) the Sanhedrin moved from the Chamber of Hewn Stone to the "stores" (Hebrew: *hanuyyot*) in the temple area (b. Shabbat 15a; b. Rosh Hashanah 31a; b. Avodah Zarah 8b). Mazar argues this is a reference to the basilica hall in the Royal Stoa (on the southern end of the Temple Mount) and believes an apse in the southern wall was constructed to accommodate for their sessions.[41] Since the Royal Stoa was the most beautifully decorated portico on the Temple Mount, this is a reasonable conclusion.[42] However, scholars disagree on whether the number forty in the Jewish sources should be taken at face value (some believe it is a symbolic figure), and thus it is unclear

whether the Sanhedrin was still meeting in the Chamber of Hewn Stone in Jesus' day. In any event, the trial occurred where the Sanhedrin normally convened, somewhere on the Temple Mount.

Luke's account of the Sanhedrin's trial is very similar to Caiaphas' interview of Jesus recorded in Matthew and Mark. In both trials Jesus is asked if he is the messiah, the son of God, and in both hearings Jesus responds in the affirmative and then makes reference to the son of man seated at the right hand of power (compare Dan 7:13). Although it might initially seem odd that the same statements were exchanged at the high priestly residence *and* in the council chamber, this is not so unusual once it is remembered Caiaphas, the ruling high priest, officiated the examination. Since Caiaphas had found him guilty of blasphemy, he

40. For a complete description, see Leen Ritmeyer, *The Quest* (Jerusalem: Carta, 2006), 371–74.

41. Benjamin Mazar, "The Royal Stoa in the Southern Part of the Temple Mount," in *Recent Archaeology in the Land of Israel*, ed. Hershel Shanks and Benjamin Mazar (Jerusalem: Israel Exploration Society, 1985), 143–45.

42. See Josephus, *Ant.* 15.411–15; Ritmeyer, *The Quest*, 90–94 for a thorough description and explanation of the Royal Stoa.

undoubtedly would have steered the investigation in such a way as to produce the same results. The tactic worked. Finding Jesus guilty of blasphemy, the Sanhedrin quickly led him off to Pilate, the Roman administrator.

JESUS IS TRIED BY PILATE (MATT 27:11-14; MARK 15:1-5; LUKE 23:1-5)

When Herod died in 4 BC, his kingdom was divided among his three sons Archelaus, Antipas, and Philip. None of them were officially proclaimed "king," but Archelaus, his oldest living son, was given the title "ethnarch" (meaning "ruler over a people") with the promise to be officially named king if he governed well. He was allotted the central, largest, wealthiest, and most difficult portions to govern: Judea, Samaria, and Idumea (Josephus, *Ant.* 17.317-320). Archelaus governed poorly, however, and in AD 6 was exiled to Vienna in Gaul (*Ant.* 17.344). From that point on (with the exception of Agrippa's short rule [AD 41-44]), Judea and Samaria were administered by Roman governors. Pontius Pilate was one such ruler.[43]

Pilate apparently ruled Judea and Samaria from AD 19-37.[44] Roman governors were primarily responsible for maintaining the peace and collecting taxes and tribute. With regard to judi-cial powers, Josephus explicitly says Augustus entrusted them with the "power to execute" (*War* 2.117).

Extra-biblical literature depicts Pilate as ruthless and vicious. Philo, for example, describes his rule as being characterized by "briberies, insults, robberies, outrages, wanton injuries, executions without trial, and endless and supremely grievous cruelty" (*Legatio ad Gaium* 301-302; compare *War* 2.177). The Gospels, however, seem to portray him as an indecisive and weak individual who did the best he could to save the innocent Jesus from execution. This ostensible discrepancy has been widely discussed, but in the final analysis, Pilate was probably "not as venal as Philo and Josephus would have us believe, nor was he as principled as Christian writers would have us believe."[45]

John 18:28 informs us that Jesus was taken into Pilate's praetorium. Although this word appears in the Greek text of the Gospel, it is a transliteration of the Latin term, which was used for the headquarters of the commanding military officer or governor (as Pilate was).[46] Mark's use of the Greek term *aule* (αὐλή) in 15:16, which in this passage clearly means palace, suggests one of Herod's royal residences.[47]

Pilate's permanent home was in Caesarea Maritima, which had become

---

43. Although Josephus and Tactitus (*Annals* 15.44.3) refer to Pilate as procurator, an inscription found at Caesarea in 1961 refers to Pilate as "prefect of Judea," which accords well with the Gospel's reference to him simply as "governor." This stone fragment confirms that Judean governors prior to Agrippa I (AD 41-44) were prefects, who were of Equestrian rank. (Equestrians, ranked below the patricians, were the lower of the two aristocratic classes in Roman society.)

44. See Daniel Schwartz, "Pontius Pilate," *ABD* 5:396-97.

45. See Evans, "Excavating Caiaphas," 338 (see the full argument on pp. 330-38).

46. Carson, *John*, 587.

47. Bargil Pixner, "Praetorium," *ABD* 5:447. The term can also mean courtyard (e.g., Matt 26:69).

Antonia Fortress (northwest view)

the capital when Archelaus was deposed. Because of the Passover Feast, however, he had come to Jerusalem to monitor the festivities, which had the potential of being riotous (*War* 5.244). Unlike the meeting-place of the Sanhedrin, the location of Pilate's Jerusalem residence has been the focus of much Christian tradition.

According to Josephus there were two main Roman fortresses in Jerusalem. One was the Antonia Fortress, adjacent to the Temple Mount on the northwest corner. Josephus states it was beautifully decorated and resembled a palace in its spaciousness (see the full description in *War* 5.238–47). Towers rose up from each of the building's four corners, and its function was to house a Roman peace-keeping cohort. Unfortunately, very little of

this structure has been found in archaeological excavations.[48] The other fortress was Herod's palace, located on the western side of the city in the area just south of today's Jaffa Gate. In typical bombastic style, Josephus describes this as an extravagant building, unsurpassed by any other. Surrounded by a wall to ensure privacy, the compound had two spacious and beautifully-decorated wings stocked with all the opulent trappings and furnishings expected of a king. The palace contained large reception halls and enough bedchambers for one hundred guests. The courtyard was landscaped with groves of different types of trees and was crisscrossed with streams and ponds (see *War* 5.176–82; 1.402; *Ant.* 15.318–19). Both the Antonia Fortress

48. See P. Benoit, "The Archaeological Reconstruction of the Antonia Fortress," in *Jerusalem Revealed: Archaeology in the Holy City 1968–1974*, ed. Yigael Yadin (Jerusalem: Israel Exploration Society, 1975), 87–89.

and Herod's Palace were burned to the ground by the Jewish rebels during the First Jewish Revolt (AD 66).

Christian tradition has located Pilate's Jerusalem *praetorium* in two places throughout history. The earliest situated it on the southeastern corner of the Western Hill, just opposite the Temple Mount. This identification may go back as far as the Pilgrim of Bordeaux (AD 333), and in AD 450 a church called the Hagia Sophia ("Holy Wisdom") was built on the site. This Byzantine church was thoroughly destroyed several centuries later, though according to historical sources it was close to the Nea Church, the remains of which have been found in the southern end of the Jewish Quarter.[49] In the Middle Ages another tradition arose locating the *praetorium* at the Antonia Fortress. As Murphy-O'Connor notes, "The basis of the conflict was simple: one group possessed churches on the western hill, the other on the eastern [i.e. north of the Temple Mount]."[50]

In the end, the Antonia Fortress won the day, and since the late fourteenth century at least (perhaps even the late thirteenth) it has been associated with Pilate's Jerusalem residence and the starting point of the *Via Dolorosa* ("the way of sorrows")—the route Jesus took to Calvary.[51] Today there are fourteen stations of the cross, the first two located near the modern church of *Ecce Homo* just north of the Temple Mount.[52] The first station commemorates the spot where Pilate condemned Jesus to death. According to tradition, this was where Pilate brought Jesus out to the Jews and proclaimed, "Behold the man" (John 19:5). In the immediate vicinity (in the basement of the Sisters of Zion Convent) are some large paving stones long thought to be the "Stone Pavement" (Greek: *Lithostrotos*; Aramaic: *Gabbatha*) where Pilate sat down on his judgment seat and delivered Jesus over to be crucified (John 19:13).[53] From here the *Via Dolorosa* continues westward to the Church of the Holy Sepulchre, where the final five stations are located.

Although the *Via Dolorosa* has left a spiritual imprint on the hearts of many Christian pilgrims over the centuries, it is, unfortunately, probably nothing more than the product of medieval historical speculation. The Roman governors, including Pilate, almost certainly stayed in Herod's palace on the west side of the city. Josephus reports this was where Florus (the Roman procurator ruling Judea when the First Jewish Revolt broke out) stayed while in Jerusalem

---

49. For a more thorough overview of this tradition, see Pixner, "Praetorium," 447-48. A summary of the remains found at the Nea Church can be found in Avigad, *Discovering Jerusalem*, 229-46.

50. Murphy-O'Connor, *The Holy Land*, 35.

51. According to Herbert Thurston, the earliest reference to the commemoration of various incidents on Jesus' journey to Calvary dates to 1285-1291 (Herbert Thurston, *The Stations of the Cross* [London: Burns & Oates, 1914], 21).

52. The fourteen stations have a long and complicated history. For a thorough overview of their development, see Jerome Murphy-O'Connor, "The Geography of Faith," *Bible Review* 12.6 (1996), 32-41; Thurston, *Stations of the Cross*, 20-44.

53. E.g., W. Harold Mare, *The Archaeology of the Jerusalem Area* (Grand Rapids: Baker, 1987), 160-66; Jack Finegan, *The Archaeology of the New Testament: The Life of Jesus and the Beginning of the Early Church* (Princeton: Princeton University Press, 1969), 156-62.

(*War* 2.301), and Philo writes that a riot nearly broke out when Pilate dedicated shields to Herod's palace in Jerusalem (*Legatio ad Gaium* 299–305). From this latter story it is clear Pilate used Herod's palace as his administrative headquarters in Jerusalem.[54] Since the Antonia Fortress was a barracks for Roman troops, it is highly unlikely the Roman governor would have lodged with them as well. Furthermore, archaeological excavations have shown that the large paving stones in the Sisters of Zion Convent date to the time of Hadrian (AD 132–135) and cannot be the Stone Pavement in John 19:13.[55] They were part of the road that led under the triple arch erected by Hadrian in commemoration of his victory over the Jews after the Second Jewish Revolt (AD 132–135).[56] Nearly all scholars today believe Pilate was staying in Herod's palace to the west.[57]

Very little of Herod's palace has survived over the years.[58] The palace was burned by the Jewish rebels during the First Jewish Revolt, and then fully dismantled in the fifth century AD.[59] Excavations have, however, uncovered traces of the outer western wall of the compound. Apparently, the entire complex encompassed an area of about 140 by 360 meters.[60] Significantly, a monumental gateway containing a large courtyard (30 by 11 meters) was found along the western periphery of this wall (about half way down). This appears to have been a private gateway leading directly into Herod's compound. Shimon Gibson, one of the excavators of the complex, has recently suggested this is the Gate of the Essenes mentioned by Josephus (*War* 5.145). Pulling together a number of pieces of evidence, he argues at length that Jesus was tried by Pilate in the courtyard of this gate. According to this suggestion, therefore, the Jewish authorities would have led Jesus out of the city on the west, then south to Pilate's tribunal set up in the courtyard of this private gate.[61]

This suggestion deserves serious consideration. But given the paucity of archaeological remains uncovered in the area of Herod's palace it is difficult to move beyond the realm of possibility. One important factor to consider, however, is the accessibility of the gate on the west. Since it led directly into Herod's compound, it was not intended for public

---

54. See Joan E. Taylor, "Pontius Pilate and the Imperial Cult in Roman Judaea" *New Testament Studies* 52.4 (2006): 575–82; Gibson, *Final Days of Jesus*, 91.

55. The paving stones run over the Struthion Pool, which according to Josephus (*War* 5.467) was still an open-air reservoir during the First Jewish Revolt] (https://ref.ly/logos4/Factbook;ref=bk.$25FirstJewishRevolt) (AD 66–73).

56. For a summary see Hillel Geva, "Jerusalem: The Roman Period," *NEAEHL* 2:764–65.

57. Pixner argues Pilate was staying in the Hasmonean palace and that the Byzantine tradition accurately commemorates this site ("Praetorium," 447–48). The historical texts mentioned above, however, make this theory unlikely. Furthermore, if Herod's palace was more lavish and luxurious (as seems to be the case from Josephus' description), why would he stay in the more modest Hasmonean Palace?

58. For a summary see Hillel Geva, "Jerusalem: The Roman Period," *NEAEHL* 2:764–65.

59. Gibson, *Final Days of Jesus*, 92.

60. Lee Levine, *Jerusalem: Portrait of the City in the Second Temple Period (538 BCE–70 CE)* (Philadelphia: Jewish Publication Society, 2002), 200.

61. Gibson, *Final Days of Jesus*, 90–106.

use (which casts doubt on it being the Essene Gate).[62] This being the case, it seems unlikely Pilate would have set up a (public) tribunal at his private entrance. Additionally, since the temple was just five hundred yards to the east, there certainly would have been an access point on the eastern side of the complex. As Chilton notes, the picture painted in the Gospels and Josephus is one of close cooperation between Caiaphas and the Roman authorities.[63] If this were the case, then it is probably more likely Caiaphas would have been accustomed to meeting Pilate on the eastern side of his *praetorium*, closer to the temple and his residence. Most likely, therefore, Caiaphas would have led Jesus to his usual meeting place with Pilate.

As the morning rays of the sun began to crest the Mount of Olives (see John 18:28), Pilate found himself staring at a man who had clearly agitated the Jewish authorities, but did not appear to be guilty of any wrongdoing. Perhaps somewhat annoyed for being troubled with this internecine dispute, he demanded to know what offense Jesus had committed. The Sanhedrin had found Jesus guilty of blasphemy, but since this was not a crime in the eyes of Rome (nor even a matter of interest), Pilate attempted to rid himself of Jesus by telling the Jews to judge him according to their own law (John 18:31). Although a precise harmonization of the four Gospels is difficult here, it seems the leadership changed their charge at this point to an accusation that would gain more traction with Pilate. Touching on his two primary areas of administration, they accused Jesus of advocating the suppression of tax payment to Rome and of seditious plotting (Luke 23:2). These allegations Pilate was unable to ignore, and thus he returned to the *praetorium* to question Jesus about his kingly ambitions. But the conversation led nowhere. Not finding any guilt in Jesus, Pilate once again went out to the Jews and declared him innocent. Unwilling to accept this verdict, the frenzied crowd continued to accuse Jesus of disrupting the peace, claiming "he stirs up the people, teaching throughout all Judea, from Galilee even to this place" (Luke 23:5). The mention of Galilee provided an out. Not only would it relieve Pilate of condemning an innocent man but Antipas would also view it as a gracious compliment.[64] Pleased with the opportunity to put an end to this early-morning crisis, Pilate sent Jesus to Herod Antipas, who was in Jerusalem for the Passover.

JESUS IS SENT TO HEROD ANTIPAS (LUKE 23:6-12)

When his father Herod died, Antipas was awarded the region of Galilee and Perea, which he ruled for 42 years (4 BC–AD 39). Since he governed Galilee and Perea throughout Jesus' entire life, Antipas figures more prominently in the New Testament than any of the other Herods. (He is simply called "Herod" in the New Testament, Josephus, and on his own coins.)[65] As the governor of Galilee,

---

62. Lee Levine, *Jerusalem: Portrait of the City in the Second Temple Period (538 BCE-70 CE)* (Philadelphia: Jewish Publication Society, 2002), 200.

63. Chilton, "Caiaphas," 805.

64. Leon Morris, *Luke: An Introduction and Commentary*, 2nd ed. (Downers Grove: IVP, 1988), 339.

65. Harold Hoehner, *Herod Antipas* (Cambridge: Cambridge University Press, 1972), 105-6.

he was familiar with Jesus and his followers (see map "Kingdom of Herod the Great" on pg. 531). It was he who executed John the Baptist, and when Jesus' fame had spread throughout Galilee, Antipas curiously mistook Jesus as John the Baptist revivified (Matt 14:1–2).

Where Antipas was staying in Jerusalem has not been the subject of Christian speculation. One possible reason for this lack of tradition is Jesus' appearance before Antipas is recorded only in Luke, and there only briefly. Luke records no dialogue and thus Antipas' role in the conviction and crucifixion of Jesus was viewed as minimal at best.

The only clue as to where Antipas may have been staying is in Luke 23:12, where Luke informs us, "Herod and Pilate became friends with each other that very day, for before this they had been at enmity with each other." This text indicates there were stiff relations between the two, meaning it is highly unlikely Antipas was staying with Pilate in Herod's palace.[66] Since the Antonia Fortress was occupied by Roman soldiers, it is likely Antipas was lodging in the Hasmonean palace (this was where Agrippa II stayed when Festus was procurator, *Ant.* 20.189). According to Josephus this building was located west of the Temple Mount, on the eastern slope of the Western Hill (*War* 2.344).[67] It seems to

have been situated close to the top of the Western Hill since it offered a nice view of the temple (*Ant.* 20.190). Unfortunately, no traces of it have been found in excavations, but some posit it was located north of the priestly neighborhood, two hundred yards or so to the northeast of Herod's palace.[68]

According to Luke some Pharisees had urged Jesus several months earlier to leave the region (perhaps Perea) because Antipas was seeking to kill him (13:31). With this in mind it is surprising to read Antipas was now "desiring" to see Jesus (Luke 23:8). The raising of Lazarus, however, almost certainly sent ripples of gossip throughout the region, and since Antipas (at one point at least) believed Jesus was a resurrected John the Baptist, his eagerness now to meet Jesus is understandable. His encounter, however, turned out to be a disappointment. Far from performing a miracle at Antipas' behest, Jesus did not even answer any of Antipas' questions (compare Isa 53:7). Frustrated by Jesus' reticence, Antipas sent him back to Pilate dressed in a beautiful robe, probably in mockery of Jesus' kingly claims.

JESUS IS CONDEMNED BY PILATE (MATT 27:15–26; MARK 15:6–15; LUKE 23:13–25; JOHN 18:39–19:16)

Pilate's position on Jesus' guilt (or lack thereof) had not changed. After receiving

---

66. The friction between Antipas and Pilate is understandable. As the son of Herod, Antipas would have resented having part of his father's territory ruled by the Romans. He may even have had his own political ambitions in the area.

67. Because of contradictory statements in Josephus and 1 Maccabees, it is unclear whether the Hasmonean palace was the same fortress constructed in the Greek Period called the Akra. For a discussion, see Levine, *Jerusalem*, 75–78. Archaeologists excavating in the Givati Parking lot of Jerusalem (near the modern Dung Gate) have very recently (2015) claimed to have found the Akra on the northern end of the Eastern Hill. See the press release at: http://mfa.gov.il/MFA/IsraelExperience/History/Pages/Has-the-Acra-from-2000-years-ago-been-found-3-Nov-2015.aspx.

68. Rainey and Notely, *Sacred Bridge*, 366.

Jesus back from Antipas, Pilate affirmed Jesus' innocence to the Jewish leadership at least three times (Luke 23:14, 15, 22), and even recalled Antipas' belief that Jesus was not guilty (Luke 23:15). He clearly was not comfortable with signing the death warrant of a man he deemed to be innocent, and thus he tried several tactics to satiate the crowd's thirst for innocent blood. First, he suggested Jesus be chosen as the one to receive the yearly gift of amnesty (John 18:39). This was a clever move on Pilate's part: it would have tarnished Jesus with the stain of guilt (thus satisfying the crowd), but would also have avoided breaking the law by executing an innocent man.

His second tactic was to give the crowd some blood and hope this would assuage their demands. Thus, after having Jesus scourged, he ordered his Roman soldiers to bring Jesus out, bloodied, bruised, clothed with a purple robe, and crowned with a crown of thorns (John 19:1–5). Again, it is impossible to be precise with the setting of this scene, but a location on the eastern side of Herod's palace is likely. The Jewish assembly outside Pilate's *praetorium* was comprised mainly of members of the Sanhedrin, and since they resided primarily on the top of the Western Hill, it is easier to envision them convening at the eastern entrance to Herod's palace than at the western gate of the compound (as Gibson argues).

John records an interesting detail in the dialogue between Pilate and the chief priests and officers. After hearing the crowd shout that Jesus is worthy of death "because he has made himself the Son of God" (19:7), John says Pilate was "even more afraid" (19:8). As Carson notes,

to the Graeco-Roman ear this placed Jesus in the category of "divine men." And since Pilate had just had Jesus scourged, he understandably experienced a spasm of fear.[69]

Talk of Jesus' claim to be the Son of God compelled Pilate to bring him back into his *praetorium* for more questioning. After some more dialogue that led nowhere, however, Pilate capitulated and went back out to the crowd to offer his official judicial decision. Taking his seat on the tribunal (the platform where official decisions were made), he marched Jesus out to the Jewish leaders and mockingly announced, "Behold your king" (John 19:14). Incredibly, the chief priests responded, "We have no king but Caesar" (John 19:15). Eager to put an end to this affair, and unwilling to stand up to the request of the Jews, the puppet prefect (on this occasion at least) delivered Jesus over to be crucified.

CONCLUSION

The arrest and trials of Jesus have for centuries been the focus of Christian tradition and theological reflection. Historically, Jesus' *Via Crucis* was paved with flagstones of irony and mystery. Only a few can be highlighted below.

First, the timing and betrayal of Jesus' arrest is riddled with irony. Although the Jewish authorities wished to rid themselves of Jesus and his teaching, they had agreed not to do so during the feast for fear of an uproar among the people (Matt 26:5). From a theological perspective, however, it was imperative for Christ to die at Passover (see 1 Cor 5:7). Thus, the Jewish authorities' attempted to delay the execution of Jesus until after the feast—

69. Carson, *John*, 600.

A Judgment Seat in Jerusalem

even though they wanted to get rid of him as soon as possible—drips with theological irony. Aside from the timing of the arrest, the arrest itself was also soaked in scandalous irony. He was betrayed by a friend with a kiss (Matt 26:50). Although normally a gesture of endearment, this was, in the literal sense, a kiss of death.

Second, and concerning the Jewish trials, it is surprising the Jewish leaders found Jesus guilty of blasphemy. This "crime" fell under the jurisdiction of the Jewish leadership and thus had no traction in the Roman court. The chief priests recognized this, yet still were unable to agree on another charge. On top of this, the Old Testament stipulates the punishment for blasphemy is stoning (Lev 24:16). If Old Testament law had been followed, therefore, Jesus would have been stoned. But given Jesus' prediction concerning the kind of death he would die (John 12:33), it was essential for him to die by a different method. In the end,

rather than being found guilty of blasphemy and then stoned, he was indicted for sedition and then crucified.

Lastly, strands of irony also surface in Jesus' trial before the Roman governor. Not wishing to defile themselves for the Passover, the Jews refused to enter Pilate's residence (John 18:28). Their pious noses high in the air, they were unaware of how soiled their purity had become by their rejection of Jesus. Pilate, on the other hand, the pagan ruler, was "afraid" (John 19:8) of the Son of God, while the Jews, the authorities on how to revere God, shouted, "Crucify, crucify." On a related note, the Jewish leadership—who several months earlier were concerned they would lose their place and nation to the Romans (John 11:48)—now announced, "We have no king but Caesar." In light of the Old Testament's repeated affirmation that God is the only true king (e.g., 1 Sam 8:7), this statement is shocking. This declaration is even more

unbelievable if the traditional conclusion of the Great Hallel in the Passover
Haggadah goes back to the first century
AD (as some believe). If this was the case,
the Jews would have concluded with the
prayer: "From everlasting to everlasting,
you are God; beside you we have no king,
redeemer, or savior; no liberator, deliv-
erer, provider … We have no King but you"
(b. Pesahim 118a).[70]

Much of Jesus' life was characterized by irony. He loved those who did
not love him, was punished for a crime
he did not commit, and ultimately was
exalted through his humiliation (Isa
52:14; 53:3-12). Even his message cuts
against the grain of society. In his kingdom, the meek are blessed, the last are
first, and the least are the greatest. The
wonder of all wonders, however, is that
God orchestrated the plan to crush Jesus
(Acts 2:23). And this he was *pleased* to do
(Isa 53:10) because Jesus' death brings life
to the world. Yet thankfully, his life did
not end in death.

BIBLIOGRAPHY

Amiran, R. and Eitan, A. "Excavations
in the Jerusalem Citadel." Pages
52-56 in *Jerusalem Revealed:
Archaeology in the Holy City 1968-1974*.
Edited by Yigael Yadin. Jerusalem:
Israel Exploration Society, 1975.
Avigad, Nahman. *Discovering Jerusalem*.
Nashville, TN: Thomas Nelson, 1983.
———. "Jerusalem: Herodian Period."
NEAEHL 2:733.
Bahat, Dan. "Jerusalem: Churches."
NEAEHL 2:799.
Benoit, P. "The Archaeological
Reconstruction of the Antonia
Fortress." Pages 87-89 in *Jerusalem*
*Revealed: Archaeology in the Holy
City 1968-1974*. Edited by Yigael
Yadin. Jerusalem: Israel Exploration
Society, 1975.
Bernard, J. H. *Theodosius (A.D. 530)*.
Palestine Pilgrims' Text Society.
London: Hanover Square, 1893.
Broshi, Magen. "Excavations in the
House of Caiaphas, Mount Zion."
Pages 57-60 in *Jerusalem Revealed:
Archaeology in the Holy City 1968-1974*.
Edited by Yigael Yadin. Jerusalem:
Israel Exploration Society, 1975.
Broshi, Magen, and Shimon Gibson.
"Excavations Along the Western and
Southern Walls of Jerusalem." Pages
147-55 in *Ancient Jerusalem Revealed*.
Edited by Hillel Geva. Jerusalem:
Israel Exploration Society, 2000.
Carson, D. A. *The Gospel According to John*.
PNTC. Grand Rapids: Eerdmans,
1991.
Chilton, Bruce. "Annas." *ABD* 1:257-58.
———. "Caiaphas." *ABD* 1:803-6.
Dalman, Gustaf. *Sacred Sites and
Ways: Studies in the Topography of
the Gospels*. Translated by Paul P.
Levertoff. London: Society for the
Promoting of Christian Knowledge,
1935.
Danby, Herbert. *The Mishnah*. London:
Oxford University Press, 1933.
Evans, Craig. "Excavating Caiaphas,
Pilate, and Simon of Cyrene:
Assessing the Literary and
Archaeological Evidence." Pages
323-40 in *Jesus and Archaeology*.
Edited by James H. Charlesworth.
Grand Rapids: Eerdmans, 2006.
Evans, Craig, and Stanley Porter,
eds. *Dictionary of New Testament*

---

70. See Andreas J. Köstenberger, *John* (Grand Rapids, Baker, 2004), 539n88.

Background. Downers Grove: IVP, 2000.

Finegan, Jack. *The Archaeology of the New Testament: The Life of Jesus and the Beginning of the Early Church*. Princeton: Princeton University Press, 1969.

France, R. T. *Matthew: An Introduction and Commentary*. TNTC. Downers Grove, IL: IVP Academic, 1985.

Freedman, David Noel, ed. *The Anchor Bible Dictionary*. 6 vols. New York: Doubleday, 1992.

Geva, Hillel. "Jerusalem: The Byzantine Period." *NEAEHL* 2:778.

———. "Jerusalem: The Church of St. Peter in Gallicantu." *NEAEHL* 5:1814–15.

———. "Jerusalem: The Roman Period." *NEAEHL* 2:764–65.

Gibson, Shimon. *The Final Days of Jesus: The Archaeological Evidence*. New York: HarperCollins, 2009.

Hoehner, Harold. *Herod Antipas*. Cambridge: Cambridge University Press, 1972.

Köstenberger, Andreas J. *John*. BECNT. Grand Rapids: Baker, 2004.

Levine, Lee I. *Jerusalem: Portrait of the City in the Second Temple Period (538 BCE–70 CE)*. Philadelphia: Jewish Publication Society, 2002.

Mare, W. Harold. *The Archaeology of the Jerusalem Area*. Grand Rapids: Baker, 1987.

Mazar, Benjamin. "The Royal Stoa in the Southern Part of the Temple Mount." Pages 143–45 in *Recent Archaeology in the Land of Israel*. Edited by Hershel Shanks and Benjamin Mazar. Jerusalem: Israel Exploration Society, 1985.

McRay, John. *Archaeology and the New Testament*. Grand Rapids: Baker, 1991.

Morris, Leon. *Luke: An Introduction and Commentary*. TNTC. 2nd ed. Downers Grove: IVP, 1988.

———. *The Gospel According to John*. NICNT. Rev. ed. Grand Rapids: Eerdmans, 1995.

Murphy-O'Connor, Jerome. "The Geography of Faith." *Bible Review*. 12.6 (1996): 32–41.

———. *The Holy Land: An Oxford Archaeological Guide from Earliest Times to 1700*. 4th ed. Oxford: Oxford University Press, 1998.

Pilgrim of Bordeaux. *Itinerary from Bordeaux to Jerusalem: 'The Bordeaux Pilgrim' (333 A.D.)*. Translated by Aubrey Stewart. London: Palestine Pilgrims' Text Society, 1887.

Pixner, Bargil. "Church of the Apostles Found on Mt. Zion." *BAR* 16.3 (May/June 1990): 16–35.

———. "Jerusalem's Essene Gateway." *BAR* 23.3 (May/June 1997): 23–30.

———. "Mount Zion, Jesus, and Archaeology." Pages 309–22 in *Jesus and Archaeology*. Edited by James H. Charlesworth. Grand Rapids: Eerdmans, 2006.

———. "Praetorium." *ABD* 5:447–49.

Rainey, Anson F., and R. Steven Notley. *The Sacred Bridge*. Jerusalem: Carta, 2006.

Ritmeyer, Leen. *The Quest*. Jerusalem: Carta, 2006.

Ritmeyer, Leen, and Kathleen Ritmeyer. "Akeldama: Potter's Field or High Priest's Tomb?" *BAR* 20.6 (Nov/Dec 1994): 20–35.

Saldarini, Anthony. "Sanhedrin." *ABD* 5:975–80.

Schwartz, Daniel. "Pontius Pilate." *ABD* 5:395–401.

Shanks, Hershel. *Jerusalem: An Archaeological Biography*. New York: Random House, 1995.

Taylor, Joan E. "Pontius Pilate and the Imperial Cult in Roman Judaea." *New Testament Studies* 52.4 (2006): 555–82.

Thurston, Herbert. *The Stations of the Cross.* London: Burns & Oates, 1914.

Twelftree, G. H. "Sanhedrin." *DNTB* 1061–65.

Winter, Paul. *On the Trial of Jesus.* Berlin: de Gruyter, 1974.

CHAPTER 47

LOCATING JESUS' CRUCIFIXION AND BURIAL

Matt 27:32-61; Mark 15:21-47;
Luke 23:26-56; John 19:17-42

Benjamin A. Foreman

KEY POINTS

- Two primary locations, each associated with a theological tradition, are posited as the crucifixion and burial site of Jesus: (1) Skull Hill and the Garden Tomb, and (2) the Church of the Holy Sepulchre.

- Based upon nearly 1,900 years of tradition and archaeological evidence pointing to a first-century tomb, modern scholarship is convinced that the Church of the Holy Sepulchre marks the general area of these two monumental events.

- Even so, the value of the Garden Tomb is its emphasis on the event rather than the location of the resurrection, whereas the Church of the Holy Sepulchre tends to conceal more than it reveals.

The cross and the empty tomb are perhaps the two most important Christian symbols. Since the days of the New Testament, oceans of ink have been spent exploring the theological significance of these two events—and rightly so. Redemption and resurrection are at the core of Christian faith. Naturally, therefore, believers have been interested in where Jesus was crucified and buried.

This is the central question of the discussion below.

GENERAL INDICATIONS

Considering the centrality of the death and resurrection of Jesus to the Christian faith, the Gospels give surprisingly few details about where in Jerusalem these dramatic events occurred. Several hints in the narrative, however, help to narrow

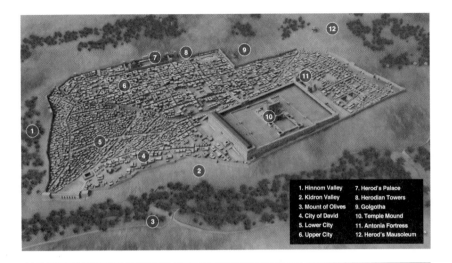

1. Hinnom Valley	7. Herod's Palace
2. Kidron Valley	8. Herodian Towers
3. Mount of Olives	9. Golgotha
4. City of David	10. Temple Mound
5. Lower City	11. Antonia Fortress
6. Upper City	12. Herod's Mausoleum

down the options. One obvious detail is that the site of the crucifixion was within walking distance of Pilate's *praetorium*—which most likely was located in Herod's palace on the west side of the city.[1] The Synoptics specify Jesus was "led" (Matt 27:31; Mark 15:20; Luke 23:26) to the place of crucifixion, and according to John, Jesus was initially forced to carry his own cross (John 19:17). His strength sapped by Pilate's flogging, however, he was unable to lug the crossbeam very far on his own, and Simon of Cyrene was conscripted to help (Matt 27:32; Mark 15:21; Luke 23:26). Jesus' weakened state after his beating by the Romans is an important point to remember since it makes a crucifixion to the east of the city, such as

on the Mount of Olives, unlikely.[2] The top of the Mount of Olives is more than two thousand yards (1828.8 m) from Herod's palace. It is doubtful Jesus, bloodied and bruised, would have been physically capable of walking more than 1.2 miles (1.9 km) across the city, into the Kidron Valley, and up the steep ascent to the top of the Mount of Olives.

The New Testament also indicates that the place of execution was outside of the city. Matthew 27:39 and Mark 15:29 relate Jesus was scorned by those who "passed by" when they saw him hanging on the cross. This implies Jesus was crucified near a road, in a visible location.[3] Simon of Cyrene was traveling on this road, and was "coming in from the coun-

---

1. See Benjamin A. Foreman, "From the Upper Room to the Judgment Seat" on pg. 483.

2. See N. F. Hutchinson., "Notes on Our Lord's Tomb," *Palestine Exploration Fund Quarterly Statement* (1870): 379-81; Hutchinson, "Further Notes on Our Lord's Tomb," *Palestine Exploration Fund Quarterly Statement* (1873): 113-15; Earnest L. Martin, *The Secret of Golgotha: The Forgotten History of Christ's Crucifixion* (Alhambra: ASK Publications, 1988).

3. The cruelty of crucifixion itself was part of a tactic to discourage others from committing the same crime. Josephus says it was the "most wretched of deaths" (*War* 7.203), and according to Quintilian (*Declamationes* 274), "Whenever we crucify the guilty, the most crowded roads are chosen, where the most people can see and be moved by this fear. For penalties relate not so much to retribution as to their exemplary effect" (quoted in Shimon Gibson,

try" (Mark 15:21) when he was shackled with the task of carrying the execution plank. The author of Hebrews is more explicit about the location, suggesting the crucifixion occurred near the city gate: "So Jesus also suffered outside the gate" (Heb 13:12).[4]

The killing site, according to all four Gospels, was called "Place of a Skull" (Matt 27:33; Mark 15:22; Luke 23:33; John 19:17), which in Aramaic is "Golgotha."[5] Why this name was assigned to the crucifixion grounds is not entirely clear, but it *may* provide a clue as to where Jesus was crucified. If the name is a description of the site's appearance, two options are possible: (1) the area may have looked like the back of a skull, implying a round knoll; (2) the site might have brought to mind the front of a skull, perhaps alluding to a rocky cliff with caves resembling eye sockets and a nose cavity. If the name relates to a topographical feature of the area, therefore, this might help us locate the site today. However, "skull" may simply have been a symbol of death pointing to the activity of the area: it was the "place of the skull" because executions were performed there.

John 19:41–42 is, without exaggeration, the most important passage in this discussion: "Now in the place where he was crucified there was a garden, and in the garden a new tomb in which no one had yet been laid. So because of the Jewish Day of Preparation, since the tomb was close at hand, they laid Jesus there." These verses provide us with two

key details. First, the place of crucifixion and the tomb in which Jesus' body was placed were in the same vicinity. This has long been recognized, and thus the discussion has centered around which tradition rightly preserves the area in which *both* of these events occurred. Second, Jesus was buried in a "new tomb in which no one had yet been laid." In other words, it was not a reused Old Testament burial cave; it was a brand new tomb, hewn in the first century AD.

Like many sacred places in the Holy Land, there is disagreement on where Jesus was crucified and buried. The debate is (only) about 130 years old and is divided along theological lines. In this time, two main candidates have been proposed.

TWO CANDIDATES

Protestant tradition locates these events two hundred fifty yards (228.6 m) northeast of today's Damascus Gate (roughly one thousand yards or 914.4 meters from the area of Herod's palace). A portion of the bedrock rises abruptly in that area, forming a hill that provides a nice view of the surrounding landscape. Several shallow caves in the face of the rock give the appearance of eyes sockets and a nose cavity, and when viewed at a certain angle the rocky escarpment is thought to resemble a skull. According to this tradition it is on top of this knoll, popularly called "Skull Hill," that Jesus was crucified. Below the hill just to the west is a two-chambered tomb identi-

---

The Final Days of Jesus: The Archaeological Evidence [New York: HarperCollins, 2009], 116).

4. Although this is an odd passage to find such a geographical detail, the author's reference to the locality of such an important event *in passing* suggests it was well-known to his readers.

5. For an explanation of the Aramaic phrase behind this name see Joan E. Taylor, "Golgotha: A Reconsideration of the Evidence for the Sites of Jesus' Crucifixion and Burial," *New Testament Studies* 44.2 (1998): 182–83.

Close-up of Skull Hill

fied as the burial place of Jesus. In the front of the cave is a channel cut into the bedrock that is thought to be the track for a rolling stone. Because John says the burial compound was in a garden (John 19:41), the site today is called the Garden Tomb.

This cave was first equated with Jesus' tomb in 1842 by a German scholar named Otto Thenius.[6] However, this identification received little attention for the next forty years, although the cave was excavated by Conrad Schick in 1867.[7] In 1881 Charles Conder also located Jesus' crucifixion on the round knoll north of Jerusalem, but identified another cave, further to the west, as the possible tomb of Jesus.[8] Although Conder was an important figure in the history of the rediscovery of the Holy Land, the area was popularized by Charles Gordon, who stayed in Palestine from January of 1883 to January of 1884. Gordon was a deeply religious individual whose faith and character had a powerful influence on Protestants in England. In the words of

---

6. See Gustaf Dalman, *Sacred Sites and Ways: Studies in the Topography of the Gospels*, trans. Paul P. Levertoff (London: SPCK, 1935), 348.

7. Conrad Schick, "Notes, Mr. Schick's Work at Jerusalem," *Palestine Exploration Fund Quarterly Statement* (1874): 125; idem, "Gordon's Tomb," *Palestine Exploration Fund Quarterly Statement* (1892): 120–24.

8. Claude Conder, "Jerusalem," *Palestine Exploration Fund Quarterly Statement* (1881): 201–5; idem, *Tent Work in Palestine*, vol. 1 (London: Richard Bentley & Son, 1878), 361–76.

Skull Hill

Franzman and Kark, "Something about Gordon rang true to the English public."[9]

His connection of the site to Golgotha eventually led to the establishment of the Garden Tomb Association in 1893, and finally to the purchase of the land in 1894.[10] Today, the property is still managed by the Garden Tomb Association, and the quiet, peaceful grounds are a striking contrast to the hustle and bustle of the surrounding city.

Located in the heart of the Christian Quarter of Jerusalem's Old City, the Church of the Holy Sepulchre has for 1700 years commemorated the location of Jesus' crucifixion and burial. The site of the crucifixion is found to one's immediate right after entering the church.

Although first-time visitors sometimes have difficulty visualizing this, the steps leading up to the Latin chapel on the right follow the natural topography of the bedrock. The traditional location of Calvary, therefore, is on a rock outcropping rising up inside the church. Visitors to the site today can reach their hand through a hole beneath the Greek altar and touch the rock. The tomb of Christ is located further inside the church to the left. In the center of the rotunda (the large circular room) sits a large wooden monument; the traditional tomb of Christ lies in the bedrock below.

Visitors to the land of Israel are faced with the question of which of the two candidates—the Garden Tomb or the

---

9. Seth J. Franzman and Ruth Kark, "General Gordon, The Palestine Exploration Fund and the Origins of 'Gordon's Calvary' in the Holy Land," PEQ 140.2 (2008): 14.

10. For more on the acquisition of the property and the circumstances leading up to the purchase, see Franzman and Kark, "General Gordon," 6–10.

The Church of the Holy Sepulchre

Church of the Holy Sepulchre—accurately commemorates the area of Jesus' crucifixion and burial. Within the academic community, however, this is nearly a settled issue. No scholar today believes the Garden Tomb was the place of Jesus' burial, and although some uncertainty remains as to *precisely* where Jesus was crucified and buried, modern research has confirmed to a high degree of certainty that these events occurred in the vicinity of the Church of the Holy Sepulchre. Two interlocking lines of evidence point to this conclusion.

THE CASE FOR THE CHURCH OF THE HOLY SEPULCHRE

EVIDENCE FROM TRADITION

The long and complicated history of the Church of the Holy Sepulchre begins with the Emperor Constantine, who ruled the Roman Empire from AD 305-337

and was the first emperor to convert to Christianity. According to Eusebius, who wrote a biography of Constantine's life, the emperor was "moved in the spirit by the savior himself" (*Life of Constantine* 3.25) to build a church near the spot where Jesus rose from the dead. In Constantine's day, however, Jesus' tomb had been desecrated by "certain impious and godless persons" who,

brought a quantity of earth from a distance with much labor, and covered the entire spot; then, having raised this to a moderate height, they paved it with stone, concealing the holy cave beneath this massive mound. Then, as though their purpose had been effectually accomplished, they prepare on this foundation a truly dreadful sepulcher of souls, by building a gloomy shrine of lifeless idols to the impure spirit whom they call Venus, and offering detestable oblations therein on profane and accursed altars.[11]

Disgusted by the pagan shrine built over Jesus' sepulcher, Constantine gave orders not only to dismantle the stone platform devoted to the goddess Venus, but to dig up the earth beneath it and remove it from the area. Once this was accomplished, Eusebius writes, Jesus' tomb emerged "contrary to all expectation ... after lying buried in darkness ... and afforded to all who came to witness the sight, a clear and visible proof of the wonders of which that spot had once been the scene, a testimony to the resurrection of the savior clearer than any voice could give."[12] Sending a letter to the bishop of Jerusalem, the emperor gave the order for a church, more beautiful than all other churches in the world, to be built at the site to commemorate the miraculous event of the resurrection (see *Life of Constantine* 3.29–40).[13] The Constantinian

building, called the "Martyrium" basilica, was dedicated in AD 335.[14]

Eusebius does not tell us who built the pagan shrine to Venus over Jesus' tomb. This historical detail is filled in by Jerome (ca. AD 346–420):

> From the time of Hadrian to the reign of Constantine—a period of about one hundred eighty years— the spot which had witnessed the resurrection was occupied by a figure of Jupiter while on the rock where the cross had stood, a marble statue of Venus was set up by the heathen and became an object of worship.[15]

This passage is important since it pushes back the building activity in this part of the city to about one hundred years after the time of Jesus (Hadrian died in AD 138).

Why did Hadrian build a temple for Venus at this particular spot?[16] One possible answer is this was simply a prime location to build a temple.[17] But while simple

---

11. Eusebius, *The Life of Constantine* 3.26 [*NPNF²*, 1:527].

12. Eusebius, *Life of Constantine* 3.28 [*NPNF²*, 1:527–28].

13. Many assume the idea to build a church on the site of Jesus' tomb came after Constantine's mother Helena visited the Holy Land in AD 326. The decision to build the church, however, seems to have been made beforehand, at the Council of Nicea in AD 325. Macarius (the bishop of Jerusalem) and Eusebius (the bishop of Caesarea) were both present at the council and both had an interest in building the church, though Macarius initially seems to have played a more influential role in convincing Constantine to build it. See P. W. L. Walker, *Holy City, Holy Places? Christian Attitudes to Jerusalem and the Holy Land in the Fourth Century* (Oxford: Clarendon Press, 1990), 275–76.

14. The plan of the basilica and subsequent architectural history of the building, though interesting, cannot be discussed here. For a brief overview, see Dan Bahat, "Does the Holy Sepulchre Church Mark the Burial of Jesus?" *BAR* 12.3 (May/June 1986): 38–45.

15. Jerome, *Letters* 58.3 [*NPNF²* 6:120].

16. Since the historical sources differ, it is hard to know whether the shrine over Jesus' tomb was devoted to Venus or to Jupiter. Scholarly opinion is divided, though for the sake of simplicity, Eusebius' word is favored here.

17. According to Walker, "In Hadrian's new city the Roman legion was placed on the highest hill; the next highest hill, which unfortunately happened to be the area of Golgotha, was chosen for the civic centre (the forum and the temple" (*Holy City, Holy Places*, 244n16).

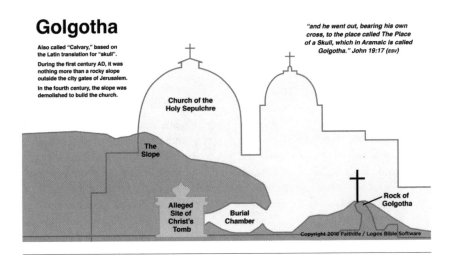

Golgotha

Also called "Calvary," based on the Latin translation for "skull".

During the first century AD, it was nothing more than a rocky slope outside the city gates of Jerusalem.

In the fourth century, the slope was demolished to build the church.

"and he went out, bearing his own cross, to the place called The Place of a Skull, which in Aramaic is called Golgotha." John 19:17 (esv)

Church of the Holy Sepulchre

The Slope

Alleged Site of Christ's Tomb

Burial Chamber

Rock of Golgotha

Copyright 2016 Faithlife / Logos Bible Software

topography may have been a factor, this does not appear to be the only reason. More likely, he built a platform there for the god he worshiped because this was the area where Christians claimed their God was crucified and raised to life. The identification of local deities with foreign ones was fairly common in the ancient world, and it is possible Hadrian took advantage of the opportunity to replace the Christian god with the deity he worshiped.[18] His construction of the platform was likely prompted by Christian tradition.

The antiquity of the tradition is confirmed by the fact that Christians in Constantine's time assumed Jesus' tomb was located under Hadrian's platform, even though it had been inaccessible to them for nearly two hundred years. Not only was it inaccessible to Christians

but it was also inside the city walls of Byzantine Jerusalem. As Walker notes, "Only a strong tradition could possibly have caused them to opt for this inconvenient and unlikely site."[19] Moreover, once the tomb was uncovered, Christians immediately accepted it as genuine. Since no miracle was required to authenticate the tomb, this lends further credence to the validity of the tradition. When the excavators cleared away the dirt and revealed a tomb underneath, it was self-evident that this was Jesus' tomb—tradition had been saying this all along.[20]

If this is correct, then the tradition locating Jesus' burial and crucifixion in vicinity of the Church of the Holy Sepulchre is nearly 1900 years old. When measured against the tradition of the Garden Tomb, the difference is

---

18. Taylor believes Hadrian was not entirely motivated by malice. She argues his platform was almost an "invitation" for Christians to come and worship Jupiter. This is possible, though it makes Hadrian quite naïve. See Taylor, "Golgotha," 198–201.

19. Walker, *Holy City, Holy Places*, 243.

20. Taylor, "Golgotha," 196–97. Significantly, Eusebius, who was generally suspicious of dramatic discoveries, also unwaveringly accepted it as the tomb of Christ. See Walker, *Holy City, Holy Places*, 243–44.

astounding. As mentioned earlier, the earliest connection of the tomb to that of Christ's was in 1842, and although others tried to argue scientifically for a similar location later on, "It was knowledge that it had been endorsed by Gordon which first gained it wide acceptance in Britain and North America."[21] Popular acceptance of the theory, therefore, was not grounded in ancient tradition, nor in scientific analysis, but in the opinion of a religiously influential individual. Many of Charles Gordon's views, however, were not based on scientific calculation, but on fanciful interpretations of biblical texts. In some of his writings he claims to have found the true site of the Garden of Eden in the Seychelles and to have pinpointed the location of the flood. As for his identification of "Skull Hill" with Golgotha, he based this not only on the appearance of the hill but also on his conceptualization of Jerusalem as a skeleton: "Zion is the body, the skull separated four times is the head, the quarries whence the stone was taken from the chest, the site of Zion the beautiful [are] the ribs of the north."[22] Gordon's deficiencies as a scholar, of course, are not enough to render the theory of the Garden Tomb invalid since the merit of a tradition might potentially be stronger than the merit of the individual popularizing the tradition. They should, however, motivate advocates of the tradition to reexamine its foundation. As we will see in the next section, recent archaeological investigations have definitively closed the door on the tradition.

EVIDENCE FROM ARCHAEOLOGY

John's detail that Jesus was buried in a new tomb in which no one had been laid (19:41) is key to this discussion. Any cave identified as Jesus' tomb must have been carved out in the first century AD.

Just a few feet north of the Garden Tomb lies a burial complex once thought to date to the Roman period (the caves are accessible only from the courtyard of the Monastery of St. Étienne). In 1974-1975 Amos Kloner and Gabriel Barkay conducted an archaeological study of the ancient cemetery and, based on the tombs' architecture, dated the entire complex to the eighth or seventh centuries BC.[23] Barkay extended his research to the Garden Tomb (the first archaeological study of the tomb since Schick examined it in 1867) and concluded it too was hewn in the eighth or seventh centuries BC, thus disqualifying it as a candidate for Jesus' tomb.[24] His argument is supported by several lines of evidence.[25]

Archaeologists today have a much better understanding of Israelite funerary practices than they did when the

---

21. Franzman and Kark, "General Gordon," 6.

22. See Franzman and Kark, "General Gordon," 5, 14.

23. Gabriel Barkay and Amos Kloner, "Jerusalem Tombs from the Days of the First Temple," *BAR* 12.2 (Mar/Apr 1986): 22-39.

24. Gabriel Barkay, "The Garden Tomb—Was Jesus Buried Here?" *BAR* 12.2 (Mar/Apr 1986): 40-58.

25. The following three paragraphs are a summary of pages 50-57 of Barkay's article. Interested readers should consult the article for more specific references.

Garden Tomb was first examined in 1867.[26] Their research reveals that not only did burial *customs* change with time, the *architecture* of the burial caves did as well. In the Old Testament period, a typical tomb had three burial benches on the walls opposite the entrance. The bodies of the deceased were placed on these benches, and to prevent the bodies from rolling off, the benches usually had horseshoe-shaped head rests carved into the rock at one end and a low rim running along the outer edge. The ceilings were flat (they were vaulted in the Byzantine period) and sometimes contained a cornice at the meeting point of the wall and ceiling. Once the flesh on the body decomposed (usually after about a year), the bones were removed from the bench and placed in a cavity (called a repository) usually carved into the rock under the bench. Although there were typically three benches in each chamber, each room usually only had one repository. The tombs were frequently reused for several generations.[27]

The distinguishing features of burial caves in the Second Temple period are burial shafts (called *kokhim*) carved into the wall of the chamber. Many of these rooms also typically contained shelves hewn horizontally along the wall. Because of the shelves' arc-shaped tops, they are called *arcosolia* (or *arcosolium* in the singular). Jesus' body seems to

have been placed on an *arcosolium* since John says Mary Magdalene saw two angels, "one at the head and one at the feet" (20:12), when she looked inside the tomb. Another typical feature of Second Temple period tombs is evidence of the use of "comb chisels." These tools were used to carve out the burial chambers and left small parallel lines on the rock surface. Second Temple burials were also carried out in two stages, though sometimes the bones were placed in an ossuary (a bone box) rather than in a bone pit.

The Garden Tomb contains none of the features typical to Second Temple tombs. The chamber inside the tomb to the right, where Jesus is thought to have been buried, is typical in appearance to Old Testament burial chambers. It is clear from a close look at the cave that it originally had three benches on the walls opposite the entrance. The benches are not visible today, however, because they were carved out in the Byzantine period to form basins, which functioned as sarcophagi (stone coffins). Additionally, in the Second Temple period the inner room of a burial tomb was usually cut *behind* the entrance chamber. The rooms of the Garden Tomb, however, are set side by side and share the same outer wall. As Barkay shows, this is the typical layout of Old Testament tombs. Finally, Barkay also reexamined the pottery found in the Garden Tomb when it was cleaned from

---

26. In 1937 several burial caves were found just north of Damascus Gate below today's Sultan Suleiman Street. Although the tombs were not published until nearly forty years later by Amihai Mazar, the pottery found there (based on a photograph taken of the vessels *in situ*) clearly dates to the eighth–seventh centuries BC. The architecture of the tomb also matches that of the cave complex studied by Barkay and Kloner. See Amihai Mazar, "Iron Age Burial Caves North of Damascus Gate Jerusalem," *IEJ* 26 (1976): 1–8.

27. The phrase "gathered to their fathers" is frequently used as a euphemism for death in the Old Testament (e.g., 2 Chr 34:28). Since the bones of the deceased joined those of their ancestors in the tomb's repository, this was literally true.

Arcosolium and Shaft Tombs

time to time, and dated some of it unquestionably to Iron Age II (eighth–seventh centuries BC). In short, not a single tomb from the Second Temple period has been found in the area (the closest is Queen Helena's tomb 600 yards to the north), the architecture of the Garden Tomb matches that of Old Testament tombs, and some of the pottery found inside clearly dates to the eighth or seventh centuries BC. The Garden Tomb, therefore, cannot be the tomb of Christ.

Today, as in the Byzantine period, the Church of the Holy Sepulchre is inside the walls of the Old City. First-time visitors to Jerusalem, therefore, might believe this disqualifies it as a candidate as well. It is important to remember, however, that the course of the walls surrounding Jerusalem has changed throughout the city's long history. According to Josephus, there were three walls surrounding Jerusalem at the outbreak of the First Jewish Revolt (AD 66; see War 5.142–155). The first wall (and most ancient) extended westward from the Temple Mount to the tower called Hippicus (today's Jaffa Gate area), around the Western Hill, down to the Pool of Siloam, then enclosed the Eastern Hill (City of David) by turning north to the eastern portico of the Temple Mount. Josephus' description of the second wall is the shortest: "[It] started from the gate in the first wall which they called Gennath, and, enclosing only the northern district of the town, went up as far as Antonia" (War 5.146). The third wall encompassed a northern suburb of Jerusalem and ended at the Kidron Valley.

The exact course of this wall is debated.[28] It, however, was built by Agrippa I (AD 41–44), about ten years after Jesus was crucified. In Jesus' day, therefore, there were only two walls surrounding Jerusalem. Unfortunately, archaeological excavations have not been able to confirm the course of the second wall.[29] It seems to have had a short span, however, since Josephus says it had only fourteen towers (War 5.158; the first wall had sixty and the third wall had ninety). Several hundred yards east of Jaffa Gate, Nahman Avigad found the remains of a gate, which he identified as the Gennath Gate.[30] If this is correct, this is where the second wall began (as Josephus indicates), meaning the area of the Church of the Holy Sepulchre was just outside of the gate in Jesus' day (see infographic "Ancient Jerusalem" on pg. 528). Interestingly, "Gennath" means garden and accords well with John's detail that there was a garden in the place where Jesus was crucified (John 19:41).

Most crucially, the Church of the Holy Sepulchre contains tombs clearly dating to the first century AD. In the Syrian Chapel (the little room west of the traditional tomb of Christ) visitors can see some of the kokhim carved into the wall of a burial complex (much of the original chamber was cut away by Constantine's workers). Other kokhim were found in the entry courtyard of the church (the

Parvis). Underneath the wooden monument marking the tomb of Jesus is a chamber containing an arcosolium. Unfortunately, the arcosolium is not visible to visitors today since it is covered by later stonework.[31]

In short, a compelling case for locating Jesus' crucifixion and burial in the area of the Church of the Holy Sepulchre can be made.[32] The tradition for the site goes back nearly 1900 years, and until 1842 it had no competitors. When the importance of the resurrection event to Christian faith (see 1 Cor 15:16–19) is coupled with the fact that Christians were never fully expelled from Jerusalem, there is little reason to believe the location could have been forgotten. Archaeology has confirmed the presence of first century AD tombs, and if Avigad has correctly identified the Gennath Gate, the tomb is located exactly where it should be, just outside the city gate. Absolute certainty is not possible, but given the strong tradition and the perfect archaeological match, the cave under the rotunda of the Church of the Holy Sepulchre may be the very tomb in which Jesus was buried.

REFLECTIONS ON THE VALUE OF THE GARDEN TOMB

Although the Garden Tomb may not preserve the correct location of Jesus' burial, the compound nevertheless continues to

---

28. See Lee Levine, Jerusalem: Portrait of the City in the Second Temple Period (538 BCE–70 CE) (Philadelphia: Jewish Publication Society, 2002), 315–18.

29. Hillel Geva, "Jerusalem, the Second Wall," NEAEHL 2:736.

30. Nahman Avigad, Discovering Jerusalem (Nashville, TN: Thomas Nelson, 1983), 69.

31. Bahat, "Holy Sepulchre," 30–32.

32. It is possible the actual crucifixion site was further south of the Church of the Holy Sepulchre. Taylor locates it approximately 200 meters (218.7 ft) to the south, in the middle of the Decumanus of Aelia Capitolina (just southwest of where David Street meets Habad Street). See Taylor, "Golgotha," 182–93.

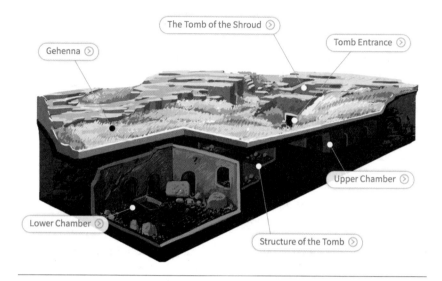

serve an important purpose. Jerusalem oozes with competing religious traditions, and in the cacophony of voices visitors to the holy city sometimes find it difficult to focus on the actual event which the tradition seeks to commemorate. Protestants in particular seem to experience this at the Church of the Holy Sepulchre. Marred by centuries of pilgrimage and construction, the Church of the Holy Sepulchre conceals more than it reveals. The tomb of Christ is not actually visible, and the traditional rock of Calvary has largely been quarried away to make room for the church. The large number of visitors, many of whom swarm to a long line snaking around Christ's tomb, also distracts the mind from focusing on the essence of the event.

All of this is stripped away at the Garden Tomb. The quiet garden, centered around an empty tomb whose stone has

been rolled away, orients the thoughts and prayers of believers toward the one mistaken for a gardener (John 20:15). It is a peaceful island amid a turbulent ocean of vociferous religiosity.

As Gustaf Dalman rightly noted more than one hundred years ago, "Our faith in the Redeemer of the world is not dependent upon knowledge of the sites of His Death and burial, least of all on the actual point at which they occurred."[33] This, the Garden Tomb Association has correctly recognized. The emphasis at the Garden Tomb is always on the event rather than the location. Although the guides suggest this *may* have been Jesus' tomb, they always remind their guests that no matter where in Jerusalem the actual tomb is located, it is, and always will be, empty. The Garden Tomb Association boldly proclaims the message that our Savior conquered death, giving hope to

33. Dalman, *Sacred Sites and Ways*, 380.

all who believe in his name. And in this there is great value.

BIBLIOGRAPHY

Avigad, Nahman. *Discovering Jerusalem.* Nashville, TN: Thomas Nelson, 1983.

Bahat, Dan. "Does the Holy Sepulchre Church Mark the Burial of Jesus?" *BAR* 12.3 (May/June 1986): 26–45.

Barkay, Gabriel. "The Garden Tomb— Was Jesus Buried Here?" *BAR* 12.2 (Mar/Apr 1986): 40–58.

Barkay, Gabriel, and Kloner, Amos. "Jerusalem Tombs from the Days of the First Temple." *BAR* 12.2 (Mar/Apr 1986): 22–39.

Conder, Claude. "Jerusalem." *Palestine Exploration Fund Quarterly Statement* (July, 1881): 201–5.

———. *Tent Work in Palestine.* Vol. 1. London: Richard Bentley & Son. 1878.

Dalman, Gustaf. *Sacred Sites and Ways: Studies in the Topography of the Gospels.* Translated by Paul P. Levertoff. London: Society for the Promoting of Christian Knowledge, 1935.

Franzman, Seth J., and Kark, Ruth. "General Gordon, The Palestine Exploration Fund and the Origins of 'Gordon's Calvary' in the Holy Land." *PEQ* 140.2 (2008): 1–18.

Geva, Hillel. "Jerusalem, the Second Wall." *NEAEHL* 2:736.

Gibson, Shimon. *The Final Days of Jesus: The Archaeological Evidence.* New York: HarperCollins, 2009.

Hutchinson., N. F. "Further Notes on Our Lord's Tomb." *Palestine Exploration Fund Quarterly Statement* (1873): 113–15.

———. "Notes on Our Lord's Tomb." *Palestine Exploration Fund Quarterly Statement* (1870): 379–81.

Levine, Lee. *Jerusalem: Portrait of the City in the Second Temple Period (538 BCE–70 CE).* Philadelphia: Jewish Publication Society, 2002.

Martin, Earnest L. *The Secret of Golgotha: The Forgotten History of Christ's Crucifixion.* Alhambra: ASK Publications, 1988.

Mazar, Amihai. "Iron Age Burial Caves North of Damascus Gate Jerusalem." *IEJ* 26 (1976): 1–8.

Schick, Conrad. "Gordon's Tomb." *Palestine Exploration Fund Quarterly Statement* (1892): 120–24.

———. "Notes, Mr. Schick's Work at Jerusalem." *Palestine Exploration Fund Quarterly Statement* (1874): 125.

Taylor, Joan E. "Golgotha: A Reconsideration of the Evidence for the Sites of Jesus' Crucifixion and Burial." *New Testament Studies* 44.2 (1998): 180–203.

Walker, P. W. L. *Holy City, Holy Places? Christian Attitudes to Jerusalem and the Holy Land in the Fourth Century.* Oxford: Clarendon Press, 1990.

CHAPTER 48

THE POST-RESURRECTION APPEARANCES OF CHRIST

Luke 24

Perry G. Phillips

KEY POINTS

- Many locations of the post-resurrection appearances of Jesus are difficult to identify with certainty.

- Textual evidence and geographical constraints help narrow down the options, though another form of evidence to consider is tradition.

- Even when tradition may suggest a site that is not authentic, we can still appreciate the spiritual and historical dimensions it points to.

W hy should any of you consider it incredible that God raises the dead?" Paul asks King Agrippa during his trial at Caesarea (Acts 26:8 NIV). Paul, of course, believed in Jesus' bodily resurrection. He was dazzled—and blinded—when he saw the risen Lord on the road to Damascus (Acts 9:3–5; 1 Cor 15:8). Other witnesses substantiate Paul: the women at the empty tomb (Matt 28:1–10), the apostles (John 20:19–29), and the five hundred who saw the risen Christ at one time (1 Cor 15:6).

Why Paul's emphasis on the physical resurrection of Jesus? According to Paul, Christianity descends to pitiful delusion without it. If Christ did not rise from the

dead, we might as well eat, drink, and be merry, for tomorrow we die (1 Cor 15:32)! To Paul, hedonism—not another religion—is the only logical alternative to Christianity.

WHERE DID JESUS APPEAR AFTER HIS RESURRECTION?

As for the "space-time" aspect of the resurrection, we know well the "time": during the early part of the third decade AD. But what about the "space" component? Where specifically did the resurrected Jesus appear to the witnesses? The answer to this question first requires an inventory of his post-resurrection appearances.

Beitzel presents detailed list of post-resurrection appearances.[1] His entries are geographical, not chronological,[2] and the locations radiate out from Jerusalem to Damascus. The following table reproduces his entries with slight modifications.

TABLE 1: SUMMARY OF JESUS' POST-RESURRECTION APPEARANCES

Person(s) to whom Jesus appears	Location	Biblical Reference(s)
Mary Magdalene	Beside the open tomb	Mark 16:9–11; Luke 24:1–11; John 20:11–18
Mary Magdalene, the "other" Mary (the mother of James and Joseph), the wife of Cleopas	A short distance from the tomb	Matt 28:1–10; 27:56; John 19:25
Peter/Cephas	Jerusalem	Luke 24:34b; 1 Cor 15:5a (reported second-hand)
Ten disciples, Thomas absent	Jerusalem (Upper Room?)	Luke 24:36–48; John 20:19–23
The disciples, Thomas present	Jerusalem (Upper Room?)	Mark 16:14–18; John 20:26–29
All the disciples	Jerusalem (Upper Room?)	1 Cor 15:7b
Stephen	Jerusalem	Acts 7:55–56
James	Near Jerusalem	1 Cor 15:7a
More than 500 believers at one time	Near Jerusalem? Galilee?	1 Cor 15:6
Two disciples	Road to Emmaus	Mark 16:12–13; Luke 24:13–31
Eleven disciples	A mountain in Galilee	Matt 28:16–20
Seven disciples	Shore of the Sea of Galilee	John 21:1–23
Disciples	Mount of Olives	Acts 1:3–11 (compare with Mark 16:9 and 1 Cor 15:5b)
Saul/Paul	Road to Damascus	Acts 9:3–9; 1 Cor 15:8

---

1. Barry J. Beitzel, *The New Moody Atlas of the Bible* (Chicago: Moody Bible Institute, 2009), 248–49.

2. Kurt Aland provides a short chronology in *Synopsis of the Four Gospels,* 10th ed. (New York: United Bible Societies, 1993), 354–55.

Traditions abound as to the locations of the post-resurrection appearances. Within these traditions, however, one finds historical evidence that enables pinning down some locations with reasonable confidence.

THE TOMB OF JESUS

Two locations vie for the historical location of the tomb of Jesus. One has a history that goes back centuries—the Church of the Holy Sepulchre. The other—the Garden Tomb, or Gordon's Calvary—is a relatively recent option, first suggested in the 1800s. Catholic and Orthodox believers favor the first, as do a number of Protestant believers.[3] Others prefer the second.[4] History and archaeology, however, support the first location.[5]

The Church of the Holy Sepulchre

Located inside the present wall of the Old City of Jerusalem (but outside the city wall in Jesus' time),[6] the site of the church has been venerated since at least the time of Constantine and his mother Helena.[7] One may question the historicity of Helena's finding the cross upon which Jesus was crucified, but this should not dissuade

acceptance of the line of witness from the time of the crucifixion to Constantine's building the original church.

Specifically, it is hard to believe that the early Christians of Jerusalem did not know the location of Jesus' tomb where they and Christian pilgrims to Jerusalem visited and venerated the site. Although numerous Christians left Jerusalem before Vespasian and Titus advanced against and subsequently destroyed the city in AD 70, a number remained in the city, and they would continue to keep memory of the site alive.

In AD 130, the Emperor Hadrian visited the city, still in ruins, and he rebuilt it, calling it Aelia Capitolina.[8] Unfortunately, two years later the Bar Kochba Revolt brought more destruction upon the city, whereupon Hadrian, to eliminate Jewish influence, expelled all Jews from the city and forbade them to enter except once a year to commemorate the destruction of their city.[9]

Furthermore, possibly as an affront to Christianity, when Hadrian had Jerusalem rebuilt, he had the area "venerated by Christians as the place of Jesus' burial and resurrection"[10] turned

---

3. The administrative sects for the Church of the Holy Sepulchre are Roman Catholic, Greek Orthodox, Armenian Apostolic, Coptic, Ethiopian, and Syriac Orthodox.

4. Before the establishment of the Garden Tomb, Christendom universally accepted the Church of the Holy Sepulchre as the original site. The idea that the Garden Tomb was the site of Christ's crucifixion is associated with General Charles Gordon who visited the site in the 1880s (Charles Gordon, "Eden and Golgotha," *Palestine Exploration Fund Quarterly Statement* [January 1885]: 78–81). However, the possibility had been suggested by travelers before Gordon in the mid-1800s.

5. See Benjamin A. Foreman, "Locating Jesus' Crucifixion and Burial" on pg. 504.

6. See Dan Bahat, *The Carta Jerusalem Atlas*, 3rd ed. (Jerusalem: Carta, 2011), 61.

7. Eusebius, *Life of Constantine*, 3.25–45.

8. Dio Cassius, *Roman History* 69.12.1.

9. Martin C. Albl, *Pseudo-Gregory of Nyssa: Testimonies against the Jews* (Atlanta: Society of Biblical Literature, 2004), xx.

10. Beitzel, *New Moody Atlas*, 229–30.

into a temple to Venus (Aphrodite).[11] Unwittingly, however, Hadrian sustained the knowledge of the location of Jesus' tomb by constructing a conspicuous landmark over the top of it. If someone asked where Jesus' tomb was located, "Under Hadrian's temple" would be the easy reply. Clearly, Constantine had good ground (literally and historically) upon which to build his church commemorating Jesus' resurrection.

Constantine's church was much larger than today's, which dates from the period of the Crusades. Constantine's church, called the "Anastasis," or "Resurrection," extended about one hundred meters from its current location east to the present Alexander Nevski Church.

The Church of the Holy Sepulchre has been destroyed and rebuilt at various times through the centuries,[12] but it has maintained a continuous witness of historical authenticity into the present.

The Garden Tomb (Gordon's Calvary)

The Garden Tomb is situated about one fifth of a mile (two hundred fifty meters), or a five minute walk, north of Jerusalem's Damascus Gate. To reach the entrance, follow a stone wall to an alley opposite an East Jerusalem bus terminal and make a right. Once inside, pilgrims immediately sense the difference between the hustle and bustle of the Church of the Holy Sepulchre and the irenic ambience of the Garden Tomb. While the church fits the history and archaeology, the garden has the character and feel. Often one hears something like, "Ah, this is more like what the garden and the tomb would have been like. I can feel it."

The Garden Tomb fits the conception of Jesus' tomb in the popular imagination; it has a tomb, a garden with a very deep cistern for water, and a hill nearby, the so-called "Gordon's Calvary," whose weather-beaten flank looks like a skull ("Golgotha" means "place of the skull"; see Matt 27:33; Mark 15:22; John 19:17).

Several factors, however, work against the garden's historical connection to the tomb. First, this site was not considered an alternative to the Church of the Holy Sepulchre until the mid 1800s, and the suggestion sometimes arose more from spiritual and typological considerations than with the evidence from history and archaeology.[13]

Second, the tomb's structure resembles that of Iron Age tombs, not tombs constructed during the first century AD.[14] Iron Age tombs surround the area

---

11. Eusebius, *Life of Constantine*, 3.26.

12. For a short history, see Jerome Murphy-O'Connor, *The Holy Land: An Archaeological Guide from the Earliest Times to 1700*, 3rd ed. (New York: Oxford University Press), 49–52.

13. Murphy-O'Connor, *The Holy Land*, 146–48. For a comprehensive discussion, see Gabriel Barkay's "The Garden Tomb: Was Jesus Buried Here?" *BAR* 12.2 (Mar/Apr 1986): 40–53, 56–57. Gordon's identification was based, in large part, on his belief that Jesus had to have been crucified to the north of the temple's altar because sacrificial victims were to be slain north of the altar according to Lev 1:11. Gordon wrote that "if a particular direction was given by God about where the types were to be slain, it is a sure deduction that the prototype would be slain in some position as to the Altar: this the Skull Hill fulfils. ... The Latin Holy Sepulchre is west of the Altar, and therefore, unless the types are wrong, it should never have been taken as the site" (Gordon, "Eden and Golgotha," 79).

14. The visitor to the Garden Tomb should take time to compare the structure of this tomb with the Iron Age tombs behind the Menahem Begin Heritage Center in Jerusalem.

of the Garden Tomb, but no Iron Age tombs are found near the Church of the Holy Sepulchre. On the contrary, a first century AD tomb resides within the confines of the church in the Syrian chapel behind the Coptic portion of the Aedicule. The Iron Age association with the Garden Tomb and the first century AD association with the Church of the Holy Sepulchre does not prove that the latter is the authentic site, but it strongly undermines the claim of the former.[15]

WHERE DID JESUS MEET THE DISCIPLES IN JERUSALEM?

Jesus is dead! Fear has gripped the disciples. First they scatter to avoid prosecution or the same fate as their leader. On the other hand, they need consoling and mutual encouragement. With Jesus they experienced purpose, fellowship, inspiration, reassurance; now they are sorely downcast. Life without Jesus is bare, baseless, and bleak. What to do?

The last time they felt assured and optimistic was during the Lord's Supper in the upper room, so the disciples wander back to the site of their last meeting for mutual support and to wait out three days hoping that their leader would return. And he did! In startling fashion that Sunday morning!

If they met in the upper room, then they met on present-day Mount Zion. Strong tradition places the upper room there.[16] Its location is a short walk from the Zion Gate and not far from the Domitian Abbey. The room is above the traditional site of David's Tomb. The present structure dates from the fourteenth century and also served as a mosque after modification in the sixteenth century. (There is a *mihrab*, or Muslim prayer niche, on the eastern wall of the structure.) This site, visited by thousands of pilgrims over the centuries is, most likely, authentic.

LOCATING EMMAUS

Imagine you're near New York City walking and talking with a friend. It's September 12, 2001. Unexpectedly, a stranger joins you and asks what you're talking about. "The events yesterday," you and your friend reply. "What events?" replies the stranger. "What!" you respond in disbelief. "Are you the only person in New York who doesn't know what happened yesterday?"

This is how the two disciples on the road to Emmaus must have felt when they first encountered Jesus.

So where was this meeting? To answer this question, we turn our attention to the location of the village of Emmaus.

Luke places Emmaus sixty stadia, or seven miles (eleven kilometers), from Jerusalem (Luke 24:13). It would appear straightforward to locate Emmaus were it not for a variant in the Greek text of Luke that places Emmaus one hundred sixty stadia from Jerusalem (slightly over

---

15. Discussing the true location of Jesus' tomb appeals to historical-geographical/archaeological geeks, but it is a moot point. "Jesus is not here; for he is risen!" (Matt 28:6 KJV)

16. See Bargil Pixner, "Church of the Apostles Found on Mount Zion," *BAR* 16.3 (May/June 1990): 16–35, 60, accessed April 20, 2016 at http://www.centuryone.org/apostles.html; Michael P. Germano, "The Ancient Church of the Apostles: Revisiting Jerusalem's Cenacle and David's Tomb," *BibArch* (website), accessed April 20, 2016, http://www.bibarch.com/Perspectives/Germano-Cenacle-Paper.pdf.

eighteen miles, or thirty kilometers).[17] Tradition and Luke's distance markers leave only four localities for Emmaus that make geographical and historical sense.

The two locations roughly sixty stadia from Jerusalem are el Qubeibeh and Abu Ghosh. Unfortunately, the traditions for both sites go only as far back as the Crusaders in the mid-twelfth century, with no record of either site being named Emmaus before this time. It appears that the Crusaders chose these sites primarily on the basis of distance, unaware of another site to the west with hundreds of years of forgotten tradition behind it: Nicopolis.

Tradition strongly supports the ancient site of Nicopolis, one hundred sixty stadia from Jerusalem, as the authentic Emmaus. First, both 1 Maccabees and Josephus mention Emmaus/Nicopolis as the site of several battles during the Maccabean/Hasmonean revolt against the Greeks (1 Macc 3:40, 57; 4:3; Ant. 12.98, 306; 13.15). Josephus also mentions the city in connection with the First Jewish Revolt against the Romans (War 5.32). Second, Eusebius points to Nicopolis as Emmaus in his Onomasticon (90.15). Lastly, the Arab village adjacent to this site bore the name "Imwas," or "Amwas," and this preserves the ancient name Emmaus.[18]

But what about its distance from Jerusalem? The tradition behind Nicopolis/Emmaus was so well established by the fourth century that it is not improbable that somewhere along the line a scribe "corrected" the Lukan account, modifying sixty to one hundred sixty. In other words, tradition trumped the preponderance of manuscript evidence for sixty stadia.

Nicopolis' distance from Jerusalem is not the only drawback to its identification with Emmaus. Luke states that the disciples "at once" got up to go back to Jerusalem. It was later in the same day that Jesus arose, and it had been almost evening when they had stopped (Luke 24:29). With a twenty mile (32.2 km) trip ahead of them, they would not have reached Jerusalem until early the next morning. From the text, the other disciples are together (Luke 24:33); they had either stayed at the Jerusalem location through the night or they had gathered together very early in the morning. Neither alternative is impossible, but they do not seem entirely plausible.

There remains one more proposal for Emmaus. Josephus mentions a place near Jerusalem named Emmaus (now called Mozah/Coloniyeh) where soldiers of the Roman Legion retired (War 7:217). This site is thirty stadia (3.5 miles, or 6 km) from Jerusalem, and the remains of a Roman road stretch out nearby. But if this is the authentic site, then one must assume Luke is giving the round-trip distance from Jerusalem to Emmaus.

Given all exigencies, probably the best location for Emmaus is Mozah, although Nicopolis is not impossible.

JESUS AND HIS DISCIPLES IN GALILEE

Less known is where Jesus met his disciples in Galilee. We know one place

---

17. Most manuscripts read sixty. Those that read one hundred sixty include Codex Sinaiticus. Sixty, however, is the preferred reading. See Bruce Metzger, A Textual Commentary on the Greek New Testament (New York: United Bible Societies, 1994), 158.

18. After the Six-Day War, for security reasons (protecting the main highway from Tel Aviv to Jerusalem), Israel removed the Arab residents of Imwas and turned the location into a park.

Pilgrims at the Mount of Beatitudes

was a mountain (Matt 28:16; Mark 16:7), and another was on the shore of the Sea of Galilee (John 21:1). It is possible that the mountain was the Mount of the Beatitudes since many people were able to see and to hear Jesus during his Sermon on the Mount. The expansive view from this site does not impede the ability of five hundred people to see the risen Jesus at one time (1 Cor 15:6).

As for the meeting at the shore of Galilee, the only candidate is the Church of the Primacy of Saint Peter by Tabgha on the northwestern shore of the lake.[19]

ASCENT TO HEAVEN

Jesus ascended into heaven on the Mount of Olives (Luke 24:50–52; Acts 1:12) east of the Old City of Jerusalem across the Kidron Valley. Where exactly the event took place, no one knows, although traditionally the Chapel of the Ascension marks where pilgrims have revered this event.[20]

CONCLUSION

Pilgrims to Israel often lament that they came to see the real thing, not traditions. But, without traditions we would not know any of the places visited by the risen Christ. The pilgrim should remember that visits to traditional locales have a spiritual dimension as well as a historical one. Although questions may arise concerning the authenticity of a site, we should be thankful that each one reminds us of the rock-bottom truth of Christianity: Jesus died for our sins, rose from the dead, appeared to many witnesses, and is presently interceding for us before our heavenly Father.

BIBLIOGRAPHY

Aland, Kurt. *Synopsis of the Four Gospels.* 10th ed. New York: United Bible Societies, 1993.

Albl, Martin C. *Pseudo-Gregory of Nyssa: Testimonies Against the Jews.* Atlanta: Society of Biblical Literature, 2004.

---

19. Murphy-O'Connor, *The Holy Land*, 285–86.

20. Denys Pringle, *The Churches of the Crusader Kingdom of Jerusalem: The city of Jerusalem III* (New York: Cambridge University Press, 2007), 74–76.

Bahat, Dan. *The Carta Jerusalem Atlas.* 3rd ed. Jerusalem: Carta, 2011.

Barkay, Gabriel. "The Garden Tomb: Was Jesus Buried Here?" *BAR* 12.2 (Mar/Apr 1986): 40–53, 56–57.

Beitzel, Barry J. *The New Moody Atlas of the Bible.* Chicago: Moody Bible Institute, 2009.

Germano, Michael P. "The Ancient Church of the Apostles: Revisiting Jerusalem's Cenacle and David's Tomb." *BibArch* (website). Accessed April 20, 2016. http://www.bibarch. com/Perspectives/Germano-Cenacle-Paper.pdf.

Gordon, Charles. "Eden and Golgotha." *Palestine Exploration Fund Quarterly Statement* (January 1885): 78–81.

Metzger, Bruce. *A Textual Commentary on the Greek New Testament.* New York: United Bible Societies, 1994.

Murphy-O'Connor, Jerome. *The Holy Land: An Archaeological Guide from the Earliest Times to 1700.* 3rd ed. Oxford: Oxford University Press, 1992.

Pixner, Bargil. "Church of the Apostles Found on Mount Zion." *BAR* 16.3 (May/June 1990): 16–35, 60. Accessed April 20, 2016 at http://www. centuryone.org/apostles.html.

Pringle, Denys. *The Churches of the Crusader Kingdom of Jerusalem: The City of Jerusalem III.* New York: Cambridge University Press, 2007.

MAPS AND CHARTS

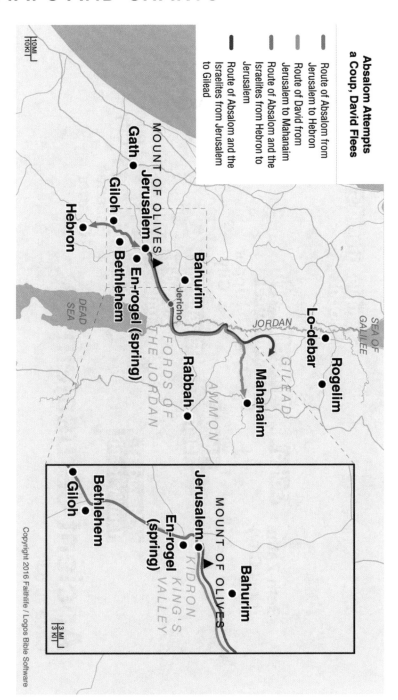

Absalom Attempts a Coup, David Flees

- Route of Absalom from Jerusalem to Hebron
- Route of David from Jerusalem to Mahanaim
- Route of Absalom and the Israelites from Hebron to Jerusalem
- Route of Absalom and the Israelites from Jerusalem to Gilead

10 MI
10 KI

MOUNT OF OLIVES

Gath

Giloh

Jerusalem

Hebron

Bethlehem

En-rogel (spring)

Bahurim

Jericho

DEAD SEA

JORDAN

Lo-debar

Rogelim

SEA OF GALILEE

Rabbah

FORDS OF THE JORDAN

AMMON

GILEAD

Mahanaim

Jerusalem

Bethlehem

Giloh

En-rogel (spring)

MOUNT OF OLIVES

KIDRON

KING'S VALLEY

Bahurim

3 MI
3 KI

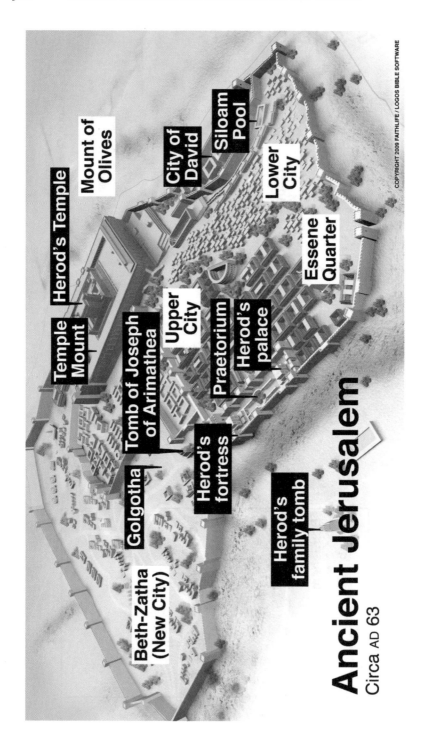

Mount of Olives

Herod's Temple

City of David

Siloam Pool

Lower City

Temple Mount

Essene Quarter

Upper City

Tomb of Joseph of Arimathea

Praetorium

Herod's palace

Golgotha

Herod's fortress

Beth-Zatha (New City)

Herod's family tomb

Ancient Jerusalem
Circa AD 63

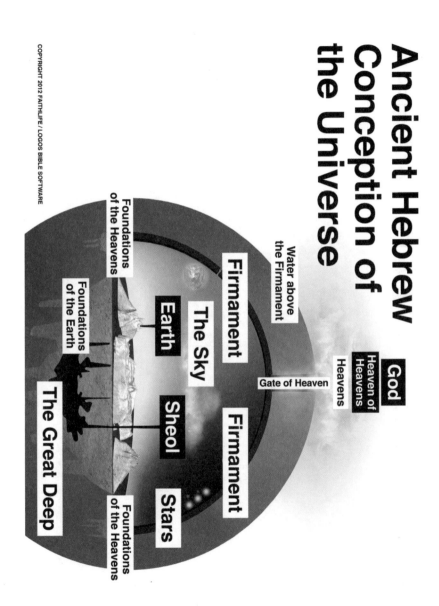

Ancient Hebrew Conception of the Universe

Agricultural Cycle of the Levant/Palestine

	SEPT	OCT	NOV	DEC	JAN	FEB	MARCH	APRIL	MAY	JUNE	JULY	AUG	SEPT
SOLAR MONTHS													
HEBREW LUNAR MONTHS		TISHRI	MARCH-ESHVAN	CHISLEV	TEBETH	SHEBAT	ADAR	NISAN	IYYAR	SIVAN	TAMMUZ	AB	ELUL
FEASTS AND FESTIVALS		TRUMPETS / DAY OF ATONEMENT / TABERNACLES		DEDICATION			PURIM	PASSOVER / UNLEAVENED BREAD	PENTECOST & FIRSTFRUITS				
SEASON		RAINY SEASON							DRY SEASON				
RAINFALL		EARLY RAINS		WINTER RAINS			LATE RAINS		DROUGHT				
AGRICULTURAL ACTIVITIES		PLOW		PLANT			HARVEST						
HARVEST							BARLEY		WHEAT	FIRST FIGS	GRAPES	DATES, SUMMER FIGS	

0 15 30 Miles
0 15 30 Kilometers

N

SIDON •

ITUREA

Damascus ◉

S Y R I A

Pharpar River

Tyre •

Litani River

Panias
(Caesarea
Philippi) •

TRACHONITIS

Kedesh •

P
H
O
E
N
I
C
I
A

Lake
Hulah

G
A
U
L
A
N
I
T
I
S

MEDITERRANEAN
SEA

Acco •

Hazor •

Chorazin •
• Bethsaida

B
A
T
A
N
E
A

Raphana ◉

Capernaum •

• Arbela
Sepphoris •
Tiberias • • Hippos

• Ashtaroth

Canatha
(Kenath) ◉

Geba •
G
A
L
I
L
E
E

Nazareth •

Sea of
Galilee

Yarmuk River

AURANITIS

Dor •

Gadara ◉ • Abila

• Edrei

Caesarea
Maritima
(Strato's Tower) •

Scythopolis
(Beth-shan) ◉

D
E
C
A
P
O
L
I
S

Sebaste
(Samaria) •

Pella ◉

• Dion

W. Fara River

Amathus •

Gerasa
(Jerash) ◉

Antipatris
(Aphek) •

S A M A R I A
• Shechem

Jabbok

Jabbok River

Joppa •

Yarkon

River

Alexandrium ◉

Phasaelis ◉

P
E
R
E
A

Tyrus •

Philadelphia
(Amman) ◉

Jamnia •

• Gophna

Emmaus
(Nicopolis) •

Jericho •

Cypros ◉

Livias •

Azotus
(Ashdod) ◉

Jerusalem ◉

Esbus
(Heshbon) •

E a s t e r n
D e s e r t

Ascalon
(Ashkelon) ◉

Betogabris
(Beth-guvrin) •

Bethlehem •
Hyrcania ◉

Medeba •

Gaza •

Marisa
(Mareshah) •

J
U
D
E
A

Herodium ◉

Callirrhoe •

• Hebron

Machaerus ◉

• Dibon

• Adora

DEAD
SEA

Arnon River

I D U M E A
Masada ◉

Beersheba •

Brook

Malatha •

Z
e
r
e
d

River

Mampsis •

N
A
B
A
T
E
A

KINGDOM OF HEROD THE GREAT

•	City
◉	Site of Herodian fortress
◉	Decapolis city
◉	Cities Herod gave to his sister Salome
▨	Boundary of Herod the Great's Kingdom
▨	Boundary of domain given to Archelaus, son of Herod, by Augustus Caesar in (4 BC), when Herod died
▨	Boundary of domain given to Herod Antipas, son of Herod, by Augustus Caesar in (4 BC), when Herod died
▨	Boundary of domain given to Herod Philip, son of Herod, by Augustus Caesar in (4 BC), when Herod died
▨	Semi-independent municipality
▨	Syrian Province

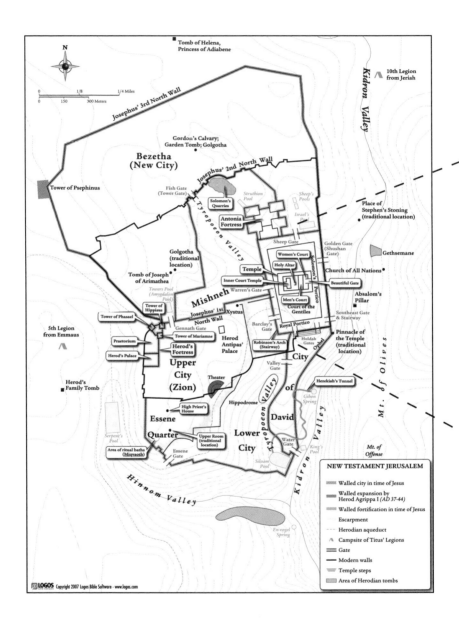

N

Tomb of Helena,
Princess of Adiabene

10th Legion
from Jeriah

Kidron Valley

0   1/8   1/4 Miles
0   150   300 Meters

Josephus' 3rd North Wall

Gordon's Calvary;
Garden Tomb; Golgotha

Bezetha
(New City)

Josephus' 2nd North Wall

Tower of Psephinus

Fish Gate
(Tower Gate)

Struthion
Pool

Sheep'
Pools

Solomon's
Quarries

Israel's
Pool

Place of
Stephen's Stoning
(traditional location)

Antonia
Fortress

Sheep Gate

Golden Gate
(Shushan
Gate)

Gethsemane

Golgotha
(traditional
location)

Women's Court

Solomon's

Church of All Nations

Tomb of Joseph
of Arimathea

Temple

Holy Altar

Portico

Beautiful Gate

Inner Court Temple

Towers Pool
(Amygdalon
Pool)

Warren's Gate

Men's Court

Absalom's
Pillar

Tower of
Hippicus

Mishneh

Court of the
Gentiles

Southeast Gate
& Stairway

Tower of Phasael

Josephus' 1st
North Wall

Xystus

5th Legion
from Emmaus

Gennath Gate

Barclay's
Gate

Royal Portico

Pinnacle of
the Temple
(traditional
location)

Praetorium

Tower of Mariamne

Herod
Antipas'
Palace

Robinson's Arch
(Stairway)

Huldah
Gates

Herod's Palace

Herod's
Fortress

Upper
City
(Zion)

Theater

Valley
Gate

City

Hezekiah's Tunnel

Herod's
Family Tomb

High Priest's
House

Hippodrome

Gihon
Spring

of

David

Mt. of Olives

Essene
Quarter

Upper Room
(traditional
location)

Lower
City

Water
Gate

King's
Pool

Mt. of
Offense

Serpent's
Pool

Area of ritual baths
(Miqvaoth)

Essene
Gate

Siloam
Pool

Hinnom Valley

En-rogel
Spring

Kidron Valley

Tyropoeon Valley

Ophel

NEW TESTAMENT JERUSALEM

Walled city in time of Jesus

Walled expansion by
Herod Agrippa I *(AD 37-44)*

Walled fortification in time of Jesus

Escarpment

Herodian aqueduct

Campsite of Titus' Legions

Gate

Modern walls

Temple steps

Area of Herodian tombs

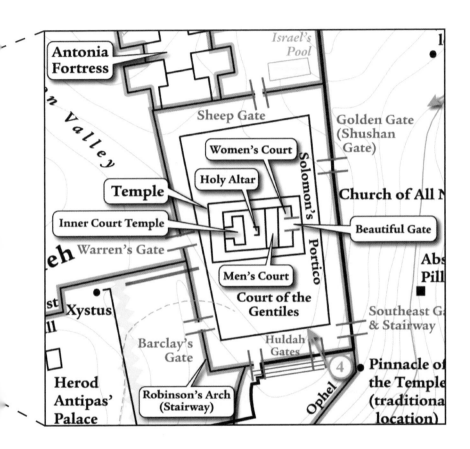

Close up of Solomon's Portico

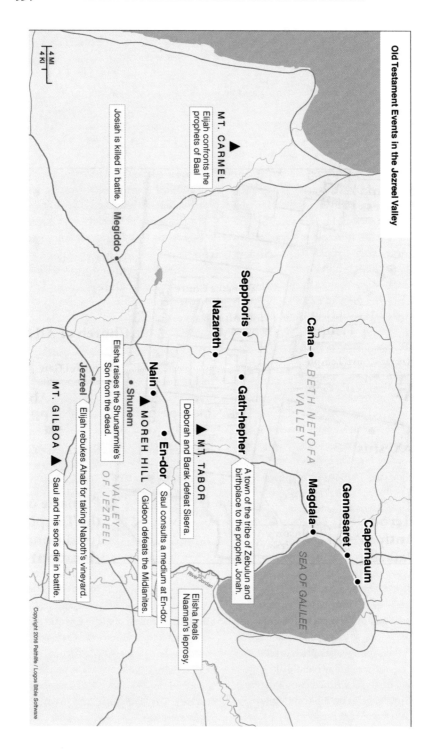

Old Testament Events in the Jezreel Valley

4 Mi
4 Ki

MT. CARMEL

Elijah confronts the prophets of Baal

Josiah is killed in battle.

Megiddo

Sepphoris

Nazareth

Cana

BETH NETOFA VALLEY

Gath-hepher

A town of the tribe of Zebulun and birthplace to the prophet, Jonah.

Magdala

Gennesaret

Capernaum

Elisha raises the Shunammite's Son from the dead.

Nain

Shunem

MOREH HILL

En-dor

MT. TABOR

Deborah and Barak defeat Sisera.

Saul consults a medium at En-dor.

Gideon defeats the Midianites.

SEA OF GALILEE

River Jordan

Elisha heals Naaman's leprosy.

Jezreel

Elijah rebukes Ahab for taking Naboth's vineyard.

MT. GILBOA

Saul and his sons die in battle.

VALLEY OF JEZREEL

CONTRIBUTORS

Dr. Barry J. Beitzel is Professor Emeritus of Old Testament and Semitic Languages at Trinity Evangelical Divinity School in Deerfield, Illinois, USA. He holds a Ph.D. in Ancient Near Eastern Studies from Dropsie University in Philadelphia. He obtained a postdoctorate in Ancient Near Eastern Geography from the Université de Liège, Belgium, and has engaged in postdoctoral archaeological work through UCLA in eastern Syria. Dr. Beitzel is the author of *The New Moody Atlas of the Bible* (Moody Press, 2009). His publications on Near Eastern geography have appeared in a variety of monographs and journals, from *Biblical Archaeology Review* and *The Bulletin of the American Schools of Oriental Research* to *Iraq: The British Institute for the Study of Iraq*. Dr. Beitzel's maps appear in *National Geographic*, *The Biblical Word: An Illustrated Atlas*, *The Holman Bible Atlas*, *The NIV Study Bible*, *The ESV Study Bible*, and in several monographs.

Kristopher Lyle obtained an M.A. in Biblical Hebrew from the University of Stellenbosch (South Africa). His research focuses on applying cognitive linguistic frameworks to our understanding of the biblical languages. He has authored and co-authored four handbooks on discourse analysis with Lexham Press and multiple articles on Biblical Hebrew lexical semantics. He received the SASNES award for his M.A. thesis in 2013.

Vernon Alexander received an M.A. in Biblical Historical Geography from Jerusalem University College and an M.A. in Christian Theology from Durham University. He is currently completing his doctoral dissertation on the subject of war propaganda in the Hebrew Bible at Bar Ilan University. He is currently Adjunct Faculty in Historical and Geographic Settings of the Bible at Jerusalem University College, as well as Adjunct Faculty in Old Testament at Belmont University. He has taught over 25 study groups on-site including for Jerusalem University College and The General Theological Seminary of the Episcopal Church, and resided in Jerusalem for six years.

Dr. John A. Beck (Ph.D., Trinity International University) has taught courses in Hebrew and Old Testament at various colleges and universities for more than 25 years. For more than 20 of those years, he has been teaching field-studies in Israel, Jordan, and Egypt which explore the relationship between geography, culture, and Bible communication. Beck spends most of his year writing and is a permanent adjunct faculty member at Jerusalem University College in Israel. His articles have appeared in numerous academic journals and books. His books include: *The Land of Milk and Honey*, *God as Storyteller*, *A Visual Guide to Bible Events*, *Zondervan Dictionary of Biblical Imagery*,

Understand Your Bible, the *Discovery House Bible Atlas*, and forthcoming *The Holy Land for Christian Travelers*. He has participated in various video production projects with Our Daily Bread Ministries, including *The Rescue of Jerusalem, a Battle of Faith*. Beck lives in Wisconsin.

Dr. Todd Bolen is Associate Professor of Biblical Studies at The Master's University in Santa Clarita, CA. For more than a decade, he lived and taught at the university's Israel Bible Extension (IBEX) campus near Jerusalem, and he continues to instruct undergraduate and seminary groups in Israel. Bolen is the creator of the *Pictorial Library of Bible Lands* (18 volumes) and the *Historic Views of the Holy Land* (17 volumes). He is currently leading a team of researchers in creating the *Photo Companion to the Bible* with the goal of illustrating nearly every verse in Scripture. He was a contributing author to *Jesus: A Visual History*, by Donald L. Brake, and he wrote the notes for 2 Kings in the *Zondervan* NIV *Study Bible*.

Dr. Benjamin A. Foreman received his M.A. from the Hebrew University of Jerusalem and his Ph.D. from the University of Aberdeen (2009). He has lived in Israel for 12 years and is a faculty member at the Israel extension of The Master's University (IBEX), where he teaches historical geography and biblical history. He also travels to Hungary on a yearly basis and is a guest lecturer of Manners and Customs and Psalms at the Word of Life Bible Institute. He has participated in several archaeological digs in Israel and is the author of *Animal Metaphors and the People of Israel in the Book of Jeremiah* (Vandenhoeck & Ruprecht, 2011).

Gordon Franz teaches at New York School of the Bible in New York City and Evangelical Missions and Seminary International in New Jersey. He studied historical geography and archaeology at the Institute of Holy Lands Studies (now the Jerusalem University College) and completed his M.A. in Old Testament Studies at Columbia Biblical Seminary in South Carolina. Gordon has also taught the field trips for the physical settings of the Bible for a number of years at several institutions in Jerusalem, including the Institute of Holy Land Studies. He developed and co-taught the Talbot School of Theology's Bible Lands program in Israel, as well as in Turkey, Greece, and Rome. He has participated in a number of archaeological excavations over the past 35 years, including Keter Hinnom where he was the area supervisor of Cave 25 where the two oldest biblical texts were discovered on two silver amulets, which pre-date the Dead Sea Scrolls by 400 years. He also worked at Kh. Nisya, Efrat, Lachish, Ramat Rachel, Jezreel, Hazor, Tel Zayit, and on Malta.

Dr. J. Carl Laney is Professor of Biblical Literature at Western Seminary in Portland, Oregon. Laney was introduced to the land of the Bible in 1973 during his studies at the Jerusalem University College (formerly the Institute of Holy Land Studies). Since that experience he has given special attention to the geographical, cultural, and historical background of the Bible, writing his Th.M. thesis at Western Seminary on "The Geopolitics of the Judean Hill Country" and his Th.D. dissertation at Dallas Theological Seminary on "Selective Geographical Problems in the Life of Christ." Laney's studies in Israel have included excavations at Tel Qasile, Tel

Jezreel, and Bethsaida. Since 1992 he has been taking students to Israel to participate in the short-term program at the Jerusalem University College. Laney's book, *Concise Bible Atlas: A Geographical Survey of Bible History*, is published by Hendrickson Publishers.

Chris McKinny is a Ph.D. candidate at Bar Ilan University (Israel) where he has submitted a dissertation focusing on the historical geography and archaeology of the town lists of Judah and Benjamin in the book of Joshua. Chris is also a core staff member of the Tel Burna Archaeological Project and is currently involved in several other writing and research projects. His past projects include *My People as Your People: A Textual and Archaeological Analysis of the Reign of Jehoshaphat* (Peter Lang, 2016) and *The Regnal Chronology of the Kings of Israel and Judah* (BiblePlaces, 2015). In addition to this academic research, Chris has served as an adjunct faculty member at the Israel Bible Extension Campus (IBEX) of the Master's University and has led numerous field tours throughout Israel for undergraduates, graduates, and laypeople.

Dr. Cynthia Parker is the Clark Assistant Professor of Biblical Studies at Biblical Theological Seminary. She holds a Ph.D. in Theological and Religious Studies from the University of Gloucestershire and teaches in churches and universities around the world. Her research interests include biblical views of place, biblical history and geography, and the correlation between theology and ecology (with particular interest in food justice). Cynthia lived in Jerusalem for five years, teaching Historical Geography of the Bible at Jerusalem University College,

and has led dozens of trips to Israel. She continues to develop innovative educational trips to Israel, seeking to inspire students of all ages through experiential education.

Dr. Elaine A. Phillips is Distinguished Professor of Biblical Studies at Gordon College in Wenham, MA, where she has taught since 1993. She holds a Ph.D. in Rabbinics from the Dropsie College for Hebrew and Cognate Learning. She and her husband, Perry (also a contributor to the *Lexham Geographic Commentary on the Gospels*), studied and taught at the Institute for Holy Land Studies (now Jerusalem University College, JUC) from 1976–79 and are adjunct faculty with JUC, serving as field instructors for the three-week course in Historical and Geographical Settings of the Bible. In addition to field study in Israel, her areas of interest and scholarly writing include the books of Exodus and Esther, biblical wisdom literature, and hermeneutics. Her book-length commentary on Esther is included in *The Expositor's Bible Commentary*, edited by Tremper Longman III and David Garland. She authored *With God Nothing Is Impossible* (Deep River Books, 2014), tracing narratives of key women in the Bible as their stories unfolded in the promised land.

Dr. Perry Phillips, after receiving his Ph.D. in astrophysics from Cornell University where he became a Christian as a graduate student, attended Biblical Theological Seminary, where he earned his M.Div. before heading to the Institute of Holy Land Studies, now Jerusalem University College (JUC), to complete his M.A. in Hebrew language. After his M.A., Dr. Phillips remained at JUC where he taught historical geography to groups of students from around the world. Dr. Phillips has taught over 60 groups in Israel, off and on, and continues to teach historical geography in conjunction with his wife, Dr. Elaine Phillips (also a contributor to the *Lexham Geographic Commentary on the Gospels*).

A.D. Riddle is a Ph.D. student at Trinity Evangelical Divinity School. His doctoral research is on the ancient road system of Lebanon. He received a graduate certificate in GIS and cartography from the University of Wisconsin-Madison, and an M.Div. and M.A. in archaeology and ANE languages from Trinity Evangelical Divinity School. Riddle has participated in excavations at et-Tell/Bethsaida, Tell es-Safi/Gath, and Abel Beth Maacah. He has traveled in Egypt, Lebanon, Israel, Jordan, Turkey, and Greece. His writing and photography appear in the *Pictorial Library of Bible Lands* and other resources from BiblePlaces.com. He has other published photographs related to archaeology and Bible lands in BAR, NEA, and various study Bibles, among others. Through his website RiddleMaps.com he has produced maps for various publications.

Aubrey L. Taylor is a Ph.D. candidate in Hebrew Bible at the University of Bar-Ilan in Israel and a member of the faculty for Jerusalem University College in Jerusalem, where she received her M.A. in Biblical History and Geography. Having lived in Israel for the better part of the last 10 years, she has taught dozens of field courses in the historical geography of the Bible for university and seminary students from all over the world. She has also lectured at the Tantur Ecumenical Institute in Jerusalem and led educational tours of Israel for lay audiences. Her current research centers on the Transjordan,

making her one of only a few scholars to focus on this region and to spend time teaching and researching in the modern country of Jordan. Interested in how space can be used for communicative effect, her work makes use of historical geography, the social sciences, and literary approaches to the Bible.

Emily Thomassen currently teaches Old Testament and Gospels at Trinity Christian College and has taught biblical history and geography at Jerusalem University College since 2011. Her teaching focuses on Bible, archaeology, history, and geography. She received her M.A. in Biblical History and Geography from Jerusalem University College. Her thesis focuses on geographic parallels between Elijah and Elisha and John the Baptist and Jesus. She is currently a graduate student at the University of Chicago and has archaeological field experience as an assistant square supervisor at Tell Keisan in Israel.

Rev. Dr. Paul H. Wright is President of Jerusalem University College/Institute of Holy Land Studies. Paul has lived full-time in Jerusalem since 1997, where he has taught classes in biblical historical geography and on the cultural backgrounds of the Bible to thousands of students in Israel. His Ph.D. was in Bible and Ancient Near East at Hebrew Union College, Cincinnati, OH. Paul has published extensively on topics related to the landed context of the Bible with the Israeli publisher Carta, and the *Rose Then and Now Bible Map Atlas* with Rose Publishing.

SUBJECT INDEX

Foster, George. 390n19

France, R. T. 13, 13n14, 27n21, 59n24, 59n28, 61n32, 189n22, 200n19, 201n22–n23, 214n84, 303n18, 312n10, 409n1, 410n4, 490n31

Franz, Gordon 125, 125n1, 169n6, 175, 204n35, 211, 211n68, 219, 219n1, 227n31, 230n47–n48, 237, 240n9, 241n15, 243n26, 264n11, 271n4, 275n23, 284n3, 314, 327, 328n3, 329n6, 331n10, 349n40, 369n5, 536

Franzman, Seth J. 508, 508n9–n10, 512n21–n22

Freedman, H. 129n16

Freund, Richard A. 272n8, 272n10, 273n12, 274n20

Freyne, Seán 150n2, 252n19

Friedberg, Arthur L. 433n3

Frier, Bruce W. 391n26

Gadara 159, 175, 178, 196–99, 199n13, 201–02, 207–15, 209n57, 209n63, 211n67, 212n73, 213n79, 214n82, 215n89, 219, 222, 225, 227–29, 231, 234, 243, 243n21, 253, 545

Gadara harbor 175, 207, 209–11, 209n63, 211n67, 212n73, 214–15, 222, 225, 228–29, 234, 243, 545

Gade, D. W. 184n1–n3, 190n25

Gadot, Yuval 321, 400n21, 448n14

Galilee xiv, xv, 2–3, 12, 19–20, 20n4, 21–23, 31–40, 39n12, 50, 54n2, 55, 66–67, 67n12, 70–81, 73n40, 75n2, 80n15, 84–90, 92, 95, 100–03, 110–12, 114, 117–23, 118n5, 118n7, 119n8, 120n12, 134–44, 141n21, 142n22, 143n23, 146–53, 147n32, 155, 157–71, 159n3, 161n7, 173, 175–81, 187–88, 196, 199–01, 199n13, 204n35, 204n37, 208–09, 210n64, 212n73, 214, 219–31, 234–35, 237–39, 241–43, 247–56,

250n11, 258, 260–68, 271–73, 278, 284, 289–92, 295–96, 300, 302–06, 309–12, 321, 330, 333, 338–39, 342, 344–45, 362, 370, 374, 376, 383, 387, 411, 415, 419, 421, 433, 459, 479, 497–98, 519, 523–24, 534, 544, 546–47, see also Sea of Galilee

Galilee of the Gentiles 33, 40, 89, 103

García Martínez, Florentino 113n6

Garden Tomb 504–16, 520–22, 520n4, 521n14, 532

Garland, David E. 118n6, 214n82, 537

Gath Hepher 103, 534

Gathercole, Simon J. 298, 298n2

Gaulanitis 23, 77, 88, 121, 121n20, 159, 159n3, 161–64, 230–31, 239, 241–43, 271, 291, 303, 309

Gaza 7–8, 27, 70

Gehenna 314–15, 323–25, 414, 428–29, 457, 457n54

Gennath Gate 514–15, 532

Gennesar harbor 224, 230

Gennesaret 103, 120n13, 139, 162, 167, 171, 224, 230, 239, 243, 249–50, 252–53, 271, 291, 534

Gentile 10, 33, 37, 40, 77, 88–90, 88n15, 96n11, 100, 103, 121–22, 121n20, 142, 146–47, 148n34, 154, 178, 183, 189, 191–94, 208, 212n73, 214, 227, 229, 231, 237, 239, 243, 243n21, 245, 247–58, 261–64, 271–72, 276, 291, 303–04, 330, 339, 351, 392, 418, 472, 472n38, 532

Gerasa 147n32, 196–99, 199n13, 201–02, 203n30, 208, 211–15, 213n77, 214n82, 215n89, 227

Gergesa 147n32, 196, 198–02, 199n10–n11, 199n13, 201n25, 205–08, 210n64, 212n74, 213n77, 213n79, 215, 215n88, 215n89, 227

Gerizim, Mt. Gerizim 95, 97n14, 98, 98n20, 339, 339n4

SCRIPTURE INDEX

Old Testament Books

New Testament Books

Septuagint (LXX)

Infancy Gospels

Latin translation of Greek

Josephus

Rabbinic Literature

IMAGE ATTRIBUTION

3D Model of Southwestern Corner of the Temple Mount
Photo by Daniel Warner.
Copyright 2004 The Virtual Bible
Used by permission.

3D Video: Jerusalem Flyover
Photo by Daniel Warner.
Copyright 2004 The Virtual Bible
Used by permission.

Aerial view of the Kursi Monastery
Photo by Barry J. Beitzel.
Copyright 2014 Faithlife / Logos Bible Software

Akeldama (within the Hinnom Valley)
Photo by פארוק.
Licensed under CC BY-SA 4.0.
Via Wikimedia Commons.

Altar in the Church of the Nativity
Photo by Darko Tepert Donatus.
Licensed under CC BY-SA 2.5.
Via Wikimedia Commons.

Antonia Fortress (northwest view)
Photo by Ariely.
Licensed under CC BY 3.0.
Via Wikimedia Commons.

Arcosolium and Shaft Tombs
Photo by Benjamin Foreman.
Copyright 2016 Benjamin Foreman
Used by permission.

Bethany
Photo by Daniel Warner.
Copyright 2004 The Virtual Bible
Used by permission.

The "Burnt House"
Photo by Amir Brener.
Licensed under CC BY-SA 3.0.
Via Wikimedia Commons.

The Caiaphas Ossuary
Photo by BRBurton.
Public Domain.
Via Wikimedia Commons.

Carob Pods
Photo by Júlio Reis.
Licensed under CC BY-SA 2.5.
Via Wikimedia Commons.

Cemetery on Mount of Olives
Photo by Antoine Taveneaux.
Licensed under CC BY-SA 3.0.
Via Wikimedia Commons.

The Church of the Holy Sepulchre
Photo by Jorge Lascar.
Licensed under CC BY-SA 2.0.
Via Wikimedia Commons.

Church of Peter in Gallicantu
Photo by Anton 17.
Licensed under CC BY-SA 3.0.
Via Wikimedia Commons.

Church of Saint Peter's Primacy
Photo by אליזבת גולדסטון.
Licensed under CC BY 2.5.
Via Wikimedia Commons.

Cistern at Qumran
Photo by David A. deSilva.
Copyright 2014 Faithlife / Logos Bible
Software

Close-up of Skull Hill
Photo by Юкатан.
Licensed under CC BY-SA 3.0.
Via Wikimedia Commons.

Colonnaded Street in Sepphorus
Photo by Oren Rozen.
Licensed under CC BY-SA 3.0.
Via Wikimedia Commons.

Dogs and Boar Statue, 1st Century AD
Photo by Pedrassani Edson L. Pedrassani.
Licensed under CC BY-SA 3.0.
Via Wikimedia Commons.

Double Gate Lintel and Relieving Arch
Photo by BiblePlaces.com (Todd Bolen).
Copyright 2009 BiblePlaces.com
Used by permission.

Elevation Profile of Jerusalem to Jericho
Image by A. D. Riddle.
Copyright 2017 Faithlife Corporation

The Golden Gate
Photo by Nikodem Nijaki.
Licensed under CC BY 3.0.
Via Wikimedia Commons.

Grain-mill
Photo by Barry J. Beitzel.
Copyright 2014 Faithlife / Logos Bible
Software

Ground view of the Kursi Monastery
Photo by Barry J. Beitzel.
Copyright 2014 Faithlife / Logos Bible
Software

Herod's Palace in Jerusalem
Photo by Daniel Warner.
Copyright 2004 The Virtual Bible
Used by permission.

Herod's Temple (Holyland Model of Jerusalem)
Photo by Juan R. Cuadra.
Public Domain.
Via Wikimedia Commons.

Herod's Winter Palace in Jericho
Photo by Daniel Warner.
Copyright 2004 The Virtual Bible
Used by permission.

Highland Plateaus of Upper Galilee
Photo by Maglanist.
Licensed under CC BY-SA 3.0.

Hippos (aerial view)
Photo by Avram Graicer.
Licensed under CC BY-SA 3.0.
Via Wikimedia Commons.

Hippos (center hill)
Photo by Daniel Warner.
Copyright 2004 The Virtual Bible
Used by permission.

House made from basalt in Chorazin, about two miles north of Capernaum
Photo by Daniel Warner.
Copyright 2004 The Virtual Bible
Used by permission.

Inside remains of the Kursi Monastery
Photo by Barry J. Beitzel.
Copyright 2014 Faithlife / Logos Bible
Software

Jerusalem Flyover (3D)
Photo by Daniel Warner.
Copyright 2004 The Virtual Bible
Used by permission.

Jordan Rift Valley
Photo by Zairon.
Licensed under CC BY-SA 4.0.
Via Wikimedia Commons.

Judean Central Hill Country
Photo by Maglanist.
Public Domain.
Via Wikimedia Commons.

Judean Wilderness
Photo by David Shankbone.
Licensed under CC BY-SA 3.0.
Via Wikimedia Commons.

Kidron Valley (looking south)
Photo by BiblePlaces.com (Todd Bolen).
Copyright 2009 BiblePlaces.com
Used by permission.

Kidron Valley (looking west)
Photo by Chris Yunker.
Licensed under CC BY-SA 2.0.
Via Wikimedia Commons.

Large Stones from the Western Wall
Photo by Gilabrand.
Licensed under CC BY-SA 3.0.
Via Wikimedia Commons.

Largest Stone in the Temple Mount
Photo by Lodo27.
Licensed under CC BY-SA 3.0.
Via Wikimedia Commons.

Location of Tel el-Araj
Photo by Benjamin Foreman.
Copyright 2016 Benjamin Foreman
Used by permission.

Map of Gadara Harbor
Image by Todd Bolen.
Copyright 2017 Todd Bolen
Used by permission.

Margins and Bosses on the Temple Mount Walls
Photo by Deror_avi.
Licensed under CC BY-SA 3.0.
Via Wikimedia Commons.

Millstone found at Capernaum
Photo by David A. deSilva.
Copyright 2014 Faithlife / Logos Bible
Software

The Mosaic at the Church of the Multiplication
Photo by Berthold Werner.
Public Domain.
Via Wikimedia Commons.

Mount Hermon
Photo by Barry J. Beitzel.
Copyright 2014 Faithlife / Logos Bible
Software

Mount of Olives (looking southeast)
Photo by Daniel Warner.
Copyright 2004 The Virtual Bible
Used by permission.

Mount Tabor and Jezreel Valley from Nazareth Ridge
Photo by BiblePlaces.com (Todd Bolen).
Copyright 2009 BiblePlaces.com
Used by permission.

Negev: Makhtesh Ramon
Photo by Andrew Shiva.
Licensed under CC BY-SA 4.0.
Via Wikimedia Commons.

Overview of Jerusalem
Photo by Daniel Warner.
Copyright 2004 The Virtual Bible
Used by permission.

Overview of Jerusalem: Temple Mount (6) and Pool of Siloam (9)
Photo by Daniel Warner.
Copyright 2004 The Virtual Bible
Used by permission.

Overview: Hinnom Valley and the Temple Mount
Photo by Daniel Warner.
Copyright 2004 The Virtual Bible
Used by permission.

Pilgrims at the Mount of Beatitudes
Photo by israeltourism.
Licensed under CC BY-SA 2.0.
Via Wikimedia Commons.

Reconstruction of Robinson's Arch
Photo by Участник.
Licensed under CC BY-SA 2.5.
Via Wikimedia Commons.

Reconstruction of the Royal Stoa
Photo by Evyatar Nevo.
Licensed under CC BY-SA 4.0.
Via Wikimedia Commons.

Remains of a Mosaic at Kursi
Photo by Anatavital.
Licensed under CC BY-SA 4.0.
Via Wikimedia Commons.

Remains of Jericho
Photo by Daniel Warner.
Copyright 2004 The Virtual Bible
Used by permission.

Remains of Robinson's Arch
Photo by Brian Jeffrey Beggerly.
Licensed under CC BY-SA 2.0.
Via Wikimedia Commons.

Remains of the Pool of Siloam
Photo by Barry J. Beitzel.
Copyright 2014 Faithlife / Logos Bible Software

Remains of the Western Wall
Photo by Daniel Warner.
Copyright 2004 The Virtual Bible
Used by permission.

Rembrandt's "Christ in the Storm on the Sea of Galilee"
Photo of painting by Rembrandt.
Public Domain.
Via Wikimedia Commons.

Sea of Galilee: Western Shoreline
Photo by Dan Lundberg.
Licensed under CC BY-SA 2.0.
Via Wikimedia Commons.

Shore of the Sea of Galilee at Tabgha
Photo by David A. deSilva.
Copyright 2014 Faithlife / Logos Bible Software

Southern Entrance to the Temple Mount
Photo by Oren Rozen.
Licensed under CC BY-SA 3.0.
Via Wikimedia Commons.

Southern Plains of the Sea of Galilee
Photo by Itamar Grinberg.
Licensed under CC BY-SA 2.0.
Via Wikimedia Commons.

Southwest Corner of the Temple Mount
Photo by Barry J. Beitzel.
Copyright 2014 Faithlife / Logos Bible Software

Tel Qatzir and the Sea of Galilee
Photo by Todd Bolen.
Copyright 2017 Todd Bolen
Used by permission.

Tombs of Hezir and Zechariah
Photo by askii.
Licensed under CC BY-SA 2.0.
Via Wikimedia Commons.

The Triple Gate
Photo by Bachrach44.
Public Domain.
Via Wikimedia Commons.

Trumpeting Stone
Photo by Ekeidar.
Licensed under CC BY-SA 3.0.
Via Wikimedia Commons.

The Caiaphas Ossuary
Photo by BRBurton.
Public Domain.
Via Wikimedia Commons.

View from Kursi Cliff looking north
Photo by Todd Bolen.
Copyright 2017 Todd Bolen
Used by permission.

View into Lower Galilee from Mount Carmel
Photo by Daniel Warner.
Copyright 2004 The Virtual Bible
Used by permission.

View of Mount Moreh from Mount Gilboa
Photo by Daniel Warner.
Copyright 2004 The Virtual Bible
Used by permission.

View of Mount Tabor, Moreh, and Gilboa from across the Jezreel Valley
Photo by Daniel Warner.
Copyright 2004 The Virtual Bible
Used by permission.

Wadi Qelt
Photo by דניאל צבי.
Public Domain.
Via Wikimedia Commons.

Wheat Field in Upper Galilee
Photo by H2o.
Public Domain.
Via Wikimedia Commons.

Wine Press
Photo by Barry J. Beitzel.
Copyright 2014 Faithlife / Logos Bible Software